GRANT WACKER

RELIGION
IN AMERICAN SOCIETY

John Wilson
Duke University

RELIGION

IN

AMERICAN SOCIETY

THE EFFECTIVE PRESENCE

Prentice-Hall, Inc., Englewood Cliffs, New Jersey 07632

Library of Congress Cataloging in Publication Data

WILSON, JOHN
  Religion in American society.

  (Prentice-Hall series in sociology)
  Bibliography.
  Includes index.
  1. Religion and sociology. 2. United States—
Religion. I. Title.
BL60.W55   301.5'8   77-16808
ISBN 0-13-773259-7

PRENTICE-HALL SERIES IN SOCIOLOGY
Neil J. Smelser, Editor

Printed in the United States of America

10   9   8   7   6   5   4   3   2   1

Prentice-Hall International, Inc., *London*
Prentice-Hall of Australia Pty. Limited, *Sydney*
Prentice-Hall of Canada, Ltd., *Toronto*
Prentice-Hall of India Private Limited, *New Delhi*
Prentice-Hall of Japan, Inc., *Tokyo*
Prentice-Hall of Southeast Asia Pte. Ltd., *Singapore*
Whitehall Books Limited, *Wellington, New Zealand*

CONTENTS

v

11

Religion and Economic Life 212.

12

Religion and the Family 237.

Part IV

RELIGIOUS DIVERSITY AND SOCIAL CONFLICT

13

A Change of View 273.✔

Part V

SECULARIZATION

18

19

Appendix

The Measurement of Religiosity   440.

Bergson : religion = "effective presence" = feeling of immanent purpose and meaning

PREFACE

In *The Two Sources of Morality and Religion,* Henry Bergson describes the essence of religion as the sensation of "an effective presence"—the feeling that all events are intended and have some significance for humans. He believed that behind the religious impulse lay the need to impose order upon a world which would otherwise be chaotic and meaningless. Bergson's insight has sociological as well as philosophical truth. Religion is itself an effective presence in society, helping shape social reality and being, in turn, shaped by it. This mutual influence is the subject of the sociology of religion with which this book deals.

This text provides a comprehensive coverage of recent literature in the sociology of religion, especially that which reports the findings of empirical research. There are two distinct emphases in how I have treated that literature. First, I have accented the problems of religious dynamics—how new religious ideas and practices arise and become institutionalized. Second, I have chosen to display the variety of sociological perspectives which ahve been brought to bear upon the topic of religion—to show how different orientations uncover different "facts" about the function of religion in society. The structure of the book reflects these twin emphases.

Part I describes the essence of religion, provides some basic sociological tools with which to investigate it, and analyzes the most widespread and taken for granted religion of all—common religion. Part II has to do with how new religious ideas and practices arise and become popular. Using the concept of institutionalization to suggest a sequence of development, new religious groups are followed from their inception to their fully organized phase. The purpose is to show the various ways in which people have attempted to resolve the dilemma with which they are faced when they attempt to share and communicate their religious experiences.

Parts III and IV of the book present an institutional analysis of religion in modern Western societies. In these parts, the second of the emphases of this text is most obvious. Sociology is characterized by several competing orientations. Two of the major orientations are used to carry out the institutional analysis of religion. Part III treats religion from a functionalist, or "pure science" perspective, while the emphasis on criticism and conflict in Part IV owes more to Marxist sociology. Although similar topics are addressed in both parts, there is no repetition, for each orientation poses its own questions and reaches its own conclusions. The aim is to provoke thought and stimulate criticism about the kind of assumptions sociologists usually make about the role of religion in society.

Part V, on secularization, returns more explicitly to the theme of religious dynamics. The possibility of a decline in the "presence" of religion in modern societies is an idea that runs through much of the research into the religious factor in political, economic and family life. In Part V this possibility is examined by using time-series data on religious beliefs and practices. One inescapable conclusion to be drawn from the studies of contemporary transformations of religion is that traditional religious forms are disappearing, and new forms are emerging. Some of these novel religions are described in the final section of the book, together with some speculations about their long-term significance. In this respect, the text comes full circle, describing the experimental and transformative religious groups with which it began.

Most of the material in this book deals with denominational America, with greater emphasis on the Protestant religious organizations than on either Catholicism or Judaism. This is chiefly because that is where so much contemporary research is directed. Non-denominational religion is thus given short shrift, except in the chapters on common religion, near-groups, sects, and civil religion—where the evidence on which to base generalizations is rather poor. For much the same reason, non-Western religion is all but ignored. This is not a sociology of world religions, but a sociology of religion as it appears in modern Western societies. Of the latter, the United States receives the most attention, simply because data pertaining to American religion are so much more abundant. Evidence from Canada and the United Kingdom is brought forward whenever possible in order to make cross-cultural comparisons. Despite the lack of comparative material, one of the aims of the book is, however, to stress the distinctiveness of American religion and its intimate connection with what is more central to American society.

The sociology of religion has made enormous strides in the past two decades. There is much excellent work reported in this volume. Yet, the more we know, the more we realize how little we know. I have attempted to stimulate further work, not only by pointing out some of the weaknesses of the research and conclusions reported, but also by providing a bibliography which, although by no means exhaustive, will furnish the reader with the means of practicing, as well as reading about, the sociology of religion.

RELIGION
IN AMERICAN SOCIETY

Part I

THE
SOCIAL FOUNDATION
OF RELIGION

1

RELIGION:
THE SOCIOLOGICAL
PERSPECTIVE

INTRODUCTION

This book is about one of the most important institutions in human societies. The creeds, cults and organization of religion are everywhere of the utmost significance, helping to form, not only the relation of man to the transcendental, but also his relation to other human beings and to the natural world. Establishing a satisfying relationship to an "Other Reality" is important even for the most modern of men and women. If hell-fire and damnation are less real to them than to their ancestors, they still firmly believe there is a God, Sunday mornings yet find them in church as often as anywhere else, and they continue to urge their children to marry within the faith. When disaster strikes them they turn to their priest. Nine out of ten Americans regard their religious beliefs as very, or at least fairly, important to them (Gallup, 1976:8), and even in a highly technological world, "a right relationship to spiritual beings and spiritual resources is presented as consummately valuable" (Swanson, 1976:viii).

Religious beliefs are universal. Humans everywhere have not only practiced religion, but also reflecting on it, have produced theologies by which to understand it better. However, a detached scrutiny of religion and a curiosity above all else about its social aspects is the concern, not of the theologian but of the sociologist. Since they began their work in the nineteenth century, sociologists have treated the analysis of religious phenomena as central to the understanding of how society works. Various assumptions have guided them. Some, like Comte, Spencer, Marx and Pareto (all strongly influenced by positivism) treated religion as an error, perhaps useful in the past but destined to diminish in importance as science becomes the chief guide to living. Others, like Durkheim, Weber, and Simmel, saw that it was precisely the non-rationality of religion which was the source of its appeal. Instead of concerning themselves with the social reasons for man's credulity, as had Spencer and Pareto, Durkheim, Weber and Simmel analyzed the source of that enduring attitude of respect with which all sacred objects are treated. Although different conclusions were bound to be drawn from such different approaches, the net result has been to keep religion at the center of sociological attention, and a rich legacy of insights has been inherited, many of which have inspired the work reported in this book.

Sociologists who study religion have two closely related objectives: one is to arrive at a complete understanding of the meaning of religion to those who practice it; the other is to make generalizations about the impact of religion on society and of society on religion. The first objective demands *empathy*, in recognition of the fact that religion is essentially a subjective phenomenon. The second objective requires knowledge of co-variation—how religious institutions and other social institutions are interdependent.

This book will attempt to describe all aspects of the relation between religion and society. But it has a special emphasis on the role of religion in cultural creativity, social transformation and institution-building. In this, it follows the lead of the German sociologist Max Weber (1864–1920), who never thought of religion except in dynamic terms. He believed that religious ideas had played a major role in determining the course of human development. Accordingly, he thought a great deal, not only about the role of religious ideas in social transformations, but also, more particularly, about the process whereby new religious ideas gain popular acceptance. He regarded the formation of a community of believers around the person of the prophet as necessary for the spread and influence of new religious ideas. This community would, he reasoned, harness "the most powerful interest of social self-esteem in the service of breeding traits" (Weber, 1946:321). The impulse behind the formation of the community lay, in his view, in the desire to protect spiritual privileges and routinize the dispensation of grace (Berger, 1971).

The lesson to be learned from Weber is that "the normal process by which the doctrine of the prophets enters into everyday life, as the function of a permanent institution," is through the "transformation of a personal following into a permanent congregation" (Weber, 2965:62).

To better describe this transformation, Weber (1946:288) contrasted the "sect" and the "church." He defined sects as "associations that accept only religiously qualified persons in their midst" and a church as "a community organized by officials into an institution which bestows gifts of grace." The sect, in other words, is a close-knit religious group at war with the rest of society and determined to change it; a church a is more formally organized association that has reached some accommodation with the rest of society and determined to change it; a church is a more tion of individual local congregations," tends to develop, by "a gradual transition," into "the typical organization of the Reformed Church" (Weber, 1965:65).

Weber clearly envisaged a constant movement of religious groups along a continuum ranging from lesser to greater institutionalization. "Groups within a society are institutionalized to the extent their functions and organizations are designed and committed to serve the common interest and to the degree that the common interest is identified and authoritatively defined" (Swanson, 1967:261). Any given religious association can therefore be viewed as more or less institutionalized at any given moment, and the sect and the church (as well as any intermediary forms) can be considered to be different "stages" of institutionalization. Obviously, churches are more institutionalized than sects.

THE PLAN OF THE BOOK

When describing religion, it is important to emphasize its dynamic character. Religious forms are always changing and always leading to change. This is true of even the most taken-for-granted and traditional of religious practices. The plan of this book is designed to emphasize this fact. The first part is taken up with the enduring needs which give rise to religious institutions and with the most informal, but, in many ways, most stable of all religious forms, common religion. Common religion is the religion of folk-ways, a substratum of widely dispersed, everyday practices which exist outside the churches. Through their common religion, people affirm the presence of divinity in their everyday world. Any changes which take place in common religion are likely to be slow and gradual, and the effect of common religion is principally a conservative one, to affirm the legitimacy of present social arrangements.

But in this common religion, there can be found the seeds of the kind of socio-religious change which is the concern of Part II of the book. Common religion possesses an antinominian element in its more esoteric parts, which functions to challenge existing religious practices and social patterns. From this very informal, rather unorganized kind of religion, there can spring movements of protest against the world, movements which are capable of inspiring the "great dramatic innovations" (Eisenstadt, 1968:xvi) which signal major social changes.

Part II, "The Growth of Religions," is concerned with how new religions form and grow. The first stirrings of revolt against traditional religious beliefs and rituals, and the social practices to which they lead often have small beginnings. It is necessary to look at the religious "underground" or "counter-culture" for the first signs of religious dissent and the portents of possible social change, and this is what Chapter 3 is intended to do. All the groups described there have challenged the status quo. But they are not themselves separate religions, nor even entirely independent organizations. The chapter concerns itself, in short, with religious protest at a rather primitive stage.

Many protest groups remain at the incipient or primitive stage; their development is stunted for some reason, and they survive on the margins of respectability. The emergence of a separate minority religious movement within but apart from the dominant religious tradition is a further, and qualitatively different, stage in the process of institutionalization. It is now that the sect, in the sense of a distinctive movement of protest against the church and society, makes its appearance. The sect, and the various forms of sectarianism in the Western world, are described in Chapter 4. Chapter 5 concerns theories about what kinds of circumstances lead to the rise of new religions and what kinds of people are drawn to them.

Sects, like most protest movements, are exclusive, in the sense that there is "no doubt about the doctrines to which an individual is committed, the authorities that he obeys, the ritual in which he participates, and the body to which he belongs, *to the exclusion of all others*" (Wilson, 1973:31). Sects provide an excellent laboratory for the observation of two essential features of religious life—conversion and commitment. The process whereby an individual comes to believe and act upon his faith, and the techniques which are used to sustain his loyalty to the faith and maintain his commitment to the fellowship are highlighted in the rarefied world of sectarianism. Chapter 6, while focusing on sectarian conversion and commitment, uses them as refined versions of the general social process of religious socialization and commitment.

Sects are highly unstable. Protest demands sacrifices for which only the most intangible rewards are given. Weber surmised that a gradual transition away from the sectarian form and toward greater acculturation and a stable, routinized organization is almost inevitable. Chapters 7 and 8 take up this idea. Chapter 7 deals with processes that, borrowing from the sociology of minority groups, might be called acculturation and assimilation. Acculturation means the change of a minority's culture to that of the host, or core, society; assimilation means that members of the minority group come to interact socially with the majority. These concepts describe the kinds of changes that take place in the relation between the protest group and the society of which it is a part, and the circumstances under which these changes are likely to occur. Chapter 8 focuses on the internal changes that occur during institutionalization as the conduct of the new religion becomes routinized and more settled practices (compatible with those of the wider society) are established. In that chapter, the study of the institutionalization process is carried through to its conclusion. The study of fully institutionalized religion can then be started.

Not only do social conditions affect the rise and spread of ideas and values, but ideas and values, once institutionalized in society, affect the actions of men and women. The relationship between religious institutions and other social institutions is the subject of Parts III and IV of this book. These parts are distinguished not by their subject matter but by their theoretical perspective. It is important to understand the reason for this. No textbook can relay all the received knowledge in its field, nor even a summary of that knowledge. A textbook is not a compendium of facts but a way of looking at the world—a perspective in which certain "facts" appear and others do not. The means by which different facts appear and disappear is the changing of one's angle of vision.

Not all sociologists look at the social world from the same standpoint. Sociology is a house divided, and, there being several angles from which to choose, it is not surprising that there are several sociologies of religion. Space forbids the exploration of more than two of these "paradigms," or perspectives, but the two to be considered are the dominant ones. The first, *functional theory*, emphasizes the contributions made by religion to the continued functioning of society, especially those unintended by the actors involved. In Part III this perspective will be used to examine the role of religion in the life of the community (Chapter 9), the contribution it makes to political stability (Chapter 10), its function as a foundation for economic life (Chapter 11), and its close links with the modern family (Chapter 12). The second paradigm, *conflict theory*, is introduced in Chapter 13 and forms the theoretical perspective of Part IV. According to conflict theory, social order is the product of coercion rather than consensus. It follows from this that religion can only be understood by relating it to major social conflicts and by examining the role it plays in the coercion of the many by the few. Part IV examines some of the implications of this paradigm: the role of religion in the allocation of life chances; the part played by religion in ethnic conflicts; and the impact of religion on political struggles.

The changing relationship between religion and society is the subject of this entire book. But it becomes the special focus of Part V, which examines the evidence for the proposition that religion is declining in the advanced industrial societies of the West. Much of this evidence suggests, not that religion is disappearing, but that changes are taking place in the form in which it is expressed in society. As old beliefs and practices falter, new ones arise from the margins of society to take their place. In a sense, then, the discussion in the book comes full circle, for it concludes on the note with which it began, that forms of new religious consciousness have obscure beginnings on the margins of social life.

The scope and aims of the book will be evident by now. It is largely an institutional analysis of religion in advanced Western societies, with its major focus on denominational America. The object is to rely as much as possible on reports of empirical research. In order to indicate the potential usefulness of the work, the implications of this particular focus should be made clear.

Most of the generalizations made here about the relationship between religion and society are applicable only to modern Western societies. These societies are pluralistic and are industrialized according to capitalist principles. Excluded from the scope of this book are the state socialist societies, where the practice of religion is severely and formally restricted, and the so-called underdeveloped countries, in which economic and social conditions are not comparable to those of the industrialized West. Within the countries of the modern Western world, the primary emphasis is upon the United States (where most of the research has been conducted), Canada, and the United Kingdom. Little attention is paid to the differences between the United States and her northern neighbor, because "careful attention to the past and present of Canada will convince observers that that nation's emergent map of religion is similar to its southern neighbor's in most respects" (Marty, 1976:3–4). like that in the United States, however, and British religious institutions Quebec will quickly indicate, but the two societies are sufficiently alike to be grouped together for the purposes of generalization. The relation between religion and society in the United Kingdom is somewhat less like that in the United States, however, the British religious institutions will be used more extensively as a basis for comparison. Insofar as there is a comparative perspective in this work, it is mainly historical. Data from the past are useful, not only for making clear what is distinctive about the present, but also for tracing the impact of tradition and custom.

"Religion" in this book refers almost exclusively to the Judeo-Christian tradition, the dominant belief system in the modern Western world. There is no description of "primitive" religions or the religions of the East, except insofar as they provide a perspective from which to view contemporary Western religion, or to the extent that they have intruded into the Western world. Certain omissions have been occasioned by a lack of reliable evidence. The churches of the Eastern rite and Catholicism among Mexican-Americans and Puerto Ricans are among the topics so slighted. Other subjects have been omitted because to treat them briefly would be seriously misleading. The religion of the American Indian, the role of Catholicism in Quebec nationalism, and Protestant/Catholic differences in Ulster have been glossed over for this reason.

Finally, the use of terms should be clarified. "Religion," "religiosity," and "the religious factor" are all used rather loosely to refer to faith in general; "religion" is also used sometimes to refer to something like Judaism or Protestantism and even to describe a specific denomination, such as Methodism. This is simply to provide stylistic variety. No attempt has been made to decide whether or not Methodism is actually a separate religion from, say, Episcopalianism. For the sake of style, the capitalized word "Church" is sometimes used as a synonym for "institutionalized religion;" at other times, however, it is used to refer to a specific ecclesia, such as the Catholic Church, but the text will make this clear. "Churches" mean the aggregate of denominational bodies (as in "the churches' stand on civil rights"). Very rarely, "church" refers to a specific building or congregation. "Mainstream (or mainline) Protestantism" is used frequently as shorthand for "the traditional, inherited, normative, or median style of American spirituality and organization" (Marty, 1976:53). The term has no exact referent, but suggests those denominations that have historically been close to the society's core values. It is not important to decide with absolute certainty whether or not a given denomination is part of, or exterior to, this mainstream.

RELIGION DEFINED SOCIOLOGICALLY

It is the purpose of this book to describe the role of religion in modern Western societies from a sociological perspective. It is assumed that religion is a distinct, autonomous sphere of social concern, related in many ways to other social concerns. It is this manifold relationship that is the target of scrutiny by sociologists; they are anxious to find out how religion is molded by social forces. Clearly, sociologists believe that it is possible to define what religion is and what it is not.

Unfortunately, the problem of defining religion in a way that would be sociologically useful is a difficult one, for religion is rich and varied in its social manifestations. Straightforward and simple definitions that refer to beliefs in gods founder on examples of otherwise apparently *a more rigorously functional definition would ask not what is believed or done, but how and to what purpose and what effect?*

10   *Religion: The Sociological Perspective*

religious groups in which dogma and creed are rejected and gods are unknown. Without entering too deeply into the controversies surrounding the definition of religion in sociology, and without attempting to embrace all the issues, two *strategies* of definition can be identified as having guided the research that will be reported in this book.

Functional Definitions

A functional definition identifies a phenomenon by its use or purpose. This is clearly illustrated by Yinger's (1971:7) definition of religion as "a system of beliefs and practices by means of which a group of people struggle with ... the ultimate problems of human life." For Yinger, it is not the substance of the belief but "the nature of the *believing* that is important." Religion is, therefore, those beliefs and practices that speak to the ultimate problems of man's existence, such as suffering, injustice, and death. Salvation religions such as Protestantism are clearly embraced by this definition, but it would also include belief systems such as Marxism and humanism. This definition characterizes as religious any person troubled with ultimate concerns.

The principal advantages of this type of definition are two. First, it conceptualizes religion not as a substance but as a form of consciousness, an orientation to life, a quest for a meaningful relationship to the "ultimate" or the "beyond." It thereby points to what, for many observers, is the irreducibly human character of man—his continual questioning, and his need for some sense of ultimate or final order and meaning. There is the additional benefit that insightful parallels are drawn between what is customarily and popularly considered religion and phenomena such as intense political commitment (as in Marxism), identity-transformation (as in sensitivity-training groups), and the ethical perfectionism of a humanist. It is a definition that commendably broadens the gaze and expands awareness.

Second, the functional definition circumvents the difficult question of whether or not religious beliefs *must* make reference to gods, or, indeed, to the supernatural at all. Durkheim (1975:78) points out the difficulty of using the concept "supernatural" to distinguish religious beliefs: "for any stranger to scientific culture, nothing is outside nature, because for him there is no such thing as nature. He multiplies miracles unconsciously, not because he feels surrounded by mysteries, but on the contrary, because nothing has any secrets for him." A definition of religion that depends upon being able to distinguish between those who believe in the supernatural and those who do not would therefore be very narrow indeed.

Unfortunately, the very features that commend the functional definition also detract from its usefulness. First, any definition that draws attention to the similarities between phenomena runs the risk of obscuring important differences between them. In the present case, the emphasis that a functional definition places on the use to which beliefs and practices are put tends to draw attention away from the religion itself. It suggests that religious phenomena can be understood without reference to their meaning. In other words, it matters not how the ultimate concern is addressed as long as it is addressed, and atheists, agnostics, and theists are all alike. This seems to be unfair, not only to the believer but to the athiest and agnostic too!

Second, the idea of ultimacy plays an important part in functional definitions. Variously used to describe concerns, problems, and even solutions, ultimacy is a quality of experience, a sense of completeness and finality. But how can ultimate and trivial concerns be distinguished? Unfortunately, there are as many difficulties in defining an ultimate concern as there are in defining what is supernatural. In fact, definitions that refer to the ultimate are no less substantive than those that refer to the supernatural, because even functional definitions refer to a thing, the "beyond," or "ground of being." Even if ultimacy is characterized purely as an attitude, the problem of distinguishing such attitudes remains, and the chances are that any list of their varieties will be "little more than a specification in sociological garb of the view of the human situation currently held by Christian theologians" (Campbell, 1971:135). Are there really universal human concerns, and is it helpful to characterize all those deeply troubled by the enduring problems of life as religious? There is an arrogance in a definition that tells people that they have unknowingly been encountering God!

Substantive Definitions

Whereas a functional definition describes what religion does, a substantive definition describes what religion is. It defines religion as a certain kind of belief, practice, or experience. For example, religion might be defined substantively as "an institutionalized system of symbols, beliefs, values, and practices that focus on supernatural beings, worlds, and forces." The attraction of this kind of definition is its familiarity (it draws on traditional Christian ideas of what it means to be religious) and its specificity. Both features make it easier to use in the Western context.

However, the substantive definition has its drawbacks. First, the definition is familiar because it rests on taken-for-granted ideas about nature and supernature, belief and action. However, these ideas stem from the Enlightenment and do not necessarily apply to all societies. Unfortunately, even in modern Western societies the religious person may make no such distinction. The definition is, therefore, rather provincial.

Second, the substantive type of definition invariably refers to the supernatural. This is a very troublesome concept. It is usually taken to mean a constraining influence for which empirical proof is not given, but this only pushes the problem back to that of defining the word empirical. Most often, this problem is solved by the sociologist deciding what is nonempirical. He or she might thus determine that extrasensory perception is empirical and not, therefore, a religious phenomenon. The room for variation here is obvious.

Thus, substantive definitions, like functional definitions, have their weaknesses. There is no present solution to this dilemma. The functional definition leaves the investigator much more open to new religious manifestations and less culture-bound. The substantive definition is easier to implement in research. Although much of the *thinking* in the sociology of religion today is guided by the functional type of definition (see, for example, Bellah, 1970), most of the empirical *research* seems to have been guided by a substantive definition. In any case, there is no need for a definition of religion-in-general, because sociologists very rarely take such a broad approach to the study of religion. Instead, they observe and seek to explain the particular beliefs and practices of particular people. The readers of this book are encouraged to think about religion substantively. In that way, the limitations imposed upon the scope of the book and the purposes of the research reported therein will have a logic to them.

Having distinguished the religious from the non-religious, one must establish some categories with which to order the enormous variety of religious practices.

RELIGIOUS DIMENSIONS

For some, religion is primarily a matter of belief, or faith; for others, it is ritual or ethical conduct; and for yet others, it is feeling, sensation, or experience. Although all of these aspects are present in all religions, their salience varies from one to another. The many-sided character of religion has led an increasing number of sociologists to attempt to isolate and measure these different dimensions. The more technical side of this work will be discussed in the Appendix, but the simple idea on which it is based explains much of the variation in religion and should therefore be clarified in this introductory chapter.

Religious Beliefs

To believe something, such as the assertion that human nature is a mixture of good and evil, is to accept it as a fact or agree that it is true. Religious beliefs are most commonly associated with statements about gods, spirits, the soul, heaven, hell, and so on. But there is no list of beliefs which are religious and another list of those which are not. All that can be said is that religious beliefs deal with the world as a totality in time and space, and with the general principles or laws that govern it by reference to a supernatural realm. They provide a general framework for order, endowing particular acts with cosmic significance. In their religious quest, people seek "to graduate beyond the immediate present, beyond the particular and the concrete to the more general categories and patterns which underlie and generate the vicissitudes of human existence" (Shils, 1975:128). Thus, abstention from certain foods is one thing for the figure-conscious and another thing entirely for the religious ascetic. *[handwritten: good example]*

Religious beliefs are not mere speculations. They organize perceptions and cognitions and provide a foundation for human actions. In other words, they are acted out and modified by experience. And yet, religious beliefs are not derived entirely from what happens in the empirical world: they are not the sum of confirmed experiences. Religious belief contains a large element of faith which, in preceding cognition, determines experiences as much as it is determined by it. For example, people do not see an ethereal object and, as a result, believe in ghosts. Rather, they believe in the supernatural realm and therefore see ethereal objects as ghosts. It is the same with faith healing. The disposition to believe, combined with correct performance, produces a cure, the cure does not produce the belief. This is why one reported healing will outweigh a thousand apparent failures, because failures and disappointments can be accounted for by the belief itself—lack of success might be due to absence of faith, the use of incorrect procedure, God's testing, or the work of the Devil. *[handwritten: nicety: conamapice]*

Of course, beliefs must be sustained by experiences, but those experiences are defined largely by the beliefs themselves. Faith is, therefore, self-confirming. Doubt is not unknown to the religious person, but it is confronted and resolved by incorporating it into a larger affirmation of faith. The power of religious beliefs to mold reality in this way lies in their rich symbolism. They are not simply factual statements about a pre-existent exterior world but pictures that help shape perceptions and that appeal as much because they "feel" or "look" right as because they are thought to be accurate. To the extent that this is true (and the extent varies from one religion to another), it is the satisfying enactment of beliefs, rather than their "proof" which is important for their continued acceptance. "Religion is embodied truth, not known truth, and it has in fact been transmitted far more through narrative, image and enactment than through definitions and demonstrations" (Bellah, 1970:44). The association among belief, ritual, and experience is therefore very close.

Rituals are prescribed, ordered enactments of the relationship of man to the Holy. Rituals are performed in all religions. Prayer, exhortation, reading, recitation, sacrifice, exorcism, dancing, singing, taboos, feasts, fasting, meetings, mortification of the flesh, and the manufacture and manipulation of symbolic objects have all played a part in religious rituals. Rituals are used to supplicate and propitiate the gods, on the occasion of important life-changes (such as marriage), during communal crises, and to mark the seasons.

The emphasis given to ritual differs from one religion to another, according to how efficacious symbolic action is thought to be. For example, the Catholic regards Mass as an important ritual in which miraculous events occur, the Anglican-Episcopalian Protestant treats it more as a commemorative rite, and the radical Protestant considers it irrelevant.[1] Religions also differ in the pervasiveness of their ritualism. Jewish ritualism, for example, fuses the whole cultural system and can become the guiding force for a complete way of life in which sanctification is achieved only by absolute separation from the profane. A wide range of taboos according to which certain things are set apart is enforced.

The purpose of ritual is to regulate the relation of humans to the divine, to properly connect the sacred and the profane: "rites are the values of conduct which prescribe how a man should compose himself in the presence of . . . sacred objects" (Durkheim, 1965:56). Any act can become a sacrament or a means of communion with the sacred. An act is designated religious when reference is made to the Holy, and when those engaged experience a reality beyond themselves. It is this "otherness" that distinguishes religious rituals from secular ceremonies.

The very idea of the Holy or the sacred implies ritual, for it is never entered or approached without special preparation. The contact of one reality with another has to be specially marked and carefully regulated otherwise the quality of sacredness will be lost. For this reason, many people abstain from mundane things of the flesh, such as tobacco, alcohol, meat, or sex as a means of purification that will facilitate their communion with the divine. Rituals will always be observed where sacred and profane meet. For example, the threshold has so many superstitions attached to it because it is the dividing line between the home, or interior regions (sacred) and the outside world, or exterior regions (profane).

Rituals involve the manipulation of a wide range of objects (most commonly the human body) for the purposes of symbolizing the rela-

---

[1]Episcopalian ministers tend to value ritual highly, whereas Presbyterian ministers attach very little significance to it (Maranell, 1974:51).

tionship of the individual and his group to the Divinity. However, ritual objects have not only allegorical uses but instrumental uses as well. In other words, they do not merely stand for something, they also do something. For example, those who take the power of the spoken word literally will believe that utterances such as "Heal!" will alone cause a return to health. In the same way, special dress, certain sequences of events, particular noises, and certain body movements can all have both allegorical and instrumental significance.

The Relation of Belief and Ritual

Beliefs are acted out in ritual and ethical conduct; practices are meaningful only because they can be set within some cosmological scheme. But given the different emphases on these separate dimensions of religion from one faith to another, it is of interest to ask whether rituals serve to remind people of their beliefs, or whether beliefs are accepted because they give ongoing rituals more profound meaning. Many authorities are of the opinion that ritual creates a disposition to believe (see, for example, Durkheim, 1965; Mehl, 1970:107; Wach, 1962; Wallace, 1966:102). And it is true that before the Reformation religion was largely a matter of practice, a mode of behavior rather than a creed. The Reformation changed this emphasis: contrast the Catholic doctrine that "God's essence is embodied in the historically existing church and in the sacraments" with the doctrine of Luther and Calvin that "God is omnipotent over his creation but his personal essence is not to be found in any created thing" (Swanson, 1967:1x). It is now possible to think with Shils (1975:155), that beliefs "could conceivably be accepted without adopting the practice of rituals associated with them . . . rituals, however, could not exist without beliefs." There is, then, no simple answer to the question of the priority of belief or ritual: in some contexts beliefs predominate: in others, it is ritual.

Religious Experience

There is a sense in which religious beliefs and rituals are merely attempts to objectify the essence of religion, an inner experience, an emotion-laden feeling of finality, wholeness, completeness and consummation. Mysticism is one kind of religion in which experience is all. The mystic "becomes aware that he is caught up in the process of the universe; he is in intimate contact with the world, the forces that underpin it, and with the basic life force of existence . . ." (Greeley, 1974a: 65). If other kinds of religion do not emphasize experience as much it is nevertheless essential to them. There are clear dangers in treating experience as a separate dimension of religion, the chief of which is that beliefs and rituals will be treated as if they were not somehow also experiences. And yet, religious experiences have suffered such neglect at the hands of sociologists (probably because they are never directly witnessed but are always mediated through beliefs and rituals) that it is worthwhile to treat them independently.

Yinger (1971:146–47) distinguishes three types of religious experience:

1. The ascetic: "the sense that one had, by withdrawal from the demands and values of the secular world and by mastery of the self, achieved contact with what is seen as ultimate reality."
2. The mystical: "the sense that by disregarding and accepting the world around one, by purging oneself of mundane interests, or by abandoning self and concentrating on ways of illumination, one has achieved union with the divine." The mystic will proclaim, for example, that love is an experience, not an idea.
3. The prophetic: "the sense that one is serving as the agent for a challenge to an evil social order in the name of ultimate standards."

Provided that it is stimulated by a feeling of being in contact with the divine, any experience can qualify as religious. A sensation of awe, a feeling of comfort and certainty, a sense of complete obligation and subservience, a joyful conviction of salvation, the feeling of vibrations, the hearing of the "music of the spheres"—these are some of the experiences that religious people report. The purest refinement of religious experience is attempted through meditation, in which the goal is pure experience, devoid of all preconceptions and in which knowledge is seen as a firsthand, encounter rather than an abstract argument based on logic.

It has been claimed that religious experiences reflect a fundamental sensitivity to the sacred or transcendental. This sensitivity is similar to an aesthetic sensibility, of which one individual might possess more than another. That a sizable number of people do report a range of contacts with the spiritual world does indeed suggest a psychic sensitivity in many persons (Greeley, 1975:31). However, it is highly unlikely that this indicates any kind of faculty or aptitude. What is more probable is that a heightened disposition to interpret sensations and experiences as contacts with the supernatural is socially learned.

Inner experiences are interpreted by beliefs and shared in rituals. There is a finely graded continuum extending from the "orthodox" experiences of the churches to the more private world in which, for instance, the individual communes with nature. There is also an imperceptible movement from the fundamental concern with the Holy in its mysterious and unfathomable aspects to the sense of mystery, the thrill of the unknown and the dread of unaccountable forces associated with phenomena such as unidentified flying objects, yeti, swamp monsters, and the Egyptian Pyramids. There are, of course, differences. Whereas the primary interest in phenomena such as the Loch Ness Monster is in clearing up the mystery, the attitude toward the Holy is always tinged with fear and an exultation in mystery; it is definitely not governed by an expectation that one day all will be revealed.

As is true of both belief and ritual, the importance attributed to experience varies from one religion to another. The Holiness movement lays considerable stress on experience: religion is felt rather than learned or performed. "The instrumental function, although not entirely absent, is secondary to the goal of expressing one's feelings" (Lefever, 1972: 89). Looking closely at a typical Holiness service of worship, it is apparent that its dominant quality is emotional rather than formal. Although a sermon may be included in the service (it is frequently omitted altogether), its role is not didactic but emotive. For this reason, it is usually chanted, there is much repetition of phrases and themes, and frequent, counterpoint interruptions from the congregation are not only tolerated but expected. A good sermon is judged not cognitively (for instance, as clever, informative, or well argued) but experientially—as "hot" or "cold."

RELIGION FROM A SOCIOLOGICAL PERSPECTIVE: WHY IS SOCIETY RELIGIOUS?

The sociologist's interest in religion is in the social forces that shape it and the impact it has on what people do. The simplest explanation for the existence of religious beliefs and practices is social learning. Religious behavior is learned as a normal part of socialization from parents, friends, and teachers. However, such an explanation really says little about why people are religious, for ideas and practices will be carried on only if they satisfy social needs. It is these needs that must be identified. Besides, social-learning theory is of little help in explaining changes in religion. A sociological explanation of religion has to identify the social forces generating and shaping the religious quest.

The solution to the problem of why society is religious is to be found in a close examination of the meaning of a concept integral to all definitions of religion—"the sacred." Religion divides the world into sacred and profane domains. Sacred things are superior in dignity and power, and a person's relation to them is by special attitudes, special respect and special precautions. This relation is sometimes full of awe and dread, sometimes loving and strongly affective, sometimes even jesting and petulant. But the constant factor is that the sacred is superior to and set apart from the mundane and the utilitarian, the seriousness of this relation is never forgotten. Profane actions are not simply routine actions, but actions in which "immediately prospective gratifications and the demands of immediate situations and of obligations to those who are close at hand play a greater part than does the link with transcendent things" (Shils, 1975:129). But the distinction between the sacred and the profane is not that between casual, carefree day-to-day living and the austerity of religious life. The sacred is the source of both severe restraint and joyful liberation. Nor is this distinction the same as that between good and evil. The sacred is the source of both the ultimately good and the ultimately evil.

There is nothing intrinsic to sacred objects which entitles them to the special attitude which is attached to them. All manner of objects can be, and have been, treated in this way. It is even possible for objects to move in and out of the sacred domain. For example, a missionary might be canonized and his bones made relics. Conversely, a burial ground might be deconsecrated and become a parking garage. What is constant is the division of the world into two separate domains and the restrictive codes of avoidance that govern relations to the sacred. Thus, if an object does move into the category of the sacred, it must be purified, and if it is moved out, it must be formally desacralized.

The clue to the real meaning of the sacred/profane distinction is to be found, not in the objects themselves, but in the attitude that is taken toward them. In other words, sacred objects are important symbolically. Their common character lies not in what they possess but in what they stand for. Here lies the fallacy of the so-called animistic and naturalistic theories of religion, which locate the origin of religious sentiments in psychological phenomena (such as dreams) or in natural wonders (such as storms).[2] As Durkheim (1965:87) pointed out, such theories put the cart before the horse. For example, the treatment of dreams as interpretable and natural objects as expressive of divinity is socially learned: it is as much the effect of religion as the cause of it.

If the origins of the sacred attitude are not to be found in the objects themselves, where do they lie: What is it that is capable of eliciting such powerful feelings of both attraction and repulsion? What is it that engenders feelings of both transcendence and subservience? What is the source of both the ultimately good and the ultimately evil? What is both uniquely individual and socially shared at the same time?

---

[2]Proponents of the animist theory argue that "primitive man's reflections on such experiences as death, disease, trances and visions, and above all dreams, led him to the conclusion that they are to be accounted for by the presence or absence of some immaterial entity, the soul . . ." (Evans-Pritchard, 1965:25).

Posing the question in these ways clearly suggests the answer. Respect is the attitude engendered by something which stands to us in the relation of moral ascendancy. Society is the only empirical reality which has this kind of moral reality. "Religious force is only the sentiment inspired by the group in its members, but projected outside of the consciousness that experienced them, and objectified" (Durkheim, 1965:261). Thus, when the faithful believe in a moral power upon which they depend and from which they derive their best aspects, they are not deceived: such a power exists: it is society. It is from social pressure that people derive the idea of a power outside themselves in dominion over them. It is from the individuality that all people derive from their social being that they obtain the idea of the divine spark within. The sacred is the moral authority of society, and the origin of the sacred is to be found in the immense value that people place upon social order, upon stable reciprocity—in short, upon morality.

It is possible to illustrate this idea by referring to Durkheim's treatment of the idea of the soul. Some of Durkheim's predecessors, such as the immensely popular Spencer, had propagated the idea that the human belief in the soul originated in dream and trance experiences in which an individual seemed to be in two places at once. Durkheim dismissed this naive kind of psychologism on the grounds that it supposed religion to be an illusion and to have no real foundation in social life. His concern was to establish the social foundation of religion, to show that something ubiquitous and profound must have an objective basis.

Durkheim saw in the belief in the soul a symbolic representation of the relation between the individual and society. He equated the soul with that part of society within the individual. The concept of the soul objectifies the social awareness that all humans internalize. But although "our moral conscience is part of our consciousness, we do not feel ourselves on an equality with it" (Durkheim, 1965: 298). It is this moral authority that is the objective referent behind the idea of the soul. Thus, when a person refers to her soul, she is referring to the social element within her—something that is both superior to her and that will live on after her in the memory of others. It is likewise with beliefs in life after death. Such beliefs are a concrete expression of the profound feeling that although an individual dies, part of her lives on in society.

The source of the sacred attitude is the sense of morality that people share. By the same token, this shared morality depends for its viability on being treated with the respect due to sacred objects. Too much emphasis on the profane weakens the bonds of social life. Precisely as religion is a manifestation of the moral ascendancy of society, so society depends on a "non-rational, supra-individual state of mind that can only be called religious" (Nisbet, 1966:251). For this reason, the sociologist assumes an interplay between religion and society; religion has an essentially social aspect, and society has an essentially religious aspect.

in short

To understand why the individual should re-present his social being to himself in religious imagery, it is necessary to understand that he does not have a *given* relationship to the world. "He must ongoingly establish a relationship with it" (Berger, 1967:5). As Durkheim (1965:240) pointed out (and as Feuerbach had before him) people "must invent by themselves the idea of those powers with which they feel themselves in connection." The individual is, in effect, compelled to impose his own order on his experience. The idea of the sacred cosmos gives to social existence an ultimate ground and validation. It establishes in an inviolable way the moral supremacy of society and of specific social forms. Although religion is not the only way society is re-presented to human consciousness, insofar as it bestows on human institutions an "ultimately valid ontological status" (Berger, 1967:33), it most effectively legitimates and ensures commitment to those institutions. The idea of the sacred is thus the most efficacious of all symbolic representations of society.[3]

The functional interplay between religion and society can be specified further. There is an isomorphism between the structure of the sacred and the structure of the social world, a congruence, expressed through religious symbolism, between particular social patterns and specific metaphysics. Even more specifically, "beliefs in gods or other spirits arise as symbols of men's experiences with the basic purposes and decision-making procedures of societies and of enduring and independent groups within societies" (Swanson, 1967:viii).

The idea of isomorphism between religion and society should not be treated simplistically. For one thing, religious beliefs and practices are not merely cognitive maps by which the social order is comprehended and rationalized. As much as anything else, religion is expressive. Hence, the congruence will be felt and enacted as much as it is thought out. Rituals "feel right" because they satisfyingly situate the individual in social relations. For another thing, religion does not satisfy because it provides an explanation for everything; it is not a full working model of social life. What is important is not that things be accounted for, but that the conviction that they *could* be accounted for be sustained. It follows

[3]Douglas (1975:xiv) writes about "imaginary powers" with which people surround themselves "to watch over their agreed morality and punish defectors. But having tacitly colluded to set up their awesome cosmos, the initial convention is buried. Delusion is necessary. For unless the sacred beings are credited with autonomous existence, their coercive power is weakened and with it the fragile social agreement which gives them being." Similarly, Becker (1975:148) refers to the "small terrors and small fascinations" with which man immunizes himself against the overwhelming terrors of life.

that the strength of beliefs, such as those concerned with faith healing, lies not so much in their proven efficacy as in their "ability to give the stricken person a vocabulary in terms of which to grasp the nature of . . . distress and relate it to the wider world" (Geertz, 1973:105). Thus, religion does not promise escape from death but it does reinterpret physical extinction; it does not promise release from suffering, but it does teach people how to suffer.

Assuming that there is an isomorphism between religion and society, which society is it?

> Is it the society we know, full of contradictions and imperfections, where injustice and falsehood prevail? Could such a society inspire the sentiments of religious idealism, enthusiasm, asceticism, and self-abnegation which the faithful have? Or is the basis of religion an ideal society, where justice, truth, and harmony prevail—a utopia?

> Durkheim answers that such a distinction is spurious and is an oversimplification of the facts. Religion is not just idealistic; it is also quite realistic. All the physical and moral ugliness we find in the profane world is also incorporated in the sacred world: war, sin, thievery, and death in one form or another have been deified. Durkheim points out that in its theology Christianity has to make a place for evil, embodied in the figure of Satan (Tiryakian, 1962:37).

The sense of sin is as essential to the maintenance of the social fabric as is the sense of good. Negative values are symbolized as well as positive ones so that people may come to some sort of terms with them. The reality of evil must be characterized and the proper attitude toward it indicated.[4]

Religion convinces the individual not only of the objective reality of social structures but also of his power to act. "The believer who has communicated with his god is not merely a man who sees new truths of which the unbeliever is ignorant; he is a man who is *stronger*. He feels within himself a force, either to endure the trials of existence or to conquer them" (Durkheim, 1965:464). Religion imparts to the person "a distinctive set of dispositions (tendencies, capacities, propensities, skills, habits, liabilities, pronenesses) which lend a chronic character to the flow of his activity and quality of his experience" (Geertz, 1973:95). Religion is important, then, not only for what it says about things but also for what it does to make action possible. Through religious action, the individual

---

[4]"Both what a people prizes and what it fears and hates are depicted in its world view symbolized in its religion, and in turn expressed in the whole quality of its life. Its ethos is distinctive not merely in terms of the sort of mobility it celebrates, but also in terms of the sort of business it condemns; its vices are as stylized as its virtues" (Geertz, 1973:131).

expresses his solidarity with his god and with his social group; he manipulates sacred symbols so as to place himself in right relationship to the sacred. As religious forces symbolize social forces, in placing himself in harmony with them the person is placing himself in harmony with society. It is humanity's desire to be "saturated with power," a power at once sacred and social which lies at the root of the religious quest (Eliade, 1959:13). In addition to providing the motive force for action, religion also guides it. Belief specified some ultimate good toward which day-to-day action is or should be moving. Indeed, religious beliefs are obligatory: if they do not lead to action, they are not "really religious" (Hoge, 1975:92).

So far, the functional reciprocity between religion and society has been emphasized. But religion is also a formulation of the ideal. It is a model *for* reality, as well as a model *of* reality. Its rites serve not only to commemorate the solidarity and continuity of the group but also to focus upon an ideal which people may seek to emulate and thereby be spiritually and morally elevated. Religion therefore has dynamic potential. It is no mere mirror image of its social context but an independent force for social change.

> Religion, once formed, is a whole world of sentiments, ideas and images which, once born, obey laws all their own . . . They attract each other, repel each other, unite, divide themselves and multiply . . . the life thus brought into being enjoys so great an independence that it sometimes indulges in manifestations with no purpose or utility of any sort, for the mere pleasure of affirming itself (Durkheim, 1965:471).

The dynamic character of religion stems, then, partly from the ideal nature of religious models (as the individual tries to transcend the inconsistencies of profane life and approximate the ideal) and partly from the transformative potential of religious beliefs as they work themselves out, independent of social structure in the imaginations of people. As Bell (1976:61) puts it: "an ideology gnawed at, worried to the bone, argued about, dissected, and restated by an army of essayists, moralists, and intellectuals becomes a force in its own right."

Although Durkheim was clearly not blind to the dynamism in religion, it was Weber who was most fascinated by it. Weber postulated a basic drive for meaning in the individual, a need to make sense of events. Consequently, he argued that the social world should be seen as a human fabrication and that religion was an important tool in the work of construction. He was extremely interested in the way in which religion legitimated social arrangements. He pointed out, for example, that without religion not even the rich are comfortable with their good fortune: "They feel the need to know that they have the *right* to their good fortune: (Weber, 1946:271). But it was the way in which religion could *destroy* social forms and build new ones that intrigued Weber the most.

Whereas Durkheim seemed to assume that the wish of people to conceive of the good society would promote consensus and stability, Weber recognized that it could also lead to conflict and change. In the attempt to come into contact with the very essence of being, to absorb the power and insight of the sacred, the individual might well breed opposition to and rejection of the established social order. The sacred, being above all nonrational and nonroutine, is thus the source of creativity and challenge. This aspect of religion is most appealing in times of stress, for then people are most sensitive to symbols and messages that attempt to articulate and make sense of events in a new way.

Religion is both world-maintaining and world-destroying, both constraining and liberating. It is capable of making the social world seem more real, more legitimate. It is also capable of making it seem illusory, a mere artifice to be rejected in favor of the real world of the spirit. It follows that both Durkheim and Weber have a great deal to tell the modern student of religion. Durkheim's viewpoint is useful because it points to the integrative role of religion. It suggests that religion can serve as a clue to how social structures work, and it circumvents tiresome and fruitless debates about the irrationality of religion by point to its objective foundation in society. The Weberian perspective is useful because it draws attention to religious movements and the nature of religious commitment in different social settings, and more particularly to the impact of religious movements on society. Thus, it is mainly to Durkheim that the studies relating particular religious beliefs to group structures are indebted. An indebtedness to Weber is recorded in the studies of the origin and development of new religious movements and their impact on the societies in which they appear.

RELIGION: AN INSTITUTION

Although the essence of religion is the experience of the Holy, and is therefore subjective, a purely private religion is as unthinkable as a purely private language. Similarly, although religious faith and commitment are essentially voluntary, they are to some degree called forth by social circumstances and therefore socially determined. And although religious symbols are apprehended in the innermost recesses of the mind, their meaning is also transmitted from one generation to another. In other words, religion is at the same time both individual and social, both interior and exterior, both singular and common, both fleeting and permanent.

The objectification, or sharing, of experiences, their articulation in truth-statements and ritual dramas, implies their institutionalization, for they become molded into accepted patterns of speech and behavior. The idea of institutionalization is that patterns of interaction and communication emerge as people attempt to solve the basic problems of human survival. The problem of rearing children has given rise to the institution of the family. The problem of relating humans to the sacred has given rise to the institution of religion.

Although it is common to use the term "institution" as if it applied to a thing or an object (sometimes literally so), the term is conceptualized more accurately as a process in which (for the sake of convenience) the pursuit of interests becomes regularized and guided by mores or laws. It is an unceasing process (never an accomplished objective), not only because the environment is continually changing but also because the individual, subjective consciousness is *always* skeptical of the precise way in which it has become objectified. In other words, a person's ways are never settled, not only because the world around her continually changes, but also because she is never contented with the way in which her ideas and visions have been made concrete. The relationship to the transcendental, in particular, is never fully understood, and can never be completely captured in human language or social forms. The institutionalization of religion thus always contains a contradiction, for it "involves the symbolic and organizational embodiment of the experience of the ultimate in less-than-ultimate forms and the concomitant embodiment of the sacred in profane structures" (O'Dea, 70:242). It is not surprising, then, that the individual is ever alert for new ways in which to articulate and express her innermost experiences and acutely sensitive to the constant encroachment of the profane onto her sacred domain.

Religious institutions slowly become less precarious as patterns of interaction and beliefs are taken more and more for granted. This growth does not occur randomly. Only certain practices and beliefs obtain sanction, *depending on the distribution of power at the time.* The direction of institutionalization is influenced by the efforts of certain groups to protect their values and encourage their realization. In the case of religion, this involves the regulation of "access' to the sacred and the emergence of a class of people as regulators—a priesthood class. It is this class and its sponsors that determine the direction and progress of institutionalization. They define offices and appoint individuals to them, they control the socialization and selection of their own successors, they develop a system of discipline in order to protect the sacred, and they specify the relationship of religion to other social institutions. The precise form that religion takes in any given context depends, then, on the distribution of power at the time and the kind of effort those with power make to secure their privileges.

Social elites will encourage institutionalization in order to legitimate their position. But there are forces, emanating from the intense idealism of religious people, that continually challenge the direction institutionalization takes. Religious beliefs assume a perfect world in comparison with which all religions are inadequate; no church can embody the Kingdom of God; no theology can convey the wondrous workings of God; no ritual can communicate the Divine Presence; no finite organization can reach infinite goals. There is always room for innovation, always an excuse for experimentation, always a just cause for a revolt against the status quo.

There is another reason why people might be discontented with institutionalized religion. For primitive man, the whole of life is capable of being sanctified: "all of man's organs and physiological experiences, as well as his acts, had a religious meaning" (Eliade, 1959:167). Modern man, on the other hand, lives in a partially desacralized world in which it is possible to speak of specifically religious institutions, institutions that are distinct from those of the family, the economy, and the polity. Where once holiness pervaded all things there is now institutional specialization. This creates the possibility of a clash between religious values and other values. The resulting compromise is always stressful for the Church, which, in the light of the universalism of its ideals, cannot be content with half-shares.

See outside

CONCLUSION

Religion demonstrates a meaningful relation between the values people hold and their general order of existence. Within the world view of religion, things do not merely happen, they happen for a reason. This is how religious beliefs and practices reinforce traditional social ties between individuals and help preserve the social structure of groups. Religion is also, however, a dynamic force; it is both a model of and a model for reality; it both communicates and constructs reality.

The motif of this book is religion in conflict and change. The most essential of all sociological concepts, institutionalization, will be used to order the discussion. Part II of the book deals with the creation of new religions and their gradual absorption into the social fabric. The functions of fully institutionalized religion are described in Part III. Part IV treats more specifically the role of religion in social change and the creation of new social forms. Part V considers the evidence for a decline in religion in modern Western societies and describes some of the responses the churches have made to changes in institutional strength.

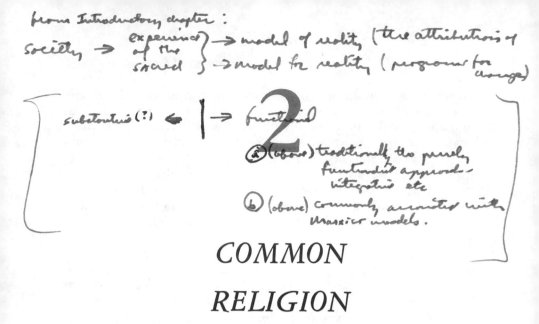

from Introductory chapter :

society → experience of the sacred } → model of reality (the attributions of → model for reality (programme for change)

substantive (?) ← | → functional

(a) (above) traditionally the purely functionalist approach - integration etc

(b) (above) commonly associated with Marxist models.

COMMON
RELIGION

Sociologists see the world in terms of rules, roles, and relationships. As a consequence, they tend to see religion as a social institution in which people occupy religious roles. Furthermore, they are inclined to think of religion as an institution that influences and is influenced by other social institutions. Unfortunately, this is a rather mechanistic view of human society. Society is not a machine and religion is not a distinct or absolutely separable part of it. Instead, religion pervades society. The sociological idea that religion is a distinct part of society seems to reflect the model of religion propounded by churchmen themselves, which categorizes people as members of this or that denomination or no denomination at all.

This "official" model is valid in many respects, but in it there is a rationality and neatness not found in real life. As well as being imposed from above in the form of creed and liturgy, religion emanates from below, in the form of folk practices and customs. This latter kind of religion does not conform to the tidy official categories and is not something one can join or organize. It is more like a "layer" of religion "beneath" denominational religion, a "subterranean theology" (Martin, 1967:74), a kind of "baseline of religiosity" that most people share whether or not they belong to a church (Towler, 1974:52).

The term "common religion" will be used to describe this phenomenon which is diffused throughout the population, permeating social divisions and denominational boundaries. Common religion belongs to *ºuning, Significance, values, upon the social order in which one lives)*

each and all. It may be used by anyone who wishes to do so, without official controls, supervision, or limitations on access. It grows informally, out of habit and custom, and is a matter of public talk and knowledge. It does, however, shade into the more esoteric expertise of occultism. Because of its ordinariness and familiarity, the common religion is taken for granted. Consequently, it involves little theology.

There has always been such a layer of religion. Even when church going was much more habitual than today and the established church was very powerful, common religion existed. Few Elizabethans, for example, questioned the influence of the supernatural upon daily happenings, even though many of them "regarded organized religion with an attitude which varied from cold indifference to frank hostility" (Thomas, 1973:204). Common religion is thus an enduring aspect of religion in social life, sometimes complementing, sometimes conflicting with, but most often simply ignoring the official religion.

It is not possible to say definitively where official religion ends and common religion begins, just as it is not possible to distinguish once and for all between official medicine and folk medicine. And yet, the distinction is real and helpful. Describing the more important features of common religion will demonstrate why.

THE CHARACTERISTICS OF COMMON RELIGION

Common religion is an umbrella term that covers beliefs and practices normally referred to as "magic," "witchcraft" and "superstition." These terms will be used in the present chapter because they are so familiar, but a word should be said at the beginning about how they will be used. In the past, much effort has been expended on distinguishing magic from religion. Why, then, include magic in a book on religion? The reason is that in many ways the distinction between magic and religion is false and misleading, the work of churchmen rather than sociologists. It has been the custom of churchmen to label as magic or superstition those practices of which they disapprove and over which they have little control. In this way, they have been able to stigmatize as nonreligion anything that threatens their monopoly over access to the sacred. In a sense, then, no belief or practice is intrinsically magical. Rather, it becomes so if the churches so define it.

This can be illustrated by looking at the readiness with which the Church has rejected the "magical" use of its ideas. For example, faith healers who imply that good health flows automatically from prayer, and who use magical practices such as stichomancy (cutting the Bible), are condemned as modern witches, for they deny that the cure of illness is a matter of faith mediated by the Church. The same attitude is taken toward the practical advice dispensed by inspirational writers such as Norman Vincent Peale, who seem to imply that material benefits and peace of mind can be achieved by right technique, without the help of the Church.

The Church has traditionally been more sensitive to the practice of white magic than black magic (Thomas, 1971:305). Although black magic does harm, the Church has a demonology to account for it and to counter it. But the practice of white magic threatens the power of the Church by promising that benefits can be achieved supernaturally without the ministrations of the clergy. It is ironic that the Church has always condemned witches for their heretical beliefs and for their alleged attempts to set themselves up as alternatives to the Church, whereas the common people have rarely condemned witches for their heresy (of which they were probably ignorant), but have done so because of their supposed harmful effects. It is indicative of the difference between official and common religion that witches are bad in the official model because of their creed, and bad in the common model because of their practical consequences.

The meaning of words such as magic and superstition must, therefore, always be carefully interpreted: one must examine the context in which they are used. These words are often incorporated into the arsenal of religious warfare and used to condemn extra-Church activities. However, this is not to suggest that there are no differences at all between official and common religion. Some of these differences must now be described.

First, official religion is given coherence by theologies and liturgies. This is a feature common religion conspicuously lacks. Common religion is not thought to stand in need of the kind of rationalization the theologian gives to official beliefs. For example, most of those who read astrology columns feel no need to know the complicated system of astrology on which the columns are based. Second, common religion also lacks a dualistic sense of there being a distinct transcendental world apart from this mundane existence. It is characteristically immanental, insofar as the spiritual is incorporated in persons, objects, places and organizations. Its orientation is exclusively toward this world and its practical problems.

Common religion finds value in the ordinary and commonplace things of everyday life.

The Jesus watches, key chains, T-shirts, yo-yo's, and bumper stickers, the religious comic books, aerosol 'Spray-a-Prayer' cans, and 'Day-Glo', velvet pictures of Jesus in the garden illustrate the disposition of popular Protestantism to sacralize practically everything . . . The extra-ecclesiastical nature of popular Protestantism is reinforced gy the portability of popular hymns, artifacts, and literature. Plaques and plates reading 'God Bless Our Home' easily adapt to the life-style of a mobile society ('God Bless Our Mobile Home,' 'God Bless Our Camper'). Picture postcards cross the country telling the legends of the 'Flowering Dogwood Tree,' the 'Crucifix Fish' and the 'Sand Dollar.' Bedspreads portray the Ascension of Jesus into Heaven . . . In various stages of planning and construction are at least five Disney Promised Lands where, for up to ten dollars a soul, you can pet the animals in the Ark, applaud the Biblical marionettes, ride an elevator up and down the Tower of Babel, spend the night at 'The Inn' and thrill to the thirteenstory fiberglass statue of Jesus Christ. (Elzey, 1975:742–743)

Third, common religion lacks the exclusivism and particularity the official model encourages. The beliefs and practices of common religion are not thought to stand in need of systematization, or of the resolution of the absolutely right and wrong way of doing things. The idea of orthodoxy plays less of a part in common religion, as does the idea of sole truth. For this reason one can practice common religion without feeling obliged to leave one's church. For example, of the subscribers to *Gnostica* (a magazine dealing with occult matters) only nine percent are not members of an orthodox church, and eighty percent subscribe to orthodox ideas about the Divinity (Hartman, 1976). Fourth, the common religion contains no overarching ethical scheme. Concepts such as judging God, and heaven and hell as places of reward and punishment are not a salient part of it. In the common religion, error rather than sin is to be avoided.

These differences should not be overdrawn. Common religion is not merely a "bundle of superstitions." It is easy to demonstrate that beneath the formal creeds and liturgies of the official religion is an informal religion which has its own coherence. A glance at some of the features of common religion will show how.

Although well-developed ideas of evil, such as "sin," are all but absent from the common religion, ideas of a moral balance do play a part. This is obscured in that magical ideas are largely mechanistic. For example, much magic works on the principle that things are separated or joined together by virtue of their intrinsic properties. But magical rites using this principle usually have a moral purpose underlying them, and a faith in that moral purpose guarantees their efficacy. Common religion thus helps order the world morally. This is evident also in working class ethics based on the assumption that we are "not so much . . . all children of God (though a form of that is there, in the background) as . . . we are all in the same boat together" (Hoggart, 1958:98).

The belief in ghosts or spirits is part of common religion. About a quarter of the American population believe they have seen a ghost (Greeley, 1975:36), and such beliefs would seem to be of a rather ad hoc kind. However, even the belief in ghosts is tied into a grander scheme of things. It is quite common, for example, for ghosts to be regarded as exemplary figures pointing out some unrequited crime, or as avengers readjusting some balance of honor. Such ideas clearly indicate that a function of belief in ghosts is one way of dealing with the guilt of unfulfilled social obligations. The belief in ghosts and like phenomena declines, not in the face of scientific challenge, but to the extent that dying comes socially disengaged. The more the young and middle-aged liberate themselves from emotional dependence on the old, and more dying itself becomes bureaucratized in retirement homes, hospitals, and funeral parlors, the less pervasive the belief in ghosts and spirits will be (Blauner, 1966:382). Belief in the spirits of the dead, a belief that is sometimes reduced to the level of a curiosity, is part of a moral universe. Ironically, the Church fosters not only a belief in ghosts but also the belief that ghosts have moral significance, because it is prone to interpret the sighting of ghosts as Satan-inspired, and to practice exorcism in the face of it.

The borderline between official and common religion is indeterminate and constantly fluctuating. A practice that from one point of view is merely superstition might appear from another point of view to be part of a larger scheme. For example, astrology, which was finally separated from orthodox Christianity only at the end of the seventeenth century, *can* be seen as proof that God works through the stars (Fischler, 1974:284). Many practitioners of common religion have no difficulty in seeing themselves as engaged in the more personalized and detailed specification of the principles of the official religion. For example, modern fortune tellers use selected objects to convince their clients that they are indeed in contact with the supernatural, and many of these objects are familiar artifacts from the official religion. "Religious statues and pictures of Christ and Mary are displayed in some offices; 'holy water' is sometimes sprinkled upon the customer as he leaves the office" (Tatro, 1974:296). Here, the practice of common religion, more adaptable to changing individual needs than the official religion, borrows some of the coherence and continuity of the more rationalized model.

Both black and white magic (and the distinction itself) rest on the assumption that there is a link between guilt and misfortune in the social world, which suggests, of course, that the universe has a moral order. It is more typical of the personalized world of common religion that good and evil are poorly developed concepts and are defined more in terms of *intention* than in terms of abstract, universal ethical categories, but a moral order is nevertheless discernible.

A distinction can be drawn between the more pragmatic, and manipulative and technical common religion on one hand, and the more elaborate cosmological schemes of official religion on the other, which enjoin the believer to petition or supplicate rather than manipulate. It is more typical of common religion, for example, that the correct utterance of a spell guarantees results. But magic is not solely technique. There is much room in magic for the wilfulness of spirits (who might take personal conduct and intentions into account in exercising their power), and there is also room for competing, evil spirits, whose countervailing power might again depend on the moral worth of the individual. Although less rationalized, then, common religion does perform many of the same functions as official religion, perhaps for different people and certainly in different ways. Common religion is best thought of as a complex of beliefs and practices, some of which are similar to, and some of which are wholly distinct from official religion.

THE VARIETIES OF COMMON RELIGION

In its more formalized aspects (such as witchcraft, magical arts, and occult practices in general) common religion merges imperceptibly with official religion. In its ideas of luck and fate, where the workings of the universe are opaque indeed, it merges with folklore. Common religion can best be conceptualized as a continuum marked by increasing complexity, greater rationalization, and growing abstractness.

At the lowest level of common religion are those efforts to organize the environment, to make a unity of experience which are prompted by the disquiet aroused by anomalies (Douglas, 1966). This level embraces not only a concern with luck and coincidences but also more elaborate beliefs—sea monsters, abominable snowmen, parapsychological events, and unidentified flying objects (Truzzi, 1974:630). Such beliefs are widespread: 54 percent of the American public and 15 per cent of the British population believe the stories of flying saucers visiting this earth (Gallup Poll, 1974). This level also includes the use of herbs, patent medicines, aphrodisiacs, and other substances that contain an element of nonrationality (Lewis, 1963:10).

The second level consists of the "extra-scientific technology" of astrology, hexing, palmistry, numerology, charms, waterwitching, and so on. This level is not only more elaborate (signs have to be interpreted by experts), but also more open to initiative on the part of the individual.

The third and most elaborate level includes beliefs in supernatural forces and spirits, the use of systems of ritual magic and witchcraft, the use of "official" religion in magical ways, such as cutting the Bible. Included also at this level are the practices associated with official religion, such as church attendance, and beliefs associated with the official teachings, such as the belief in God, which are given a personal interpretation by common people.

These various levels all manifest the essential characteristics of common religion. To show how, it is convenient to begin with that kind of common religion which is closest to the official model, church attendance and orthodox belief. It might seem perverse to begin a description of unofficial religion with a discussion of highly orthodox practices. But appearances are often deceiving, and it cannot be assumed that people go to church or hold supernatural beliefs in exactly the manner prescribed by the official model. Unfortunately the data on this level of common religion are poor. While the records on who practices religion are quite good, what is not clear is the meaning of these practices to those involved.

Church Attendance and Rites of Passage

Going to church (or its equivalent) at least once a week is part of the normal life of about half the American population. The figure, which has risen steadily during the twentieth century, presently stands at 40 percent. There are interfaith differences in this practice: 55 percent of Catholics are weekly attenders compared with 37 percent of Protestants and 16 percent of Jews (Gallup, 1975:3).

Not all kinds of people are equally likely to be regular church attenders. Women are more frequent and regular churchgoers than men, blacks more than whites, married people go more often than the single, the inhabitants of small towns and villages show higher attendance rates than city dwellers; high-status people are seen in church more often than those of low status. Churchgoing increases steadily with age until physical disability sets in, at which point, attendance declines. Similar demographic profiles are not available for the United Kingdom, but there is no reason to expect major differences. As in the United States, there are denominational differences in church attendance rates in the United Kingdom. Only 16 percent of the Anglicans (who make up 64 percent of the population) go to church at least once a month, compared with 45 percent of the members of the Free Churches and 73 percent of the Catholics (Butler and Stokes, 1969:125).

These variations in attendance reflect the impact of major social forces on religious practice. The higher attendance rates of women, the middle-aged and the married reflect the influence of the family on churchgoing, and in particular suggest that the church is seen as a general socializing agency for the children (for more on this see Chapter 12). The rural/urban differences, besides reflecting the greater impact of modernity on the cities, also shows the extent to which regular churchgoing is tied to the life-style of the stable, close-knit, homogeneous type of community (see Chapter 9). Higher rates for the black population reflect the traditional importance of the church in that community. The different attendance rates of high- and low-status people are difficult to interpret. Doubtless, the higher rates of the middle class reflect their greater propensity to become involved in voluntary associations in general. However, the exact meaning of such attendance rates is not clear at this time. This topic will be taken up again in Chapter 11.

Although weekly church attendance is the practice of a minority of the population of both the United Kingdom and the United States, in any given year nearly everyone participates in some kind of religious service. Thus, in the United Kingdom, where only 15 percent of the population attend church weekly, a further 40 percent go to church at least once a month (Martin, 1967:43). In the United States 40 percent of the people attend church weekly, while 95 percent attend services occasionally (Glock and Stark, 1966:236). Many people are occasional attenders, going to church when they feel a personal need. Many others, not conscientious in their Sabbath observance, nevertheless accept invitations to baptisms, marriages, and funerals officiated by the Church.

The willingness of people who are otherwise unreligious (by the official model) to solemnize life-passages is nothing new. It was noted as long ago as the eighteenth century that many more people availed themselves of church weddings and funerals than attended church regularly. The majority of people have always seemed readier to believe that the Church should provide benefits than to believe that it should impose duties. When people draw on the Church to mark life-transitions in this way, they are drawing on beliefs and ideas that they have rarely examined or seriously considered and that are only vaguely in tune with orthodox Christian doctrine. Baptism has always had "superstition" attached to it, perhaps because people feel the burden of moral responsibility for others keenly and they are anxious about securing the baby's future. There is a widespread belief that an unbaptized child has been deprived of something and will experience misfortune in later life (Sissons, 1973:260). Fichter (1951:37) observed that dormant Catholics still followed the practice of having their children baptized. Indeed, parents who omitted having their children baptized were subject to greater sanction by other Catholics than those who failed to attend Mass. The marriage ceremony also has "magical" aspects. The ring, used to symbolize union and possession, also serves to protect against infidelity: losing the ring is thought to bring bad luck. The persistence of funeral rites reflects the need to "do the right thing" for the deceased, in regard to whom some barely conscious feelings of guilt might be held. Although 25 percent of his sample did not believe in life after death, Gorer (1965:33) found that 98 percent buried their relatives to the accompaniment of religious rites. Such rites of passage are clearly a part of the common religion as it has been defined here, and their observance bears little resemblance to the image conveyed by the official model. Most of this behavior, being motivated more by vague feelings of "luck," "insurance" and social obligation, is rationalized at a fairly low level of sophistication.

Religious Beliefs

Religious beliefs are distinguishable by their assumption that there is a reality that does not belong to this world but nevertheless affects it. The belief in some miraculous guiding Force, Being, or Principle behind the working of the universe appears to be ubiquitous. More particular beliefs, such as the idea that there is life after death, or the idea that there is a Paradise awaiting sojourners here on earth, or the idea that there are spirits and demons at work in everyday life, are found with less consistency but are nevertheless widespread.

Although these popular ideas appear in a certain form in the official religion, they are not necessarily part of a rationalized cosmology, and they are therefore legitimately considered part of the common religion. Like church attendance, the affirmation of belief in a supernatural world is a folk phenomenon and does not necessarily have the theological significance attributed to it by the official model.

The conviction that there is a God, or First Cause behind the workings of the universe, and to whom mortals are accountable, is an established part of Western culture. It is officially represented in Christian and Jewish teachings concerning God the Father, Creator and Preserver, but the common people have long adhered to some such notion without necessarily having learned Christian or Jewish teaching.

The countries of the modern Western world differ quite widely in the proportion of their populations affirming a belief in God, ranging from 94 percent in the United States to 65 percent in the Scandinavian countries; the United Kingdom, at 76 percent, falls between these two extremes (Gallup, 1976:13). Woman are slightly more likely than men to believe in God, and the belief is more widespread among the old than among the young (Gallup, 1976:12) and more common among lower status groups (Maranell, 1974:62). The impress of social forces on religious belief is clearly discernible here. Belief in God is more widespread among the less secure social groups, such as the poor, older people, and women.

Reluctance to affirm the existence of a Supreme Being does not signify a lack of any supernatural beliefs. A 1968 survey of the English population discovered that 37 percent held a personalized image of God, but another 42 percent believe that there is a Life-Force, Spirit, or Principle running events (*Independent Television Authority*, 1970:16–20). This probably explains the differences between Southern Baptists and Congregationalists in the United States. Ninety-nine percent of the former group but only forty-one percent of the latter affirm the existence of God (Stark and Glock 1968:28). However, the Congregationalists, rather than denying the existence of any supernatural guiding force, are probably rejecting the implied personalism in the traditional conceptualization of the Diety and affirming instead of belief in God as Principle or First Cause.

Rather surprisingly, belief in life after death is less common than belief in God. Seemingly, many people use the concept "God" not to make a supernatural reference at all, but to refer to a Force or Principle. Apparently, many people are able to believe in "God" without also believing in the possibility of eternal life. A firm belief in life after death is held by 69 percent of the American population, and a further 11 percent are unsure. In the United Kingdom, 43 percent firmly believe, and a further 22 percent are unsure (Gallup, 1976:17). Not surprisingly, belief in immortality increases with age (Stark, 1973:54).

The official model—for instance, the orthodox Christian teachings on the after-life—uses concepts like purgatory, heaven and hell to describe life beyond the grave. There is considerable variation in belief even within official Christianity—Fundamentalists still tend to believe in hell as an actual place, whereas Modernists are more inclined to view hell as a state of mind—but there is even greater variation in the minds of the people for whom these ideas have an obscure and uncertain place. Among the English, the hold of orthodox ideas about heaven, hell and Judgment Day is weak. Only 18 percent of the population believe there is such a place as hell. Those who believe in heaven picture it in rather unspiritual terms that seem to owe little to theological teachings. One of Gorer's (1955:257) subjects saw heaven as a world "more peaceful than the present one with no cold wars, or washing up. I hope there will be animals, music and no towns: a kind of ideal earth in heaven. I hope everyone will be able to remain at the age at which they were happiest on earth." An archetypal symbolism runs through people's ideas of heaven, where "natural beauty prevails, the opposites are harmonized and change is brought to rest" (Blum, 1970:63). This symbolism owes little to the official model of religion although it does not contradict it. In America, belief in both heaven and hell is more widespread, but the discrepancy remains. Ninety percent of the population believe in heaven, but only seventy percent believe in hell (Alston, 1972a).

Just as the belief in some kind of ultimate motivating force, or Godhead, is common, so is the belief in an ultimate source of evil. Indeed, handling the problem of evil could be said to lie at the core of all religion. The personification of God and triumph of monotheism in the Judeo-Christian tradition demanded a complementary Prince of Darkness to explain suffering and sin, and the figure of Satan, God's grand cosmic antagonist, plays an important part in the official model. The idea is also present at the more popular level in the fascination with possession, exorcism and the diabolic, as well as in the folk beliefs about evil Spirits and Forces influencing everyday life. The hold of the official model is uncertain about half of the American and one-fifth of the English population believe in Satan (Harris, 1974; *Social Surveys*, 1974) which suggests that the need to personify evil in traditional terms, or balance the idea of God or Creative Source with a diabolic Force is now rather weak. Later on, some of the less rationalized explanations for evil will be described, but at this level, at least, such ideas are not very important.

It comes as no surprise to learn that more people believe in heaven than in its logical counterpart, hell, or that more people believe in a personal God than in his natural antithesis, Satan. Nor is it surprising that there is little consistency between belief and practice. For example, 25 percent of those who believe in the Deity, never pray to him, and, conversely, 25 percent of those who do not believe in the Deity, *do* pray to him! (*Mass Observation*, 1948:53). It is a feature of common religion that it lacks the rationalized dogma and creed of official religion: it has no overall logic or symmetry.

Common religion shows all sorts of inconsistencies of this kind. Private devotionalism, for example, is much more widespread than some of the more superficial measures of religiosity would indicate. In the United States, where only 40 percent of the population regularly attends church, all but 4 percent occasionally pray (McCready and Greeley, 1976:77). The same is true of the English, of whom 15 percent attend church weekly, but 43 percent pray regularly (*Social Surveys*, 1965:46). Nor is religiosity confined to those who are members of a denomination; 39 percent of Americans who are *not* church members believe in life after death (Hyanson, 1975), 20 percent believe in heaven (Alston, 1972a) and 20 percent feel they have at one time been "in the presence of God" (Vernon, 1968a:222). Religious practices clearly do not fit the neat and tidy official model of religion. Furthermore, the practice of common religion, although it bears surface similarities to the official model, does not always carry with it the significance attributed to it by theologians and priests. People bring their own, personal meanings to official observances. This can be seen more clearly in the second level of common religion, the "parasitic vagaries of popular devotion" which are an accretion to official religion, added to it by the people for their own use (Thomas, 1973:305).

ACCRETIONS TO OFFICIAL RELIGION

Common religion consists, in part, of those aspects of official religion which are treated in a magical way. Durkheim (1965:49) noticed that there are many religious rituals which "work by themselves, and their efficacy depends upon no divine power, [for] they mechanically produce the effects which are the reason for their existence." Official religion is most likely to be treated in this magical fashion where it is immanental, fatalistic, and where practical needs are brought to bear on it. Magical ideas have long been associated with the Catholic Mass, for example, because the Catholic laity has connected the theology of transubstantiation with folk ideas about the pronunciation of words that effect a change in the character of material objects. Magical ideas also occur in the religion of nominal Protestants. Pope (1965:87) reports

> a strong admixture of magic . . . in the popular religion of the Mill workers [of North Carolina]. They trust devoutly in the power of prayer to get results and believe that the results will be precisely those they pray for. . . . When petitions are granted, they mark well the ritual by which they were made; a group of men in one church believe that prayer at 'the white spot'—a bare place in an old field—has special efficacy, and go there frequently to pray.

The magical treatment of religious ideas is also found in attitudes toward the clergy. Smith (1968:183) describes various Victorian beliefs about the supposed magical power of the clergy, one of which is that the right hand of the bishop is lucky, the left unlucky. The Catholic priest is especially subjected to such treatment because of his singular status as a celibate, his special training, his use of a foreign language, and his elaborate dress. Catholics have also been prone to treat their saints in a magical fashion, regarding them as particular helpers offering special miracles.

Common religion is also represented in the popular inspirational literature, which is a modern form of the magical treatment of religious ideas. This literature is devoid of theological content: there is no dogma, no doctrine of salvation, no prophecy, no concept of sin, and no denominational discipline. God is a beneficent force, to be harnessed by the use of right technique to solve practical and interpersonal problems. There is little reference to God's will because this implies a gap between a knowing ruler and an unknowing subject, a gap that does not answer the everyday practical needs of the readers of the literature. Instead, the unity of man and the divine, and the possibility of unmediated contact with power and knowledge, is promised—much in the manner of the technician.

The inspirational literature reduces God to a resource and religious practice to a technique. Norman Vincent Peale, for example, offers a kind of spiritual technology: he instructs his leaders to "learn to pray correctly, scientifically," and urges them to employ "tested and proven methods." The thing to be avoided is not immorality or bad conduct, but "slipshod praying." Schneider and Dornbusch (1958:68) underline the magical character of this religion. It provides "a set of things to do which may be done on occasions when 'one's heart isn't in it.'" Peale thus transforms spiritual problems into problems of technique, and the Bible becomes a manual. Peale's teachings are a popularization of the core of Puritanism, an intense moral zeal for the regulation of everyday conduct. He has reduced this core, however, to a "catchpenny opportunism" tuned to immediate practical problems largely removed from ultimate values (Bell, 1976:59).

Peale has a black counterpart in Dr. Frederick J. Eikerenkoetter, II, better known as "Reverend Ike," who teaches "self-confidence and self-reliance" to the black community by using much the same ideas as Peale. The Reverend Ike mixes more obviously magical ideas, such as the use of "prayer cloths" for healing purposes, with more orthodox religious ideas about salvation by faith and the material benefits of right thinking (Snook, 1973:86). Both Peale and the Reverend Ike display the contractual attitude toward the Deity so typical of common religion—the idea that if the individual keeps his side of the bargain, the Deity is bound to keep his.

One aspect of the teaching of both Peale and the Reverend Ike is faith healing. Faith healing is in some respects a legitimate part of the official model, but it is also a manifestation of the common religion, for the means used do not always conform to the official rules. Working on the vague borderline between orthodox religion and "magic," faith-healing revivalists such as Oral Roberts and the late A. A. Allen have cleverly exploited the potential of the electronic mass media in building a vast personal following (Harrell, 1971:33). Denying that ordinary doctors can cope with the demons who cause sickness, they teach that miraculous healing is a major "gift of the spirit," one that can and should take place frequently.

When they proclaim the immediate, almost automatic effectiveness of their ministrations, popular faith healers make highly questionable interpretations of Christian teachings, which emphasize more strongly the necessity of faith before healing can occur, and admit more explicitly the possibility that a cure will be denied. The most successful of the faith healers manipulate official teachings in order to reflect more accurately the practical, everyday needs of their listeners. They transform faith, or belief in impossibilities, into a cause: having sufficient faith will cause the desired result. It is for this reason that Oral Roberts can successfully initiate a "blessing-pact plan" in which he offers "to earnestly pray that any gift given to his ministry will be returned 'in its entirety from a totally unexpected source' " and to promise that "if, after one year, this has not happened, he will refund you the same amount immediately and no questions asked" (Harrell, 1973:31). In 1964, A. A. Allen began selling pieces of his original revival tent, which he called "Prosperity Blessing Cloths," with the promise that they would bring healing and economic security to the purchaser (Morris, 1973:31). The numerous faith healers in the United States, constitute a vibrant and popular part of the common religion. They have their own "house organ" (*The Voice of Healing*), an informal network of professional relationships and an immense following. By means of the mass media as well as their continuing tent and stadium revivals, they reach many people who are untouched and unmoved by the orthodox denominations.

BELIEF SYSTEMS SEPARATE FROM OFFICIAL RELIGION

The miraculous cure of illness and supernatural assistance with the solution of personal problems exist on the margins of official religion. However, they are also associated with witchcraft, which is clearly outside the official religion. The late 1960s and early 1970s witnessed a considerable renewal of interest in witchcraft and magic—part of a general "occult revival," the social significance of which is not yet clear. What is clear, however, is the willingness of the public to give credence to occult techniques and practices, and its continued fascination with the esoteric.

Alfred (1976:180–183) provides an excellent descriptive summary of witchcraft in the United States today:

The contemporary practice of witchcraft in the United States is arrayed along two orthogonal dimensions. First there is a continuum between the practice of black magic and the practice of white magic. Although witches of either stripe generally make more of this distinction than is warranted, there are some genuine differences. Practitioners of black magic are more willing to employ their arts for ends regarded as evil by the surrounding society, consider themselves more in league with demons and dark spirits, and call more upon satanic tradition for both ancient technique and the legitimation of modern innovation. White witches and warlocks (the technical term for male witches) are careful to dissociate themselves from magic employed for any but supposedly beneficial ends, ritually protect themselves from the influence of evil demons (even when these are invoked for the performance of certain functions), and call more upon the European witchcraft tradition, which seems to be an underground survival of pre-Christian paganism and nature worship.

At right angles to this dimension is a continuum involving degrees of organization. At one end, we find individuals (with perhaps a small, local, and informal following) practicing magic as a folk craft. At the other, we find organized groups practicing canonical witchcraft according to a specified tradition. Among white witches who practice individually are those who have earned or learned their witchcraft status through kinship with or apprenticeship to another solitary witch, those who have picked up the art from reading or more tenuous media contact, and those who have "invented" their practices, usually inspired by highly visible cultural archetypes and often with the aid of psychedelic drugs. . . . Typically one finds them casting spells for the health and success of family and friends and celebrating nature festivals, such as plantings and harvests, and astronomical and astrological events, such as new and full moons, new years, solstices, equinoxes, eclipses, and the appearance of comets. . . .

Organized or canonical white witchcraft groups are usually called covens and consist theoretically of precisely thirteen members, although they usually range from ten to fifteen. Estimates of the number of these groups in the United States today range from fifty to three hundred. . . .

Those involved in black magic include solitary Satanists who believe they have made a pact with the Devil. Relatively unorganized black magic groups include not only sexually oriented groups but also the highly publicized, though rare, Acid Satanists of the Charles Manson variety. Such groups are almost completely nontraditional and revolve around the hypnotic or charismatic nature of the cult leadership.

Truzzi (1972:26) estimated that the number of witches in the United States in 1970 was about 3,000, although he notes that "the popular interest of the general public toward this kind of occultism is very superficial." Witches, and those who consult them, can stand for all those who sustain an interest in the esoteric, including those who concern themselves with astrology, divination (for example, the I Ching, Tarot), fortune telling and so on. No doubt Ellwood's (1974:192) skeptical remarks that most occultists are merely "thrill seekers" rather than people seriously interested in sacred concerns contain some truth. Nevertheless, the evidence of sustained concern suggests more than a faddish curiosity.

Those who serve as modern shamans also include astrologers. Astrology is based on the assumption that "the stars have special qualities and influences which [are] transmitted downwards upon a passive earth" (Thomas, 1973:337). There are four spheres of astrological activity:

1. general predictions
2. nativities—telling an individual's character or fortune on the basis of the structure of the heavens at the time of his or her birth
3. elections—choosing the most propitious moment for action
4. deciding guilt, responsibility, or blame.

Astrology is appealing because it projects the unresponsive, absurd side of society onto the heavens, and because it firmly locates the person in the center of the universe. It is a mixture of fatalism and free will that symbolizes the relation of the individual to society. "Inasmuch as the social system is the 'fate' of most individuals independent of their will and interest, it is projected upon the stars in order to thus obtain a higher degree of dignity in which the individuals hope to participate themselves" (Adorno, 1974:20).

Interest in astrology is quite pervasive in the United States, especially among women and the young. Three quarters of the population know their "sign," and 22 percent actually believe that astrological predictions are accurate (Gallup, 1976b:27). About four in ten of those between 21 and 30 claim to have at least a fair amount of knowledge of astrology (Wuthnow, 1976:159). Most people today obtain their astrological guidance from newspaper horoscope columns (the first of which appeared as long ago as 1642 [Thomas, 1973:406]) or women's magazines, but specialist horoscope magazines also sell very well.

The astrology column is an example of "secondary superstition," in that the individual has no primary experience of the occult, which is mediated by the newspaper and by the professional (Adorno, 1974:14). The typical astrology column dispenses rational advice (where rationality means making the best of prevailing conditions for one's personal interests) according to a system that is "entirely abstract, unapproachable and anonymous" (Adorno, 1974:20). The column contains no theology, no "solemn speculations about the fate of mankind at large," but concentrates instead on practical, interpersonal problems, all of which can be surmounted "if only one chooses the right time" (Adorno, 1974:43). Astrology is not fatalistic, because it always leaves the ultimate choice to the individual. Rather, it reifies the irrational, opaque and anonymous forces of society in the concept of fate, while assuring the reader that these forces need not be threatening—as long as the advice of the column is followed. Although devoid of metaphysics and grand ethical systems, astrology is quite capable of dealing with the inconsistencies of existence. For example, the contradictory requirements of social life—

conflict and harmony—are dealt with by the simple expedient of "distributing these requirements over different parts of the same day" (Adorno, 1974:43). The reader is thus enjoined to be aggressive in the morning, and loving and companionable in the afternoon; in other words, act in a certain way when the time is propitious for doing so.

Not enough is known of the extent of astrological beliefs in the United States and what part they play in everyday life. However, Greeley (1975:11) has investigated what he calls belief in the "paranormal," which includes belief in the ability to fortell the future by supernatural means. He discovered that 30 percent of the population had "often," or "several times," had feelings of déjà vu, 32 percent felt that they had achieved mental communication with someone who was far away, and 12 percent claimed to be clairvoyant. It should be noted that the individual who claims to be clairvoyant is also likely to be the person who claims to have had feelings of déjà vu (in other words, the above percentages are not cumulative). Greeley's data describe only those who have actually had paranormal experiences, not those who are willing to believe others have had them. If this latter group is taken into account, the number of people willing to believe in the paranormal must be quite high. Clearly, such experiences hover on the borderline between official religion and what is labeled magic. Greeley found that people who had such experiences were slightly less likely to go to church than the average American, but slightly more likely to hold orthodox beliefs.

Common religion operates at the level of astrology, palmistry, and clairvoyance. This level also includes the modern shaman, or healer. Much like the "cunning man" of old, this person, who is known as an "adviser" or "conjuror," works for a fee and intervenes with the supernatural forces on the client's behalf. Hill (1973:851) reports that healers are still active among the rural black poor, offering cures for burns, toothaches, warts, back pains, intestinal disorders, dizzy spells, and so on. These "root doctors" sell amulets or "mojos" that cure or ward off spells or curses; they even sell "court spells" to be used to obtain favorable trial verdicts (Whitten, 1962). Forbidden to write down their knowledge, these conjurors are an important part of black oral tradition. This folk religion is not confined to rural areas, however, for blacks who migrate to the cities preserve such beliefs as that

> the dead can return to the living in spiritual visitations that are not necessarily ill-intentioned or dangerous. Children born with teeth or as twins come under an ominous sign. Conjuring is the cause of insanity. Many maladies must be attributed to the insertion of a snake in the human body by a conjuror in the service of some enemy. Frizzled chickens should be kept to dig up any conjure bag an enemy may place near your house (Genovese, 1974:217).

Healers and advisers are also consulted by whites who need help with interpersonal problems, such as a drunken husband, a faithless wife, a difficult child, or an unjust employer. The cure of psychosomatic illnesses caused by worry over some personal problems usually involves the identification of the evildoer who has put a "fix" on the victim. The cliente has probably already defined her complaint as "unnatural" and therefore incurable by normal means (Snow, 1973).

Fate, Luck, and Omens

Common religion converges with the kinds of beliefs that refer to fate or luck. Strictly speaking, official religion, with its well-developed ideas of human responsibility and divine will, is antithetical to ideas such as luck, but everywhere they exist side by side. Such beliefs help bridge the often wide gap between religious principles and everyday needs. Superstitions, for example, are a subtle combination of supernatural forces at work in the world, on the one hand, and human instrumentality on the other. They consist partly of "avoiding actions," which "prevent a magical effect" (Mauss, 1972:58), such as not walking under a ladder, and avoiding polluted or unlucky days and numbers; partly of cleansing actions, such as throwing salt over the shoulder after it has been spilled; and partly of protective actions such as touching wood. Omens, such as having a black cat cross one's path, or breaking a mirror, seem to admit of no human intervention (except that one should be very careful after they have appeared), although they can be contradicted by other omens. Popular acceptance of omens gradually shades into beliefs in "pure luck" or a fate that is "blind." At this level, only the slightest hint of a moral order is present, and the idea of human responsibility has all but disappeared.

Common religion can be described, as above, as a continuum moving away from the more rationalized and general belief systems of the official model. All common religion is characterized by a focus on the immediate, the detailed, the practical, and the personal. A mixture of knowledge of natural processes, traditional religious ideas, and folklore, common religion is oriented above all else to practical needs. Operating beneath official religion—which, although it offers eventual and total release from world suffering, gives little comfort and guidance here and now—common religion works because only the religious virtuoso could consistently relate the grand scheme of things devised by clergymen and theologians to daily problems. Most people, if they are religious at all, are religious in a personal, practical sense. Uninterested in rational systematization, they are influenced by religion "because of their mundane expectations rather than because they have any concern with great religious ideas" (Bendix, 1962:92).

Common religion finds its purest expression among social strata who are governed by practical needs, but for whom irrational forces render life circumstances unpredictable. The lack of individual power among these strata "contributes to the massive survival of beliefs in fate, in luck, in a universal moral homeostasis and in superstitions of every kind" (Martin, 1969:177). It is significant that superstitiousness varies inversely with social class (Maranell, 1974:163). None of this is surprising. The culture of the lower strata is everywhere "dense and concrete," geared to a life "whose main stress is on the intimate, the sensory, the detailed and the personal" (Hoggart, 1958:89). These lower strata probably have had some experience of the Church (as children), they have formed a clear image of the Church and its function in society, and they hold some kind of religious belief and engage in private devotions. But they do not identity with the official model, with its formal ideas of commitment and obligation and with its predominantly middle-class mores. Working-class people, though not avoiding the great themes of existence, such as birth, sex, and death, are not concerned with becoming involved in associations organized around them. Working-class culture, like common religion, is not so much unreligious as unidealistic, its horizons confined by the demands of expediency.

WHAT IS THE FUNCTION OF COMMON RELIGION?

Despite the consistent emphasis on the practicality of common religion in this chapter, we must not forget that common religion makes reference to the supernatural. Common religion has two functions—to do something and to say something. In order to understand how this is so, we must look in more detail at how common religion works and in what situations it is used.

Common religion, as described in this chapter, is so heterogeneous that a complete description of its structure and function is out of the question here. The focus of the ensuing discussion will be upon what is referred to as magic, as a kind of archetype of common religion. Mauss (1972:63) described magic as "a gigantic variation on the theme of the principle of causality," and set out to abstract from the various manifestations of magic its principal varieties. He uncovered three "laws" upon which the practice of magic is based.

1. CONTIGUITY. This law states that "things in contact are and remain the same." It follows that the part (for instance, teeth, hair, or nails) can stand for the whole person; that the whole can be detected in the part (for example the hair of a man contains his life force, the bones of a corpse contain death); and that power is contagious (for instance, a man is to be "found" in the food he has left, in the clothes he has cast off, in the bath water he has used, or in the house he has occupied).

2. *SIMILARITY.* This law states that like produces like. It follows that supernatural power can "leak" from object to object if they are similar. The use of dolls and drawings of people in casting spells upon them indicates that the likeness need only be schematic or conventional. When objects are chosen for their similarity, only a particular quality will be relevant. For example, a lump of clay might be chosen for its softness, its pliability, its color, its coolness, or when fired, its hardness.

3. *OPPOSITION.* This law states that like drives out like in order to produce the opposite. For example, water might be used to drive away rain and bring the sun.

Each of these laws is an example of the principle that the subjective association of ideas reflects an objective association of facts. The association of ideas is not random, but part of the received tradition. For example, for any given ritual it will be known in advance just *which* quality of clay is relevant, and the effect of the magical transference is similarly known. Thus, the hardness of clay might be used to suggest a cure for the spine of a client, but it is not supposed that he will become hard all over. In magical rites, "two objects are seen as having resemblances and differences and an attempt is made to transfer the desirable quality of one to the other which is in a defective state" (Tambiah, 1973:222). Magical association applies not only to objects but also to words. This is evident in the inspirational literature cited above according to which bad thoughts produce bad health and good thoughts produce good health.

Common religion focuses sharply on achieving material results through the kind of techniques illustrated above, and in many respects bears striking resemblances to secular technology. Both magic and technology are directed at practical problems, both are based to some extent on experience and experiment in the natural world, and both assume some kind of mechanical cause-and-effect relationship in their operations. Indeed, some practitioners of common religion feel a greater affinity with science and technology than with religion. For example, many astrologers, particularly those practicing professionally, do not regard their profession as being within the province of the 'occult.' Instead, they argue that "astrology is a science, open to all who wish to study it, and not secret, mysterious or 'occult' " (Hartman, 1976:178). In the same fashion, not all dowsers see themselves as magicians; they prefer, instead, to use a scientific theory, such as magnetism, to explain their results. Those who consult dowsers, for their part, are probably as mystified by the theory of magnetism as they might be by magical lore.

These similarities between magic and technology are described in order to emphasize the fact that for most people common religion merges with the secular and mundane world of the scientist and technologist. Yet, the function of magic in society cannot be reduced to that of a mere variant on technology. To say that people often adopt the same attitude toward magician and technologist is not to say that these two individuals work in the same way. The practitioners of magic do not attribute immediate causal significance to a given practice. They do not argue that their various actions "make" rain or that their spells can make a person fertile in the same way that cooking transforms food. Magical action is always mediated by another reality.

Both magic and technology use analogical modes of thought—but the modes are different. In magic the rites conducted are "performative acts" by which a property is "imperatively transferred to a recipient object or person on an analogical basis" (Tambiah, 1973:199). In science, analogy is used merely to make known instances serve as models for incompletely known phenomena: it is used as a basis for making predictions which are then tested experimentally.

Although magic may be a mode of thought separate from technology, in one important respect it is still oriented to the same kind of problem—the reduction of cognitive anxiety and the production of material results—and this is the clue to its first function. Magic is appealing because of what it promises to do. Nothing could be further from the truth than to claim that magic is a kind of false or naive science. As shown above, magic works according to its own laws, and these do not contradict but can coexist with scientific laws. However, people resort to magic, as to science, when they feel unable to control their environment. Thus, those in hazardous situations are more likely to practice magic. For example, superstitious beliefs are more common among lobstermen, whose livelihood and personal safety are constantly at risk, than among textile workers (Poggie and Gersuny, 1972). They are even more common among fishermen who have spent a long time at sea (Poggie *et al.*, 1976). Astrological interest is more common among the lonely, those having problems at work, among those in poor health, and among those troubled by the death of a loved one (Wuthnow, 1976, 162).

According to this model, magic and technology are both resorted to in the same situation—that of uncertainty and stress. But they do not compete with each other, and it is possible for magic to accompany technology. It is quite common, for example, for water witching to be practiced at the same time that geological surveys are being conducted (Vogt and Hyman, 1959:189). Magic will tend to play a greater part if a single important decision is being made (rather than a series of minor, trivial choices). In such a situation, magic clearly functions on the same principle as the toss of a coin: to alleviate the anxieties caused by having to choose between two equally attractive (or unattractive) alternatives. In this important sense, then, magic appeals because of what it is thought to do.

Another function of magic is that it *says* something. Two themes that run through all common religion are power and classification. Magical rituals, for example, both do things and say things. Common religion is not a bundle of superstitions and left-over pagan practices bearing no relation whatsoever to social structure. Ideas about magic, magical power, and magical persons all say something about social structure. Common religion is something people use to think about their society. Thus, it is no accident that witches are stereotyped as old women, for being old and female is an ambiguous social category that is considered threatening to the social order. In the same way, the idea of fate conveyed in astrology columns symbolizes the interdependence of anonymous social forces against which people must somehow make their way. The "superstitions" attached to rites of passage demonstrate the individual's continuing need to mark these important life changes. The advice and guidance of the healer reaffirms social obligations and symbolically restores just social relationships, giving stability and coherence to social interactions for people unsure of their rights and obligations.

Magical practices both say and do. The performance of magical rites before an event does not necessarily mean that the practitioners believe that the rites cause the event. Rather, such rituals say something about the event, as grace before a meal indicates that the meal is about to begin. Many superstitions are chiefly a way of saying that the individual is in control; they do not necessarily hinge on the idea that they produce an outcome. This is one reason why magical practices are judged not so much in terms of their proven results as in terms of their validity, their correctness, or their legitimacy. The conditions of their performance—their structure and style—is as important as their perceived effect.

A great deal of common religion "is an attempt to force experience into logical categories of non-contradiction" (Douglas, 1970a:192), to fit life, as far as possible, into categories with which men and women have grown to be comfortable. Much of the "magic" and "superstition" has this affirmative character, restoring order in the midst of apparent chaos. However, reality will not fit so neatly into the categories which humans would impose upon it. Bits and pieces of reality are always ambiguous with regard to human logic—and this is the source of another kind of fascination present in common religion, the positive attraction toward anomalies and abominations which is present in much witchcraft and magic and a great deal of popular religion. But the function is the same, for even the latter helps mark off the anomaly as something special, even something sacred, and thus guarantees more forcefully that things are as they seem and that an order does underlie the universe.

CONCLUSION

The object of this chapter has been to describe the common religion and to try to account for its appeal. Although common religion is situated "beneath" the official religion of churches and memberships, it is partly manifested in orthodox measures of religiosity such as church attendance, denominational membership, and belief in the supernatural. On the assumption that it would therefore be wrong to portray common religion as being apart from the official religion, some data were presented on patterns of attendance, membership and belief.

Common religion is chiefly situated, however, at the level of "low" culture or everyday life, where the practical demands of specific situations have created a complex of beliefs, convictions, and practices both public and private. The theme that runs throughout this complex is that of classification: events and people are given order and placement—right and wrong, good and evil, cause and effect—in categories that have emanated from the people rather than from those seeking authority over them. However, as Weber pointed out long ago, there is a chronic tension between official and common religion, which is due to the individual's constant tendency to rationalize his classifications into an all-embracing cosmology. The official religions seek to either de-legitimate or co-opt the common religion. Nevertheless, the common religion persists, because of the necessary interstices between the religious principles of the theologian and the practical, everyday demands of the individual.

Part II

THE
GROWTH
OF RELIGIONS

3

THE

SEEDS OF CHANGE

INTRODUCTION

The second part of this book describes how new religions come into being, how they grow and in the process help change society. Sociologists have learned that social changes have their origins on the margins of society, in the less visible noninstitutional sphere of social life which is not publicly legitimated or rewarded. It is here that deviant, genuinely transformative ideas and practices will be found, and the transformation of consciousness, which is the beginning of all new religions, is made possible.

Normative, institutionalized religion contains little potential for really fundamental change. The Church, by virtue of its indispensible association with an infinite, "other reality," is mystified by tradition and made impregnable by its association with sacred things. Religious institutions are perhaps the most enduring of all social institutions. Nor is common religion a source of fundamental change. Although it is deviant, it does not challenge the existing order; and although it can incorporate innovations (like television), only in a limited sense does it actually challenge the orthodox religions.

Because religious change begins on the margins of society, it is not easy to locate. It begins in the small and unstable groups and amorphous social movements that constitute the underground or counter-culture of religion. Some of these little groups are destined to cause major social changes; most simply disappear. What happens to those which do survive is the subject of the next six chapters.

The common religion described in the previous chapter is situated on the margins of official religion. Since it is from the margins of the normal that the abnormal and novel appear, it would seem reasonable to begin the search for the seeds of religious change there. However, much of common religion does not challenge official religion in any coherent way, but merely co-exists with it, a kind of deviant subculture loosely supervised by the churches. For example, something like astrology is used in an almost casual way to cure mundane problems and make normal life easier. It does not challenge the churches and its impact is chiefly a conservative one. The constant appeal of astrology columns is to find fault with oneself rather than with given social conditions. The rule of astrology is to adjust oneself continuously to the commands of the stars, the effect being "to enforce the requirements society makes on each individual so that it might function" (Adorno, 1974:35).

But although there is a conservative side to common religion, there is also an antinomian, liberating side. Common religion can be both comforting and challenging. We can illustrate this duality by using astrology again. Although it has a conservative side, astrology also provides an antirationalist, antipositivist sort of theorizing for those who are not content with the way things are. Innocent stargazing can take on a "clandestine aspect as occultist astrology in the doctrinal teachings of secret societies and esoteric sects" (Fischler, 1974:284).

When people begin to interest themselves more intensively in the occult, the enormous potential for change in religious systems becomes clear. Religion is concerned above all with power, variously called *mana* or *charisma*. Direct access to this power provides a shortcut to knowledge and leadership and thereby threatens the authority of the established denominations. In its most radical form, this means more than the opposition of one structure to another. Mana or charisma are, above all, antistructural: antithetical not to specific structures only but to "all that . . . holds people apart, defines their differences, and constrains their actions" (Turner, 1974:65). A search for the sacred is a search for *communitas*—total, unmediated relations between one individual and another. Laws are replaced, not by other laws, but by love. The experimental search for hidden knowledge conducted on the margins of the unknown (which makes up a large part of common religion) thus has enormous potential for change.

THE IMPORTANCE OF THE GROUP IN NEW RELIGIONS

Although new religious ideas and practices are born in the minds of individual men and women, religion is essentially a communal affair. Behind the faith of every individual believer is the cult. Thus, even the most radical and antistructural new religion gives birth to structure, however simple. Indeed, for most religious groups the period of anti-structure or *communitas* is very brief indeed. Laws are gradually devised to guide relations once governed by love alone and spontaneity is supplanted by discipline. A snapshot taken of the beginnings of religious change thus shows a world of "near-groups" or incipient religions which are amorphous, fragile, dynamic, and volatile.

The origin of all new religious groups is to be found in movements of dissent from established religion. These movements are found within all established religions, sometimes crossing and sometimes remaining within denominational boundaries. Not all of them seek to break away from or overthrow the existing denominations or fundamentally alter social behavior, but they might well give rise to more radical groups that do. These movements and near-groups have the important characteristic that they exist as religious phenomena in their own right, yet they also have the potential to develop into or motivate sectarian groups that desire absolute autonomy and challenge the established churches. In a sense, they represent a presectarian phase of protest. They dissent from the established churches but have not broken with them to form their own organization. Yet often they command loyalties and influence behavior as powerfully as autonomous groups. It is here that the seeds of change are to be found.

Four "primitive" forms of protest can be identified:

1. *Social movements* within a specific church, seeking to reform some particular practice or re-orient the church in its relation to a society. Examples are the Evangelical and Oxford movements in the Anglican Church, the Fellowship of Concerned Churchmen in the American Episcopal Church, and the Cursillo movement in the American Catholic Church. Social movements occasionally crystallize into parties, most often when the church in question is closely allied with the state.
2. *Religious orders*, which are groups of religious *virtuosos* who have voluntarily set themselves apart from the ordinary church member in an attempt to realize more fully certain values of the church. They are usually authorized by the parent church, but live under strict controls. Orders are reformist groups within the church, but their influence is limited.
3. *Collegia pietatis*, groups who desire to revive the church from within according to some principle they believe is shared by all sincere church members. Such groups have distinct separatist tendencies. Their members are likely to consider themselves a highly select group in the vanguard of the church. For its part, the church's elite is likely to try to control the group, either by ignoring it or by setting restrictions on its activities. The Charismatic Renewal movement in the modern Catholic Church and the Moral-Rearmament movement in the Anglican Church are two examples of such groups.
4. *Pan-church movements* which, rather than secondarily attracting followers from several different churches (as some of the above groups do), aim primarily to negate all denominational boundaries. This category includes

broad movements of opinion and thinking, such as the Fundamentalist movement.

Because all these groups operate on the margin of institutionalized religion, membership (if such a term is appropriate) can mean many different things. It might mean, for instance, that a follower of a party will leave one congregation in order to attend a nearby church of the same denomination where sermons more agreeable to him are preached; it might mean that a follower will spend more time working in the movement organization than on the affairs of her church; it might mean that an individual identifies himself primarily as a member of one of these near-groups and only secondarily as a church member. Needless to say, such attitudes can cause considerable tension within the church and do, on occasion, lead to schism.

Some idea of the kind of structural and ideological tensions involved in the formation and growth of near-groups, and some of the consequences of this kind of dissent, can be gained by considering an example of each in more detail. The following accounts are necessarily sketchy: the idea is to provide enough information about each kind of near-group to demonstrate the part it plays in religious change.

SOCIAL MOVEMENTS

The Oxford movement will serve to illustrate this kind of near-group. Although its origins lie in Victorian England, the effects of this movement are still visible in the Church of England and, to a lesser extent, in the Episcopal Church in the United States. The Oxford movement was sparked by the Electoral Reform Act of 1832, which had the effect of admitting more Catholics and Non-Conformists into Parliament and thereby bringing into question the propriety of having the Anglican Church under the dominion of the state. The major concern of the members of the Oxford movement was to free the Church of England from state control in a way that would not undermine the church's traditional role as spiritual leader of the nation.

The movement was not merely an effort at minor ecclesiastical reform. It was concerned, more than anything else, with returning to the kind of holiness, asceticism, austerity, and demanding discipline which the Church of England seemed to have lost. It was part of a call for self-denial and spirituality inspired by the Romantic Revival. Its opposition to the 1832 Reform Act was based not only on the Act's threat to the autonomy of the Agnlican Church, but also to its enfranchisement of the bourgeoisie, a class associated, in the Romantic mind, with materialism and modernism.

The wave of protest that began in the 1830's had all the features of a modern social movement. Its "propaganda" was broadcast in "Tracts for the Times," a series that began in 1833. Its leaders—Newman, Keble, and Pusey—were all charismatic figures heavily influenced by the heroic imagery of the Romantic movement. The "doings of the Anglo-Catholics were accompanied by unseemly and disgraceful riots in various places" (Neill, 1960:268). Many clergymen were tried in a blaze of publicity before ecclesiastical courts for allegedly Romish practices. Those convicted responded by rejecting the authority of the courts which, they argued, were an arm of the state rather than the church.

The Oxford movement originated as a reform movement within the church. However, it aroused the antagonism not only of Anglicans who feared the Catholic tendencies in the movement (the ornate ceremonial, the renewal of monastic life, the experiment in liturgy) but also of Anglicans who sought to prevent the further separation of church and state. This opposition, combined with Newman's studied indifference to social pressure, threatened for some time to bring about a formal break. Ironically, the departure of Newman to the Church of Rome prevented the break and ensured that the movement would remain part of Anglicanism.

The movement eventually settled down as a moderate, reform-oriented association of Anglican clergymen whose major goal was to fight for the independence of the church from the state and the prevention of its contamination by Evangelical ideas. It has since become more like a party within the Anglican Church. Its first party-like organization was the English Church Union, formed in 1860. The "high" Anglo-Catholic faction it still represents stresses not only formal, Catholic-like ritualism, but also a doctrine that the church is the Divine Society and not a mere creature of the state. It is opposed to the "Low" Evangelical Party. Party loyalties are reflected in the decision whether or not to wear vestments, in the choice of theological college and the "living" to which one is appointed. Anglican parishes are still identified as "High" or "Low." Party factionalism spread to the Episcopal Church in the United States, whose General Convention is the annual proving ground of party strength. The "High" American Church Union has been active in opposition to prayer book revision and the ordination of women.

Although religious parties resemble their political counterparts, the idea of a "loyal opposition" is not fully legitimated in religious organizations. For this reason, parties are unlikely to maintain a permanent organization unless, like the Church Missionary Society (which is "Low"), it serves an ancillary purpose. They are seldom cohesive or self-conscious enough to establish a permanent organization. Parties wax and wane in organizational strength as particular issues come and go. Party organizations may be set up during periods of great strife and they might well form the nucleus of a breakaway group. but generally they fade away once the controversy has died down. In the interim, party loyalties are kept alive through informal friendship networks, in the religious press, and in theological colleges.

RELIGIOUS ORDERS

The religious order is a near-group because, although it is oriented to changing the church (usually by attempting to reinstate tradition), it lacks complete autonomy or independence from the church. The religious order is

> an organization recognised by the church, either centralised and hierarchically governed, or locally governed but bound to uniformity of rule and observance, of priests, or laymen, or priests and laymen, or laywomen, who have committed themselves to the goals of the organisation and who live in segregation and community— the degree of which will vary between different orders—and who accept as binding on themselves more exacting moral injunctions than those propounded by the church at large (Hill, 1973b:21–22).

Religious orders nearly always originate as lay movements gathering around a religious virtuoso. Although an order is definitely reformative, it seeks reform by return to tradition. Its legitimacy rests on a claim to live by rules that have always been present in the church but that have lately been neglected. Its principal strategy is to isolate itself in order to be more authentically religious, thereby keeping alive the spirituality of the church. However, the order does not expect that all church members should imitate it and does not, therefore, recruit a wide following.

As movements of dissent within the church, religious orders occupy an ambiguous position. The church sanctions the order, thus showing its "appreciation of a virtue requiring acknowledgement," but also segregates it, showing its "apprehension of the disruptive nature of intense and concentrated charisma" (Shils, 1975:131). Not all movements are so authorized, and some become schisms—the Waldensians are a case in point.[1]

In authorizing a religious order, the church is institutionalizing reform within limits. How closely this reform is supervised varies from one case to another. The Dominicans and Jesuits are closely supervised,

---

[1] Peter Waldo petitioned the Third Lateran Council in 1179 for permission to preach repentence and apostolic poverty. Although a few years later a similar petition by Francis was granted, Waldo's was not. He nevertheless embarked on his mission of preaching and attracted a considerable following despite the church's vigorous opposition. Only a few Waldensians remain.

whereas the Cistercians and Trappists enjoy considerable freedom. Tension between the order and the parent church is almost inevitable, but an order is not sectarian, for its dissent is against the parent church only and not against the total society. The order has no desire to leave the church, but seeks to restore it. Furthermore, although both order and sect regard themselves as an elect, a gathered remnant, *the order tolerates a double standard of religiosity, and it is willing to admit that some will be saved outside the order.*

Church officials are presented with a delicate problem whenever they authorize an order. Unwilling to surrender their own control over religious affairs, they will seek to impose even greater controls on the activities of the order. However, these controls may prove so irksome to members of the order that they break away and attempt to form a new community or, indeed, break with the church altogether.

No new Catholic orders have been instituted for many years, but they remain a powerful force within the church and function as a legitimate source of criticism and innovation. Several orders, for both men and women, were established in the Anglican Church in the nineteenth century. They have been officially recognized by the church's hierarchy, but they are controlled quite closely. Although the stress on superior holiness remains in both Catholic and Anglican orders, these orders have more recently assumed special missions in more socially oriented fields, such as education, health, and welfare. In some respects, the modern counterpart of the religious order is the college campus and seminary, which are somewhat segregated from normal religious life and tend to be more reform oriented than the denominations.

COLLEGIA PIETATIS

New religious ideas are sometimes articulated by quite small religious groups that Wach (1962:174) refers to as *collegia pietatis*. Such groups form in protest against a compromise the church is alleged to have made with the world and aim at the reform of certain practices or the reassertion of certain principles. Although there is a tendency for members of such groups to see themselves as superior to other church members, *their desire is not to leave the church so much as to elevate it to their own standards.* They are the "leaven of the lump," the core of spirituality around which other, lesser church members are scattered. They differ from the religious order in their lack of toleration of a double standard of religiosity.

Collegia pietatis are dissent groups at the "presectarian" phase, during which "a movement is being called out, and its leaders have not yet worked out the implications of their activities" (Wilson, 1970:29). During this phase, the group is neither inside nor outside the church. The group itself, claiming to represent the central tenets of the church, is naturally opposed to leaving it. It is only when the opposition of the parent church is felt keenly enough for the group to begin vigorously defending its principles, followers and leaders that a sect is born. In arguing its right to exist, the *collegium pietatis* will emphasize the distinctiveness of its teachings, the autonomy of its leaders, and the independence of its members.

Many social movements (such as Holiness) have now entered the presectarian phase, and many sects (such as the Seventh Day Adventists) did, at one time, pass through it. A movement that seems to be passing into its presectarian phase today is neo-Pentecostalism, and its appearance within the Catholic Church can be used to illustrate this stage.

Groups urging a "charismatic renewal" in the Catholic Church began forming during the 1960s, having first appeared in the Protestant Episcopal Church in 1960. Members from these scattered groups came together for the first time in 1967, on the campus of Duquesne University. However, there was no real organization until the Charismatic Renewal Conference of 1968 (O'Connor, 1971:15). The movement enjoyed remarkable growth; the mere 100 attending the first conference expanded to over 22,000 at the 1973 meetings (Harper, 1974:322), which drew charismatics from approximately 1,250 separate Catholic Pentecostal groups around the country (Harrison, 1974a:50). In the same year, six percent of all Catholics polled reported having attended a Pentecostal prayer meeting in the last two years (Greeley, McCready and McCourt, 1976:30).

Catholic Pentecostal groups focus their devotion on the Paraclete (the Holy Spirit) and seek a return of the Catholic Church to the message of the Pentecost contained in the Scriptures. They believe that the gifts of the Holy Spirit are freely given to those who have sufficient faith. Consequently, their meetings center in the experience of spirit baptism and the signs following, such as speaking in tongues. They differ from traditional Pentecostalists in their more sedate behavior: there is less shouting, gesticulating, emotional display, and disorderly prayer in their services.

The neo-Pentecostals appear to be little interested in bringing about structural reform within the Church. In fact, they are quite conservative theologically and socially (Fichter, 1975:53). However, they are interested in obtaining greater freedom for the laity within the Church and in obtaining liturgical reforms that would facilitate the realization of individual spirit baptism by all Catholics. The Ambivalence of groups in the presectarian phase is clearly demonstrated here. The neo-Pentecostals have no desire to leave the Catholic Church. They are not the liberal middle-class Catholics who will leave the Church if it does not become more progressive, and they are not the traditionalist working-class Catholics who would rather leave the Church as it is. Instead, they seem to be devout Catholics who have rejected not so much the spiritual side of the Church (which they are trying to revive), but the social controls of the Church (which they are trying to break down).[2]

This ambivalence is reflected in their attitudes toward the Church and toward the groups they have formed. They remain loyal to the Church, being frequent attenders, and loyal to their priests, constantly urging one another to avoid elitism or separatism (Fichter, 1975:28). Yet nearly half of them admit that they would not obey a Bishop's injunction for them to stop their meetings, and their beliefs are quite heterodox, with a strong infusion of Protestant Pentecostalism.

These signs of disloyalty and heresy have, not unexpectedly, led many Catholic bishops and priests to look askance at the movement—but they too are ambivalent. The gifts of the Pentecost are clearly part of the Christian tradition, and in many ways the movement signals a commendable return to piety on the part of church members who are all too often rather unspiritual in their church affiliation. Yet the groups pose a real challenge to the authority of the priesthood because of their emphasis on the authority of the Scriptures (and not the priest) and their tendency to treat charisma as directly accessible (rather than mediated by the church). Although the Catholic Church has endeavored to play down the significance of the neo-Pentecostal groups, bishops have been forced to take a definite position regarding them. Most typically, they have sought to co-opt them. In 1969, the National Conference of Bishops decided that the movement should "not be inhibited but allowed to develop"—with appropriate pastoral supervision (O'Connor, 1971:21). A Charismatic Renewal Committee was formed in 1972, and the Church even set up a "charismatic parish" in St. Charles, Illinois.

"Tongues-speaking" groups have also appeared among Episcopalians, Methodists, Lutherans, Baptists and Presbyterians. These denominations, though being more receptive to such outbreaks on theological grounds, have nevertheless treated their appearance with caution. Whereas the Lutherans have applauded the zeal of the neo-Pentecostals, the Southern Baptists have taken a more negative position. For example, during 1975, assemblies affiliated with the Southern Baptist Convention were advised to either disavow or take disciplinary action against congregations and ministers who openly supported the movement.

A form of religious protest often confused with the Charismatic Renewal movement, but similar only in its presectarian characteristics, is the Underground Church. This is the name given to a loose association

---

[2] Harrison (1974a:51) estimates that half of Catholic Pentecostals are college graduates and just over half have professional or technical jobs. Fichter (1975:72) estimated that only three in ten Catholic Pentecostals are blue-collar workers.

of groups united in their protest against the social conservatism of the churches. They condemn particularly the churches' sluggish social action programs, the careerism of the ministry and the preoccupation of most laypeople with trivial organizational affairs. In response, the Underground Church groups encourage involvement in civil rights actions, liturgies in which laypeople participate fully, and worship that ignores denominational boundaries. Their prayer meetings feature "contemporary music, reading from Scripture and modern literature with discussion, impromptu prayers from the congregation, the Lord's Supper with a prepared or improvised Canon, a kiss of peace, communion with leavened bread and wine, and a concluding prayer and/or hymn" (Boyd, 1969:129).

Some of the ambivalence found in the Charismatic Renewal groups is also found in the Underground Church. Members do not see themselves as sectarian but as the nucleus of church unity and renewal. On the other hand, far from regarding themselves as marginal, they are inclined to dismiss church leaders as irrelevant. This kind of attitude is most threatening to the Catholic hierarchy, for the movement thus challenges the traditional authority of the priest and the bureaucratic discipline of the Church. Although group members might claim that the celebration of Mass in the home means a faithful return to the original community of the Disciples, it also means a loss of control by the Church's hierarchy.

The rise of the Underground Church in Catholicism can be traced party to the civil rights agitation of the 1960s, but its chief inspiration was the Second Vatican Council (Steeman, 1969). For many Catholics, the Council's proposals to replace Latin with the vernacular, offer Mass with the priest facing the congregation, have the congregation join in making the responses to the priest, and allow the Mass to be celebrated at home only opened the way to further changes. Underground Church groups also provide many Catholics with feelings of sharing and belonging not found in the modern parish (they are particularly common in urban areas where parish boundaries have become meaningless). Many Underground Church groups look upon themselves as a kind of floating ecumenical parish.

Underground Church members see themselves on the periphery of the official hierarchy, but they do not see questions of doctrine and authority as irrelevant—they have not withdrawn to their own private religion. They manifest a need for theological and liturgical exploration, for a more communal religious life, and for the greater social engagement of their church. The official church appears to them irrelevant, but not expendable.

Yet the Underground Church must pose a threat to the established churches because it tends to reduce the distinction between clergy and laity to one of different kinds of service rather than different positions in a divinely ordained hierarchy. In addition, by their own admission many Underground Church members, both Protestant and Catholic, feel "closer to Jews and humanists who share their commitment than to fellow church members who do not" (Boyd, 1969:xiii).

The Underground Church has never explicitly set out to replace the established denominations, partly because it is opposed to all structures, which it considers irrelevant. Its protest has been more indirect. "The disillusionment with the institutional Church has produced an unwillingness to deal with it" (Boyd, 1969:125). The Underground Church probably appeals because of its marginality, its attempt to synthesize the old and the new, its attempt to make novel use of traditional symbols without altogether losing sight of their older meanings. It has been more progressive than neo-Pentecostalism and more prepared to see the Church as "historically conditioned, imperfect morally and religiously, a learning community being taught by the Spirit through continuing historical experiences" (Bianchi, 1970:31). But although more radical than neo-Pentecostalism, the Underground Church has shown no more signs of seceding. For example, at no time has it attempted to ordain leaders outside the Church.

For their part, the established churches have tried to co-opt the spirit of reform. They have set up coffee shops, communes, and community centers designed to appeal to younger people. Disapproved of by many lay people, these ventures operate on the periphery of the churches and function much like missions, which the churches (now focusing on the young) once sent out to the poor.

PAN-CHURCH MOVEMENTS

Pan-Church movements deliberately transcend denominational boundaries and challenge the elites of individual denominations in the belief that the principles for which they stand make such boundaries irrelevant. These movements occur on a larger scale than any of those discussed above, and, *although they do not form discrete organizations in their own right, they can provide the fuel for new religious groups.* A number of these movements can be identified, the first of which is fundamentalism.

Fundamentalism

Of all the divisions that separate American church people from one another, there is none as profound as that between the modernist and the fundamentalist (Wilson, 1968:103). The division has been strong enough to spawn many schisms. For example, the Presbyterians split over Fundamentalism in 1936, when the Presbyterian Church of America left the Presbyterian Church in the United States. The schismatics were themselves rent by Fundamentalism in 1937. The Presbyterian Church in the United States suffered another split over fundamentalism in 1973. Schismatic groups in Methodism, such as the Free Methodists, and in Baptism, such as the Conservative Baptists and the Regular Baptists, show that fundamentalism has been a divisive movement in those denominations also.

Fundamentalism is a pan-church movement in two senses which are common to all those described in this chapter: it seeks a return to basic principles; and it is associated with broader social concerns. Fundamentalism is an attempt to cleanse and purify the churches by reasserting the indispensability of certain "Fundamentals" of Christian teaching: Virgin Birth, Miracles, Satisfaction Theory of Atonement, Resurrection of Jesus, and Inerrancy of the Bible. As a formal statement of beliefs and a call for reform, the Fundamentals were first published between 1910 and 1913, but a groundswell of concern to restore the original teachings and oppose the modifications and reinterpretations begun by German Higher Criticism and evolutionism began as early as the 1870s. Fundamentalism was in many ways a grass roots effort to preserve and promote a particular version of Christianity.

Fundamentalism had achieved a wide following by the 1920's but its victorious temperance crusade probably marked the peak of its success, and the beginning of decline can be seen in the humiliation of the Fundamentalist William Jennings Bryon by Clarence Darrow during the famous Scopes Trial in 1925. It remains, nevertheless, a powerful minority movement in the churches. As a source of controversy, it is absent only in denominations which are so conservative as to admit no change whatsoever, or so liberal as to have no Fundamentalist members at all.

Fundamentalism is also a *social* movement. Its origins lie in the anxieties caused by the decline of white, Anglo-Saxon Protestant power which began in the 1890s and which were exacerbated by an influx of Catholic immigrants. It is also a counterpoint to the Social Gospel which modernist theologians supported so warmly (Cole, 1931; Furniss, 1954). In fact, Fundamentalism is incomprehensible without reference to the modernist and the kind of liberal social action programs he supported.

In contrast with Fundamentalists, modernists treat the Scriptures as largely mythological, seek to integrate religion and science, dismiss many of the reports of miracles as irrational, and warmly embrace the idea of the churches' social action programs. Modernists see their God as immanent in everyday affairs and their religion as grounded in the human condition rather than in some supernatural world.

The Fundamentalist movement as a whole has never separated from the established churches. Its ideas have been kept alive by small groups (often acting covertly), by periodicals, and, later, by loose associations of assemblies and ministers. By the 1920's, the Fundamentalist movement was strong enough to sponsor organizations designed to foster its ideals within Protestantism. Some of these organizations spanned the churches—the World Christian Fundamentalist Association (1916) is an example. Others spoke for the Fundamentalist cause within individual denominations—the League of Faith (1925) in Methodism, the New Testament Tract Society (1921) in the Disciples of Christ and the Bible Baptist Union in the American Baptist Convention. By the 1930s, the Fundamentalists had their own colleges, seminaries, publishers, and periodicals.

Since the turn of the century, almost all church conflict has pivoted on this Fundamentalist/Modernist axis. Marty (1970:178) believes that for this reason it is possible to speak of Protestantism as a whole having a "two-party system." Generally speaking, although the Fundamentalists have lately been in the minority, they have continued to be a source of considerable strife. The American Baptist Convention, for example, has almost been rent in two by this conflict. Between 1910 and 1920, in particular, "their disagreement extended not only to theological differences but also to the method of achieving denominational goals, the nature of the goals themselves and the particular personalities who should lead the denomination. It was during this period in the history of the Convention that a system of party politics almost reached the point of formal development" (Harrison, 1959:161). The Fundamentalist movement proved to be so troublesome to the Convention's elite that the Convention amended its bylaws in 1946. Thereafter, the number of delegates any church could send to the Annual Convention was contingent upon the percentage of the benevolent funds that the church contributed to the Convention. The Fundamentalists, who directed a high percentage of their funds to specifically Fundamentalist causes, such as missionary societies, were especially hurt by this move.

Since 1940, a growing differentiation has been taking place within the Fundamentalist movement, reflecting, in part, growing political differences. One segment of the movement, led by Carl McIntyre's Bible Presbyterians and loosely clustered together in the American Council of Christian Churches (1941), continues the strict Fundamentalism now associated closely with right-wing politics. A more moderate Fundamentalism, calling itself Evangelicalism in an effort to disassociate itself from the strident militancy of the conservatives, is exemplified by the Christian Churches, Billy Graham's Evangelical Association, and the Campus Crusade for Christ, and is gathered together loosely under the umbrella of the National Association of Evangelicals (1941). The Evangelicals are more open to cooperation with liberal churchpeople, they impose less rigorous standards of morality, and they are more intellectualist in their approach to Scriptural study. During the 1960s, a newer form of Evangelicalism arose, one that deemphasized Bible inerrancy and showed much greater concern for social issues. In reaction, the old guard Fundamentalists have become more defensive, quicker to withdraw from social involvement, and more pessimistic about the future (Marty, 1976:80–105).

This constant flux and ferment within and across the denominations reflects different interpretations of basic teachings and varying responses to social and political changes. It shows that religious institutions are in constant turmoil. However, much of this turmoil does not reach the level of formal separation, but remains relatively unorganized and unplanned—a matter of feeling and disposition as much as membership and commitment.

Holiness

Fundamentalism courses through the great majority of Protestant denominations and has provided the fuel for a great number of schisms. In addition, it continues to exert pressure for change as a movement in its own right. No understanding of modern Protestantism is complete without an account of its work. The same is true of the Holiness movement, which arose at about the same time as Fundamentalism. The Holiness movement teaches that the individual can be sanctified by salvation. Like the Fundamentalists, followers of the Holiness movement see themselves as reasserting an essential but neglected tenet of the Protestant faith. Initially, the movement received the endorsement of a variety of denominations, including the Methodists and Congregationalists. However, the very strong emphasis that Holiness preachers placed upon the possibility of absolute cleansing from sin through the salvation experience began to suggest to more orthodox church leaders the heresy of antinomianism and the movement was condemned. The result of this condemnation, as is so often the case, was the intensification of the conflict, and it was not long before autonomous Holiness groups began to form, a prominent example being what is now known as the Church of God.

Not all Holiness advocates left their denominations, however, and even those who did so have set up the most ephemeral of religious organizations. Holiness people reject formal association, exclusive membership and federal structures; *they continue, in short, to constitute a social movement rather than a denomination*. The Holiness movement, although spurned by many churchpeople, has been slow to take on the characteristics of a sect and it remains a near-group. The main reason for this is the intense individualism and subjectivism of the Holiness message, which demands no formal church structure. This means that to a large extent it can be ignored as a political force within the churches. The movement has coexisted with the churches for a long time, hovering rather uneasily on their boundaries. This is especially true in England where the Keswick Convention (founded by Holiness-influenced Anglican clergymen in 1875) continues to operate, neither a separate sect nor a part of the church (Warburton, 1969:137). The story in the United States has been rather different; there, separate Holiness sects have formed more readily, but the Holiness movement has not become confined to such sects.

The Keswick Convention has its American counterpart in the Cursillo movement in the Catholic Church. The Cursillo is a three-day weekend retreat during which thirty or forty people gather to talk, study, and engage in spiritual exercises with a view to obtaining emotional release and personal strength. Begun in 1967, the Cursillo has gradually emerged as a self-conscious movement with its own organization. It has the blessing of, but is also being watched carefully by, the Church's hierarchy (Snook, 1973:123).[3]

Revivalism

Revivalism has been an enduring source of reformism in the Protestant churches. *Although in itself it is a nonsecessionist form of protest* (Wach, 1962:159), *its influence has often been secessionist,* and it is responsible for the spawning of many new religious groups. Revivalism means both a return to religion and an awakening to religion on the part of those who were not previously church members. Revivalism has both a periodicity and a continuity. In other words, there are times when revivalist fervor sweeps the country ("Awakenings"), and periods in between, when mass evangelism is carried on almost as a regular form of worship.

There have been four Great Awakenings in the United States. Each centered around a theological controversy, each took place during a period of great social upheaval, and each is associated with the work of one or two charismatic figures.

The Awakening of 1725 to 1750 was sparked by the infusion of Arminianism into the strict Calvinism of the original American settlers.

---

[3] Pentecostalism has more readily spawned sects. Neo-Pentecostalism has exhibited a similar tendency. One example is the Christian Growth Ministries, which sponsors an extensive teaching organization. CGM began as a pandenominational Pentecostal movement, but it has gradually crystallized into a separate organization with its own team of evangelists and "shepherds" who function like pastors.

Preachers such as Jonathan Edwards and George Whitfield taught that salvation was attainable by faith and that true religion was an essentially emotional, "heart" experience. Their message appealed particularly to the lonely, hard-working, illiterate frontiersman and filled a need for emotional expression, individual comfort, and pragmatism that was not met by the traditional Churches.

The Awakening of 1800 to 1835 spread the Arminian theology of heart religion into the growing cities. Its most prominent evangelist, Charles Finney, saw the corruptness of the new cities as stemming from individual sin and sought to return his listeners to a more pious way of life. Finney spoke against the evils of the developing industrial revolution with its emphasis on credit, profit, and impersonalism. He contrasted plain, simple Christian living with the cosmopolitan, skeptical, impersonal, and amoral life of the big city.

The Awakening of 1875 to1914 saw the revivalist movement really reach the cities. Dwight Moody began his revivalism in England in 1874 and attracted audiences of thousands night after night in successive campaigns. He returned to America in 1876 to repeat his success in cities such as New York and Chicago. Moody managed to transfer the excitement and drama of the frontier to the new frontier—the city.

Moody's message was a simple one: crime and unrest were increasing because the nation had turned from God; the established churches were of little help because they had compromised too much with the world and had forgotten the message of individual redemption. Moody urged abstinence from the habits of the city—dancing, theater going, immodest dress, drinking, and swearing—as part of the preparation for salvation. In many ways, Moody sought to *return* to the old frontier and rural life; he "took little heed of the fierce complexities of the industrialised world" in which the old ways were becoming increasingly redundant (Weisberger, 1966:230). Moody probably appealed most to recent migrants to the city who were anxious about the loss of small-town values.

The Third Awakening was furthered by Billy Sunday, who began to attract large big-city audiences in 1910. Sunday preached a gospel entirely free of modernism or the Social Gospel, and firmly linked Fundamentalist Protestantism to the central American value of self-reliant individualism. He thus spoke attractively to those who were anxious about the growing twin powers of monopoly capitalism and trade unionism. His message, like Moody's, was that the necessary return to the old, simple ways would be effected by an awakening to the redemptive power of Jesus Christ.

The Fourth Awakening began in 1945 and lasted until about 1960. The greater sophistication of the mass media meant that this Awakening was associated much more vividly with the name of a single figure, Billy

Graham, than previous Awakenings, but other preachers, such as Oral Roberts and A.A. Allen, also played a part in its growth. Those same media opportunities, and the adroit use of advertising, enabled Graham to address huge audiences. His 1954/1955 English campaign drew 2.75 million people, and in 1957 he attracted 2.0 million in New York alone. Graham's campaigns are famous for their careful advance planning, bureaucratic organization and exploitation of the mass media, but the message is much the same as in previous Awakenings—a return to the unchanging fundamentals of the Christian faith is necessary to alleviate personal and social ills. Evangelists such as Oral Roberts and A. A. Allen have introduced a greater emphasis on faith healing than Graham (betraying their Pentecostal backgrounds), but otherwise their message is identical, and they may well have been more successful in their sustained evangelism in reaching large numbers of people. Each has been able to build an organization of complexity and wealth that rivals Graham's (Morris, 1973:5; Harrell, 1975:58).

Revivalism warrants treatment as a single movement throughout American history because certain themes have endured. Let us briefly consider six of these themes.

INDIVIDUALISM. Revival religion speaks to personal woes and personal salvation. Listeners are urged to look inside their own souls, to assess their own spirituality in the light of what they hear, and to make their own decisions for Christ.

EMOTIONALISM. Revivalism is a religion of the heart, not of the head. Conversion is an emotional experience. Only a little of the intense emotionalism of the old frontier camp meetings has disappeared.

MORALISM. Revivalism teaches that the Christian life must be lived. The quest for redemption means recognizing one's sinfulness and following the path of righteousness despite all temptations. Others should be judged by their intentions, not by their status, and by their morality, not by their learning.

CONSERVATISM. Revivalists seek a return to fundamentals. They preach reform, but they are restorationists. Change is suspect, new ways are unpopular.

NON-DENOMINATIONALISM. The revivalist ignores denominational ties and regards church membership as irrelevant to the attainment of salvation. Revivalists do not dismiss the established churches altogether. Indeed, they seek their support and endorsement and urge their listeners to attend the church of their choice, but it is the Church, mystically conceived, the body of saints, that is most real to them. Revivalism transcends denominationalism: it has become "a national religion without destroying either the technical separation of church and state or the independent self-government of the individual denominations" (McLoughlin, 1959:523).

There has long existed a tension between revivalism and the denominations: revivalists have occasionally been anticlerical. But in the main, revivalists have preferred to ignore the churches rather than attack them, seeking to channel church members' excess religious energy into moral crusades against social evils that can be run on a nondenominational basis. Thus, revivalism has long been associated with mission work and with agencies such as the YMCA, which are also run on nondenominational lines. For their part, the established churches have looked upon revivals with mixed feelings. Some ministers have objected to the threat to their authority over their congregation posed by the charismatic figure of the evangelist; other ministers dislike the idea of promising listeners direct, unmediated access to God, which seems to make the priest superfluous; and others feel that congregants who have attended a revival campaign will never be able to settle down to the routine of weekly services. Many ministers have welcomed the revivalist, however, especially if they share his fundamentalist leanings.

THE EVANGELIST. Although revivalism in the United States is associated with famous names such as Whitfield, Finney, Moody, Sunday and Graham, the revivalist movement is populated with hundreds of itinerant evangelists. Revivalism is intrinsically bound up with the figure of the evangelist—he or she is indispensable to the successful revival. On the other hand, it is not true that the evangelist alone makes the revival. Finney was not successful until he was in his fifties; Sunday's popularity had waned by 1914, twenty-one years before his death; Aimee Semple McPherson spent seven fruitless years on the Eastern seaboard before making her successful move to California.

It is common to liken the evangelist to a salesman or huckster. Indeed, both Moody and Graham were traveling salesmen before they began full-time preaching, and without doubt the most successful revivalists have used many of the tricks and techniques of the successful circus manager. By their oratory and personal magnetism, evangelists help focus and give excitement to a revival campaign. On the other hand, the revivalist is an intermediary, more of a prophet than a messiah, interested more in listeners than in followers, content to inspire rather than govern. Thus, Graham refers to himself as "The Western Union Messenger of God," and Aimee Semple McPherson discounted her own importance by declaring, "I am only the office girl who opens the door and says 'Come In'" (quoted in Steele, 1970:21). For these reasons, evangelists are unlike sectarian leaders; although they are interested in reform, they are anxious to avoid separation. The long-term impact of revivalism is, however, often very different.

Revivals are powerful social movements, related not only to specific theological re-orientations, but also to major social changes. Revivals have led to major changes in the churches, have sometimes led to schism, and have also spawned sects seeking to carry on the revivalist fervor. However, modern revivalism has both a conservative and a radical consequence.

The response of many denominations to revivalism has been to seek to co-opt it, the result of which has generally been to eliminate its potential for change. Assuming that revivals do indeed reawaken religious fervor, many denominations have sought to use them for their own promotional purposes. In a sense, the very character of movements such as Methodism and the Disciples of Christ was cast by their birth in revivalism. For example, not only did the Methodists evolve the circuit rider system to sustain the revival-induced fervor, but they also stressed that ministers should be preachers first and foremost, and pastors only secondarily. Both the Baptists and the Disciples also exhibit signs of the influence of revivalism—their emotionalism, their emphasis on conversion, their camp meetings. Revivals also influenced the growing Holiness and Pentecostal movements, in which individual services as well as annual camp meetings continue to emphasize personal experiences, the quest to save individual souls, enthusiasm, intense preaching, salvation for all who seek it, complete reliance on a Bible literally true, frequent and involuntary motor activity, and the "presence" of the supernatural (Bloch-Hoell, 1964).

Co-optation has taken its toll on the spontaneity of revivalism. Even the Church of England and the Catholic Church have instituted week-long parish missions in imitation of the camp meeting, and many other denominations organize retreats in which the same influence is obvious.

Much contemporary revivalism functions quite explicitly as a "pump-priming" device for the denominations. Billy Graham's audiences are mainly white and middle class and already churchgoers (Whitam, 1968:118; Clelland *et al.*, 1974:49). In Graham's 1970 Knoxville campaign, thirty-one percent of his listeners came to the meeting as part of an organized church outing, and seventy-one percent were already church members (Clelland *et al.*, 1974:51). Of those making the "decision for Christ" in his 1957 New York campaign, 93.8 percent were already church members (Whitam, 1968:123). Clearly, a sizable proportion of Graham's converts, like many of the converts of Moody before him, are not new church adherents at all (McLoughlin, 1959:200).

"Pump-priming" clearly refers, then, not to the attraction of more church members, but to the evangelist's inducement of increased attention and heightened morale among those already in the church. There is little doubt that evangelists are well aware that they are not actually expanding the number of the faithful. Indeed, Graham has taken to calling for "rededication" and promising *assurance* of salvation. People who are already church members go to revivals partly because they function as a spectacle, providing entertainment on a fairly regular basis for those who feel they cannot attend the cinema or theater, partly because they provide an opportunity for emotional display and release, and partly because they function as a kind of rite of passage. On this last point, Wimberley *et al.* (1975:165) note that about three quarters of those who make the "decision for Christ" are in their teens or younger. It is possible that this event acts as a kind of confirmation service, watched over by proud parents.

Revivals have themselves become more and more institutionalized and more and more consciously managed.

> The essence of the old revival tradition can be seen in Jonathan Edwards' almost incredulous wonderment in 1735 at the 'surprising work of God' which brought about the conversion of many hundred souls in Northhampton in the opening phase of the First Great Awakening. Exactly one hundred years later Charles Finney wrote quite matter of factly after the stirring awakening in which he had participated from 1825 to 1835 that a revival "is not a miracle or dependent on a miracle in any sense. It is purely a philosophical result of the right use of the instituted means" (McLoughlin, 1959:85).

Finney's popular *Lectures on the Revivals of Religion* is less a work of inspiration than a handbook on revival technique.

The earliest explicit manipulation of the revival as a religious organization (rather than as something that just "happened") had a strong theological rationale. By Finney's time, Protestant theologians were arguing that the individual was not a passive, determined part of the system of nature, but "a free, rational, moral and creative cause" (Ahlstrom, 1975,I:510). The idea of instigating and directing the revival was thus legitimated. For example, Finney prolonged his meetings in order to generate emotional stress, used extensive advertising to ensure good crowds, deployed confederates in the crowd to urge hesitant listeners to the front and to act as examples, and invited converts into "inquiry rooms" after the decision for Christ had been made. Moody, who introduced many of the budgeting and administrative techniques of the corporate business, only continued this line of development. The revivalists of today have centralized control of finance, sophisticated accounting methods, highly specialized staffs, carefully planned recruitment programs, and skilled mass media departments (Winter, 1968:38).

Modern revivalism has in large part become absorbed by common religion. Organizations such as the Allen Revival Movement and Oral Roberts' Evangelical Association, using both the old-style mass meeting (now in football stadia) and the resources of television, sustain the religious life not only of the regular church member but also of those who rarely go to church. In this sense, revivalism speaks to the personal and immediate needs of those unwilling or unable to become part of organized religion.

Over time, then, revivalism has been partly co-opted and partly absorbed by the common religion and has thereby surrendered its potential for change. However, revivalism has always posed a serious threat to institutional religion—and continues to do so. The impetus for change in revivalism takes two forms: First, revivals dramatize and intensify theological debates, much as political demonstrations dramatize political conflicts. To attend a revival is to take sides in a religious issue. The revival is no mere show, but an enactment of firmly rooted beliefs, a statement of principle, and a declaration of faith. The revival is thus a source of polarization and mobilization, helping to organize and energize the contending parties in a dispute.

Second, revivalism is opposed to all organization. The evangelist attributes lack of spirituality to the stultifying effects of organized religion. Indeed, anticlericalism is only barely concealed beneath the surface of revivalism. The evangelists themselves are either not ordained at all (for example, Moody) or wear their ordination very lightly (Graham, among others). Many of the nineteenth century evangelists attacked the clergy as a class, decrying "hierarchies, seminary professors, dry learning, 'hireling ministers,' unconverted congregations and 'cold' formalism" (Ahlstrom, 1975,I:575). The evangelist is a populist, lauding the simple, unaffected and democratic religion of the common person against the "Godless religion in the Christless Church" (Morris, 1973:42). In turn, revivalists (especially those who conduct faith healing) have always been opposed by some denominations (and by many sects besides), by the medical profession, by local community leaders (who do not want "peace disturbed")—and even by the Internal Revenue Service.

The repeated revivals of the last three centuries have created many schisms. The Presbyterians have suffered especially from waves of revivalism, perhaps because the tension between their traditional Calvinism and the more popular Arminianism of the Baptists and Methodists was exacerbated by the evangelists' preaching. The Presbyterians divided in 1801 and again in 1837, and in both cases the occasion was a wave of revivals (Weisberger, 1966:41). Schisms occurred in English Methodism in 1818, 1819, and 1820, and in each case the spark was revivalism. The secessionists were poorer people warming to the evangelists' preachings against the cold formalism of the parent church (Currie, 1968:58). Revivalism has also caused schisms among the Baptists and the Congregationalists (Littel, 1962:35).

Revivalism can cause schisms to occur in already established denominations, but it can also lead to the formation of entirely new sects. Like the revival campaign itself, these sects show little initial interest in building up a permanent organization. Instead, they function as a kind of sustained camp meeting, offering a constant round of activities to maintain interest in and guarantee the effectiveness of the evangelist's message of personal salvation. Their overflowing and entertaining services, exciting and daring new evangelistic projects, and charismatic leaders contrast vividly with the perhaps rather boring routine of the regular denominations.

A sect born of revival crystallizes only slowly because the evangelist urges above all else individual sanctification. "If salvation may be attained by a 'Heart experience' what need could there be for bishops, priests, sacraments and ceremonial?" (Wilson, 1970:48). This means that an evangelist can attract a loyal following and build an effective organization without establishing an entirely new sect. Thus, Dwight Moody very nearly started his own sect, but stopped just short. Operating out of the Moody Bible Institute (organized by the Chicago Evangelization Society), Moody built an army of "gapmen" to fill the breach between the organized churches and the laboring poor they were not reaching. For reasons that are not clear, but that probably have to do with his favorable reception by the churches, Moody did not start his own sect. However, William Booth, who had much the same idea in England, did establish his own organization—the Salvation Army.

Whether or not an evangelist does found a new sect depends partly on his own desire for independence and partly on the attitudes of the leaders of the established churches. William Booth, who began his career in interdenominational mission work (as had Moody), found that although he was quite successful in attracting the unchurched, his efforts were either ignored or condemned by leaders of the established churches. Although reluctant at first, he was gradually led to see the need for an organization of his own. One of America's most famous women evangelists, Aimee Semple McPherson, followed a similar path. After some years of unsuccessful preaching in the East, she moved to Los Angeles, where in 1918 she established her Angelus Temple—a kind of permanent revival tent. As "pastor" of the Temple, she gradually shifted to a version of Pentecostalism she called "The Foursquare Gospel," but she still claimed to appeal to members of all churches. Gradually, however, she gathered a following loyal specifically to her and began to appear as serious competition to, rather than help for, the orthodox ministry. She maintained all the features of traditional revivalism—highly florid and dramatic revival meetings, faith healing, speaking in tongues, emotional display—and attained charismatic stature. She also gradually built up an organization that would promote her revivals. McPherson's expulsion from the Los Angeles ministers' association only formalized her break with the established churches; she had started her own sect, now known as the International Church of the Foursquare Gospel.

Revivals can lead directly to the formation of new religious groups, which usually consist of the following of a particular evangelist. The connection between revivalism and new groups may be less direct, however. Most evangelists have little desire to build an organization that will sustain the fervor they have created. However, the aftermath of a revival is a time of great religious unrest and speculation, and history has shown that it is also a time when many new sects appear. The origins of the Mormons, the Seventh-Day Adventists, and the Oneida Community can be traced with confidence to periods of revivalism. Moreover, growing sects seem to draw strength from the interest in spiritual concerns that the evangelist inspires. The spurts of expansion enjoyed by the Shakers, for example, coincide directly with waves of revivalism.

SCHISM

The concluding section of this chapter will describe the process of schism and specify some of the conditions under which it occurs. Not all new religious groups are the product of schism. Some are formed when people gradually drift away from a denomination only to regather later in another, independent sect. A helpful distinction is that between *secessions*, which are formal breaks, splits, or divisions within a church that lead to two or more different churches, and *offshoots*, which originate as the following of a popular preacher and which, although they might draw the bulk of their membership from a particular denomination, do not formally divide it (Currie, 1968:54).

Schism occurs when a minority group in a denomination comes to feel that the denomination is no longer pursuing the proper goals and that a break is the only course open to it. The schismatics usually charge that the denomination has become too worldly and unspiritual, but it is not unknown for groups to secede because they think the denomination has become irrelevant to social concerns. The actual issues over which separation takes place are usually organizational, for although disagreement at the level of general goals can be lived with, differences in regard to specifying means are harder to reconcile. Schism usually involves fundamental conflicts of values: they do not occur over novel issues, but result from the intensification of long-standing, perhaps inherent contradictions in a denomination's teachings. The factionalism which precedes schism probably occurs because people enter religious groups for very different reasons and read different meanings into their teachings.

Schism is rarely a sudden break. Rather it is the culmination of accumulated hostility and antagonism between dissidents and denominational leaders. Yet the actual break may take place against the wishes of both parties. The dissidents will feel no great urge for independence if they hold to the belief that people will be called out" at the proper time. They will not want to separate into yet another minority group if they feel their message transcends sectarian divisions (and, indeed, if like Theosophy they stress that they are *not* a sect, even though others so regard them). They will not seek separation if the very thing they abhor is the proliferation of denominations and the organization that attends it. And they will be reluctant secessionists if they remain firmly convinced (as do many Pentecostals) that their message is perfectly orthodox and not distinctive at all. Thus an early Pentecostal plaintively wrote, "We declared we were not a sect and not an organization, and then we turned right round and organized. Whether we admit it or not we in a measure are a sect. But that does not mean we are going to have a sectarian spirit" (quoted in Hollenweger, 1972:31). For their part, the denomination's leaders are placed in the dilemma of causing a break if they are firm in their control of deviance in the church or of losing control of the church if they are tolerant.

That schism can occur despite the wishes of the parties involved means that social structural forces play a large part in bringing about the actual break. Insofar as conflict is endemic to all religious organizations, the explanation of why schism, an actual breakdown of integration and consensus, takes place must lie in the structure of the group. The following considerations would seem to be important:

Schism is more likely when a denomination allows the formation of factions. In turn, the formation of factions is more likely when ties of kinship, community, and so on make themselves felt in the church and function as competing loyalties. Schism will then take place along kinship, community, regional, racial, or ethnic lines.

Schism is more likely in highly centralized denominations because the opportunities for grass-roots dissent *within* such denominations are limited.

Schisms are more likely when there is no charismatic leader. This is not simply because the charismatic leader acts as a unifying symbol, but also because the leader, being a kind of "totem" for the group, is the prize for which factions fight. As long as a faction retains its loyalty to the leader, there is little sense in leaving the group.

Schism is more likely when the structure of the group has not become encrusted in religious legitimation. Where organization is regarded as a mere expedient, its dissolution is not threatening.

Schism is more likely if the group has no deliberative assembly and no other means of institutionalized conflict. In the absence of such a structure, conflicts tend to escalate to a point where compromise is impossible.

Schisms are more likely when the denomination's elite vacillates in its treatment of the dissidents. Schism rarely occurs when the authorities act strongly to stifle all group dissent or when the denomination is so decentralized that there is hardly anything to break away from. If the elite engages in "erratic reformism," now ridiculing, now accommodating the dissidents, hopes are alternately raised and dashed, which gives rise to the greatest frustration and the greatest desire to break away altogether. Paradoxically, a weak elite will lessen the chances of schism because the dissidents will be confident of wresting power from within.

CONCLUSION

The subject of schism, open separation, brings this chapter to a close, because none of the groups described in it are separatist. The purpose of this chapter has been to describe the seeds of religious change. They are barely visible in movements and organizations such as those we have considered. Many movements and little groups soon die out. Others continue to operate as reform movements for some time, perhaps affecting some change through their constant agitation. Still others become semi-independent religious organizations, operating ambiguously on the margins of institutionalized religion. But no instance of actual secession has been described, for all of these groups stop short of complete autonomy. The next stage, that of the sect, is described in Chapter 4.

4

SECTS

Religious groups that secede or "come out" of the existing churches—and less commonly, groups that are formed of previously unchurched people—are referred to as sects. Although a sect is a specific group, there is also a "sectarian" orientation to the world, which denotes feelings of apartness, exclusiveness, total commitment, purity, and uniqueness. Sectarian attitudes are more common than sect groups. As the previous chapter has demonstrated, it is possible for a group to adopt sectarian attitudes toward their denomination and thus comprise a nucleus of especially highly committed members without forming an independent body (see Berger, 1958; Demerath, 1965; Dynes, 1957). Nevertheless, sectness is a property of groups and is not reducible to a constellation of attitudes. Demonstrating that sectarian attitudes are found among some church members does not deny the existence of sects as a distinctive type of religious association.

There is much debate about the true meaning of the concept "sect" and about whether or not this concept, taken from Christian ecclesiology, has any sociological utility (see Beckford, 1976; Eister, 1973; Goode, 1967; Johnson, 1963; Johnson, 1971; Snook, 1974). At the present stage of theoretical development in the field, the advantages of using it seem to outweigh the disadvantages, especially if the concept is kept simple.

Wilson (1970:26) has suggested that all groups called sects have the following characteristics:

1. They are joined on a voluntary basis. Commitment to sect membership is made of the believer's own volition. He is neither born into it nor forced to become a member. Joining a sect is not taken lightly, however, for it means a break with the ordinary and a deeper commitment to religious life. In turn, the sect is free to choose whom it shall admit, and is under no obligation to proselytize universally.

2. Becoming a member of a sect is conditional upon passing tests set by the sect. Some demonstration of merit—sufficient faith, knowledge, experience or ritual expertise—is mandatory for full membership.

3. Members of sects regard themselves as of superior spiritual worth and are exclusive. They see themselves as an elite group possessing the one true doctrine, and they exercise strict discipline over one another in order to ensure that members do not fall below the demanding standards set. Measures are taken to protect group members from worldly influences that threaten their spiritual purity.

Furthermore, sects strongly emphasize *communitas*, the ties that bind sect members together. These ties originate in common religious experience, not in functional necessity. This is true even if the sect is somewhat impersonal. *Communitas* does *not* necessarily mean democracy. In fact, many sects have strongly hierarchical power structures, usually controlled by charismatic leaders, and take the form of some kind of patrimonial community.

Sects are movements of social protest that reject the authority of established religious leaders (and sometimes the authority of secular leaders too) by claiming to have direct access to religious experience, knowledge or power. Sects condemn the established churches ("the Whore of Babylon") while claiming for themselves a divine mission and guidance. Most sects devise a method of obliterating the priesthood/laity distinction: the Disciples of Christ sought to make no man a priest; the Mormons made every man a priest.

The challenge a sect makes to the established churches is often implicit. Any group that, for instance, affirms the value of the "heart experience" or the "gifts of the Spirit" is proposing a criterion of spiritual worth over which the officials of the established churches have little control. The challenge may be unintended. Indeed, some groups seem to become sects in spite of themselves. They have no intention of establishing an independent church, but are forced into this position by the existing churches.

Although all sects are trying to bring about social change, they do not have to break absolutely with tradition in order to make their protest effective. Indeed, it is probably wiser if they do not. Typically, a sect, even while condemning established religion, will reaffirm some of the traditional ideals of the Church. For example, although the Shakers castigated the churches of their day, they traced their ancestry through the Quakers, the Cathars, the Waldensians, the Bogomils, the Manicheans—indeed, all the way back to the original Christian martyrs.

The rejection of the world and withdrawal are essential to sectness. A disgruntled minority removes itself from a "corrupt" and "complaisant" majority. Sect members typically separate themselves from others with respect not only to their religious beliefs, but also to marriage, friendship, work and play. However, this separation is always a matter of degree. Few sects demand absolute separation from the world. Christian Scientists, for example, do not spurn the material goals of this world, although they do advocate deviant means of securing them. Other sects, such as the original Baptists and the modern Jehovah's Witnesses, reject certain forms of church government while remaining indifferent to forms of secular government—except to the degree that they interfere with religious life.

TYPES OF SECT

Little of meaning can be said about the "chaos of cults" that make up the world of sectarian religion, until the various groups have been categorized. The most parsimonious way of doing this is to look at the teachings of each group and discover how it answers the fundamental problem, "What shall we do be be saved?" It is in the way they answer this question that sects

> necessarily establish their conception of the world and of the supernatural, and how to behave toward them. Their response to conditions reflects their response to this ultimate religious concern. Their doctrine, their social ethic, relations with other groups, posture to the outside world, and their conception of what is expedient to do in their meeting together reveal what the sectarians think is the way to be saved (Wilson, 1970:36–37).

On the basis of different conceptions of salvation, it is possible to distinguish seven types of sect.

Conversionist

Conversionist groups are convinced that the world is evil and that salvation can be achieved only through profound change in oneself—for instance, by being "born again." The purpose of this type of sect is to effect individual consciousness of guilt, bring about conversion, and secure redemption. The group tends to place most of its emphasis on proselytizing and its meetings are inclined to be emotional, because the desired end is, above all else, right feeling in the relationship between the worshiper and her Savior. Such "heart religions" tend to reject formal ritualism. Examples such as early Methodism and Baptism and, later, Pentecostalism and Holiness suggest that conversionist sects, in their heavy emphasis on the state of grace of the individual, are largely indifferent to social institutions. However, other examples, such as the Salvation Army, indicate that it is possible to combine an interest in individual salvation with an interest in social welfare.

The focus of conversionist sect life is the worship meeting. Conversionist sects stress preaching or "exhorting," because their chief objective is to bring about and sustain a change of heart, which requires an emotion-charged atmosphere. Although the degree to which worship services are characterized by emotional display varies, Holiness sects are not untypical. The meetings of these sects are remarkable for the form of the sermon and the singing that encapsulates it. The message of early Methodism was sung as much as it was spoken or read, and modern conversionist sects such as Holiness continue this tradition. In addition, the sermon, seldom written or prepared in detail in advance, serves as much to intensify emotion as it does to impart knowledge. Typically, the preacher begins in a normal conversational tone, introducing a passage from the Scriptures and elaborating on it so as to fit it to the circumstances of the congregation. Moving on to an application of the text to today's morals, the preacher begins to change voice and use a more dramatic, tense style. His words might now take on the cadence of a chant, rhythmically punctuated by audible gasps. As he reaches the climax of his delivery, the preacher may well become virtually incomprehensible, the chief impact being his emotional involvement and dramatic display. Toward the termination of the sermon, however, the preacher will begin to return to a normal conversational tone, using measured phrases to bring his audience down from their peak of emotional involvement. Throughout, the congregation will have been very active, crying "Amen," "Yes, Sir!." and "That's right!" They are active participants in the sermon, helping to create the close emotional bond and atmosphere necessary for them to "make their decision for Christ" or, through testimonial, to affirm their faith. In a sense, worship offers nothing new. "The congregation enjoys the sermon *because* it knows what is coming next," and in the emotional heat of the meeting it undoubtedly hears what it wants to hear (Rosenberg, 1974:145). The meeting concludes as it begins, with well-known, often repeated, simple, but attractive hymns that are appealing as much for their rhythm as for their music and words.

Several contemporary denominations, such as Methodism, Baptism and the Disciples of Christ, originated as conversionist sects, and many other religious groups, such as the Salvation Army, have been able to perpetuate much of their conversionist fervor. Conversionist sects continue to crop up. A recent example is the Jesus Movement, which began to appear on the West Coast of the United States in 1967, probably as a result of Pentecostal evangelizing among hippies (Petersen and Mauss, 1973:264). The Jesus People believe the world to be totally corrupt. In the words of one adherent, "America is on the road to Hell! The condition described in Revelation and Acts paints a pretty clear picture of America today" (quoted in Petersen and Mauss, 1973:268). The only solution, they maintain, is individual redemption through the acceptance of Jesus as the Savior. The chief activity must therefore be the "street work" of bringing people to Christ. Apart from evangelizing the focus of life in this sect is the worship meeting, at which "praying, testifying, preaching, instrumental music, dancing and wiggling about, and interjections of 'Praise God' and the like," are used to engender the kind of experience which makes meaningful a commitment to a life of Christ (Petersen and Mauss, 1973:266).

As a whole, the Jesus Movement has crystalized only here and there into sect form. It is made up chiefly of "communes" and "houses" between which there is some communication and mobility. However, that it is capable of becoming a distinct and separate sect is suggested by the more extreme Children of God, who share most of the conversionism of the movement in general but are distinctive in their pervasive sense of impending doom, their feeling that isolation from the world is necessary to ensure righteousness, and their ascetic way of life. They spurn both the established churches as too cold, informal, and worldly, *and* many of their fellow Jesus People for their "hang loose" approach to conversionism.

Recruits to the Jesus Movement have been mostly young middle-to upper-middle-class white people, so it is not a sect born of the oppressed. However, Jesus People do tend to have histories of dropping out of school or college, drug use, and drifting (Petersen and Mauss, 1973:264). The movement seems to offer a new identity, a new and stable meaning for a life previously marked by much change, mobility, and superficial ties. It also offers a set of simple answers to personal and social problems depressing in their apparent complexity, and a sense of prestige and group acceptance to people who have previously drifted from one social group to another. They hear that Jesus provides a guide and source of comfort and that the group can help them meet their Savior. Thus, like all conversionist sectarians, the Jesus People have come to accept that the root of their problems lies in individual guilt and that the solution to those problems lies in confession to Christ and acceptance of him as their Redeemer.

Introversionist

Introversionist sects believe that the world is evil because of a lack of holiness, and that only by withdrawing from that world and drawing strength from one another in community will individual holiness be sustained. The chief object of an introversionist sect is to create a haven for the cultivation of personal holiness. Members are taught that doctrine is not as important as inspiration and "sustained moral rectitude" (Wilson, 1970:43). Over time, the community itself takes on sacredness and the people within it absorb some of this holiness.

Groups such as the Amish, the Rappites, the Amana and the Doukhobors are not utopian sects (as is often supposed); they are introversionist, because their chief object is piety, and the vicinal segregation is merely a means to that end. Unlike utopian sects, they do not necessarily practice some form of communism. They may adopt communitarianism as an expedient, shunning the world in order to cultivate a deeper spirituality. On the other hand, community life in utopian sects is adopted as a deliberate end-product of a religious vision. In order to sustain the community, introversionist sects assume utopia-like distinctiveness in matters of speech, dress, marriage, friendships, eating and drinking habits, and political behavior. They tend to be little interested in proselytizing, seeing themselves as "strangers and pilgrims" in the world, and they will even go so far as to be hostile to visitors fearing that their standards will be lowered. Not surprisingly, there are variations in the strength of this kind of sectarianism. Both the Amish and the Mennonites are introversionist but the latter have accommodated more to the world, showing a greater willingness to accept technological change and secular education.[1]

Perhaps the clearest example of introversionism is provided by the radical wing of the Mennonite tradition, the Old Colony Mennonites, who have successively migrated from the Ukraine, Canada, Mexico and Bolivia in order to preserve the freedom to follow the life of piety they seek. The Old Colony Mennonites believe that only those who turn to God in confession and commitment on the basis of faith and live in strict obedience to God's commands can be called members of the Kingdom of God. Their goal is to lead an exemplary life in matters of personal piety and daily activities. Punishment is sure for those who fail to remain pure in the world. On the other hand, God is a great benefactor and will take care of those who have faith in him and lead lives of righteousness. Members of sects such as this have a very strong sense of exclusiveness and electness and take satisfaction in their life apart from others.

[1] For a description of the Amish, see Hostetler (1963).

Although individual piety is the core of their faith, introversionist sects interpret their relationship with God in terms of the people of the Government, which means that the purity of each affects the chances of salvation of all. Group norms, then, become the guide to salvation and conformity to those norms becomes one means of signaling redemption—hence the salience of commitment to the group, obedience to its demands and avoidance of the world. To maintain group purity, the Old Colony Mennonites segregated themselves vicinally, allowed few visitors, provided their own education, practiced endogamy, made many activities communal, and restricted contact with the outside world by prohibiting phones, radios, and televisions. Yet, although they have undoubtedly stressed sharing and cooperation, the Old Colony Mennonites have never been communistic (see Redekop, 1969).

In their search for a life of holiness, several religious movements that originated in the East and have become popular in the United States in recent years conform to the introversionist type. One example is the International Society for Krishna Consciousness, led by guru A. C. Bhattivedanta Swami, which was introduced into the United States in the 1970s. Krishna Consciousness is an extension into Western society of the Vedic cult of Krishna worship. Its goal is to change the polluted atmosphere of material society so that the pure love of Krishna dominates. "Each individual strives to cleanse his soul in order to obtain release from the endless wheel of birth and rebirth and to achieve liberation for his soul" (Daner, 1976:I). Guru Bhattivedanta Swami is worshipped as a pure devotee of the Lord, the latest in a long line of disciples since Krishna's original appearance thousands of years ago. He does not claim to be God, but his knowledge of God entitles him to the same treatment as that given God.

> Krishna Consciousness claims to be the revival of the original consciousness of the living being—the conscious awareness that one is eternally related to God, or Krishna. The true self (soul) is thought to be eternal, ever existent, but due to the ignorance of material contamination, the soul is forced to assume a continuous succession of material bodies. When one body dies, the soul immediately assumes another body and is born again . . . The individual forgets his past life and identifies with his present body, which is for a devotee simply a temporary covering for the soul. This false identification with the temporary body must be overcome and the person must realise his true position, namely that of the loving servant of Krishna (Daner, 1976:33).

The devotee is expected to perform loving service (*bhakti*) to the supreme Lord, and it is the function of the group to teach him *bhakti* and help him to perform it. The focus is thus on individual piety and the efforts of the group are concentrated on bringing this way of life to the attention of others and helping them follow it. This is also true of the Divine Light Mission, led by guru Maharaji-ji, whose members "perceive an enhanced 'loving' quality to their interpersonal relationships as emanating automatically from the deepening of their inner spiritual awareness." They "tend to view improvement in interpersonal relations as resulting from improved spiritual 'intuition' rather than the reasoned application of invariant moral principles" (Robbins, 1976 et al:117).

Revolutionist

According to members of sects such as the Jehovah's Witnesses, the world is evil and must be overturned totally and supernaturally. Those who have sufficient faith and belief will be saved when the overturning occurs and the new world is ushered in. Meanwhile, the responsibility of the faithful is to prepare the way and be ready to help bring about the End. For this kind of sect, salvation seems to hinge ultimately on knowledge of and faith in the word and obedience to the commands of God—hence the heavy emphasis on prophetical scripture.

Revolutionist sects teach that present tribulations are "necessary," that historical sequences are leading toward a cataclysm, and that the faithful must be "called out." Their meetings have little of the emotional fervor of the conversionist type and are more likely to take the form of Bible study or a sermon giving exegeses of prophetical writings. Revolutionists tend to proselytize aggressively because they connect spreading the word with the successful culmination of God's plan. There are variations within the type. Some sects, such as the Mormons, cast themselves in a very active role: they were helping to build the coming kingdom. More typical of contemporary society are the Seventh-Day Adventists, who adopt an attitude of patient expectation, emphasizing obedience to God's commands as a means of preparing the way for Christ's return.

The Seventh-Day Adventists trace their origin to the Millerite speculations of the Nineteenth Century. William Miller, a Baptist preacher, gathered a following in New England in the 1830s on the basis of his prophecies that the Second Advent would occur in 1844. Not all of the followers were discouraged by the failure of this prophecy. A group of them gathered around Ellen White, who revised Miller's biblical reasoning on the basis of a series of visions she began having in the 1840s. White managed to convince her followers that they were indeed living in the final, critical period of the history of the world, to which all of society's ills could be attributed. She also reconfirmed their belief that the End was near, but declared that no firm date could possibly be set.

Instead, she taught, the faithful should devote their energy to preparing for the return of Christ, for as he taught, prior to his return, the life of every person, dead or alive, will be "reviewed." Only after it has been decided who deserves to survive will the "sanctuary be cleansed." Salvation (contingent on this final decision) is granted the individual who pleads a sinless life. Appropriate guidelines were set down by White herself, who imposed ascetic standards on her followers, including strict observance of the Sabbath on the seventh day. The Seventh-Day Adventists have since grown to be a world-wide organization with an American membership of 500,000. Although some of their millenial fervor has been lost, it has always been an important part of their teachings and remains a vital element in their appeal (see Schwartz, 1970).

The Jehovah's Witnesses are an equally well-known revolutionist sect. They too, have undergone some changes. The disconfirmation of the prophesied End in 1914 followed by the death of the founder, Charles Russell, two years later, led the witnesses to look inward. Their new leader, Joseph Rutherford, "stimulated a resurgence of evangelical fervor among Bible students by giving them specific tasks on specific days, organizing coordinated sales campaigns, appointing service Directors to administer evangelism in local ecclesias and publishing a magazine which has geared toward the recruitment of new workers for the Watch Tower cause" (Beckford, 1972:30). These changes are testimony to the difficulty of sustaining millenial expectations among a large group. If adventist hopes have receded into the background, then the sect could be said to have either shifted altogether outside the category of sect, as did mainstream Christianity, or become a different kind of sect as in the two cases cited here.

Another well-known sect with revolutionist overtones is the Lost Found Nation of Islam, better known as the Black Muslims. This sect originated during the depression of the 1930s when many proposals to radically reconstruct American society were in the air, but did not receive national attention until the civil rights movement of the 1960s, when its intense nationalism and outspoken hostility toward whites won the approval of many blacks. It is the belief of Black Muslims that "America's so-called Negroes are the 'lost Nation of Islam in North America.' They have now been found, and a Messenger has been sent to prepare them for their day of destiny, for 'judgement of the world has arrived and the gathering together of the people is now going on'" (Lincoln, 1973:72). The eschatology of the Black Muslims is elaborate and differs from that of the Seventh Day Adventists and other revolutionist sects, chiefly in its overt racialism. The Muslims teach that the "white devils have been given 6,000 years to rule. The allotted span of their rule was ended in 1914, and their 'years of grace' will last no longer than is necessary for the chosen of Allah to be resurrected from the mental death imposed upon them by the white man. This resurrection is the task of Muhammed himself" (Lincoln, 1973:79–80).

The Black Muslims originally rejected Christianity as a white person's religion, spurned the orthodox black denominations as the hand-maidens of white Christianity, renounced racial integration as a social goal, and made frequent predictions about the insurrection that would befall the white power-holders in American society. They announced that they planned to retire from it until by supernatural means the whites were destroyed. They therefore took an often militantly dismissive attitude toward mainstream culture. In recent years, however, this stridency has waned. The death of the founder and sole leader of the movement, Elijah Muhammad, in 1975 was followed by a modification of some of the separatism of the movement, including a decision to admit whites for the first time.

Utopian

Utopians believe that the world is an evil system, filled with competition and jealousy, and that salvation can be achieved by only returning to the basic organizational principles revealed in the Scriptures. They are convinced that only in a rebuilt world will righteousness reign. Inspired by the idea of human perfectability, Utopians believe that people are basically good but have been corrupted by society. To realize this perfection, they seek to create a purified, spiritual society founded on the fundamental , communistic principles of the primitive church, a society in which harmony and close fellowship can be achieved. Thus, Utopians are distinctive not simply because they are convinced of earthly corruption or simply because they envision a better world. They are also distinctive because they believe the Kingdom of God will be established on earth by human action under divine tutelage and surveillance. Their object is to establish a new order of society, which in its perfection will convince others of its divine provenance and inspire their emulation.

Three themes run through religious utopianism:

1. A desire to unite body and mind, flesh and spirit. For example, physical labor is considered to constitute a condition for mental well-being, and sexual activity is seen as a manifestation of a supreme spiritual state.
2. An urge to experiment—with diet, birth control, drugs, dress, sexual relations, childrearing, architecture, and crop-planning.
3. A sense of uniqueness and coherence as a group that is an end in itself—a search for complete unity of purpose, group-bondedness, and sharing.

In order to realize these ideals, utopians try to avoid divisive life-styles (such as monogamous pairs) and attempt to institute an orderly system in which centralized, communal activities and joint decision-making absorb the individual in the group.

The United States has witnessed many utopian experiments, and they seem to occur in waves. Special conditions are required for its occurrence. There must, for instance, be a considerable degree of religious liberty and personal autonomy to facilitate the segregation required. There must also be a heightened awareness of the mutability of social structures and of the impress of those structures on human development and awareness that occurs only during times of rapid social change. These conditions seem to have existed in the expanding frontier regions of America in the middle of the nineteenth century and again during the 1960s, and both of these periods witnessed intense utopian speculation and activity.

Despite the similarity in stimulating conditions, there are some interesting differences between the utopias of the past century and those of the present day. These differences suggest that, although there are elements integral to the utopian quest, its objective expression is influenced by its social milieu.

1. Twentieth century utopian sects tend to be small, and typically look upon themselves as "families," whereas the experiments of the previous century were often conducted on a large scale (potentially at least) and tended to look upon themselves as embryonic societies.
2. Modern utopias place more emphasis on personal growth within the group than on the earthly salvation of the group as a whole. In this respect, they reflect the contemporary concern with problems of meaning and personal identity.
3. Specific groups are more likely today to be looked upon almost as temporary expedients for individuals with quite specific and perhaps transitory problems. The life time commitments of the nineteenth century are not as common. The higher mobility rates and looser kinship ties of today facilitate the higher rate of membership turnover.
4. Whereas the nineteenth century utopian sects sought by careful design and divine guidance to properly lead the individual toward a completely righteous life, the modern utopias have an opposite emphasis—the escape from planning and programming.
5. Finally, whereas the nineteenth century utopias were in some respects an escape from the urban world and were located in often remote rural districts, the utopian groups of today are found equally in the cities, where they attempt an adjustment to urban life (Kanter, 1972:166–169).

New Utopian sects in the style of the Hutterites or the Bruderhof are rare. Contemporary utopian sects tend to be more service-oriented. In other words, they are established not according to some divinely inspired master plan but for the purpose of, for example, facilitating a greater awareness of the truth, or enhancing individual spirituality. An example described by Kanter (1972:196) is Cumbres, established in rural New Hampshire in 1969 by Cesareo Palaez. The purpose of this sect was to enhance human potential through the use of a combination of humanistic psychology and Eastern spiritualism, mainly Zen. Palaez demanded that jobs be shared and rotated, that group members live ascetically, and that meals be taken communally. He also discouraged monogamy. However, community life was not merely a means to individual ends, for *communitas* itself was a major goal of the sect. Palaez was unable to secure sufficient funding for the group—which never became self-sufficient as had the Hutterites—and the sect disbanded in 1971.

Although most of the nineteenth century utopian sects have disappeared (like the Rappites), or (like the Oneida) transformed themselves into something altogether different, a few have persisted and indeed continue to grow in numbers. One such group is the Hutterians, named after their sixteenth century Anabaptist founder, Jacob Hutter. The Hutterians are one among many religious sects that migrated to North America from Europe during the second half of the nineteenth century in order to be free to practice their religion. The main body of Hutterians moved from Russia to the Dakotas in 1874, and some of them moved on to Manitoba at the end of the First World War.

The Hutterites adhere formally to the fundamental principles of the radical wing of the Protestant Reformation—justification by faith alone, believers' baptism, pacifism, and a church composed only of those who have freely and determinedly chosen to be Christ's disciples. In addition to these principles, they continue the practice of community of goods, which they believe has an equally authentic pedigree in Christian teachings, reasoning from Acts 2:44, "And all that believed were together, and had all things common." Communal living is not, then, merely an expedient to the Hutterites but rather a vital sign of spiritual fellowship. The Hutterite colonies are intentionally kept small and are so arranged as to sustain a strong sense of community: colonies jointly buy and sell produce, there is much working in groups, and where a division of labor is necessary it is jointly agreed upon; property is held in common; decision-making is widely diffused; endogamy is practiced; eating and most recreational life is communal; and a colony can sanction deviants by the practice of "shunning" them. The spiritual welfare of the individual is bound intimately with the welfare of the community as a whole. The Hutterites have been extremely successful in their utopianism. In the opinion of Peters (1971:186), they are as close now to their founding ideas as they have ever been in their colony life.[2]

[2]For a description of the Hutterites, see Hostetler (1974) and Hostetler and Huntington (1967). There is a good description of another utopian sect, the Bruderhof, in Zablocki (1971).

Manipulationist

Manipulationist sects believe that salvation can be attained by the employment of supernatural means summoned by special knowledge and techniques. In this type of sect, the attraction is, above all, the acquisition of special, usually secret knowledge, which can be used to manipulate the world for the individual's benefit. "Worship" meetings tend to be unemotional and emphasize learning and technique. They are oriented to a Divinity seen not as a Redeemer but as an "abstract idea of great power" (Wilson, 1970:44).

Manipulationist sects do not emphasize rejection of the world. Rather they are likely to attempt to use their power to manipulate the world in order to reap more benefits from it. Members are provided with an exclusive, semiesoteric means of achieving generally desired ends. Nor do such sects really reject established religion. Rather, they reinterpret it. For example, the suffering, death, and resurrection of Christ might be seen not as efficacious in itself, but as an allegory of the initiation process through which all adepts must pass. Moreover, orthodox rituals are not completely rejected. Rather, they are examined for new symbolic significance in the light of new knowledge.

Manipulationist sects are distinctive in at least three other ways. First, meetings are educative—" the gathering of an association of like-minded and like-instructed people, who use a common method in coping with the world" (Wilson, 1970:141). For example, the Christian Science practitioner does not so much officiate at a meeting as provide a service or consultation, much as a doctor would.

Second, the sense of community is minimal and participation tends to be segmentary. There is little of the all-embracing gemeinschaft of the utopian or conversionist sect. Sects such as Unity survive almost entirely by means of highly impersonal communications through the mail. Other sects, such as New Thought, might have local fellowships, but members attend these much as they might attend a clinic, for specific services; they probably belong to other groups or attend other clinics as well. Membership, where it is recognized at all, might be marked simply by dues-paying and might be granted on the basis of level of understanding of the sect's teachings. Manipulationist sects do not fulfill the whole range of human requirements. As a result, it is common for members to engage both in "seeking"—drifting from one like group to another—and in multiple affiliations—taking up with one group without relinquishing affiliation with others. This kind of sect does not typically present a system of ethics for members to follow, and exhorting from the pulpit or platform is definitely discouraged. Instead, addresses from "the practitioner" are applied by each individual to his particular circumstances.

Third, teachings are syncretistic: they combine not only several religious traditions but also ideas from philosophy, Eastern thought, the hermetic tradition, and even modern science. Manipulationist sects display an ambivalent attitude toward orthodox science, rejecting it in its popularly accepted and institutionalized forms but imitating much of its method of work and style of investigation. There is no hesitancy in incorporating scientific findings where they are thought to be relevant, for *all* thought systems are believed to be ultimately subsumable under the gnosis the sect has revealed.

Christian Science (no longer truly a sect), was once a manipulationist type of sect. A contemporary example is Scientology. A system of lay psychotherapy called Dianetics was developed in 1950 by L. Ron Hubbard, but Scientology itself did not begin until 1954, when Hubbard parted from some of his followers and developed his original ideas into a more complete and more clearly religious system. Hubbard taught that each person has an essentially persistent element called "operating Thetan" which transmigrates at death. The chief activity of Scientologists is "processing" by which the "thetan" can be retrieved from the obscurity caused by "bad thoughts" and the individual restored to her full human potential. Processing requires the use of an electro-psychogalvanometer, and this "clearing" is a step-by-step process through which the individual is guided by expert "auditors." The later stages of processing are closely guarded secrets, available only to the inner circle of Scientologists. Scientology promises adepts that they can realize their potential (for example, they can solve their personal problems or achieve their material goals) by undergoing the clearing process and achieving a better mental approach to life. The sect thus resembles closely older sects of this type like Unity and New Thought. Because his teachings so closely resemble popular psychology, Hubbard has been the object of frequent government investigation. He moved the headquarters of his sect from California to England in 1959 as the result of an Internal Revenue Service investigation. Due to frequent harassment by the British Government, he has since left that country and set up a floating headquarters aboard a number of ships in the Mediterranean.

Many manipulationist sects have drawn their inspiration from the Orient. Sects such as Theosophy are appealing not only because they are exotic, esoteric, and syncretistic, but also because they provide a means of transcending institutionalized religious forms. More fundamentally, the Eastern religions offer a different kind of totality and order. In uniting spirit and biology, believers leave behind the clash of matter on matter and mind on matter.

Not only syncretistic sects like Theosophy but actual sectarian "imports" like Vedanta have taken a hold in the United States and the United Kingdom. Vedanta, for example, teaches three fundamental truths: "that all man's real nature is divine; that the aim of man's life on earth is to unfold and manifest this Godhead, eternally existent in man, but hidden; that truth is universal" (Ellwood, 1973:224). The implication of these teachings is that all gods are but particular manifestations of the Universal Being, and, of course, that all religions and churches are thereby equally true. The eastern sects have therefore approached the Western denominations in a spirit not of rejection but of embrace, an approach usually spurned by those denominations.

In attempting to secure knowledge and insight more recent Eastern imports such as Zen and Subud use nonverbal means such as drugs, meditation, music, and communal life to a much greater extent than the older groups such as Vedanta. This trend reflects two basic changes in American society. First, the newer groups became popular during the 1960s, a decade that placed great emphasis on nonverbal communication and intuition as against learning and reasoning. Second, the older movements, themselves children of their age, tended to portray learning and novitiation as a preparation for distant future rewards—a version of the Protestant Ethic—whereas the newer groups promise immediate access to desired rewards of a more personal and nonmaterial kind.

These manipulationist sects seem to speak to a need for a faith based upon esoteric experiences, a faith that mainstream Protestantism by and large excludes. Their devotees are looking for spiritual reality in expanded states of consciousness, and to that purpose engage in interior exploration. These sects offer few sermons, lectures, or even written words, for the emphasis is above all on meditation and nonverbal communication (usually in imitation of some exemplary person), by means of which a new spiritual harmony with the cosmos is achieved. The virtues valued most greatly are love and sincerity. It is not unknown for this type of sect to institute an intensive group life but this is done only to enhance the possibility of greater spiritual awareness and personal adaptation.

Thaumaturgical

Thaumaturgical sects practice what might be called a form of magic. The ills of the world, it is believed, can be cured by "magical dispensation by supernatural agencies from the normal laws of causality" (Wilson, 1970:39). The concept of salvation is least developed in this type of sect, for there is little sense of sin and redemption, but rather the feeling that special powers (oracles and miracles) are available for the solution of specific problems. Consequently, there are no worship meetings in the usual sense and minimal ritual. If the example of a spiritualist group is called to mind, it can be seen that the most important feature of a thaumaturgical sect is the client/medium/spirit relationship, and the most important objective is the acquisition of spirit guidance for personal problems.

The intense individualism of thaumaturgical sects is tempered somewhat by "the need for protection, the desire to acquire prestige beyond the local level. . . and the benefit to all practitioners from joint sponsorship of propaganda" (Wilson, 1970:168). The cluster of sects referred to as spiritualist groups have experienced this tension between the individualistic demands of the clientele and the felt need for more formal association on the part of practitioners and others. Modern spiritualism can be said quite confidently to have begun in 1848, when "rappings" were heard at the home of the Fox family of Arcadia, New York. The two Fox daughters established a system of communication with spirits by means of the rappings. Various clergymen attempted to exorcize the spirits. They not only failed, but also gave the Fox girls' claims greater credibility thereby. The first spiritualist circle grew up around the Fox family, and a public investigation in Rochester, in 1849 gave the circle wide publicity. The interest in contact with the spirits of the dead spread rapidly throughout the United States and became somewhat of a craze. The first New York circle was founded in 1851 and by that date there were already 6 or 7 magazines devoted to the subject being published (Nelson, 1969:8). The various mediums and their circles attracted a great deal of opposition from both churchmen and politicians (Alabama made the holding of séances punishable by a fine). But for a while, this controversy only added to the numbers interested in the subject and anxious to attend the séances. In England, attention was first drawn to spiritualism by the visit of the medium Mrs. Hayden, and several circles were formed in the 1850s. As a topic of popular curiosity, spiritualism probably enjoyed its greatest appeal during the 1850s. Although public interest declined there after many small groups continued to meet. The first national organization of spiritualists in England was founded in 1865 and, the first such organization in the United States was established in 1898 (Nelson, 1969:25).

The chief focus of this kind of thaumaturgical sect is on communication with spirits. Meetings are characterized by "rappings," automatic writing, trance speaking, clairvoyance (the ability to see spirits and transmit their messages), and spirit healing. Although communication with spirits is the center of the spiritualist life, it is not important that anything profound be transmitted. What most devotees look for is the reassurance that the spirits indeed exist and are watching over mortals here on earth. There is little concern with doctrine, apart from a vague belief in the existence of God and the immortality of the human spirit, spiritualism is compatible with a wide variety of religious traditions. Spiritualist sects seem to appeal mostly to those who are not deeply committed to a specific religious tradition or church but who draw comfort and reassurance from any proof of individual immortality. Spiritualist activity removes much of the fear of death, of a Devil incarnate, and of hell, as well as providing guidance in making personal decisions.

A version of spiritualism is found among the many black sects in urban areas in which a medium claims to be in contact with spirits and to be able to provide healing and advice. These sects differ from the more staid, usually white middle-class spiritualists in that they combine some traditional voodooism with Catholic attitudes toward holy objects and Pentecostal attitudes toward spiritual healing. Like their white counterparts, however, they are overwhelmingly utilitarian, offering communication with spirits for the purpose of success in love, marriage, gambling, employment and healing (Washington, 1972:113).

Despite loose alliances between thaumaturlogical groups and among their leaders, they tend to be the most ephemeral of all sects as far as organization is concerned. Any desire for dominance by a particular medium tends to be obstructed by the counter-assertion (necessary to thaumaturgical sectarians) that, in principle, contact with spirits is open to all because of the divine spark within each body. Any given medium attracts and keeps a following not through organization but because of credibility of performance.

Another example of the thaumaturgical type of sect is the so-called flying saucer cult. This is an example of modern spiritualism in a new technological guise, for group members believe that saucers and their passengers might be regarded as spirits performing particular services. Ellwood (1973:132), describes a group he visited in 1968 called Understanding Inc., which was organized around a medium named Chief Standing Horse. This person claimed to be a full-blooded Indian who had traveled to Mars, Venus, "Orean," and "Clarion" with the help of "saucerian" friends. He brought back the message that unidentified flying objects were sending "energy beams" to those who would open themselves to them, and that these beams would provide the insight and power sufficient to overcome all personal problems. The "saucerians" were, in fact, spirits (perhaps past inhabitants of the Earth) who were acting as intermediaries for the "Infinite Intelligence" or "Great Guiding Force."

The meeting of UFO groups commonly feature a lecture, which usually consists of a recounting of a contact's experiences in space and what he had learned there. The elaborateness of these lessons varies from group to group. Whereas Understanding Inc. seemed to offer in its "energy beams" an open-ended power, another group described by Ellwood (1973:147), called the Amalgamated Flying Saucer Clubs of

America, proposed, through its contactee Gabriel Green, sweeping economic reforms. Other UFO groups, such as the Aetherius Society, founded in England in 1954, resemble revolutionist sects in their message of the impending doom awaiting the world from which only the saucerians can save us.

Reformist

Members of reformist sects believe that the world is evil but can be improved if they act in accordance with the dictates of conscience (that is, insights derived from the apprehension of the divine). Reformists tend to see themselves as "the leaven of the lump," and they stress above all else right living as a manifestation of proper spiritual guidance. Their intention is to improve by example. Thus, rituals count for little among them. Instead, they are intent on improving social conditions under religious auspices. Wilson (1970) offers only one example of a reformist sect, the Quakers, but there must be serious question that this group represents true sectarianism at all. Rather, it might be considered a form of attenuated protest.

CONCLUSION

The current membership of these various sects is but a small minority of the religious population. The amazing variety of these groups, their obviously precarious existence, and their unorthodoxy make it tempting to regard them as exotic flowers, worthy of the attention only of those with specialized interests. Yet they have been the breeding grounds of many new religious, political, and economic ideas. They are also important because many of the principal social processes in religious behavior can be seen clearly in them. The conversion of the individual to religious life, her commitment to a religious group, the stresses, strains and benefits of religious community life, although these processes appear in exaggerated form in sects, they are the universals of the religious experience in modern society. With this in mind, we may now look at some of the theories that have been proposed to explain new religious movements—why people join them, how people become committed to them, and how they organize themselves. These theories speak not only to sectarian religion but to all organized religious life.

5

THEORIES
OF RELIGIOUS CHANGE

The near-groups described in Chapter 3, and the sects described in Chapter 4, are all movements of protest, and have the potential for inspiring major social changes. Each rests on a claim to be in effective contact with that which is most vital, most powerful and most authoritative in the universe, and each, therefore, is antipathetic to established forms of authority. Their appearance is usually treated as a sign that "the times are out of joint." They seem to appeal mostly to those who have been led by social disturbances to become disaffected with social arrangements and disillusioned with the churches' attempts to cope with their anxieties. Just what is meant by times being "out of joint" and who is most likely to be attracted to new religious ideas and practices is the topic of this chapter.

Sociological theories of religious movements can be formulated at two levels—the structural and the individual. The first attempts to answer the question: Why do religious movements occur? The second tries to answer the question: Why do certain individuals join them? Each type of theory rests on the assumption that new religious movements are a protest against the existing socio-religious order and are closely associated with times of social upheaval, conflict, and widespread social dislocation. A second assumption they make is that new religious ideas and practices will appeal principally to those members of society who are discontented with their lot and seek, through religion, to improve it.

STRUCTURAL THEORIES

Structural theories seek to relate sectarian manifestations to sources of strain within the system (see, for example, Smelser, 1962). These strains may be temporary (for instance, an economic depression), in which case the emphasis is on a certain *period*, or they may be chronic (for instance, urbanization), in which case the emphasis is on *place*. Structural theory seeks to identify times and places of structural strain and relate them to variations in the rate of sect occurrence.

Period: The Burned-Over District

A period of intense sectarian activity occurred between 1800 and 1850 in upper New York State. Cross (1950) tried to relate this activity to structural changes occurring at the time in a way that will illustrate this kind of theory. The first half of the nineteenth century saw such a flurry of sectarian activity in New York, so many "luxuriant new growths," that the area earned for itself the name of "Burned-Over District." "Few of the enthusiasms or eccentricities of this generation of Americans failed to find exponents here. Most of them gained rather greater support here than elsewhere. Several originated in the region." (Cross, 1950:3). This upsurge of sectariansim started, as so many do, with a wave of revivalism which began about 1800. All the major denominations (with the exception of Episcopalianism) were affected. The second Great Awakening, with its camp meetings, itierant preachers and inter-denominational missions, reached its peak in this area between 1825 and 1837. Not only did new members flock to the established denominations, but many splinter Baptist and Methodist groups were also formed. In addition, and more significant for Cross's analysis, it was also a period of widespread religious experimentation. Not only did marginal groups such as the Shakers attract renewed attention, but new sects were formed at this time, including the Mormons, the Millerites, and various spiritualist circles. Added to this was the ferment caused by the widely popular temperance, abolitionist, and anti-Masonry movements that swept the area during these years.

It is hard to unravel the many complex forces which contributed to this remarkable upsurge of sectarian activity. Certainly the Yankee migrants had brought a piety and moralism to the area, but this accounts for neither the radical nature of the movements nor the willingness to experiment. Undoubtedly, the frontier conditions made interdenominational ventures attractive and ensured that denominational memberships would mean little, but again, the innovations cannot be accounted for by this alone. Indeed, the areas in which religious interest and fervor were the greatest were not precisely on the frontier. Sectarianism in upper New York State was not immediately related to high mobility, extreme social isolation or severe hardship. In fact, sectarian activity did not peak until after the completion of the Erie Canal had provided some economic stability for New York State, and then it tended to occur in areas of the state that had begun to settle into stable farming communities. Sectarianism was characteristic of neither the growing towns nor the sparsely settled western regions of the state. Furthermore, this religious upsurge did not really get under way until the second generation had established itself economically, and it was among these more permanent folk that the interest in new religions was greatest (Cross, 1950:76).

Roughly speaking, for the data are sparse, the intensification of sectarianism coincided with an economic *boom* in the area, or, more accurately, with the onset of economic fluctuations in the area as it became an exporter of agricultural produce to the cities. It seems that the exalted expectations and repeated disappointments generated by the new market economy made attractive religious innovations and reforms. One example of this mood was the extreme *optimism* of the millenial movements during this period. Finally, it is significant that the decline of religious enthusiasm in 1836 coincided more or less with the onset of the economic depression of 1837.

Obviously, such a brief review of a very complicated case cannot hope to cover adequately the multitude of factors that created the Burned-Over District. The structural theory proposes, however, that *vicissitudes* in the economy, the uncertainties marked by its various and unpredictable ups and downs, generate a willingness to try new religious forms. From a structural viewpoint it is not accurate to associate sects with periods of economic depression. Rather, they are correctly associated with strains in the system caused by change with which it cannot cope.

Cross's analysis associates sectarianism with economic fluctuations and the anxieties and speculations resulting from them. The implication is that any period of economic (or political) upheaval will be accompanied by sectarian multiplication. This certainly makes the upsurge of sectarianism during the 1960s more comprehensible. However, the difficulty with this kind of theory is deciding what amount of strain is sufficient to generate more sectarianism. There seems to have been as much economic fluctuation in the period 1929–1939 as there was in the periods 1825–1837 or 1960–1970, but the Depression years are not known for having been a period of great sectarian activity—although in

California, where the Depression hit hardest, there was a flurry of sects. The theory is plausible, then, but rather hard to test.

Place: Surrogate Communities

One structural theory that emphasizes *place* rather than time might be called the surrogate community theory. According to this theory, industrialization and urbanization have disrupted the traditional ties of the family and of small town life causing a loss of personal relationships, moral guidance and prestige among those most affected—the industrial worker and the rural migrant to the city. Sects, it is argued, provide a new ethic of brotherliness, in which emphasis is placed upon an immediate and simple kind of helping relationship, one that is more typical of the closed, agrarian society that industrialization and urbanization are destroying.

One of the first to use this theory was Holt (1940:741), in his study of the spread of the Holiness movement in the South during the 1930s. Holt believed that Holiness sects were "largely the product of the social disorganization and cultural conflict which have attended the over-rapid urbanward migration and concomitant urbanization of an intensely rural and among other things, religious fundamentalist population." He observed that Holiness had spread most rapidly where the pace of urbanization and industrialization was fastest. It was here that the "culture shock" of modernization was most profound: "a loosening of mores from a strict social control, a liberation of the individual from his group, an increasing impersonalism, as against the personal character of the rural environment, an increasing mobility as contrasted with the old stability and isolation, and on top of these changes, a lasting disruption of personal and occupational habits and status." The combination of fellowship and strict moralism found in Holiness sects seemed to serve the new city dweller as "a defense of the old standards and modes of behavior."

The same theory has been used to explain the "storefront churches" that began to appear in the northern cities as blacks migrated from the South during the 1930s. They provided a transplanted rural community and a means of escaping the disturbing anonymity of the cities (Frazier, 1974:51). Those who joined them were not so much newly religious as religious in a new way. Blacks continue to migrate north and new sects continue to form. Williams (1974:162), noting that modern black ghettos lack traditional communal ties, regards the Holiness sects that thrive there as a necessary form of personal association. Each member feels part of a hierarchy and feels an affinity with a concrete social group, which is symbolized by its name, the life-style, and dress of the members.

These sects do not enable blacks to ignore the fact that the city is a world where the struggle for survival is bitter and intense. But they do provide a more limited arena in which such struggles can be conducted, and they are a source of intensive solidarity, sufficient to compensate for the individualism of the wider society and to temper the internal squabbles among sect members.

The theory that sects are surrogate communities and that they are most likely to arise in areas of high mobility and impersonalism has also been used to explain Pentecostal sects among the Puerto Ricans of New York City (O'Dea and Poblete, 1970:188) and among Italian immigrants (Parsons, 1965:185). Members of these sects speak of their isolation and loneliness prior to joining and their warm sense of being cared for once they became members. However, sects are not simply havens for those searching for a return to the past in a context of warm fellowship. First, sects perform a *bridging* function: they help preserve some of the old communal ties, and at the same time they help the migrant adjust to the new urban way of life by teaching asceticism, the value of hard work, and the importance of respectability. Besides furnishing a new community, they also help form a new personality. Second, sects build upon and help reaffirm family ties, which are challenged but rarely completely disrupted by urbanization. The sects function somewhat like an extended family, not so much replacing a family that has been lost as confirming the family's continued usefulness and worth (Moore, 1974:127).

Some sects do act as substitutes for the family, and they are clearly identifiable. Sects such as the Children of God, Hare Krishna, and the Unification Church seek to replace the bonds of kinship with those of faith and loyalty to the group. Young members of the Jesus Movement typically had family backgrounds "fraught with turmoil and conflict." In the communes of California and Oregon, they had found a new "family" of "brothers" and "sisters," to act as a substitute for the family life they had lost. There were also many drifters in the movement, people who had dropped out of high school or college, left the parental home and wandered from one region of the country to another. They lacked a sense of firm social anchorage and had found in the movement a replacement for the primary group ties they had spurned. (Petersen and Mauss, 1973:274)

Of course, the surrogate community function is not something exclusive to sects or new religious movements. For example, although sectarianism is more common among recently arrived Puerto Ricans in New York City than among those who have been in the city for ten years or more, the same could be said of Catholicism among Puerto Ricans. The more recently arrived Catholics also tend to go to church more frequently than those who have been in the city for some time. Migration to the city does seem to be associated with an increase in religiosity (especially attendance), but there is little to suggest that this must be sectarian. The established denominations, if available and open to the newcomer, and if active and warm at the local level, can perform the surrogate community function equally well (see Garrison, 1974). Kloetzli (1961:98) agrees: he found "a significant number" of recent arrivals from the countryside in the urban Lutheran congregations he studied.

Thus, it seems that family dislocation and migration are not sufficient conditions for sect formation, although they may be necessary. Being a surrogate community is a function the denominations can equally well perform. Yet, it could be argued that, although sects are not *alone* in their ability to provide a community surrogate, it is a role for which they are particularly well suited, and one in which the denominations, because of their size, often fail. It is within sects that the emphasis on *communitas* and an ethic of exclusivism is strongest. It is significant that, although all urban churchgoers have close friends, it is only among sectarians that all these close friends will be fellow members of the congregation (Stark and Glock, 1968:167).

There is, in sum, considerable evidence to support the surrogate community theory. The communal or familial appeal of many sects is evident in their use of the terminology of "brother" and "sister," in the sincere, warm, and loving relationships manifested and prized by sect members, and in the sharing and sense of exclusivity that sets them apart. Also, it is well-known that sects have long been popular among migrant peoples—especially those moving from the country to the town.

So sweeping a theory must, however, be modified in some particulars in the light of accumulating sociological research. First, not all sects seek to perpetuate or recreate the parish, village, or family structure that has been lost. Some sects have adapted with supreme efficiency to modern city life. Manipulationist sects, for example, are as impersonal and efficiency minded as their urban milieu. A revolutionist sect such as the Jehovah's witnesses shows few more signs of being a surrogate community. "The highly affective quality of the bonds uniting members of other minority religious groups is . . . lacking in the Watch Tower movement." There are frequent complaints from ex-members that "congregations are rarely warm or friendly enough to prevent some members from feeling lonely and dispirited." (Beckford, 1975:86)

Second, the very same sects, such as Pentecostalism, that are said to be especially attractive to the migrant and common in urban areas seem to appeal equally to those still living in rural areas. They also recruit from those who have lived in the city for many years and have presumably had time to adjust.

Third, migration, and its attendant disorientation and isolation, is surely not a sufficient condition for the rise of sects. Calley (1965:143) argues that the Pentecostal sects among West Indians in London provide a surrogate community for the new immigrants. However, it is equally true that immigration is a time of great falling away from the churches. About 70 percent of the total population of the British Caribbean attend church regularly, compared with about 4 percent of the West Indians in London (Hill, 1970:38). On the basis of figures such as these, it is hard to argue that the experience of migration is pushing people into religious experimentation.

Fourth, the evidence as to whether or not people who join even communally oriented sects have actually experienced loneliness and isolation is inconsistent. Although Petersen and Mauss (1973) found personal histories of drifting among Pentecostals (who are quite similar in many respects), histories of disrupted families were no more common than usual, and members reported no pathological relationships. Nor did Pope (1965:133) validate the surrogate community thesis in his study of Gastonia, North Carolina. Although he was observing an industrializing region of the South in which sects were proliferating, he found no evidence that sect members were more likely to have been recent migrants to the area from the hinterland. Similarly, Dynes (1956:28) could find no association between recency of migration to the city and sectarianism. Nelsen and Whitt (1972:231), using an anomie scale intended to reveal some of the tensions attendant on migration, failed to find any association between anomie and sectarianism.

Clearly then, the surrogate community really cannot be used to point to chronic sources of social strain underlying sects, because the flourishing of sects among migrants and other mobile people has not yet been convincingly related to such strains. This is not to deny any truth to the argument whatsoever. The enormous emphasis placed upon family and community by many sects would surely indicate a need for community, and this can be related plausibly to the stresses of migration and urban life. Just as surely, however, the loss of community is not the only reason for th existence of such sects.

Transvaluation

A slightly different structural theory about the origins of sects is that large scale social changes such as industrialization and urbanization create "pockets" of powerlessness and poverty, and it is to the people in these pockets that sects, in offering an alternative source of power and prestige, make their chief appeal. The sects make a promise for the future, offering a special function or mission to those who will have faith and join. Sectarians are thus encouraged to reject altogether the source of their discontent. "What they cannot claim to *be*, they replace by the worth of that which they will one day become" (Weber, 1965:100). On joining a sect, even the least socially acceptable can imagine themselves among the elect, even the least powerful can look forward to exercising government.

The sectarian does not seek to escape the world of hierarchy and status. Indeed, it is perhaps among sectarians that such concerns are most marked. The difference is that the criteria of status are now religious and not secular. In place of the class concerns of the mundane world, the sect offers multiple grades of spiritual status—saved, sanctified, baptized with the Holy Ghost, baptized with water, and so on. In this way, a sect does not so much improve the status of its members as enable them to transcend ordinary status. Thus, a group such as Hare Krishna can spurn the whole stratification system based on material rewards and replace it with a reward system based on degrees of devotionalism. A Baptist or Pentecostal can ask, "What matters then, if a Methodist has more money but has never been baptized with the Holy Ghost?" (Pope, 1965:137).

The application of this theory, the guiding thesis of which is that sects offer a means of transvaluation, requires the location of those pockets of powerlessness and low status that seem to have been prone to sectarianism. For example, women have long been thought to be especially susceptible to sectarian appeals because of their minority position. This was not so much the case before the nineteenth century (although Ann Lee of the Shakers shows that there were exceptions), but during the last century, when women began to enter the work force (often out of the necessity of having to support a household) new economic pressures began to bear upon them. Unable to operate legitimately in occupations such as teacher, counselor and nurse, women sought to exercise the leadership denied them in secular and religious life by moving into groups that operated on the margins of education, health care, and orthodox religion. In particular, "mind cure" sects such as New Thought, Theosophy, Christian Science and spiritualism attracted large numbers of women, many of whom came to occupy leadership positions in them. No doubt this occurred in part because these manipulationist and thaumaturgical sects, in their optimistic belief in the individual, were quite positive about the status quo, and seemed to males to offer no challenge to it, and in part because these sects merged easily into the more acceptable, growing female occupations of teaching and nursing. However, women were also prominent in the Holiness movement, which coincided with the agitation for women's equality. To some extent, the Holiness movement's emotionalism and its rejection of formal education as an ideal for ministers made it easier for women to gain acceptance in the movement. The same theory that accounts for the high rate of sectarianism among women will also be used to explain sectarianism among the poor, among ethnic minorities, age groups and so on. For example, Balswick (1974:30) argues that the Jesus people were engaged in a generational rebellion against parental authority which they saw symbolized in the power structure of the churches. The common denominator in sectarianism is powerlessness.

ACTION THEORIES

Structural theories have in common a certain "distance" from the individuals with whom they are concerned. They seek to identify structures and processes that seem to be correlated with places and times of intense sectarian activity. Structural theories do not provide much of an understanding of the meaning of becoming a sect member to those involved. A full account of why new religions appear must surely describe how the actors concerned interpret their social circumstances, and what meaning sect involvement has for them. It is this kind of understanding that action theories seek to provide.

It has long been supposed that sects are drawn principally from the more deprived segments of a given population, because sects typically reject the dominant values of society and because the more deprived have little to lose by experimenting with new ideas and practices. But it has become increasingly clear that the most destitute or powerless in a population do *not* form new religious movements; they are the most fatalistic and apathetic of a population. The straightforward assumption that sects are populated by the "disinherited" has gradually been abandoned in the face of mounting evidence not only of the fatalism of the most destitute but also of the obvious appeal many sects have for people who are manifestly not poor. Christian Science, for example, has never appealed to manual workers, the poor, or to the uneducated. Its principal consistency has always been the middle-class office worker, teacher, and small businessman—and even a few aristocrats. "Its appeal is certainly most direct to those who have the blessings to enjoy in the world, and for such enjoyment the system provides a rationalization" (Wilson, 1961:212). Christian Scientists are likely to be, not those without hope, but those who would strive in the world and are uncertain about that striving, those who are inclined to take an optimistic, evolutionary view of the fate of humanity, but need further legitimation for that attitude. Sects that are removed even further from the American mainstream, such as the Children of God and Hare Krishna, also recruit from the middle class. The young members of sects such as these (embracing, perhaps, a poverty they have never known before) have been led by their affluence to question the value of material success and the priority placed by American society on the accumulation of possessions. Joining the Children of God or Hare Krishna provides a more coherent, stable, ascetic and less open-ended life style (Judah, 1974:112; see also Peterson and Mauss, 1973).

It is clear from these examples that what is important in joining a new religious movement is not one's objective circumstances, but the attitude of mind taken toward those circumstances (see Glock, and Stark, 1965:246; Aberle, 1966). The concept used to describe the condition of feeling dissatisfied with one's circumstances is *relative deprivation*. It denotes a conscious experience of a negative discrepancy between legitimate expectations and present, or anticipated, actuality. Strictly speaking, relative deprivation may arise from a false definition of the situation and may therefore by illusory, but for an enduring and widespread feeling to grow, it must to some degree be tied to objective conditions. The important idea is the perception of injustice or intolerable conditions. Thus, even those who are well off will feel discontented if they have been convinced that they are not as well off as they *should* be.

Relative deprivation varies with the dimension of status with which it is associated (class, power, and so forth), and it varies in magnitude, degree and frequency. It is, therefore, something to which careful measures should be applied (see Runciman, 1966). The use of this concept in a theory of sectarianism has great potential—which is yet to be fulfilled, as the following review will indicate.

The purpose of the concept of relative deprivation is to measure social psychological attitudes. Unfortunately, it is often invoked simply as a post hoc structural interpretation of what "must have happened." In other words, the investigator fails to gather any information about expectations and feelings of injustice or discontent and instead infers such feelings, either from an analysis of the sect's teachings or from an analysis of the structural conditions prevailing at the time of joining the sect (see, for example, Petersen and Mauss, 1973:267; Hine, 1974:653). This is clearly a most improper use of the concept.[1]

A more assiduous use of the concept of relative deprivation is exhibited in Schwartz's (1970:41–42) careful participant observation of an urban Pentecostal sect. His analysis illustrates some of the potential and

---

[1]Hine (1974:653) is careful to point out that deprivation "must be conceptualized as relative and it must be perceived or felt." However, she tests the theory by comparing socioeconomic status with acceptance of the belief in the Second Coming of Christ and frequency of tongues speaking. In fact, no correlation exists between either belief or practice and socio-economic status, but in neither case does this say anything about relative deprivation because no social psychological data are provided.

some of the pitfalls of using this concept. Schwartz's working hypothesis was that "if a person decides to resolve his status problems (those which involve his self-respect with regard to his standing relative to others in societal, economic and prestige systems) in religious terms . . . then his sect affiliation can be predicated both by his objective position in societal occupational systems *and* by his subjective assessment or expectations of the probability of future upward mobility in the socioeconomic system." This hypothesis contrasts explicitly with the idea that sectarianism is most common among the *absolutely* deprived.

Schwartz believed that Pentecostals are oriented most of all to status concerns, and that it their exclusion from the respectable middle class that disconcerts them the most—rather than, say, income inequalities. They are, he argued, concerned above all with securing respectability and achieving acceptance of the view that religious and moral qualities, rather than differences in wealth, are the proper measures of respect. Joining a Pentecostal sect, he hypothesized, is caused primarily by status anxiety resulting from actual or anticipated status loss.

In order to test this hypothesis, Schwartz (1970:183) conducted a number of scheduled interviews in which he examined the "status trajectory" of members of the sect—their view of "where they have been, where they are now, and where they hope to go in the occupation system." He found that upper-, upper-middle, middle-middle, and lower-class people were altogether absent from his sample; his subjects were members of either the lower middle class or the stable working class. In order to test his hypothesis about relative deprivation, Schwartz concentrated his interviewing on "those motives which are related to the problem of adaptation for a particular niche in the socioeconomic order." He discovered that his subjects had low or nonexistent occupational aspirations, either for themselves or for their children; they were little interested in their job and saw scant opportunity for learning skills in it; and they showed little inclination to expand their level of autonomy by, for instance, becoming self-employed.

Schwartz concluded that Pentecostals were distinctive in their lack of mobility aspirations, their lack of interest in their job, their failure to take any concrete steps to improve their job marketability (such as education), and their failure to map out their children's future. He therefore judged that the Pentecostals had "tacitly abandoned any realistic efforts to rise in the occupational order, and that they do not seem interested in having their children attempt what they have failed to accomplish or avoided confronting." The sect members had devoted themselves instead to achieving moral status through religious observance, which both compensated for their failure economically and promised them acceptance into the solid middle class. Schwartz therefore judged his hypothesis validated.

The concept of relative deprivation would seem to have been very useful in this case. But a closer examination of the actual use to which it was put in Schwartz's analysis points up some of its pitfalls. Having made the "justifiably naive assumption" that Pentecostals suffer from status deprivation and see in their sect membership a means of reversing status positions, Schwartz was encouraged to confine his investigation to "those motives which are related to the problem of adaptation for a particular niche in the socioeconomic order," even though he admitted that there are many motives for joining sects. In other words, he examined only those motives that seem rational in the light of the life circumstances of the Pentecostals—motives that were purely his own invention. Having thus decided which motives to study Schwartz proceeded to interpret them—in the light of the supposed experience of deprivation. For example, because he believed that Pentecostals desire to "escape from a world with few prospects of radical improvement," he decided that one reason for becoming a Pentecostal is "to escape from a world with few prospects." Furthermore, because he sensed "a fear of losing a rather precarious status advantage," he could understand the motivation behind the intense concern that Pentecostals show for rescuing others from degrading ways of life: they are trying to protect their own status (Schwartz, 1970:166).

Unfortunately, Schwartz was unable to provide any evidence that his Pentecostals had indeed "abandoned" efforts to rise in the social order (as opposed to never having made such efforts at all, which seems more likely). Likewise, he presented no evidence that his subjects felt a sense of deprivation at their inability to realistically plan for career advancement by their children. In other words, the "justifiably naive assumptions" with which Schwartz began became an article of faith to him and he concluded by seeing Pentecostalism as *a solution to a problem he had invented.* He read into the life experiences of Pentecostals motives that were meaningful in the light of the relative deprivation he supposed but for which he provided no evidence.

The difficulties of analyzing sectarianism are clearly illustrated in Schwartz's work. It appears that he assumed relative deprivation but did not demonstrate it, and thereby blocked out other possible explanations. Not only did he confine his interviewing to the younger members of the sect (on the ground that status concerns would be more salient to them), but he also restricted his interrogation to status questions. He further confined his investigation by interpreting each statement about jobs and status as if they did indeed reflect status deprivation. For example, he reported Pentecostals to have "sought rebirth in the Holy Spirit" because they felt their lives were "going down the drain." Schwartz (1970:165) explained that "Pentecostal converts wanted to escape from an inner state over which each could exercise little control and which entailed sinking to a lower level than he felt his better self should be." He then construed this to imply that the average Pentecostal" sees himself in an ambiguous position in the status system of the larger society." In fact, Schwartz presented no evidence to support this argument, or to show this is the way the metaphor of "going down the drain" is to be interpreted. Indeed, according to Schwartz's own report, Pentecostals are indifferent to rankings of occupation or prestige.

Schwartz's research comes close to exhibiting a rigorous and correct usage of the relative deprivation concept. Schwartz did indeed concern himself with how his subjects saw the world around them, and how *they* connected life circumstances with sect membership. However, relative deprivation is a very broad concept and there is a great temptation to make up one's mind about what it actually means in any given situation before observation begins. The use of concepts of status to measure relative deprivation is especially dangerous, for the imagery of the ladder thus connoted tends to narrow people's concerns to a restricted set of goals and means. Schwartz's subjects, unlike their investigator, did not see the social world in terms of one ladder or hierarchy. They were inclined instead to think in terms of individual integrity and respectability, important concepts that have meanings independent of, although to some extent related to, social class concerns. Perhaps, then, Schwartz closed his analysis prematurely. Yet, he did interview and observe his sectarians, and it is only in this way that the most important theory in this field will be truly tested. Invoked in a *post hoc* fashion, the theory tends to be tautological because the only evidence for the cause of the sect (relative deprivation) is the existence of the sect itself. Invoked during a structural analysis, the concept is meaningless because the all-important data are missing. Used to guide in-depth interviewing and prolonged observation, the concept can be very useful, as long as the fact that it is an *assumption* is always remembered.

This review of the various theories of why new religious movements arise and who joins them makes clear both their conceptual development and their tendency to focus on a single cause. It is obvious that sects make multiple appeals, and that sectarians have a variety of motives for joining. Each sect makes available to its members a wide array of rewards. This can be illustrated, by way of conclusion, by considering the Jehovah's witnesses.

The Jehovah's witnesses are a strongly Adventist (or revolutionist) sect and would, according to most explanatory models, appeal to those who have little to gain from this world and would like to see it replaced by another. But observation has shown that the movement "does not stand in any specific relation to a social class: it recruits from a wide range of social classes, although the range does not effectively include

the extremes of privilege and disprivilege" (Beckford, 1975b:153). The
reason is that <u>many meanings can be attached to becoming a witness</u>.

A close examination of the rewards offered to those who are "publishers" in the Watch Tower movement suggests why there should be this
diverse appeal. First, membership in the sect involves, above all else,
"publishing work," which entails door-to-door magazine sales (with back
calls), cell-group study in order to prepare for the door-to-door visita-
tion, and congregational meetings four times a week. This activity is
connected only remotely with the coming of the Kingdom of God. Instead, it provides the witness with a kind of "salvation by works"; his
spiritual status is measured by how well he performs his publishing
work, and the measures are there for all to see. Second, being a witness
means the acquiring of new knowledge through intensive doctrinal
study and class leadership. This learning not only furnishes a new sense
of power but also provides an interracial, even international, community
of acceptance based on shared knowledge. Additionally, the classwork
provides valuable speech and interactional training. Third, witnesses are
expected to conform to a strict moral code, which in many ways resembles that of the Puritan middle class. This code provides an unambiguous guide for living, and the community of witnesses furnishes the support necessary for full conformity to it. The witness is not only assured of
being on the right path but is also helped in following it. Fourth, witnesses are taught that their organization has absolute authority in religion
and that it should be the sole reference for them. The individual witness
thus associates himself with a positive symbol and acquires a new sense of
self-respect and dignity in his relationship to it (Cooper, 1974:707).

This list of rewards could be extended. It is long enough, however, to
indicate that sects present a number of different faces to prospective
converts, and that sect membership is capable of taking on a variety of
meanings for those involved. This does not mean that the various
theories are wrong as much as it means that each must be carefully
related to a particular facet of sectarianism, and that the search must go
on for further dimensions of this kind of religiosity.

Much of the inadequacy of present theories of religious change is due
to their failure to take into account actual *mobilization problems*. The decision to join a religious movement is, of course, affected by background
factors, but it also has a lot to do with the kind of contact established
between the movement and the prospective member. Studies of Pentecostal sects, for example, show that new members have almost always
been recruited by a friend, relative or neighbor (Harrison, 1974b). Even
the Jehovah's witnesses, who do a great deal of door-to-door evangelizing, draw about half of their new members from families, friends, and
workmates (Beckford, 1975b:160). The more established the sect, the

more likely the initial contact is made through a relative—usually the spouse. The more ephemeral the sect, the more likely the contact is made through a friend (Gerlach and Hine, 1970:80).

Frequent personal contact with someone regarded positively who is already a sect member is a much surer basis for predicting the conversion of an individual to a new religious movement than any measure of deprivation or social isolation (Gerlach and Hine, 1970:85; see also Bibby and Brinkerhof, 1974b). This is implied by the fact that if ideological appeals alone were sufficient to generate sects and attract people to them, there would be a much higher proportion of people converted by means of mass propaganda than is presently the case (see Lofland, 1966:63–191). It should be obvious by now that sects are not simply statements of dissatisfaction with the social order in religious guise, and they are not merely reflections of social imperatives. Sects are a rich, symbolic world within which a wide variety of new identities can be formed. The crude tools of sociological analysis described in this chapter are only partly successful in enabling us to understand this world.

THE LEADER

Dramatic and inspiring figures are often associated with the birth of new religions, but how essential are they to religious innovation? This is a difficult question to answer, but what does seem clear is that the fiery prophet in the Old Testament mold is not essential, and that new religious communities commonly form around reformers who are quite unprophetic (Weber, 1965:46). And yet, many movements, including most of the better known and the more successful, *have* been inspired by a prophetic or charismatic figure. It is of considerable interest, then, to examine this figure and the role he plays in mobilizing new religious groups.[2]

The significance of the prophet lies in his claim to have made contact with the sacred—God, the Supreme Being, the Ultimate Force—and to have come forth with a new path to redemption. In making this claim, the prophet preaches truly radical change, for he has gone to the very roots of human understanding to find his vision of the world. Few indi-

---

[2] James Wilson (1973:197) faults existing theories of social movements on the grounds that they fail to explain how the original charter members of a group come together, when the hopes of reward are so slim. He proposes that greater attention be paid to the role of the associational entrepreneur, the individual who is willing to take risks and defer immediate gratifications in the expectation of future reward. These rewards will probably not be monetary (as in the case of a business entrepreneur), but they might well be measured in terms of prestige, power, and ideology: "either he will respond to different rewards. . . or he will have a more distant time horizon than his followers."

viduals have the imaginative and creative powers to maintain contact with ultimate concerns. Prophets are therefore rare. But many people are looking for gifted individuals to deal with their ultimate concerns for them—to make contact by proxy with the sacred. If the times are propitious, then, the prophet will be heeded. He calls the people out—he creates, reveals, liberates and demands that his listeners flee the tired and taken-for-granted routines of established religion.

The prophet who attracts a group of disciples who become personally devoted to him on the basis of announcements he makes about having discovered or having had miraculously revealed to him a new plan of salvation is called a *charismatic* leader. The concept of charisma was introduced into sociological use by the German sociologist Max Weber, writing before the First World War. Weber borrowed the concept from a work by Rudolf Sohm (*Kirchenrecht*) in which "charisma" was used to refer to the "gifts of the Spirit" described in the Scriptures—wisdom, knowledge, faith healing, miracles, prophecy, distinguishing true and false spirits, and ecstatic utterances and their interpretation. Weber used the term to describe the qualities of a certain type of leader, which he defined as follows: ". . . he is set apart from ordinary men and treated as endowed with supernatural, superhuman, or at least specifically exceptional powers or qualities. These are such as are not accessible to the ordinary person, but are regarded as of divine origin or exemplary, and on the basis of them the individual concerned is treated as a leader." Although the emphasis in Weber's (1964:358–59) definition seems to be on the personal attributes of the individual leader, it was not his intention to define charisma as an aspect of a person's character. Rather, he meant to describe a relationship between the leader and his followers, one in which the right to lead is granted on the basis of perceived attributes. An amplification of some of the points in Weber's definition should make this clearer.

First, the charismatic leader gains a following because he is thought to possess exemplary qualities, which manifest themselves in feats of prophecy, divination, heroism, and exceptional endurance. The important thing to note is that these qualities are imputed to this individual by other people; sociologically, it does not matter whether he actually has these characteristics or whether they in fact symbolize what he claims they symbolize. Charismatic recognition is not tied, therefore, to an objective set of personal attributes, but is a function of (1) the qualities demanded or looked for by the group to whom he makes his appeal, and (2) definite acts on his part. The particular qualities selected as exemplary are those that are consonant with the group's circumstances and goals.

To be accepted as a charismatic leader, the individual "must articulate

thoughts and aspirations in a community to which he speaks . . . he articulates what it is that others can as yet only feel, strive towards and
imagine but cannot put into words or translate explicitly into action"
(Burridge, 1969:155). Through his exemplary qualities, the charismatic
leader assures the acceptance of new ideas. These qualities are not ob-
tainable by merit or endeavor; they are derived from some transcendental source of power and knowledge: "What is important is that the
charismatic leader's message should appear to come from a source
beyond common sense experience. It must be a relevation. Usually the
message is claimed, or presumed, to have been revealed in a dream or
vision or some other mystical experience. Whatever the cultural idiom,
the message is taken to be beyond man's wit to devise. It is a divine
revelation, it transcends the capacities of man acting alone" (Burridge,
1969:155).

It has been quite common for charismatic leaders to be credited not
only with superhuman powers but also with divinity. George Baker,
founder and leader of the Kingdom Peace Mission, is an example. The
sect he founded in New York in the 1930s appealed chiefly to poor
blacks who were attracted to the movement by the benefits to be reaped
from the communistic system he established as a central element of sect
life. By far the most powerful appeal of the sect, however, was George
Baker himself, who claimed to be God and, being so believed, assumed
the title of Father Divine. Baker was thought to have healing and
prophylactic powers and he put himself forward as "the only redemption of man" (Cantril, 1963:132). Like Jesus, he was thought to have
miraculous powers of feeding the hungry masses. Charismatic stature is
not confined to males. Ann Lee, founder of the Shakers claimed to be
the female counterpart of Christ (Whitworth, 1975:224), and Mary
Baker Eddy, founder of Christian Science, was believed by many of her
followers to be the "Woman of the Apocalypse" (Wilson, 1961:144). This
list could be extended greatly if we also included those who claimed to be
in such close contact with the divinity that they themselves were touched
with divinity. John Noyes, founder of the Oneida utopian sect, pro-
claimed that he was commissioned to inaugurate the Kingdom of God on
Earth and had been given special powers and privileges to do so: Elijah
Muhammad, leader of the Black Muslims, placed himself in a long line
of semidivine prophets who called their people to redemption.

A second point in Weber's definition is that charismatic leadership is
essentially tied to new obligations and thus entails a radical reorientation
on the part of the followers. It is incorrect to label a merely popular
figure as a charismatic figure, for the truly charismatic person seeks to
escape the mundane world and preaches the overthrow of the present
social order. Charisma transforms all values and breaks all traditional

and rational norms. The prophet's new knowledge does not rely on precedent but flies in the face of it: Jesus said, "It is written but I say unto you . . ." It is a major source of internal transformation, a means by which an individual can articulate the pre-existing discontents of a group and accentuate their sense of being in a predicament to which there is only one solution—the leader himself. Yet although the charismatic leader is revolutionary, he must also appeal to tradition, for only by doing so can he establish communication with his group of followers. Traditional concepts, symbols, and images, albeit reinterpreted, are used to facilitate the acceptance of the radically new. Even Mormonism, which began with Joseph Smith's visions of the Golden Plates in 1830, and later developed into a church of more than a million totally outside the Protestant mainstream, claims to be a divine restoration of the Apostolic Church after centuries of apostasy. It has revived many Old Testament practices (such as polygamy), and committed itself to the establishment of an Israelitish Kingdom of God on Earth. Smith and his followers completely rejected the authority of the established churches without (in their view) abandoning the rock upon which those churches stood. The implication of Smith's teachings, however, were completely sectarian and resulted, of course, in an absolute break from orthodoxy.

The third point to notice in Weber's definition is that there is a special quality to the relationship between the charismatic leader and his followers. Weber tried to summarize this quality with words such as "trust" and "duty." Charismatic leadership cannot be bestowed. It requires an initiative on the part of the leader to make clear his conviction in his mission and therefore in his solemn and inescapable *duty* to lead. Because the charismatic leader takes himself seriously, he seizes power, his is not a choice but a call. On the other side of the charismatic relationship, the followers deposit complete trust in their leader. Although charismatic leadership is not in the power of lesser mortals to give, it is very much a function of recognition made manifest in overt declarations of love, respect, obedience, deference, and sacrifice: an unrecognized charismatic leader is a contradiction in terms. Although there are obvious similarities between the charismatic relationship and, say, the relationship between a popular figure and his "fans," there are significant qualitative differences, which can be grasped by contrasting a love relationship with a relationship between two friends.

Charismatic leaders have played a pivotal role in the birth of many religious movements. Despite the prominence of the prophet, however, there should be no "Great Man" theories in sociology that imply that heroic figures are the sole cause of social changes. New religious movements arise not because great men will them into being, but because specific needs have arisen among groups of people. Explaining religious movements means identifying these needs and describing how the movement, through its leader, promises to satisfy them. Therefore, the necessity of the prophet should not be exaggerated. Not all religious movements have a single undisputed leader: in some cases, like-minded people successfully institute a sect without an individual, or even a group of individuals, coming to dominate the decision-making. This is especially true where the sacred is thought to be widely accessible, or, to put it another way, where charisma is widely dispersed—as in Holiness and, for different reasons, spiritualist sects.

CONCLUSION

New religious movements adopt a "new mode of measuring man, a new integrity, a new community" (Burridge, 1969:13). How are they to be made sociologically intelligible? Whatever else is said, it has to be clearly remembered that there is something which is beyond sociological analysis in the creative act itself: how or why a particular message is received or why it seems appropriate to others is something about which very little is known. On the other hand, the spread of new ideas and practices does not take place randomly. There is a pattern to religious change, and it is this pattern which the theories in this chapter have tried to explain.

New religious movements do not arise out of stable contexts, rather they arise out of a changing social order. The changes are important because they create or intensify discontent, anxiety or isolation. But sociologists are a long way from linking specific kinds of change to particular consequences, and even further from the goal of predicting where and when social change will result in new religious movements. Too many of the explanatory models described in this chapter are monocausal; they state necessary, but not sufficient conditions. Too many of the theories fail to give an understanding of the kinds of needs to which new religious movements address themselves, or make intelligible to the outsider what it means to become newly religious. Lastly, too many of the theories simply fail to treat religious movements as part of a total social whole in which the operation of a transcendent power is a vital part. They tend to ignore, and thus explain away, the actual content of the new religious message, the re-statement of basic cultural assumptions which gives to it popular appeal.

6

BECOMING RELIGIOUS:
CONVERSION
AND COMMITMENT

INTRODUCTION

Becoming religious means assuming a particular kind of identity, a process more broadly conceived as socialization. Beginning at birth, and throughout life, individuals internalize culture and learn how to be active participants in society. For most people, becoming religious is part of this socialization process, as natural and as taken for granted as learning sex-roles. The chief source of recruitment, even for sects, is likely to be the children of existing members (Bibby and Brinkerhof, 1974b). Children are aware, for example, of their religious identity (Protestant, Catholic, or Jew, for instance), by the time they are five—although they tend to equate religions with national and racial identities and consider them mutually exclusive. By the time they are nine, they are able to distinguish between religion and irreligion, and they can identify denominations by their practices. A knowledge and comprehension of beliefs has normally been acquired by the age of twelve. Much of this learning "comes naturally" in the home and among friends, and some of it is imparted by means of formal instruction (see Elkind, 1964).

The family is undoubtedly the strongest source of religious socialization. The mother is the most frequently cited influence on the transmission of religious beliefs, especially among Catholics (Croog, 1967:97;

Argyle and Beit-Hallahmi, 1975:30). Children of religious parents are more likely to be religious than those of non-religious parents (Landis, 1960:344) and family religiosity is the strongest single predictor of a college student's religious attitudes and behavior (Hoge, 1974:113). Of the three major faiths, the influence of the family on a child's religiosity is perhaps the strongest among Jews, who are subject to a flow of influence starting with Jewish parental religiosity and extending to Jewish education, attendance at synagogue, involvement in Jewish organizations, and Jewish education for one's children—at which point the generational cycle starts once more (Lazerwitz, 1973:213).

Primary socialization is followed by secondary socialization in adolescence and adulthood. Attendance at church, for instance, leads to greater knowledge of religious teachings. Schooling is also important: "In the long run, . . . attendance at parochial school and a strong family religious background may combine to form adults who are more religiously committed, informed and active than those who lack one or the other ingredients" (Johnstone, 1975:87). School and family work together to socialize people religiously:

> While young people are in parochial schools, the religious atmosphere of the school does have some considerable effect on their religious attitudes and behavior, with the increment being particularly strong for those whose religiousness was not previously developed in the family environment. However, when the young people graduated from school then the school's impact seems to be reduced, if not completely eliminated, in those younger people for whom the religiousness of the school has not been prepared and reinforced by religiousness of the family. Adult life then leads to a substantial erosion of the impact of parochial schooling on the religious development of those whose family backgrounds are not religious, but little or no erosion of the effect of parochial schooling takes place in those graduates who come from religiously oriented families (Greeley and Galen, 1971:293).

More often than not, teenage conversions are a matter of heightened commitment to already known religious beliefs. Such adolescent conversions can be understood partly "in the context of a rebellion [against the parents,], which is expressed in a 'holier than thou' demonstration against their superficial religiosity" (Argyle and Beit-Hallahmi, 1975:59). These conversions need entail no change of life-style, but merely a more systematized and profound grasp of an already pious life.

This chapter takes much of this kind of religious socialization for granted: for most people it is indeed true that religion is learned on their mother's knee and in Sunday school. Instead, the discussion here will focus on the more extreme case of religious conversion, the purpose being to highlight the way in which a new religious identity is formed.

CONVERSION

Religious conversion can mean a total change of identity, a wrenching of the personality, and is therefore a subject worthy of study in its own right. This concept is also important, however, in understanding the formation of sects. For although conversion is not confined to sects, it is not normally considered possible to become a member of a sect unless one has undergone conversion, and becoming a sect member is perhaps the purest expression of the kind of rebirth suggested by the concept. The following discussion of conversion will focus on this pure form, in which an individual totally changes his world view, as when he becomes a member of a religious sect or changes from one faith to another. At the conclusion of the discussion, the concept of alternation will be introduced, a concept that helps us understand less drastic switches from one denomination to another.

Conversion is usually described as a change of identity, one that is vastly different from, say, merely switching jobs or altering spending habits. Lincoln (1973:114) describes what this means for the Black Muslim:

> The true believer who becomes a Muslim casts off at last his old self and takes on a new identity. He changes his name, his religion, his homeland, his 'natural' language, his moral and cultural values, his very purpose in living. He is no longer a Negro, so long despised by the white man that he has come almost to despise himself. Now he is a black man-divine, ruler of the universe, different only in degree from Allah Himself. He is no longer discontented and baffled, harried by social obliquy and a gnawing sense of personal inadequacy. Now he is a Muslim, bearing in himself the power of the Black Nation and its glorious destiny. His new life is not an easy one: it demands unquestioning purpose. He may have to sacrifice his family and friends, his trade and profession, if they do not serve his new-found cause. Be he is not alone, and he now knows *why* his life matters. He has seen the truth and the truth has set him free.

Not all sects place so much emphasis on securing some kind of conversion at time of entry. The Muslims are perhaps among the more extreme in this respect. In all new religious movements, and in those that permit only adult membership, some kind of conversion is a necessity, but the amount of change varies. Conversionist sects, such as the Holiness and Pentecostal movements (and the Methodists before them), lay great stress on the need for conversion and are diligent in their proselytizing. But not all sects see this as the kind of work they should be doing. Introversionist sects such as the Amish have "little interest in evangelizing others, since inner illumination or inspiration is not readily communicated to outsiders who may, indeed, be regarded as contaminating the faithful" (Wilson, 1970:43). Reformist sects, believing themselves to be the "leaven of the lump," are not active in conversion work either.

A Step-Sequence Model of Conversion

The conversion process comprises a number of stages, and an individual may drop out at any one of them. Lofland (1966:57) distinguishes between the "verbal convert," whose interest and disposition is guaranteed but whose commitment is uncertain, and the "total convert," who has become a "deployable agent" of the group and who has totally identified with it. Gordon (1967:218–25) makes a similar distinction between the "pro-forma" convert and the "authentic" convert.

A step-sequence model is most useful in explaining conversion. One precondition of conversion is the experience of "enduring, acutely felt tensions" stemming from some kind of deprivation, an experience that impels the individual to search among other religious groups for the satisfaction of her needs (Lofland, 1966:7). Religious conversion will follow if these tensions are already seen in a religious light. In fact, only a fraction of the converts to sects are former non-believers, this is true even of sects that appeal to the "unchurched." Pope (1965:133) found that at least 80 percent of the membership of Gastonia's sects were former members of other orthodox denominations.

A second precondition for conversion is the experience of some "crisis" or "turning point," a "moment when old lines of action were completed, had failed, or had been or were about to be disrupted" (Lofland, 1966:50). Rather than speak of crisis, Beckford (1957b:165) talks of "a context of mental, and occasionally physical, anguish" as a precondition for conversion to the Jehovah's witnesses. Those he interviewed cited anxieties about illness, sexual problems, and other personal problems; concern for the stability of important social institutions, such as the family; the danger of nuclear war; a general anxiety concerning the future, especially as it affects one's children; and apprehension about major social problems of the day, such as crime, violence and urban decay. Beckford, much more than Lofland, sees the crisis as being a social rather than a personal one. In other words, conversion need not stem from any sense of personal inadequacy or from a crisis on one's life (although it may), but might be caused instead by a sense of social crisis.

Sects actually play upon this theme, urging the need to convert by pointing to society's moral decay or to the sins in an individual's past life. A misspent life and the crisis to which it has led is a common subject of the testimonials that are such an important part of demonstrating loyalty to the sect. In giving a testimonial, the individual strips himself of his old identity under the guidance and with the help of the group. He describes how " a sinner" was led to "see the light." A dramatic event or "leading" usually plays an important part in this tale.

Unfortunately, the concept of crisis is rather vague, and crises are hard to recognize in real life. The idea that conversion is always preceded by a crisis, the presence or absence of which can always be demonstrated, is hardly tenable. It is more appropriate to treat the idea of crisis as part of the "vocabulary of motives" of the convert, one way in which the convert prepares herself for and makes sense of her change of life. Even so, a study of converts to Mormonism found little evidence that converts saw their transition as being connected with life crises they had experienced (Seggar and Kunz, 1972). Perhaps the salience of the crisis, and the degree to which conversion is seen as being related to crisis vary from one group to another.

A third precondition of conversion is the severing or weakening of previous social bonds—to family, friends, and community. Gordon (1967:33), interviewed forty-five interfaith converts and was told by thirty-eight of them that "there had been but little communication not only between their parents and themselves, but with siblings as well," prior to the conversion. The converts to the Unification Church studied by Lofland (1966) were mostly "loners" living on their own and away from their families. To some extent, the process of conversion *must* entail the weakening of previous social relationships, as will any change in group membership, but its significance should not be overestimated. Again, it is probably a means by which the convert learns to make sense of what he has already done, rather than the cause of what he is about to do. The sect he joins will be anxious to portray previous loyalties in negative terms because these old attachments compete with commitment to the sect. The process of conversion is thus partly a coming to see old friendships as valueless.

More important than the weakening of old ties is the establishment of affective bonds with the prospective group (see Hine, 1969). To many, conversion requires stressful experience and group support in order to be carried through. It is other group members who help to describe, explain, and then legitimate what is being experienced, and it is they who offer the necessary emotional support and encouragement. The convert looks to the group for guidance along an already partly formed path.

Conversion is a movement *toward* rather than a departure *from*, a matter of growing conformity rather than increasing nonconformity. Conversion frequently means "coming to accept the opinions of one's friends" (Lofland, 1966:52). It is a positive step, one that is taken after a prolonged period of denying changes that are, in fact, gradually taking place, a matter of "coming home" (Tamney, 1970). As often as not, it is a final admission that change has indeed occurred. Most of the Mormons interviewed by Seggar and Kunz (1972) felt that their prior establishment of warm, friendly relations with Mormons had been the most important factor in their conversion to that faith—more important than their knowledge of Mormon teachings, of which they had scant knowledge at the time of their conversion.

The step-sequence model of conversion conveys a vivid imagery of people being pushed and pulled from one religious group to another. If this suggests that the convert is the helpless victim of social forces, then it is misleading. The individual plays an active role in conversion: she is not converted, but converts. She engages in a process of interaction in which she negotiates a new identity for herself.

The step-sequence model is most applicable to situations in which conversion involves a fundamental change of identity, where it is a matter of adopting a deviant role and moving across considerable social distances. Conversion to the Unification Church, to Mormonism, or to the Jehovah's witnesses would seem to be suitable cases, but what about the Presbyterian who becomes an Episcopalian?

Travisano (1970:598) argues that "conversions" are not all alike and that the simple "alternation" should be distinguished from the more complex conversion. Conversion is a radical break—from Jew to fundamentalist Christian, from Catholic to Protestant, from Methodist to Hare Krishna devotee—it is "a radical reorganization of identity, meaning and life" (Travisano, 1970:600). The convert is referred to as an "apostate," or "heretic," and is placed under heavy pressure to change his mind.

Alternation means a change of religious affiliation, but it does not, like so many conversions, mean the assumption of a deviant role. On the contrary, alternation is a common, almost expected, kind of religious accomodation to altered social circumstances, part of a general change of life-style. Thus, a Pentecostal might become a Methodist or a Methodist an Episcopalian as she moves up the social ladder in conformity to social expectations that she will change the kind of voluntary associations to which she belongs as her circumstances improve. Such changes are fairly common, are associated with no crisis, entail no real transformation of the self, and require little or no renunciation of friends. Some are almost routine, as when an adolescent finally affirms her membership in the church and formally enters it, or when a spouse changes denominations in order to keep a marriage homogeneous.

Alternation occurs more frequently than conversion. Within Protestantism, denomination switching is especially common. For example, 46 percent of a sample of Protestant church members in California had once belonged to another denomination (Stark and Glock, 1968:184). Congregationalists and Presbyterians are more likely to have switched than Episcopalians, Lutherans or Baptists. It is possible by inference to substantiate these findings by citing a national sample gathered by the National Opinion Research Center in 1965 comparing father's and subject's religious affiliation. Forty percent of those presently Protestant reported that their father's denomination differed from their own. Converts to Catholicism and Judiasm were far fewer, and converts from Catholicism and Judaism were also scarce. Eight-six percent of the Catholics and 98 percent of the Jews in the sample reported that their father was of the same faith as themselves (Stark and Glock, 1967:196). Among Protestants, Baptists and Lutherans have the lowest proportion of converts among them; Congregationalists, Presbyterians, and Episcopalians have the most. It is likely that the more liberal the denomination theologically, the larger the proportion of converts in its membership. For example, 89 percent of the ultra-liberal Unitarian-Universalist Association once belonged to another denomination (Tapp, 1973:17). Not all estimates of switching are this high. A *Catholic Digest* survey in 1965 reported that only 20 percent of its respondents had switched denominations (Marty, Rosenberg and Greeley, 1968:306). Counting the number of new Protestant church members in a western Canadian city, Bibby and Brinkerhof (1973:280) discovered that an even lower proportion, 9 percent, were actual converts. Most of the remaining were new only to a church in that city, having reaffiliated after moving there.

The occasions of such alternations seem to be fairly standard. The most common occasion for switching to another denomination seems to be either marriage or moving to another city or community in which no congregation of one's original denomaination is nearby (Fichter, 1951:40; Bibby and Brinkerhof, 1973:280; Marty, Rosenberg and Greeley, 1968:206). As for the direction of alternation, Stark and Glock (1968:187) maintain that "people who change their church tend to move from more conservative bodies to theologically more liberal ones." Mueller (1971), having reanalyzed Stark and Glock's data, argues that the picture is not so simple. People tend to move to churches that are convenient to get to, similar in liturgy to the denomination they have just left, and that have the same kind of social composition. The theological position of the denomination or the pastor is a minor reason for alternation.

The application of the step-sequence model to such switching can only be partial. This sort of behavior does not entail the kind of identity transformation and deviance the step-sequence model identifies as typical of sectarian conversion. On the other hand, there are some respects in which the model does seem to fit. Although obviously not the emotional crisis the model anticipates, marriage *can* be an enormously stressful experience and *can* function as a "turning point" in the individual's life, sufficient at least to induce him to change to the religion of his spouse or suggest that they both change to a third religion. Similarly, migration to another community need not entail the often abrupt and bitter severance of old social relationships that accompanies conversion to a sect, but denominational switching is no doubt encouraged by the loss of old friends and acquaintances upon moving and by the strangeness of the new location, especially if there is no congregation of the original denomination accessible. Personal relationships also seem an important factor in alternations. For example, about half of the adult Lutherans sampled by Kloetzli (1961:188) reported that their first contact with their present church was "some form of personal contact." It makes sense, then, to keep the model in mind when examining all forms of change from one religious denomination or faith to another. The only danger stems from exaggerating the conditions or forces necessary for the change and attaching too much significance to the change involved.

COMMITMENT

All social groups require some degree of commitment from their members if they are to survive and accomplish their objectives. A person who is committed to a group is one who defines his own needs as coextensive with that group's necessities and acts in a consistent manner with respect to them. The problem of securing and maintaining commitment is felt more urgently in marginal groups such as sects, than in more orthodox denominations. This is partly because a more intense commitment is expected, but it is also because commitment is harder to sustain in deviant groups. This is especially true where, for instance, entry to the sect is a ritually important event which is accompanied by and expected to produce great changes. The heightened expectations of the noviate increases problems of subsequently sustaining loyalty. Yet, although the issue of commitment may loom larger in sects than in other kinds of religious organization, the problem is a perennial one. Commitment processes witnessed in sects are the more exaggerated forms of those found in all religious associations.

Sects provide a particularly interesting arena in which to study commitment processes because they have to defend themselves not only against orthodoxy, but also against antireligion as well. Furthermore, in sects, it is possible to observe commitment mechanisms in the process of formation. The degree of commitment varies with the type of sect. The utopian and introversionist types perhaps demand the most commitment because of their goal of totally encapsulating the member; the manipulationist and thaumaturgical types demand only partial commitment.

Once a person has been persuaded to join a religious group, she must be induced to maintain her loyalty to it despite frequent and perhaps hostile challenges from the outside world. Actually, it is easier to maintain commitment than to secure an initial conversion, particularly if membership carries the stigma of deviance and exposure to social censure, for joining creates cognitive dissonance. As the convert asks herself whether being associated with the sect is really worth the loss of friends, social status, and perhaps even a job, she is constantly assailed with doubts about the wisdom of her choice. One ready way to assuage these doubts is to inflate the perceived rewards of sect membership by stressing the importance of the sect and its mission, and de-emphasizing the significance of its critics. This process is facilitated by the highly supportive behavior of other sect members, who "prime the pump" by impressing on the new member the importance of the group and the rightness of her decision to join.

The core of commitment is a reciprocal relationship between what a person is willing to give the sect and what it, in turn, expects of him. A sect holds its members most firmly when its social requirements reflect their self-interests. Commitment means that an individual renounces his own "selfish" interests, voluntarily restricts his range of choices, and withdraws his investments in objects other than the group itself. Becoming committed is facilitated if the individual stakes "something of value to him, something originally unrelated to his present line of action, on being consistent in his present behavior." Then the "consequences of inconsistency will be so expensive that inconsistency . . . is no longer a feasible alternative" (Becker, 1960:35). Commitment is therefore cumulative: its strength is measured by the number of "side bets" the individual is prepared to make on his original decision. The sect is interested in multiplying the number of these "side bets."

Commitment varies not only from one religious group to another but between various members of the group. The responsibility of defining what level of commitment may be considered appropriate lies with the leaders of the sect. It is they who decide what membership entails. It is therefore possible to suffer as much from overcommitment as from undercommitment; members may seek to invest *too* much in the group. The signs of undercommitment are easy to recognize. They include apathy, lack of task motivation, abated idealism, and an unwillingness to make personal sacrifices. The signs of overcommitment are "a penchant for the spectacular rather than the efficient and a tendency to grapple with the first task at hand instead of considering other tasks with more delayed but more important effects" (Demerath and Theissen, 1966:685). A sect rejects commitment greater than it has the resources to handle. Fanaticism may not be welcomed, for instance, if it presents to outsiders an exaggerated image of the kind of self-sacrifice demanded of noviates. The Catholic Church handled over-commitment by instituting monastic orders. They insulated the drastically spiritual elements from the steady operation of the ordinary religious community.

The kind of commitment demanded depends a lot on the teachings of the sect. Introversionist sectarians, for example, typically demand total commitment because they tend to see themselves as the *vessels* of divinity. They attempt to regulate their lives in such a way as to conform to their particular image of an ideal world-hence their intense concern with interpersonal relationships. Manipulationist sects demand only partial commitment because they do not offer an exclusive path to salvation. They seek only to uplift their members' lives in certain respects and are willing to tolerate multiple membership and a variety of ethical standards.

Religious groups do not expect that all members will be able to or willing to make the same commitment to the group, and they acknowledge this by instituting different grades of membership. Usually, sects use their own jargon to make a distinction between full and associate members. Thus Shakers distinguished between "Noviate," "Junior," and "Senior" church orders. Jehovah's witnesses separate "Pioneers" from "Publishers." Mormons elevate "Deacons" above the rank and file. The Children of God refer to the newer, untried members as "Babes" to signify that full performance is not yet expected of them. A new member later becomes a "Younger Brother" and finally an "Elder Brother." Not all distinctions are so formal, of course, but most religious groups have some kind of "onion-skin" arrangement: the few highly committed members composing the core of the sect, while those evidencing lesser degrees of enthusiasm are relegated to the gradually enlarging number, at the periphery, who make little sacrifice and expect fewer rewards.

Commitment cannot be secured by coercion. It is essentially a personal, voluntary decision. The decision is made on one of the three following grounds (Kanter, 1972:69). More accurately, it is made *principally* on one of these three grounds, for commitment always involves all three.

1. *Instrumental:* The individual decides that the material cost of leaving the group would be greater than the cost of remaining in it.
2. *Affective:* The individual feels bound to the group by strong, seemingly unbreakable emotional ties, which exceed those felt toward any other person or group.
3. *Evaluative:* The person judges that the demands the group makes upon him are right and just and that his conformity to group norms is most likely to realize the values he holds.

In principle, therefore, commitment is a fusion of material interests, emotion and values. Although the first may play a minor part in religious associations, it is not an unimportant one, for many religious groups appeal partly on the grounds that they will help improve the economic fortunes of their adherents.

Sectarians are quite conscious of the fact that maintaining commitment is a problem. Many have purposely instituted mechanisms to induce greater commitment, while, in other cases, practices that were originally intended for other purposes perform this function latently. A list of some of these mechanisms, with special reference to utopian sects, has been provided by Kanter (1972). This list can be of general usefulness as long as its utopian-like assumption that total commitment is the natural good of a sect is borne in mind.

Sacrifice

"The process of sacrifice asks members to give up something as a price of membership. Once members have agreed to make the 'sacrifices' their motivation to remain participants increases" (Kanter, 1972:76). The Children of God, for example, surrender all possessions on entering the sect (Davis and Richardson, 1976:334). It might seem strange to begin a list of commitment mechanisms with sacrifice. At first glance, commitment would appear to rely most on the positive benefits which might accrue from involvement. But the *costs* of membership also bind the individual to the group. A person tends to see a course of action as valuable if she has paid highly for it. For example, tithing instills in the giver greater loyalty to the group because membership is something for which a price has been paid. By the same token, the individual has a lesser stake in the other goods that money could have bought.

All sects require that their members make sacrifices of some kind. The consumption of certain foods, drinks, and drugs might be banned or certain pastimes such as dancing, light reading, theater going, music making, and playing games might be prohibited. Members might also be asked to give up free time by devoting many hours to working for the group. The Jehovah's witnesses, for example, impose such an arduous work-load of house-visits and back calls that little time is left for other pursuits. Members of the Unification Church devote most of the day "to activities such as 'witnessing' on the street, giving and listening to lectures, and attending other functions" (Robbins *et al.*, 1976:115). Note, however, that sects often appeal to those who are already deprived, and the "sacrifice" they make might be largely symbolic. Poor people might take a vow of poverty, swearing to avoid indulgence and excess; the powerless might declare that a time of trial and tribulation must be endured before the good times come. The impact of all sacrifice, whether material or symbolic, is to make involvement in the group so costly as to encourage the belief that membership *must* be valuable.

Sacrifice is made when a person has to "lay himself on the line" for the sake of his beliefs. A simple, public profession of belief, or the public enactment of ritual, may be enough to do this if the group is stigmatized by the public, because the individual intentionally draws the stigma on himself and sacrifices prestige. For example, "In a society where public display of intense emotion is reserved for spectator sports, and where the appropriate background for spontaneous and uninhibited self-expression is the cocktail party, the abandonment of the Pentecostal to a joyous outflow of unintelligible vocalization and possibly some nonconsciously controlled physical behavior is considered indecent if not insane" (Hine, 1969:224). Authentic membership of a Pentecostal sect carries with it the expectation that the individual will be open to, and display, the gifts of the Spirit. It also carries with it the probability that he will be ridiculed and thought unable to properly control himself in public. In other sects, it is not mere lowered prestige or ridicule that membership brings, but the risk of arrest. For example, members might be expected to openly use controlled substances like

LSD and marijuana or illegally handle poisonous snakes and thereby enter the criminal underworld.

Investment

The individual who gives up something in order to join a group makes a sacrifice. But he might contribute something to the group in the expectation of greater return in the future, in which case he makes an investment in the group. This investment constitutes a bond which ties him to the group until he reaps his reward. The greater the investment, the greater the commitment. Investment varies in degree and kind from one religious group to another: (1) members might be encouraged to invest all of their resources in the group, or they might be permitted to retain personal control over much of what they own; (2) a sect might hold all invested property in trust, or make it available for communal use, or exchange it for facilities (land, buildings, etc.) which are of use for the whole group; (3) the investment might be long or short term, fixed of fluid. The larger and more fixed the investment, and the more it disappears into the communal facilities of the group, the greater the commitment. The investor will have contributed to the "capital equipment" of the group, ready to identify with its fortunes and discount the demands of the world at large.

Renunciation

Sects, and to a certain degree all religious groups, demand of their members an exclusive allegiance to fellow members, which means that ties with kin and friends, indeed, all forms of involvement with "the world," be renounced. Renunciation takes several forms:

ISOLATION. The most complete form of removal from the world is absolute vicinal segregation: the group attempts to be a world unto itself, furnishing its members with all their wants and obviating any need for contact with unbelievers. This strategy, confined almost exclusively to utopian and introversionist sects, is practicable only in sparsely populated areas and is becoming increasingly difficult to follow. Hawthorne (1955:24) describes how, for the Doukhobor community of seventy years ago, "the individual found his friends, his work and subsistence, his family life, the answer to all questions of justice, meaning and value, and the direction even for the details of his existence. . . . Illiteracy. . . . safeguard against change, as did the development of a protective shell of evasion in dealing with queries and conversations with non-Doukhobors. . . . the *mir* supplied all needs, there was no satisfactory life for an individual leaving the sect, no role or occupation, no niche for a displaced individual." The "protective shell" is much more fragile today, when the mass media and an interventionist State play so large a role in daily life. Sects like the Old Colony Mennonites and the Bruderhof have migrated from one country to another to escape the encroachments of the outside world on their religious community.

INSULATION. A milder form of renunication is to carefully regulate the interaction between sect members and the "unclean." This means imposing restrictions on the entry of nonmembers into the life of the sect and setting limits on sect members' involvement in the outside world. For example, the Hutterites welcome tourists, salesmen and customers into their community, but only authorized sect members are allowed to talk to them. The Exclusive Brethren do not welcome outsiders at their meetings of worship, nor do they meet many non-members in the outside world, for their excursions into profane society are carefully regulated. The sect does little evangelizing; Brethern are reluctant to occupy dwellings in which non-Brethren also live; children are discouraged from playing with or making friends with non-Brethren children; adolescents are not encouraged to go to college; and adult Brethren are not permitted to belong to a trade union (Wilson, 1967:326–329).

The Shakers, too, designed an elaborate set of rules to minimize interaction between members and nonmembers. The faithful were expected to obtain permission to leave the "territory," and those who did leave were expected to "cleanse" themselves by confession on their return. Only the trustees were allowed to deal with strangers, and even their conversation was monitored. All incoming news was censored, and letters were routinely opened (Whitworth, 1975:29). Because the essence of sectarianism is its apartness, examples of insulation can easily be found. More recently, urban sects have instituted some of these insulation techniques. Father Divine, leader of the Kingdom Peace Mission, strictly forbade his "children" to have direct contact with those outside the sect, wherever this could be avoided, and prohibited their reading anything not written by him (Cantril, 1963:128).

Sects that proselytize vigorously, such as the Jehovah's witnesses, experience considerable difficulty in securing an adequate degree of insulation. The witnesses' answer to this is to carefully regulate the necessary interaction between "publisher" and the public: "They are trained only to distribute literature and to engage members of the public in set pieces of conversation. The interaction between witnesses and audience is therefore highly structured in advance and delimited in the accepted scope of its content" (Beckford, 1975a:80).

In addition to the restriction of direct contact between members and nonmembers, insulation takes other, more symbolic forms. The sect encourages its members to clearly distinguish between "us" and "them," between the "clean" and the "unclean," and thereby lessen their desire to make contact with the unsaved except under carefully controlled circumstances. The Shakers, for example, were taught that the world is an intrinsically evil place, an antechamber to perdition to be avoided at all costs.

Some sects demand that special apparel be worn, and in that way set their people apart. The colorful European costumes of the Amish and the saffron robes or *dhoties* of Hare Krishna are more than mere display: they help preserve the distinctiveness and solidarity of the group. A similar function is performed by the use of special language or dialect. The "Pennsylvania Dutch" spoken by the Amish is actually a German dialect which they have preserved since the time of the European settlement. The Hutterites, too, speak German and view the world entirely through German thought patterns and from a perspective "common in medieval Europe before the dawn of modern science" (Hostetler, 1974:149). The insulating function of language is enhanced by controls on education. Thus, both the Amish and the Hutterites limit their children's formal education to the elementary grades, after which, learning is "on the job" which, for these largely agricultural people, is nonverbal. Most sects, even if they do not speak a separate language or dialect, will develop an argot. They will use standard English terms in nonstandard ways which are ambiguous or incomprehensible to the outsider but to the insider convey specific and valuable information (see Zaretsky, 1974a).

THE SEVERANCE OF NON-SECT RELATIONSHIPS. Renunciation means that all relations with people outside the sect are to be subordinated to relations with fellow members. Workmates, friends and even family might be forsaken in the interests of the sect. There is no shortage of examples of such practices, from the venerable and solemn vow of the nun as she becomes "the bride of Christ," to the sudden disappearance of the modern teenager who becomes one of the Children of God. Even if the convert is not specifically commanded to stop seeing family and friends, she will tend to do so, simply because she now has less in common with them and receives less approbation from them. The experience of this Black Muslim is probably typical:

When you start going to the temple four or five times a week and selling the newspaper, you do not have time for people who are not doing these things. We drifted—the friends I had—we drifted apart. . . . All the friends I have now are in the Nation. Another Brother and I get together regularly and read the Koran and other books. . . . We read and talk about the things we read and try to sharpen our thinking. I couldn't do that with my old friends (Quoted in Howard, 1971:456).

The Muslims are one of the many sects that encourage new members to change their name, not only to symbolize their rebirth but also to set themselves apart from the unclean. They begin their withdrawal and detachment from "normal" society by denying their "Negroness" in a ceremony in which the traditional stereotypes about black people are denounced. The initiate drops his "slave" or last name and replaces it with *X* or some other symbol given him by the leader. In this fashion, Malcolm Little became Malcolm X, and Cassius Clay became Muhammed Ali.

DISSOLUTION OF DYADIC RELATIONSHIPS WITHIN THE GROUP. The object here is the same: to prevent the growth or perpetuation of ties that might compete with the primary loyalty of the individual to the group. Sect members are encouraged to relate to one another principally if not solely on the basis of their common spiritual fellowship. This means that family relationships and friendships in the sect should take second place. To accomplish this, sects implement a variety of rules, including celibacy, free love, planned sexual relations, a ban on friendships and the regular disruption of work groups and study sessions.

Communion

Beliefs are more plausible if they are known to be shared. The more one engages in positive interaction with those who hold similar beliefs, the more plausible those beliefs will appear to be. For this reason, intense feelings of brotherhood, comradeship, fellowship, and the reality and power of the group greatly foster strong commitment to the sect. Sects have developed a variety of ways to encourage this kind of communion:

ENSURING MEMBERSHIP HOMOGENEITY. The more uniform the religious background, social status and ethnic origin of members, the greater the sense of communion among them. This homogeneity can be achieved either by deliberate selection or by subsequent socialization.

All other things being equal, socialization and selectivity can frequently be substituted for each other, on the simple ground that if the organization can recruit participants who have the characteristics it requires it does not have to develop these characteristics through training or education. On the other hand, if the organization has to accept every individual who wishes to join, or every member of a specific but large and unselected group, it has to turn to socialization to produce the desired characteristics (Etzioni, 1961:158).

By definition, sects are highly selective concerning who they allow into full membership. The Shakers, for instance, cognizant of the rigors of utopian life, obliged each candidate for admission to undergo a long probation during which he could learn the ways of the sect without having to make the sacrifice of spouse, children, and property demanded of full members (Tyler, 1962:150). Similarly, the Hutterites ask each initiate to spend one year living in the community, and only at the successful completion of this year is full membership granted. Other sects impose some kind of test, examination or ordeal in order to sift out those unlikely to conform to the demands of the group, or they reserve full membership only for those who show they are capable of living a spiritual life.

Sects that do not select carefully are more scrupulous in their socialization practices so as to ensure membership consensus. Sectarians typically shield their children from the outside world so that they grow to at least adolescence before being exposed to competing norms and values. Adult members are submitted to a constant barrage of propaganda information about the accomplishments of their leaders, the success of their rallies and meetings, testimonials from converts; occasionally, plaudits from nonmembers. Socialization may become formalized in schools, Bible institutes, and correspondence courses (the Black Muslims have their own university), and it almost certainly becomes part of the regular routine of the sect. The Jehovah's witnesses, for example, attend a weekly "drill" during which questions are asked on all aspects of the sect's work. Even spiritualists, who have not felt any strong urge to set up elaborate organizations, have had Sunday schools since the 1890s (Nelson, 1969:174).

THE SHARING OF PROPERTY AND TASKS. A sense of community is also generated by cooperative work, a feeling of a task jointly accomplished, and by sharing and helping among members of the group. Sect members generate fellow-feeling from the idea that they are commonly subject to urgent demands that they can fully meet only by cooperation. This notion is especially effective if faith is supplemented by a daily regimen of work. It is these demands made jointly that transform sect membership from a leisure-time pursuit to actual commitment. Speaking of a black, Holiness sect, Williams (1974:91) comments on the enormous amount of work which went into the preparation of periodic feasts; what was important about these feasts was not only the communal eating but the cooperative endeavor they symbolized. Members of this sect also stressed the importance of helping activities, such as assisting a fellow member in moving.

REGULAR GROUP CONTACT. *In its most extreme form, this consists of* communal living, eating, and recreation, as in the several utopian and introversionist sects. Thus, in writing about the Unification Church, Robbins *et al.* (1976:115) note that "when one joins the family one generally gives up one's other instrumental and expressive involvements and takes up residence in a communal 'Unification center' henceforth devoting most of one's energies to the movement. . . ."

RITUALS. Often aimed specifically at bolstering a sense of community, rituals provide an opportunity for the members of the group to come together to reaffirm their faith and strengthen their fellow-feeling. The worship services, with their communal singing, joing prayer, and perhaps the collective experience of speaking in tongues; commemorative rites, such as baptism, marriage and funerals; feasts, picnics, and outings to other churches; rallies and conventions—all serve to unify the sect. These rituals not only gather sect members together physically but also provide an opportunity for the meaning of sect membership and the importance of faith in the group and its leaders to be reasserted in a dramatic and memorable way.

The group is also pulled together by rituals that test one's faith, for through the common witness of an ordeal, the meaning of sect membership is dramatized and the witnesses vicariously draw strength for challenge to their own faith. One of the most notorious ordeals is the ritual of snake handling among some of the fundamentalist sects of the American South. At the meetings of these sects, poisonous snakes (representing the Devil) are handled as a test of faith. It is hard to imagine a more dramatic way of publicly demonstrating faith.

> The din of rhythmic guitars, shouting and singing, clapping and stamping become more insistent. Several worshipers are dancing 'under the power,' whirling about and moving vigorously in time with the music. A young man about twenty-five, sitting on the

edge of the platform and holding a pair of copperheads in his cupped palms, allows two older men to drape eight or ten rattle snakes and copperheads about his head and shoulders. At the same time, a woman removes her shoes and pokes her feet at a large yellow rattler she has placed on the floor. The serpent coils, raises its tail, and rattles menacingly, but does not strike. Another devotee, holding two rattle snakes, one in each hand, close to his body at about waist level, slowly lifts and turns his hands so that the reptiles' swaying heads are brought within a few inches of his face. When the rattlers stop moving and dangle 'limp as shoestrings, the worshiper exclaims, 'Glory to God! The mighty power!' and passes the serpent to other believers (Kane, 1974:296).

Although these proceedings seem chaotic, they follow a fairly well-defined pattern which is familiar to all members of the sect. They know what to expect and demand that the same sequence be repeated in each service. The ordeal is part of a regular ritual of dedication and commitment to the group and the faith for which it stands. The occasional deaths from snake bites or strychnine poisoning only add to the power and awesomeness of the ritual.

GROUP SOLIDARITY. Sects also generate ideological communion by continually emphasizing the ultimate value of love, fellowship, and solidarity, and by fostering the idea that "power" or "blessings" are more likely to be received in group settings characterized by these values. Sectarians are enjoined to treat one another and the group as ends in themselves rather than merely as means to other ends, and solidarity rather than individualism is promoted as an ideal goal. Those who promote harmony in the group are symbolically rewarded. The sect may also play on the sense of apartness and perhaps persecution that members come to feel because of their involvement in the group. The sect may, for example, contrast the wickedness of the world with the goodness of those in the sect, and point up the dangers of disloyalty and disunity.

Mortification

Like sacrifice, mortification is a form of bonding to a group that is often neglected in the preoccupation with the rewards of sect membership. But it is undeniable that one of the most powerful sources of commitment to a group is the feeling of degradation that the sect member feels as he is made to submit to the group. "Mortification processes provide a new set of criteria for evaluating the self; they reduce all people to a common denominator and transmit the message that the self is adequate, whole, and fulfilled only when it lives up to the model offered by the community" (Kanter, 1972:103). Mortification can be achieved in a number of ways:

CONFESSION. The individual humbles himself before the group, baring his innermost being, and is brought to recognize that he must judge himself according to the standards of the group. The more a sect emphasizes "heart experience," repentance and sanctification, the greater the importance of this confession. The Shakers, for example, not only expected converts to give up all for the communal life they established, but also dwelt upon the sinfulness of a past life that had tolerated sexual relations. They attributed great importance to the act of confession as a sign of true commitment.

> The convert was required to describe his past life and sins in great detail, and confessions were frequently deemed insincere or insufficient and had to be repeated. Confession was believed to expiate sins and to purify the convert, while symbolizing his rejection of the world and its temptations. Further, the act of confession mortified the convert and so encouraged the development of humility and submissiveness (Whitworth, 1975:18).

Although the Shakers were perhaps an extreme case, the initiation procedures of most sects involve some kind of open confession of past errors or sins and acknowledgement of wasted years.

TESTIMONIALS. A public proclamation of conversion and commitment makes evident to all the significance of group membership and the power of the sect over the individual—as well as increasing the social pressures on the individual to sustain his commitment. Testimonials are extremely important in conversionist and introversionist sects which place great value on having the right experience and expect to see the results of salvation in behavior. Through accumulated personal testimonies, sect members are able to see how well their hitherto private experiences fit into a common pattern. "This initial testifying objectifies subjective experience 'fixes' it as a reality, both for the convert and for his group" (Gerlach and Hine, 1970:136).

SANCTIONS AND MUTUAL CRITICISM. Through public denouncements, temporary removal of membership and other means, the individual is disciplined by the group. The form of sanctioning depends a lot upon the political structure of the group, but for commitment purposes, sects endeavor to generate mechanisms of censure in which it is clear that the individual appears before the group as a whole. One important form of sanctioning is mutual criticism, which was practiced in the Oneida sect. John Noyes, leader of this sect, explained the function of "the Criticism" in the following way:

> The system takes the place of backbiting in ordinary society and is regarded as one of the greatest means of improvement and fellowship. All of the members are accustomed to voluntary benefit of this ordinance from time to time. Sometimes persons are criticized by the entire family; at other times by a committee of six, eight, twelve, or more, selected by themselves from among those best acquainted with them, and best able to do justice to their character. . . . This ordinance is far from agreeable to those whose egotism and vanity are stronger than their love of truth (Quoted in Nordhoff, 1961:289).

This practice has been perpetuated in some of the communes of the contemporary Jesus movement, especially those influenced by sensitivity training.

Other sanctions include the withdrawal of love, friendship, and material benefits, and at the extreme, "shunning" or "avoidance" culminating in excommunication. Avoidance is a very common means of sanctioning, because sect members derive great satisfaction from close group involvement and thus feel its withdrawal keenly. Furthermore most sects believe that for purity to prevail, the avoidance of the impure is necessary. Therefore, the technique of shunning as if the deviant individual were tabooed is particularly appropriate. Zablocki (1971:196) describes "the exclusion," a finely graded sanctioning system practiced by the Bruderhof.

> There are various grades of exclusion. The mildest is exclusion from the *Gemeindesthunde* (the meeting for prayer), either just once or indefinitely, until reform is demonstrated. For more serious offenses, a person may also be excluded from Brotherhood meetings. . . . Next there is small exclusion . . . in which the Brother is allowed only minimal contact with the other community members during the daily routine; and great exclusion . . . in which he has absolutely no participation in the daily life of the *hof*. The most severe form of exclusion is to be sent from the Bruderhof completely, to make one's own way in the world.

Many utopian and introversionist sects practice avoidance as a means of mortifying the individual and impressing on him his dependence on the group. Its strength, of course, depends on at least some prior commitment. For example, the link between confession and penance is contrition, which is an inward state. Although the sect may seek to control behavior, the transformation that makes sanctions work is entirely subjective—from acknowledgment of sin to feelings of guilt, to contrition, to confession and penance, and finally to some sense of cleansing and absolution. None of this can be achieved unless the individual is already persuaded of the normative basis of the sanction and of the agent of social control.

REWARDS. Members are instructed that they can avoid mortification and receive rewards by committing themselves to the sect. Inasmuch as sects are voluntary associations, commitment must stem first from inducements rather than sanctions. Those who conform and perform well receive the approbation of the elders and move up the hierarchy of prestige in the group as well as furthering its claim to superiority over the unregenerate outside the sect.

The principal rewards available to sect members are the promise of higher spiritual status and greater group deference. Of course, the sect itself does not grant higher spiritual status, but it does establish the signs by which it might be recognized, and it is the means of assurance for the individual concerned about his status. A sect might also offer material rewards to those most committed to it, but these rewards must always be interpreted in terms congruent with the sect's values. In a sense, a hierarchy of spiritual status within the sect, supplemented by a mechanism whereby fellow sect members or, more often, sect leaders are able to determine movement up and down this hierarchy, is a way in which the sect can exercise control over its members and induce their greater commitment. "Skillful control of the process can convince the seeker that all he will ever need to know will eventually be made clear to him and he can be induced to develop an even greater commitment to the organization in terms of personal identity and (not least) money" (Campbell, 1972:128). The manipulation of symbols in this way is extremely important for sects that must rely principally on persuasion to activate and sustain commitment. David and Richardson (1976:328) noticed, for example, that the Children of God use titles "in a curiously free way . . . so much so that nearly every full-fledged member can win some rank."

REMOVING THE BASIS OF PERSONAL PRIDE. Requirements of uniform dress (as in the Hare Krisha sect), simplified naming (such as addressing fellow sect members as "brother" and "sister"), communal eating and the removal of privacy (as in the Children of God) effect a de-individuation in which the sectarian's concept of self is defined solely in terms of the group.

Transcendence

Commitment is intensified in proportion to the sect's success in fostering a belief in its own power and significance. Attaching the group to ultimate concerns enhances its stature and legitimizes its demands on the individual. The sect nourishing a sense of transcendence is not "just another group." There are a number of ways in which this feeling can be encouraged:

1. Members are led to believe that they are capable of extraordinary feats.
2. The sect itself is portrayed as divinely planned, guided and supervised. Thus, an ex-member of the Bruderhof explains, that "regardless of an individual's status within the Bruderhof, as a Bruderhof member he is elite. He is given a rationale that allows contempt for all non-members plus a masking benevolence toward them. The individual also gains a sense of power-gratification from the assumption that the Bruderhof way of life will eventually be forced on the rest of the world." (Quoted in Zablocki, 1971:261).
3. The leader of the sect is surrounded by a mystique and perhaps accorded charismatic status, and the decision-making in the sect is kept secret or made to appear irrational. This associates the sect with the awesome and fascinating world of the secret and hidden.

CONCLUSION

Although the preceding list of commitment mechanisms is a lengthy one, Kanter's (1972:137) investigation, confined as it was to utopian and introversionist sects, hints that there are possibly many more such mechanisms. This chapter has merely summarized some of the more important and successful techniques for sustaining commitment and has provided some examples. But although there may be other ways in which commitment can be maintained, a given technique can perform a number of different functions. Thus it is not always necessary for a religious group to institute every commitment mechanism in order to be successful.

Commitment mechanisms do not guarantee that a religious fellowship will become a viable association of strongly committed individuals. But it does seem that the more commitment mechanisms a group institutes, the greater the chances of its success. To the extent that a religious group does not seek to institutionalize communal, primary, and expressive relations, such mechanisms will be considered neither desirable nor necessary. In some sects, primarily manipulationist and thaumaturgical ones, it is clear that these mechanisms are neither instituted nor allowed to develop. Such sects simply do not seek to embrace all of the social roles of an individual. The same holds for denomination, for they too do not make total demands on their membership. Nevertheless, no religious group is free of the need to sustain commitment, and mechanisms to that end, even if only vestigial, will always be present.

7

SECT TO DENOMINATION: EXTERNAL RELATIONS

There is no private religion. Even the most personal religious experience generates a need for outreach and mutual affirmation. The "creation of communities" is an essential aspect of the development of religion in society and an important topic in the sociology of religion (Weber, 1965:176). This chapter and the next one take up once more the theme begun in Chapters 3 and 4—the way in which new religious ideas and practices gain adherents, who then form communities to propagate and defend their new religion. Protest begins in the near-groups of the kind described in Chapter 3 and, if the conditions are right, leads to the formation of the sects described in Chapter 4. It is now time to ask what happens when a sect grows, when "the inspirations of a few become the conviction of many" (Bendix, 1962:259). Chapter 7 looks at the changes in the relationship between the sect and the outside world; Chapter 8 describes what happens to the organization of a religious group as it expands and the routine demands of everyday life begin to have their effect.

THE CONCEPTS: CULT, SECT, DENOMINATION AND CHURCH

The following account of religious dynamics draws on the work of Weber (1965:65), Troeltsch (1931, II:993), and Niebuhr (1957). It is they who first pointed out that sectarian fervor does not last and that sects gradually develop into more church-like forms of religious organization. Their ideas have guided much subsequent research in the field of religious organizations and have generated considerable debate (see, for example, Eister, 1973).[1] It is necessary, then, to begin this account of religious dynamics by carefully elucidating the meaning and purpose of the concepts to be used.

In religious circles, the word "sect" is used to refer to a heretical and sinfully divisive group. It is contrasted with the "Church," which is the upholder of the true faith and moral guardian of all the people. Clearly, churches are normal and good, sects are deviant and bad. Troeltsch and Weber borrowed these concepts but not the value judgments. Sociologically, a sect is merely a movement of religious dissent; a church is an organization which, emphasizing sacrament and creed, strives to be coextensive with society.

Troeltsch and Weber, both Europeans, tended to think in terms of the polar opposites, sects versus church, there being either orthodoxy or dissent in European societies. Niebuhr, an American, could find little use for this dichotomy because the United States has no established church, no single orthodoxy against which all dissent must be sectarian. He therefore proposed an intermediate type—the denomination. Subsequent research has indicated that even this third type does not exhaust all the social forms of religious organization, and a fourth has been added. Robertson (1970:123) provides the best description of the conceptual scheme most commonly used by modern sociologists.

1. *The sect:* a group that considers itself the sole true religion and, seeking to preserve its spiritual purity by remaining apart from the world, exercises close control over its membership.
2. *The established sect:* a group that is willing to tolerate the truth claims of other religious groups, but is nevertheless exclusive in its membership and remains aloof from the world except for the purpose of spreading its message.
3. *The denomination:* an association that tolerates the truth claims of other religious groups and has liberal membership requirements.
4. *The church:* a body that claims a monopoly on the truth, but has a broad, all-inclusive definition of membership.

This scheme is merely an ordering device, and makes no predictions. However, religious groups typically pass out of the sectarian form (or phase) and into one of the other three. This movement is usually associated with numerical growth, and it customarily involves an increase

[1] Eister (1973) reviews a considerable amount of critical writing on the church sect scheme, but there are many who believe that it remains a useful sociological tool. See, for example, Budd (1973:73), Fallding (1974:155), Hill (1973a:47), Johnson (1963:542), Johnstone (1975:111), Mehl (1970:144), Nottingham (1971:230), O'Dea (1966:68), Scharf (1970:115), Schneider (1970:163), Schwartz (1970:65), Swatos (1976), Towler (1974:113), Wach (1962:197), and Wilson (1966:181).

in organizational complexity. It is clear from the scheme that such a movement would also imply an attenuation of protest.

At this point, something should be said of the familiar concept "cult," which does not appear in this scheme. Most of the groups referred to as cults are merely sects that have no firm locus of authority above the individual. The cult is not a different type of religious group but merely one form in which new religious movements appear. Some sults become sects, and some of these sects become denominations. The term "cult" might be applied to thaumaturgical groups such as spiritualist circles because they are so eclectic, so little differentiated from the surrounding cultic milieu, so transient, and so undemanding of their clientele that they can hardly be said to constitute a separatist group at all.

A group assumes this cultic form (which is highly unstable) when there is no locus of authority above the individual. In other words, no single individual or elite group has authority, and religious truth and expertise remains open to all. Only when one person or one subgroup manages to establish its authority above the rest and proceeds to endow the group with a unique status as a mode of access to the truth, does a sect appear (Wallis, 1975b:41). Thus, the Mormons' transition from cult to sect was effected by Joseph Smith's efforts during the 1830s to reserve to himself the right to receive revelation and thereby to establish his supremacy over those few (such as Oliver Cowdrey) who had been with him from the start. Smith also set up a High Priesthood (with himself at the head), membership of which was strictly controlled by him, in order to guarantee stable direction for the group and continuity of command (O'Dea, 1957:159).

THE MEANING OF ACCOMMODATION

The first use to which the conceptual scheme will be put is to throw further light on what happens over time to the relation of a sect with the outside world. Niebhur argued forcefully that the original fervor of the sect would fade and that compromises with the profane world would occur. He was pointing to dilemma faced by all sects. Although sects reject the world and seek to change it, they must live in it and with it in order to do so. They must avoid on the one hand the ineffectualness that aloofness brings and, on the other hand the loss of principle that follows from too close an intimacy with the profane world.[2]

[2]The sect takes literally the injunction: "Be not conformed to this world, but be ye transformed by the renewing of your mind that ye may prove what is that good and acceptable and perfect will of God" (Romans, 12:1). Rejection and withdrawal are integral to sectarianism; a disgruntled minority is removing itself from a "corrupt" and "complaisant" majority. Sectarians typically separate themselves from other people not only with respect to their religious beliefs but also with respect to marriage, friendship, work and play. Not

No matter with what fervor sectarians begin their protest against the world and with what determination they set themselves apart from it, they gradually relent and learn to live with it.

> Life cannot go on without routine, which is constantly reasserting itself. Thus, the charmistic founders of a new society might have elevated a particular norm of conduct—e.g., equality or saintliness—to a dominant position, to the practical exclusion of all others. As time passes, personal and primordial attachments, considerations of expediency, and loyalties within particularistic corporate bodies become more prominent again. The norms of equality or saintliness might still be respected, but not exclusively respected (Shils, 1975:133).

Instead of waiting for and effecting the transformation of the world, the sect begins to see *itself* as the transformation, less as a leader and more as a gathering place, not so much an arena of struggle but a place of safety. It ceases to give testimony and becomes an agency of advice.[3]

History exaggerates what proportion of sects become denominations because the sects that do not follow this course remain small and anonymous or disappear altogether. Many well-known contemporary denominations, such as the Presbyterians, Baptists, Congregationalists, and Disciples of Christ, were once sects. However, many sects of the past, such as the Diggers, Levellers, and the Rappites, are heard of no more except in history books. Many of the sects being formed today will suffer the same fate. Further, some sects, such as the Jehovah's witnesses and the Seventh Day Adventists, have vigorously sustained their independence without suffering a decline in membership. Accommodation is, then, more of a tendency than a law. Only under certain conditions will it take place.

The history of Methodism will serve to illustrate the accommodation process. The Methodist sect originated in Wesley's concern with the lack of spirituality in the Church of England and with its complaisant support

---

all sects enjoin *absolute* separation from the world or demand the rejection of all worldly pleasures. Sects like Christian Science do not spurn the material goods of this world, although they do advocate deviant means for securing them. Other sects, such as the original Baptists or the Jehovah's witnesses, reject certain forms of church government while remaining indifferent to forms of secular government, except to the degree that they interfere with religious expression.

[3]Although accommodation means a growing acceptance of and identification with orthodoxy, not all change in sect doctrine or practice is accommodative. Religious groups are constantly modifying their doctrine in the light of the teaching of other churches, and even of secular organizations, without necessarily lessening their protest against them. Nor should it be supposed that accommodation takes place uniformly: it might occur with regard to certain practices (for example, community organization) but not others (for example, family life).

of many of the corruptions and injustices of political and social life in eighteenth-century England. Wesley's earliest followers were drawn from what would now be called the counterculture of England. He spurned the pulpit for the open field, and his listeners were artisans rather than the respectable middle class. The growth of the Methodist movement during the nineteenth century brought about some major changes in its relationship to society, however.

> As the nineteenth century progressed, the search for respectability increasingly affected Methodists. They demanded better chapels; abandonment of biblical and doctrinal crudities; nice singing; 'a good time'; modest pleasures; and a cheerful, happy, unambitious society. They eschewed everything drastic and extreme; they sought to avoid all conflicts; they held up the ideal of respectability and moderation in religion and life. . . . Rising prosperity had weakened denominational commitments. The decline of hell marked the supersession of rigid denominational boundaries and a reduction of the severity of religious conflict. A modestly aspirant Methodism sat loosely to its beliefs and practices (Currie, 1968:140).

What is most noteworthy about this description is the "search for respectibility" with which the Methodists becomes increasingly preoccupied. The attenuation of sectarianism begins the moment the group places the values of the wider world on a par with its own.

In the space of less than one hundred years, Methodism went from a sect on the outer fringes of English religion to a denomination at the core of Victorian middle-class society. But its history only repeated that of the Baptists during the sixteenth century and the Quakers during the seventeenth. The pattern was to be repeated during the twentieth century by the Salvation Army. In the United States, the tendency is even more pronounced. Methodists, Baptists, Disciples, and even Holiness sects, all once associated with the unwashed and illiterate, have entered the ranks of religious respectability. A Disciple became President of the United States in 1963 and a Southern Baptist followed in 1977.

WHY ACCOMMODATION OCCURS

One cause of accommodation is that the more influential members of the sect obtain an increased "stake" in the world. A steadier job, a more stable family life, a wider circle of friends, greater political freedom, will change the priorities of members from challenge to comfort, from change to stability, from being different to being normal.

It has also been argued that accommodation is stimulated by the succession of one generation of sect members by another (Niebuhr, 1957:54). During its first generation, a sect will attract people who share its rejection of the world and wish to associate with others of like kind. The voluntarism of the sect and its practice of screening applicants' intensity adds to the members' sense of apartness. However, a sect's second generation, the children of original members, will not necessarily share either the social background or the experiences of the first generation. They will have only dim memories of the issues behind the formation of the sect, and having neither decided to join the sect nor passed a test to gain admission, they do not share the radical fervor of the first generation.

Niebuhr's argument is quite plausible, but there are some weak links in it. First, it cannot be assumed that children of sect members will join their parents' church. Second, sects do not typically waive their entrance requirements for children of sect members, as Niebuhr implies. As long as tests of membership are applied, generation will have no effect on the strength of protest. Third, as long as sects proselytize they will continue to recruit new first-generation members, and with these new members they can expect to sustain the radicalism of the group. The generational thesis is not universally valid, then, but applies only under certain circumstances—where there *is* a high rate of internal recruitment, where few new members are entering who share the original radicalism of the group, and where, for one reason or another, tests of membership are dropped.

The feeling of exclusiveness with which a sect begins is likely to weaken as sect members accrue more possessions, secure more prestigious jobs, establish settled communities or obtain more political power. These changes shift members of the sect closer to the center of society, a shift that will be accelerated by the second generation. However, the shift will not occur at all unless other people tolerate the group and its activities. The public must cease regarding it as a deviant organization and begin treating it as one group among many, competing equally with other religions. Pluralism, in turn, furthers the process of accommodation because it encourages each competing group to gravitate toward the mean and eliminate any "peculiarities" which might impair its ability to "sell itself" on the "open market."

Pluralism has fostered the rapid accommodation of many American religious movements. In the United States, the practice of religion takes place within a legal framework of toleration for all religions, and is highly competitive. Each new religious movement in America can "aspire to the top," assured of toleration, of the right to compete equally with other religious groups, and of the legitimacy of the voluntary principle. Moreover, Americans are encouraged to think that religion is less a matter of doctrinal revelation and more a matter of commonly received opinion. Thus, they feel it right that different religious groups should rise and fall in popular opinion.[4] Such attitudes are less common in societies where there is an established church because the contrast which is drawn between conformity and nonconformity restricts the mobility of new religious groups.[5]

Accommodation is a process of interaction in which both sect *and* society are likely to change. Accommodation can mean the elimination of distinctive practices and beliefs: the Mennonites soften their discipline of "shunning"; Pentecostals relax their sanction against wearing cosmetics; the Jehovah's witnesses reconsider some of their prophecies; or the Amish come to accept some technological developments they had hitherto spurned on principle. In all these cases, something is given up. In other cases, however, accommodation means that society moves closer to the sect and bestows respectability upon it: the Church of England came to accept many of Wesley's evangelical ideas and thus made Methodism respectable; the state altered its policies on social welfare and thus legitimized the work of the Salvation Army among the poor; the state furthered the emergence of a ministerial stratum among the Christadelphians by treating their ministers on a par with ministers of other

[4]Pluralism stimulates accommodation, but even in the United States the boundaries of toleration are limited. They do not include groups like the Oneida, the Mormons, the Jehovah's witnesses, the Seventh Day Adventists, the Divine Light Mission, the Children of God, or the Unification Church, each of which has, at one time or another, been subject to suppression by the mainstream churches.

[5]Pluralist societies cannot be dichotomized into orthodoxy and dissent because there is no firm center of religious authority. Thus it is conceivable that some American sects protest, not against the mainstream, but against other part of the counterculture. For example, the Children of God teach a nineteenth-century brand of Christian asceticism. Even sects such as Hare Krishna enjoin a life of hard work without sex, drugs, liquor or meat. Both sects reinforce their teachings with tight group discipline that contrasts vividly with the "hang loose" ethic of the hippie counterculture on the one hand and the strong-minded political materialism of the New Left counterculture on the other. In this sense, they have recaptured some of the vestiges of the Protestant Ethic of mainstream America. They have turned away from the antinomianism of the hippies (rising out of the feeling that the conventions of society are oppressive) and express a desire for moral rectitude reminiscent of the appeals for law and order which the respectable white middle class began making in the 1960s. This is not to say, of course, that sects like the Children of God and Hare Krishna see themselves as returning to the fold of denominational religion. While their chief target has been the counterculture of the hippie and political radical, they have also rejected the hypocrisy, complaisancy, formalism and superficiality of the orthodox denominations. Like all sectarians, they see themselves as returning to the very roots of religious faith, as truly wrestling with the really profound human problems, a fight the denominations had chosen to avoid. Thus, while there is no "center" against which these sects reacted, nor have they fully aligned themselves with the mainstream culture. Yet, in terms of latent functions, they are much closer to the center than they are to its periphery. Thus it is possible to speak of sects without introducing ideas of Established Church or Dissent.

denominations for the purpose of conscientious objection. Ironically, a sect may not welcome being treated equally by the state if it fosters an accommodation the sect does not seek.

THE RANGE OF ACCOMMODATION PROCESSES

Two separate but related areas of change are discernible in the accommodation process: (1) a change in the meaning of membership; (2) a change in the relationship of the sect to other religious groups and to secular organizations.

The Meaning of Membership

ADMISSION STANDARDS. Accommodation means a decline in entrance requirements. "Sects require an act of subscription. But when sects persist for a very long time, such tests of merit become nominal." (Wilson, 1970:30) Sect members begin to look upon the salvation or special redemption that drew them together as in principle open to all rather than being confined to the chosen few, albeit within the church. Relaxed standards are especially appealing to the second generation of sect members, who have obtained their membership more or less by birthright. In this sense, the sect begins to change from a *dissent* group to a *descent* group. Belonging to a religious group by virtue of parental membership implies less radical fervor than belonging out of deliberate choice.

There are numerous instances of this decline in admission standards. In the early days of Methodism, religious achievement was measured in terms of the "witness of the spirit" made manifest in worship and in personal efforts to live a moral life and work hard at one's job. An unmistakable heartfelt experience of salvation was considered necessary for chapel membership, and each chapel exercised close surveillance over the moral and devotional life of each of its members. Offenders were disciplined by the rest of the members of the chapel. Attendance at class meetings on a regular basis was an important measure of commitment to the faith. During the nineteenth century, however, there was a conspicuous decline in these observances and a relaxation of the rules concerning them. Salvation came to be looked upon not as a public, instantaneous event but as a progressive growth of grace, not necessarily marked by an outward, dramatic change. Religious achievement began to be measured more and more in terms of institutional support, such as tithing; conscientious Methodists came to be those who propped up the institutional fabric of the denomination with time, money, property, and expertise (see Brewer, 1952; Chamberlayne, 1974).

The requirement that full communicant status be predicted on a personal religious experience is relaxed during the process of accommodation. The well-known institution of the "Halfway Convenant" (whereby individuals are granted provisional membership until the experience of full regeneration) is an attempt to deal with this problem, as is the "birthright membership" of the Society of Friends. The once strict demands made upon prospective Baptists (Campolo, 1971:34), Pentecostals (Pattison, 1974:446), and Jehovah's witnesses (Beckford, 1975b:88) are also disappearing.

LEVEL OF COMMITMENT. In its pristine state, a sect imposes rigorous discipline and demanding standards of behavior on its membership. Over time, however, discipline becomes lax and standards are lowered. An intense concern with spiritual purity is hard for a fellowship to maintain, especially if withdrawal from the competing attractions of the profane world is not possible. As a consequence, once strict requirements concerning prayer and worship, creedal assent, ethical performance, loyalty to the leaders and commitment to the group are relaxed. In this way, religious membership becomes less rigorous, less stringent (Isichei, 1964).

The meaning of membership also changes during the accommodation process as the result of a redefinition of roles. The sectarian's roles are all fused into one—or at least his religious role dominates his other roles. During the process of accommodation, he begins to differentiate more clearly among his social roles, and he begins to look upon his religious role as one among many. Furthermore, the sectarian's religious role is consummatory—an end in itself. During the process of accommodation, the religious role assumes an increasingly instrumental character: it becomes a means to other, social ends, such as social respectability. In either case, religious action is reduced to the level of action in other spheres, such as politics and economics, and the chances are increased that religious norms will be subordinated to secular norms.

Changes in the meaning of membership during the accommodation process are also reflected in the increasing variety of motives that are "available" for church attendance. The sectarian's reasons for church attendance are stated in unequivocally religious terms, such as a desire to be "near God." Fellowship tends to be considered in predominantly religious terms—communion with an elect or "truly" Christian group. Some of these motives remain during accommodation, but others begin to appear; setting an example to one's children, having the opportunity to make new friends, and generally enhancing one's social life, or simply habit, become the most important reasons for attending church. By the same token, the measure of church membership for the sectarian is typically interpreted in special religious terms, such as "born again" or "accepting Jesus Christ as Savior." As accommodation takes place, the meaning of church membership changes to incorporate conformity to broad moral qualities such as decency and integrity, which the sectarian shares with other members of the society.

Relations with Other Social Groups

As a group passes from sect to denomination, its members begin to regard it not as unique, but as "one of a set of acceptable religious vehicles" (Robertson, 1970:124). They place less emphasis on the distinctive teachings of their fellowship and become more tolerant of other religious groups and the society in which they live. The formerly strict boundaries around each congregation are gradually eroded, and members are allowed to live more "in the world."

One sign of this aspect of accommodation is a willingness to enter into fellowship with similar religious groups (shown by many formerly independent Pentecostal assemblies); another is the decision to participate in ecumenical organizations (which the Disciples of Christ have done); and another is the unification of formerly schismatic groups (as in Methodism). Accommodation also means that the relation of the group to the secular world changes: avoidance and hostility are replaced by cooperation and sufferance. The groups shows a greater willingness to work with state and voluntary agencies to provide welfare for those in need; members are allowed to avail themselves of secular services such as medicine, insurance, and legal help; the group becomes more conscientious in its observance of civil law and social custom. The longer a religious group survives, the more it is compelled to develop this more intimate association with society. Only if the group meets sustained opposition, and only if it is able to maintain the strict boundaries around its membership, will it become an established sect. Where new land, new labor, and new capital abound, where geographical and social mobility is common, where the churches espouse values of pluralism, competition, and development—in short, where society is "open"—the transition of the sect to denominational status is highly probable.

DO ALL SECTS BECOME DENOMINATIONS?

The forces that encourage accommodation are so strong, and the number of religious groups that have undergone the process are so numerous, that it is an excusable error to suppose that all groups must experience this fate. Religious dynamics display a wide variety of forms, and there is nothing inevitable in the sequence outlined above, as a consideration of the following indicate:

First, the motives leading to accommodation are strong, but so are those working against it. Unlike other people, sectarians have deliberately submitted themselves to new kinds of discipline and community, by which they are set apart from wider society. In many cases they have "burned their bridges behind them." Their distinctiveness has special meaning for them. It is unlikely that moves to diminish the original sense of exclusivity will be unopposed.

Second, it is not necessary to suppose that a small, struggling sect will survive at all. Many, if not most, near-groups have failed to carve a distinct identiy and establish a viable organization. Many have remained movements, never developing beyond a leaderless stage, consisting of little else than a vague sense of common beliefs and purposes. It might well be that the Jesus movement will never reach the stage of a separate sect. It organization is extremely weak, and its "hang-loose" ethic encourages not only a high turnover rate in the groups that do form, but also fosters repeated divisions and mergers. The movement as a whole is held together only by members wandering from one commune to another and by a few underground newspapers.

Third, even if a distinct sect does emerge, it may not survive. It might fail to replace lost members, to agree on a permanent organization, or to adjust to some change in the outside world. History hides its failures. Many of the "retreat communes" of the 1960s did not last, partly because they failed to establish means of engendering commitment, lacked a clear chair of command and were ritually impoverished (Kanter, 1972:188).

Fourth, if a sect *does* succeed in attracting a loyal following, it need not become a denomination. It is quite possible for sects to survive in more or less their original form for a long time. Some alterations are inevitable, but the group cannot therefore be said to have become a denomination. Wilson (1961:10) calls the outcome of this kind of development an "established sect" because it "offers a different sort of accommodation from that of the spontaneous, emotional and unstructured group. The established sect provides an objective social environment for the individual, and imposes constraints upon him, for ultimately the moral codes of the group are identified with the behests of God, acknowledged as external, transcendent and impersonal in their authority." The established sect fits the description given by Zald and Ash (1966:333) of a "perfectly stable" movement organization as "one which over time always seemed to be getting closer to its goal without quite attaining it." This outcome is most likely if the sect feels no *great* urge to reach out into the world, but nevertheless condemns it. For example, many introversionist sects such as the Old Order Amish, have remained relatively small and have preserved primitive forms of group life in which the stress is on piety and the importance of maintaining emotional ties. Many sects have survived as such for a long time. Harrell (1971:27) has gathered information on some of them. The Congregational Holiness Church, operating in Georgia and South Carolina, was founded in 1921 and claimed 4,859 members in 1969. The Church of God of Prophecy, which is scattered through the South, was founded in 1923 and claimed 43,441 members in 1969. The Primitive Baptist Church, founded in the early nineteenth century, today numbers 792,000. Also, many single-congregation groups have survived for many generations. Some of them have joined together in associations such as the World Baptist Fellowship and the Bible Baptist Fellowship, but even so, they have remained fiercely independent and completely autonomous in belief and practice.

Fifth, it should not be assumed that the development of an elaborate formal structure is necessary for the survival of a religious group. For example, in many spiritualist associations, argot implements a stratified system of sect roles and statuses, each known by its occupants' use of certain argot terms. This rather than some structure of offices and rules ties spiritualists together. As Zaretsky (1974) points out, however, reliance on an informal structure such as argot is possible only if great significance is attached to the power of words and if part of the mystique of the group lies in its hidden and secret knowledge.

Sixth, a surviving sect may well change its form, but only to become another kind of sect. For example, a revolutionist sect might fail to sustain interest in its eschatology, only to take on the characteristics of a conversionist sect (as was the case with the Seventh Day Adventists). The Christadelphians, having also weakened their commitment to Adventism, have transformed into an introvesionist sect. The Quakers have changed from introversionism to reformism. Utopian sects are likely to turn to a kind of introversionism or to exemplary reformism. In the first case the sect becomes preoccupied with the practical side of communal life and with devotional matters. In the second case the utopians come to see themselves as the vanguard of social progress and seek to disseminate a message of "Do as we do."

Seventh, it is possible for a movement to reverse the denominationalization process. A movement may instigate a return to values in which an effort is made to return the group to many of its original ways. The Shakers underwent a revival after the Civil War in reaction to the compromises and unspirituality of their second generation. The Quakers underwent a revival in the late nineteenth century. Sects can experience such marked swings in activity and attention because they have multiple and vague objectives. It would therefore be an oversimplification to see them as being united behind a single, clear purpose. A period of intense evangelism might be followed by a period of concern for internal order and individual spirituality.

Finally, denominationalism affects not only sects but churches too. The church is the nation organized for worship. Any loss of absolute conformity will encourage the restoration of a voluntary principle of membership, loosening the ties to the state, relinquishment of the claim to represent all the people and enforcement of higher standards of commitment for the loyal few. The Oxford Movement signaled the beginning of denominationalization in the Church of England in the 1830s; the Anglican Church in Canada began its contraction in the last quarter of the nineteenth century; and "indifferentism" (the belief that all Christian groups operate in good faith) began to spread among American Catholics at the beginning of the present century. The Second Vatican Council accelerated the denominalization of the Catholic Church. The changes wrought by Vatican II suggest "a kind of spiritual disestablishment, at least in the sense that the Church will now tend to rely upon the persuasive powers of its messages and the call of its epiphany rather than upon alliance with other institutions or even reliance upon established tradition." (O'Dea, 1968:29) And, to anticipate the subject of the next chapter, this has been accompanied by internal changes, most noticeably the democratization of the church. "Now the Pope is supposed to listen to the college of bishops, and the clergy is supposed to listen to the laity." (Fichter, 1974b:81)

There are, then, a number of possible forms of sectarian development: continuation at the incoherent, presectarian stage; survival as an established sect; change to another form of sect; movement toward a denomination followed by a reversal of this trend; and dissolution. Each represents a response (not always voluntary) to a dilemma which confronts all religious organizations. They either strive hard to maintain some significant personal meaning to their adherents (but in the process lose any kind of relationship to man's larger history) or, in struggling to attain historical relevance, they lose contact with the personal needs of their membership.

8

SECT
TO DENOMINATION:
INTERNAL RELATIONS

Christianity began as a small, eschatological community living in expectation of the *parousia*. The image of the original band of disciples gathered at the feet of Jesus has encouraged the view that all religious movements have their origin in small, distinctive, homogeneous and largely self-sufficient groups, in which members relate to one another informally, acting with a great degree of spontaneity, and wearing the few rules and regulations very lightly. Enough evidence has been gathered to show that this assumption is not always warranted. Not all religious movements begin as primary groups; the amount of direct, emotional, spontaneous and equalitarian interaction which takes place in many religious movements, even in their earliest phases, is very small—Unity, New Thought, and Scientology would be examples.

What *is* true of all religious movements, however, is that structure is *emergent* within them. They are structures-in-the-making. Whether they have deliberately rejected routine in the interest of obtaining more authentic social relationships, or they are without structure simply through lack of precedent, religious movements tend to begin with minimal structure. Tasks are only vaguely differentiated, lines of authority are obscure, and rules of behavior are extremely general. The reason is the freshness of the group, and exceptions occur solely where the group has taken over, ready-made, the organizational structure of another group, or has simply absorbed the sex, age, and economic categorizations of the wider society.

Whether the original informality is prized or lamented, a desire to establish the operations of the group on a more formal, routine basis soon arises. All that remains to be decided is the form this routine will take. The need for "a coherent system of expression" is very strong (Douglas, 1970b:19) especially where ultimate values are concerned, and this need is powerful enough to overcome the feeling that authentic inner experiences might be deadened by the cold hand of formalism.

The emergence of structure is no "iron law" that determines the behavior of people in religious groups regardless of their will: it reflects common solutions to common problems. The original enthusiasts are anxious to tell others of their beliefs and experiences, they feel a need to learn more from one another about their faith and secure validation for their beliefs, they must decide who should be able to join the group and who should not, and both they and their leaders need assurance that their right to make decisions on behalf of the group is firmly based and clearly understood. They also feel a need to settle among themselves the basic principles of their faith, to agree on the rituals they should follow, and to find a reliable means of support. Thus, a sect might arise partly in protest against the clericalism of the established churches and refuse to make distinctions between "clergy" and "laity," but it soon finds itself with the task of deciding not only who should organize meetings and lead discussions, but also who should be the "spokesman" for the group in its relations with other groups. A sect may not want a ministry, but it may have to organize one if, for example, it wishes to enter into alliances with other minority religious groups, to obtain conscientious-objector status or immunity from prosecution under laws prohibiting fortune-telling and quackery.

Thus, even in religious fellowships that do not deliberately set out to routinize their religious life, this process is likely to occur. According to Fichter (1975:35), the sequence is already under way in the charismatic groups which sprang up in the Catholic Church in the United States in the late 1960's, groups that hardly intended to elaborate autonomous structures.[1] The growth of structure in religious groups creates insoluble dilemmas as essentially subjective and private experiences are shared and then made public. These dilemmas are the cause of frequent and

---

[1]Edward Plowman writing in *Christianity Today* (10/10/75) reported a dispute within the neo-Pentecostal movement over authority and discipleship. "Powerful figures in the movement have built up a chain of command linking many groups around the country to themselves, in some cases involving the relaying of tithes up through the system. . . The main guiding forces of the charismatic movement seem to emphasize discipleship, 'teaching' and 'community' at the expense of evangelicalism as a top priority. . . The ecstasy of one-in-the-spirit fellowship is wearing off among people who have been in the movement for a long time, and emotional love-and-worship sessions are increasingly giving way to Bible study. As a result, many charismatic Christians are discovering—or rediscovering—doctrinal distinctiveness."

intense debates over issues such as the locus of control in the group, the proper degree of formality in its administration, the correct definition of membership, and the most efficient division of labor.

To illustrate the kinds of changes in internal relations involved in the progression from sect to denomination, it is convenient to turn once again to Methodism. The first Methodist missionaries to the United States were sectarians. Few in number, rigid in discipline, and highly exclusive, they held services characterized by dramatic emotional display and minimal ritual. Their chapels were humble and sparsely furnished. Two centuries later, American Methodists number over ten million; in certain regions of the country they have become the dominant religion; they have invested heavily in real estate, stocks and bonds; they require lengthy and demanding training for their ministers; they have relaxed their criteria of membership and discipline; they have constructed a complex administrative apparatus; and they have negotiated a close working relationship with other Protestant denominations (Brewer, 1952). What the Methodists achieved in two centuries, the Pentecostals are achieving in under one hundred years. Many Pentecostal fellowships are well on the road to denominational status.

The growth of sects into denominations has been so common in the United States that some scholars (such as Greeley, 1972) characterize America as the "Denominational Society." Indeed, that form of religious organization seems to be the one toward which most groups gravitate. The normal course of religious development in the modern West is for a fellowship to adopt increasingly rationalized forms of administration and, partly as a consequence of this, to centralize its decision-making. However, the degree to which any given sect adheres to this normal course is variable, for as Rudge (1968:39) has pointed out, "a church conceived along [bureaucratic] lines has no foundation in the New Testament; there is nothing to give validity to such points as rationalization, the mechanistic structure and relationships."[2] The purpose of this chapter, then, is to outline the sequence of development of religious organizations and to indicate some of the variations commonly found.

---

[2]Of all types of sects, the conversionist is most likely to follow the sequence to be outlined in this chapter. Intent on competing for souls, the conversionist sect quickly develops "elaborate agencies to promote missionizing, Bible colleges and the publication of literature" (Wilson, 1970:91). Manipulationist sects are also likely to move in this direction because the practitioner/client relationship encourages the adaptation of rational procedures. The ease with which manipulationist sects assimilate a scientific ethos also opens the way for efficiency-oriented administration. Introversionist sects are the least likely to follow the sequence because their inspirationalism is antithetical to the development of rational, hierarchical control. Nor will revolutionist sects take this course, for their apocalyptic teachings discourage the institution of elaborate organizations.

The first sign of increasing bureaucratization is that positions within the fellowship become functionally specialized, impersonally defined and related to other positions by universalistic rules.

There are two key indicators of this process. First, religious functionaries become increasingly identified as administrators and spend more and more of their time on administrative chores. To the traditional duties of preacher, priest, pastor and teacher are added those of organizer and administrator (Hall, 1973:58; Paul, 1973:216; see also Blizzard, 1965a, 1965b, 1958), and time spent on these new duties begins to mean less time spent on the others (Quinley, 1974:239; Hall, 1973:58; Fukuyama, 1972:13). Increasingly, the training of religious functionaries stresses preparation for administrative responsibilities (Rudge, 1968:8). A growing proportion of religious functionaries become identified primarily as administrators and the number of available nonpastoral roles in the church increases.[3]

Second, separate and functionally specialized administrative departments begin to make their appearance. These usually have their origin in voluntary efforts to help the denomination perform special tasks, such as Mission, Education, Ministry Training and Social Work but, in the process of rationalization, their responsibilities are formally determined, membership is established on a legal basis, and competing jurisdictions are settled. As the denomination grows, these agencies tend to attract a greater proportion of personnel and expenses.[4] They also tend to become more independent, as they generate their own source of income and establish links with similar agencies in other denominations. This is a new administrative structure to set beside the structure of ministerial authority (Winter, 1968:25).

The more formalized the departmental structure becomes, the more lines of communication within the denomination are defined by function, and the more priorities shift from the problems of the laity to the management and budget problems of the executive. This tendency is encouraged by the natural inclination of the executive to promote the idea that organizational needs are the most pressing. If this view is accepted, these same executives become the most qualified to occupy decision-making roles in the denomination, which, in turn, enables them to solidify their power.

---

[3]In 1945, only 0.4% of Presbyterian ministers were classified as executives. By 1965, this proportion had risen to 3.5%. During that period, Presbyterian church membership rose by 50%, but the number of executives working for the denomination increased twelve times (Demerath, 1968:407).

[4]For example, about 70% of the annual budget of the Presbyterian Church in the United States is spent on administration (Balk, 1968:27).

There is considerable evidence of the widespread occurrence of this kind of functional specialization and administrative growth (Winter, 1968). But religious groups contain powerful impediments to the full flowering of rational administration, the most important of which ought to be briefly described.

First, many religious groups attribute great significance to their circumstance of origin and soon generate a veneration for tradition. Part of this tradition is that authority is attached to positions within the group which were established at the time of its origin. Such positions are defined more by habit and custom than by rational competence. Traditionalism will mean that arrangements have to conform to precedent rather than to abstract rules of efficiency and that re-arrangements have to take into account traditionalistic considerations such as seniority, loyalty and blood relationships as much as optimal system performance. Furthermore, rules governing relationships between positions will not be rational. Instead, they will be based on what is required by a particular person or what the value of a particular purpose is.

Second, religious groups tend to stress spontaneity, even a spirit of play, which runs counter to the rational, pragmatic discipline of a bureaucracy. This is one reason why many religious people regard rationalized administration as oppressive. Thus a Baptist complains that a "system, whether it be hierarchic or organization, has a constant tendency to impose itself as an obligatory channel of mutual service" (Harrison, 1959:41). This attitude is more common in sects founded by a charismatic leader because the pragmatism of the bureaucrat will be seen as a threat to the sacred itself. However, if a sect already stresses impersonalism and efficiency and if its meetings are more like a clinic than a love feast, no impediment to bureaucratization will exist.

Third, religious professionals do not simply work at a job, they follow a vocation. A vocation occupies the whole of a person's life, entailing total commitment to the work. In addition, a minister's obligations are diffuse and the demands made upon him all-embracing. The minister cannot be encapsulated in the bureaucratic office. His training, too, is vocational: he is expected to withdraw from society during his period of training; he cultivates broad spiritual ideals; he is given a liberal arts education; and he is equipped with a broad range of skills such as teaching, nursing, and counseling. This kind of training does not provide the specialized, function-oriented preparation expected of the bureaucrat. Once in his job, the minister, like most professionals, feels a greater loyalty and affinity to his fellow ministers than to his organizational superiors, a sentiment that undermines the hierarchy of control upon which the bureaucracy rests. And, in many cases, ministers have a kind of tenure, which further removes them from bureaucratic control. To this official tenure is sometimes added the nonrational ties between minister and congregation or church: ministers cannot be likened to sales agents and switched according to organizational need, for they develop familial ties to their flock. Religious professionals are not expected by their laity to give more priority to administration than to the pastorate (Strommen, 1972:165; Ward, 1961:56; Smith *et. al.*, 1974:33). At the same time, however, these same laity make virtually impossible organizational demands on their minister (Schroeder, 1964:187).

The second sign of increasing bureaucratization is that a system of rational economizing is devised.

Rational administration depends upon a predictable revenue (for example, tithes replace dues, or fees replace irregular donations) and a methodical system of disbursement (for example, cash allocations come to be determined by functional need rather than in response to ad hoc requests). Whereas a *sect* might, for instance, hear a "call" for more missionaries and solicit funds only after appointments have been made on the assumption that "the Lord will provide," a *denomination* is more likely to carry out a survey to assess the likelihood of sufficient funds being donated and only then recognize a need as genuine. The epitome of rationalized accounting is the trained bookkeeper and the professional fundraiser. A denomination is also more likely to conduct surveys to find out, not only what the laity is thinking (a tacit admission of the possibility of divergence of opinions within the group), but also studies of the social environment (a tacit admission that the world, to some extent, has to be adapted to).

Considering that a once poverty-stricken sect such as the Disciples of Christ had a national budget of over thirty million dollars in 1962 (Winter, 1968:125), it is hardly surprising that rational systems of accounting have been adopted. However, in all religious groups, there are forces at work preventing the full rationalization of how the group earns and spends money. Wherever tradition and ultimate values are of central importance, material support tends to be based on need and tied symbolically to spiritual worth. This contrasts with the regular, salaried form of support given full-time workers in a bureaucracy. Whereas a *denomination* employs salaried officials, a *sect* is more likely to fund its functionaries through offerings, which are unpredictable in amount and timing. The amount of support a functionary receives, furthermore, is indicative of his symbolic worth rather than his functional efficiency.

A rationalized administration assumes a freedom to choose incentives and impose sanctions on a rational basis that many religious groups do not have. Religious organizations are *normative*, in that they strive to generate positive and intense commitment to cultural goals. Such commitment can be generated only by inducements and sanctions that are symbolically related to the values of the group. For this reason, the severest sanction a sect can impose is denial of access to highly valued privileges, such as participation in rituals. This means that incentives of the bureaucracy—salaries, commissions, fines, and bonuses—are largely irrelevant in the sect. Only if such incentives are carefully interpreted so that they express cultural goals will they be acceptable.

A third sign of increasing bureaucratization is the introduction of empirical means of determining goals and assessing performance.

Denominationalization betokens greater control, more planning, and more elaborate organizational programs. It also involves a desire for a clear statement of the goals of the church, more explicit criteria for measuring the progress of the group, and set procedures for deciding priorities. For the religious professional, this means an increased emphasis on the training, rational selection, promotion, and deployment of personnel. It makes little difference that "bonuses are disguised as 'allowances' " (Paul, 1964:99). Furthermore, job performance is evaluated more and more in measurable empirical terms—fund raising, property maintenance, membership expansion—and less and less in traditional, less tangible terms, such as pastoral work and preaching. Although ministers are still expected to feel "the call," more empirical testing and selecting procedures are introduced in the screening of applicants (Fichter, 1961:9; Campolo, 1971:32).[5] A further sign of this aspect of bureaucratization is the organization of a central placement bureau to make more efficient and less costly the mobility of ministers between congregations. The fitting of ministers to congregations is thus removed from reliance on an "old boy network" and other traditional forms of personnel selection, and a more rational market for ministers is created.

Denominationalization also entails a decline in the importance of the transcendental goals of fellowship and the ascendancy of intermediate, empirically measurable goals. Sectarians are not alone in tending over time to allow the goals of preserving the organization itself to become more important than the goal for which the organization was set up. The evaluation of church programs in terms of their contribution to the

---

[5]The rationalization of ministerial roles means a more methodical attitude toward all personnel matters. Although ministers are expected to "feel the call" to the vocation, ministerial recruiters become increasingly active, and they tend to look for ability to lead, organize, and "sell" the "product" (Fichter, 1961:9). Increasingly, technological procedures for selection are used. Many seminaries of the American Baptist Churches, for example, now use the Minnesota Multiphasic Personality Inventory testing device to screen applicants for admission (Campolo, 1971:32). Surveys are carried out to discover the sources of low ministerial morale (see, for example, NORC, 1972) and of high turnover rates in the ministry (see, for example, Judd *et al.*, 1970).

maintenance of the congregation rather than their fealty to original values is an example of this way of thinking.

To settle on empirical, short-term measures of progress might be very satisfying for the congregation, but if such measures are given too much emphasis, they destroy the essential purposes of the church, which are ultimately transcendental. It is not surprising, then, that many church members are uncomfortable with these developments and oppose them. The concern of religious groups to realize ultimate values, which cannot be rationally calculated, limits the extent to which empirical measures can be applied to group performance. Religious groups certainly develop intermediate goals (such as building sanctuaries, raising money, and recruiting new members), and it is possible to measure the success or failure of these goals in empirical terms, but the relation of the group to ultimate values is always symbolic. The performance of the church must be seen to exemplify or act out its values. Religious groups must be so organized that, in their own operations, they do not contradict the ultimate ends that give them their purpose.

On its way to becoming a denomination, a group changes the criteria it uses to judge the performance of the religious professional. But there is a limit to how objective and empirical such criteria can become. The religious professional is expected to have heard "the call." He must be "fit to serve," not only by having the right objective qualifications but also by having the right intention (Fichter, 1961:304). This subjective component is not reducible to empirical measures. Just how true this is depends a lot on the minister's conception of his role. If a minister feels a need to prove himself in terms comprehensible to the laity, there is a good chance he will allow empirical criteria to be applied to his performance, for, in this sense, he is much like the employee in an organization (Hagstrom, 1957:59) or a professional who works for a set fee.

A further implication of the idea of the call is that a religious professional is not supposed to judge himself primarily by empirical criteria, or be motivated by practical incentives. Indeed, he is not really expected to be ambitious at all (as ambition is normally understood). To some extent, success is always "given" to the minister; and it is not something to be won entirely by his own efforts. In addition, the highly personalized role requirements of the minister are all but impossible to attach specifically to performance criteria: it is hard to judge how well a minister is doing. In any case, the proper concern of a minister is how a job gets done rather than how much of it is accomplished. Religious organizations do have career lines, of course, but advancement must always be mediated supernaturally if it is to be genuine.

The professionalism of the clergy will also inhibit the adoption of pragmatic criteria to assess group performance in the sense that the clergy's cosmopolitanism makes them much less interested in organizational maintenance and much more interested in their rather diffuse and hard to measure performance to clients. If the bureaucrat works to maintain the organization, the minister works to make a difference to individuals' lives and tends to regard bureaucrats as "parasites rather than necessities to the church" (Judd *et al.*, 1970:29). The minister tends to be much more interested in, and committed to, the pastoral and preaching side of his job. This he sees as most satisfying, while the organizational side, which is most time consuming and for which he has least training, is the most dissatisfying (Fichter, 1965a:186).

A fourth sign of increasing bureaucratization is the emergence of "a firmly ordered system of super- and subordination in which there is a supervision of the lower offices by the higher ones" (Weber, 1946:197).

Denominationalization means a gradual centralization of decision making and the loss of autonomy by local ecclesias. This process of oligarchization is common in voluntary associations, however democratic they may appear on paper. Decision making soon becomes concentrated in the hands of the few who have the time, skills, experience, money and commitment necessary for the acquisition and deployment of power.

The motives behind centralization are a desire to control the budget, a wish to reach and enforce agreement on doctrine, a desire to determine the appointment, deployment and discipline of personnel, and a wish to establish relations with other religious organizations and with secular agencies. The most sensitive index of degree of centralization is the source of control over the budget.

The conditions most conducive to centralization are as follows (Zald and Ash, 1966:339):

1. There is a base of support for the movement that is independent of membership sentiment—for example, investments and property.
2. Membership is not inclusive; thus, members retain some loyalty to the outside world, thereby diminishing their "stake" in the church and increasing the likelihood that they will leave the administration of the church to a few.
3. The leaders have been co-opted or "recognized" by the authorities or have been invited into alliances by other religious groups. In either case, the motivation of the elite to centralize control is increased.

The process of centralization can be seen clearly in the case of the Disciples of Christ, a denomination whose original principles firmly stipulated a decentralized church structure. However, the Disciples' desire to establish missions (and then Bible Schools for the training of missionaries) has, along with other outreach programs, necessitated greater and greater centralization of budgeting. The Disciples have decreased the proportion of total funds raised that is available for spending by local congregations. They have increased the proportion of money raised at the local level that is spent at the national level. They have increased the proportion of the total budget raised by the center itself through investments. The proportion of funds allocated to enterprises such as education and missions, which are controlled by the center, has also been raised. And the whole structure of promotion and fundraising has been unified and placed under the control of the central staff. This central staff has doubled in size between 1940 and 1965 while the overall Disciple membership was stagnant. Exactly the same developments have taken place in the Methodist and Presbyterian churches (Winter, 1968:27), and to a lesser extent in Quakerism (Isichei, 1968).

Many religious groups have experienced this kind of centralization while striving for more control and more efficiency. However, religious groups are unlike other organizations in that they espouse an *ecclesiology*—a theology of the church. Part of this ecclesiology is a political doctrine outlining the principle by which power within the church is allocated and exercised. Because "commitments to the formal polity are stronger and more enduring than the commitments to organizational efficiency and stability" (Takayama, 1975:17), it is quite possible that the desires of church members to realize their values in their church conflict with the imperatives of efficient coordination. This is especially likely if the doctrine of the church is congregational and prohibits the kind of centralization and hierarchization upon which the bureaucrat relies. The consequence is that many religious groups do not follow the sequence of development outlined above.

It is customary to distinguish three forms of political structure in the religious groups that appear in modern Western societies (Moberg, 1962:61–62):

1. *Episcopal*, which emphasizes "the role of bishops, other hierarchical personnel, and the clergy as their representatives [and] rests upon such beliefs as authority through apostolic succession and the supreme importance of the church as God's representative on earth." Only the Roman Catholic Church truly approximates the Episcopal form in its sense of the bishop's authority not being derived from the church itself. The Church of England holds to a modified form of the episcopacy, taking the view that the church actively chooses the man to be bishop, although he is then, in turn, responsible to God in the exercise of his authority.
2. *Presbyterian*, which "stresses control of the church by a presbytery or equivalent body of clergymen."
3. *Congregational*, which "places highest authority in church government in the hands of the local congregation." Strictly speaking, this local control includes supervision of doctrinal conformity, the hiring and firing of ministers, and management of the budget.

This typology is based on locus of control, which ranges from highly centralized in the episcopal form to highly decentralized in the congregational form. Thus, for example, if centralization is measured by who actually owns church buildings, who is empowered to authorize the establishment of new congregations, and who appoints ministers, the Protestant Episcopal Church is the most centralized, the Presbyterians next, with Methodists, Unitarians, Congregationalists and Baptists following, in that order (Makler, 1963:9).

The reasons for a given religious group's adoption of one kind of polity over another cannot be entered into here. Suffice it to say that the choice reflects deep-seated beliefs about the nature of religious experience, the relationship of the individual believer to God, and the status of the community of believers in the world. It also reflects to some extent circumstances of origin. In the case of sects whose major constituent parts preceded the founding of the overall organization, it is more common for some kind of congregational system to evolve and for decision making to be decentralized. On the other hand, in the case of sects that grew around one leader or group and subsequently established "branches," it is common for a more corporate structure and centralized decision-making to develop. The polity is thus tied closely to the values and tradition of the church, and is something about which church members typically have strong feelings. The laity can be relied upon to articulate the proper church doctrine, even though they might be ignorant of the actual operations of the church as an organization (Davidson, 1969:317).

Many churches in the Reformed tradition are highly democratic in their church doctrine. For example, the democratic and highly decentralized polity of the Baptists is believed to receive strong legitimation from the Bible (Harrison, 1959:59). The Baptists are highly resistant to the formation of any structures above the congregational level because their original secession from the Church of England was designed to "pulverize ecclesiastical authority and power" (Harrison, 1959:59). Members of the Southern Baptist Convention have experienced these feelings more intensely than Baptists in the North. They refuse to speak of the Baptist Church at all (the correct expression is "Baptist churches"), and they do not send delegates, but rather "messengers," to Convention meetings. Each local assembly is an autonomous church, subject and inferior to no other church. Any union of churches is looked upon as a completely voluntary organization with no binding power whatsoever. The Convention itself, which originated for the purpose of fostering mission activity, is not an ecclesiastical organization or even a federated structure. The "messengers" merely report back and forth. The Convention has no real voice and little binding power. For example, its Christian Life Commission, concerned with such issues as gambling, temperance, and "blue laws," is looked upon as an internally oriented, educative body. It is by no means unusual, then, for sizable groups to withstand the centralization tendency. Even more interesting, some groups have fought against it and reversed it. Both the Mennonite Church and the Brethren in Christ began shifting in the middle 1970s from a form of synodal polity in which regional conferences through their bishops exercise considerable authority over local congregations to a brotherhood-like congregational polity (Kauffman and Harder, 1975:185).

Resistance to centralization on the basis of values supporting local control is strengthened by regional and ethnic factors. The Missouri Lutheran Synod, which is the most ethnically pure of all the synods (it is German), has not followed the pattern set by the other Lutheran bodies in allowing national structures to dominate those at the regional and local levels. Within that synod, communication tends to rely less on bureaucracy and more on strong, ethnically based networks of social relationships (Winter, 1968:32).

Thus, it is the absence of a locus of authority above the individual or his local congregation that causes religious groups to resist centralization. This is true of manipulationist sects like spiritualism and of introversionist groups like the Quakers. Methodists, Catholics, and even the Disciples of Christ, on the other hand, seem to be more highly conscious of their church as a social structure and more concerned with the problems of establishing it as a viable organization.[6]

Just because a religious group pursues congregational ideals does not mean that it will be successful. As soon as some fellowship of independent congregations is established, a process of concentration of authority (typical of all voluntary associations) has begun. This occurs because the committee work and other organizational tasks become concentrated in the hands of the few who have the time, leisure, skill, money and expertise necessary. Concentration is even more likely if the supra-assembly structure that a movement eventually does institute is unwieldy, as is probably true of the Southern Baptist Convention. This organization makes a concession to centralization in the form of its Annual Convention. However, this affair is attended by upwards of 10,000 "messengers." An informal (and probably self-perpetuating) elite is almost certain to arise in such situations.

[6]The Churches of Christ, a schism from the Disciples of Christ, have firmly resisted centralization. While the Disciples started a Bible college only eight years after their foundation in 1832, formed a missionary society in 1849, joined the Federal Council of Churches in 1909, and began to discuss a merger with the United Church in the 1970s, the Churches of Christ have resisted all such moves toward denominational status. All attempts to set up a national convention have failed.

It is that part of the ecclesiology that stipulates how power is to be distributed in the church that provides the most powerful obstacle to centralization, especially if the ecclesiology is congregational. Ecclesiology will also temper the drive toward centralization if it is used to resist the shift of power in a denomination from the "charismatic" or ministerial line of command to the "rational-legal" or bureaucratic line of command. An increase in organizational complexity usually leads to an increase in the size and power of the bureaucratic line. The greater the power of this bureaucratic line, the less the power of either the clergy or the laity—and this is true whether the denomination is episcopal, presbyterian or congregational. It is not important that this shift of power might well happen by default; the ministry lacks the expertise, and the laity lacks the time to tackle the increasingly complex administrative problems. The result is the same, the evolution of a *dual structure of power*.

A dual structure of power is one in which two bases of authority are legitimated, one conforming closely to the church doctrine (and supposed to be dominant) and the other conforming strictly to rational-legal principles. An executive line of command thus rises to parallel the pastoral or charismatic line. These lines coexist uneasily. The minister who favors revivals, for example, will strongly resist the constraints imposed by the executive line. A sustained pastoral concern for the teaching and the proclamation of faith to the community of believers, a work grounded in faith, does not gel with the work of agencies that stress organizational efficiency and stability.

Dual structures can be seen in nearly all the denominations in the United States. Methodism, for example, exhibits an organizational development "starting from what might be called 'a preacher's church' through the lines of organizational structure—conference (preachers) and board (lay)—[creating] parallel organizations" (Winter, 1968:27). These two lines are not completely separate, of course. The General Conference admitted lay delegates in 1872, and boards have always included ministers among their members. Nevertheless, they do reflect different bases of authority and do provide the source of tension within the church. The Lutheran Church of America, to take another example, has developed a dual structure that matches that of the Methodist Church. Judaism and Catholicism have also experienced the development of dual structures, as have groups such as the Jehovah's Witnesses (Wilson, 1970:237; Beckford, 1975b:39), Christian Science (Wilson, 1961:143), and even in the Jesus movement communes (Simmonds, 1974:245).

Dual structures may emerge horizontally rather than vertically. Rationalization may occur at headquarters but meet resistance at the local level. For example, Methodism has developed a strong, rational organization that coordinates affairs at the national level, but at the level of the chapel fund raising is still carried on in traditional ways, such as fetes and bazaars (Moore, 1974:137). Pentecostals have largely resisted the bureaucratization of their assembly structures, but there has been little to prevent missions from becoming highly rationalized. Principles of "worldly business efficiency" are applied quite easily to the structure and methods of propaganda of organizations such as the Full Gospel Businessmen's Fellowship (Hollenweger, 1972:7). These kinds of groups demonstrate that formalization of regional or national structures can proceed while local services and activities retain their informality and spontaneity.

The existence of dual structures reflects the failure of a religious movement to completely rationalize its affairs: the bureaucrat cannot achieve complete control of the group. Even though church executives have specific spheres of competence delineated for them, and even though they perform their tasks within universalistic and impersonal rules, their authority cannot be purely rational because the ministerial line always retains an important residue of power. This means that the church executive differs from the typical bureaucrat in three ways. First, he retains some sense of his job as being a calling rather than merely a career. Second, although he is appointed on the basis of (and is valued for) his ability to prodcue organizational efficiency, this concern must always be subordinate to his fealty to church values. Even if the top-priority goals *are* organizational, this will rarely be admitted, so his power will always be largely informal. Third, his sense of hierarchy will always be mediated by the presence of another (and in principle, superior) line of authority. Thus, for example, the bishops who sit with him on board committees are a permanent obstacle to the full rationalization of the operation of those boards.

Although they are primarily executives, the administrators in modern denominations retain some nonrational, charismatic elements which distinguish them from secular bureaucrats. This is clearly illustrated by the behavior of an executive in the American Baptist Convention, a denomination that has been hostile to both formalization and centralization.

> Under the present institutional arrangement the executive professionals of the denomination have no alternative but to depend on the strength of their personal ability and the extension of their individual influence in order to compensate for a lack of rational-legal authority. A State secretary described his method of operation in the following manner: "I don't have any right to tell the church what to do with respect to any issue just because I'm the State secretary. I can't do a thing if the people don't want me to . . . Let

me give you an example. If I know that one of my churches is going
to appoint an uneducated minister from one of the Bible schools, I
write to the pulpit committee and ask them if they want me to
preach. I always want to preach to these people before I talk business with them . . . When I get to the church I don't talk about the
work of the State Convention from the pulpit. I preach straight
from the gospel and try to give them a real inspiring sermon. Then
I've got them!" (Harrison, 1959:76–77).

Clearly, this official sees the execution of his bureaucratic tasks as resting
ultimately on his charismatic claims. His legitimacy is thus of a mixed
type. The same is true of the state secretary of the Disciples of Christ.
"Sociologically, he occupies a status for which there is ambiguous and
shifting definition. His role behavior, then, is likely to depend upon
whether he possesses attractive personal qualities" (Whitley, 1959:191).

What is so threatening about agency domination of a church is that
the goals of the staff line and those of the ministerial line often diverge.
Asked to rank the importance of the highly rational expedient of long-
range planning for the church, Methodist superintendents (positioned
on the ministerial line) ranked it sixth, whereas secretaries of agencies of
the General Boards (in the staff line) ranked it first (Leiffer, 1969:136).
The staff line members also viewed centralized decision making more
positively. In the eye of the bureaucrat, policy initiation and determination should take place at the center and be carried out by technically
trained, full-time officers.

The bureaucrat meets with opposition from the laity as well as from
the ministry. There is a strong antipathy between bureaucracy and the
kind of democratic freedom of conscience that many religious groups
espouse. Bureaucrats are reluctant to sacrifice their expertise to the
inspired judgments of laymen. In addition, the bureaucrat is, strictly
speaking, not elected from below but appointed from above, a procedure that fosters the self-perpetuation of executive elites. It is highly
probably that as bureaucratization takes place in a religious movement,
lay control weakens, especially if bureaucratization is covert, for then a
shift of power is known to be occurring but few can pinpoint its location.

The concentration of a religious group's power in a bureaucracy is
cumulative. The bureaucrat, once appointed, is in an excellent position
to assume effective policy-making responsibilities, even though the denomination or sect may have an "official" democratic polity. Such executives tend to have much greater detailed knowledge of the kinds of issues
that come before the decision-making bodies, and they usually influence
what actually is discussed. In contrast, American Baptist Convention
delegates, the official decision makers, are a mixed group totally lacking
the kind of communication facilities available to executives. The power

of the bureaucrat may extend even to determining the composition of the boards, for they have the power of nomination. In this sense, they are able to appoint their bosses (Harrison, 1959:113).

The covertness and informality of the church bureaucrat's power make it greater. When a denomination, sect or church claims to have no supralocal or national structure and yet operates on a national scale, then the executive line will be able to exercise considerable influence over budget decisions and personnel practices, an influence perhaps greater for the fact that the bureaucrat, when challenged, can claim that he really makes no decisions at all. Bureaucratic domination is recorded by Harrison (1959) in the case of the American Baptist Convention and by Judd *et al.* (1970:83) in the case of the United Church. There is further evidence in Winter (1968), enough, at least, to suggest that bureaucratic domination is extremely common.

There are limits to the power of the bureaucrat. The various agencies cannot manage entirely without voluntary support. Thus they must always legitimize their policies partly by reference to church values, and they must always obtain popular support for these policies. Furthermore, the very covertness of the operation of the church bureaucrat that works so often to his advantage also means that there are constant behind-the scenes struggles for supremacy in decision-making. Moreover, the representation of the laity or the ministry on the boards represents *some* intrusion into the purely rational operations of the executive line. Finally, it is important to note that in many denominations the occupants of bureaucratic positions are very often ministers who, because of their training, lack the skills necessary to rationalize procedures completely.[7]

CONCLUSION

In concluding this review of the varieties of religious group development, it is necessary to examine the relationship between the external and internal aspects of the movement from sect to denomination. It is usually argued that increasing organizational elaboration and accommodation go hand in hand. As the organizational "presence" of the church increases, so the church will temper many of its demands. As it seeks further accommodation, its organizational needs become more

---

[7]Although the doctrine of the church shapes organizational development, ecclesiology is, in turn, modified by practical demands of administration. As a sect expands or modifies its attitude toward the outside world, it has occasion to re-examine its founding principles. These principles usually turn out to be rather vague and suggest a variety of forms of organization from which to choose. The sect thus has the freedom to choose several different doctrines of the church in order to suit organizational exigencies.

complex and more important. There are enough examples to suggest a causal relationship: the Quakers, for one, have amassed sizable financial holdings, which has induced a kind of conservatism among them. According to one sympathetic critic, "We acquired too big a stake in commodity markets and the stable structure of capitalism and in consequence lost 'our concern with the exploited and underprivileged' " (quoted in Hubbard, 1974:141).

The actual relationship between accommodation and routinization can best be seen as a kind of dialectical progression. Beckford (1972:22) offers a concise description of this process as it occurred in the Jehovah's witnesses:

(a) The initial phase was characterized by the emphasis given to the instrumental function of publishing and distributing millenialist literature. The purely instrumental phase lasted for about fifteen years.

(b) The second phase was characterized by a relaxation of the prohibition on forming groups of Bible students and by a willingness to offer advice on how each group should be constituted and administered. The reasons for relaxing the prohibition were . . . such considerations as the fear of losing subscribers if they lacked social support for their ideas; the financial advantages accruing from group involvement in evangelism and sales of literature; the greater ease of checking doctrinal dissent if believers were grouped together for study and discussion; and the likelihood of greater commercial stability if the subscribers become a kind of permanent membership. This phase lasted about ten years.

(c) The third phase opened around 1905 and can be considered both as a reaction against the previous phase and as a synthesis of the two earlier phases. The danger of allowing local ecclesia to assume unrestricted expressive functions was reflected in the members' reluctance to remain committed to evangelism rather than to worship and study. The desirability of revamping the pristine image of a straightforward publishing concern was tempered by the realization that the expressive functions had become institutionalized and could no longer be ignored. The attempted resolution of the problems took the form of heightened central control over all aspects of the local companies. The Society even began dictating officially acceptable ways and means of fulfilling expressive functions.

In this case, the shift away from millenialism and the outreach toward the idea of gathering and preparing the "remnant" went hand in hand with the increasing organizational elaboration of the movement and the centralization of control. In the case of the Jehovah's witnesses, the beginnings of denominationalism can be seen in the idea that evangelism is conducted to benefit the movement rather than the movement existing to help evangelism. Proselytizing becomes important because it is work to be doing rather than because it is a necessary means to an end.

There are a number of reasons why bureaucratization in itself should promote accommodation in a religious group. First, administrators tend to become more concerned with preserving the organization and their own office within it than with maintaining and increasing the impact of the church on the individual and society. This concern resonates with the wishes of laity who find "survival goals," such as recruiting new members, raising more funds and erecting grander buildings more tangible and meaningful. In their view, these goals are easier to measure, they are not value-laden and therefore help avoid conflict among members (and among members and nonmembers) and, insofar as a contribution to such goals is easy to see, they tend to generate greater trust among members.

A second reason why bureaucracy tends to conservatism is that the emphasis of the bureaucrat on routine, predictability, set procedures, and stability inhibits any desire to change. Indeed, the collection of money and other resources in a routine manner requires that the denomination cultivate popular indifference to its cause if the public cannot be persuaded to endorse it enthusiastically. Thus, the drive to organizational security encourages a moderate position on issues.

There is another side to this picture, however, one that indicates that the development of a bureaucracy does not always encourage accommodation and amelioration. The development of a complex denominational bureaucracy funded from surplus revenues can provide not constraint but freedom, not closer control of church officials but autonomy. In this case the bureaucrats of the denomination are the most radical in the movement, simply because they have the freedom and resources to lift them above the everyday concerns of the laity and the ministers closely associated with them. "Obviously, a staff has the freedom to explore new objectives only when organizational maintenance problems have been solved; hence, the apparent paradox that it is in associations that have managed to win obvious respectability and assured member loyalty where one often finds elites willing, indeed, eager, to take on new political tasks" (James Wilson, 1973:209). During the 1960s, it was frequently found that the church people most likely to be active in the civil rights and anti-war movements were the "bureaucrats." The entire administration of the United Presbyterian Church in San Francisco was taken over by liberal priests in the 1960s, and their attitude towards civil rights issues diverged markedly from that of the more conservative laity and parish priests. Their executive power enabled them to turn a minority position into the official policy of the synod (Lee and Galloway, 1969:54).

The Jehovah's witnesses are another exception to the rule that bureaucratization leads to accommodation—although for entirely different reasons. The Jehovah's witnesses have centralized their decision-making and standardized their code of behavior (Beckford, 1975b:92). However, the group has lost little of its original fervor and has not developed other ancillary functions, such as social service. Though achieving a high level of administrative rationality, they have managed to sustain their protest against a highly rationalized world. The main reason would seem to be that decision making in the Watch Tower Society is highly centralized (policy-making at the lower levels not being tolerated), which means that original goals can be defended more easily against the temptations of day-to-day existence.[8] Other reasons (and these are found in other groups too) include the specificity of the original goal of "publishing" the Word, the decision not to employ non-witness administrators, and a continued refusal to cooperate with other religious groups or secular organizations.

This mention of the Jehovah's witnesses provides a fitting end to these two chapters on the development of religious organizations. Superficially, the witnesses are so obvious a case of a revolutionist sect that has become an accommodating and somewhat introverted denomination in conformity with the common trend. But on closer inspection, they exhibit a highly complex mixture of organizational styles. Although they have rationalized their administration, this has not attenuated their protest against the world. Thus, although it is true that most religious movements do follow the sequence outlined above, exceptions are common and significant enough for the extreme generality and simplicity of the outline to be painfully obvious. Much more study of religious organizations is needed.

---

[8]The Jehovah's witnesses are a highly unusual case. They have always had a bureaucracy at the heart of the movement in the form of the Watch Tower Publishing Company, whose goal, publishing the Word, has always been paramount. Over time, this bureaucracy has been sanctified; ritual and opportunities for emotional expression have been *added* in the form of local ecclesias in which groups of witnesses can meet.

Part III

RELIGION
AND
SOCIAL INTEGRATION

9

CIVIL RELIGION
AND THE
FAMILY OF GOD

INTRODUCTION

The revivals, sects, and other religious movements described in Part II show clearly the way in which social changes are continually reshaping religious ideas and practices. In Part III, the process whereby religious beliefs and practices become institutionalized is not a major concern. Instead, the focus is on the relation of religion to other social institutions.

All social institutions are historical realities that exist outside and independent of the human beings within them. Institutions are the impress of the past upon the present. The values and norms learned in childhood strongly influence adult behavior. It is valid to speak of an institutional "presence" in society and this "presence" is not reducible to individual opinions, attitudes, and actions.

The interplay between religious institutions and other social institutions is highly complex and open to a number of different interpretations. Part III of this book concerns *the function of religious institutions in meeting important social needs*, paying special attention to the integrative consequences of religion.

The reason why religion is necessary is apparently to be found in the fact that human society achieves its unity primarily through the possession by its members of certain ultimate values and ends in common. Although these values and ends are subjective, they influence behaviour, and their integration enables this society to operate as a system (Davis and Moore, 1945:244).

The emphasis is on the social consequences of religion and, in particular, on the role of religion as a locus of significant symbols, values, norms and supernatural sanctions for conduct, all of which have the function of promoting conformity of expectations and performances, acceptance of the distribution of rewards, agreement on the boundaries of society, collective self-definitions and the tie of the periphery to the center (Shils, 1975:x).

Many social scientists have concerned themselves with the functions of religion, and they all draw their inspiration from Durkheim, who was the first to argue that a group's experience of its collective power as sacred is the necessary basis for cohesion in society (see Chapter 1). Religious symbols express "the social unity in a material form" and fuse "all particular sentiments into one common sentiment" (Durkheim, 1965:262). Religious ritual is "a means by which the social group reaffirms itself periodically" (Durkheim, 1965:432). Accordingly, it is possible for Warner (1961:248), a follower of Durkheim, to see in Memorial Day ceremonies "rituals comprising a sacred symbol system which functions to periodically integrate the whole community with its conflicting symbols and its opposing, autonomous churches and symbols." Commemorative rites reaffirm the community's commitment to basic values, and the symbols employed invoke mutual sacrifice on behalf of community ideals.

Durkheim tended to emphasize rituals in his functional analysis, and it is indeed easier to see the integrative function of religion in the "effervescence" of periodic rites. But religion also promotes social solidarity through the sharing of values and beliefs. This might best be illustrated by a seemingly paradoxical case—the Protestant's exaltation of the individual. As Durkheim pointed out, Protestantism places enormous emphasis on the state of grace of the individual believer, obliging him to continued introspection concerning his intentions and motivations. The Protestant Reformers thus made self-fulfillment of the individual paramount. Yet this does not result in anarchic egoism, but in a strong ethic of individualism to which all Protestants subscribe. *They are united in their individualism.* Thus, religion does not have to destroy the individual in order to bring about social integration.

Building on Durkheim's insights, other sociologists have added to the list of functions religion performs. Religion helps make a society's values seem more consistent by locating them within an all-embracing belief system in which ultimate ends and intermediate ends are coherently related; it thus helps foster social *consensus*. Religious institutions are in part responsible for the *transmission of values* from one generation to another. The rituals, parables, and myths of religion help to *reinforce values* by periodically rehearsing their meaning and the penalties of ignoring them. Religious teachings provide a reinterpretation of social failure in spiritual terms; they set individual problems in a new and more satisfying context, offering universally available values (such as salvation) in the place of scarce values (such as material success) and thereby *compensating* for lack of value-realization. Finally, religion functions as an agent of *social control* by means of its system of rewards and punishments, its censorship, its moral concern, and its power to legitimate specific social arrangements. To the extent that religion attaches the misfortunes of this world to guilt that must be expiated supernaturally, it will operate as a powerful reinforcer of existing social norms.

An important point to be remembered from Chapter 1 is that the social reality reflected in religious symbolism is not the way society actually operates, but is an ideal society. Religion replicates the normative structure, not actual conduct: "a religious institution is more demonstrably functional with respect to a specific image of the ideal society than with respect to an existing system of events, and thus the organizational 'needs' which functional analysis must postulate are 'needs' chiefly with respect to a particular ideal image" (Wallace, 1966:37). The object of functionalism must be to investigate the extent to which religious systems actually do replicate the norms of society. In fact, it is better to assume that religion is a function of kinship, economic and political institutions—which in turn are a function of religion. In other words, assume that all parts of the social system are interconnected.

The most distinctively functional analysis of religion is that in which religious beliefs and practices are examined from the standpoint of their contribution to the maintenance (or disruption) of some sociocultural system. Thus, for example, Malinowski (1948:53) saw in funeral customs a way in which the needs of group solidarity and morale were met at a time when the death of a member of the group threatened the group with dismay, demoralization, and disintegration. Difficulties in specifying system "needs," and even greater difficulties in attaching particular social practices to these needs in a causal way, have resulted in a more tentative kind of functionalism, one in which the object of study is the reciprocal relation between religious and other social institutions, and the part played by religion in integrating the total culture.

The most sophisticated and ingenious modern exponent of the Durkheimian model of religion is Guy Swanson, who in two books, *Birth of the Gods* and *Religion and Regime*, has attempted to apply Durkheim's model without becoming trapped in the conceptual apparatus of "needs" and "system maintenance" that has ensnared others. His work is complex and painstakingly detailed, and therefore almost impossible to summarize without loss. It would be difficult to improve upon Towler's (1974:98–101) summary of the argument in *Religion and Regime*, however, and it will be quoted here.

Religion and Regime is about the Reformation. Swanson contrasts European religion and politics before the Reformation, then in 1490, and again in 1780 when the movement had concluded. Swanson focuses in particular on the notion of *immanence*, which he considers crucial to the difference between Catholic belief and the various Protestant creeds.

> In Catholicism, [Swanson] points out, God is not only present in the world in the person of Jesus, but remains accessible through the Church. The sacraments, the relics of the saints, the priestly hierarchy, shrines, holy water and a hundred other things provide the faithful with tangible aspects of divinity which are ever present. The world of the Catholic is shot through with God, who is met at every turn, and who is no less immanent in the world than he is transcendent beyond it. Leaving aside various intermediary religions, such as Anglicanism and Lutheranism, at the other extreme we find that Calvinism presents a pattern which is the sharpest contrast with Catholicism. According to extreme Protestant beliefs, when Jesus ascended into heaven the world was left without a trace of him. The disciples are simply the disciples of the Lord, not themselves sacred in their own right. The Lord's Supper is a memorial containing nothing sacred in itself apart from the memory which was recalled. God, for the Calvinist, is utterly transcendent, *Deus absconditus*.

Swanson sets himself the problem of explaining just what it is in men's experience of their social world that corresponds to this religious contrast. He points to differences among the political regimes which were emerging at about the same time as the Reformation, and makes use of the distinction, drawn by David Easton, between "the polity of an organization as an association and its polity as a social system." Polity in the first sense involves decisions taken in the interests of the several parties concerned. The good of the organisation of state is equated with the sum of the interests of the various members. Polity in the second sense concerns decisions taken in the interests of the organisation or state *qua* institution. Here the interests even of an overwhelming majority of the members may be disregarded in the interests of the organisation itself. Decisions in matters of state include the authority "to make war or conclude peace, to create magistrates, to establish a system of judicial appeals, to pardon adjudged offenders, to coin money, to have allegiance or fealty or homage, to grant patents including those of monopoly, and to convoke and control the militia of the state."

Following Easton's distinction we see that decisions such as these, which affect the interests of the state, may be thought of in two quite different ways. It will be clearer if we take as an example the decision as to whether or not war should be declared. On the one hand the decision may be taken so that the best interests of all the subjects of the state are followed. The landowners may want peace, while tradesmen, the army and the church want war. The decision will depend on the balance of power and the balance of interests between these various parties. On the other hand it may be that when all these various interests have been consulted a further consideration is introduced: what will most effectively preserve the integrity of the state as an autonomous community and advance its position vis-à-vis other states? This is an altogether separate matter, although in practice the long term interests of the citizens may be best served by attending to the immediate interests of the state as a well-ordered community. Bearing in mind these two types of consideration we can see that, at the extremes, there are two contrasting ways of deciding whether or not to go to war. . . .

In Swanson's view this distinction is crucial. On the one hand, the state may be thought of solely as the composite of its members. On the other hand it may be thought of as an entity separate from its members and above them, with interests of its own which must be accorded primacy of place in all decisions. He argues that experience of the respective types of political arrangement which enshrine these two contrasting conceptions of society will influence what kind of god will be found credible in the society.

In societies where the authority for matters of state is clearly exercised as separate and independent of the interests of the subjects, this will predispose people to believe in a god who is immanent in the world. Just as the authority and purposes of the state are separate and visible, no matter how detestable they may happen to be, so the presence and purposes of a god will be deemed to be visible and knowable. Conversely, the society in which there is no conception of the state as separate from, and above, its members, and has political machinery to adjudge no interests beyond the composite interests of its members, will predispose its members to belief in a god who is transcendent, invisible and inaccessible. . . .

Many of the political forms which emerged for the first time in the sixteenth century, Swanson points out, vested authority for decisions in matters of state in representative assemblies. In such assemblies landowners, craft guilds, the professions, and so on were all represented, and their representatives exercised authority in the interests of their constituencies. The interests and authority of the state as such effectively disappeared from view, and while a distinction might still be drawn in theory, in practice the good of the state came to be equated with the good of the several constituent members. The authority of the state, *qua* state, had become an authority *absconditus*. So Swanson argues that the notion of a God immanent in the world has no social experience from which it might be rendered meaningful under such a political arrangement. Just as the state cannot be distinguished as a separate entity, so neither can God, who thus becomes totally transcendent and fundamentally unknowable and unapproachable.

Swanson has caught nicely the spirit of Durkheim's thought and added precision to it. It is particularly important to note the metaphorical aspect of the relation between religious and political structures and the indeterminancy of the relation. Assumptions of crude, deterministic isomorphism should be avoided.

RELIGION AND SOCIETAL INTEGRATION

Durkheim has been interpreted as saying that a society is integrated to the degree that its members possess a common religion. "Religion provides the obfuscating but necessary rhetoric of public harmony" (Martin, 1967:107). But it is incorrect to interpret Durkheim's position as meaning that religion is the *cause* of integration, because this presents a much too mechanical view of the relation between religion and society. Remember from Chapter 1 that not only does religion have a social aspect, but society has a religious aspect. "The state of perpetual dependence in which we find ourselves in the face of society inspires in us a feeling of religious awe" (Durkheim, 1975:93). In other words, it is not that "religion produces the cohesive society, but rather that the phenomenon of cohesion has a religious quality about it" (Hammond, 1974:116).

Rather than argue that religion causes the integration of American society, it is more accurate to say that, at its highest level, American society has a sacred character. The symbols of cohesion and unity have assumed sacred significance, transcending the petty divisions of denominational religion. A national figure such as Lincoln thus becomes "each year less profane and more sacred," moving with each successive generation away from "the Man of the Prairies" toward identification with deity and "ultimate godhood" (Warner, 1961:273). Culture heroes, symbolizing virtues such as industry, ambition, humility, and sacrifice, enable Americans to realize themselves and see their common purpose. As Durkheim originally suggested, these heroes acquired sacred stature in the process.

This is an argument that social cohesion has a religious quality about it rather than an argument that religion causes social cohesion. It is tantamount to saying that all societies (which, by definition, have acquired some cohesion) have a sacred aspect. Its most forthright contemporary exponent is Robert Bellah, who claims to have discovered what he calls a "civil religion" in America, in which is located the sacred and integrative dimension of American life.

CIVIL RELIGION

Civil religion is a faith not confined to the denominations, but one which emerges from the life of the folk and is manifested in loyalties, values, and ideas expressed in everyday life concerning the national purpose, society's values, its morals, and its traditions. It exists concretely in "shrines" at Gettysburg and Arlington and in "sacred" anniversaries such as Memorial Day, Thanksgiving, the Fourth of July, and the birthdays of Washington and Lincoln. Wallace (1966:77), among others, had referred previously to a "religio-political cult," which amounts to a "nondenominational, theistic faith used to rationalise and sanction political, military, and other secular institutions, such as schools. . . ," and Mead (1975:30) has referred to a "religion of the Republic," which, by his own account, is the same as Bellah's "civil religion."

Bellah offers as a clear example of the operation of the civil religion presidential inaugural addresses. The separation of Church and State and the existence of a large number of different denominations in the United States means that the tie between politics and religion must always be indirect. Bellah found, however, that religion has constantly been used by political authorities as a means of legitimating their actions and policies—although on close inspection it is a peculiar kind of religion. Presidents do indeed invoke the name of God in their inaugural addresses (a time of close attention to the issue of unity), but the references typically come only at the beginning and the end of the address, and even then the Deity is mentioned only in a cursory fashion. Furthermore, an appeal is made to God (not Christ), a God of no particular church or faith. So consistent is this practice that Bellah rejects the idea that it is an example of hypocritical piety on the part of a politician keen to ensure future support and re-election. He also rejects the view that it is a case of pure rhetoric or unthinking conformity. Furthermore, he dismisses the view that it is an attempt to reach a kind of lowest common denominator religion, a synthetic version of the major faiths. Instead, he holds that there is a separate religion, reducible to neither the pseudo-religious patriotism of politicians nor the common tradition of the mainstream denominations. It is a religion that articulates all that is held sacred about American experience. In the absence of an established church, it is a source of powerful sacred symbols that functions to promote national solidarity and sustain individual commitment of a religious intensity toward national goals. It is a linking of national fortunes and destiny with the transcendental, "a set of beliefs and rituals, related to the past, present and/or future of a people ('nation') which are understood in some transcendental fashion" (Hammond, 1976:171).

There is a crude manifestation of the civil religion in "an Ameri-can Legion type ideology that fuses God, country and flag" (Bellah, 1970:182), but the true civil religion is by no means captured in these unsubtle forms. It is present in the minds of all who have faith in democracy (as defined by the American system), in which the goals of freedom, equality, and justice are sacralized. It is present also in the Protestant civic piety, which promotes a strong work ethic, a confident pragmatism, a moralistic attitude toward politics, and a firm belief in the responsibility of the individual for his or her own fate. Civil religion means, then, that the ultimate dimension of American life is sacralized—a fact that can be recognized in the frequent public ceremonies which mark important national anniversaries.

In order to understand the relation of the idea of civil religion to Durkheim's work, it is important to note two things. First, Bellah is not equating religion with the churches, and certainly not with Christianity. Rather, he sees the civil religion as an interpretation of the major faiths in the light of political experience. It exists alongside the organized churches rather than being a part of them. Of course, it draws on much the same tradition as those churches, and it has an effect on them—it has encouraged, for example, a moralistic rather than a contemplative denominationalism—but it cannot be reduced to the sum of the major denominations. Second, although the relation between religion and politics in the United States has been "singularly smooth" (Bellah, 1970:180), this does not mean that civil religion is some kind of "establishment" religion. There is an inevitable tension between civil religion and politics. This is an important point and should be elaborated upon.

Civil religion is a celebration of American ways—but it is also prophetic. What does this mean? First of all, civil religion, as exemplified in presidential addresses, functions to engender support for core political values and institutions. Furthermore, politicians rarely lose the opportunity to impress upon their constituents the social importance of a kind of "religion-in-general" and the national value of religious practices. This is done without in any way establishing a particular religion. Politicians are capable of maintaining that religion ought to be a force in the life of every American while at the same time defending the right of all Americans to choose the particular church in which they worship.

There are, then, close ties between political loyalties and religious commitments in the United States. But civil religion is neither a spiritualized State nor a politicized religion. It does not present the Church as an agent of redemption, but the nation and its people. By virtue of its appeal to tradition, to the founding principles of the nation-state, and to national values, civil religion has the potential not only to exist alongside and tacitly support political institutions, but to challenge them as well.

A central tenet of the civil religion is that the nation is not an ultimate end (an assertion that might be found in the more vulgar versions of religious nationalism), but stands under transcendental judgment concerning how well certain principles and values are being realized. In other words, civil religion teaches that there is a law higher than the national interest that must be obeyed. *This is the Durkheimian idea that the sacred symbol system refers to the ideal society.* In the civil religion, the nation presents an idealized picture of itself to itself.

In a most important sense, then, the civil religion can be prophetic and, as Lincoln's articulation of it at the time of the Civil War demonstrates, even divisive. It is not the celebration of society as it is, but as it ought to be. It invokes not actual practices but abstract principles—"All men are created equal." These abstract principles, futhermore, are variously articulated in popular theologies, which lead to conflicts over civil religion itself. The idea of civil religion is not, then, a necessarily conservative one.

Bellah has extended and refined the Durkheimian thesis to read as follows: a sacred dimension being considered an inherent part of all social life, the integrative function of religion can be detected even where formal religious unity is absent. This is done simply by locating the source of commonly held feelings of ultimacy and unity. Anything about which people feel a sense of ultimacy is thereby religion. This, of course, makes it very difficult to see any relationship between "religion" and "society," or to see them as separable at all. Bellah, like Durkheim before him, seems to be more interested in the moral foundations of social cohesion than in religion as such, and seems to have dealt with the problem of the relation between religion as defined in this book and other social institutions by explaining it away. Religion cannot "cause" cohesion because religion *is* cohesion. This would seem to be a less than satisfactory way of coping with the problem of religion in a complex society.

Two further reservations about Bellah's interesting thesis are in order. First, it is quite conceivable that there is little new in this idea of civil religion: it may merely be another name for the link between religion and patriotism that has more or less been endorsed by the mainstream churches throughout history. Bellah denies that civil religion is simply a spiritualized patriotism, but does admit to there being "vulgar" versions of it that are. The vacuity of the religious references in this civil religion ("go to the church of your choice;" "Worship any God you please as long as you worship some God") also suggest that this civil religion is nothing more than the expression of a mainstream "American" religion upon which all can agree and "beneath" which people can attend their different denominations for the social satisfactions they provide. Again, Bellah denies that civil religion is a kind of "common denominator" religion, but there is no doubt that this "religion in general" provides a unity at the level of values while legitimizing a need diversity of lifestyles.

A third reservation is that there is some question as to whether this civil religion can be located quite as easily as Bellah implies. A content analysis of newspaper editorials on "Honor America Day" (4th July, 1970) uncovered few references to the themes mentioned by Bellah as characteristic of civil religion: "Of the twelve statements selected as integral to the thesis of American civil religion, only 5, or less than 50%, received any mention at all. There were themes which were *similar* to those described by Bellah, but they were secular. For example, frequent reference was made to the Bill of Rights, but no mention made that they were God-given" (Thomas, 1972:222). On the other hand, Wimberley *et al.* (1976:893) in factor-analyzing questionnaire responses from persons who attended a Billy Graham crusade, did discover a separate civil religion dimension. Responses which clustered together under this heading included "We should respect the President's authority since his authority is from God"; "To me, the flag of the United States is sacred"; "God can be known through the experience of the American people." A later study (Wimberley, 1976) of a more heterogeneous sample uncovered a distinctive civil religious dimension related to but independent of both church religiosity and political commitment. Contradictory results such as these are perhaps to be expected from just one or two tests of such a complex thesis. Evidently, though, the existence of a separate civil religion has not been disproved, and there is much impressionistic evidence to support the idea.

Bellah has provided a valuable insight into the way religion can function to promote social integration in modern societies, despite their pluralism. He manages to do this without saying simultaneously that specific religious beliefs and practices must necessarily be tied to specific aspects of social structure. If this thesis applies at the national level, does it also apply at the local level? Is the image of the small town held together by its main-street church a realistic one? Some sociological research has addressed this question, which will be the topic of the remainder of this chapter.

THE CHURCH AND THE COMMUNITY

The bond between territory and religious identification has always been very strong. The parish system long used by many denominations is an obvious manifestation of this bond, and even today, in a highly mobile society, the majority of churchgoers live within a mile of their church (Dynes, 1959:264). The idea of the church serving the needs of the community in which it is located in return for support and loyalty from that community is very old. This situation fits neatly into functionalist assumptions about the role of religion in society.

The concept of community will be used here not in any technical sense, but to refer simply to "the outermost limits of what may *personally* be experienced or encountered by the individual in his everyday life" (Berger and Berger, 1975:111). The idea of community has a deep hold on the American mind, even though national forces have increasingly come to shape the lives of modern Americans. Communities persist in the United States in the following respects: (1) the small town and rural community have not entirely disappeared although, of course, their cultural preeminence, autonomy, and independence have been much reduced; (2) urbanization has not destroyed community life, but transformed it—urban villages have appeared; (3) new-style communities have arisen in the suburbs. In considering the functions of religion in the community, we must consider each of these survivals.

The Small-Town Church

Functional theory suggests that community solidarity is in large part a function of religious activities. This is but an elaboration of an idea long accepted and frequently verified in empirical observation. For example, Pope (1965:89), in his study of the mill villages and small towns of North Carolina, argued,

> There is no doubt that mill village churches have been among the most powerful agencies in community organization. . . . the church in the mill village is a community center; in the comparative absence of other social institutions, it is the focal point around which economic life in the village largely revolves. Natural leaders among the workers find in it almost their only vehicle for expression of leadership. . . .

Pope observed, further, that the church was the "center of most 'worthwhile' community enterprises, including recreational activities."

The rapid urbanization of the South demands that we use caution in applying these ovservations of the 1920s to the remaining small towns of the modern South—and Earle *et al.*'s (1976) follow-up study throws no fresh light on this particular aspect of Pope's work. Yet Hill (1966:172) argues that in the South as a whole, the church, more than the town hall or the school, is still "the unchallenged center" of community life. Having observed the social life of "Springdale," a small rural community in upstate New York in the late 1950s, Vidich and Bensman (1960:231) concluded that churchgoing was probably the most important, visible community activity, church related functions occupying about fifty percent of all organized social life in the town. Studies of the black community suggest an even greater functional importance for the church as a means of social integration (Frazier, 1974:40). The presence of several competing denominations does not seem to have prevented religion from being generally supportive of community values, and a community project may be one of the few occasions when the several denominations join together.

For most Protestant Americans, the nature of their involvement in their local church is more or less the same, whatever the denomination. The parish or congregation is presided over by a church council led by a minister. Annual meetings are held, at which the entire congregation is entitled to make inputs into the running of the church. The congregation also votes in council members. Although there are variations on this theme, all American denominations by and large replicate the traditional town meeting. This becomes especially clear when the typical structure of small-town politics. These parallels extend even further: members of with particular responsibilities, such as finance, education, welfare, evangelism, and maintenance, in a way that replicates the ideal structure of small town politics. These parallels extend even further: members of the council tend overwhelmingly to be older males (although the congregation is typically predominantly female); they are also more highly educated, and they hold jobs that are of higher prestige than those of the rest of the congregation. In other words, the character of the politics of the church reflects that of local community politics. Additionally, middle-class people (who make up the bulk of the most active church members) tend to be those who emphasize most strongly the values of community stability, solidarity, and cooperation. The church is seen by them as an agency for achieving these ends.

Intense involvement in the local congregation of mainstream Protestant denominations can be seen in most communities as an expression of commitment to and consciousness of that community. In smaller towns, where the sense of community is presumably strongest, rates of church attendance tend to be higher (Nelsen *et al.*, 1971:393). The usually positive relationship between social status and frequency of church attendance is enhanced among those with a strong sense of community (Roof, 1974a:305) and "traditional religious beliefs and private devotional activities are disproportionately found in rural and small-town settings" (Roof, 1976:203). For the church to function as a basis of community feeling, however, it probably has to be present in ways other than a place of attendance. Church programs would seem to be of great importance in this regard. Besides providing additional means of community interaction, these programs reflect community roles; there are separate programs for different community categories, such as the young and the old, and different programs to meet different community needs, such as welfare and recreation. This is particularly true of the black community, where the church has traditionally played a direct and instrumental role in catering to community needs. For example, some black churches include in their Sunday service announcements of jobs available for the unemployed.

The community role of the church as a aource of stability and integration need not be intended or even recognized. Only in exceptional cases do church members see themselves (as church members) reaching out into the community, helping preserve community morals and standards. Church members tend to rate their churches most highly as a context in which to make new friends and a place to become involved in fund raising and plant construction. Offering specific services to the community or mounting evangelical campaigns in the community are typically given low priority (Metz, 1967:62). The integrative function of the churches is thus latent.

The integrative role of the synagogue is evident among Jews. Jews attend religious services much less frequently than Protestants or Catholics: only seventeen percent attend more than once a month (Sklare, 1971:118). However, the synagogue is by far the strongest agency of the entire Jewish community; up to eighty percent of the Jewish community will be affiliated with it in one way or another. A closer look at the way the Jewish synagogue operates reveals the important communal function it performs. Synagogues are formed by local initiative and are largely free to determine their own programs. This not only provides an opportunity for grass roots action, it also makes it more likely that the synagogue will be oriented to community needs. All synagogues are regarded as equal, which makes them useful for incorporating mobile Jews. Each synagogue has a center, which is the focus of local Jewish activities and culture. Finally, synagogues typically sponsor adult study programs and other services that are useful to the community.

In addition to providing a kind of structural underpinning for community life through their programs and organizations, the churches also heighten community consciousness by solemnizing community events. The point is not so much that the specific community is celebrated as that churches help people celebrate as a community. Anniversary days such as the Fourth of July do not celebrate the community as such, but they do provide an opportunity for the community to become aware of itself. The gathering of the community for services on Memorial Day indirectly strengthens the community by its theme of "the sacrifice of the soldier dead for the living and the obligation of the living to sacrifice their individual purpose for the good of the group" (Warner, 1961:249).

The denominations also help symbolize community solidarity by cooperating with one another in welfare and recreational programs, by playing down denominational differences during community events and by, for example, agreeing not to conduct fund-raising drives on the same weekend. Indeed, communities tend to define as religious *that which is integrative*. People are inclined to feel that something has to keep the community together, that the churches are the best agents for this, and that, therefore, they should not be controversial.

These cooperative efforts notwithstanding, the integrative function of community churches should not be overestimated. Veiled beneath a cloak of public harmony and fraternity, the separate denominations may carry on an intensive evangelical competition. There is also the danger that, given the multiplicity of churches in any given community, what is everybody's business becomes nobody's business, and the decisions affecting the quality of community life are left to secular agencies (Obenhaus, 1963:213). Finally, religion has not been a *sufficient* bulwark against the breakup of the rural community. As rural areas have felt the pull of the city and become depopulated, so the rural church has declined. Its most frequent recourse has been the merger of parishes, which hardly enhances the position of the church as the focus of community solidarity. In the absence of recent community studies, the role of the church in the community, and the validity of the functional thesis today, are matters open to considerable doubt. Although the functional argument is probably overdrawn, the continued centrality of religious institutions in small-town life cannot be disputed. However, further research into the institutional presence of churches in community life is urgently needed.

The City Church

In the United States, the ancient parish system has been modified only slightly by the congregational system. There remains the same pattern of regular attendance, communal worship and organizational activity geared to community needs. Congregationalism did, of course, chip away at the territoriality of the parish system. Even rural church studies reveal that, given the means of mobility, people will travel long distances to their church in order to be with worshipers of the same ethnic and occupational background. The tie between a specific locality and a church is thus threatened by the rise of new occupational communities under industrialism and the mobility afforded by modern technology (see Bultena, 1944).

A much more serious threat to the traditional parish system, however, has been urbanization. The growth of the cities has seriously undermined the close link between a specific territory and a specific church. In few urban parishes today are the residents and the congregants entirely the same. The rupture has been exacerbated by the tardiness with which churchpeople have responded to urbanization. Protestant churchpeople in particular have tended to regard the city as something alien and therefore as mission territory, unsuited to traditional modes of religious organization, an attitude that cannot fail to weaken the solidarity functions of the church. This is not so true of Catholicism, which has always been more of a city church in the United States. In Canada, however, Catholics *have* been "prone to equate virtue with ruralism and tradition" (Fallding, 1971:112).

The reasons why city life must alter the traditional link between church and community are obvious. In the city, the traditional correspondence between residence and workplace almost invariably breaks down. The identification of the individual church member as both consumer and producer within the community, an identification upon which the traditional church based its appeal to common values, is thus broken. The city also precludes a strong sense of territory. Its multioccupancy buildings and rapidly shifting land-use patterns separate people and place in a way that makes dysfunctional the church's identification of the available congregation with a stable residential unity. City neighborhoods are also typified by a high rate of turnover and heterogeneity in the population. The churches reflect rather than modify these characteristics. City churches have a high rate of turnover and a heterogeneous membership. This seriously impedes the churches' ability to perform their traditional integrative functions. The city is also a place that encourages impersonal, associational relationships—some urban parishes number over 10,000 inhabitants. It is hard to conceive of the church, operating in ways established in small towns, coping with this kind of massness.

None of this means that the churches have ceased to operate in the cities. It does mean, however, that the contribution of religion to urban living has to be examined very carefully. It soon becomes apparent, for example, that the church, though not absent from the city, has adapted to the decline of the community rather than preventing it. The downtown church has become separated from its geographical base and can no longer function as the territorial focus of a neighborhood. Inner-city churches tend to hold onto members who are moving out of the district,

> placing in leadership positions the most successful business executives (who often live in the suburbs) and attempting to set up a program with a wide appeal for those groups which can guarantee financial support. In the end, the lower-class population group takes over the neighborhood, and the congregation, having excluded it from membership, finds that its only remaining alternatives are to die or to flee (Kloetzli, 1961:105).

This process is even more likely in the presence of class and racial differences. It is accelerated by the fact that many congregations in inner-city areas comprise a disproportionately large number of older women, who are unable to prevent the continued decline of their church but are nevertheless most reluctant to allow the dissolution of a congregation with which they have long been associated. The result is that many churches have failed to adapt to inner-city life at all, either departing altogether or floating above the community in which they are situated and drawing their congregation from other areas. The Anglican Church, among many others, has *never* really adapted to inner-city life and has little contact with it. For example, in the Battersea (London) Deanery in 1965, less than one percent of the population covered by the deanery were to be found in an Anglican church on an average Sunday (Paul, 1973:178).

The downtown church, like the area in which it is situated, often tends to be rather impersonal. Congregants are typically church members of long standing who, as often as not, now travel a considerably way to the church. It could be argued, of course, that inner-city life has no communities on which to build. However, it is not clear whether the association between inner-city life and the decline of the church in the inner city is due to the loss of community or to the church's failure to answer the needs of the *new kind of community* that inner-city life has created.

The mainstream churches have made many attempts to adapt to inner-city life, some of which have been quite successful. They include creating artificial parishes in order to compensate for the lack of territorial divisions of a manageable size—including the treatment of housing projects as "parishes"; setting up interdenominational special-purpose missions to skid-row areas and blighted neighborhoods; forming groups within parishes or congregations, such as study groups and house churches, in order to overcome feelings of impersonalism; organizing retreats and conferences, in order to periodically re-create the sense of community that has been lost; and becoming involved in community organizations, in order to help rebuild urban neighborhoods. The churches are not, then, without the resources to adapt to urban life and to continue to provide a sense of community and unity. That this can be done is also expressed in multi-staffed urban parishes and in adjustments such as those made by the Mormons, who subdivide their "wards" whenever they approach becoming a population of 1,000 (O'Dea, 1957:180). The functionalist thesis should not, therefore, be tied too closely to the traditional parochial concept and should not be allowed to conceal functional alternatives to the parish system.

The traditional parish system would seem to have an uncertain future in urban areas. There is little evidence that a church's parochial structure actually helps in any way to sustain urban community consciousness. Fichter (1973:44), observing a Catholic parish, clearly does not feel that the parish makes much of a contribution to the integration of people at the community level: "there was a closer social bond in sharing the same occupation than there was in sharing the same religion." The church of the urban parish appears to function more than anything else as a kind of service station where people go as individuals to have their personal needs met. The churches are aware of this development, of course. One Catholic solution has been the ethnic parish—a combination of territorial and ethnic bonds. In the cities, the Catholic parishes have long functioned as bases for ethnic solidarity for entering immigrants, operating as a center for all sorts of organizations. The Catholic priest performed an important mediating role for the ethnic immigrants, helping them with legal, occupational, welfare, and marital problems. It is significant that where the Catholic Church has refused to institute an ethnic parish (for example, among New York's Puerto Ricans), it does not play a large part in the life of the community. The same is true of Mexican American Catholics, amongst whom attendance is very low, compared with other Catholics (Grebler *et al.*, 1970:474). The links among territory, community, and church demand a stability and homogeneity not typically found in urban areas. The churches have largely failed to create this stability, and where they have refused to build on preexisting community ties they have become largely irrelevant. These failures, contrasted with the success of the churches in small towns where the sense of community is already high, suggests that *the churches are as much a consequence of community solidarity as they are a cause of it.*

Suburban Religion

By and large, suburbanization has consisted of the movement of the better off (usually white) to the less densely populated areas at the periphery of the cities, and the movement of the poor into multi-occupancy dwellings adjacent to the downtown business district. This process, which has been under way since the 1890s, reflects the growing affluence of the middle class, the migration of the rural-born poor whites and blacks to the industrial cities, and the influx of large numbers of European immigrants into the cities.

The impact of suburbanization on the churches has been a desertion of the inner-city areas and a movement to the suburbs. An analysis of membership trends in the United Methodist downtown congregations in seventy-nine cities across the United States showed that seventy percent of the churches had lost membership between 1960 and 1973, a time when overall church membership remained steady (Jones and Wilson, 1974:viii). In 1963, fifty-seven percent of the suburban United Church congregations in Canada reported net increases in membership, whereas forty-nine percent of the inner-city congregations reported net losses (Crysdale, 1965:11).

As the churches have moved to the suburbs, they have changed their character. The inhabitants of the suburbs tend to be middle class and mobile. They are well-integrated economically: they share the same kinds of jobs, consumption patterns, and lifestyles. But they have few other ties because their work place and residence are separate and the turnover of residents is high. Furthermore, the number of social institutions in the suburbs being low because of their newness, the churches are forced to take on a greater number of functions. The job of the churches becomes that of creating a community where none existed before. The most important change they undergo is to acquire a host of social services, as opposed to explicitly religious functions. The modern suburban minister "is a religious leader possessing a B.D. or its equivalent, a rudimentary knowledge of how social organizations work, and hopefully an M.A. in psychological counselling" (Newman, 1976:269).

Sociological observations of suburban churches reveal that they do indeed stress fellowship above all else. In the "Park Forest" suburb of Chicago, for example, people ranked their criteria for choice of church as follows: (1) the minister; (2) the quality of the Sunday school; (3) the location; (4) the denomination; and (5) the quality of the music. The minister was looked to primarily for counseling and the Sunday school was seen as a useful place for children to make friends (Whyte, 1957:407). The suburban church seems to be an important ground for community identification. It tends to be very highly family-oriented, typically having a higher proportion of complete families as members than inner-city, small-town, or rural churches (Kloetzli, 1961:96).

The functional theory that the church provides a sense of community in the suburb is supported by the findings of Carlos (1970:756), who discovered that Catholic attendance was higher in the suburbs than in the inner city, even with class, age, sex, and ethnicity held constant. The suburban Catholic church seems to operate as a quasi-community, drawing people of a common background together in more personal relationships. The Catholic pastor in a suburban parish usually lacks clerical assistants but, reflecting a greater communal role, often has lay assistants. The suburban Catholic priest is also expected to be more of a joiner and to be generally sociable.

In the case of Jews, the picture is less clear. Suburban Jews show a much lower rate of weekly attendance than their urban counterparts (Goldstein, 1968:230). Perhaps this is because the kind of Jew who moves to the suburbs is the kind of Jew who attends infrequently anyway. But it could also mean that the synagogue per se does not, and perhaps never has, served integrative functions for Jews. Solidarity among Jews might be more a matter of residential propinquity than formal religious adherence. It is important to remember, however, that although few Jews attend services regularly, nearly all (ninety-three percent) maintain "membership" in the synagogue—albeit a term loosely defined.

Research suggests three patterns of relationship between church and community. In tradition-oriented small towns and rural areas, the churches symbolize and affirm a strong sense of community. In the suburbs, the churches play a more active role, helping to create a new sense of community. In the inner city, the churches either reflect the impersonalism of the city and have little to say about community at all, or they provide a kind of surrogate community, a context in which to relate to other city dwellers independently of workplace or residence.

The function of the churches as surrogate communities is hinted at in patterns of friendship choice. Anderson (1968) compared friendship choices in three different cities, one predominantly Protestant, one heavily Catholic, and one with a Mormon majority. He found that friends are indeed chosen by religion, particularly if the religious group is in the minority. For example, although thirty-four percent of the Protestants in "Protestant City" would by chance be expected to choose their three closest friends from among other Protestants, fifty-eight percent actually did so. But in "Catholic City," where the chance percentage was only five percent, forty-one percent of the Protestants made their friendship choice by religion. Interestingly, the discrepancy between expected- and actual-choice percentages (the measure of the degree of religious choosing) was greater in communities where Catholics are dominant, suggesting that the beliefs and structures of Catholicism are more conducive to a sense of community, even in urban areas. This is probably due to a combination of the Catholics' minority status historically, their rules of endogamy, their lower social status, and, of course, their parochial system. Laumann (1973:91) found that "Catholics are likely to have more ethno-religious [friendships] than Protestants, but this relationship tends to weaken as we move from low to more highly educated groups." Such friendship patterns say nothing directly about how well the church supports a territorial community. The thesis that religion fosters a sense of community *among its adepts* is much more defensible than the thesis that wherever church and community coexist, religion will preserve and sustain community boundaries and identification. The latter thesis is valid only if the community is relatively stable and well integrated (Eister, 1957).

CONCLUSION

It is clear from the evidence presented in this chapter that religion is not essential to social integration. Nor does it always perform a socially integrative role. Religion is likely to promote social integration only where (1) "suprasocial authority" is granted precedence over other forms, (2) religious and other social institutions support the same values, (3) tradition is greatly revered, and (4) there is consensus within the religious community itself (Glock and Stark, 1965:180–81). In other words, religion is integrative only where specific religions and specific communities are coterminous in a relatively stable situation. These restrictions on the scope of the functionalist thesis are not as severe as they might appear, for two reasons. First, situations in which religion and community or territory are coterminous are not rare. Southern Baptists in Texas, Mormons in Utah, Catholics in Rhode Island are examples. Second, the existence of religious divisions may be deceptive, for the different denominations in the American community share a common religious tradition and culture, which, at the very general level, as Bellah has shown, does unite all church members in the society.

10

CHURCH AND STATE

INTRODUCTION

Political activity consists of contests for the power to make and enforce laws. Political institutions express interests and demands, make decisions on law and its enforcement, and implement those decisions. In modern societies politics is the world of parties, interest groups, legislative assemblies, and the State; it is an arena of campaigns, caucuses, votes, and elections. What relation does religion have to this world?

At one time, religious collectivities and political collectivities were one and the same. This is no longer true, but many sociologists assume that, religion being the source and defender of ultimate values and the State being the repository of legal force within a territory, the two must be compatible. In other words, religious practices which threaten the State will not long be tolerated, and a State that does not have the sanction of religious institutions will have difficulty maintaining its legitimacy. This idea flows naturally from the assumption common to functionalist sociologists that "structures which endure in social systems have effects which, in general, help other structures to perform or contribute to the maintenance of these other structures" (Skidmore, 1975:130). There is nothing mechanical or inevitable about this. A pattern of behavior such as religion is molded to another pattern such as politics if, for political purposes, it is found satisfying and deliberately encouraged or, without planning at all, it gives satisfaction and is allowed to stand. The sociological task is to show how and why religious and political behavior are related.

It is by no means the case that political activities are confined to the workings of the State, but the importance of the State in modern societies (and limitations of space) requires that the focus in this chapter be entirely on the problematic relation between Church and State in the United States and the United Kingdom. The formal separation of Church and State is a familiar fact to students of religion and politics in the United States; in the United Kingdom, there lingers an Erastianism that sees the Church as one aspect of the State. Nevertheless the two cases are quite similar.

THE DEVELOPMENT OF
CHURCH-STATE RELATIONS IN THE UNITED STATES

The founding of the American Republic was an experiment in new approaches to the relation between Church and State. Specific ties between the State and a particular faith were prohibited, as was church interference in the running of the State. The First Amendment of the Bill of Rights (1791) declared, "Congress shall make no law regarding an establishment of religion, or prohibit the free exercise thereof. . . ." The Fourteenth Amendment to the Constitution (1868) extended the free-exercise guarantee of the First Amendment to the states. All the states, too, have their constitutional separation of Church and State, although in reality, "the law of the State constitutions closely followed the interpretation of the Supreme Court under the United States Constitution" (Sorauf, 1975:26). In the twentieth century, the Supreme Court has broadly interpreted the Bill of Rights to mean that the State must remain neutral not only between religions but also between religion and irreligion.

With a few exceptions, the early American settlers did not advocate freedom of worship as a general principle, but only freedom from control for themselves. The exclusivist Puritan theocracy that grew up in Massachusetts illustrates this. The Bill of Rights, however, ratified a growing sentiment (evident in the decline of the hegemony of the Bay Colony) that, given the multiplicity of the competing faiths, church establishment on a formal basis would be a permanent barrier to a stable union.

Although the Bill of Rights prohibited Congress from establishing a particular Church, Church and State were not thereby unequivocally and finally sundered. The line dividing Church and State was not made clear then and has remained obscure ever since. Guidelines which appeared reasonable in one period become anachronistic in another. At the state level, the issue of disestablishment was (as in England) always tied closely to party politics. Some states had abolished State tax support for churches by the time of the Revolution, but the progress of disestablishment, first in the South and later in New England, was closely associated with the defeat of the Federalists—a party much more concerned than the Jeffersonians with maintaining the values and patterns of behavior of colonial times. Vistiges of this link remain in the association between Episcopalian and Republican forces. The final state disestablishment did not come until 1831, when Congregationalism finally lost its hold in Massachusetts.

Because separation was not laid down definitively at the founding of the Republic, the relationship between Church and State has constantly fluctuated. What is more significant for our present purposes is that, as an issue, the separation of Church and State seems to be more important now than at any other time in the nation's history. The Supreme Court considered the meaning of the First Amendment clause with respect to religion only six or seven times before 1940, but since then has reviewed it some forty times. In fact, between 1951 and 1957, eleven Church-State cases were heard; between 1958 and 1964 twenty-two were decided; and the period 1965 to 1970 witnessed thirty-four decisions, as did the period 1971 to 1974 (Sorauf, 1975:360).

Clearly, Church-State relations have become more problematic, not less so. The frequency with which the issue comes before the courts appears to depend on such things as the activism of particular justices and the prevailing public sentiments concerning the limits of pluralism. The overall rise in the number of cases heard also probably reflects a declining Protestant hegemony, combined with a rise in the power of the Catholic community at a time when the ability of the Catholic Church to sustain its educational institutions without state aid is considerably diminished. In the period 1971–1974, the issue concerning Church-State relations that appeared most frequently before the high appellate courts was that of state aid to parochial schools (13 times) while similar issues, such as grants to attend religious colleges (5 times) and grants for construction of buildings at religious colleges (3 times) also cropped up frequently. The questions of state supported busing for parochial-school students, shared-time programs in schools, and the uttering of religious invocations at high school commencements illustrate the extent to which Church-State problems have pervaded the sphere of education (Sorauf, 1975:261).

Over time, the State has shown itself willing to permit a freer exercise of religion. The Supreme Court has more and more subscribed to the view that religious rights prevail unless they violate *compelling* State interests (Burkholder, 1974:36). Although this increased liberalism of the State toward religion could be interpreted rather cynically as a recognition that religion is now less salient than before, the point is that the separation of Church and State in the United States has not been a constant or settled aspect of social life. The "wall" between the two has constantly been raised and lowered.

REASONS FOR THE SEPARATION OF CHURCH AND STATE IN THE UNITED STATES

The motives behind the separation of Church and State in the United States are extremely varied and intricately interrelated. A simplified list of them follows:

1. The United States was originally settled by groups such as the Mennonities, the Catholics and the Puritans, who were seeking freedom from the religious persecution they suffered in Europe.
2. The dominant values in the infant nation were liberalism and pluralism. Both emphasized freedom of choice and individual responsibility, an emphasis that extended into the area of religion.
3. Most of the earliest immigrants came from England, where (after the revolution of 1688) religious toleration was practiced to a greater degree than in other European countries.
4. The sheer number and variety of religious groups present by the time of the founding of the independent nation made some sort of accommodation to pluralism necessary if a united nation was to be established. In addition, the voluntarism of most of these groups (which emphasized the fact that the true church is the community of the faithful) paved the way for religious pluralism and militated against a church in which citizenship and religious affiliation would be synonymous.
5. At the time of the framing of the Constitution, only one in eight Americans were church members. This made it necessary to make provision in the Constitution for tolerance of irreligion.
6. The colonial experiences of states such as Rhode Island, Pennsylvania, and Virginia, which had successfully practiced some degree of religious toleration, acted as a model for the nation as a whole.
7. The First Great Awakening, which began in 1734, strengthened the nonconformist spirit in the United States and helped break down the constraints of the old parish system upon which the Anglican Church largely depended.
8. The need to attract settlers and trade made it economically attractive to prohibit religious barriers to migration.
9. The framing of the Constitution was much influenced by French pre-Revolutionary ideas of egalitarianism and deism.
10. Freemasonry, popular among many moving spirits of the American revolution, strongly advocated religious toleration.

Clearly, the principle of separation of Church and State in the United States is not a simple one. Rather, it fuses many different motives concerning the practice of religion in a free society. These motives continue to guide Americans' attitudes toward Church and State, and they contribute to the frequent debate concerning the exact line of demarcation between these two spheres. The issue of separation was definitely not settled when the Constitution was written. Although it would not be correct to say that religious and political forces are formally allied in the United States, neither has it ever been true to say that they are independent of each other. It is true, however, that the formal disestablishment of religion in the United States *is* something that separates it from European societies. Informally, there may be religious "establishments." The Mormons in Utah, the Catholics in Rhode Island, and the Southern Baptists in Texas are conspicuous examples. In fact, in a region like the South, not only is there almost total domination by Baptists and Methodists, but other Protestant denominations that manage to gain a foothold there, such as the Presbyterians and the Disciples of Christ, have moved closer to the dominant denominations in form and style. However, such regional emphases aside, the separation of Church and State is far wider in the United States than in Europe.

Actually, European societies have come to separate Church and State to some degree, and they all practice religious toleration. However, in these countries "the freedom is conceived as belonging to minority sects or religious groups, often with the qualification that they be officially recognized by the State; it is, in other words, a corporate rather than a personal freedom. In the United States from the very beginning the freedom was deemed to belong to the individual rather than to any group to which he might or might not belong" (Pfeffer, 1974:13).

One consequence of the separation of Church and State in the United States (and to a lesser extent in the United Kingdom) is the absence of the kind of anticlericalism associated with a link between Church and Party found in many European countries. The combination of political protest and irreligion that stimulates anticlericalism is largely missing in America: because, first, the pluralism of American religion prevents any one group from being identified too closely with the State, and, second, the voluntarism of American religion prevents domination by a priestly class. There is a kind of anticlericalism in the United States, or at least a popular guardedness about the clergy as a body, but it lacks altogether the class and political connotations of its European counterpart. It is more likely to take the form of the egalitarian sentiment that "the minister should be a good fellow and one of us" (Ahlstrom, 1975, II:324). There is no marked anticlericalism in the United Kingdom, except among the left-wing members of the Labour Party. The probable reason for this is that at the time socialism was beginning to grow in strength, the churches as a whole began to lose political impact. The clerics in the United Kingdom are not so much attacked as ignored.

THE LINKS BETWEEN CHURCH AND STATE
IN THE UNITED STATES:
THE STATE USES RELIGION

Despite the constitutional separation of Church and State in the United States, the links between them are very close. One way of looking at this relationship is to see each institution as being functional for the other. In other words, religion has positive consequences for the State and vice versa. The First Amendment to the Constitution demands that there be (1) no establishment of religion, (2) no interference in the internal affairs of a church, and (3) no discrimination between churches by the State. Yet, the State cannot achieve its purposes without violating these principles—at least in part. The question, then, becomes that of deciding precisely how the State modifies the practice of religion in order to achieve its own ends.

The State is forbidden by the Constitution to legitimize or authorize any single religion. This means that no religious group can be declared illegal because of its religious beliefs and practices. Yet, for one reason or another, some religious groups *are* defined as a threat to social order by the State and are consequently controlled. Thus, although the State is officially neutral with regard to religious practice, it is continually defining what religion is and which religions can legally be practiced.

The State decides, first of all, which groups actually are religious: for example, Scientology is declared not to be a religion, but Transcendental Meditation is even though it claims to be a science. A coalition of parents, conservative Christian clergymen, and religious libertarians filed suit in the U.S. district court in Newark, New Jersey in 1976 to halt the teachings of TM in New Jersey's high schools. The plaintiffs alleged that the TM program violates the constitutional doctrine of separation of Church and State. TM leaders insist that TM is not a religion, but merely a technique for expanding awareness. Conversely, New York State authorities in 1977 denied the Unification Church tax-exemption on the grounds that it was actually a political group, despite the Church's protest that it was a bonafide religion.

The State also decides what restrictions should be placed on religious behavior: for example, snake handling is forbidden. The State decides what restraints should be placed on religious principles: for example, draft exemption on grounds of conscientious objection is granted only to certain "religious" groups. The State decides what amount of autonomy a religious group will enjoy: for example, it limits the extent to which church members can educate their own children. The State, finally, decides by what means a religious group will obtain financial support: for example, it decides what kinds of income are tax-exempt. In a very practical sense, then, the State decides what religion is practiced.

The State interferes in the internal affairs of the churches (their ritual and organization) and in their external affairs (their mode of evangelism, their ethics, and their relation with other institutions) in the interests of social order and welfare as defined by the State. This interference can rarely be construed as the deliberate manipulation of religion for the State's purposes. Rather, it is a necessary consequence of the State's operations. For example, the State may find itself discriminating in favor of a church without having intended to do so. In the *Everson* v. *Board of Education* Supreme Court decision of 1947, the state of New Jersey's authorizing local authorities to give tax support for expenses incurred in traveling to parochial schools was upheld, on the grounds that this was not so much aid to the school (and by implication the church) as aid to the child. The Court therefore chose not to see this as a case of State discrimination in favor of a given church, even though its consequences were exactly that. Other cases can be cited: providing good school buses in the interests of traffic safety benefits poor parochial schools; Sunday closing laws, which are justified on the grounds of rest and recreation, discriminate against Jews, Seventh Day Adventists and others who observe Saturday as the Holy Day of the week. It is extremely hard, then, for the State to avoid "interfering" in religion, even if only inadvertently.

The State control of religion is not always inadvertent, however. Religious groups rarely encounter State hostility because of their theology, but more often if they seem to threaten "strongly held national values" (Pfeffer, 1974:14). In other words, the ties between politics and religion *of a certain kind* are close, but, because of this, there are minority religions that threaten the solidarity of this tie, and *these* are closely controlled. Some examples should illustrate this point:

Mormons have not been permitted to threaten values supporting the monogamous family by practicing polygamy. A Mormon was arrested for having more than one wife as recently as 1946.

Jehovah's witnesses have not been permitted to threaten national security or weaken patriotic values by refusing to salute the flag. A decision endorsing saluting the flag in school was handed down in 1940 against the witnesses. However, this ruling was reversed in 1943 in *Barnette* v. *West Virginia Board of Education*, and the sect once again enjoyed the right to refrain from pledging allegiance in school or saluting the flag. In the

United Kingdom, some Jehovah's witnesses' claims for conscientious objector status have been refused. In Canada, the Hutterites' refusal to bear arms, hold political office, pay taxes for the purposes of war, or take an oath has likewise been opposed by the State.

The claims of the sect I AM to provide healing power have consistently been opposed by the State, and its founder and leader, Guy Ballard, has been convicted of making fraudulent claims. In fact, Ballard was convicted not on the basis of whether or not he actually succeeded in healing, but on the basis of whether or not he believed he could heal: the U.S. Supreme Court eventually decided that he was insincere, and thus convicted him of fraud. On the basis of this ruling, the status of the thousands of other faith-healers in the United States is placed in extreme jeopardy! The same kind of control has been placed on Scientology. In 1958, the U.S. Federal Drug Administration seized and destroyed 21,000 tablets of a compound known as "Dianazene," which had been marketed by Scientology as a preventive and as a treatment for radiation sickness (Wallis, 1975c:92). In 1963, Scientology again became the target of government control: charges of making false and misleading claims were filed against it for its use of "E-meters" as a cure for diseases. The charges were dismissed in 1967 on the grounds that, Scientology being a religion, the effectiveness of the meters could not be proved. The same year, however, the status of the sect was once more brought into question, this time by the Internal Revenue Service, which ruled that Scientology was *not* a religion but purely a profit-making organization. Faced with these conflicting rulings (but probably feeling that of the IRS much more keenly), Scientology moved its headquarters outside the United States. Scientology has also been attacked by both the British and Australian Medical Associations, and in Australia it was banned by a special act in 1965. In England, no law was passed, but in 1968 restrictions were placed on the entry of nonresidents for the purpose of learning Scientology techniques.

The Black Muslims have not been allowed to undermine the value of racial equality by preaching race hatred. They have been challenged as being political rather than religious because of their advocacy of racial separation—a charge that could be made just as easily against many white fundamentalist sects! Muhammad Ali claimed recognition as a conscientious objector on the grounds of his Muslim faith. This claim was ruled against in 1968, but the decision was reversed by the Supreme Court in 1971.

Hasidic Jews and the Old Order Amish have not been allowed to challenge educational values by breaking compulsory school attendance laws. Here again the courts have generally sought a compromise whereby a mixture of educational systems is allowed (Pfeffer, 1974:25).

The Jehovah's witnesses, for whom blood transfusions are prohibited, and Christian Scientists, who are precluded from vaccination, have not been allowed to challenge orthodox values of the sanctity of life by refusing available medical treatment. Cases concerning this issue have been decided in favor of the State on the grounds of the State's superior claim to uphold life. The counter argument, still powerful, is that the State should interfere only when such practices threaten *public* health, welfare, or morals (Burkholder, 1974:41).

The State has been cautious in allowing deviant practices in a religious context. It will generally do so only if there is no perceivable threat to dominant values. Thus the Navahoes of the Native American Church have been allowed to eat the illegal drug source peyote in their services, but Timothy Leary's attempt to gain legal sanction to ritually consume LSD as part of his League for Spiritual Discovery was unsuccessful, probably on the grounds of his guru status in the hippie subculture.

The State has demanded that its law and order exigencies supersede the confidentiality of the minister/laymen relationship. In 1974, a clergyman of the American Lutheran Church was ordered jailed for contempt of court because he refused to answer questions before a grand jury investigating the occupation of Wounded Knee, South Dakota for two months in 1973 by militant Indians. The minister claimed that such questions would violate the confidence entrusted in him by the members of the group (the American Indian Movement) for whom he acted as spiritual advisor.

In all of these cases, what is most noticeable is that the State is much more likely to be indifferent to, or neutral about, forms of worship and evangelism than it is about ethics. The State is concerned above all to make sure that the churches conform to and help sustain consensus on dominant values. Aside from this, however, the State (at least in the shape of the Supreme Court) has become increasingly tolerant of religious practice. The Court has taken a particularly liberal view of what religion is. For example, in a 1970 conscientious objector case, the Supreme Court ruled that even if a registrant did not himself describe his beliefs as religious, the Court could so characterize them if they seemed to occupy a sincere and meaningful place in his life in a manner equivalent to that of orthodox religion (Burkholder, 1974:48).

Clearly the State has a great deal of influence on what kinds of religious practice become institutionalized. Religious expression is controlled so as to remain within what is defined as the national interest. But only in a few cases is there much need for close supervision and constraint. Popular religion has always been fervently patriotic and supportive of dominant political values. This can be seen clearly in popular religious forms such as revivals. Turn-of-the-century revivalism was "virtually reduced to ritualistic mass commitments to social conformity defined in terms of the 'American Way of Life' " (McLoughlin, 1959:362). Billy Sunday's preaching, in particular, expressed ardent patriotism, not to say xenophobia. Later, in the 1920's, revivalism became associated with even greater nationalistic excesses, such as the "Red Scare" and the Ku Klux Klan.

The tie between national interests, as defined by the State, and Church interests became especially close during the First World War, particularly after America's entry in April, 1917. During this period,

> The churches not only became willing agents for . . . important tasks [such as stimulating patriotism and the spirit of sacrifice, selling and buying Liberty Bonds, recruiting, conserving the food supply and mounting propaganda campaigns] but felt for the most part flattered that the government took them into partnership. The clergy, who were honoured with government positions, writing pamphlets, making speeches over the country, or four-minute ones between acts at the theatres, positions as chaplains, special agents for commissions, or as secret agents, all had an increased prestige, both real and imaginary (Abrams, 1969:79).

Many churches became recruiting stations and organized Liberty Loan Sundays. Any qualms churchmen might have had about such a close association with the government were eased by the thought that war efforts on the part of the churches were purely voluntary. Denominational differences became less and less important, and the fusion between orthodox Christianity and Americanism became stronger. The nearly 4,000 conscientious objectors who claimed exemption on religious grounds (mainly Mennonites, Jehovah's witnesses, Dunkers, Seventh Day Adventists and Quakers) received "brutal treatment" C. Abrams, 1969:135).

During the Second World War, the churches' attitude toward the conflict was more "realistic" (Abrams, 1969:264), and the intense, often hysterical nationalism of 1917–1918 was not repeated. There was none of the "Holy War" rhetoric of 1917, and there was some degree of toleration for those who opposed the war on religious grounds. During the Vietnam War, the churches placed themselves at an even greater distance from the State. By and large, the position of the churches on Vietnam reflected the fundamental division the war created within the country: some denominations were "hawkish" and others were in the vanguard of the peace movement.

The State has solicited the help of the churches for purposes other than war. For example, President Kennedy used the churches to recruit and deploy personnel for the Peace Corps and to help organize summer work programs for VISTA volunteers. In the late 1960s, the Office of Economic Opportunity funneled an estimated 90 million dollars through the churches for community action programs (Adams, 1970:45), and President Johnson made use of black clergymen in quelling the urban riots of the 1960s. In addition, the State has encouraged the community action programs of the churches themselves, anxious to promote the kind of personalized and gradual change such programs promise.

The tie between the State and religion is not limited to the help that the churches provide on specific projects. Clearly, the State also sees religion in general as a valuable device for maintaining social order and consensus. Religion and politics are fused whenever political leaders use religious imagery or cast their appeals in religious terms. They merge whenever religious affirmations are made in connection with State functions. There is little evidence that this intimate association is weakening. The phrase "under God" was inserted in the Pledge of Allegiance in 1954, and the motto "In God We Trust," present on the coinage since 1865, was at the same time made the national motto.

The close ties between religion and politics in the United States, tempered by the principle that the State should support no specific church, have resulted in the linking of irreligion with political disloyalty. The extreme manifestations of this notion are the association between "un-Americanism" and "Godless Communism" and the prejudice against atheists running for political office. The bonds between religion and politics also encourage the State to promote the idea that religion, in general, is a "good thing." Thus, President Eisenhower was able to say, "Our Government makes no sense unless it is founded in a deeply felt religious faith—and I don't care what it is" (quoted in Herberg, 1960:84). State support for religion-in-general can be seen in a number of other ways:

First, churches are granted exemption from taxation on property used for worship, on their assets, on businesses in which they participate, on gifts made to them, and on inheritances and contributions they receive. Churches are not required to file a declaration of assets, income, or financial dealings. The State does not look upon this tax exemption as a favoring of religion. In fact, it takes the opposite view. In 1970, the Supreme Court ruled that tax exemption for churches was justified on the grounds that taxing church property would involve the State excessively in religious matters. The State has garnered widespread support for the privileges it grants to religion: seventy-eight percent of the Protestants, eighty-one percent of the Catholics and eighty percent of the Jews polled in 1965 supported the idea of tax exemption for religious organizations (Marty, 1968:270). Ironically, some church members feel that this privilege has been extended too far, and some of the more liberal denominations have been trying to eliminate the tax exemption of church-owned businesses and to get the denominations to pay their share of the municipal services they use, such as fire and police protection.

Second, the State provides for and pays chaplains in the armed forces and in prisons. Chapel attendance is compulsory at the military academies. Tuition payments are made to veterans even if they choose to attend theological college.

Third, the State authorizes clergymen to solemnize marriages, and even allows them to have special automobile license plates.

Fourth, although prayer in public schools has been declared unconstitutional by the Supreme Court, it continues to be imposed by school authorities all across the country, especially in the South (Sorauf, 1975:287). The two landmark decisions by the U.S. Supreme Court were made in 1962 and 1963, prohibiting the recitation of prayers and devotional readings of the Bible in public schools. Two surveys conducted in 1960 and 1966 showed a marked reduction in religious observances in schools, but the practice continued, especially in the South. For example, in 33 percent of the school systems polled in 1960, all schools included regular devotional services in the daily curriculum. By 1966, this proportion had fallen to 8 percent. In the Southern school systems, the figures were 60.5 percent in 1960 and 26.0 percent in 1966. Even in 1966, 13 percent of the school systems reported that at least some of their schools were conducting devotional Bible reading, and 26 percent were conducting released time programs (Dierenfeld, 1967). Opposition to these practices has come not only from secularists but also from some religious groups. For example, Catholics object to the use of the King James Version of the Bible; Jews oppose prayers in schools because they are both ineffective and compulsory; and many minority religions are fearful of the establishment of a Protestant national church.

Many politicians and religious leaders promote the idea that being religious is a sign of good citizenship and that religious commitment also implies commitment to and involvement in the political system. A number of sociologists have examined the relationship between religiosity and political loyalty, with interesting results. Those who attend church regularly are "more likely to vote than those who are less involved in the churches" (Lenski, 1963:184). In addition, members of the denominations that are tied most closely to the political establishment historically (for example, Congregationalists, Presbyterians and Methodists) record higher rates of voting and campaigning than the fringe groups—even with level of education held constant. It has long been supposed that Catholics (consisting mainly of more recent immigrants) are less involved in the political process than Protestants. However, as much as this may have been true in the past, it is no longer. The religious groups most likely to vote are Catholics of Slavic and Polish descent, and Irish Catholics are the most active political campaigners: they are twice as likely to be active as the nearest Protestant group (Greeley, 1974b:134). The increase in the political activity of Catholics probably has a great deal to do with the passing of the immigration trauma. As they enter the mainstream of American life and enter the middle class in increasing numbers, so they absorb the lifestyle of the older white, Anglo-Saxon Protestant group, part of which is a higher rate of voting. It is unlikely that religion alone determines the level of political commitment; religious affiliation is one of a number of constituents of social identity which serve to generate political interest and loyalty.

THE LINKS BETWEEN CHURCH AND STATE IN THE UNITED STATES: THE CHURCH USES THE STATE

The wall between religion and politics is frequently and purposely crossed by the churches themselves. The breaches take three forms: (1) majority churches try to use their traditional ties with the State to control minority religions of which they disapprove; (2) minority religions try to use the neutrality of the State to guarantee fair competition; and (3) the power of the State is used to further church social programs and shape society to the image favored by the churches.

Breaches by the Majority Churches

Protestant churchmen have traditionally looked to the State to protect their traditionally privileged position and help them preserve the identity of the American people as, not only a Christian people, but a *Protestant* people. Because the Catholic Church is international in scope and made up primarily of the more recently immigrated ethnic groups, it has been perceived as the principal threat to Protestant hegemony, and has been subjected to the greatest hostility. For example, the American Protective Association, founded in 1887, sought to have the government place restrictions on immigration and prohibit parochial schools. Later, in the 1920s, the American Protestant Alliance sought an amendment to the Constitution that would have barred from citizenship anyone acknowledging allegiance to the Pope. Similar legislative drives, usually aimed at bringing religious loyalties into line with political loyalties, have been mounted against Jews, Mormons, Jehovah's witnesses, the Black

Muslims, and even the Jesus People. The practice of labeling ministers in minority religions as political deviants is one of long standing. During the turbulent 1780s, the Shakers were charged with sedition and were widely suspected of being traitors: "Ann Lee [was] once. . . . stripped by a mob who at first maintained that she was a male British agent in disguise" (Whitworth, 1975:16). Jewish rabbis and Catholic priests have frequently been linked with internal conspiracies and foreign powers.

The mainstream churches have also sought to use the apparatus of the State to control religious movements which they feel threaten not only religious, but also political and familial values in their aggressive proselytization. The Unification Church and the Children of God have both been accused of "brainwashing" young people and "kidnapping" children away from their parents. The mainstream churches have supported legal action against these movements (Davis and Richardson, 1976:324).

The majority churches also assert their hegemony by using the State's power of education and law enforcement. The Protestant denominations supported the institution of a nondenominational public education system in the nineteenth century, but only because it implicitly buttressed the Protestant position—that the Bible can be used without ministerial guidance. This idea did not suit either Catholics or Jews, who failed to appreciate the "neutrality" of the scheme. Moral crusades, such as the one that culminated in the Prohibition Amendment, were also predominantly Protestant efforts.

The mainstream churches have used the State to combat not only minority religions but also irreligion. In the United States, the mainstream churches have allied themselves with the State in the battle against "rising atheistic Communism." This alliance is singularly reminiscent of the alliance between the Anglican Church and the British Government at the time of the French Revolution. In both cases, the antagonist is irreligion, in both cases irreligion is associated with political dissent at home, and in both cases the result has been to draw Church and State closer together—if only for a time. In each case, there is a decided class element, a widespread fear that irreligion will spread among the working class and thereby threaten middle class interests and social stability in general and a belief that the government should join the churches in the fight. Such fears explain some of the vituperation directed at plaintiffs in cases of Church-State separation. The desire of these individuals to separate Church and State is often interpreted as a move toward the official toleration of irreligion—and atheistic communism. These people have been subjected to verbal and written abuse, their children have been beaten, and they have been socially ostracized. The issue has usually been transformed into one of Godless Communism versus God-fearing Americanism, and the tensions are high because the upbringing of "innocent children" is usually involved (Sorauf, 1975:152).

Breaches by the Minority Churches

Minority religious groups use the State mainly for defensive purposes, looking to it to regulate competition and make sure that none of the major denominations gain an unfair advantage. Two kinds of claims for recognition by the State can be made by minority churches in the interests of defense. The first is "claims for exemption from a positive requirement of the State (e.g. military service, jury duty, the flag salute)" (Burkholder, 1974:35). Claims for exemption from *benefits* should also be included here. For example, the Amish reject government farm subsidies and social security in their effort to remain separate, and in doing so they make the same kind of claim for special government treatment. The Seventh Day Adventists and the Southern Baptists have refused the state aid to their elementary schools to which they are entitled (Sorauf, 1975:52). The second kind of claim is "for permission to carry out a religiously-conceived obligation (e.g. polygamy, snake handling, child labor, sacramental use of wine and drugs) that is prohibited by the State" (Burkholder, 1974:35).

The call that denominations make for protection by the State is always ambivalent. Minority churches tend to stress equality of treatment by the State, for that is the only chance they have of competing successfully with the larger denominations. Thus, a group zealous in its work on behalf of the separation of Church and State, the Religious Liberty Association, is made up primarily of smaller religious groups, such as the Seventh Day Adventists, the American Jewish Committee and American Jewish Congress, the Baptist Joint Committee on Public Affairs, and the association of evangelical denominations known as the Protestants and Other Americans United for Separation of Church and State. These churches look for the State to play an active role in guaranteeing religious freedoms, and at the same time they ask for particular exemptions for themselves. The larger denominations tend to favor a State that supports religion-in-general, but they do not like the State to be too active as this would favor minority religions. These contrasting attitudes are reflected in the changing positions of the Catholic Church, which in some contexts is a minority religion and in others a majority religion.

> In situations where the Catholic church is under direct attack . . . the clergy and professional leadership usually interpret the Bill of Rights and American freedom as that of protection of

minorities against the caprices of an unjust majority. Where Catholics find themselves in a majority, however, the principle of majority rule over community morals is more frequently and generally advanced (Underwood, 1957:154).

The Churches' Influence on the Political System

The churches seek to mold the State itself in their own image and to use the power and resources of the State in their efforts to shape society to their ideals. This is evident in, for example, the shaping of American politics, which bears the impress of Protestant thinking, and in the educational system, which has evolved as a cooperative effort between churches and the State.

The dominant strain of Protestantism that reached the shores of the United States was Puritan. It has long been argued that there is a specific tie between Puritanism and the democratic political structures that have evolved in the United States. The Puritan religion (and the denominations such as Presbyterianism and Congregationalism that flowed from it) provided a self-restraining value system designed to inhibit the tyranny of the majority. It "emphasized voluntary association for chosen impersonal ends, rested on consent of Church and State, put legal limits on all powers, envisioned a necessary political life for the Saints, and carefully distinguished between the realms of the Church and State" (Strout, 1974:12). Puritanism also provided something of a training ground for democrats: "By making each man God's agent, ascetic Protestantism made each individual responsible for the state of morality in the society; and by making the congregation a disciplining agent it helped prevent any one individual from assuming that his brand of morality was better than others" (Lipset, 1963:96). The democratic temper of the country was thus formulated by its Puritan founders.

The zeal to protect religious freedoms that the early settlers brought with them also spilled over into a concern to protect political freedoms. There is, in both American religion and politics, "a tendency to think of rights rather than duties, a suspicion of established (especially personal) authority, a distrust of central government, a deep aversion to acceptance of obviously coercive restraint through visible social organization" (Williams, 1960:446). Thus, in addition to its impact on democratic structures, religion also helped pave the way for the establishment of a pluralistic system of politics (Elazar, 1961). Those espousing ideas about the equality of faiths, and willing to compete with each other on that basis according to agreed-upon rules, had little difficulty in accepting a political system run along the same lines. The denominationalism of American religion and the pluralism of its politics each reflect values of equality, growth, mobility, competition, self-improvement, and achievement. Denominationalism has also favored the traditional liberal view of the State as a "night watchman" concerned only with the security of its citizens and their property.

The integration of religion and politics runs even deeper than this. There is a moralism about American politics that owes a great deal to the Puritan interpretation of God as a moral being who demands purity, and is severe with the unclean. American politics "have always been characterised by an extraordinary emphasis on utopian moralism, which provokes Americans to view social and political dramas as morality plays within which compromise is virtually unthinkable" (Lipset, 1975:142). This view has been stoutly defended by Protestant denominations such as the Baptists and the Methodists, who teach people to follow their conscience in the faith that the individual is perfectible and capable of avoiding sin. In the absence of an established church, the consequence of this attitude is that religious groups are regarded as purely voluntary associations whose job is to safeguard public morality. They are given an active role, but one that is primarily ethical in orientation.

It is possible to see here a reciprocal relationship between religion and politics. Although it would be far from the truth to say that American political life is informed by a specific Christian ethic, it is correct to say that American religion has given to politics a strong moral concern that to a large extent obscures economic conflicts. On the other hand, the liberal philosophy on which American politics rests has shaped the expression of religion.

> In the main drift of religion in America the theological and liturgical and mystical and contemplative move into the background; the historical and communal give place to the individualistic, the traditional to the immediate, the authoritarian to the freely decided, the appeal to the mind and the aesthetic sense to the appeal to the will, the awareness of the ultimate to the concern with the practical life. The penumbra of beyondness, absoluteness, and mystery fades away, and leaves—at the core of what Americans think religion to be—the moral (Miller, 1961:94).

This piety has admittedly been given more of a political character by the idea of America as a "new Jerusalem." But the more collectivist interpretation of this message in the utopian communities of the nineteenth century failed to take hold, and the more individualistic idea of social progress through individual improvement has dominated. The frequent reform efforts of the churches, the moral crusades against drink, sex, gambling, abortion, and so on, should thus be seen more as efforts to realize more widespread individual morality than as attempts to bring about structural change. The occasional political campaigns of the churches do not, then, contradict the thesis that religion and politics are fused in a redemptive quest for progress and improvement.

Besides molding the shape and conduct of politics to suit their vision, the churches have sought to harness the resources of the State in their effort to mold children in their image. Many denominations and sects seek to provide their children with education that conforms to their values. The Catholic Church is best known for this work, but conservative and ethnically conscious Protestant bodies such as the Lutheran Missouri Synod, and many smaller Protestant sects, do likewise. Whereas some denominations have sought only freedom from State interference, others have tried to use the State to serve their own parochial ends.

Public opinion is quite mixed with regard to whether or not church schools have the right to government support. Catholics tend to be more favorable and the Jews the least (Marty, 1968:192). Opinions are more favorable concerning the more indirect method of State support for parochial education—the "released time" arrangement whereby public school pupils are allowed to spend part of their school day receiving parochial education (Marty, 1968:196).

The most direct and meaningful form of assistance the churches can extract from the State is financial aid. The most vigorous proponents of such aid have been Catholics, who find it extremely difficult to accept the idea of religion being a private concern about which the State must be neutral. Catholics argue that financial aid for their parochial schools is legitimate because to some extent these schools serve the public interest: they admit (in principle, at least) all students, irrespective of religion and they save the taxpayer money. In addition, fee-paying Catholics believe they are being doubly taxed. Others, not only Catholics, argue that the principle of Church-State separation is not breached by financial aid if this is distributed proportionately. However, this argument cannot hold, for however much the State attempts to treat the different denominations on an equal basis in this regard, the effects of its actions will always be unfair, since not all churches are alike in their approach to education. For example, if the government decides to give equal aid to all elementary educational institutions run by the churches, it will benefit the Catholic church over the Southern Baptists, because the former places greater emphasis on child socialization and has developed an elaborate network of organizations to that end. In similar fashion, government aid to church-run hospitals would disadvantage sects such as the Jehovah's witnesses and Christian Science, who have little faith in modern medicine.

Many churches have consistently sought to use the resources of the government to further their teachings and educational institutions. The signs are that these efforts are meeting with increasing success. State aid to parochial education seems to be increasing. Yinger (1971:445) sees a number of factors behind this:

1. The growing political and economic power of Catholics, the group lobbying most energetically for State aid.
2. The increasing need for funds created by the escalating costs of providing parochial education as more and better-trained teachers are hired.
3. An increase in the number of parochial schools outside Catholicism, in Lutheranism, Jewish and Southern Protestant bodies.
4. An overall Americanization of the school system, which is making it more homogeneous and drawing closer the parallels between parochial and public education.

In 1971, the Supreme Court ruled that State grants to Catholic colleges for secular building purposes were not a breach of separation because colleges are not intended principally for religious indoctrination (elementary schools supposedly are) and because, in any case, college students are less susceptible to religious influences and mission (Sorauf, 1975:23).

The increasing State aid for parochial education may also have been facilitated by greater sophistication by the churches in the manner in which they attempt to make use of State funds. During the 1970s, for example, several states were induced to propose a voucher plan whereby a state would issue vouchers to parents equal to the average cost of education at local public schools, to be used (if the parents so chose) to pay tuition at parochial schools. States have even been persuaded to offer direct subsidies to parochial schools—only to have this form of aid rejected as unconstitutional by the courts. State support seems to be most acceptable if it is disguised in secular terms. Financial aid to a Catholic school is acceptable if it is used for the purchase of school buses, which would improve traffic safety in the community.

In the United Kingdom, the ties between the State and the Church of England have been so close that the impact of the churches on education has been more profound. Heresy from Anglican doctrines was long considered a criminal offense and was usually punishable by execution carried out by the State. This affected early reformers such as Tyndale, the Anabaptists, the Unitarians and the Quakers. Blasphemy continued to be a criminal offense until 1930; the last person to be jailed for this crime was imprisoned as late as 1921 (Myers, 1960:17). Until well into the nineteenth century, the State tolerated only certain forms of religious dissent. Groups such as the Quakers were subject to close surveillance, and efforts were made to prevent them from turning their religious dissent into political protest. Until the nineteenth century, Quakers were not allowed to vote, give evidence in criminal cases, serve on juries, or hold offices of profit (Myers, 1960:11), and much more severe restrictions were placed on Catholics and Jews.

Even today the links between the State and the Church of England are strong. Several examples can be cited:

1. The head of the Church (the Archbishop of Canterbury) crowns the sovereign as head of State.
2. By the Accession Declaration Act of 1910, the sovereign must declare himself a faithful Protestant who will uphold the Protestant tradition.
3. The Archbishops of Canterbury and York and twenty-four other Anglican bishops have seats in the House of Lords.
4. A Bishop conducts daily prayers in the House of Lords, and the House of Commons Speaker's chaplain must be an Anglican minister.
5. Anglican clergy are given precedence over other faiths on national ceremonial occasions.
6. All of the Anglican Church's chief officials are Crown appointments (made, in practice, by the incumbent prime minister) and the monarch has still the power of disposal of six percent of the Anglican incumbencies.
7. All matters relating to change in ritual in the Anglican Church, or modifications in its doctrines, are subject to approval by the Parliament.

In these, and many other ways, the ties between the State and the Church of England are manifested. Although moves to disestablish the Church of England have been under way for a long time, its official and traditional position is still that of the church of the nation. Though some of these linkages that remain are symbolic only, they retain a great deal of power. And although Anglicans' hopes of ever completely dominating the religious life of the United Kingdom were shattered by the exclusion of dissenters during the reign of Charles I, they still count themselves first among equals.

The dissenters who broke with the Church of England in the sixteenth century have become an increasingly influential force in English life. Nonconformist denominations such as the Methodists, Congregationalists, Presbyterians, and Baptists have maintained the position that independence, competition, variety and self-reliance are the essential ingredients of religious institutionalization. These denominations began to effectively undermine the domination of the Church of England in the second quarter of the nineteenth century. The repeal of the Test Act in 1828 (which had relegated dissenters to the status of second-class citizens by means of its restrictions on baptism, marriage, burial, education, and political life) marked the beginning of the political and economic emancipation of those not within the Established Church. Considering not only the growth of Nonconformity but also the increasing strength of the Catholic Church in England around the middle of the nineteenth century, the United Kingdom had become effectively pluralist by the end of the Victorian age. The Nonconformist denominations, significantly, began to call themselves Free Churches, thereby symbolizing not only their escape from a minority position but also their freedom from State control.

English churches have also sought to use the State to further their educational aims. In the nineteenth century, the Nonconformists attempted to use the State to provide a secular educational system because Anglicanism dominated what few educational institutions there were. The Church of England, on the other hand, sought to use the State to preserve its monopoly on the education of children. At the same time, other Nonconformists and Catholics sought State financial aid for their parochial schools. The result was a compromise, expressed in the dual system set up by the Act of 1870, in which government aid was given both to new secular schools and to church-related schools. In 1902 52.5 percent of the pupils in State-financed schools were still in church-related or "voluntary" schools. The Act of 1902 abolished the old "Board" (State) and "Voluntary" (Church) system and established Local Educational Authorities, to be run by city or county governments—but aid was continued for both State and Church schools. The voice of the Anglican Church remained influential well into the 1940s. For example, the Education Act of 1944 increased State control over church schools in return for increased aid, but this measure was accompanied by a *quid pro quo* arrangement that made religious instruction a compulsory part of the curriculum of all State-aided schools.

CONCLUSION

The links between Church and State are close in both the United States and the United Kingdom. In the United States, the Church's impress upon the State must always be more indirect because of the Constitution. For example, no Church can formally lobby in Congress on pain of losing its tax-exempt status. In any case, the churches rarely advocate specific legislation directly (Prohibition is a notorious exception). Rather, they speak to the morality of an issue, usually through "spokesmen" who speak not for the churches but for themselves.

However, the churches are not inactive in Washington. They evade lobby laws by registering as educational institutions, in which role they help to "educate" Congressmen about church members' desires. More than a dozen church-related agencies have offices in Washington that operate essentially as lobbies (Adams, 1970:247). The *formal* separation of Church and State is not, then, an *actual* separation. Neither body is indifferent to the other, and each tries constantly to bring the other into closer conformity to its own needs.

11

RELIGION

AND

ECONOMIC LIFE

INTRODUCTION

Economics has to do with the getting and spending of wealth. Economic institutions are the rules, roles, and groups within which this getting and spending is carried out. The ideas that men and women have about their work, the occupational communities to which they belong, the market where they go to buy essential goods—in short, the economic aspect of life—are shaped by noneconomic forces, one of which is religion. Religious ethics have practical consequences for economic life and thereby help shape economic institutions. Sometimes these consequences are direct, as in the case of an Amish farmer who refuses to buy on credit. Most often they are indirect, as in the case of the largely unacknowledged ideals of asceticism that influence how a woman judges a fair day's work, or how a man distinguishes between a pressing need and a luxury.

Sociologists have long been interested in the impact of religion on economic action—and no less interested in the impact of economics on religion. There has been a tendency to assume a congruence between religious and economic institutions. That is, dominant religious and economic values will be similar and religious and economic roles will be compatible. The basis for this assumption is Durkheim's theory that religious ideas are a reflection or projection of existing social relationships, including economic and technological forces, which are experienced as external to individual people. That this assumption is sometimes false and that religion can foment economic conflict rather than harmony will be demonstrated in Chapter 14. However, there are strong grounds for making this assumption of functional compatibility, and the present chapter will show why.

RELIGIOUS ETHICS AND ECONOMIC IDEAS

It is hardly to be expected that a society should achieve a tolerable level of integration and stability *without* there being homology between two such important institutions as religion and economics, for "a given type of structure in any major part of the society imposes *imperatives* on the rest" (Parson, 1951:178). Nor is there any mystery about *how* religious ethics and economic ideas become congruent: "As soon as a group of adherents is attracted to a particular idea or ethical system, which in origin is purely concerned with problems of salvation and ultimate meaning, they will begin to 'elect' those features of the original idea with which they have an 'affinity' or 'point of coincidence' " (Hill, 1973a:108). In a survey of the development of religious ethics and economic ideas in the United States, it comes as no surprise then to find them closely associated.

Protestantism (especially its evangelical wing) has imparted to American economic life a morality striking in its individualism, activism and pragmatism. In its achievement orientation toward God and its exploitative attitude toward nature, American religion has furnished a rationale for the perseverance, unremitting labor and repeated effort so central to the idea of work and success in the modern capitalist system. Competing religious themes, such as those that encourage a detachment from the world and an exploration of inner space, have never really gained a hold on the American mind (Marty, 1970:148). This extremely close association between dominant religious and economic ideas can be easily demonstrated.

The Protestant emphasis on the personal achievement of grace has reinforced the goal of personal achievement in economic life.

> Classical economic theory posits the existence of a society composed of autonomous, competitive, profit-seeking individuals; classical liberalism conceives of an atomised society in which individuals are free to pursue their private ends, including the acquisition and enjoyment of property; traditional Protestantism . . . views man as a free actor who is able through personal actions to affect his own destiny (thereby adding a measure of responsibility to the emphasis on individual action) (Quinley, 1974:95).

Revivalists of the nineteenth century popularized this religious and economic individualism. Moody told his audience that "being a friend of Jesus solved a man's personal problems and once a man was right with God he was right with the world" (McLoughlin, 1959:252). He believed that economic failure was a sign of spiritual unworthiness and assured the more impoverished of his listeners that whosoever was saved who did remain poor was merely being "tested." He had no compunction about attributing poverty to laziness and excessive drink—both of which could be eliminated by conversion.

The more Calvinist of the revivalists even dismissed charity as a waste of time and money because it contributed nothing to the self-improvement of the destitute. But many others as a result of their greater sense of confidence in man's perfectibility and their more intense millenial expectations showed a more disinterested benevolence. In consequence, they were more disposed to temper Protestant individualism with social reformism. They aimed at improving the lot of the poor by regulating factory employment practices and easing crowded living conditions.

Popular preachers of a later era, reaching much wider audiences through cheap, mass-produced books and magazines, the radio and, eventually, television, continued to espouse a religion which was almost nothing but an adjunct to business. Billy Sunday, Aimee Semple McPherson, Emerson Fosdick and Bruce Barton in the 1920's, Fulton Sheen in the 1930's, and Oral Roberts, Norman Vincent Peale and Billy Graham after the Second World War helped perpetuate the idea that, by following the appropriate religious exercises, the rationality and efficiency necessary for economic achievement would be realized. The most popular religious spokesmen of their day would draw their examples of the rewards of Christian uprightness from the business world and would promise that the proper prayer, positive thinking ("faith") and persistent endeavor grounded in vaguely apprehended Christian teachings, would ensure the worldly success they assumed their followers desired. There was also enough in their ideas about "service" and "stewardship" to meet the desires of the wealthy and powerful to justify their wealth and power.

To most modern Americans, it is natural that religious ethics and economic principles should go hand in hand. The American Business Creed, which espouses the value of competition, the dignity of work, the rights of the individual in the market place, the desirability of material possessions, the need for a practical approach to life, and a willingness to take risks and condemn the welfare state, government regulations, and labor unions, is strongly supported by a majority of the members of the mainstream denominations. Among those who are highly religious, Catholics are the most ardent supporters of this creed (Photiadis,

1965:98). Most church members have the Horatio Alger dream of ascending from rags to riches in their own lifetime by their own skill and effort (Lenski, 1963:105).

The congruence between religious and economic thinking is manifest not only at the cultural level but also in the conduct of religious life itself. American denominationalism, with its implicit belief in the survival of the fittest faith, repeats the economic principle that superior efficiency will result from competition. The struggle for souls, the obsession with organizational growth, the anxiety about appearing acceptable in the community—these denominational concerns are also economic concerns. The bureaucratization of religious associations, largely in imitation of the modern business corporation, has strengthened this relationship.

Economic forms and economic thinking have undergone continued development, and by and large religious thinking has shifted to accommodate these developments. The most significant recent change has been the shift from competitive to monopoly or corporate liberal capitalism, which occurred at the turn of the century.

THE DECLINE OF THE PROTESTANT ETHIC AND RUGGED INDIVIDUALISM

In the individualism of the nineteenth century evangelists there lingered the association between Puritan asceticism and the importance of hard work and self-restraint that Max Weber pointed to in his essay, *The Protestant Ethic and the Spirit of Capitalism*. This association thrived in a world of small businesses, high mobility and cohesive communities—in short, the world of early capitalism. The rise of large-scale corporations, mass-production technologies and labor unions at the turn of the century called into question the economic principles about which the Protestant Ethic spoke most eloquently and demanded instead a set of economic mores oriented more toward life in large-scale organizations and mass consumption markets. These changes caused what Whyte (1957:184) calls a "Social Ethic" to replace the Protestant Ethic and a new model worker, an "organisation man" to replace the old entrepreneur, who would tend to see personality development and achievement as attained through working *with* others rather than against them. Reisman (1961:45) sees the "other-directed" economic actor as having almost totally replaced the old "inner-directed" type. Economic success today "depends less on what one is and what one does than on what others think of one—and how competent one is in manipulating others and being oneself manipulated."

Modern economic forces have greatly altered the image of the successful businessman.

> Until recent times, senior officials of the mature corporation were inclined to assume the mantle of the entrepreneur. They pictured themselves as self-reliant men, individualistic, with a trace of justifiable arrogance, fiercely competitive and with a desire to live dangerously. These characteristics are not readily reconciled with the requirements of the technostructure. Not indifference but sensitivity to others, not individualism but accommodation to organisation, not competition but intimate and continuing co-operation are the prime requirements for group action (Galbraith, 1967:92).

The precise strength and pervasiveness of the old entrepreneurial ideal in America and the extent of the changes described by Galbraith are open to debate, but there can be little doubt that technological and accompanying political changes greatly altered work and its context at the turn of the century.

Changes in work were accompanied by changes in consumption which, under the old Puritan doctrine, was something that should be restricted to necessities. The mass-production capabilities of the new assembly lines, the drive for expansion inherent in the capitalist system, and the growth of installment buying and advertising all placed such a premium on continual consumption as a social and individual good that the old ideas of restraint in buying and the control of impulse in consumption came to be viewed in increasingly negative terms. What was once a quality became a defect. This process was hastened by the coming of the automobile and the mass media. Each helped to break down the isolation of the small communities, in which the old economic principles were followed most closely.

It is highly significant that these changes in modes of production and consumption have been paralleled by changes in religious ethics. Religious leaders have placed increasing emphasis on the need for social adjustment and conformity. Beginning with theologians such as Walter Rauschenbusch and Martin Buber, and popularized by Harvey Cox, John Robinson and Martin Van Buren, a new ethic has emerged in which God and man are seen as co-equals, mutually dependent on each other for the performance of common tasks—God is no longer the divine judge, but a loving God, nurturing human beings as persons. Churchgoers are more and more likely to hear that "the best way of living acceptably to God is to nurture one's fellow men in a cooperative endeavor" (Winter, 1974:1149). Churchgoing, it is argued, will bring you peace of mind; God is a "good neighbor" or helpful "colleague" who will assist you in times of trouble. The esteemed minister is one who is sociable, mixes well, offends no one, and is a good organizer. The models to be emulated which are touted in Bible-study classes are individuals who show superior ability to get along with others and work as a member of the team.

The spirit of entrepreneurial capitalism is by no means dead, however, and neither is the Protestant Ethic. Although the room for individual achievement through free competition may have diminished with the rise of large-scale corporations, government bureaucracies and trade unions, bastions of traditional capitalism survive. Small businesses, farms, and professions such as law and medicine are areas in which individualism and competition remain primary values. The churches, too, continue their promotion of ideas of self-reliance, personal responsibility, and competitiveness. They proclaim equal opportunity for salvation while at the same time admitting that, because of insufficient individual effort, not all will achieve it. In other words, they teach "The American Way": each person shall have an equal right with others to develop his or her talents and virtues, and there will be equal rewards for equal performance. They not only reach these values, they also bear witness to them in their own actions. Ministers behave very much like entrepreneurs developing and "marketing" their "product" in an intense competition for souls. Their message is tuned to whatever the market will bear and unattractive messages are "dropped."

THE SOCIAL GOSPEL

During most of the nineteenth century, dominant Protestant ideas about the sanctification of work resonated with bourgeois ideals of industry and thrift. However, Protestantism is not a narrow class belief, and has readily accommodated to the modifications in economic behavior and thinking that began to occur toward the end of the century. When the value of unrestricted competition and absolutely free labor began to be questioned in what was eventually to become the Progressive Movement, the Protestant churches were able to reinterpret the Scriptures to suit the new work ethic—and the Social Gospel was the result.

In fact, churchmen had begun to agitate for some kind of reform of the economic system as far back as the middle of the century. The revivalists dramatically expressed the shock of many churchmen at the degradations of the industrial system and urged that the greed and inhumanity that were creating the excesses of the industrial system be curbed by ameliorative reform (Smith, 1957:151). The early reformers inspired the YMCA, the Sunday school movement and some early settlement houses. The connection between this early, revival-inspired reformism (which was also related to the abolition movement) and the later Social Gospel is unclear. There is no doubt that much of this revivalist reformism was rather conservative. For one thing, it sought to replace the evils of the industrial system by turning the clock *back* and restoring the old agrarian world. For another it espoused a highly individualistic kind of reformism, tracing the root of social evil to the individual soul rather than economic conditions; reform would come about, not through social action but through conversion. Nevertheless some of the ideas of the mid-century revivalists were taken up by the Social Gospel reformers of the 1890s.

The Social Gospel movement, which began to gather strength in the 1890s, moved away from the intense individualism of Finney and Moody toward a policy of ameliorative reform. Attacking with equal zeal the cruelty and exploitativeness of employers and the corruption and violence of the unions, Social Gospelers placed themselves in the middle of the two warring camps in an attempt to protect the "innocent" and "silent majority" caught between. They concentrated their own efforts on settlement houses and inner-city missions, but leaders like Washington Gladden also gave their vociferous support to attempts to legislate unemployment insurance, codes of minimum wages and maximum work, child and female labor laws, more progressive taxation, the right to collective bargaining and public works programs to relieve unemployment.

The Social Gospel movement eventually led to the formation of ginger groups like the Christian Socialist Fellowship and the Church Socialist League. By 1901, the Congregationalists and Episcopalians had each set up new committees to deal specifically with labor issues, and their example was followed by the Presbyterians in 1903 and the Methodists in 1908. Even more important, the Federal Council of Churches, formed in 1908, took on as one of its first tasks the reformulation of a social creed for the mainstream churches so as to better equip them to deal with the realities of industrial life.

The rise of the Social Gospel was heavily influenced by the Progressive movement. The Progressives' advocacy of greater State intervention in the regulation of the economy, and their general strategy of trying to curb some of the excesses of the capitalist system in order to improve its performance was clearly echoed in the Social Gospelers' self-identification as mediators. Like the Progressives, Social Gospelers were mainly middle class and liberal, and they appealed to the same constituency—those beginning to feel squeezed between big business on the one hand and big labor on the other.

The Social Gospel stood for reforms which would preserve the basic mechanisms of the free enterprise system—private property, wage-

labor, and the market. The preferred strategy for obtaining these reforms was education and voluntary services rather than government
action, which was reserved for measures that would free the system to
work more efficiently. In this way, the Social Gospel movement, with the
Progressive, fostered the development of welfare capitalism, in which
the business community began to take on some of the social responsibilities of their economic actions. As a result of the Social Gospel
movement, public services to some extent modified the pursuit of profit,
and industrial "families" replaced the warring camps of labor and capital
(Underwood, 1957:362).

The churches, though condemning many business practices for their
inhumanity, did not look favorably on the rise of the unions. Their usual
response to industrial unrest was to urge the restoration of peace—
which meant a return to the *status quo ante*. The moderate reformism of
even the more radical of the Social Gospelers did not combine easily with
"the hard-bitten realism produced by the violent history of left-wing
labor" (May, 1949:261). Most church leaders were unable to reconcile
themselves to the unionists' assertion of rights over their theme of sacrifice, and they naively overestimated the possibilities of harmony in the
industrial sphere.

The Social Gospel was a predominantly Protestant movement. The
Catholic Church adopted much the same position, even though
Catholics were the largest single religious group represented in the
American Federation of Labor between 1900 and 1918 (Karson,
1974:165). The Catholic Church favored an economic arrangement in
which neither management nor labor would dominate, and in which the
Church would play a mediating role. The encyclical *Rerum Novarum*
(1891) had expressed strong support for private property, opposed
socialism, and accepted unionism on the condition that it was clearly
indoctrinated with Catholic social principles. The Catholic Church favored a kind of guild system, which in fact resonated quite well with the
rather conservative craft unionism of the time. Overall, the position of
the Catholic Church reflected its conception of politics in general—a
"device for taking the risk and uncertainty out of urban life" (Ahlstrom,
1975, II:509). It is probable that the Catholic hierarchy was gradually
pushed into an acceptance of some kind of unionism by the threat of
socialism. Catholics were urged to "take an active part in the regular
trade union instead of forming separate organisations" in order to fore-
stall their take-over by more radical elements (Karson, 1974:177). It is
also probably true that the economic attitudes of the Catholic Church
were heavily influenced by a ghetto mentality and strong ethnic concerns. Once these began to break down after the end of the First World
War, Catholic bishops began to associate themselves more vigorously

with broader economic concerns. In advance of the New Deal, they began to speak out for a minimum wage, protection of the right to organize, insurance against the hazards of unemployment, accident and old age, and the construction of public housing.

The Social Gospel movement was part of the turn-of-the-century struggle between Modernists and Fundamentalists. The mainly middle-class Modernists supported the Social Gospel proposals for reform, whereas the Fundamentalists either wanted no part of the economic system or were keen to preserve it. Modernism did not, however, precede economic changes. It was,

> a self conscious effort to *adapt* religion to its surrounding culture by emphasizing social activity and cooperation with an immanent God, rather than the definition of theology or tradition. The modernist, instead of challenging contemporary thought, proposed to find relevant patterns in its achievements, confident that democracy and the sciences could supply the guiding ideas that theological tradition no longer provided (Strout, 1974:211).

Modernism was part of an effort to prevent the spread of the belief that economic processes follow their own laws; it was an adaptation to the growing compartmentalization of life in which economics and religion were separate concerns. "The gospel of wealth, the gospel of steward-ship, and even the gospel of service that were to appear in the 'twenties' were all efforts to preserve the fabric, or at least the illusion, of a society unified by morality, of a culture informed by religious meaning and morals" (Meyer, 1960:27).

The Social Gospel was most ardently supported by the more liberal churchmen, those most acutely aware of the unprecedented needs created by the growth of monopoly capitalism, but it was only one form of adjustment the churches made to economic developments at this time. Fundamentalism was another contrasting form of adjustment, speaking to those churchpeople most anxious to preserve the hegemony of Puritan, small town life. Its flowering was the temperance movement and Prohibition (Gusfield, 1969). Most churchgoers fell somewhere in between these two extremes, almost as reluctant as the Fundamentalists to recognize the decline of the old Protestant Ethic but not half so willing as the Social Gospelers to endorse welfare capitalism. The 1920s saw a decline of both movements. Prohibition proved to be a pyrrhic victory for the Fundamentalists, and the Social Gospel lost its popularity during the prosperous twenties. In fact, businessmen enjoyed great popularity during the 1920s and this is reflected in the popular theology of the time. For example, in Bruce Barton's best seller *The Man Nobody Knows*,

Jesus and the Biblical heroes were made over into typical American business executives.[1]

THE NEW DEAL

Ironically, although the Social Gospel was condemned by many and considered by others to be a failure, several of its proposals were incorporated in the New Deal, the series of economic reforms instituted by Roosevelt for the purpose of alleviating the distress caused by the Great Depression. During the Depression, American economic thought shifted further to the political left than at any time before or since. To some degree, the churches followed this trend. In 1932, the Federal Council of Churches (FCC) "drastically revised the social creed it had adopted in 1912, now affirming the need for government action and social planning" (Ahlstrom, 1975, II:413). By that time, also, the official position of most of the Protestant denominations on unionism had passed from outright condemnation to "understanding." Some even attempted to ally Marxism and Christianity. The Fellowship of Social Christians, which Rheinhold Neibuhr helped organize in the 1930s, engaged in a kind of Marxist analysis of the ills of capitalism and saw as inevitable the eventual rule of the proletariat.[2]

Not too much should be made of these changes, however. Although the churches, along with other social institutions, began to look more favorably upon social planning and government provision of welfare, and began also to take a more tolerant attitude toward labor militancy, this shift was a guarded one. Thus the New Deal received almost unfailing support from the FCC, but "while the Council did suggest economic planning, the substitution of cooperation for competition, and the end of the real abuses of the present economic system, it did not launch a crusade to wipe out private ownership in favor of some form of doctrinaire socialism" (Miller, 1958:89).

The unionism that the churches supported (even that of the slightly more radical Congress of Industrial Organizations) was not unionism of the European variety, which reflects a greater awareness of class solidar-

---

[1]The English counterpart to the Social Gospel was Christian Socialism, which had its origins in campaigns to extend the welfare work of the churches into the cities. Christian Socialists, espousing rather vague notions of brotherhood and progress, joined the liberal campaign against the aristocratic monopoly on land and the evil of factory owners (Jones, 1968:447).

[2]Toward the end of the 1930s, however, even this critique of capitalism became muted. Niebuhr shifted to a more pessimistic neo-orthodox theological position and began to interpret the reforms of the New Deal as irrelevant to man's spiritual well being.

ity and the potential for political conflict. The American unionism that the churches helped form was more an attempt to improve the worker's market capacity by introducing controls on the supply of labor than it was a political movement—a unionism much more committed to the free enterprise system than its European counterpart. Moreover, in the New Deal, as in the Progressive Era, the churches functioned to legitimize what was already taking place. The creation of organizations such as the Council for Social Action by the Congregationalists in 1934 was no doubt partly a response to the growing popularity of Socialists such as Norman Thomas.

A final point on the changes in religious ethics that took place during the New Deal era: like the Social Gospel reforms, the New Deal reforms obtained the support of only a minority of churchpeople. "Almost all of the sources of Protestant opinion *implied* support for Hoover rather than Roosevelt in 1932" (Miller, 1958:120). Many churchpeople preferred the more individually therapeutic offerings of a Norman Vincent Peale, who argued that the way out of poverty was positive thinking grounded on faith: "one had only to think about things in the right way, not to change them" (Meyer, 1960:407). It is significant that the main growth in church membership during the 1930s took place not in the liberal churches, which supported the New Deal, but in the conservative denominations, which were largely indifferent to it (Strout, 1974:266). The Southern Baptists were probably not alone in rejecting resolutions in favor of the regulation of child labor but enthusiastically endorsing a resolution deploring the use of tobacco (Bailey, 1964:125).

The priorities of the Southern Baptists testify to the continued strength of the old Protestant Ethic in American denominations. Many Christians continue to insist that the exercise of private and personal rights is tantamount to social wealth, and that the practice of private virtues is the totality of their public responsibilities. Today, however, a much wider range of economic attitudes are tolerated by American churches. The more theologically conservative tend to be the strongest supporters of the free enterprise system; the more liberal tend to favor some kind of welfare state—although they stop far short of socialism (Hadden, 1969:77). The major economic upheavals of the 1960s, including the many reform movements that sprang up, were almost wholly secular. Indeed the economic crises of 1880–1910, 1929–1939, and 1960–1970 have been attended by a growing separation of religious ethics and economic thinking.

In more stable times, the continued close ties between religion and economics are revealed. One reason for this is that the churches are themselves an important *part* of the economy and would stand to lose a great deal if it were greatly disrupted. The churches are buyers, sellers, employers, investors and propertyholders. Every year, the churches receive and spend vast sums of money, and each major denomination is an economic force in its own right (see Larson and Lowell, 1969). The occasional instances of a denomination permitting ethical considerations to modify its economic behavior (such as a decision not to invest in armaments industries) are the exceptions that prove the rule.[3]

Another reason for the close tie between religion and economics is the circulation of personnel between the two institutions—or at least the fact that they recruit from a common pool. It is particularly significant that the clergy of the mainstream denominations (not including Catholics) tend to come from families with above average incomes (Smith and Sjoberg, 1961:292), and that boards of trustees tend to be upper-middle-class. This relation is even stronger in the United Kingdom, where recruitment of clergy by the Church of England is overwhelmingly from those groups that have a large stake in the economic system. As a result, the economic ethic of the Anglican Church is suffused with class bias: the clergy has, at the very least, given tacit support to the principle of competitiveness even when proposing reform (Norman, 1976:231–32). The elite public schools of England, although small and few in number, provide about forty-five percent of the clergy of the Church of England (see Coxon, 1967).

RELIGION AND SOCIAL STRATIFICATION

Functionalists argue that "no society can maintain itself without a certain, although undefinable, minimum of *consensus* among its members, and that religion, by acting as an agency for value integration and social control, is an important aid in securing this consensus" (Nottingham, 1971:60). Enough has been said to demonstrate that the churches provide a moral legitimation for economic arrangements and lay the groundwork for consensus about economic obligations and rewards. Setting economic arrangements (including inequalities) within a cosmological scheme so that all appears "natural" is one way in which this function is performed. But the churches go a great deal further, as an examination of the relation between religion and social stratification will reveal.

Denominational membership is not randomly distributed across social strata. Church divisions tend to follow social divisions, and religious affiliation is popularly associated with certain levels of social affiliation.

[3]In 1977 fifteen Protestant and Catholic groups, owning nearly ten million dollars in bank stock, filed stockholders' resolutions with five major U.S. banks opposing their South African investments (*Christian Century*, 2/16/1977).

To a large extent, church membership is a badge of social status. Consequently, the denominations, by their divisions and their hierarchies, tend to legitimate socioeconomic rankings and thus perpetuate them.

It should come as no surprise that the denominations perform this function, especially in the United States, where status hierarchies based on ascription are not important, where the culture places a premium on personal achievement (which means that people will continually look for signs of advancement and confirmation of their status), and where there is no established church (which means that religious identification is available as a deployable mark of status). The high rate of mobility that prevails in the United States only increases the likelihood that churches will be used as synthetic communities of neighbors who, lacking the *natural* features of neighborliness, create through their local church a surrogate community *based largely on similarity of occupation and life style.* Choosing a church on the basis of status compatibility therefore comes naturally to the American.

Social Class and Church Attendance

Church attendance is not randomly distributed across class lines. Where, how often, and with whom someone attends church reflects her social status (Demerath, 1965:10–14). This is entirely to be expected in a society in which religious commitment and loyalty to the community are almost synonymous, and in which the traditional association between credit worthiness and church membership (Weber, 1946:311) has only recently been made redundant by the rise of computerized banking. A person's churchgoing signals her membership in a status group, and the overall pattern of churchgoing repeats the pattern of status differences in society as a whole.[4]

However, more recent research on the relation between social class and church involvement calls for at least a modification of these assumptions. Once it is recognized that social class is a composite of a number of social characteristics capable of varying independently, the complexity of the relation between social class and attendance becomes more apparent. Data from a national survey in the United States in 1965 reveal that attendance at Sunday church does vary by social class, but the pattern of variation differs from one measure of social class to another (Marty et al., 1968:213–14).

---

[4] In the past it was important not only which church one attended but where one sat in the congregation. The pew rent system, now defunct, was a way of segregating classes within a congregation. "There was often a complete gradation, from large and prominent pews near the front through cheaper lettings in less eligible positions, down to free seats in remote corners or behind pillars" (Mayor, 1967:23).

TABLE 11:1

ATTENDANCE AT SUNDAY CHURCH
(in percent)

	Don't Attend	Once a Month or Less	About Twice a Month	About Three Times a Month	Every Sunday
EDUCATION					
College graduate	26%	17%	6%	10%	41%/100%
1-3 years college	24	17	6	8	45
High school graduate	28	13	8	11	40
1-3 years high school	37	13	8	9	33
Eighth grade or less	42	9	7	9	33
INCOME					
Upper	26	13	9	11	41
Middle	30	14	7	9	40
Lower	38	12	8	9	33
OCCUPATION					
Professional	26	17	6	8	43
Proprietor or Manager	22	16	7	11	44
White collar worker	27	13	7	10	43
Service worker	44	12	6	5	33
Manual worker	35	12	8	11	34
Farmer	31	13	13	10	33

Along each dimension of social class, attendance is positively related to higher social status. The relationship is especially marked for the occupation dimension, where there is a clear break between the white collar and blue collar groups. Gallup Poll data from 1974 (Gallup, 1975:3) do not confirm the income and education relationships (little variation along either dimension was reported), but they do substantiate the white collar/blue collar differences:

TABLE 11:2

CHURCH ATTENDANCE DURING AN AVERAGE WEEK

Occupation	National	Protestant	Catholic
Professional, Business	42%	41%	64%
Clerical, Sales	40%	35%	63%
Manual	35%	32%	46%

It might well be that the apparently weaker relationship of income and education to attendance in able 11:1 is a function of the failure to control for sex. More women than men go to church regularly, mainly, it seems, because of their feelings of responsibility for the moral upbringing of their children. However, women also tend to have lower incomes. This might explain in part the lack of a clear relationship between income level and rate of church attendance, for women's religiosity is less influenced by socioeconomic factors. The church participation of the male correlates much more closely with social status than does that of the female (Mueller, 1975:797). Were males only to be included, the relationship between income and attendance would probably be a lot stronger.

The weakness of the correlations between education and income and attendance, compared with that between occupation and attendance, might also reflect the greater functional interdependence of occupation and church participation. Church attendance is perhaps the most formalized, organized, and public side of institutional religiosity. It is not surprising that it is linked most closely with that aspect of class that concerns not how much one knows or the size of one's income, but with such things as the organizational and interpersonal skills required by a job, the kind of friendship and colleagueship networks built at work, and the amount of leisure time afforded by the job. It is reasonable that the more organized side of religion should be most consonant with the more organizational side of class.

The 1974 Gallup Poll data also suggest that the relationship between occupation and attendance is stronger for Catholics than for Protestants. This is borne out in a more detailed analysis by Lazerwitz (1964:431).

TABLE   11:3

**FREQUENCY OF CHURCH ATTENDANCE
BY OCCUPATION OF FAMILY HEAD**

	Frequency of Church Attendance			
Religious Groups	*Regularly*	*Often*	*Seldom*	*Never*
PROTESTANTS				
Professions	47%	23%	23%	7%/100%
Owners, managers and officials	41	22	30	7
Clerical and sales	43	23	29	5
Skilled	35	21	36	7
Semi-skilled	34	23	36	7
Unskilled	35	27	31	7
Farmers	44	30	20	6

ROMAN CATHOLICS

Professions	81	11	7	1
Owners, managers and officials	83	8	5	4
Clerical and sales	81	11	5	3
Skilled	68	15	13	4
Semi-skilled	66	16	13	5
Unskilled	62	21	11	6
Farmers	67	9	20	4

Here again, a fairly clear break between white collar and blue collar workers appears in both faiths (farmers are more like blue collar workers). The assumption that the higher the status of a person, the more likely he is to attend church regularly seems to be borne out. This assumption will crop up again in this chapter when we examine variations within denominations. The evidence is not plentiful, but it does seem from Lazerwitz's data and from the 1974 Gallup Poll that the relationship between social class and attendance is stronger for Catholics than for Protestants. Jews show no relationship at all between attendance and social class, but then synagogue attendance on a weekly basis is rare anyway.

A positive association between social status and church attendance is also found in England (Glock and Stark, 1965:193; figures for 1957):

TABLE 11:4

CHURCH ATTENDANCE DECLINES WITH SUBJECTIVE CLASS

Self-Rated Class	Percentage Attending At Least "Now and Again"
Upper	73
Upper-middle	71
Middle	56
Lower-middle	52
Working	39

The same relation is found if occupation is used as a measure of status.[5]

From all reports, the English worker's habit of attending church did not survive his migration to the cities and factories. Although a boom in churchgoing occurred in the mid-Victorian period, it was caused by the

[5]Sissons (1973:120) found little difference in church attendance by social class in Scotland. However, he did find that people in professional occupations were much more likely to be involved in church-related societies.

expansion of the middle class, not by a return to religion on the part of the working man. By the end of the nineteenth century, the poorer districts of cities such as London showed very low rates of church attendance compared with the wealthier areas. The few manual workers to be found in church each Sunday were largely individuals from the upper ranks of the working class "whose existence was relatively secure and who wished to find a meaning in life beyond the daily round" (McLeod, 1974:55), and who were probably upwardly mobile.

Income Ranking and Denomination

It has long been recognized that "individual churches are overwhelmingly affiliated with a particular social class" (Pope, 1965:71; see also Hoult, 1950). This is as true within the black community as within the white (Washington, 1964:129; Blackwell, 1975:78–88). It is to be expected, then, that there will be differences in average income between the various denominations, to the extent that the income hierarchies in the community will be replicated in denominational hierarchies. A survey in California in 1964 shows this to be so (Stark and Glock, 1968:97):

TABLE 11:5

| Denomination | (No.) | Members' Annual Income | | | | |
		10,000+	9,000–7,000	6,000–5,000	4,000–	No Answer
Congregational	(151)	64%	15%	10%	6%	5%
Methodist	(415)	52	26	10	5	7
Episcopalian	(416)	47	23	13	10	7
Disciples	(50)	46	26	10	14	4
Presbyterian	(495)	48	24	11	12	5
American Lutheran	(208)	44	24	19	9	4
American Baptist	(141)	39	28	16	10	7
Missouri Lutheran	(116)	41	29	16	7	7
Southern Baptist	(79)	26	33	17	14	10
Sects	(255)	22	30	23	20	5
Catholic	(545)	34	28	23	9	6

Although each denomination contains all income groups, and although the differences between some denominations are small, the overall pattern is clear. Clustering by income is further indicated by the fact that none of the Southern Baptists, but a full 23 percent of the Congregationalists, reported an income of over $16,000 a year.[6]

---

[6] Socioeconomic differences also separate the branches of Judaism. Orthodox Jews tend, on the average, to have lower incomes than Conservative Jews, whereas Reform Jews have the highest average income of all.

Occupational Rank and Denomination

In his study of a California community in the 1940s, Goldschmidt (1944:348) found that the community's occupational elite (its managers, proprietors, professionals, farmers, and white collar workers) tended to be members of the Congregationalist and Methodist denominations, whereas the manual workers were more likely to attend sects such as the Church of the Nazarene and the Assembly of God. In his community study of "Maizeville," Schroeder (1964:36) discovered the same kind of association between occupation and church membership: the Congregationalists and Presbyterians were two-thirds white collar workers, and the Baptists, Lutherans and members of the Christian Churches were two-thirds to a half blue collar. Although each denomination had members from all occupational categories, a hierarchy of occupational prestige obviously existed. This pattern persists, even in times of greater mobility. Earle et al. (1976:108) found an occupational stratification of churches in Gastonia quite similar to that observed there nearly forty years before by Pope.

Goldschmidt discovered that the least occupationally homogeneous of all the denominations in his community was the Catholic Church. The Catholics probably do represent a wider range of occupations than any Protestant denomination. However, there are grounds for supposing that at the level of the individual church, the Catholic Church is as finely graded by occupational status of members as any Protestant denomination. Underwood (1957:200) found that in "Paper City," the parochial system had accentuated class divisions within the Catholic churches. Catholic congregations tended to be more occupationally homogeneous than Protestant congregations, and the Catholic parishes were more class sensitive than the city's political wards. The parish helped structure marriage patterns, educational institutions, recreation habits, and political behavior in such a way as to accentuate class differences in parish of residence. What the Protestants express in their denominational divisions the Catholics express in their parishes.

It is no secret that denominations are ranked in terms of their social status. It is significant that when people are asked to identify the denomination most like their own, they tend to choose the one that is closest in social status. It is also significant that members of lower status churches, when they do not choose a church of a similar rank, tend to choose a higher status denomination—but this is not reciprocated by members of higher status churches (Schroeder, 1964:70). Ironically, it is usually the elites who not only sit atop the hierarchy but also determine the criteria by which placements in the hierarchy are made—hence the importance they attach to objective criteria such as wealth, size, tradition, continuity, and architecture when judging the merits of the church.

These are all criteria that the elites find easier to meet than do those below them.

Religious Participation and Socioeconomic Status

The degree of involvement in religious institutions varies with socioeconomic status. In the general population, frequency and regularity of church attendance are greater among higher-status groups (see Bultena, 1949; Burchinal, 1959; Lazerwitz, 1961). However, this is the case only because lower-status persons are less likely to declare any religious affiliation at all and are, therefore, less likely to participate than higher-status persons. What if church members alone are observed? Does social status influence their rate of participation?

There is considerable evidence to suggest that within each denomination, higher status members show the highest rates of participation (David, 1932:426; Finney, 1971:155; Schroeder, 1964:49; Kersten, 1970:43; see also Demerath, 1965). The strength of this association varies according to the dimensions of status employed: the net influence of income is small, that of occupation the greatest (Mueller and Johnson, 1975:791). However, these findings should not be taken as evidence of greater religiosity on the part of higher status people. It is well known that such people have high rates of participation in *all* kinds of voluntary associations, and their more frequent church attendance may merely reflect this disposition rather than greater religiosity.

Controlling for members' non-church organizational involvement does indeed reduce some of the status differences in rates of church participation (Glock and Stark, 1965:188; Goode, 1966;110; see also Estus and Overington, 1970). But "the shifts in magnitude attributable to this control are not large and the data suggest that the modest SES-religious participation relationship is not primarily a function of general social participation" (Mueller and Johnson, 1975:794). Thus, something about the separate socioeconomic groups, especially something about their occupation, produces slight variations in rates of church attendance.

Social status has a bigger impact on who occupies positions of leadership in the church. It has long been known that boards of trustees and other such committees are drawn mainly from the middle class (see Davis, 1932), and contemporary data show that committee membership is much more common among those of higher status than those of lower status. The explanation for this fits neatly the functional theory of religious participation: "as roles within the congregation become better examples of the symbolic values of congregations, social class position plays an increasingly determinate part in role allocation as we move from indicators of participation such as worship or attendance to offices held"

(Estus and Overington, 1970:767). Middle-class church members use committee memberships to express their middle class status; lower-status church members either fail to put themselves forward or are not looked to for this purpose.

That socioeconomic status does influence rate of attendance and has a much bigger impact on church leadership indicates that it is the organizational aspect of religiosity that attracts the middle-class individual. This is not merely a reflection of his enthusiasm for "joining" and "organizing"; it also indicates that he tends to "see" his religion differently (see Stark, 1972). The middle class person "does" his religion and looks upon it as a public activity that is bound up tightly with other aspects of his life (see Fukuyama, 1961). The lower-status person, on the other hand, has a more private religion, one that is oriented more to devotion. Even when a congregation is largely working-class, it is the middle class that will occupy its leadership positions (Demerath, 1965:15). The higher-status groups look to religious participation to legitimate their status publicly; the lower-status groups look to religion in a more private way to provide moral support, catharsis, and comfort.[7]

Socioeconomic status is thus of some importance in determining patterns of religious life in the United States, and it is obvious that religious participation plays a part in cementing differences in social status. However, it is very important to note that "the combined influence of the three SES indicators [is] only one percent of the total variance in religious participation: the addition of non-religious participation, race, religion, gender, marital status and presence of children [increases] the explained variance another five percent" (Mueller and Johnson, 1975:798). In other words, social status is not very important as an influence on religious participation; nor are many of the other social characteristics that might be thought influential. Clearly, more research on factors which cause church attendance variations (such as parental habits) is needed.

Considering the functionalist thesis concerning the relation between religious behavior and social stratification, three conclusions seem warranted: (1) specific denominations *are* identified with specific status groups—although the relation is not strong, it is probably sufficient for the pattern of religious affiliation to confirm status differences; (2) religious involvement is yet another arena in which different status groups act out their different life styles and thus reaffirm their differences; however, (3) status considerations play a minor part in determining dif-

[7]Although members of the middle class are over-represented in church leadership positions, they judge this activity as less important for them than do the few working-class people in such positions. For the middle-class person, membership on the church board of trustees is probably one of several such positions; for the working-class person, it might be the only opportunity to exercise power (Stark, 1972:493).

ferences in religious behavior, at least as this has been measured in conventional survey research.

Social Mobility and Religious Membership

Although it is not possible to go as far as Winter (1961:101) and declare that "the sacred organisation becomes the means to sanctify one's position on the economic ladder," enough evidence has been produced to demonstrate that religious identity and social status are closely related. It follows from this relation that when an individual changes social status, she might well change her religious affiliation as well. It is a common supposition that as an individual moves up the social ladder, she will change her religious affiliation to a higher status church (Moberg, 1962:225; Frazier, 1974:83).

The idea that denominational change is a natural accompaniment to social mobility has some plausibility, and it is a common belief that it occurs widely. Unfortunately, there is little evidence to support this idea—and a considerable amount to refute it. Movement up and down the stratification ladder has little or no effect on current denominational preference, and the more religious the individual, the more likely is this to be so. Denominational switching as a consequence of occupational mobility seems to be the practice of only a small minority of those who are mobile, and most of this small group are only marginally religious (Finney, 1971:24). Only those who are mobile over a large range of occupations tend to change their denomination, and they are just as likely to drop their religious affiliation altogether as to join a higher status denomination (see Lauer, 1975). Nelsen (1976) found that in rural areas, where religion is perhaps more likely to enter into the prestige ranking of individuals, religious mobility did parallel social mobility. In urban areas, however, where religion is a more private experience, there is no relation at all.

It is possible for an individual to be both religiously and socially mobile if his denomination *as a whole* experiences upward mobility. In this case, switching becomes unnecessary. The acquisition of property and investments, coupled with growing organizational sophistication, might mean that a denomination and its members become more middle class together. The Disciples of Christ and the Mormons have clearly undergone this transformation. However, such cases are rare, and play only a minor part in establishing the pattern of relations between religion and economics.[8]

[8]Some denominational mobility occurs in England, but compared with the American experience, the process is very slow (Wilson, 1966:111). Denominational mobility of this kind does not necessarily mean that all the members of the denomination become middle class. As a denomination adopts more middle class ways, the working class members may drop out and be replaced by middle class people who now begin to find the denomination attractive.

The Function of Sects

The thesis that religion serves to legitimate the economic system is invalidated by neither religious nor economic diversity, for it is through this very diversity that the system of inequality is rationalized. One possible contradiction to the thesis is the sect, which rejects not only the economic system but the usual criteria of religious respectability as well. The sect would appear to have little to contribute to integrating the economic system.

It is possible, however, to see sects as performing an *adaptive* role in society, helping to buttress the economic system in a way different from, but just as effective as, denominations. First of all, sects teach an otherworldly religion, which transfers attention away from this world and leaves economic institutions unchallenged. Second, by appealing to those who are "temporarily dislocated" within the system, sects can act as a mode of adjustment to it and a means of absorbing marginal groups back into the system (Wilson, 1966:105).

If some sects function to socialize marginal economic groups into the mainstream, others perform a similar function with respect to generations. Thus, many of the sects within the Jesus movement clearly operated as means of rehabilitating and reassimilating drug addicts, alcoholics, school drop outs, and delinquent gang members. Through their "soup kitchens," "pads," and other settlement-house operations, as well as their more ambitious communal experiments, they resembled in many ways the Salvation Army of old, functioning to socialize a "lost" generation. They allowed the "drop out" to combine some counter-culture and mainstream values (for example, allowing them to see the "high" of the drug culture in the same light as getting "high" on Jesus), and in this way functioned as a sort of decompression chamber for adolescent rebellion, reconciling young persons to their inevitable return to a "normal" way of life in traditional institutions (see Robbins et al., 1974). From this perspective, the marginal sects affirm rather than deny existing economic arrangements.

Although sects, loudly denouncing the worldliness of others, would appear to be dysfunctional for economic integration, a close examination of what they actually say and do reveals a different picture. The rejection of worldliness is usually coupled with proscriptions on drinking, gambling, dancing, attending amusements, fornicating, and conspicuous consumption, and frequent enjoinders to work hard and seek the approval of others. Their doctrine of spiritual equality of opportunity, furthermore, fits nicely with economic ideals of equal economic opportunity and self-improvement (Garrison, 1974:320). Such teachings function, in short, to socialize the marginal people to whom they appeal into a middle-class way of life. The emotional display often witnessed in sects does not contradict this thesis: emotionalism is probably necessary to draw new members in and provide them with a warm and rewarding group context in which they will learn the values important for adequate performance in an urban, industrial society.

The majority of American sects share the pragmatic values held by most Americans and focus the attention of their membership not on the next world, but on the task of achieving competence within the prevailing economic system. Accordingly, they suppress the irrational, the erotic, the aesthetic, the risk-taking impulse in people, and foster instead a calculating and cautious ideal more appropriate to middle-class life styles. This ethos carries over into attitudes toward welfare; the sects commonly take a highly individualistic attitude toward helping the unfortunate, bestowing charity only as need arises and basing the award upon the merits of the recipient as they perceive them.

Referring specifically to sects, Zaretsky (1974a:xxvi) observes that "rituals are clearly used in many of the churches to uplift daily life and to return the individual to his occupation. In this sense, groups wish to transform people's lives so that they have a greater ability to function in society." Unable to make a frontal assault on the bastion of the middle class because their members lack the necessary skills, sects allow their membership to slowly absorb and internalize the values necessary for economic advancement and social respectability.

This thesis also applies to sects among blacks, membership in which "facilitates and stimulates identification with economic values long linked with the middle class" (Lenski, 1963:131). Holiness sects, which began to spread in the black community after 1886, teach that the only real problem is that of sin, which is to be overcome by an encounter with God and the special experience that results from it. The search for perfection sanctification orients blacks to a personalized idea of right conduct and individual achievement. This theme is found even in the more extreme sects, such as the United House of all Prayer: Daddy Grace taught his followers to expect "participation in those benefits of society which symbolise power (e.g. land, money, buildings, etc.) rather than directing their attention to the next world, and instructed [them] in habits of frugality, hard work and honesty" (Washington, 1972:12). In a similar fashion, the Jehovah's witnesses teach blacks a kind of asceticism and work-discipline that makes them desirable employees in the industrial world. They are commanded to put in a fair day's work for a fair day's pay, that honesty is the best policy, and that unions are a destructive force. They are also made content with low pay by the teaching that the consumer culture is false and evil.

Sects are much more likely to perform this kind of integrative function if the economic system is relatively open, and in any case it is to be admitted that they are much more likely to appeal to "those groups most conscious of striving, seeking new ways to move at cultural goals" (Wilson, 1961:332). The contribution of sects to the economic integration of society is clear. They help socialize their members into dominant values *and*, in the opportunities they provide for organizational involvement and leadership, supply an important learning experience for those anxious to inculcate middle-class ways.

CONCLUSION

This chapter has attempted to unravel the complex relationship between religion and economics in modern Western societies. The guiding thesis has been that religious and economic institutions are functionally related—that there is an "elective affinity" between religious ethics and practices and economic behavior. Drawing on functional theory, we have argued furthermore, that in the main, the churches function to legitimate the dominant economic values and conduct in society. This is consonant with the view elucidated in Chapter One that religion, as part of a social system (society) tends to legitimate the values of that system. It is also consonant with the view that society is a system of which religion is a part, and that the development of both religion and economics will not take place haphazardly but within constraints that each imposes on the other. Note that the thesis says nothing about intentions, but merely points to the consequences of what people believe and do.

At the level of values, it is possible to see a congruence between dominant economic ethics and the teachings of what can justifiably be called the religious mainstream. This mainstream stands foursquare behind the principles of bourgeois capitalism. The various important shifts in economic thinking that have occurred during the last one hundred years have not undermined this close relationship, although they have occasioned some strain. By and large, the teachings of the mainstream churches have accommodated to these changes. Value consensus is replicated at the structural level by the interchange of elite personnel between the economy and religious organizations, and by the operation of the major denominations as important corporations within the economic system.

The second half of the chapter demonstrated that the stratification system in the United States, its economic hierarchy, also receives direct legitimation from the religious system. Commitment to the economic system and commitment to religion, at least in the sense of regular church attendance and zealous organizational work, tend to go hand in hand. At the same time, the various denominations in the United States are clearly ranked in objective terms of economic privilege, and tend to be associated in the popular mind with different status groups. Denomination function, therefore, not only as focuses of differential association, where one meets one's own kind, but also to dramatize and express the American status hierarchy as a whole. The apparent abnormality of the sects does not negate the functionalist thesis, for they too serve to legitimize—and, indeed, strengthen commitment to—the status system as a whole. In Chapter 14 we will look at certain aspects of this religion-economics relationship in a different light. The presence of a "prophetic" or radical American religion and the enormous religious diversity in the United States are two obvious reasons why this apparently close relationship between economic ethics and religious teachings should be suspect. Nevertheless, there is obviously a large element of validity in the functionalist thesis with which this chapter began.

12

RELIGION

AND THE FAMILY

INTRODUCTION

The family has three basic functions: to regulate sexual relations, to ensure the comfort and protection of the parents and children during procreation, and to provide primary socialization for the offspring. The way in which the family performs these functions is best communicated by the concept of the *life cycle*, which is a way of looking at different ages and the family positions associated with them as different stages in social maturation, each with its own rights and responsibilities. The life cycle is marked by transition points such as birth, puberty, marriage, parenthood and retirement, the timing and significance of which vary from one culture to another. On one's passage through the life cycle, the values and norms of society are transmitted from one generation to another. A very important source of these values and norms is religion. Religious definitions of right and wrong and the meaning of personal identity help shape the life cycle. The impact of religious beliefs and practices on passage through the life cycle is the subject of this chapter.

Functionalist theory suggests that two institutions as basic as religion and the family are bound to modify and influence each other. Examples can be found of conflict between kinship obligations espousing an exclusive "community of believers" and religious ideals, as a result of which an individual will feel the contradictory pulls of family and religious commitments. But these are exceptional cases, and as often as not they are an attack not upon the family as such but upon certain forms of kinship.

The principal focus of this chapter is the impact of religion on the family—but it should not be forgotten that the influence is mutual. The family is an important buttress of the Church, helping inculcate attitudes conducive to committed church membership and the support of religious principles, just as the Church provides legitimation for dominant family values and practices (see Chapter 6).

"The family that prays together stays together." This aphorism attests to the popularity of the idea that religion has integrative consequences for the family. While Church and family may not be as close as they once were, the continued popularity of baptism, church marriage, and funeral rites is a sign that families still look to the Church to commemorate important transitional periods of their life cycle. Of course, the actual family structure condoned by religion varies from one faith to another, and from one time to another. For this reason, the relationship between religion and the family should always be considered as part of a total social whole. For example, economic changes might bring about modifications in both family and religious structures. For some time now in Western societies the bisexual, monogamous, nuclear family (with some extended kin obligations) has been the norm. By and large, the churches support this norm. Only the more liberal denominations even entertain the idea of debate on such issues as homosexuality, extramarital sex, freer divorce, abortion, birth control, and group marriage.

For most denominations, rules of family living are the most demanding part of their ethical system, although Jews and Catholics have traditionally had more to say about proper family life than Protestants. Among Catholics, a strong positive correlation between degree of involvement in the family and degree of involvement in the church indicates a mutually supportive relationship (Lenski, 1963:248). It is even harder to separate the sacred and secular side of Jewish life: "to marry and establish a family is a *mitzvah*, a religious commandment" (Sklare, 1971:74). The more conservative Protestant denominations, such as the Lutherans (see Kersten, 1970) and many smaller sects, similarly fuse the sacred and the secular in the family. These variations notwithstanding, all denominations support the family as a vital social institution and provide rituals such as baptism and marriage to solemnize important family occasions. They also enjoin devotionalism in family settings (such as grace at meals) partly to co-opt the family for the purposes of religious socialization, but also to reinforce family values and promote harmony in the family.

How common is devotionalism in the home? Unfortunately, data are scarce on this topic, but Moberg (1971), summarizing a number of studies, is forced to conclude that despite the urgings of the churches, only a minority of families bring religion into the home. Regular family devotions are reported by a quarter of Methodist families, less than half the Congregationalists, a quarter of Presbyterians, and two in five Baptists. Jews conform even less to their stricter norms. Even though for the traditional Jew "the synagogue is, in a sense, merely the lengthened shadow of his home," family practices among Jews are at a "low level" (Sklare and Greenblum, 1967:50). The Jewish family seems to be losing its sacred character. Those family rituals that do survive (such as the celebration of the Passover in a Seder) tend to be those that enable the Jewish family to accommodate itself better to its Gentile environment. Family devotions are probably most common among sectarians. For example, eighty percent of the Mennonites say grace before meals (Kauffman and Harder, 1975:178), compared with sixty-nine percent of the general population (Gallup, 1972:1779; the first figure is from 1972, the second from 1962).

Clearly, religion no longer suffuses family life. Today the functional relationship between religion and the family usually takes more subtle and indirect forms. The family still looks to the church to legitimize and clarify values and beliefs concerning family roles. Religion teaches that entrance into family life is a sacrament, or ordinance, the vows in which are sanctioned by God and into which God enters as a third party. The family thus becomes a moral system with a divine foundation. Exactly what this means for the fulfillment of family roles has not been adequately explored. However, a considerable amount of data is available on the relationship between religion (usually by major faith) and various family practices. In order to describe the impact of religion on the family, the rest of the chapter will follow a kind of life-cycle model, starting with marriage, passing on to the number of children wanted, expected, and born, and then proceeding to the way in which those children are socialized and their sex roles determined. Along the way, it will be possible to describe the influence of religion on the choice of spouse and the impact of religion on family stability.

THE DECISION TO MARRY

It is the norm in American society that one marries. This norm is religiously sanctioned by Scriptural passages such as, "And the Lord God said, 'It is not good that a man should be alone; I will make him a help meet for him' " (Gen., 2:18). However, there are religious differences concerning both the strength of support for this norm and the degree of conformity to it. Of the three major faiths, Protestants are the most likely to be married, followed by Catholics and then Jews. The differences are never greater than ten percent, however, and variation in marriage rates *within* the faiths (for example, by ethnicity) are as great as those between them (Greeley, 1974:46). It is more indicative of the influence of religion that those with no religious affiliation show the lowest rate of marriage—67 percent—although, as Greeley points out, those with no religious affiliation tend to be younger and may show a lower rate of marriage for that reason. It is also quite possible that rather than church affiliation encouraging marriage, as these figures suggest, marriage encourages a renewal of religious identification. Whichever is cause and whichever is effect, religious affiliation is associated with being married, albeit with minor variations between and within the faiths.

THE DECISION WHOM TO MARRY

Religion helps define the field of eligible marriage partners. For most churchpeople, marriage with a person of another faith is a deviation from a norm. The Catholic Church is especially firm in its stand against mixed marriages, discouraging them in the interests of the unity of the family and the future of the children. The Church will countenance a mixed marriage only under the strict conditions that all children born to the pair be raised as Catholics, that a Catholic priest officiate at the wedding, that the Catholic partner be considered in no danger of losing the faith, and that the Catholic spouse try to convert the non-Catholic spouse to Catholicism. Endogamy norms are equally strong in the more conservative Protestant denominations. The Southern Baptists, for instance, hold that marriages between Protestants and Catholics are "nothing else than a token of weakened faith" and are "unpleasing to God" (Kelsey, 1973:157).

One purpose of the rule against mixed marriage is to promote family solidarity, but the rule is also aimed at sustaining commitment to the Church. In fact, mixed marriages weaken the ability of the family to transmit the faith where members of that faith are in a minority. For example, "youths who have one Catholic and one non-Catholic parent are much more likely to adopt a religious orientation more characteristic of non-Catholics" (Trent and Golds, 1967:187). It is also the case that the majority of the children of intermarried Jews will be Gentile (Sklare, 1971:202). In the light of these correlations, it is tempting to assume that mixed-religion marriages will always result in the apostasy of the children away from the minority religion. But it is hazardous to leap from correlation to cause. It might well be that mixed-marriage parents are more liberal, and transmit enough of this liberalism to their children to allow them greater freedom of choice—including the freedom to choose their own religion. Nevertheless, a "leakage" in mixed marriages as children depart the faith certainly occurs.

Besides leading to the "loss" of children, mixed marriages are the most common occasion of apostasy by adults. Vincent (1964:56) estimates that 30 percent of those who leave the Catholic Church do so at the time of marriage to a non-Catholic person. Here again, correlation does not mean cause. Although marriage to a person of another faith may be sufficient cause to prize an individual away from her religion-by-birth, it is just as likely that the least religiously committed persons (and therefore those who are most probably apostates) are most likely to enter into a mixed marriage in the first place. Thus, Lazerwitz (1971:60) argues that "the basic threat to Jewish continuity does not stem from intermarriage. Rather intermarriage (without conversion) is but a symptom of diaspora Jewry's growing dissatisfaction with contemporary Jewish institutions and cultural forms."[1]

Interestingly, although the Catholic Church takes one of the strongest stands against intermarriage, the Catholic laity are more tolerant of mixed marriages than Protestants. Two thirds of Protestants approve of mixed marriages, compared with 85 percent of Catholics (Erskine, 1965:329). Moreover, Catholics are becoming more tolerant: the proportion of Catholics who think it "very important" for young people to marry someone within their own religion fell from 56 percent in 1963 to 27 percent in 1973 (Greeley, McCready and McCourt, 1976:34). The greater tolerance of Catholics might indicate that, given the safeguards they feel are written into mixed marriages on their behalf, such unions are less threatening to their faith. The Protestants, who are without such protection, are less confident. It is noteworthy that although younger Catholics would be willing to marry a Protestant, they would not be prepared to change to the faith of their mate. Young Protestants, on the other hand, although less willing to make a mixed marriage, would be more willing, if they should marry a Catholic, to change to the faith of their mate (Rosten, 1975:561).

Seventeen percent of white marriages in the United States are religiously mixed (see Alston et al., 1976). Catholics are more likely to marry outside the faith than Protestants. Calculating the percentage of individuals in a population who were married to a partner of another faith, Besanceney (1970:64) found that 31 percent of Protestants and 39 per-

---

[1]It is one thing to say that, of those who lose their faith, a sizable minority do so because of their involvement in a mixed marriage, and another thing entirely to say that mixed marriages most often end in one of the partners relinquishing his or her original faith. In fact, while half of the American men who do change their religion do so at the time of marriage, 90 percent retain their religious preference when they marry. And, although the occasion of a mixed marriage is likely to have been the cause of conversion among those who have changed, most mixed marriages involve no change at all.

cent of Catholics were so married in 1961. Using the same method of computation, Sklare (1971:187) discovered that outmarriage among Jews between 1958 and 1964 never rose above 18.5 percent.

Conforming to norms of religious endogamy is obviously stronger among Jews than among either Protestants or Catholics—the boundary line between Jews and Gentiles remains clearly marked and difficult to cross. Analyzing data from Canada, Mueller (1974:262) detected the same pattern. His method of computation was different (he calculated percentage of marriages of members of a religious group that involved a member of another group), but it is the proportions that are important. In 1965, Canadian Protestants exhibited an outmarriage rate of 26.8 percent, Catholics a rate of 23.2 percent, and Jews a much lower figure of 14.4 percent.

In trying to gauge the strength of endogamy norms in various religious faiths, one should remember that some outmarriage will occur by chance whenever one faith makes up more than half of the population. To obtain an accurate assessment of the impact of religion on the decision whom to marry, it is necessary to control for the relative strength of members of any given faith in the total population. The significant point is that calculating exogamy in this way alters only slightly the relative standing of the three major faiths. The Jews still have the lowest rate of exogamy, at 12 percent of random expectations; Protestants and Catholics are now about equal at 55 percent of random expectations (Mueller, 1974:261).[2]

TRENDS IN INTERFAITH MARRIAGES

Since at least the 1930s, there has been a virtually uninterrupted rise in the proportion of individuals in each faith marrying outside the faith. This is true of all three major faiths in both the United States and in Canada. The following table, adapted from Bumpass (1970:254), shows

[2]The computation of mixed marriage rates is beset with all sorts of problems. Some concern the lack of information about the religious affiliation of those getting married. Some concern different ideas about what constitutes a mixed marriage. Church affiliation does not clearly indicate the distance which might separate two marriage partners. Is an Episcopalian further apart from a Southern Baptist than she might be from a Catholic? There are also problems with the computation of marriage rates. The figure for mixed marriages in a given population is different from the figure for individuals in a given population involved in a mixed marriage. The proportion of individuals in a sample involved in a mixed marriage will always be lower than the proportion of mixed marriages. For example, if, out of 100 marriages involving a Protestant, 30 are mixed (that is, a mixed marriage rate of 30 percent), only 18 percent of all the Protestants will be religiously inter-married because those 30 mixed marriages bring into the sample 30 non-Protestants, and 30 as a percentage of 200–30 is 18 percent.

the changes in the proportion of white women in each faith and marriage cohort married to a spouse of another faith.

TABLE   12:1

**PROPORTION OF MARRIED INDIVIDUALS IN INTERFAITH MARRIAGES,
BY MAJOR RELIGIOUS GROUP AND MARRIAGE COHORT: WHITE WOMEN
MARRIED ONCE, 1965 NATIONAL FERTILITY STUDY**

| Cohort | Total | *Current Religion* | | |
		Protestant	Catholic	Jew
1960–65	.14	.11	.20	.10
1955–59	.12	.09	.18	.06
1950–54	.10	.08	.14	.14
1945–49	.09	.07	.13	.08
1940–44	.07	.05	.12	.08
1935–39	.07	.05	.12	.05

The rate of increase is about the same for Catholics and Protestants;
the Jewish trend is less regular, although this might be due to the small
number of Jews in the sample used for analysis. Bumpass estimates that
about half this trend is artifactual.[3] Therefore, the rise is probably not
quite so steep as it might appear, but the trend remains nevertheless.
The rate of increase in Canada has also been uniform and, if anything,
more rapid. In 1927, 5 percent of Protestant brides and grooms were
marrying spouses of a different faith. By 1967, this proportion had risen
to 17 percent. For Catholics, the 1927–1967 rise was from 7 percent to
16 percent, and for Jews, the increase was from 3 percent to 10 percent
(Bumpass, 1970:254). A variety of other studies confirm that interfaith
marriage is increasing (see, for example, Abramson, 1973:77; Mueller,
1974:26; Sklare, 1971:188). A number of factors can be adduced to
explain these rising intermarriage rates: the waning influence of religion; the decline in the number of first-generation immigrants; the
increase in the number of people in college; the increase in the number
of women at work; changing family values, including greater equality of
the sexes, weaker extended kinship ties, and greater popularity of the

[3]The National Fertility Study data (1965) used by Bumpass pertain only to white women
who have been maried only once. In consequence, there is a danger of overestimating the
intermarriage trend. Mixed marriages are less stable, which means that a lower proportion
of all mixed marriages of earlier than that of later cohorts will be intact in 1965 and thus
included in the sample. The result is that a bigger trend is recorded than that which
actually exists. Furthermore, some of those who marry a spouse of a different faith eventually adopt the faith of that spouse, which means that the later cohorts will appear more
heterogeneous than the earlier cohorts.

romantic love ideal; and increased urbanization, which raises the rate of religious intermixing.

DIFFERENCES IN INTERMARRIAGE RATES WITHIN THE MAJOR FAITHS

What do intermarriage patterns look like if some of the denominational differences within the faiths are examined? Before taking a look at some of the more detailed intermarriage patterns, we must say something about how the intermarriage rate should be calculated. It is well known that a large number of people change their denomination just prior to marriage in anticipation of the event. Any analysis that looks only at presently mixed marriages (and those in the previous section would be included) is likely to understate the extent to which people have gone outside their faith in choosing their mate. For example, in a survey carried out by Babchuk (1967:553), 84 percent of the couples were of the same religion at the time of the study, but in 74 percent of these cases, one of the spouses had changed religion at the time of marriage. True endogamy is the proportion of people who marry someone whose original denomination was the same as their own and both of whom now practice the same religion.

Endogamy rates calculated in this way, showing the proportion of individuals in each respective group who married someone whose original denomination was the same as their own, are supplied by Greeley (1971:88) who analyzed 1968 National Opinion Research Center data:

TABLE   12:2

Presbyterian	15%
Methodist	30
Lutheran	34
Baptist	35
Catholic	75
Jew	94

The figures show much closer conformity to endogamy rules by Jews and Catholics, but they also show interesting variations within the Protestant faith, with Baptists more than twice as likely to choose a spouse from the same denomination as Presbyterians.

Obviously, many Protestants marry outside their denomination, but where do they turn? How likely is it, for example, that a Baptist will marry a Presbyterian? Of the members of the various Protestant denominations, which are most likely to marry Catholics? Using Census data, Monahan (1971:89) computed the ratio of actual mixed marriages to the number to be expected by random choice. Note that, unlike Greeley in Table 12:2, Monahan controls for the population distribution of each religious group. However, he does not, as did Greeley, allow for conversion at the time of marriage. He therefore underestimates the extent of exogamy.

TABLE 12:3

RELIGIOUS ENDOGAMY IN THE UNITED STATES, 1957:
THE RATIO OF ACTUAL TO EXPECTED RANDOM MATINGS
BY RELIGIOUS COMBINATIONS (WHITES ONLY; TABLE ADAPTED)

	Baptist	*Lutheran*	*Methodist*	*Presbyterian*	*Catholic*	*Jew*
Baptist	5.20	.08	.31	.20	.11	—
Lutheran	.09	9.92	.18	.21	.30	.03
Methodist	.31	.21	5.64	2.50	.18	.03
Presbyterian	.19	.18	.24	12.57	.15	.03
Catholic	.10	.29	.16	.17	3.25	.05
Jew	—	.06	.04	.14	.07	26.21

As with the figures for overall interfaith-marriage rates, controlling for population distributions here alters the endogamy rankings of the various religious groups. Jews retain their high rate; they are twenty-six times more likely to marry other Jews than would be expected had they randomly married. This far exceeds the endogamy rate of the next most inmarrying group, the Presbyterians. Catholics show the *lowest* rate of endogamy when their relatively smaller numbers are controlled for. The table also reveals some interesting facts about the patterns of outmarriage exhibited by the various Protestant denominations. The denomination most likely to marry into the Catholic faith is the Lutheran, which is not surprising in view of the historical linkages and theological and ecclesiastical similarities between them. This reasoning might also apply to the pattern of Presbyterian-Methodist marriages. However, social class considerations might also be relevant, for people marrying outside their group look to the one above it in relative social status. This might explain why Baptists who outmarry are most likely to marry Methodists, and why Methodists who outmarry are most likely to marry Presbyterians. Unfortunately, there is no way of accounting for the discrepancy between Greeley's and Monahan's data—the different outmarriage rates for Presbyterians are most remarkable. Clearly what is needed is interfaith marriage data which contain information on both the original denomination of respondents and enables controls to be imposed for the distribution in the population of the respective religious groups.

WHO MARRIES OUTSIDE THE FAITH?

Many factors have been adduced to explain why some individuals break the religious norm of endogamy. Most of the sociological research on intermarriage treats it as a form of deviance and concentrates on facilitating conditions (for example, city life, where there is more social mixing) or upon disposing conditions (for example, higher amounts of education). The objective here is to stipulate those conditions under which an individual is most likely to break the norm and marry outside the faith.

Unfortunately, not all of the various studies to be reported investigate all of the alleged conditions. Nor do they all demonstrate the relevance of the conditions to one another. In any case, the importance of a single factor is likely to vary from one religious group to another. In short, there is no theoretical model of intermarriage to guide thinking on this subject. In the absence of such a model, it seems best to proceed in chronological order, treating each of the alleged factors as they "occur" in the life of the individual.

1. The chances of marrying outside the faith are greatly enhanced if members of the faith constitute only a small proportion of the population. For example, the number of mixed marriages is as high as 75 percent among Catholics in Raleigh, North Carolina, Savannah, Georgia, and Atlanta, Georgia, where Catholics make up only 2 percent of the population, but as low as 8 percent in places like El Paso, Texas and Providence, Rhode Island, where over half of the population is Catholic (Monahan, 1971:86).

2. Outmarriage is also affected by the culture into which one is born. In the case of Protestants, there are variations by denominations; in the case of Catholics, there are variations by ethnic group.

3. Raising children is the responsibility mainly of the family, and part of that responsibility is to ensure that religious endogamy rules are internalized and obeyed. Intermarriage can therefore be looked upon partly as a breakdown of social control in the family. This breakdown is most likely to occur when:

a. the parents themselves are not religious (at least in the sense that they do not regularly attend church and do not attribute much importance to religion);
b. the parents are separated or quarrel frequently;
c. the parents are of mixed faith;
d. the parents have been geographically and socially mobile;

e. parent-child relationships have been distant and unsatisfying;
f. ties with extended kin, such as grandparents, uncles and aunts, are weak (Besanceney, 1970:135–48).

However, although outmarriage might be regarded as deviance by the parental family and thus viewed negatively, it is likely to be seen by the outmarrying person as a positive step, a means of escaping a "spoiled identity" and gaining a new and more acceptable one. "Such people often deliberately seek out marital partners from other religioethnic groups" (Lazerwitz, 1971:59).

4. Changes in the rate of exogamy over time suggest that intermarriage increases with greater acculturation. More recently immigrated Americans should show lower rates of exogamy than third- or fourth-generation Americans. Among both Catholics and Jews, exogamy correlates positively with length of time a family has lived in the United States (Abramson, 1973:77; Goldstein, 1968:169).

5. In some cases, being a man or a woman influences the chances that a person will outmarry. For Protestants, gender makes no difference. Among Catholics, however, women are more likely to marry outside the faith. Besanceney (1970:78) suggests as a reason for this that

> Before a mixed marriage at which a Catholic priest officiates, the Catholic and non-Catholic party must each have agreed that the children of the union will be raised as Catholics. Since the early training of children is necessarily entrusted to the mother and she typically provides the religious influence in the family, such an agreement gives some security to a Catholic woman in a mixed marriage.

The Catholic man marrying a non-Catholic woman may feel less secure in this matter and avoid a mixed marriage.

Jewish men marry outside the faith more often than Jewish women. This is probably because men have greater freedom to marry women who are beneath them economically. Given the economic superiority of the average Jew over the average Gentile, Jewish men can look to Gentile women more easily than Jewish women can look to Gentile men. This pattern may also reflect the fact that children usually take the status of the father rather than that of the mother, which makes it easier for the man to take the risk of marrying out.

6. A child born late in the birth order is more likely to marry out than the first or second born, probably because such children are subject to weaker discipline than their older siblings (Heiss, 1960:53).

7. Intermarriage depends on the opportunity to mix socially, and this

opportunity is enhanced in an urban setting. Intra-Catholic marriages occur less frequently in urban areas (Abramson, 1973:75).

8. Level of education has no influence on the chances of a Protestant marrying outside the faith, but among Catholics, the greater the amount of education, the greater the likelihood of intermarriage (Abramson, 1973:77). Among Jews, a curvilinear relationship is found: those with medium levels of education are the most likely to marry out.

Warren (1970:147) argues that absolute level of education is not as important as relative level in determining outmarriage.

> If a man obtains more or less education than the mode for his religious group, he is less likely to marry a girl who shares his religious preference than a man who obtains the typical educational level of the group. Since at the time of mate selection educational attainment sorts people into different social and geographical spaces, it follows that the ratio of girls of the same religious preference to girls of all other preferences will be reduced in the locations of those men who obtain more or less education than is typical of their religious group.

When relative rather than absolute education is measured, it is found that Protestants too are influenced by education.

9. As would be expected, the relation between level of religious education and chances of marrying outside the faith is reversed. Religious socialization facilitates the internalization of norms. Thus, for example, attendance at a parochial school and a denominational college is positively associated with endogamy for all faiths (Goldstein, 1968:169; see also Heiss, 1960).

10. It is to be expected that rate of church attendance would be positively correlated with endogamy. However, the only study of intermarriage to have demonstrated any relation at all is that of Goldstein (1968:169), who found that exogamy was more common among those who only rarely attended synagogue.

11. Income level does not have a uniform effect across all three faiths. Among Protestants, income appears to be no factor at all in determining intermarriage rates. High-income Catholics are more likely than other Catholics to marry outside the faith, but the reverse is true for Jews: the richer they are, the less likely are they to marry Gentiles (Besanceney, 1970:80). This may well reflect the "retentivism" of Jews, which, given the greater freedom of choice wealth bestows, will make them more zealous in adhering to endogamy norms. Richer Catholics, on the other hand, are more likely to use that freedom to marry "up" into Protestant and Jewish ranks.

12. Occupational prestige is positively related to exogamy rates among Catholics. But among Protestants, the higher the occupational prestige, the less likely is an individual to choose a non-Protestant partner. These findings probably reflect the influence of old WASP values on both faiths: upwardly mobile Catholics will be keener to marry out of their predominantly lower status faith, whereas upper-status Protestants will be less keen to leave a faith that has traditionally been tied to the nation's elites (Besanceney, 1970:82).

The *relative* impact of social class factors and religious factor on choice of marriage partners is by no means clear at this time. The accumulated research seems to suggest that in those categories of social class in which a particular religious group is underrepresented, class endogamy will work against religious endogamy; otherwise, it will reinforce religious endogamy. In other words, upper-status Catholics, who are underrepresented in the sense of not filling the same proportion of upper-status "places" as their numbers in the general population would warrant, tend to choose spouses above all from within their own class, even if this means going outside their own religion. In the lower status ranks, where Catholics are overrepresented, religious considerations will be dominant.

In the light of findings such as these, the trends in interfaith marriages described earlier can be better understood. Where *social class* factors are superimposed on religious factors, the crossing of religious lines at the time of marriage is less likely. Some of the rise in intermarriage rates can be accounted for, then, by the recent socioeconomic leveling of the three major faiths, particularly the catching up of the Catholics in the areas of education and income. The increasing affluence of the Catholic community might account for their willingness to look outside what was once thought to be a very closed community. Intermarriage is inhibited where *ethnic* considerations are added to those of religion. It is reasonable to expect, then, that any decline in the strength of ethnic consciousness will encourage a rise in intermarriage rates. Thus the national decline in the proportion of individuals of prime marriage age (15–25) and of foreign birth or parentage from 36 percent in 1930 to 16 percent in 1960 might well have contributed to the rise of intermarriage rates (Bumpass, 1970:257). The increasing rate of intermarriage might also reflect simply a secularization of American and Canadian cultures and a decline in the importance of religion as a factor in marriage choice. However, the question of whether or not those cultures are indeed secularizing is much debated and we will take up this issue later. Therefore, not too much reliance should be placed upon it as a way of accounting for what looks like a major trend in Western society.

RELIGION AND FAMILY SIZE

The number and frequency of children born into a family is influenced very much by religious considerations. Along with other social influences, such as level of education, church teachings contribute to the determination of how many children a couple will have and how they are spaced. The relation between religion and fertility is extremely complex, and the ensuing discussion cannot fail to over-simplify it, but Freedman et al. (1961:608) provide a concise starting summary:

Jews: (1) have the lowest current fertility (2) expect to have the fewest children (3) want the smallest families (4) approve the use of contraceptives most strongly (5) are most likely to have used contraception (6) are most likely to use the effective appliance method of contraception. On all these aspects of the fertility complex, Catholics differ most from the Jews, and Protestants have an intermediate position.

This summary indicates how complex the idea of fertility is.

As of 1965, the average number of children desired by Catholics was 3.7, compared with an average of 3.0 among Protestants (Ryder and Westoff, 1971:69). These differences in the number of children desired diminish after the birth of the first child, which suggests that Catholic ideals are somewhat attentuated by the trials of actually having children (Bouvier, 1975:72). The average number of children born per family as of 1965 was 2.8 for Catholics, 2.3 for Protestants and 2.1 for Jews. The higher average number of children ever born to Catholics is "almost entirely due to the larger percentage having more than four children and the small percentage having less than two" (Bouvier, 1975:58). Catholic women tend to continue their child-bearing longer than Protestants, and fewer have no children at all.

There are minor differences in fertility within the faiths. Among Protestants, the members of the more conservative denominations and sects have the highest fertility rates. This is almost certainly due to the fact that such sects draw disproportionately from the lower classes, where fertility tends to be higher. However, class would not appear to be a factor where fertility is highest of all—among the Mormons, Hutterites, and Mennonites who lay great stress on the regeneration of the community of believers, and who have created close ties between kinship and religious roles. The number or children per Mennonite woman 35 to 44 years old and ever married is 3.7, compared with 3.0 for the

general population (Kauffman and Harder, 1975:178). Canadian Hutterites report a figure of 745 children 0 to 4 years of age per 1,000
women 15 to 44 in 1971, compared with 292 for Canadian Jews, 358 for
Anglicans and 403 for Catholics (Kalbach and McVey, 1976:238). Within
Catholicism, there are differences in fertility among the various ethnic
groups: Catholics of German ancestry and Spanish-speaking Catholics
have the highest rate, 3.1 children per woman ever married, compared
with a low 2.3 among Slavic Catholics (Greeley, 1974b:42).

The injunction "Be fruitful and multiply and replenish the earth" is
enunciated most firmly by the Catholic Church. The official teachings of
the Catholic Church, as set out in Pope Paul VI's 1968 encyclical
Humanae Vitae is that "a reciprocal act of love which jeopardizes the
responsibility to transmit life which God the Creator, according to particular laws, inserted therein, is in contradiction with the design constitu-
tive of marriage, and with the will of the Author of life." Pope Paul did
not thereby rule out all regulation of family size, for he allowed that "the
physical or psychological conditions of the husband and wife, or . . .
external conditions" might demand the use of contraception so as to
interfere with the procreative process, but he did exclude all forms of
"artificial birth control" in favor of "natural" means, such as continence
and the rhythm method. While the Catholic Church, because of its size,
is the best-known opponent of artificial birth control, it is by no means
the only denomination to take this position in the United States; the
various Orthodox churches and the Mormons also oppose contraception
by any means other than periodic abstinence. The various Protestant
denominations either tacitly support contraception in the interests of
population limitation (for example, the Presbyterians) or refrain from
making binding declarations in this area (for example, the Baptists).

Denomination policies are echoed by the laity. Only 30 percent of
Catholics see their church as telling them how many children to have
(which, indeed, it does not), but *all* are aware that their church prohibits
artificial birth control used to limit family size. A small minority (20
percent) of the most religious Protestants recognize any denominational
direction on contraception, and the the proportion is only slightly higher
(30 percent) among the more religious Jews (Westoff, 1963:83).

But although the Catholic Church takes a clear and unequivocal stand
on the propriety of contraception, and although all Catholics are aware
of this stand, fewer and fewer lay Catholics find themselves able to agree
with this position. The papal encyclical of 1968 ran strongly counter to
the opinion of the laity. In a Gallup Poll conducted in 1971, 58 percent
of the Catholics interviewed agreed that one could ignore the pope's
encyclical and still be a good Catholic (Rosten, 1975:393). Indeed, only
40 percent of the *priests* surveyed in 1969 agreed with the encyclical, and

opposition was almost unanimous among the younger priests (National Opinion Research Center, 1972:103). The proportion of Catholics supporting the traditional view continues to decline: by 1973, 83 percent of all Catholics had come to favor the idea of artificial contraception (Greeley et al., 1976:35).

The most volatile contraception issue in recent years has been the attempt to broaden the grounds on which an abortion is legal. Abortion became more of an issue during the 1970's, when states such as New York passed more liberal abortion laws, the constitutionality of which was upheld by the *Roe* v. *Wade* Supreme Court decision of January, 1973. Subsequent attempts to pass a constitutional amendment outlawing abortions (except under the most stringent conditions) obtained the vigorous backing of the National Conference of Catholic Bishops.

Despite the intense heat of the campaign against more liberal grounds for abortion, and despite the unprecedented lobbying by the Catholic Church, the attitude of the Catholic laity toward abortion is becoming more like that of Protestants. A Gallup Poll conducted in March, 1976, reported that 48 percent of the Protestants surveyed were opposed to any constitutional amendment concerning abortion—but so were 42 percent of the Catholics polled. Catholics continue to be less tolerant of abortion than the more liberal Protestant denominations, such as the Episcopalians, the Presbyterians and the United Church, but on the other hand, they are as tolerant as, if not more tolerant than, members of the more conservative Protestant denominations (Ryder, 1971:278; see also Hertel, 1974). For example, at their annual conference in 1976, the Southern Baptists urged their members not to use abortion as a means of birth control. The stronger opposition of conservative religious groups remains even when controls are imposed for socioeconomic status (Petersen and Mauss, 1976:246).

In the light of all that has been said about changing attitudes toward birth control, it is not surprising that Catholic *practices* should be changing too. An increasing number of American women favor fertility control, and "the greatest change has occurred among Catholic women, many of whom have moved away from exclusive endorsement of the rhythm method" (Ryder and Westoff, 1971:137). The shift is especially noticeable among the better-educated Catholics, who are coming more and more to approximate Protestants in their use of contraceptive techniques.

The proportion of women in the Catholic community using the various kinds of contraception is shown in the following table, adapted from Westoff and Bumpass (1973:42):

TABLE 12:4

**PERCENTAGE OF WHITE, MARRIED CATHOLIC WOMEN AGE 18 TO 39
WHO HAVE NEVER USED ANY METHOD OF CONTRACEPTION OR
WHO MOST RECENTLY USED RHYTHM OR SOME OTHER METHOD... DATA
FOR 1965 DIFFER FROM EARLIER DATA BECAUSE "STERILIZATION
FOR CONTRACEPTIVE REASONS" WAS NOT PREVIOUSLY INCLUDED
AS A FORM OF CONTRACEPTION**

	Women Per Year			
Most Recent Method	*1955*	*1960*	*1965*	*1970*
None	43%	30%	21%	18%
Rhythm	27	31	28	14
Other	30	38	51	68
	100	100	100	100

In other words, the percentage of Catholic women using a contraceptive technique other than the approved rhythm method has more than doubled in 15 years, the greatest increase coming in the last 5 years. The decline in the proportion using no method at all is particularly marked.

Among Catholic women under 24, the proportion not conforming has risen from 30 percent to 78 percent in fifteen years. As Westoff and Bumpass (1973:43) point out, "It is not surprising that women tend to adopt more effective methods as they grow older; as a cohort ages, increasing proportions have had all the children they want and thus face the risk of unwanted pregnancies." Remarkably, even the proportion of younger Catholics using artificial methods has risen sharply. Catholics are now indistinguishable from the general population in their contraceptive practices, including, according to one small study (McCormick, 1975) their willingness to abort. This change does not necessarily mean a *general* decline in Catholic commitment, of course. It may simply mean a refusal to follow the Church on this particular issue, combined with the availability of the more efficient and easy-to-use contraceptive pill (Westoff and Bumpass, 1973:44). It probably also reflects changing preferences. The number of children desired by Catholics fell from 3.3 in 1967 to 2.8 in 1971, and this decline was greatest among young Catholic women (Bouvier, 1975:84).

Thus, Catholics seem to be moving closer to Protestants in their fertility. However, two important differences remain. Catholics are less likely than Protestants to use the most efficient method of contraception—the pill (Bouvier, 1972:517). Second, Catholics are less willing to use birth control techniques of any kind before the birth of their first child, and they experience a shorter interval before its birth (Bouvier, 1975:62).

The use of the contraceptive pill is more common among working Catholic women than among those who do not have a job outside the home. Catholic women who work outside the home are also more likely to combine the use of the pill with support for more modern sex roles, which stress the independence of women. Interestingly, this does not hold for nonworking Catholic women, among whom there is a negative correlation between pill use and support for modern sex roles. It is hard to account for this. As Scanzoni (1975:185) questions, "Do younger, more modern Catholic wives prefer to experience familistic costs earlier rather than later; or does reduced contraceptive rigor somehow stimulate equalitarianism?" In any case, as the pill has become more widely available, as more modern sex roles have been diffused, as the number of women in the labor force has increased, and as the level of education of Catholics has risen, the contraceptive practices and fertility rates of Catholics and Protestants have moved closer together.

FACTORS AFFECTING THE RELATION BETWEEN RELIGION AND FERTILITY

Religion is not the only determinant of family size. Social class considerations, among others, influence the number and spacing of children in a family. Furthermore, the extent of conformity to religious norms such as those of the Catholic Church appears to vary from one social group to another. It is important to ask, then, why the relation between religion and fertility should vary.

Strength of Religious Commitment and Fertility

If the object of investigation is conformity to a religious norm, it is to be expected that variations in strength of religious commitment will be important. Among Catholics, regularity of church attendance is positively associated with the number of children a couple expects to have (Ryder and Westoff, 1971:72). Conformity to church doctrine on birth control is also strongest among those frequently attending Mass and receiving Communion (Ryder and Westoff, 1971:188; Bouvier, 1975:146). Among Protestants and Jews, for whom religious injunctions on birth control are not as important, there is no relation at all between strength of religious commitment and number of expected children (Finney, 1971:46). Only among Lutherans and Presbyterians has some slight positive correlation between regularity of church attendance and number of expected children appeared (Finney, 1971:185). Among Protestants as a whole, fertility depends much more upon social status factors. For Catholics, social status considerations do help shape fertility patterns, but strength of adult commitment to religion is far more important (Finney, 1971:193). Scanzoni (1975:87) found that among Catholics, religious devoutness and traditional attitudes toward sex were mutually supportive: "Wives who have been more traditional have been more devout, which in turn reinforces and perhaps increases traditionalism, and so forth. Acting together, both elements have evidently resulted in larger families."

Regularity of church attendance is one sign of religious commitment, and among all Catholics and some Protestant denominations it is positively related to fertility. This association is probably a reflection of the mutual reinforcement of strong orthodox religiosity and traditional attitudes toward the family. It is also to be expected that conformity to Church-inspired norms of fertility will be influenced by level of religious education. Students at Catholic schools receive explicit instruction in the philosophy of the family as seen by the Church, and are encouraged to internalize Church values on marriage and the family. Catholics attending mixed schools are exposed to divergent views. It has been found that "Catholics who were educated exclusively within church-related schools expressed preferences for larger families and exhibited less control over fertility than Catholics whose education was in the public schools" (Westoff, 1963:94).[4] Does this mean that attending parochial school causes an individual to conform more closely to orthodox teachings concerning the family? Not necessarily, for the more devout (and the more fertile) Catholics are more likely to send their children to parochial school in the first place. It is likely that both family background and schooling increase conformity (Finney, 1971:49). Ryder (1973:66) explains the relationship as follows:

> Certainly some of the excess of Catholic over non-Catholic fertility has been the consequence of the Church's disapproval of all means of fertility regulation, except the notoriously ineffective rhythm method, but this explanation bypasses the point that Catholics have, at least until very recently, accepted this limitation on their exercise of reproductive rationality. Moreover, Catholics have always reported that they want more children than non-Catholics. Probably the predominant source of support for this desire for relatively more children, and of acquiesence to restrictions on effective fertility regulation, is the subcultural emphasis on family solidarity as the bedrock of the social order, as can also be seen in

[4]Secular education tends to reduce Catholic fertility (Finney, 1971:126).

the strength of the Catholic opposition to premarital contraception, to divorce, and to equality for women. The Catholic family, like the Catholic Church, retains a patriarchial structure. Commitment to spiritual values competes with secular interests that would promote lower fertility. And finally, the Catholic community provides consolation and reassurance for those who have more children than they can support.

The independent effect of the family and especially its conjoint effect with parochial education should not be underestimated when the causes of fertility are being measured.

Social Class, Religion, and Fertility

Although variations in the strength and nature of religious commitment are obviously of great importance in explaining differences in fertility rates, there are also social class factors to be considered. Social class is commonly acknowledged to be an important influence on fertility. It is necessary, then, to establish the relationship among social class, religion, and fertility.

Overall, there is a negative association between fertility and income level. But for Catholic women, fertility is positively related to level of living (Westoff, 1963:130; Ryder and Westoff, 1971:79). The more dollars their husbands make, the more children they plan to have. Catholics seem to feel that the financial costs of additional children should be borne, and that a couple should have as many children as they can afford (but no more). Another measure of class, educational attainment, is negatively related to fertility in all three faiths, as the following table, adapted from Goldstein (1968:119) shows:

TABLE 12:5

NUMBER OF CHILDREN AT TIME OF INTERVIEW BY FAITH AND AGE GROUP

Husband's Education	Catholic		Non-Catholic		Jew	
	18–29	30–39	18–29	30–39	18–29	30–39
Under 12 years	2.4	3.3	2.1	2.9	—	—
12 years	2.1	3.1	1.8	2.5	1.8	2.2
Over 12 years	2.0	3.1	1.5	2.5	1.4	2.3

All three faiths show somewhat of a decline in fertility with higher levels of education, although in the older cohorts this difference has disappeared in the case of Jews and is not as marked among Catholics as among non-Catholics. Thus, there are both religious differences *and* class differences in regard to fertility. This raises the question as to the relative weight of these two factors. Freedman et al. (1961:610) believe that the differences in fertility between the two faiths that do not have firm positions on birth control (Protestants and Jews) are reducible to class differences. Thus, the lower fertility rates of Jews compared with Protestants are attributable to the concentration of Jews in superior educational, occupational, and income categories. The higher fertility rates of Catholics are not completely reducible to class differences, however, for Catholics are represented in every occupational, educational and income group (Argyle and Beit-Hallahmi, 1975:159). Although the changes in fertility described above suggest a decline in the impact of religious teachings, religiosity appears to have had a stronger effect historically on overall fertility rates than social class (Westoff, 1963:131). No student wishing to understand the forming and functioning of families can afford to ignore its influence.

RELIGION AND MARITAL SATISFACTION

So far this discussion of religion and the family has looked at the decision to marry, the choice of a marriage partner, and the begetting of children. It is appropriate to turn now to the impact of religion on the marital satisfaction of the parental couple. The assessment of marital satisfaction is beset with measurement problems, but it does seem that the more religious a couple is, the more likely they are to report their marriage a happy one. Landis (1960:342) found that college-age children who saw their parents as more devout tended to see them as more happily married. More directly, however, it has been discovered that "the marital satisfaction scores for both husbands and wives who were church members or who were regular or occasional in their church attendance were consistently higher than the scores of the husbands and wives who were not church members or who did not attend church" (Burchinal, 1957:308). This does not necessarily mean that regular church attendance or church membership causes greater marital satisfaction. People who become church members and attend church regularly are quite likely to be sociable and conformist. Such people are also likely to make tolerable and tolerant marriage partners. Nor does regularity of attendance or even membership say much about religious beliefs and teachings. Thus, it is not clear whether this greater marital satisfaction is the result of shared and internalized norms or merely the consequence of having common voluntary association memberships and social habits. These reservations notwithstanding, the association between strength of orthodox church commitment and marital satisfaction remains.

RELIGION AND DIVORCE

Religious groups differ quite widely in their position on the permanence of the marriage union. The orthodox Catholic attitude toward marriage is that it is a sacrament and therefore indissoluble short of death.

> The ideal situation is that in which two Catholics living in the state of grace receive the sacrament of matrimony at a Nuptial Mass in their own parish church with the intention of preserving a permanent, monogamous, fruitful union. Any deviation from that situation must be considered a deviation from the ideal proposed in the Catholic religion. In varying degrees, therefore, the following fall short of the ideal pattern: afternoon weddings, mixed marriages, civil or religious unions "outside the church," separation, divorce, adultery, birth control, and abortion (Fichter, 1951:96).

Many other religious groups take an equally firm stand on the permanence of the marital union. Although for all Protestants marriage is not a sacrament but an ordinance, some denominations take very seriously Matthew's injunction, "And I say unto you: whoever divorces his wife, except for unchastity, and marries another, commits adultery." Other groups, although they may legitimize certain grounds for separation or divorce other than infidelity, impose strict requirements on the marital pair to sustain the union and forbid the remarrying of a divorced person. Thus, although all the denominations take the position that the family unit, once begun, should be permanent, there is sufficient variation in the strictness with which this is interpreted for the variations in divorce rate by religious group to come as no surprise.

The evidence on whether or not those with religious affiliations are more or less likely to become divorced or separated suggests that religious marriages are on the whole slightly more stable. Vernon (1968b) summarizes the findings of a number of surveys showing that those with no religious affiliation are as much as three times more likely to obtain a divorce than, say, Catholics. More sophisticated data from the 1970 National Fertility Study confirm these findings by and large. Significantly, however, this study found that differences are much reduced when controls for social class are imposed. In other words, the apparent correlation between lack of religious affiliation and likelihood of divorce is in large part attributable to the fact that those without religious affiliation tend to be of higher status, and higher-status people also tend to have higher divorce rates. Thus, when controls for class are imposed, the rate of marital disruption among women who reported they had no religious preference during childhood dropped from six points to only two points above the grand mean, at which point the divorce rate of religious "nones" was found to be lower than the rate for Episcopalians, Baptists, and Fundamentalists. Therefore, it cannot be concluded that religious affiliation, per se and in all cases, enhances the possibilities of a lasting marriage (Bumpass and Sweet, 1972:756).

Differences in divorce rates are to be expected between those of different religious affiliations. Somewhat surprisingly, considering the much stricter Catholic injunctions on this, Catholics have a divorce rate that is 3 percent higher than that of all Protestants. Jews have the most stable marriages: their marital-instability rate is almost seven points below the grand mean. Within Protestantism, the highest rate of marital instability, when all other important influences on marital stability are controlled for, is found among Episcopalians: their rate is eight points above the grand mean. The most stable group of Protestants are the Lutherans. Within Catholicism, there are differences in divorce rates by ethnic group. The Irish show the lowest rate of marital instability (1.8 percent), followed by the Italians (2.0 percent), and the Germans (3.2 percent). The Spanish-speaking Catholics have the highest rate of all—6.6 percent (Greeley, 1974b:46).

The separate analyses of Bumpass and Sweet and Greeley each show that Jews have the most stable marriages. There are only minor differences in the divorce rate of Protestants and Catholics. The different denominations within Protestantism and the different ethnic groups within Catholicism constitute a complex mosaic: some Protestant groups score higher in marital instability than some Catholic groups, even though Protestants as a whole are slighly more stable than Catholics. As with fertility, then, Catholics seem to be becoming more like Protestants in the matter of divorce.

Two questions remain about interfaith differences in divorce rate. There is some reason to believe that rates of divorce and desertion among Catholics are underreported. The very strong injunctions against divorce in the Catholic Church probably dispose many Catholics to leave the Church at the point that they begin to think about leaving their spouse. The result is, of course, that the number of Catholic unions sundered is underreported. Although this kind of behavior no doubt occurs in all the churches, it is reasonable to suppose that it happens more frequently where the injunctions are the strongest. It is also probable that the distribution of desertions to divorces in the Catholic community is different from that found among Protestants. The prohibition of divorce on all but the narrowest of grounds probably means that the severing of a Catholic marriage is more likely to take the form of desertion than divorce. For this reason, although the overall rate of marital instability may be quite similar among Catholics and Protestants, the desertion rate of Catholics is probably higher. One study has indeed found this to be so. Monahan and Kephart (1954:464) found that Catholics were overrepresented among cases of desertion by 40 percent, Jews by 40 percent, and Protestants by only 25 percent. This suggests that much of the marital disharmony among Catholics is not expressed in crude divorce rates but remains hidden.

The divorce rates for members of all three faiths have been rising, and attitudes toward divorce are changing in the direction of extending the number of grounds on which a pair may legitimately and permanently separate. Accompanying this issue is the question of whether or not remarriage be permitted. The changes have been most marked among the Catholic laity, who, as in the case of birth control usage, seem to be moving in advance of the official position of the Church. By 1971, a Gallup Poll was showing that 60 percent of Catholics disagreed with the official Church position that a divorced Catholic who remarries is living in sin (Rosten, 1975:492). A 1973 survey showed that 73 percent of Catholics approved of remarriage after divorce (Greeley, 1976:35). Even a majority of priests are in favor of divorce being available on more liberal grounds (National Opinion Research Center, 1972:117). If this trend continues, the remaining differences between Protestants and Catholics will disappear, and only smaller, more conservative groups such as the Mormons will continue to uphold the stringent requirements of marital permanence.

THE FATE OF MIXED MARRIAGES

From all that has been said so far, mixed marriages would seem to have a poor chance of success. Is this true? Many people certainly believe so (Marty et al., 1968:262). College students contemplating marriage feel that religious differences are much more difficult to handle in a marriage than economic, ethnic, or educational differences, and second only to racial mixing in their threat to marital happiness (Gordon, 1964:37). Research has indeed shown that "disharmony and instability are markedly more frequent among religiously mixed couples than among couples sharing the same religious affiliation: (Crockett, 1969:464). The chief source of controversy is, not surprisingly, the upbringing of the children (Rosten, 1975:561).

Accumulated data on the fate of mixed marriages warrant the following generalizations:

1. Protestant-Catholic mixed marriages are less stable than religiously homogeneous marriages. They are about five percentage points less stable than Protestant-Protestant marriages, eleven points less stable than all-Catholic marriages, and sixteen percentage points less stable than intra-Jewish marriages. The marriage in which a Catholic woman marries a non-Catholic man is slightly more likely to last than the reverse (Bumpass and Sweet, 1972:764; see also Burchinal, 1963).

2. When a Catholic marries outside the faith, one of the important determinants of marital stability is the faith into which he or she marries. Burchinal (1963), using a rather limited set of data from Iowa, uncovered a pattern of increasing Catholic outmarriage instability as the denomination into which the individual married became further removed theologically and ecclesiastically. Thus, Catholic-Lutheran marriages are the most stable, followed by Catholic-Presbyterian and Catholic-Methodist, with Catholic-Baptist the least stable. Unfortunately, these comparisons are not controlled for class, and class-mixing also makes marriage unstable, but the suggestion is nevertheless there that marriage between spouses of different religious subcultures (as with the Baptist-Catholic union) are less stable.

3. The lowest rate of marital stability of all is found among Catholics who marry those of no religious faith (see Burchinal, 1963).

4. There is no general support for the proposition that interdenominational Protestant marriages have higher instability rates than intradenominational marriages. However, *some* interdenominational marriages are considerably less stable than marriages between spouses of the same denomination, less stable, in fact, than Protestant-Catholic marriages. For example, social class and all other variables being controlled for, marriages between Baptists are fourteen percentage points more stable than Baptist woman-Lutheran man marriages (Bumpass and Sweet, 1972:765).

5. The evidence on the importance of religious mixing relative to mixing by age or class is inconsistent. Burchinal (1963:362) found that "the marital survival rates for interreligious marriages in the same age and status subsample exceeded those for religious homogeneous marriages in other age and status subsamples." This would seem to suggest that the influence of religion on the behavior of marriage partners is declining. Interestingly, though, Bumpass and Sweet (1970:765), in their analysis of much sounder national data, conclude that although age and educational differences influence marital stability, the mixing of religious faiths is still the most threatening factor of all.

The data on the consequences of intermarriage remain crude and scanty, and the grounds on which to base any kind of interpretation are therefore flimsy indeed. It is tempting to adopt the obvious theory that all mixing in marriage (especially if it includes a clash of values) threatens the stability of the marriage. Therefore, marriage between religiously dissimilar spouses will be a high risk. But it need not be assumed that religious mixing causes instability, even though the association is admitted. It is quite likely that those who enter into mixed marriages are different anyway. They are likely to be less committed to the values of their group, less able to compete in the marriage marketplace (and therefore, it might be reasoned, less likely to be able to sustain a marriage), or simply more liberal and therefore more likely to be willing to countenance separation or divorce in the event of discord.

In accounting for the instability of mixed marriages, one must also recognize that intermarriage, like all marriage, occurs within a network of roles. The success or failure of a marriage depends a great deal on the religious behavior of significant others, especially kinfolk. An interfaith marriage is more likely to end in separation or divorce when the faiths of these significant others are widely divergent and strongly espoused.

RELIGION AND CHILD SOCIALIZATION

All denominations have something to say about the proper relationship between parents and children, about how children are to be brought up, about sex-role development, and about how children should behave with regard to the adult world in general. Religious training is something that all but two percent of American parents feel they should give their children (Marty et al., 1968:208; Scanzoni, 1971:286). Thus it is legitimate to see it as a normal part of the upbringing of any child.

The significance of religion in socialization is further indicated in the attitude most parents take toward the church. They see it as a place of character building for their children, and a means of helping to keep the family together (Fairchild and Wynn, 1961:177). Children are frequently the most important consideration in choosing a particular church—ahead of the minister, the location of the church, its programs, and even the denomination of which it is a part (Campbell and Fukuyama, 1970:59; see also Berger and Nash, 1962).[5]

---

[5]Sharot (1976:150) observes of the Jews that, although the synagogue might be used infrequently for worship, "many parents join in order that their children should attend the congregational classes, absorb a sense of Jewish identity, and associate with other Jewish children."

The influence of children's needs on churchgoing points to the impact of the life cycle on religious practices. It has been long recognized that there are age variations in church attendance (Anders, 1955:56), but it has become increasingly clear that these variations are a function not so much of age per se as of movement through the life cycle. Couples with growing children have the highest rate of church attendance (Weldon and Johnson, 1975:794). The relation between children's needs and patterns of attendance by age is especially strong for women (Glock et al., 1967:54).[6]

It has been assumed in the past that frequency of church attendance by parents levels off after children enter adolescence and declines after middle age. Using data from a longitudinal study, Blazer and Palmore (1976:84) were able to show that there is indeed a decline in religious activities amongst those over sixty, particularly those in nonmanual occupations—perhaps because their attendance rates were already high. The decline accelerates among those over seventy, probably because of deterioration in health, vision, and hearing. However, the feeling that religion is important to oneself increases with age, as does certainty of the existence of God (Moberg, 1965:80).[7]

The detail in which a church actually stipulates appropriate child-rearing methods varies from one denomination to another. Groups as disparate as the Catholic Church and the Seventh Day Adventists take a close interest in the way members' children are brought up, whereas other denominations, such as the United Church and the Presbyterians, seem to use a more indirect approach. Unfortunately, little evidence exists concerning the impact of church teachings on methods of child rearing. It is known that theologically more conservative parents adhere more strongly to more traditional methods of child rearing which emphasize authority and obedience (Kersten, 1970:159). And yet, Kunz (1963) found that Mormon parents were no different from others in how they reared their children, despite the traditional, strict methods

---

[6] Although parents with children of Sunday school age are the most regular church attenders of all those who pass through the normal life cycle, it is those without children who are the most frequent and regular attenders of all (Glock et al., 1967:73).

[7] Bahr (1970), drawing on life history interviews, arrives at a different conclusion about the relation between aging and church attendance. He discovered that with advancing age church attendance becomes steadily less important as a source of voluntary affiliation. Wingrove and Alston (1974:330), using cohort analysis, found so much variation in the relation between age and church attendance among five different age cohorts that generalizations on this score were impossible. They conclude that, although church attendance does vary slightly with age, it is influenced more strongly by social events. For example, it is clear that the attendance peak for all age cohorts occurred during the religious revival of the 1950's, and attendance rates for all age cohorts declined after 1960 (Wingrove and Alston, 1974:326).

enjoined by their church. Clearly, much more data are needed in this area before firm conclusions can be drawn.

SEX ROLES

Religion is probably the single most important shaper of sex roles. The traditional notion of woman's inferiority to man has been consistently legitimized by the Church: the Talmud, Canon Law, and the Bible—indeed, the whole corpus of Western religious literature—affirms this relation. The Reformation, though theoretically modifying the Catholic domination of women, merely changed the mode of subjugation by confining the woman to the home (where lay her special calling) and allocating to the man the more instrumental vocation of producer outside the home. Only sects such as the Quakers and Unitarians dissented from this view.

Christian theology has associated original sin with the temptation of Adam by Eve, and casts women in the role of the evil principle to be avoided except as a tool for procreation. Equally as a means of avoidance and subjugation, women have been desexualized and venerated as spiritual beings (Mariolatry is one manifestation of this attitude). In this way, they are robbed of any status as economic producers or political actors. At the same time, theologians, especially Catholics, have applied to the man/woman relationship the same operation/cooperation relation found in the Christ/Mary relationship.

In the Catholic tradition,

> the Eternal Woman is said to have a vocation for surrender and secrecy; hence the symbol of the veil. Self-less, she achieves not individual realisation but merely general fulfillment in motherhood, physical and spiritual. She is said to be timeless and conservative by nature. She is shrouded in "mystery," because she is not recognised as a genuine human person. (Daly, 1970:127)

One implication of this notion of the "Eternally Feminine" is that women are made into something "totally other," impossible to identify with or enter into a normal relationship with. Women are thereby transformed into a caste, and in this sense they share the same fate of blacks and Jews. The Catholic Church expresses this ideal not only in its family ethics but also in its own structure—the celibacy of the all-male priesthood, the denial to women of even minor liturgical functions, the refusal to admit women as Mass servers, and the injunction that women cover their heads while in church. The Eastern Orthodox Churches are identical in this regard.

It is to be expected from this glance at the Catholic position on sex roles that they would conform most closely to traditional notions of masculine and feminine behavior, and this is indeed the case. Catholics are more likely than Protestants to believe that the man should have authority in the home, that women should not go outside the home to work, and that the chief role of the woman is motherhood. This finding is especially true for Catholic men (Scanzoni, 1975:34,42). Significantly, however, among younger women there are no religious differences in sex-role images. Younger Catholic women are just as likely as Protestants to have modern ideas about the position of women.

If broad interfaith differences in sex-role images are disappearing, this does not mean that religion no longer makes a difference in how the roles of men and women are perceived. It is to be expected, for example, that theologically more conservative church members, whatever their denomination, will be more in favor of traditional sex-role images. For instance, many conservative Protestants are more traditional than the majority of Catholics. The Southern Baptists are probably typical of the more conservative Protestant denominations in their position that "the submission of the wife is not a demand on the part of the husband"; rather, "it is a response in accordance with the Divine intent and the wife's basic need" (Kelsey, 1973:163).

Many Protestants believe, as do many Catholics, that each sex has a definite role and function—one the child bearer and the other the bread winner. This position follows logically from the story of the "first marriage ceremony in the Garden of Eden" (Graham, 1975:423). The sexes are mutually complementary: "Man, biologically and emotionally strong, needed the seasoning of tenderness that woman alone could provide, and she in turn required man's strength and leadership qualities to complete her, to give her fulfillment."

According to prominent Protestants such as Billy Graham, Christianity, far from helping subjugate woman, has been her only chance of spiritual fulfillment and contentment. Social equality, however, is out of the question, for "the Lord God decreed that man should be the titular head of the family." It stands to reason that where views such as these prevail, the women's liberation movement will be anathema.

What has been the position of the denominations on the issue of women's rights? Although the Catholic Church has given vigorous support to organizations *opposing* the Equal Rights Amendment, and although fraternal organizations like the Knights of Columbus have also been actively opposed, the Catholic laity are more likely than Protestants to favor the amendment (Gallup, 1974b:17). The strength of traditional views of the woman's role in large denominations such as the Southern Baptists and the Mormons, not to mention the numerous fringe groups such as the Hutterites (Hostetler, 1974:145) and Jehovah's witnesses (Beckford, 1975b:54), is sufficient to weight against the opinions of the more liberal Protestant denominations. There are no overall interfaith differences, then, in support for the women's movement.

One reason for this lack of crude Protestant/Catholic differences, beside the conservatism of many Protestants, is the increasing liberalism of many Catholics. Indeed, the Church itself has been changing its official view in recent years, at least to the extent that a broadened woman's role outside the home and greater equality within it are recognized (Daly, 1968:77). The laity, on their part, are becoming more receptive to a greater role for women in the Church. A little less than a third of the Catholics polled in 1973 would approve the ordination of women as priests (Greeley et al., 1976:29). However, the Pope repeated his opposition to this idea in 1977. Attitudes are also changing in the Protestant denominations that are associated most closely with the Catholic Church. The Episcopal Church began ordaining women in 1977, joining the Canadian Anglican Church in this respect. However, the Church of England has rejected the idea. Even the Jews, who hold strongly patriarchial religious attitudes, have begun to change their attitude toward women. The Rabbinical Assembly, the representative voice of the Conservative branch of Judaism, voted in the early 1970s to henceforth count women for a *minyon*—the minimum number of adults (ten) needed for communal worship. However, women have a long way to go before equality is achieved. Only 1.8 percent of the ministers in the United Methodist Church in 1971 were women, and these were more likely to be part-time workers, paid lower salaries, employed in rural areas and in smaller churches. Only one in 506 District Superintendents were women, and there were no female bishops (Smith et al., 1974:14,17).[8]

RELIGION AND THE REGULATION OF SEXUAL BEHAVIOR

Although the family performs important economic and political functions, its chief function is the regulation of sexual relations. In an important sense, kinship structures *are* the definition of normal sex. Thus rules prohibiting incest regulate sexual competition among close kin and pre-

[8]Whether or not a denomination ordains women says as much about its theory of the ministry as it does about its views of women. This is one reason why a theologically conservative denomination such as the Southern Baptists will agree to ordain women, but a theologically liberal denomination like the Episcopalians will be reluctant to do so. Relations with other denominations also play a part in the decision to ordain women. For example, many Anglicans are reluctant to ordain women because they fear that it could impede union with the Catholic Church.

pare children for entry into their own mature sexual life. The churches have traditionally played a large part in the determination and enforcement of the norms regulating sexual behavior, usually working through the family, the primary agent of socialization.

Argyle and Beit-Hallahmi (1975:153–54), reviewing a number of studies concerning the relation between religion and sexual practices, conclude that, overall, religious people are much more likely to subscribe to and conform to traditional sexual norms concerning the monogamous, sexually exclusive family unit than nonreligious people. However, there are variations by strength of religious commitment and by faith. There is a negative correlation between the degree of religious involvement and the attitudes held by young people concerning sexual behavior as shown by data from a 1967 study of college students conducted by Ruppel (1970:652):

TABLE   12:6

RELIGIOSITY AND SEXUAL PERMISSIVENESS BY ACADEMIC CLASS

Religiosity	High Permissiveness	
	Freshman	Senior
Low	68.2%	83.7%
Moderate	45.9	32.6
High	18.9	18.2

Conformity to traditional sexual norms is clearly much lower among the less religious—a relationship that becomes stronger during the college career. Although the Catholic Church has the public image of being more conservative in its ideas about sexual behavior, Catholics are much more likely to have engaged in premarital sexual intercourse than Protestants. The Protestant/Catholic differences are about the same for men and women; but Jewish men are more like Catholic men in their higher rates of premarital sexual activity, while Jewish women are more like Protestant women in showing lower rates (Blood, 1972:112). Of all groups, the negative correlation between religiosity and premarital sex is strongest for men (Landis, 1960:345).

In recent years, some churches (especially the more liberal Protestant denominations) have changed their approach to the regulation of sexual conduct, moving from appeals to Biblical texts and simple· punitive prohibitions to the use of sociological and psychological arguments concerning the effects of premarital and extramarital sexual activity on community stability and individual mental health. A version of this approach, "situation ethics," which stresses above all that two individuals be fully aware of the implications of their act toward each other and not exploit each other, became very popular during the 1960s.

RELIGION AND JUVENILE DELINQUENCY

In addition to sexual conduct, the impress of church teachings should be visible in other areas of morality. Unfortunately, very little is known about this subject.

> What is known about delinquency, crime, and religion is as follows: The relationship of religion and deviant behavior is obscure; early studies . . . can only be accepted as quasi-scientific attempts to measure the problem; wide debate exists as to whether religious principles are distinctive and can be measured discretely from other values; little is known about the role of the clergy or chaplain in the correctional process; and research into the proper function of religion in prevention of crime and delinquency is nonexistent (Knudten and Knudten, 1971:148).

According to two studies, church attendance has a weak, positive relation to respect for police authority, but is otherwise unrelated to support for moral codes (Hirschi and Stark, 1973:77; Burkett and White, 1974). A study of tenth graders in Atlanta, however, uncovered a negative relation between church attendance and juvenile delinquency—perhaps a reflection of differences between the North (where the two earlier studies were conducted, and the South, where church attendance might say more about moral behavior in general (Higgins and Albrecht, 1977). It is hard, then, to discover any consistent influence of religion on youthful moral behavior. Whether this is actually the case, or merely reflects faulty research methods, is a question which cannot be settled without further work in this area.

CONCLUSION

The impress of religion on the family is evident throughout the life cycle. In turn, religious behavior is to some degree a reflection of the different interests and demands of the individual at various stages of that life cycle. Religion clearly influences the decision whether or not to marry, and has a marked (but now declining) influence on the definition of the field of eligibles from whom the future marriage partner will be chosen. The barrier between Jews and Gentiles is stronger than that between Protestants and Catholics. Indeed, Catholics show a greater willingness than several Protestant denominations to break what are for them quite strong prohibitions against intermarriage. Those who do break endogamy norms seem to be distinctive on a number of counts. Most obviously, they are not as religious as those who conform to the norm. They also tend to live in areas where fellow church members constitute a small proportion of the population, they tend to come from families in which social control has been weak, and social class considerations may have promoted their outmarriage. It is certainly the more marginal church members who marry out and, in this sense, the churches have remained firm on the issue. Mixed marriages are much more likely to result in marital instability, the chief cause of which is disputes over the upbringing of the children.

Assuming that marriage takes place, the next step in the life cycle is the bearing of children. Religion has a clear and marked effect on the size of families. As is popularly supposed, Catholics do indeed have higher rates of fertility, but these rates are falling as the Catholic community becomes more highly educated and better assimilated into American society. Although social class considerations also help determine family size, religion remains an important, if not the most important, influence.

The churches also have an impact on the permanence of the marital union. Marriages in which both partners are religious seem to be happier and in general have a greater chance of enduring. Jews have the most stable marriages of all, but no overall comparisons between Protestants and Catholics can be made because of their internal differences. Among Protestants, Lutherans have the most stable marriages, but the Episcopalians' rate of divorce far exceeds that in the Catholic community.

Relatively little research has been conducted on the impact of religion on child socialization. The churches promote clear conceptions of sex roles and offer explicit teachings on proper sexual behavior. The Catholic Church and Judaism have been thought of as having the more traditional notions of sex roles and sexual relations, and indeed Catholics do tend to be more traditional in both respects. Here again, attitudes seem to be changing and younger Catholics are closer to Protestants in their views on these two issues. Finally, on the basis of even more limited data, it is possible to conclude that the impress of church teachings on the moral behavior of adolescents in areas other than sex is not really visible. There is no relationship between religiosity and juvenile delinquency. However, this might well reflect the inadequacy of the research as much as the actual state of affairs. The considerable variations in American family life can in some part, then, be attributed to the impact of religion, although religious differences (and therefore, perhaps, the salience of religion itself) seem to be waning.

Part IV

RELIGIOUS DIVERSITY
AND
SOCIAL CONFLICT

13

A

CHANGE OF VIEW

Of the many integrative forces working in society to offset the dislocating impact of competing interests, religion is surely one of the most important. The Church provides an overarching scheme of values which sanctifies political and economic objectives and integrates one social institution with another. It also identifies the individual with the group, gives support in times of personal crises, and offers a means of overcoming guilt and alienation. Religion is a powerful antidote to social dislocation at the individual level, at the level of the family, of the community and of the nation.

Religious diversity is, of course, a fact of modern societies, as is a considerable amount of social disharmony. But neither of these facts weakens the functionalist argument about the role of religion in society. Religious diversity in the context of genuine pluralism enhances rather than destroys social integration. According to the functionalist model, society is a network of organized groups and associations, reflecting the diversity of social identities and economic interests present. No single organization or group of organizations can dominate, since no organization has exclusive control over all the resources necessary to do so. It is a system of checks and balances. The laws and customs of the land reflect the equilibrium reached in the group struggle at any given moment. Religion, as a differentiated base of interest, helps distribute power and influence among several social groups and thus inhibits the polarization of society, establishing at the same time, cross-cutting ties to ensure that no single loyalty predominates, except that to the nation as a unit. The latent consequence of religious diversity is, then, to enhance social integration. The few irreligious people in society constitute no threat to this finely equilibrated system.

This is the perspective that has informed Part III of this book. From this standpoint, religion does indeed appear to contribute a great deal to the proper socialization of people into the ways of society, and to the strengthening of a society's institutions. In Part IV, a change in the angle of vision occurs. Some of these functionalist assumptions are going to be challenged. In the process, the emphasis is going to shift—from equilibrium to imbalance, from harmony to conflict, from order to disorder, from values and norms to interests and power. Functionalism tends to play down religious conflict and its relationship to social conflict, whereas the view to be adopted in Part IV emphasizes just these features. In its emphasis on the consequences of a pattern of belief and behavior for the maintenance of society as a whole, functionalism has a distinct (although not inevitable) tendency to see only the integrative side of religion. The functionalist's stress on the harmonizing, integrating, and psychologically supportive consequences of religion rather than the disruptive, disintegrative and psychologically disturbing effects follows from their tendency to exaggerate the harmony between culture and social structure. As Geertz (1973:144) points out, culture and social structure are capable of a wide range of modes of coexistence, "of which the simple, isomorphic mode is but a limiting case—a case common only in societies which have been stable over such an extended time as to make possible a close adjustment between social and cultural aspects."

The functionalists' consensual view of society has two consequences, both of which need to be questioned here. First, in the functionalist view, religious diversity is of interest because of its contribution to pluralism. The diversity of religious traditions and groups found in modern society is of interest because it demonstrates the way in which members of society, through a web of group affiliations, build a sense of loyalty to the society as a whole and to no one group in particular. They are also more likely to resist the concentration of power in a single, homogeneous group at the top. There is no doubt that this is a plausible model of how a system with religious differences might work. It is equally obvious, however, that religious differences are *not* always integrative, especially when they coincide with other social differences, such as class, ethnicity, race, and politics. The extremes of conflict witnessed in Ulster, and to a lesser extent in Belgium, the Netherlands and Canada—not to mention the United States in various times and places—are sufficient to indicate that religion can intensify conflict, sharpen hatreds, and promote disharmony.

Second, functionalists are wont to write about religion promoting consensus on a society's values. But society is not a harmonious whole, and consensus on values and societal objectives cannot be assumed in this way. Society is a world in which order is the product not only of normative agreement but also of coercion applied in the course of constant and bitter struggles for power. It makes little sense, from this perspective, to refer to religion-in-general sanctifying values-in-general. Religion functions not for "society" but so as to legitimize the demands of specific groups. To some extent, this function accounts for the differences among religious groups. Religious diversity is a sign not of pluralist harmony but of conflict between different social groups, each of which finds legitimation for its own interests and values in a different religion. The existence of religious hegemony, a situation in which the majority of the population apparently subscribes to the same broad religious principles, is no obstacle to the adoption of this contrary view. The dominance of a "mainstream" can be attributed to the power of elite groups to ensure the acceptance of religious ideas that are most congenial to their interests. In short, by shifting out of the functionalist framework and using a conflict model, one may appreciate the ideological character of religion.

The contrasting perspectives just outlined represent two competing paradigms in sociology. The first, the functionalist perspective, is challenged by the second, a "conflict-oriented" or Marxian view. The "assumptive legacy" of this conflict theory is Marxism. Its major tenets are as follows (Jonathan Turner, 1974:80).

1. Although social relationships display systematic features, these relationships are rife with conflicting interests.
2. This fact reveals that social systems systematically generate conflict.
3. Conflict is therefore an inevitable and pervasive feature of social systems.
4. Such conflict tends to be manifested in the bipolar opposition of interests.
5. Conflict occurs most frequently over the distribution of scarce resources.
6. Conflict is a major source of social change in social systems.

Assumptions such as these contradict functionalist ideas about the bases of social order and demand that different kinds of questions be asked about institutions such as religion. It is the purpose of Part IV of this book to use the "assumptive legacy" of Marxist sociology to ask additional questions about the role of religion in society.

More than anything else, this change in the angle of vision means a different view of the relationship between religion and social class. To the more conflict-oriented theorist, social inequalities reflect the differentiation of competing interest groups in a society on the basis of productive relations. To the functionalist, social inequality means the multi-dimensional differentiation of individuals in terms of social superiority and inferiority as measured by the dominant value system of the society. In Part III religious diversity appears as one way in which status differences are symbolized and affirmed. Different levels of status reflect different positions in a race for a common prize. That different religious groups tend to finish "ahead" means merely that some have run the race (or even started it) with an advantage. However, it is possible to see social inequalities in a rather different light and consider their relation to religious differences from another viewpoint altogether. It is equally plausible, for instance, to regard the unequal distribution of life-chances in modern society as meaning that the access of legitimate individuals to elite positions in society is severly restricted. In other words, it is reasonable to assume that the major socioeconomic division in society is between the few and the many. The imagery of the "status ladder" comprising many finely graded rungs up and down which status-seeking individuals move is abandoned in favor of a conflict-group imagery that stresses the importance not of individuals, but of positions, group ties and group consciousness. Models of class conflict break down the stratification system into a few basic groups differentiated by radical discontinuities in wealth and power, and anticipate that elites will use all means (including religion) to maintain their position and prevent those below from undermining it.

By invoking the concept of ideology and by stressing the importance of power differences in society, the conflict model challenges the functionalist view that religion functions as a promoter of neutral integrative values. The difference is partly one of perceived priorities. Functionalists are not disposed to believe that technology and economic institutions are sufficient to engender social order. Social stability can be achieved, they argue, only through a morality that rests ultimately in religion—although this need not be orthodox religion. Functionalists thus tend to see religion, or values in general, as causal agents. Conflict theorists on the other hand see economic forces as a sufficient cause for social order (not necessarily consensus). Their interest in religious beliefs is in their power to legitimize present economic arrangements. Conflict theorists are therefore likely to see ideological elements in religious beliefs and practices (see Birnbaum, 1973). The "consensus" that religion engenders becomes, in the conflict model, "hegemony," because it is a set of dominant ideas reflecting the interest of the ruling class. These ideas condition members of subordinate classes to voluntarily support the political and economic institutions that guarantee ruling class domination. Assuming this, one may then ask what kinds of interests are furthered by the unity established by religious socialization. It is also possible to query the economic political interests expressed in the religious diversity in America. It might well be that religious "pluralism" is a technique whereby a variety of life styles and attitudes are accommodated under one dominant value system and "real" social conflicts are masked. If this is so, the existence of a limited religious diversity beneath a "mainstream" orthodoxy assumes a rather different meaning. That a very small group of church people do not belong to this mainstream and that among this group there are a few who criticize certain social practices (in order to preserve the general scheme of things) does not undermine this assumption.

The assumptions of the conflict theorist will largely guide the analysis in Chapters 14, 15, 16 and 17. In Chapter 14, the relationship between social class and religion will be examined. The object will be to investigate the extent to which religion buttresses major social class divisions in the United States and serves as a means of controlling access to elite positions of power and wealth. To some extent, the data presented in Chapter 11 will have to be reinterpreted because the close links between economic and political elites and certain forms of Protestantism have already been hinted at. In Chapter 14, the data on economic differences between Protestants, Catholics and Jews will be presented in much more detail. The major questions to be dealt with are these: Is there a Protestant establishment? In other words, are there high-echelon groups, linked by tradition and values to historical Protestantism, who use religion to sustain their position of dominance? This thesis is partly substantiated if significant differences in socioeconomic level among Protestants, Catholics, and Jews can be found. However, the thesis is not invalidated if small differences in status criteria fail to appear, if at the same time it can be shown that significant differences in wealth and power remain.

A further thesis of conflict theorists is that religion can operate so as to mask real divisions by substituting unreal ones. For this reason, it is important to look at the relationship between religious and racial and ethnic differences. Race and ethnicity are two ways in which class differences are broken up or (more cynically) masked. To the extent that religious identification and identification with other ascriptive groups like ethnic community coincide, class conflict will be attenuated. Conflict theorists favor a model of ethnic pluralism in which one group is perceived as controlling (and usually oppressing) another rather than the simple assimilation or melting pot model. Chapter 15 will look at the role of religion in ethnic and racial conflict.

Finally, in Chapters 16 and 17, the focus will once more be upon politics. Again, a tradition of party loyalty is associated with religious identification in the United States. Chapter 16 will examine the contemporary strength of this association and the extent to which it modifies class voting. Chapter 17 will examine the extent to which the churches have, on the other hand, encouraged people to act politically in their economic interests in their championship of radical causes.

THE EXTENT OF RELIGIOUS DIVERSITY

The persuasiveness of the functionalist thesis is seriously undermined by the presence of many competing religious groups in all modern Western societies, but especially in the United States (see Eister, 1957). Part IV considers the consequences of this diversity. It is important in making the transition to the next four chapters to gain some idea of the extent of this diversity. Just how many religious groups are there, what is their relative size and strength, and how significant are the differences between them?

Of course, the mere presence of different religious organizations in a society need have no greater significance than the presence of different sports teams. The reason religious differences are so important is that religion is much more than a voluntary association of people with a common hobby or pastime. A denomination, sect, or church is also a community of people who intermarry, worship together as a family, choose their friends along religious lines, and socialize their children according to the teachings of their faith. Each faith, even each denomination, is a separate subcommunity as well as a voluntary association. It is a way of life, with social clubs, athletic leagues, insurance companies, professional societies, publishing houses, veterans groups, and even movie-rating committees. This communality means that "conflicts between socio-religious groups contain a potentiality for disruptive violence unmatched by any other kind of intrasocial conflict, with the possible exception of those based on class differences" (Lenski, 1963:61).

Conflict between socio-religious groups is exacerbated and prolonged by these parallel institutions. Chief among them is education. Educational agencies not only perpetuate ideological differences in their teachings—students who attend Catholic colleges, for example, "arrive more religious and leave more religious" (Trent and Golds, 1967:203)—but also foster common religious friendships. Thus, Catholics who attend all Catholic schools are much more likely to have all Catholic friends (Trent and Golds, 1967:144). In the United States in particular, the Catholic Church has developed an elaborate array of parallel organizations, including fraternities such as the Knights of Columbus (founded as a counterpart to Freemasonry, which excluded Catholics) and a Catholic press, which comprises about 600 separate magazines and newspapers.

The history of Anglican/Catholic/Nonconformist relations in the

United Kingdom and Protestant/Catholic/Jewish relations in the United States has been marked by persistent, often extremely bitter and occasionally violent conflict (see Chapter 15). To most evangelical and fundamentalist Protestants in both countries, the most important foe has always been and remains the Catholic Church, and the greatest evil that faces them, greater even than communism, is the papacy. In America, the Southern Baptists, for instance, "are genuinely afraid of and excited about the Catholic Church as a political institution and a political threat in American life" (Kelsey, 1973:18). Even moderate Protestants find it impossible to accept Catholic teachings on papal infallibility and the cult of the Virgin, although they are slightly less disposed to connect these beliefs with antidemocratic, "un-American," or treasonous attitudes.

For their part, many Catnolics regard Protestants as a deviant, breakaway minority who must be brought back within the fold, to be sympathized with for their hopeless fragmentation outside the church. Jews have for centuries been the target of persecution by both Protestants and Catholics (all in the name of God) on the pretext that Jews murdered Christ and are therefore subject to God's eternal wrath. Furthermore, in both countries the Jewish minority has been associated by the churches with economic and political conspiracies against society in such a way that their persecution has increased.

In addition to these lines of conflict among the three major faiths, various minority groups, such as the Quakers, the Mennonites, the Hutterites, the Mormons, the Christian Scientists, the Jehovah's witnesses, and, more recently, the Children of God and the Unification Church, have been subject to harassment (extending sometimes to murder) in the name of religious principles. This has been especially true for groups that have been linked to political dissent.

To appreciate the potential for socio-religious conflict in modern Western societies, one must obtain some idea of the extent of religious diversity found within them. As this entails assessing the comparative size of different religious groups, and as such assessments are very difficult to make, only the crudest outlines can be presented here. However, they will be sufficient to show the potential for religious conflict.

The religious pluralism of the United States is a well-established and frequently commented upon fact. However, there is no such thing as a list of all the religious groups in the United States, let alone any judgment of their relative sizes. Two kinds of data are available. The first, perhaps more accurate as a measure of affiliation, is derived from social surveys in which respondents declare their religious affiliation. This kind of data rarely documents the complete range of religious groups, however, as the samples are so small. Nevertheless, they do give some idea of the relation size of the *major* religious groups. A 1964 National

Opinion Research Center survey recorded the following distribution, expressed as percentages of the total population (Stark and Glock, 1968:8):

Catholic	25.8	Congregationalist	2.2
Baptist	19.3	Other Protestant	16.0
Methodist	13.0	Jewish	3.9
Lutheran	8.8	Non-Christian	0.5
Presbyterian	5.8	No Religion	2.5
Episcopalian	2.9		

This kind of list, whatever its shortcomings, at least permits the conclusion that the United States is almost exclusively a Christian country. For two reasons, however, such a list does not show the true extent of religious diversity in the United States. Denominations lumped together in this list are denominations that in real life find it hard to coexist. Examples are the American Baptist churches and the Southern Baptist Convention and the United Presbyterian Church and the Presbyterian Church (South). Second, the list is enormously abbreviated, as there are approximately 280 different religious bodies in the United States, and the survey approach just does not have the scope to capture this range.

A different method of assessing the nature and extent of religious diversity in the United States is to look only at those Americans who are church members and see where their loyalties lie. The *Yearbook of American and Canadian Churches* not only furnishes information on church membership but also provides more detailed figures for the many smaller groups that usually fail to obtain statistical representation in social surveys. There are all sorts of problems in interpreting the figures given in the *Yearbook*. Each denomination has its own method of enumerating its membership. Many of them (including the Christian Scientists) do not number their membership at all. Denominations also differ widely in their ideas of who should count as a member. Moreover, not all the denominations that do count their membership do so annually. Thus, the figures in the *Yearbook* do not all apply to the same year. Those that do number their membership do so in ways that vary widely in their sophistication and accuracy, whereas some groups use computers, others rely on ministers' estimates. Finally, even though the list of separate bodies given in the *Yearbook* is long, there is no doubt that many smaller groups are not represented at all, either by choice or simply through omission. Nevertheless, the *Yearbook* is the best available source of data on membership and it does give a rough idea of the relative strength of the various religious organizations in the United States.

The list that follows is taken from the 1975 *Yearbook*. It is not a complete listing (over 280 separate groups are recorded in the *Yearbook*), but it does show all groups reporting a membership of over 50,000. The list is divided into various "families" of denominations, and also includes some of the religious groups that have frequently been mentioned in this book. Altogether, the religious organizations shown here make up 91.33 percent of all church members in the United States in 1974.

THE MAJOR DENOMINATIONS IN THE UNITED STATES AS A PROPORTION OF THE TOTAL NUMBER OF CHURCH MEMBERS (131 MILLION) IN 1974

PROTESTANT (predominantly white, mainstream) (37.13%)

United Methodist Church	7.0%
Episcopalian	2.2
Churches of Christ	1.83
United Church of Christ	1.4
Christian Church (Disciples)	1.0
Reformed Church in America	0.2
Unitarian-Universalist Association	0.1
National Association of Congregational Christian Churches	0.05
Evangelical Covenant Church of America	0.05
Friends United Meeting	0.05
Free Methodist	0.04
Presbyterian Churches (2.86%)	
United Presbyterian Church in the USA	2.14
Presbyterian Church in the USA	0.69
Cumberland Presbyterian Church	0.07
Presbyterian Church in America	0.03
Lutheran Churches (6.49%)	
Lutheran Church of America	2.3
Lutheran Church-Missouri Synod	2.1
American Lutheran Church	1.8
Wisconsin Evangelical Lutheran Synod	0.29
Baptist Churches (13.79%)	
Southern Baptist Convention	9.3
American Baptist Churches	1.47
National Primitive Baptist Convention	1.25
American Baptist Association	0.76
Conservative Baptist Association of America	0.22
General Association of Regular Baptists	0.17
Free Will Baptists	0.16
Baptist Missionary Association of America	0.15
Baptist General Conference	0.08
United Free Will Baptist Church	0.07
General Baptist	0.05
North American Baptist General Conference	0.03
Independent Black Denominations (8.22%)	
National Baptist Convention of the USA	4.2
National Baptist Convention of America	2.0
African Methodist Episcopal Church	0.89
African Methodist Episcopal Zion Church	0.78
Christian Methodist Episcopal Church	0.35

Holiness/Pentecostal (major groups only) (1.84%)	
Assemblies of God	0.8
Church of the Nazarene	0.3
Church of God (Cleveland)	0.23
United Pentecostal Church International	0.21
Church of God (Indiana)	0.12
Pentecostal Church of America	0.08
International Church of the Four-Square Gospel	0.06
Church of God of Prophecy	0.04
CATHOLIC (37.34%)	
Roman Catholic	37.0
Other Catholic	0.34
JEWISH CONGREGATIONS	4.6
ORTHODOX CHURCHES (3.02%)	
Greek Orthodox	1.48
Orthodox Church in America	0.76
Other Orthodox	0.78
MISCELLANEOUS GROUPS	
Church of Jesus Christ of Latter-Day Saints	1.6
Reorganized Church of Jesus Christ of Latter-Day Saints	0.12
Jehovah's witnesses	0.36
Seventh Day Adventists	0.30
Mennonite/Amish/Brethren	0.26
Salvation Army	0.20
International General Association of Spiritualists	0.12
Buddhist Churches of America	0.04

Obviously not all religious groups are shown in this list and the criteria for inclusion of the miscellaneous groups were somewhat arbitrary. The list groups the various bodies into "families" according to historical tradition. Such a grouping says little or nothing about how closely linked in theology and social ethics they are today. The American Baptist Churches today might be "closer" to the United Church of Christ than to the Southern Baptist Convention, with whom they are linked historically.

The list contains some interesting items of information:

1. Although only 55 of the over 280 different religious bodies are identified in this list, they comprise all but about 9 percent of the 131 million church members in the United States. The Catholics, the Methodists, the Episcopalians, the Churches of Christ, the United Church, the Disciples, the various Presbyterian denominations, the Lutheran Churches, the Southern Baptist Convention, and the American Baptist Churches, alone account for over 70 percent of the total membership. Religion in the United States is not quite so pluralistic as it would at first appear.

2. The Catholic proportion is reported as 37.34 percent. There is some suspicion that this overestimates the number of Catholics. This figure has to be contrasted with that of 24.7 percent which Greeley (1974b:42) arrives at on the basis of a summary of the surveys carried out by the National Opinion Research Center between 1963 and 1972. The latter figure is probably a more accurate indication of the strength of the Catholic Church in the United States.

3. The strength of the Baptists in the United States is clearly shown by the list. It is true that they are greatly fragmented, but in the Southern Baptist Convention they have the largest single denomination among the Protestants, and in all, the Baptists constitute almost one seventh of the church members in the United States.

4. Racial segregation in the churches is reflected in the 8.22 percent of all church members who belong to the independent black denominations. Furthermore, this figure as certainly under-reports the membership as the Catholics figure over-reports their numbers. Of all the major denominations, the independent black churches enumerate least often—some of their figures in the 1975 *Yearbook* date back to the 1950s. Although this in itself does not denomstrate underreporting, it does add substance to the evidence from social surveys that record a higher percentage of blacks in the church-membership population. For example, Greeley (1974b:42) found that blacks make up 13.9 percent of all church-affiliated Americans and that no more than 1 or 2 percent of them are to be found in white-run churches. It has to be concluded, then, that about 10 million of the church members in today's churches are blacks who belong to all-black denominations.

5. Percentage figures can be misleading as an assessment of institutional strength. It is generally agreed that there is a Protestant religious mainstream consisting of Episcopalians, Presbyterians, the United Church, Methodists, Baptists, Lutherans, and the Disciples of Christ. This body makes an impact out of all proportion to its numbers. The several denominations are united in a fairly uniform historical and cultural heritage and a common set of theological and ecclesiastical assumptions that no amount of wrangling over the priesthood, congregational autonomy, or the Trinity can disguise.

6. The list reveals an interesting corollary of the preceding point. Some groups have a "presence" on the American religious scene out of all proportion to their numbers. whereas other are largely invisible despite a huge membership. The most conspicuous case is that of the Jews, a highly visible minority who make up only 4.6 percent of the total church membership. The United Church of Christ has a long and venerable history on the American religious scene but its members are now outnumbered by the Mormons. In contrast the Orthodox churches make up 3.02 percent of the total church membership (and they count

adult males only!), but their "presence" is disproportionately small—perhaps because of their greater reluctance to assimilate. And if one counts only the larger of the Pentecostal/Holiness associations, their proportion is almost as great as that of the Episcopalians.

7. The various established sects, such as the Seventh Day Adventists, the Jehovah's witnesses, the Salvation Army, and the spiritualists, which have attracted a great deal of attention from sociologists, constitute a miniscule proportion of the church population of the United States.

The list demonstrates the unwisdom of referring to "the Church" in the United States; outside of the Catholic Church, only the Southern Baptists can claim even a tenth of the total church population. There are no signs that this diversity is diminishing. The newer religious bodies, such as the Holiness and Pentecostal sects, seem to be growing at a faster rate, which thus redistributes church membership. Mergers, such as those in the United Church, the Methodist Church, and the Lutheran Churches, are counterbalanced by schisms in the Presbyterian Church and the growth of the newer groups. Two studies conducted in 1952 and 1971 (*Yearbook*, 1975:264) show that Pentecostal/Holiness groups like the Church of God (Cleveland) and the Pentecostal Holiness Church grew by 120.9 percent and 75.0 percent respectively, while the general population was growing by 34.9 percent. During the same period, the Mormons recorded a 98.0 percent growth rate. At the other end of the scale, the United Methodist Church, although gaining 5 percent more members, was obviously losing ground relative to the increase in population, and the United Church suffered a gross loss in membership, as did the American Baptist Churches and the Disciples of Christ.

Religious diversity in comparable Western societies can only be described very crudely in view of the paucity of data. However, some figures exist for Canada and the United Kingdom, and these will be considered briefly.

Religious Diversity in Canada

Unlike the American Census, the Canadian Census contains a question on religious affiliation. It is possible to obtain from this a fairly accurate and comprehensive picture of religious heterogeneity in Canada. Canadian society has been subject to almost as much religious diversity as American society, but the merger of many of the separate denominations in the United Church of Canada and the presence of a larger French-Canadian Catholic population have reduced the variety. According to the 1971 Canadian Census, as reported in the *Yearbook of American and Canadian Churches* (1974:255), the Canadian population is 46.2 percent Roman Catholic, 17.5 percent United Church of Canada,

11.8 percent Anglican, 1.3 percent Jewish; and 4.3 percent of the population have no religion. Catholics bulk much larger in Canada than they do in the United States. Furthermore, between 1961 and 1971, Catholics increased from 30 percent to 33 percent of the total Canadian population; during the same period, the membership of the United Church declined from 26.3 percent to 21.8 percent (See Stone, 1975). The Catholic population is, of course, heavily concentrated in Quebec, and, to a lesser degree, New Brunswick. Thus, numerical strength is regional rather than national.

Religious Diversity in the United Kingdom

There is less religious diversity in the United Kingdom than in the United States because of the political power of the established Church of England. Since the Reformation, the Church of England has dominated religious affairs in that country, the Church of Scotland (a more Presbyterian version of Anglicanism) has been the dominant force north of the border, and a Protestant minority has held power in Ireland (later, Ulster). Since the nineteenth century, the strength of the Anglican Church in Wales has been greatly weakened by the rise of Nonconformity, especially Methodism.

Unfortunately, the data on religious-group populations in the United Kingsom are mixed in quality and date. According to a Gallup Poll conducted in 1965, of those claiming some sort of religious affiliation in England, 67 percent belonged to the Church of England, 13 percent were Nonconformist, 9 percent were Catholic, 1 percent were Jewish and 4 percent were affiliated with other religious groups (*Social Surveys*, 1965:9). The Church of Scotland does not enjoy quite the same supremacy as the Church of England: it draws 36.1 percent of the total adult population, the Free Church members make up 6.5 percent and the Catholics a further 15 percent (Highet, 1972:225). Notice that the figures for England are for all those claiming church affiliation, whereas the figures for Scotland are for the total population. In Ulster, Catholics dominate numerically, with 34.9 percent of the total adult population, and Protestants make up the remainder: Presbyterians, 29 percent; Church of Ireland, 24.2 percent; and Methodists, 5 percent (Ward, 1972:296).

Religious Diversity in Western Europe

Similar religious heterogeneity is found in Western European countries. For example, about half the West Germans belong to the Evangelischen Kirchen in Deutschland and 44.1 percent belong to the Catholic Church (Kehrer, 1972:192). In the Netherlands, the main church bodies are the Catholics, with 28.3 percent; the moderate Calvinists, 28.3 percent; and the strict Calvinists, 9.3 percent (Laeyendecker, 1972:330). Eire, France, Italy, Spain and Portugal, on the other hand, have extremely large Catholic majorities, small Protestant minorities, and an undetermined but probably quite sizable number of unaffiliated people.

CONCLUSION

The interest in the chapters that follow is not so much in these religious differences themselves but in the extent to which they are aligned with and intensify other social differences, for "when Catholics are mostly Irish and Italian and mostly working class; while Protestants are mostly *nth* generation Americans of English and Middle European backgrounds, and are white collar workers or farmers, then the potential lines of cleavage in society coincide" (Coleman, 1964:92). Most modern Western societies are crisscrossed by lines of division representing status, income, power, ethnic, and racial as well as religious differences. Many vertical divisions, such as ethnicity, are differentiated horizontally by other divisions such as income. The most important question to decide is the extent to which these cleavages overlap. One way of approaching this problem is to construct a "scale of communality" (Yinger, 1971:239): at one end of this scale there is complete coincidence of religious, class, ethnic, and regional divisions; at the other end, religious differences vary independently of other social divisions. The United States has no religious/political parties, and few political issues are linked exclusively with specific churches. Yet in America there are religiously homogeneous ethnic groups and religiously homogeneous regions, such as the South, where about 90 percent of the population is either Southern Baptist or Methodist. The United States might be said to occupy a midpoint position on Yinger's scale, moving, perhaps, toward a position of greater independence between religious and other social divisions.

The coincidence of cleavages is not, however, stable. Nor is a linear development toward or away from total coincidence or freedom plausible. Instead, there is likely to be a constant movement toward and away from coincidence. The heightening of social tensions is often marked by an alignment of social cleavages as events make religious issues more salient and tend to polarize people's perspectives. For example, during the 1960s, the modernist/traditionalist differences that usually lie dormant in Protestantism were made explicit once more in the position of different churches on the civil rights. Contrary to the functionalist argument, religion does not promote harmony in a time of conflict, disharmony in society is likely to intensify disharmony in the churches, which in turn exacerbates social conflicts.

The most important alignments are those between religious affiliation and political allegiance and between religious affiliation and social class. In the United States and the United Kingdom, religion is not correlated as closely with political division as it is in, for example, the Netherlands, which is remarkable for its organization along denominational lines and in which trade unions and political parties are explicitly aligned with churches. In a country where even sports clubs are religiously identified, the impact of religion on politics cannot be overestimated. In other European countries, national religious differentiation is a mask for local alignments. For example, in Germany there is religious homogeneity within political regions. Schleswig-Holstein is 88 percent Protestant, the Saar 74 percent Catholic (Kehrer, 1972:193). Similar regional and religious alignments exist in Canada where Catholics form significant minorities in Quebec, Ontario and New Brunswick. In the United States, religio-political alignments are more subtle, but there *are* such alignments, as the Protestant South and the heavily Mormon state of Utah demonstrate. There is also an urban/rural split that has a political impact. Both Jews and Catholics are mainly urban people. A third of American Catholics, for example, live in cities of over half a million people (Abramson, 1973:35).

There are also religion/class alignments. Class structuring receives considerable impetus where status-group membership (such as church affiliation) is tied to economic organizations (Giddens, 1973:112). It has already been demonstrated that in the United States social classes are to some extent mirrored in different denominations. Although this is not so much the case in the United Kingdom (in accordance with a more general European pattern), there is a striking relationship between lower class membership and a complete absence of church affiliation. These economic and political issues will be taken up in the chapters which follow.

14

RELIGION
AND CLASS CONFLICT

INTRODUCTION

Religious beliefs and practices draw Americans together by sanctifying a common set of values and establishing a common sense of identity (see Herberg, 1960). Religion in America is integrative not despite denominational differences but because of them. Denominational pluralism (which is but a variation on a single theme) and the preference of different social strata for different denominations *replicate* a certain image of the social stratification system in the United States (see Chapter 11). There is much evidence to support this idea that religious stratification and economic stratification are functionally adapted. However, this chapter, informed by a Marxian model of economics, will present a rather different view of this relationship. In order to understand this view, we must contrast functionalist and Marxian theories of social inequality.

Functionalists tend to treat social inequality as mainly a matter of stratification, or "the ranking of units in a social system in accordance with the standards of the common value system" (Parsons, 1954:388). This system of stratification is seen as performing the vital social function of role allocation, the differential rewards accruing to each rank being the means by which society allocates people to needed jobs (see Davis and Moore, 1945). This model is highly compatible with a view of denominational pluralism in which the denominations are seen as playing their part in legitimizing the stratification system, and thus helping allocate people into jobs.

Marxian sociologists take a different view of social inequalities in capitalist societies, which they see as dominated by one fundamental cleavage—that between the propertied capitalist class and the property-less working class. There are other economic groups, but bourgeoisie and proletariat are the decisive classes. A class (not a stratum) is a group in conflict with another class (not a different "rung on the ladder"). Marxian sociologists also take a different view of the role of social ideas such as religion. Whereas a functionalist might stress the importance of a normative agreement in maintaining social order (and assign religion a functional role in securing it), a Marxian sociologist stresses the role of coercion in maintaining social order and looks upon religion as a coercive weapon.

The task of describing the relation between religion and economics, though assuming a basic class conflict in society, is greatly complicated by the obscurity of the lines of cleavage in modern capitalist societies. Although America is certainly not as pluralist as many commentators have claimed (Hamilton, 1972:34–36), there is no denying that in the United States differences in income, occupation, education, ethnicity, region, and religion crisscross in a confusing manner. There is the further difficulty that most of the research on social inequalities in the United States has used the functionalist model, ignoring class divisions and accentuating stratification differences in income, education and occupation. Most of the data have little to say about class characteristics such as property holdings, occupancy of elite positions, and class consciousness. This chapter will therefore have two objectives: (1) to examine the relation between religion and inequality according to the data collected, with the idea of assessing the extent to which religion helps obscure the real class conflicts in American society; (2) to look more closely at some of the data on class differences that do exist, to see what role religion plays in structuring class conflict.

There is considerable concentration of wealth in the United States. The top five percent income bracket gathers in 19.1 percent of all income, receives 63.5 percent of all dividend income, and holds 75.1 percent of all the stock owned in the United States (Rossides, 1976:131). The survey and census data do not say much about what part religion has played in the creation of such inequalities. What they do say is that there are small and diminishing religious differences in socioeconomic status in the middle strata, but what they only *suggest* is that religious differences remain quite marked at the upper end of the ladder. In other words, most of the data purportedly measuring class (the finely graded socioeconomic differentials) show little of religious relevance.

The scant data on real class differences (as indicated, for example, by property holdings) show much greater religious differences.

The idea of there being social inequalities among Protestants, Catholics and Jews makes little sense without reference to the works of Max Weber. In his *The Protestant Ethic and the Spirit of Capitalism*, first published in 1903, Weber argued that certain forms of Protestantism had a special affinity with the spirit of capitalism that now rules the Western world. Adherence to the Protestant faith seemed to bestow advantages over Catholics in the competition for economic achievement. Werner Sombart, a contemporary of Weber's, tried to make the same case for Jews in his *The Jew and Modern Capitalism*. Both Weber and Sombart could draw on evidence showing that Protestants and Jews had been more successful than Catholics. Although neither argued that Protestantism or Judaism would *continue* to enjoy this advantage, subsequent sociological work has been predicated on this assumption, the most famous example being Gerhard Lenski's *The Religious Factor*, published in 1963.

Weber was as much concerned to establish a connection between the Protestant Ethic and the spirit of capitalism by comparative means as he was to show a social psychological association between them, but it is the latter focus that has been adopted by most of his followers in this field. These individuals have assumed a connection on the basis that the attitudes of Protestantism are compatible with the attitudes of the typical capitalist entrepreneur. Weber identified the following themes as important:

1. The Lutheran concept of "the calling," the idea of laboring in one's station in life as God's instrument or steward on Earth, gives to work a positive virtue.
2. The Calvinist doctrine of predestination encourages the belief that "by their fruits shall ye know them," and generates an intense concern to detect signs of grace or electness.
3. The ascetic life enjoined by the Puritans provides an armor against fleshly temptations and mitigates against the kind of waste and self-indulgence that might hinder the accumulation of wealth.
4. The Protestant Reformers "de-mystified" the world, stripping it of mysteries and miracles and encouraging a methodical, pragmatic attitude toward the world.

At no time did Weber suggest that these attitudes were purposely fostered in order to legitimate capitalism, but he was convinced that there was a strong "elective affinity" between these attitudes and the economic outlook of the capitalist. A consideration of the capitalist attitudes he thought to be most important seems to warrant this conclusion:

1. Work is a worthwhile activity in its own right, not merely a means of subsistence.
2. The aim of work is constant increase.
3. Economic choices should be made on purely rational grounds in the interests of efficiency, and without regard to tradition.
4. All forms of personal indulgence and display are distasteful: life should be lived in moderation.

No discussion of the relation between religion and economic conflicts can ignore this penetrating thesis, for it clearly suggests that Protestants are much more likely to be capitalists than Catholics. This chapter will focus almost entirely on these broad interfaith differences and will attempt to determine the extent to which they are found in modern American society. The aim is to see to what extent capitalists are more likely to be Protestants and to what extent entry into the capitalist class is contingent on the adoption of Protestant views.

SOCIAL INEQUALITY AMONG RELIGIOUS GROUPS

The first step is simply to look at the average socioeconomic status of the major religious groups. The second step is to isolate the religious factor from other possible causes of social inequality.

TABLE   14:1

**EDUCATION, OCCUPATIONAL PRESTIGE, AND INCOME
FOR DENOMINATIONS
(Blacks and Spanish-Speaking People Excluded)***

Denomination	Number of Years of Father's Education	Number of Years of Own Education	Occupational Prestige Score	Income
Protestant				
Baptist	8.17	10.70	37.21	8,693
Methodist	9.50	11.86	41.23	10,103
Lutheran	8.84	11.24	38.90	9,702
Presbyterian	10.69	12.66	46.39	10,976
Episcopalian	12.18	13.47	48.19	11,032
Other Protestant Denominations	8.62	11.19	38.33	
Protestant, no Denomination	9.81	11.29	40.62	
Catholic	8.58	11.50	40.40	11,374
Jew	10.24	13.98	48.89	13,340

*Data from National Opinion Research Center studies conducted between 1963 and 1970 and reported in Greeley (1976:43).

Jews enjoy a consistent advantage on all three measures of social inequality. However, no simple Protestant/Catholic contrast is possible. Protestant denominations such as the Presbyterians and the Episcopalians are better educated than Catholics, but Catholics are better educated than Baptists and Lutherans. The same pattern prevails for occupation. Catholics are much higher than the national average in income, earning more than not only Baptists and Lutherans but also Methodists, Presbyterians, and Episcopalians (Rossides, 1976:170).

The socioeconomic differentials between members of different religious denominations cannot be safely attributed to religion itself until the possibility has been ruled out that other social factors are responsible. One obvious source of income differences is occupation, and it is known, in turn, that occupation is greatly determined by educational achievement. As education precedes occupation, which in general "precedes" income, the best way to isolate the impact of religion is to, first, examine the relation between religion and education, holding family background constant because *that* is a determinant of educational achievement; next, look at the relation between religion and occupation, but with educational level held constant; and, finally, examine the relation between religion and income, holding both education and occupation constant. In all cases, given the close association between being black and Protestant and being black and being of low socioeconomic status, it is necessary to eliminate the race factor. In the studies cited below, this was usually done by eliminating blacks from the sample.

Education

Table 14:1 shows up to three years difference in the average education of the membership of different religious groups. But before this kind of gap can be attributed to religious influences, it is necessary to eliminate other possible causal factors. It is well known, for example, that family background is an important influence on educational achievement and, as the first column in the table indicates, members of religious groups vary widely in the kind of home they come from. It is certainly true that much of the variation in educational achievement between religious groups can be attributed to differences in family background. Greeley (1976:50) claims that controlling for father's education eliminates all differences, and research by Fox and Jackson (1973) supports this claim. However, Warren (1970:141), using different data and controlling for father's occupation, finds that "sizable differences . . . among some religious groups remain." His data, gathered in 1962, show Jews, Episcopalians, and Presbyterians at the top of the educational ladder—even with differences in family background eliminated.

Catholics did not drop to the lowest rung, however; that was occupied by the Baptists. Religious differences persisted even among those with the same number of siblings. Evidence gathered in other studies is not consistent, but most of it would seem to support Warren's conclusion. Trent and Golds (1967:49), for example, discovered that holding father's occupation constant did not alter the fact that Catholics tend to acquire less education than Protestants. In other words, there *is* a religious factor in educational achievement.

Many factors are likely to have contributed to the formation of this pattern of educational disparities among religious groups, not the least of which is the culture of the respective groups. Since their arrival in the United States, and before continued education became the norm, Jews have placed a high value on education, have been willing to undergo sacrifices to obtain it, and, once in the educational system, have had the perseverance to stay (Sklare, 1971:58). The conduciveness was not one of content (for Talmudic learning is antithetical to modern secular education) but one of orientation: "Jewish intellectual traditions facilitated the *transition* from an archaic system of religious instruction to modern secular education" (Steinberg, 1974:62). So great was this veneration of learning among Jews that "the process of mobility through education became endowed with quasi-religious significance."[1]

The success enjoyed by most Protestants in the schools should come as no surprise as in many respects it is *their* system.

> Until the beginning of the twentieth century American higher education had an unmistakably Protestant cast. Most of the leading colleges had been founded by religious denominations, often with the specific purpose of training missionaries and producing an educated ministry. The intellectual and moral climate was heavily tinged with Calvinism, and the main purpose of a college education was understood to be the cultivation of mental and moral discipline. Compulsory prayers and church services occupied no small portion of the student's daily regimen and religious revivals were commonplace. The vast majority of faculty and students were also Protestant. (Steinberg, 1974:62)

Over time, American colleges have become less Protestant, but there is no doubt that the outlook and expectations generated by the kind of learning they provide have placed Protestants at an advantage. The only exception to this pattern have been fundamentalist Protestants, who are

[1] Jews moved quickly into the nation's colleges. "By 1908 a government report showed that 8.5 percent of the male student body of seventy-seven major institutions of higher learning were composed of first- and second-generation Jews (Jews at this time made up about 2 percent of the population)" (Glazer, 1972:81).

highly anti-intellectual and hostile to formal, secular education (Elinson, 1965:410). Fundamentalists plan on attending college with much less frequency than any other religious group (see Rhodes and Nam, 1970).

The secularization of secondary education did not immediately better the position of the Catholic community. In the opinion of many (such as Trent and Golds, 1967; Steinberg, 1974), the culture of the Catholic is not conducive to successful performance in the secular educational system. Some of the reasons given for this are (1) the strong belief among Catholics in the unity of intellectual, moral, and physical development; (2) repressive child-rearing practices which inhibit attitudes necessary for educational achievement; (3) authoritarian attitudes on the part of the priest; and (4) a "ghetto mentality," fostered by residential seclusion and minority status that restricts horizons and lowers expectations.

To these cultural factors must be added structural conditions. First, most Catholics emigrated from areas in which secular education was minimal, literacy rates low, and respect for learning almost absent. Second, Catholics, unlike Jews, set up their own educational institutions because they feared that mixed education would weaken ethnic ties and because public education was heavily tinged with Protestantism. These schools were small, poorly staffed, and inadequately equipped. Third, Catholic immigrants tended to be less wealthy and less skilled than, say, Jewish immigrants.

In view of these impediments, it comes as no surprise to find Catholics underrepresented in the nation's colleges, and the better the college, the greater their underrepresentation. Furthermore, Catholics are underrepresented most at the faculty level and least at the undergraduate level. Jews are overrepresented at all levels. However, Catholic performance in the educational system is beginning to improve. Age-cohort data show, for instance, that among younger faculty, Catholics are present in almost the same proportion as their numbers in the general population (Steinberg, 1974:105).

There can be little doubt that both cultural and structural changes have been taking place that are working to the advantage of the Catholic. Most important, Catholics are beginning to overcome the disadvantages of their immigration experience—lack of skills, illiteracy, and poverty—to perform as well as or better than Baptists and Methodists. However, they still lag behind Jews and the Episcopalian, Presbyterian, and Congregationalist denominations. Thus, religious differences in education persist, although they are not as great as they once were.

Occupation

Table 14:1 shows clear differences in occupational prestige between Baptists and Lutherans on the one hand, and Jews, Episcopalians, and

Presbyterians, on the other. Such differences cannot be attributed to religion, however, until other possible causes have been eliminated. For example, the heavy concentration of Jews in high prestige occupations and the low occupational prestige of Baptists might be due to the fact that Jews, unlike Baptists, tend to dwell in the city where the higher prestige jobs are concentrated. In fact, holding place of residence constant does reduce some of these differences in occupational prestige, but it does not totally eliminate them (Means, 1962:227; Glenn and Hyland, 1967:71; Goldstein, 1969:624; Jackson et al., 1970:56).

The religious factor does disappear, however, when controls are imposed for father's occupation and individual's own education (Warren, 1970:143). In other words, if one compares members of different religious groups who have had the same amount of education and whose fathers held roughly the same job, no differences in occupational prestige appear. If religion does affect the kind of job one gets, it does so not directly but through education. Nor does religion directly influence job selection (contrary to what might have been expected from Weber's thesis). Catholic college seniors show, if anything, a slightly greater disposition than Protestants to opt for a career in business (Trent and Golds, 1967:142), and if they choose to go to graduate school, they are just as likely as Protestants to enter physical or social science programs (Greeley, 1963:182).

Income

The income differences reported in Table 14:1 are almost as misleading as the occupational differences. Using other data, Goldstein (1969:629) and Gockel (1969:642) independently concluded that any differences in income among members of religious groups are actually the result of differences in education. In other words, whichever religious group one belongs to, more education means more money. However, Gockel found that the association between income and religion did not disappear entirely when controls for education were imposed and that an interesting pattern emerged. Warren (1970:151), who found the pattern in his data too, describes it as follows: "initial religious preference has an influence on income that is not accounted for by father's occupational status, the respondent's education, or occupational achievement"—among certain groups. When controls for education and occupation are imposed, higher income levels for the Congregationalists, Episcopalians, and Jews remain. It is as if members of these denominations are able, because of their religion, to "use" given units of education to supply disproportionately more income. In summary, much of the difference in income among people of different faiths is not due to religion at all, but to socioeconomic factors. However, religion does have a direct effect on income for certain groups, as well as an effect on income through education for all groups.

Ethnicity

All the evidence cited so far suggests that family background is an important coproducer with religion of socioeconomic differences. The importance of family background is emphasized by recent studies of ethnicity that make it possible not only to further separate family background factors from those of religion alone but also to look within the social categories identified by faith. For example, if the Protestant and Catholic communities are broken down by ethnicity, the category that ranks second in income to the Jews is the Irish Catholics. And although a Catholic group (the Spanish-speaking) has the lowest income of all non-black groups, a Protestant group (the Irish Protestants) has the next lowest (Greeley, 1974b:42–43). In other words, when ethnic background is taken into account, much of the Protestant advantage in income disappears; such differences can be attributed more to circumstances of origin than to religion as such.

Holding ethnicity constant also eliminates many of the religious differences in occupation and, even more important, in education. Controlling for ethnicity reveals that, although there are indeed many Catholics in low status occupations, most of them are Spanish-speaking and Eastern European Catholics. Irish Catholics hold jobs only slightly inferior to those of Protestants of British ancestry (Greeley, 1974b:54–55). The same can be said for education. When Americans are broken down into ethnic as well as religious groups, Jews continue to show the highest educational attainment, but the Irish Catholics rank next—just above Protestants of British ancestry. Of all Gentiles, Irish Catholics have the highest rate of college attendance (Greeley, 1974b:50). Thus, the religious differences in socioeconomic status are reducible in part to family background differences (as measured by father's status) and in part to ethnic differences. It is the distinctive ethnic experience of Americans, as well as their religion, that causes these patterns.

If much of the socioeconomic variation among religious groups is reducible to ethnicity, it is likely that as the immigration trauma recedes, the apparently religious differences will dissappear. Greeley (1974b:68) offers evidence that indirectly supports this hypothesis. Having conducted a crude cross-sectional analysis in which the population was divided into age cohorts and each ethnic group was compared with the mean score for its own age group, Greeley found that Italian Catholics over sixty are almost a full year beneath their cohort mean in education, but that Italian Catholics in their twenties are about one tenth of a year above the mean. Similar generational differences were found among

Polish and Slavic Catholics. The Catholics furthest removed from immigration were doing decidedly better; they were performing as well as their Protestant compatriots. In Canada, where religion is so closely associated with ethnicity and language, it is probable that the same reason can be given for the fact that Protestants enjoy higher income than Catholics; it is ethnic differences which cause the inequalities as much as religion (Fallding, 1971:110).

Three conclusions can be drawn from this evidence on social inequality among religious groups. First, much of the difference is indeed due not so much to religion per se but to circumstances of family origin, such as father's occupation and ethnic background. Second, many of the differences seem to be disappearing. This is due to the waning impact of immigration, and probably to a decline in the importance of the religious factor. Third, there *are* remaining differences in socioeconomic status—at the upper reaches of the stratification hierarchy. In other words, for a number of reasons, Catholics now rank on a par with the Methodists, but the superiority of the Episcopalians, Presbyterians, and Congregationalists—the old Protestant establishment—remains. This fact will be discussed at greater length below, for it points to a continuing function of religion as a buttress of elite position. But the same conclusion is reached by the research on religion and social mobility, to which we turn now.

RELIGION AND SOCIAL MOBILITY

Social mobility, defined here as differences between father's and son's socioeconomic status, is much more likely to be experienced by Protestants than Catholics, according to Weber. Although defenders of Weber's thesis can still be found (Lenski, 1963:84; Anderson, 1970:143), and although, as the concluding section of this chapter will show, there is *some* evidence pointing to the continued success of Protestants in moving into the higher echelons, most of the recent work in this field shows little difference between Protestants and Catholics in regard to social mobility.

Data reported by Jackson (1970) show that a manual worker's son who is a Catholic is *more* likely than a manual worker's son who is a Protestant to move into a white collar job. Bode (1972:60) goes further, arguing that Catholics "have rather strikingly exceeded Protestants in terms of occupational mobility." Significantly, however, Catholics are less likely than Protestants to move into professional and business occupations—given the same point of origin. In other words, Catholics are as mobile, or more so, than Protestants in regard to short-range mobility (blue-collar to white-collar), but they are not as successful in moving into higher-status, decision-making jobs.

As the rate of mobility among Catholics nears that of Protestants, a change in the relation of religion to socioeconomic status takes place. In 1943, a higher proportion of Protestants than Catholics were white collar workers, but by 1965 the Protestants had lost this advantage (Glenn and Hyland, 1967:75). Catholics have shown a greater ability than Protestants to capitalize on the expansion of the white-collar sector during this century. Since 1910, the proportion of white-collar jobs in the national labor force has increased from 22 percent to 38 percent, but the proportion of Catholics with white-collar jobs has increased from 24 percent to 43 percent (Abramson, 1973:41). Part of this realignment may be due to the influx of the mostly Protestant southern blacks into the blue-collar jobs of the northern cities, but there is nothing here to suggest that Catholics find it harder than Protestants to move out of a blue-collar job and into a white-collar job.

This realignment of the occupants of white-collar jobs also reflects the structural downward mobility of the Protestant community. The Protestants suffered from the transition of the United States from a nation of small, independent entrepreneurs to a nation of employees: "The Catholics who always had been concentrated among the wage earners were now joined by many Protestants in the same type of employment. Members of the two religious groups worked in the same blue-collar and white-collar organizations, receiving similar wages and sharing in a similar way of life" (Kosa, 1970:17). This kind of structural mobility was accelerated by the sharp reduction in immigration after 1924. From 1925 on, the Catholic community ceased to be annually replenished with a fresh supply of uneducated and unskilled workers with the exception of Spanish-speaking Catholics.

Mobility rates among different faiths are also likely to move closer together as family structures (which are shaped by religion) become more alike.[2] In view of traditional differences in fertility among the faiths, it is reasonable to suppose that "each Jewish child would enjoy a greater investment of time and capital than each Protestant child, and Protestant children more than Catholics" (Anderson, 1970:150). In other words, the greater number of siblings of the average Catholic child has placed her at a disadvantage to the Protestant and Jewish child. However, not only are family-size differences diminishing, but the number of relatives living in the Catholic home (an inhibitor of mobility) is moving closer to that of Protestants. Thus, an indirect religious effect on mobility is also disappearing (Lenski, 1963:215; Goldstein, 1974:113).

[2]Lenski (1963:225) found religious differences in the rationale which parents give for the directives they give their children. Protestants were more likely than Catholics to use the kind of future-oriented rationale most conducive to the formation of capitalist attitudes.

If increasing rates of mobility among Catholics are associated with the passing of the immigration trauma and the assimilation of the Catholic community into the American mainstream, there should be differences in mobility *within* the Catholic community by generation—the more recent the immigration, the lower the rate of mobility. Unfortunately, the data are not consistent on this issue. Abramson (1973:44), discovering ethnic differences in mobility within Catholicism, uses this finding to support the generation hypothesis. For example, the Italians (early immigrants) have higher rates of mobility than newer immigrants, such as Spanish-speaking Catholics. On the other hand, Kosa (1970:22) found that the newer ethnic stock had higher rates than the older.

Two interpretations of the relation between immigration generation and mobility are possible. One, favoring Abramson, sees the rate of high mobility as being associated with degree of assimilation—which implies that the Catholics who have been in the United States the longest will have the higher rates of mobility. The other, favoring Kosa, sees the later-arriving Catholics as enjoying the benefits of the expanded economic opportunities of mid-century America. Each of these interpretations is plausible, and data are not now available to settle the issue. In any case, the conclusion stands that Catholic mobility rates are becoming more like Protestant mobility rates—except at the higher levels, where upward mobility continues to be easier for Protestants than for Catholics.

IS THE PROTESTANT ETHIC DEAD?

These studies of the relation among religion, social class, and social mobility are all inspired, in one way or another, by Weber's thesis concerning the effect of the Protestant Reformation on the rise of capitalism. When assessing the relevance of these studies to Weber's original argument, one must separate the question of how well his thesis has stood the test of time from the question of how useful it is today in predicting the impact of religion on social inequalities. A great deal of attention has been paid to the first question (see, for example, Green, 1959; Eisenstadt, 1968; Nelson, 1973), but resolving this issue is essentially a matter of going over historical data on the origins of capitalism to make sure that Weber's theory is empirically confirmed. The studies in this chapter address not this issue but the problem of whether or not Protestants still enjoy an advantage over Catholics.

The Puritan ethos, generally agreed to be a vital element in the origins and growth of capitalism as a new economic system, is not necessary for its continued existence. Indeed, Weber clearly stated his conviction that the motivations giving rise to the system would not be the same as those sustaining it. By his own time, Weber saw that the role of the Protestant churches had changed, although they still had a vital part to play in the economic system. He observed that church membership was still an important means by which Americans established the kind of trust upon which economic dealings depended. The question "To which church do you belong?" remained a pertinent one in a nation of traders looking for obvious signs of an individual's respectability and dependability. Since Weber's time, the computerization of the credit system has to some extent altered this picture, but church involvement continues to be a sign of respectability, at least in the small community. The Protestant Ethic survives at least in this particular.

The Protestant Ethic also survives, in part, in the modern "organization man." This might seem a paradox in view of Riesman's (1950) description of the change from the inner-directed to the other-directed personality, and in view of the remarks made in Chapter 11 about the shift away from the entrepreneurial idea to that of the bureaucrat. But vestiges of the Protestant Ethic are to be found in even the most modern of executives. They too are imbued with a rational drive for economic gain. Even their concern for "teamwork" and organizational harmony is consistent with the Protestant Ethic, for the Puritans were not the obstinate individualists they are often made out to be, but placed great emphasis on fitting in with the group and conforming to group standards.

The Protestant Ethic also survives in secular form, as Weber predicted it would. It survives in everyday injunctions such as "Anything that is worth doing is worth doing well." It is also manifest in the bourgeois disdain for "unnecessary" and "frivolous" expenditure and contempt for the "idle rich," as well as in the widespread ambivalence about enjoying leisure time and the fear of being taken over by one's possessions. In many ways, the importance of the Protestant Ethic today lies not in its actual relation to socioeconomic achievement, but in the *belief* that this relation exists. Although hard work does not guarantee success, although chances of upward mobility of great magnitude are low, contrary beliefs are widespread, especially among members of the middle and upper classes. These individuals are also much more disposed to argue that the poor owe their condition to lack of initiative and ambition, and to see their own success as proof of their possession of those attributes (Huber and Form, 1973:107). Welfare is approved only insofar as it recreates the individual for worldly, instrumental activism so that the country does not "waste its human resources" and thereby decrease productivity. However, these beliefs have lost a great deal of their specifically religious meaning, and they are now found equally among Protestants and Catholics.

The equal presence of a secularized version of the Protestant Ethic among Protestants and Catholics is demonstrated by Schuman (1971), who used 1966 data to examine the possibility of different attitudes toward work between the faiths. His conclusions are as follows:

1. Protestants are more likely than Catholics to rank the feeling of accomplishment a job provides as most important when choosing a job. But the five-percentage-point difference is not very significant. Only between high status Protestants and Catholics are significant differences found.
2. Only insignificant differences exist between Protestants and Catholics with regard to attitudes toward work. Just as many Catholics as Protestants take a positive attitude toward work, stressing its intrinsic rewards and its moral dimension. Featherman (1971:217) did find that Protestants responded more strongly to the intrinsically rewarding aspects of work, while Catholics tended to emphasize the material outcome of the job, but he attributes this attitude to work as a source of future economic goods to the relative economic deprivation of Catholics rather than to their religious ethic.
3. On the assumption that capitalist achievement requires a degree of asceticism, attitudes toward consumption were investigated. No interfaith differences appeared in such matters as approval of installment buying, attitudes toward saving, and emphasis on the "productive" as opposed to the "indulgent" use of leisure time.

The conclusion to be drawn from Schuman's analysis, and from the many studies summarized by Bouma (1973:148), is that no significant differences exist between Protestants and Catholics in regard to work and consumption. Equally important, Featherman (1971:221) concluded that such attitudinal differences as do exist are of minor importance in adult life. Schuman's data contain too few Jews for analysis, but Featherman (1971:217) found that they have "positive motivations toward work *both* as an instrumental activity (extrinsic value) and as a terminal activity (intrinsic value)."[3]

That Protestants and Catholics are becoming more alike in their attitudes toward work and consumption means three things. First, vestiges of a Protestant Ethic remain, but there is nothing distinctively Protestant about them anymore. Thus, self-interest has taken on new meaning. For most people, the idea of the self now lacks "any larger identification with social and religious realities," and the concept of interest is now without "any encompassing context of loyalties and obligations" (Bellah, 1975:xiii). This common sense utilitarianism provides no coherent sense

[3]Data on Protestant/Catholic economic differences in the United Kingdom are sparse. However, Sissons (1973:240) found that Catholics display an "emphasis upon income, security and an easy-going atmosphere at work," whereas Protestants were more dedicated to work itself, the possession of responsibility and the opportunity of working with or serving other people.

of economic morality. Second, attitudes toward work and leisure are becoming increasingly secularized; members of different faiths can share these attitudes without violating their religious principles. Third, the Protestant Ethic has indeed been made redundant, to a large extent because the economy no longer calls for such rules of conduct. This last point is important and needs some elaboration.

Technological and economic changes have made "inner asceticism" irrational in many contexts. The injunction to be thrifty is unwise when inflation is permanent and relatively cheap credit is widely available. Thriftiness also makes less sense when savings are imposed on the typical wage-earner by the reinvestment policies of major corporations and the tax programs of the State. Furthermore, corporate marketing trades heavily on the glorification of consumption—the consumption of more and more goods—and fosters an attitude of "Buy now, pay later." As a result, the American population is not thrifty: most Americans have few savings and many are chronically in debt.

The Protestant Ethic has also been made redundant by the growth of large-scale corporations. The traditional assumption that economic success is a direct result of hard work and self-discipline is undermined as more and more people become functionaries in large-scale organizations where their individual initiative is severely restricted and their productiveness is secured by external controls and the machine. About 80 percent of the white-collar population was self-employed in 1800, compared with about 15 percent today. Thus, the room for the "self-made person" has become severely restricted. In any case, "Much of the variance in sales, earnings, and profit margins can be explained by factors other than the impact of management. Hence it is difficult, if not impossible, for the manager within a large complex corporation to determine to what extent, if any, his individual efforts influence corporate profits or loss" (Winter, 1974:1139).

Three other changes that have taken place cast further doubt on the value of hard work and self-discipline. First, technological improvements now enable the worker to increase his productivity without greater personal effort. Second, trade unions have brought increased economic benefits through collective rather than individual effort. Third, the need for self-reliance has been diminished by the introduction of the welfare State. This last change is perhaps the most important of all. The Great Depression, in particular, "revealed that the self-made man did not guarantee the good order of the economy . . . and that the harmonic local community was not the model of the national community. Self-help failed to help the multitude of selves . . . Ascetic self-denial, perseverance, the power of the will—none prevailed" (Meyer, 1960:218).

A considerable portion of the economy is now politically determined by state spending, particularly for defense and social security. Whatever motivation the Protestant Ethic continues to provide, its impact on the economy must surely be slight. For it to have any consequence at all, the consumer would have to be sovereign (setting levels of demand for goods and their price), and if she ever enjoyed this position, she no longer does. Today, the corporation is sovereign, for it chooses which goods are to be marketed and in what quantities. The corporation, through advertising, has in many ways taken over from the churches the function of determining the correct way to behave and what conformity to group norms means. Advertising also engenders a fun morality, in which having fun (through consumption) is almost an obligation, and in which traditional ascetic ethics are replaced by new consumption ethics.

Ironically, the increasing technological and organizational complexity of life means that virtues such as hard work and thrift may be obstacles rather than aids to economic fortune. For instance, profitable farming operations rely increasingly on the use of expensive heavy machinery. Yet the purchase of such equipment, necessarily on credit, runs counter to the values many farmers have of self-reliance, hard work, and thrift. In fact, those farmers who conform most closely to the Protestant Ethic tend to make less rational decisions concerning the use of machinery and ultimately make less profit (see Goldstein and Eichhorn, 1961).

Thus, there is no simple answer to the question: Is the Protestant Ethic dead? There is little doubt that the puritanism described by Weber is a thing of the past, along with the entrepreneurial capitalism associated with it. Today, rags-to-riches stories continue to be told, and, ironically, a version of the Puritan Ethic does live on in groups such as the Mormons (O'Dea, 1957:143), the Seventh Day Adventists (Budd, 1973:105), the Black Muslims (Edwards, 1968; Tyler, 1966), the Jehovah's witnesses (Cooper, 1974) and Holiness sects (Johnson, 1961). But self-made individuals are so few and these religious groups so small that they are societally insignificant. A secular version of the Protestant Ethic, one that is largely stripped of transcendental references, is widely diffused but just as likely to be found among Catholics as Protestants (Hunt and Hunt, 1975:600). In a society increasingly dominated by large-scale planning and instrumental rationality and consumption values, no interfaith differences in economic ethos appear to be all that relevant.

Religious concerns seem to be becoming increasingly detached from economic considerations. Glenn and Hyland (1967:84) argue that parental status, not religion, is the key to economic success; Jackson et al. (1970:61) believe that "any religious effect can be ignored in building a theory of occupational achievement in contemporary society"; Huber and Form (1973:115) found that religious factors were irrelevant to how people see and justify the stratification system; and Ploch (1974:279) failed to find any trace of religious influence on economic attitudes. The gradual equalization of the faiths, *at least according to the very crude measures used* by the various researchers, suggest a growing secularization of economic life.[4]

CONCLUSION

Conflict theorists start with the assumption that property and property relations play the most important role in forming the contours of social inequality.

> In each type of society, there are two fundamental classes. Property relations constitute the axis of this dichotomous system: a minority of "non-producers," who control the means of production, are able to use this position of control to extract from the majority of "producers" the surplus product which is the source of their livelihood (Giddens, 1973:28).

Private property is the basis of the economic system in capitalist societies, and the advantages it affords some are the limits it imposes on others. The capitalist elite is composed of the occupants of the topmost positions within the dominant corporations, the senior managers and directors. The capitalist class also includes, not only major stockholders but also those who sell their labor at a great premium, such as top professionals and high state officials. The non-propertied class includes not only those who are forced to sell their labor but also individuals such as small shopkeepers who, although formally independent, are almost entirely at the mercy of big business for their success. If this is the basic cleavage within the capitalist system, what does religion have to do with it?

[4]The usual crude distinction between Protestant, Catholic and Jew does not afford a fair test of the Weber thesis because it ignores the theological differences within the faiths. Weber's original thesis concerned only the most Puritan wing of Protestantism, and was not intended to include either the Church of England or the Episcopal Church. Subsequent developments have probably included a shift in the location of the Protestant Ethic as Weber described it. The more pietistic Lutherans, for example, adhere more closely to the Protestant Ethic today than the more Calvinist Presbyterians (see Schuman, 1971). Southern Baptists are popularly identified with the Protestant Ethic, but their discipline of the body and the senses, unlike that of the Calvinists described by Weber, is treated, not as a means to an end, but as an end in itself. Their taboos against hard drink, loose sex and gambling are goals in themselves; they do not necessarily lead to a more acquisitive spirit. Finally, Weber's own work was largely interpretive, involving painstaking and detailed analysis of documents and diaries in the interest of understanding the meaning of religion and economics for the Puritan. Contemporary approaches to this problem are both crude and trivial, losing in depth of understanding what they might have gained in breadth of scope.

Unfortunately, the data presented in this chapter do not really address this problem, although they provide certain clues. One reason for this inadequacy is that no data are available on the association between wealth (rather than yearly income) and religious affiliation. Although there is some association between wealth and income, figures on income say little about the possession of property and savings, which not only make life more comfortable but also create vast inequalities of opportunity. About one half of one percent of the adults in the United States possess about one third of the nation's wealth: the tenth earning the most income holds about three quarters of all net savings, the bulk of which is inherited (Anderson, 1974:134).[5] The real inequalities appear, not in the area of "small wealth," but in the larger holdings which are, of course, the most significant. Small wealth (such as cars, appliances, and houses) is income-using wealth; big wealth is income-producing. In addition, big wealth means control over corporate activities, whereas small wealth means merely that a few thousand dollars worth of stock can be withdrawn if company performance is unsatisfactory. Extreme inequality in the holding of wealth is well documented, but there is no information on its association with religion.

A second reason for the inadequacy of the data reported in this chapter is that they do not provide information on the occupational elite. In most surveys, capitalists are disguised within the general category of "professional, managerial, and sales." Who gets the country's top jobs—the chief executive positions—is not really clear. It is known, for example, that 85 percent of the occupants of the topmost positions in the 200 largest corporations during the 1950s were Protestants—and in manufacturing, mining and finance corporations the proportion was 93 percent. Moreover, the individuals referenced in works such as *Who's Who* and *American Men of Science* are nearly all Protestant (Anderson, 1970:143).

The data presented earlier on occupational prestige is singularly unhelpful in deciding the religious composition of the occupational elite. Some of it is actually misleading: although 40 percent of all Jewish males are either managers or proprietors (Goldstein, 1968:78), the exclusion of Jews from top executive positions in corporations (except retail) is well documented (see, for example, United States Equal Opportunity Commission, 1968; Baltzell, 1964:322; Burck, 1976). The apparent equality of Catholics is also deceiving. Reporting that "the real mystery is the failure of Catholics to penetrate the top ranks of business," a 1970 survey found that only nine percent of the chief executive officers in the *Fortune*

[5]In his study of "Paper City" Underwood (1957:244) discovered that although the city was between 80 percent and 90 percent Catholic, Protestants owned the major textile and paper manufacturing concerns, the banks and the insurance companies.

500 corporations were Catholics (Diamond, 1970:320). Protestants made up 93 percent of the top officers in banking and insurance corporations. The individual net worth of 80 percent of these individuals ranged from 300,000 to 6 million dollars. A 1976 survey of chief executive officers reported that Catholics are still greatly underrepresented in proportion to their weight in the whole population. Episcopalians, Presbyterians and Congregationalists are greatly overrepresented. Baptists are underrepresented, and Methodists and Lutherans are represented in numbers equal to their proportion in the total population (Burck, 1976).

Further evidence suggesting that a Protestant occupational elite exists is the underrepresentation of Catholics and Jews in top political jobs such as the Presidency, member of Congress, and State governor (Rieselbach, 1973:33; Gaustad, 1968:125).[6] Catholics and Jews are able to secure government posts, but these tend to be relatively minor. The major government tasks of "foreign affairs management . . . policing . . . and stabilizing the economy" are performed by Protestants: the government in Washington is the basic field of operations of the dominant political group in the United States, a group that happens to be very disproportionately white and Protestant" (Hamilton, 1972:223).

A third reason the data in this chapter are inadequate as a test of the Marxian model is that they do not describe ability to enter elite positions. The data do show that at the lower levels of the stratification system Catholic rates of short-range mobility are as high as those for most Protestants. In fact, given the same point of origin, Catholics are likely to experience more educational mobility than Protestants. It is significant, however, that Protestants still enjoy higher rates of occupational mobility into elite positions (Greeley et al., 1976:50–51). Greeley (1977:64) brings out the ethnic differences within the major religious groups: "At the very top of the prestige scale (categories running from 88 to 99 on the hundred point scale) are 16 percent of the Jews, 9 percent of the Irish Catholics, 5 percent of the British Protestants, 4 percent of the Italians, and 2 percent of the Poles." As Catholics are not below Protestants in

[6]The Congress sitting in December, 1976 continued the overrepresentation of elite Protestant groups. For example, Presbyterians, who comprise 3 percent of the church members in the United States, comprised 11 percent of the Congressmen and 14 percent of the state governors. The figures for some other groups are equally striking: United Methodists, 7 percent of the church member population were 14 percent of the Congressmen and 2 percent of the state governors; for Episcopalians the figures were 2.2 percent, 11 percent and 8 percent; United Church, 1.4 percent, 4 percent and 6 percent; Unitarian, 0.1 percent, 2 percent and 4 percent. Certain groups were underrepresented. For example, Lutherans, who comprise 6.4 percent of all church members were 2 percent of Congressmen and 6 percent of state governors; Eastern Orthodox, 3.0 percent, 0.7 percent and 2.0 percent; Catholics, 37.3 percent, 24 percent and 30 percent. Other groups were fully represented: Jews, 4.6 percent, 5 percent and 4 percent; Disciples of Christ, 1.0 percent, 0.9 percent and 2 percent; Mormons, 1.7 percent, 2 percent and 2 percent (Christianity Today, 12/3/1976).

income, it seems unfair to attribute this finding to lack of ambition or willingness to work. Rather, it must be attributed to discrimination. Despite improved educational performance, Catholics still suffer from a combination of their identification as "ethnics," the foreignness of their religion, and their traditional association with lower-status groups. Mobility is clearly not as open to them as many of the studies reported in this chapter would suggest. Religion seems to have something to do with this, but more data on elites would be needed before we could say what this role is.[7]

This concluding section has dwelt so far on the kind of information that would be needed to really examine the religion/social class relationship from a Marxian point of view. What sense does the Marxian model make of what data there are?

First, there is so much overlap between Protestants and Catholics in regards to socioeconomic achievement, and so much variation within each religious group, that *broad interfaith comparisons are meaningless*. Irish Catholics perform as well as, or better than, all but a very few Protestants, and Baptists have an average income, occupational prestige score, and educational achievement level below all but the Spanish-speaking Catholics. Furthermore, this within-faith heterogeneity is becoming more marked over time. Yet, religious differences in socioeconomic status do exist, particularly at the level of the upper middle class, where real economic power begins to be felt.

Second, short-run mobility is not really affected by religion any more. Protestants and Catholics now compete for middle class jobs. However, a Protestant elite survives. Entry into elite positions is still difficult for Catholics, but less so for Jews. To some extent, religion still marks the boundary between the capitalist and the non-propertied classes, but the use of religion in this way is declining.

[7]Featherman (1971:213) sees no evidence of in-career discrimination against Catholics. "If one adjusts the gross differentials in sub-group achievement for both social background and prior socioeconomic attainments (where education is antecedent to occupational achievement, which in turn precedes economic achievement)," no statistically significant religio-ethnic differentials in occupation or economic achievement remain. In other words, socioeconomic differences between adult Protestants and Catholics are entirely due to social origins, schooling, and early career attainment differences.

15

RELIGION,

ETHNICITY AND RACE

INRODUCTION

Social conflicts in the United States do not form around a division between property owners and wage laborers. The most fundamental cleavage in the United States is racial, and to a lesser extent ethnic. This cleavage crosscuts class lines. Insofar as religion is an integral part of ethnicity, and insofar as separate religions have always marked the boundaries between the races in the United States, religion has helped add a *caste* system to American society, a system that attenuates pure class conflict while adding bitter conflicts of its own.

The purpose of this chapter is to describe the impact of religion on ethnic and racial conflicts in the United States. The tie between religion and ethnicity is very close. The first step, then, is to see to what extent religion has furthered or hindered ethnic acculturation and assimilation. This entails an examination of the "melting pot" thesis and a cursory review of the history of religio-ethnic conflict in the United States. The second topic of the chapter is the link between religion and race conflict. A brief overview of the impact of the churches on the formation of race relations in the United States is followed by an examination of institutional racism in the churches themselves. The chapter concludes with a discussion of the relation between religion and racial prejudice.

RELIGION AND ETHNIC CONFLICT

An ethnic group "consists of those who conceive of themselves as being alike by virtue of their common ancestry, real or fictitious, and who are so regarded by others" (Shibutani and Kwan, 1965:47). Ethnic identity consists of feelings of (1) community—through neighborhood, peer-group, and leisure-time pursuits; (2) association—participation in work, educational and charitable organizations dominated by people of a common ancestry; (3) tribalism—a sense of peoplehood and common origin, a feeling of primordial ties; and (4) common religion.

Ethnic boundaries in the United States are more permeable than those of race, but they are still clearly marked and difficult to cross. For example, residential segregation by ethnicity is common (see Guest and Weed, 1976). Indeed, there is almost as much residential segregation between Norwegian and Russian immigrants as there is between Russian immigrants and blacks—although blacks are, as a whole, much more segregated (Greeley, 1974b:3). The ethnic group, with its own particular class position, its own close-knit marriage patterns, its traditional party loyalties, and its culture, is a firmly established part of the development of the United States, and no person can understand present-day social conflicts adequately without recognizing this.

The role of religion in creating and perpetuating ethnic divisions has been an important one. Religion is a part of ethnicity. Ethnic groups perpetuate folk religions, binding particular peoples to particular religions by means of language, community organization and patterns of interaction. A desire to defend and preserve ethnic heritage goes hand in hand with preserving religious traditions. On the other hand, commitment to distinct religious traditions no doubt rationalizes and helps sustain ethnic differences. "The survival of ethnic identities seems to be only meaningful in the context of the survival of religious identities. Religion provides an essential mediation between the ethnic group and the larger culture of the modern world" (Bellah, 1975:108). This can be seen most clearly in the case of the Jews—who have created a subcommunity in which parallel institutions for health, education, community organization, and charity splay out from the synagogue—but it is also visible in the ethnic divisions within the Catholic and Eastern Orthodox Churches. Religion can have an important impact on the number of characteristics that separate ethnic groups, on the clarity of distinction made among them (the most profound differences between people are cultural), on the degree of solidarity within them, on the amount of mobility among them, and on how much the whole system of ethnic stratification is taken for granted.

The Herberg Thesis

Although the tie between ethnicity and religion in the United States has always been very close, it is the opinion of some that the ethnic factor has become less important in recent years. This is thought to be due to the reduction of the yearly number of immigrants to about 400,000 (most of whom are North Europeans), and to the gradual disappearance of the first-generation immigrants of the pre-1920 era. As the older, established immigrant groups have begun to acculturate, it is argued, the bond between religious affiliation and ethnic identity has loosened. The once-sharp ethnic distinctions are gradually being replaced by much more general feelings of identification with one of the three major American faiths—Protestantism, Catholicism and Judaism (Herberg, 1960:34).

During the late 1950s, this thesis attracted considerably support. It seemed to explain why, during the 1950s, church attendance boomed while interest in and knowledge of specific church teachings remained low. Herberg argued that the three major faiths had become the princi-pal sources of American self-identification, more important for that purpose than either class or ethnicity. Furthermore, he maintained that the three major faiths were but different cultural manifestations of the same fundamental unity. They represented a common subscription to a dominant set of values that he labeled "the American Way of Life," which included a positive evaluation of religion itself, a faith in the democratic system, a belief in progress, and a sense of national mission. Herberg's argument not only elevated meaningful religious commit-ment to a very general level, one that far transcended old denomina-tional boundaries (which he saw as increasingly redundant), but also denied the future significance of ethnicity as a factor in American life. As it is the purpose of this chapter to explore the continuing relation between ethnicity and religion, a consideration of Herberg's thesis is obviously important.

Herberg's far-reaching thesis met with two initial and obvious criti-cisms. First, he ignored the impact of secular humanists on the forma-tion of American identity. Although small in number, these individuals have played an important role in determining moral, ethical and cultural standards in the United States. Second, he ignored altogether racial divisions. For the present purposes, however, five other criticisms of Herberg's kind of thinking (for in his use of the "melting pot" theory

Herberg was by no means alone) are more relevant to an understanding of ethnicity.

First, Herberg ignored class factors. He seems to have assumed that ethnicity is free of status connotations. But, of course, ethnic labels are commonly used to place people socially. For instance, there is a clear status ranking within Catholicism. The Irish have dominated the Catholic community because they immigrated earlier and because of their familiarity with English. For example, they make up 17 percent of the American Catholic male population but 34 percent of the active Catholic priests and 49 percent of the Catholic Bishops (National Opinion Research Center, 1972:88). Ethnic insignia retain their social importance because of their class connotations.

Second, the argument that ethnic identification is less important for those born in the United States than for first-generation immigrants reflects the "melting pot" theories popular in the 1950s. At that time, it was assumed that although uneven progress was to be expected, all immigrant groups would gradually blend into a common type especially now that immigration had ceased. However, the 1950s were a time of great national insecurity and conservatism, in many ways similar to the early 1920s, when immigration restrictions were first imposed. There is reason to believe that the pressure to conform to a common "Americanism" was especially strong during that period. What Herberg saw as a trend, then, was probably only one particular fluctuation. The resurgence during the 1960s of a greater ethnic consciousness belies this trend. The 1960s suggest that acculturation was proceeding much faster than assimilation. In other words, the different ethnic groups were perhaps gaining a greater measure of ability to speak and write the dominant language, but they were not necessarily assimilating, in the sense of forming friendships with different ethnics, marrying them or tolerating them in the same neighborhood.

Third, at no point did Herberg provide any factual evidence that a meaningful source of identity for American people is something so amorphous as "Protestant," "Catholic," or "Jew." He is on firmer ground in the case of the Jews, precisely because they are an ethnic group. Surveys cast serious doubt on Herberg's contention that denominational memberships are becoming meaningless. Differences in religious outlook among the members of various Protestant denominations are "both vast and profound" (Glock and Stark, 1965:116). Nor can divisions within Catholicism be denied, especially since they tend to fall along ethnic lines. Many parishes are still ethnic enclaves. In Gary, Indiana, 25 of the 45 parishes are drawn along ethnic lines. In Chicago, there are 43 ethnic parishes for Poles, 27 for Germans, 12 for Italians, 10 for Lithuanians, 8 each for Bohemians and Slovaks, 7 for Greeks, 5 for French Catholics, 4 for Croations, 2 each for Slovenians, Hungarians and Mexicans, and one each for Dutch, Belgians, Melkites, Chaldeans, and Chinese; a total of 135 ethnic parishes out of 279.

Fourth, Herberg's thesis assumes a third generation return to religion measured, in part, by higher rates of attendance. But the evidence on rates of attendance by generation since immigration is mixed. "Three groups show steady and continuous decline over the three generations: the French-Canadian Catholics, the Jews, and the North European Protestants. . . . Two other groups, the Anglo-Saxon Protestants and Irish Catholics, also show signs of declining church attendance, but not as strongly" (Abramson, 1975:166). Among Polish and Italian Catholics, "it is the *children* of the immigrants who rise . . . in religious association, but it is the *grandchildren* who fall away" (Abramson, 1975:167).

Finally, Herberg's thesis also ignores: (a) the fact that different ethnic groups entered the United States at different periods and therefore do not share the same immigration experiences; (b) ethnic differences in country of origin, and the fact that strength of loyalty to ancestors differs from one culture to another; and (c) the different regions of settlement of ethnic groups, each providing its own opportunities for assimilation.

The Herberg thesis, the most important element of which is the present irrelevance of the tie between religion and ethnicity, must collapse under the weight of these criticisms. In any case, its stimuli—rising church attendance and waning ethnic visibility—have disappeared. Ethnic identity remains strong, and religion continues to play an important part in its expression.

The History of Religious and Ethnic Conflict

In the history of American inter-group conflict, ethnicity and religion have been inextricably intertwined. The association of Anglo-Saxon ethnicity and Protestantism, the tie between Catholicism and mainly Italian-, Irish-, Polish-, and Spanish-speaking immigrants, and, of course, the inseparable unity of ethnicity and religion among the Jews, constitute an important part of American social history.

Data taken from seven National Opinion Research Center surveys conducted between 1963 and 1972 show that the country of origin of an individual's parents and his own religion are associated quite closely. Those whose parents were Italians, Poles, Slavs, French, or Spanish-speaking are 100 percent Catholic; those with Irish parents 38 percent Catholic; and those with German parents 20 percent Catholic. Those of British or Scandinavian background, on the other hand, are 100 percent Protestant. They comprise 53 percent of all non-black, non-Oriental

American Protestants. The Irish, the eastern and southern Europeans, and the Spanish-speaking make up 51 percent of all Catholics (Greeley, 1974b:42).

In the light of this superimposition of religion and ethnicity, it is hardly surprising that ethnic conflict in America has always carried religious overtones. The Protestant Anglo-Saxons (who made up the great majority of the early settlers) have dominated the economic, political, and cultural life of the country. Only since the last quarter of the nineteenth century have Catholics and Jews assumed any importance. The history of ethnic conflict in the United States is, then, very much a tale of oppression by WASPs over other religio-ethnic groups.

ANTI-CATHOLICISM. For most of American history, prejudice and discrimination against Catholics has been heavily tinged with ethnic hostilities, so much so that it is impossible to say where one leaves off and the other begins. Initially, anti-Catholicism was devoid of ethnic connotations, for the Protestant settlers brought with them hostile attitudes toward the Catholic Church that they had developed in Europe untinged by ethnic considerations. The constitutions of many of the original states contained clauses excluding Catholics from office. However, most of these were rescinded by the 1820s, when the major influx of Catholic immigrants began.

During the 1940s, the Catholic population in the United States doubled, mainly as a result of emigration from Ireland. This surge of Catholics was greeted by the rise of the Know-Nothing Party (1849–1861), membership in which was restricted to white, American-born Protestants without Catholic parents or wives. Know-Nothings feared that the newcomers, loyal to a seemingly autocratic and alien church, would endanger American security and political freedoms. In addition, the alien culture of the vast majority of the Catholics provided a convenient target of blame for the increasing problems of poverty, unrest, and crime caused by the growth of the nation. "The Catholics, somewhat like the Jews in the next century, provided a great foil for extremist purposes, because this visible body of ethnic immigrants was connected with images of secret, exotic and conspiratorial institutions" (Lipset and Raab, 1970:49). The Know-Nothing movement was preceded by a "craze for disclosures" which included such notorious publications as *Six Months in a Convent* (1834) and *The Awful Disclosures of Maria Monk* (1836) (Myers, 1960:92).

The American Party (the proper name for the Know-Nothings) was no mere fringe group. In 1854, it seated 8 of the 62 senators and 104 of the 234 representatives in Congress, and put 9 governors in state houses (Myers, 1960:144). The collapse of the American Party at the onset of the Civil War was as rapid as its rise, but this short-lived movement found a successor in the American Protective Association, founded in 1887. This later movement was inspired in part by the rise of a Catholic *nouveau riche* and in part by the growth of Catholic political power in the form of the urban Democratic party machines. A new wave of disclosures appeared; these emphasized the links among "Rome, Rum and Rebellion" (see Kinzer, 1964).

One of the most vocal manifestations of anti-Catholicism was the Temperance movement. The goal of the more moderate Temperance advocates was to better socialize new Americans into the old Protestant virtues of self-control, hard work, impulse renunciation, and sobriety— virtues that were also functional for an emerging industrial labor force. This assimilationist drive was quite humanitarian, and was linked not only with the abolitionist movement but also with early feminism. The coercive side of the Temperance crusade drew a heavy line between two distinct subcultures—the traditional, rural and small town, old middle class of the Anglo-Saxon Protestant and the modern, urban, new middle class of the non-Anglo-Saxon Catholic. This side of the Temperance movement took a much more militant line against the lifestyle and values of the new urban dwellers and was more overtly anti-Catholic. It was symbolized in the formation in 1896 of the Anti-Saloon League, which not only defined itself by what it opposed but also specifically attacked the saloon, the symbol of the urban, ethnic, Catholic, lower-class leisure style. Rum, Romanism, and rebellion were pitted against prohibition, Protestantism, and patriotism.

The passage of the Eighteenth Amendment marked the culmination of the attempts by Anglo-Saxon Protestants to preserve their grip on the morality of a growing America, but Prohibition foreshadowed their decline. The repeal of that amendment signaled the consolidation of both the urban and the Catholic culture as normal and acceptable parts of American life. The era of Prohibition was, however, a time of extreme anti-Catholicism and ethnic differences in general. The upper classes excluded Catholics from clubs, business associations and resorts to an extent that was "little short of incredible" (Domhoff, 1967:29).

The Protestant middle class gave their support to a revived Ku Klux Klan. Basically a political movement, the Klan feared the Catholics' "foreign allegiances," their desire to unite Church and State, their undemocratic ecclesiology, and the power of the priest. For this and many other reasons, including racial hatred, the Klan became very popular during the 1920s. By 1922, it was operating in all states and had a membership of five million. The Klan comprised eight million members in 1925, but after this year it began to decline (Myers, 1960:241).

The upsurge of anti-Catholicism in the 1920s was generated by a number of social forces. These included:

1. the residue of nativism generated during the First World War;
2. the rapid growth of the Catholic community, especially its augmentation by the non-Anglo-Saxon southern Europeans—between 1891 and 1910, 8 million of the 12.5 million immigrants came from eastern and southern Europe (Krickus, 1976:42);
3. a fear of new entanglements with the Vatican at a time of increasing isolationism;
4. hostility toward the growth of cities, with which Catholics and non-Anglo-Saxons were associated.

The anti-Catholicism of the 1920s included a movement to reduce immigration, aimed especially at reducing the number of non-WASPs entering the country. The subsequent decline in large-scale immigration after the passage of quota laws brought about an abatement of militant anti-Catholicism in the later years of the decade. Indeed, it was possible for Al Smith (a Catholic) to become the Democratic candidate in the 1928 presidential election. However, he did lose the election, and there can be no doubt that he lost some votes because of his Catholicism, especially in the South (see Bailey, 1964:92–110).[1]

Anti-Catholicism weakened during the Great Depression, in part because the Protestant work ethic lost much of its credibility in the face of massive unemployment and high inflation. However, fringe groups and demagogues such as Gerald K. Winrod remained active, fanning the embers of religious and ethnic bigotry. Hostility toward Catholics rose again during the late 1940s and early 1950s. The most prominent political figure of this time, Joseph McCarthy (himself a Catholic), caught a tide of cold-war isolationism and xenophobia to stir up suspicion of all foreign entanglements and allege countless cases of disloyalty. Catholics as well as Jews suffered from this resurgence of prejudice. More extreme Protestant groups, such as the American Council of Christian Churches, did not hesitate to link Catholicism with Communism (see Curry, 1972).

Organized anti-Catholicism lives on in groups such as the Americans and Other Protestants United for Separation of Church and State. Much of the desire of this group to maintain separation of Church and State stems from its anxiety about growing Catholic power. Although it concerns itself with all Church/State issues, it is much more likely to become involved in cases concerning perceived Catholic "encroachments" (Sorauf, 1975:60). Just as they did during the Temperance crusade, Protestants continue to mobilize against practices that are closely identified with the ethnic Catholic groups. For example, they vigorously condemn gambling, knowing full well that it is the major source of

---

[1] Although Smith lost the election, the significance of his Catholicism is unclear. Not only was he a Catholic, but he was also identified as an Irish "city slicker" who was opposed to Prohibition (see Silva, 1962).

income for many Catholic, working-class parishes in urban areas (Underwood, 1957:132).

Both Catholics *and* Protestants believe that Catholics are discriminated against in politics. Protestants believe that Catholics engage in "undemocratic" bloc voting. Catholics believe that Protestants discriminate against them in employment. Kersten (1970:86) found that Lutherans, especially in the more conservative denominations, are very suspicious of Catholics. As many as 37 percent of the members of the Wisconsin Synod feel that Catholics are getting too much power. This kind of fear and hostility is the result not of disagreement over teachings, but of differences in lifestyle and community, differences of a "noncognitive, emotive" character (Schroeder, 1964:73).

A great deal of anti-Catholicism is directed at the Catholic system of education, which is seen as an alien institution teaching un-American loyalties. Ironically, Catholics who attend Catholic schools are no different in their political loyalties from Catholics who attend mixed schools. They are just as likely to be interested in community affairs and just as likely to have non-Catholic friends. They also show greater tolerance toward non-Catholics than do Catholics who attend mixed schools (Greeley and Rossi, 1966:137). Whatever the beliefs of Protestants, then, the Catholic educational system does not appear to be "subversive."

American anti-Catholicism is now muted, but it survives, especially among the more fundamentalist Protestants who are less educated, relatively poor, and living in small communities in the South (Lipset and Raab, 1970:44). Much of this remaining hostility is, as it always has been, tinged with ethnic prejudice, but it would be a mistake to think that religion causes ethnic prejudice in this case. What is much more likely is that Protestantism, and the manner and morals associated with it, is less the motivation for ethnic prejudice than the excuse for it. It serves to rationalize feelings of hostility already present.

ANTI-SEMITISM. Jews have been the target of prejudice and discrimination for centuries. It is impossible to separate the ethnic and religious components of this prejudice. It is of interest, however, to try to assess the impact of religion on the treatment of the Jews, for Jewish-Gentile conflict has been one of the hardest fought of all social divisions. The object here is to see to what extent religion has added to the virulence of the conflict.

There is some evidence that, overall, religious people tend to be more anti-Semitic than nonreligious people. For example, college students who belong to religious clubs are more anti-Semitic than those who are not affiliated with any religious society (Blum and Mann, 1960:99). Nationally, the stronger the religious commitment a person has, the stronger the anti-Semitism (Lipset and Raab, 1970:441). Hostility toward Jews by Protestants and Catholics has a long history, and has been more virulent than the hostility shown by Protestants and Catholics toward each other. Jews have always had difficulties gaining entrance into top corporate-management positions, government posts, and political office. They have been systematically discriminated against in social life. For example, a survey by *Rights* magazine discovered that 67 percent of social clubs practice some form of religious discrimination against Jews, most of them in covert and hard-to-oppose ways (Mack, 1963:98). Jews have been discriminated against in other elite areas, such as resorts (see Baltzell, 1964).

Whatever other reasons there might be for this kind of discrimination, the fact that Jews and Christians are religious rivals of long standing has no doubt played a part. This hostility has been intensified by the fact that the Jews, unlike the majority of Catholics, have been "retentivist": they "reject the idea that assimilation is the end toward which they should strive" (Sklare, 1971:4). The form and substance of anti-Semitism has varied enormously from time to time. Like the Catholics, American Jews have been linked with conspiracies to undermine the democratic system and enslave the American people to an alien power. But more than the Catholics, the Jews have been linked to nefarious concentrations of economic power. Whereas the Catholics have been suspected of political corruption and sedition and of attempting to take over the school system, the Jews have more typically been suspected of economic manipulation, exploitation, and graft.

Research into the impact of religion on prejudice and discrimination against Jews is guided by two contradictory assumptions. The first sees in mainstream American religion an ethic of brotherly love and charity that would seem to work against anti-Semitism. The second sees the long history of Jewish/Gentile religious warfare and expects Christians to harbor feelings of fear, resentment, suspicion, and anger toward the "Christ killers." The precise nature of the impact of religion on anti-Semitism has provoked a great deal of discussion among social scientists.

Most of this debate centers on the results of a 1964 national survey reported by Glock and Stark (1966). On the basis of these data, the authors concluded that there is indeed a religious factor at work generating and sustaining anti-Semitic attitudes—a conclusion that not all social scientists have accepted. Middleton (1973:35) summarizes Glock and Stark's complex argument succinctly:

They argue that orthodox religious faith leads Christians to take a particularistic view of their religious status, which in turn leads them to hold the historic Jew responsible for the crucifixion of

Jesus. Religious hostility to the historic Jews breeds in them hostility toward the modern Jew. If the individual accepts norms of religious libertarianism, however, the causal sequence may be partly broken at any of these earlier steps. In the final link in the causal chain those who view the modern Jew as an unforgiven crucifier being punished by God also tend to develop secular anti-Semitic beliefs.

Glock and Stark do *not* maintain that religiosity in itself leads to anti-Semitism, but only that a certain kind of religious bigotry does. The more religiously bigoted the individual, the more likely he is to hold anti-Semitic beliefs. Controls for race, education, region, and sex do not alter this relationship. It is important to repeat, however, that there is no simple cause and effect relationship between religious orthodoxy and prejudice. Hostility toward present-day Jews is strongly related to religiosity only if religious hostility is also present—which is not always the case.[2]

The Protestant clergy are less likely than the laity to be anti-Semitic. For example, only 10 percent of the clergy agree that Jews are more likely than Gentiles to cheat in business, compared with a third of the laity. However, the clergy do manifest considerable *religious hostility* toward the Jews. They are as likely as not, for example, to agree that "the reason the Jews have so much trouble is because God is punishing them for rejecting Jesus" (Stark, 1971:52).

The more theologically conservative a clergyman, the more likely he is to express religious hostility toward Jews. This holds true even when controls for socioeconomic status, sex, age, and political preference are imposed. The clergy are prone, then, to express fear and distrust of Jews in a religious context, but they are not as ready as the laity to make the transition to secular anti-Semitism.

ANTI-PROTESTANTISM. Because they are the majority group, Protestants have not been thought of as the object of prejudice and discrimination. However, relations among the faiths and among the various ethnic groups with which they are associated have undoubtedly been soured by religious hostility toward WASPs. Catholics feel a keen sense of rivalry and betrayal toward Protestants, a sentiment that spills over into a generalized hostility. They condemn Protestants for being a breakaway group, patronize them for being disunited and conflictive, and distrust

[2]Glock and Stark's measure of religious bigotry includes: (1) a firm belief in God, the Devil and life after death; (2) strong feelings of particularism (for example, that Christians are God's chosen people and that salvation is impossible without belief in Jesus); (3) negative attitudes toward religious libertarianism (for example, regarding favorably restrictions on speech and assembly of atheists); (4) belief that the historic Jews crucified Jesus; (5) a belief that the modern Jews are being punished by God.

them because they support groups such as the Ku Klux Klan and the White Citizen's Councils. Moreover, Catholics regard Protestants as intolerant and clannish (Lenski, 1963:67). Probably for the same reason that few studies have been done of prejudice by blacks toward whites, no studies seem to have been done of the attitude of Catholics and Jews toward Protestants.[3]

Declining Religious Differences?

The extent to which religion can intensify or inhibit ethnic conflict depends a great deal on the amount of difference there is among the various religious groups that have traditionally been aligned with ethnic groups. There is some evidence that the three major faiths are becoming more alike in several important respects, and to the extent that this is so, the contribution of religion to any ethnic conflicts that might remain would surely be reduced.

As the number of Catholics in the population of the United States has increased and, as their general level of affluence has risen, they have tended to Americanize. They are no longer quick to see themselves as a foreign group, and they have come to regard themselves as competitors for the top positions in society. At the same time, they are beginning to question the value of some of their separate institutions. This is evident in some of the changes which have recently taken place in Catholic colleges: (1) curricula have been opened to new subjects such as social science; (2) colleges have begun to make self-studies and employ outside consultants to advise them on more efficient performance; (3) faculties have been upgraded according to universalistic criteria; (4) lay control over the administration of colleges has been increased; (5) faculties have been given greater autonomy, and their right to collective bargaining

---

[3]In the United Kingdom, the major religio-ethnic polarity is between the Anglo-Saxon, Anglican center and the Celtic Nonconformist and Catholic periphery. This is clearly so in Ulster, but it is also true in Wales, where the Celtic, Nonconformist native tenant has long been subordinated to the Anglo-Saxon Anglican absentee landlord. In England, the proportion of nonconformists in the population in 1851 was about ten percent; in Wales it was about 30 percent. In 1961, the proportions were 14 percent and 39 percent (Hechter, 1975:176). The formal establishment of the Anglican Church in Wales has always been regarded by the Welsh as an adjunct to English political domination. The campaign to disestablish the Anglican Church at the end of the nineteenth century became a "symbolic focus of ethnic and economic oppression" (Martin, 1967:95). Hechter (1975:338) found that higher rates of Nonconformity tend to be associated with lower per capita income, suggesting a pattern of religio-ethnic discrimination. Religion is also used as a means of emphasizing ethnic differences in the United Kingdom. Even where Englishmen in Wales originally shared the Nonconformity of the Welsh, "contact between individuals of different nationality often led to religious re-identification on the part of Englishmen, so that mutual statuses between the two groups were minimized. This, in turn, created antipathy to the English migrants, and was probably a stimulus to the development of nationalist sentiments in the Celtic periphery" (Hechter, 1975:191).

recognized; (6) course requirements and residence rules have been relaxed; (7) censorship has been reduced. In other words, during the 1960s, a time of great upheaval in all educational institutions, Catholic colleges came more and more to resemble their secular counterparts.

The Catholic Church in America has become more characteristically "American." The acculturation of the Catholic Church got under way before the First World War with the formation in 1917 of the National Catholic War Council, which coordinated the war effort of American Catholics. The Church thus acquired a new and distinctively American voice. Moreover, this was a voice that spoke of patriotism and love of country, a bonus for a church often suspected of foreign entanglements and the exercise of hidden powers. In 1919, this Council grew into the National Catholic Welfare Council, a purely voluntary association of bishops that was accepted only grudgingly by the Vatican. The important thing, however, was that American Catholics now appeared to be Americans first and Catholics second. In 1966, the NCWC was dissolved as a result of Vatican Council II initiatives, and was replaced by two bodies that further established the autonomy of the Church in the United States. The National Conference of Catholic Bishops focuses mainly on internal affairs, and the United States Catholic Conference gives the Church a lobbying voice in American politics. The Church has thus acquired an increasingly distinct and autonomous American identity, one that makes possible its competition with other American denominations on a more or less equal footing.

American Catholicism has gradually accommodated itself to American pluralism. Protestants have traditionally been more disposed to believe that religious beliefs can, and should, be propagated competitively. Therefore, they have encouraged a healthy rivalry among the separate faiths in the search for adherents, a competition that is conducted in a spirit of mutual toleration and respect—ideally at least. For many years, the Catholic minority found this idea congenial in practice but distasteful in theory. However, since Vatican II, there has developed in the Catholic Church a greater spirit of toleration toward other faiths in the United States. The Declaration of Religious Freedom issued by the Council signaled a more positive attitude toward religious pluralism and a significant advance on the pre-Conciliar attitude of grudging toleration. The net result is that the Catholic Church in America has moved closer to the Protestant denominational form.

An equivalent process of homogenization is affecting the Jewish community.

> There has long been an over-all development of new forms of
> Jewish identity and expression, with an emphasis on those aspects

that are congruent with Americanisation. Religious commitments are retained when they are functionally integrated within a secular context and where retention of Jewish identity is possible in a form that is expected and conditioned by the majority of the community (Goldstein, 1968:229–30).

Furthermore, Jewish practices, always emphasizing the community as a whole, have increasingly taken on the congregational principle of religious organization, especially in the suburb (Glazer, 1972:134). Even the rabbinical function has become Americanized. The emphasis is less on "scholar-saint" and more on the role of leader of public worship, director of educational and social services, community representative of the Jews, and pastoral counselor.

The Jewish Americanization experience is marked to some extent by the shift in Judaism from the traditionalism and orthodoxy of Conservative Judaism to the liberalism of Reform Judaism (Glazer, 1972:46). Reform Jews make up 12 percent of the first generation Jews but 35 percent of the third generation (Goldstein, 1968:177). Jews and non-Jews are becoming more alike in a variety of ways. In other words, the Jewish middle class is becoming more like the Protestant middle class than the Jewish working class—although intermarriage remains low. The productive aspect of class and religious differences are decreasing in importance, but wide differences in consumption remain.

RELIGION, RACIAL PREJUDICE AND RACIAL CONFLICT

The most fundamental division within the United States today is racial. The relations between black and white have usually been hostile, unfailingly stressful, and very often extremely violent. Although the ethnic divisions just described have been marked by grave injustices and severe oppression, it is only blacks (and, to a lesser extent, Indians, Orientals, Mexican-Americans, and Puerto Ricans) who have been placed in the position of a pariah caste. The color barrier has proved much more difficult to surmount than that of strange language, new customs, and social exclusion (see Blackwell, 1976). Additionally, the stigma of slavery, family disorganization, chronic poverty, political disbarment, and a more or less complete break with their past has severely impaired the ability of blacks to work singly or together to assimilate (see Taeuber and Taeuber, 1964; Appel, 1970).

The precise contribution of the churches to the development of this caste system has been much debated. On the one hand, ethics of equality and brotherhood have inspired Christians to break down racial barriers and fight discrimination. On the other hand, the denominations are largely segregated, and many have long espoused and defended racialist beliefs and practices. The focus of this section will be on the role of the denominations in perpetuating racial conflicts. The attempts of the denominations to eliminate the caste system will be the subject of Chapter 17.

The relation between religion and race was established early in the history of the United States. A few churchmen attacked slavery, others did not see it as a religious issue, but most supported it. The Methodists and the Baptists, who at first attacked the slave system, were prompted by their growing affluence (and ownership of slaves) to "recede from their position in the face of general opposition to their stand" (Frazier, 1974:29). By the end of the eighteenth century, the institution of religion itself had become firmly segregated as independent black denominations were formed in the North and local assemblies were segregated in the South. Blacks were attracted chiefly to the Methodist and Baptist preachers, from whom they learned that they "were expected to accept their lot in this world and if they were obedient and honest and truthful they would be rewarded in the world after death" (Frazier, 1974:19).

The church provided a haven for blacks in a hostile white world. But is served also to perpetuate the caste system. It is significant that much of the impetus for segregation has come from black churchmen. Despite the slow but gradual desegregation of secular institutions, blacks have exhibited no strong desire to integrate their own institutions or surrender their religious autonomy. It is almost as if they believe that "such a movement would serve to undermine the resources necessary to withstand the white world" (Washington, 1964:248). The independent black denominations (such as the American Methodist Episcopal Church, the National Baptist Convention of America, the National Baptist Convention of the USA, and the Progressive Baptist Convention of America) may well be among the last social institutions to integrate, for they are a powerful source of self-esteem for the black people, a source they are most reluctant to surrender.

After the Civil War, black religion was augmented by schisms of black church people from white denominations as Jim Crow laws began to take effect. For example, the Colored (later Christian) Methodist Episcopal Church was formed in 1870, and later became the "Central Jurisdiction" of the United Methodist Church in the grand union that took place in 1939. Black denominations such as this have tended to strengthen a belief in the invulnerability of whites and the vulnerability of blacks. In addition, they have fostered a sense of separatism by their own internal stratification, which has become more marked with black migration to the cities. Upper class blacks, few in number, have inclined toward membership in predominantly white denominations, especially Episcopalianism. Middle class blacks have remained loyal to the independent Methodist and Baptist denominations. With urbanward migration, many working class blacks lost the churchgoing habit and others joined the sects and storefront churches (see Blackwell, 1975:78–88). Blacks have thus established elaborate religious parallels to white institutions. It is not surprising that Frazier (1974:75) calls religion "the most important institutional barrier to integration and the assimilation of Negroes."

White churches have run the gamut from fierce and aggressive segregation to liberal integration, the modal point being passive acceptance of institutional racism combined with an attack on prejudice at the individual level. The segregation of the mainstream denominations is probably a result of neglect as much as anything else. Orthodox theologians have simply ignored race as an issue: "It is as if Black people do not exist—indeed have never existed" (Lincoln, 1974:143).

Historically, denominations have mirrored prevailing racial attitudes. Before the Civil War, all denominations, with the exception of a few small groups like the Quakers, supported slavery and were segregated. The Methodists (1844), the Baptists (1845), and the Presbyterians (1858 and again in 1861) all divided into pro- and anti-slavery factions around the time of the Civil War. The Presbyterians actually split first over the "Old School versus New School" controversy. However, about one third of the more conservative Old School membership was located in the South, and the schism had distinct racial overtones. The New School split in 1858 and the Old School in 1861, this time explicitly over the issue of slavery, and the supporters of slavery went on to form the Presbyterian Church in the United States. This division persists, and the racial overtones remain. "In 1958, when [the Presbyterian Church in the United States] refused re-union with the northern church, the votes in its presbyteries correlated markedly with black-and-white population ratios in the respective districts" (Ahlstrom, 1975,II:106). The Episcopalians, Lutherans, and Catholics escaped division partly because their conservatism led them to offer tacit support for slavery and partly because their diocesan structure enabled them to head off conflicts at the highest levels by making regional arrangements. Other churches avoided schism only because, like the Unitarians and the Congregationalists, they had few members in the South or, like the Disciples of Christ and the Jews, they were so highly decentralized.

Religion was used by both North and South to justify their respective positions during the Civil War: "for violence of statement and ultimacy of appeal, the clergy and the religious press seem to have led the multitude" (Ahlstrom, 1975,II:119). After the war, the southern churches consistently supported the establishment of a nonslave but caste system, symbolized in the Jim Crow laws. The strongly evangelical religion dominant in the South, stressing a pristine, moral kind of church, became part of a conservative worldview, an integral part of which was an adamant defense of white supremacy. During Reconstruction, American Protestantism "in its best moods was capable of genuine charity, but in its average performance and typical expression, it strengthened nativism, contributing in many ways to extreme manifestations of intolerance" (Ahlstrom, 1975,II:328).

Racial Segregation in the Churches

It is not easy to answer the question of whether or not the churches of today are less segregated than they were at the turn of the century. It is fairly certain that the situation had not changed much by the time of the 1954 Supreme Court decision declaring separate-but-equal educational facilities unconstitutional, although, at that time, practically every major denomination, including those in the South, *did* express their support for the Court's decision. In the intervening years, the churches had moved from a position of either indifference to or outright support for racial segregation to a position of public and unequivocal rejection of it. By 1954, the deliberative assemblies of all the principal religious bodies were on record as opposing racial segregation. It is, however, "a giant step from the lofty ideals of national and regional conventions to the realities of a segregationist convenant back home," and there is little convincing evidence that the churches practiced what they preached (Campbell and Pettigrew, 1959:2).

Without saying that any of the major religious bodies practice racial discrimination, the existence of racial segregation in America's churches today is patent. In 1970, blacks constituted about 11 percent of the population of the United States. A Gallup Poll conducted in 1971 showed that Episcopalians are 93 percent white, all the Lutheran Synods together are 99 percent white, the Presbyterians 98 percent, the Catholics 97 percent, and the Jews 99 percent (Rosten, 1975:448). Obviously, this is not straightforward racial discrimination because many other factors are involved: Episcopalians have few black members because they have few poor people; Lutherans are heavily concentrated in the Midwest, where blacks are a relatively small proportion of the population; Presbyterians, although a relatively liberal group, "lost" the blacks to the Baptists and Methodists as long ago as the eighteenth century; Catholics are not well represented in the South, where the concentration of blacks is high; and, of course, Jews are a heavily ethnic group—there are few nonethnic Jews in Judaism. Nevertheless, the existence of racial segregation seems hard to deny.

Gallup reported much larger proportions of blacks in the Methodist and Baptist Churches: Baptists were 27 percent "nonwhite" (all but 8 percent of whom are black) and Methodists 11 percent "nonwhite." These figures are deceiving, however, as Methodists and Baptists long ago completely divided along racial lines; blacks now have their own denominations. The figures are more revealing if separate denominations are scrutinized. For example, just 4.2 percent of the members of the "white" United Methodist Church are black (Christianity Today, 6/18/76).

What is more important than national aggregate figures such as these is evidence of segregation at the local level, where social interaction actually occurs. Thus, although the American Baptist churches might show few overt signs of racism in its figure of 11 percent blacks, the congregations of the ABC are overwhelmingly segregated. Those 11 percent blacks are segregated in assemblies of their own, enclaves largely out of touch with the white-run denomination to which they nominally belong (Campolo, 1971:50). Similarly, although the United Methodists might point to their black constituency as evidence of lack of segregation, 88 percent of all their congregations are totally white (Christianity Today, 6/18/76). A survey conducted in 1977 showed that 54 percent of whites attending church did so in churches with no black members at all; in the South the figure was 66 percent (Gallup, 1977:3). There is little evidence, then, that religious worship is conducted regardless of race. Only 10 percent of all American blacks were worshipping with whites in 1964 (Reimers, 1965:178).

The civil rights movement of the 1960s has undoubtedly had an effect on religious denominations, especially at the national level. This impact is signaled by such moves as the ABC's election of a black as its president in 1969. However, within each organization, discrimination on racial grounds continues to be the norm. For example, the Episcopal Church had appointed six black bishops by 1974, but they accounted for only 4 percent of all the bishops in that denomination (Rosten, 1975:379). Similarly, only 5 percent of the professional staff of the United Methodist Church in 1970 was black (Ebony Handbook, 1974:355a).

The turmoil of the 1960s did not seriously affect the pattern of discrimination at the local level except under the following unusual circumstances: (1) the proportion of blacks in the local population was small; (2) the congregation was situated in a large city or near an academic center; (3) the community was in transition (Washington, 1964:242–43). Otherwise, the forces of residential segregation, interaction networks, and denominational loyalties combined to keep 11 A.M. to 12 noon on Sunday the most segregated hour in America.

The Catholic Church has been slightly more tolerant at the local level (Lamanna and Coakley, 1969:153). Forty percent of Catholics, compared with 60 percent of Protestants, reported attending all-white churches in 1977 (Gallup, 1977:3). But there have always been, and still are, all-black parishes in the Catholic Church, and in 1972 there were still only 200 black priests in the United States (Rosten, 1975:378). Catholic fraternities, such as the Knights of Columbus, have always been racially segregated. Nevertheless, Catholics have shown a greater willingness than Protestants to open their institutions to non-whites. In 1957, for example, 77 percent of Catholic colleges in the South were biracial compared with only 29 percent of Protestant colleges (Bailey, 1964:147).

Racial Prejudice in the Churches

Patterns of institutional racism do not necessarily indicate strong racial prejudice or even deliberate discrimination among the individuals in those institutions. Interaction patterns, tradition, residence, and social class differences can all play a part in determining the racial mix of a church. It is important, then, to try to assess the extent of racial prejudice in today's churches and its impact on segregation.

Are religious people more or less racially prejudiced than nonreligious people? It has not proved easy to answer this question. There are many sociological studies of this problem . After reviewing these studies, Gorsuch and Aleshire (1974:283) asserted that church members *are* more prejudiced than those who have never joined a church. The same could not be said of church attendance, however, for the occasional attender, rather than the frequent attender or the nonattender, expresses the greatest prejudice.

But Campbell (1971:49), who also reviewed studies of this problem, came to a different conclusion:

> In acceptance of interracial contact, the perception of discrimination, support of the black protest and positive response to legal and economic programs of aid, Protestants and Catholics who are closest to their church do not differ from those who are furthest away. Church attendance, with whatever exposure to church doctrine this may imply, apparently has no influence on these attitudes, but it does reduce the acceptability of strong-arm or violent actions by whites in response to black protest.

It might well be that Gorsuch and Aleshire, who examined *membership*, have more to say than Campbell, who discusses the somewhat more tenuous topic of affiliation. It is conceivable, for instance, that the feelings of ethnocentrism that contribute to racial prejudice *will* be more common among the members of a church than among those who express an affiliation. It is also significant that in studies of the kind of support that third-party movements such as George Wallace's American Independent Party receive, it *is* the occasional-attending Fundamentalists who give their support more than those who go frequently or not at all. The suggestion then is that the first set of conclusions are more plausible. However, the argument is probably not reconcilable at this level, where crude categorizations such as membership, affiliation and attendance are made.

Variations in Racial Prejudice by Religion

Catholics are slightly more racially tolerant than Protestants. For example, 58 percent of Protestants, but 65 percent of Catholics, support government programs that help blacks avoid discrimination in housing (Campbell, 1971:47). Even these small differences would probably disappear if controls were imposed for place of birth and income, for a higher proportion of Protestants live in the traditionally more racially intolerant South, and Catholics tend to occupy the higher-income brackets, whose members display less racial prejudice.

Using data gathered in 1968, Greeley (1974b:194) showed that most Catholics are indeed more racially tolerant than Protestants, although the Jews are the most tolerant of all.

TABLE 15:1

**RACIAL ATTITUDES AMONG ETHNIC GROUPS
FROM THE NORC INTEGRATED NEIGHBORHOOD STUDY (ADAPTED)**

Religio-Ethnic Group	Favor School Integration	Would Bring Black to Dinner	Oppose Keeping Blacks Out of Neighborhood	Oppose Laws Against Intermarriage
Western European Protestants	70%	59%	45%	42%
Irish Catholics	82	79	68	61
German Catholics	79	68	60	57
Southern European Catholics	80	69	54	56
Eastern European Catholics	78	57	43	59
Jews	100	92	79	75

Clearly, this evidence does not support the stereotype of the "hard hat" ethnic denying blacks the advancement they have begun to secure for themselves. The widely reported clashes between blacks and mainly

Catholic ethnic groups in many of the larger northern cities in the early 1970s should not be construed to mean that Catholics are more prejudiced than Protestants. Greeley (1974b:199) convincingly attributes these events to, as much as anything else, the conflicts that have continually occurred in the larger cities of the North as poorer incoming groups (in this case, blacks) come into contact with neighborhoods formerly occupied by European ethnic immigrants (in this case, Catholics).

It appears that generalized statements about the relation between religious faith and racial prejudice are not possible. It is much more likely that racial prejudice is correlated with theological differences along a conservative-liberal continuum than it is with broad faith or even denominational memberships. This is distinctly suggested by findings that members of the theologically more liberal denominations, such as the Unitarians, Presbyterians, and members of the United Church, exhibit lower rates of prejudice than members of the theologically more conservative denominations, such as the Southern Baptists and Lutherans. The differences are not large, and they may be due as much to regional and social class factors as they are to theological orientations, but at the denominational level there are nevertheless some differences along the conservative/liberal continuum (Hadden, 1969:133). Adding substance to this position, Kauffman and Harder (1975:138) found that support for restricted covenants in housing is stronger among the more orthodox and conservative Mennonite churches than among the liberal bodies. The same relation between conservative theology and racial prejudice is found among the clergy. Within each denomination, the more conservative a minister is theologically, the more likely he is to express racially prejudiced statements. For example, conservative ministers are most likely to agree that "Negroes could solve many of their own problems if they would not be so irresponsible and carefree about life" (Hadden, 1969:111). To substantiate this point, Kersten (1970:74) found that among Lutheran ministers prejudice against blacks is positively related to theological conservatism.

At the extreme conservative end of the theological spectrum are the fundamentalists. It was the more fundamentalist ministers who displayed the strongest segregationist sympathies in Little Rock in 1957. They were "armed with the firm conviction that God intends the races to be separate" (Campbell and Pettigrew, 1959:24). Surveying the research on racial prejudice and religion, Lipset and Raab (1970:434) conclude that "the most prejudiced of all are the fundamentalists and those with strong religious commitment who have not been educated beyond the eighth grade."

Not all sects are segregationist or themselves segregated. The very poor, uneducated people who attend single-congregation churches or follow faith healers are often "color blind," and their assemblies are racially integrated. Sects associated with the new urban middle class in the South (admittedly few in number) tend to take a quite liberal view on race, for their members feel little economic threat from blacks. "The most rigid defense of racial prejudice and custom has come from the stable and well-established sects, composed of successful farmers, skilled labourers, [and] petty bourgeoisie" (Harrell, 1971:116). These people are concerned to raise themselves permanently above the black population and are preoccupied with the maintenance of a "respectable" life. The sects to which they belong are not integrated. Two of the largest Pentecostal sects, the Assemblies of God and the Pentecostal Holiness Church, have always been white. There are only white sects in the major Pentecostal alliance, the Pentecostal Fellowship of North America.

The more established sectarians find in their religion a justification for racial separation and a negative attitude toward the civil rights campaign. They believe, for instance, that the separation of the races is enjoined in the Scriptures; they are convinced that suffering, each person in his or her own way, is an integral part of the Christian life and are therefore capable of interpreting the miseries of blacks as "testing"; and their principle of noninvolvement in political issues makes them wary of civil rights activism. These attitudes are coherent and widespread enough to lead Harrell (1971:77) to conclude that "sectarian literature since 1945 is a mirror of Southern racist thought."

Differences in Racial Prejudice between Clergy and Laity

There is growing recognition that, "there is little if any relationship between the attitudes of the priests and those of their parishioners on . . . social issues" (Glock et al., 1967:153). The clergy, who tend to be more liberal, cannot lead where their flocks will not follow. But rank-and-file conservatism may well have less social impact if it is not reflected in the policy positions and programs of the major denominations. It is important, therefore, to obtain some idea of the magnitude and extent of clergy/lay differences in regard to racial issues.

There is little question that the clergy are more liberal (usually much more liberal) than their congregations on racial issues. They are much more likely to approve of campaigns to secure equal rights for all regardless of race (Glock et al., 1967:153) and to support government intervention to secure equal treatment of minority groups in employment and housing (Fukuyama, 1972:86).

Predictably, these differences generate considerable tension between pastor and flock. For example, of the California Protestant ministers who supported fair-housing legislation, "63% reported that they met with private opposition in their actions, 47% lost contributions, 32% had their positions publicly attacked before their church boards, and 11% faced efforts to have them removed from their parish positions" (Quinley, 1974:212). The more liberal and outspoken a minister, the more likely he was to have suffered a decline in church membership; the ministers who had opposed the fair-housing legislation or had not spoken out at all experienced little change.

Why Are Religion and Prejudice Related?

The knowledge that religious people are not less prejudiced than the non-religious, but are perhaps more so, and that certain kinds of conservative theologies seem to be highly correlated with racial prejudice has occasioned a great deal of speculation about the precise nature of this relationship and the reasons for it. According to Stark and Glock (1973:95), there are three reasons why religion might lead to prejudice:

SPECIFIC TEACHINGS: for example, the Christian teaching that the Jews are the murderers of Christ and have been sentenced to eternal damnation, or that blacks are descendents of the condemned tribe of Ham. The reasoning here is that religious hostility engenders secular hostility. Glock and Stark (1966) showed this to be true of Protestant laity, and Stark (1971:81) found that Protestant clergy were only slightly less likely to associate the two kinds of hostility. As attractive as this theory might be, sufficient contrary evidence has been brought to bear against it that it cannot be accepted as valid (Middleton, 1973:41; Maranell, 1967:359; Ploch, 1974:290). There is just too much evidence of a *lack* of association between religious orthodoxy or dogmatism, taken alone, and racial prejudice, for this theory to be supported.[4]

Particularism: the idea that one's own religion is uniquely true and legitimate and all others are false. This, it is reasoned, is likely to engender an intolerance for deviants, a strong we/they dichotomization of the world, and a feeling of elitism.

Conservatism: chiefly the idea that people are in control of their individual destinies, that individual salvation should be the principal concern of each person, and that the poor and the powerless are to blame indi-

[4]Not only have others failed to replicate Glock and Stark's findings, but there is also serious question as to the validity of their measures. Their Religious Bigotry Index, for example, and their measure of anti-Semitism almost fully reduce to a correlation between two measures of prejudice, since the former instrument is strongly contaminated with anti-Semitic content (see Dittes, 1967). Furthermore, the distinction Glock and Stark make between religious hostility and secular hostility toward Jews, although conceptually proper, is not psychologically warranted. The correlation between the two is virtually a tautology.

vidually for their plight. The association between conservatism and prejudice consists, in part, of a particular kind of ethicalism, according to which the most important criteria of performance concern the relation between man and God rather than man and man. For example, members of the theologically more conservative denominations are much more likely to be concerned with their personal conduct before God than with right conduct before their fellow humans. Thus, the number of Southern Baptists who look upon swearing as a barrier to salvation (27 percent) is greater than the number who think that discrimination against other races would have this effect (Stark and Glock, 1968:70).

Prejudice is related to religion if it is *highly particularistic and theologically conservative*. The precise relationship is not a simple one of cause and effect, however. Instead, both religion and prejudice are part of a subculture of in-group solidarity and intolerance toward out-groups. This is implied in Lenski's (1963:173) conclusion that a combination of church membership and communal involvement leads most directly to prejudice. The same pattern of association was uncovered by Kersten (1970:74) in his study of Lutherans:

> the higher one ranks on the Associational Involvement, Religious Practice and Religious Knowledge Indexes, the less apt is he to hold prejudiced attitudes toward Negroes. In relation to communal involvement, however, the opposite pattern prevails. . . This finding suggests that race prejudice is fostered by and supported within one's primary group relationships—that is, by his close friends, family and relatives.

In other words, it is the religious subcommunity rather than the involvement in church affairs or religious beliefs per se that perpetuates racial prejudice.

Religious orthodoxy is not, of course, irrelevant, but it is its combination with community, or a *localistic* view, that forms the foundation of prejudice.

> Individuals with localistic orientations may be induced to hold intolerant, authoritarian attitudes generally, and especially against those who are perceived as threatening or competitive. Religious beliefs obviously come into play in world-view constellations; however, specific doctrines and teachings may function less to cause than to legitimate sentiments that originate elsewhere (Roof, 1974b:661).

Localism is associated with limited perspectives, simplistic beliefs, and an ignorance of abstract cultural systems. In combination with low education and religious orthodoxy, it constitutes a world view in which various kinds of prejudices, resentments, and defensive attitudes toward minority groups are a natural part.

People who go to church regularly score high on associational rather than on communal measures of religiosity.[5] It is this group that manifests the least prejudice. In fact, the relation between frequency of church *attendance* and prejudice is curvilinear. The very frequent church attenders and the non-attenders have the lowest amounts of prejudice; the most prejudiced are those who attend occasionally (see Bagley, 1970).[6]

This pattern of association between *occasional* church attendance and racial prejudice points to the same conclusion that is arrived at when religious orthodoxy is examined: prejudice is associated only with a certain *kind* of religiosity in certain kinds of context. Thus, Allport (1966:455) distinguishes between the "extrinsic" religion of the occasional attender and the "intrinsic" religion of the regular attender.

> While there are several varieties of extrinsic religious orientation, we may say they all point to a type of religion that is strictly utilitarian; useful for the self in growing safely, social standing, solace and endorsement of one's chosen way of life. As such it provides a congenial soil for all forms of prejudice. . . . By contrast, the intrinsic form of the religious sentiment regards faith as a supreme value in its own right. It is oriented toward the unification of being, takes seriously the commandment of brotherhood, and strives to transcend all self-centered needs.

Two kinds of religiosity are also distinguished by Allen and Spilka (1967:205), who identify a "committed" and a "consensual" religion, which parallel Allport's "intrinsic" and "extrinsic" religion. Committed religion "utilises an abstract, philosophical perspective; multiplex religious ideas are relatively clear in meaning and an open and flexible framework of commitment meaningfully relates religion to daily activities." Consensual religion, on the other hand, is "a typological, concretistic, restrictive outlook on religion. While verbally conforming to the 'traditional' values and ideals, these are vague, nondifferentiated, bifurcated and neutralised or selectively adopted." Consensually religious individuals are more prejudiced than those who are disposed to the more committed kind of religion.

Strommen (1972:140) finds much the same kind of bifurcation among Lutherans. "Law-oriented" Lutherans (whose religion is extrin-

---

[5]For an explanation of these terms, see the Appendix.
[6]Church attendance is not related to racial prejudice among blacks (Noel and Pinkney, 1964:615).

sic) are more prejudiced. They exhibit a fear of the future, proceed cautiously while remembering the past, favor a traditional family structure, believe strongly in individual responsibility, subscribe to a strong moral code, are concerned to keep the traditional church liturgy and dogma, and have a strong feeling for the spiritual purity of the church. The minimal emphasis in this law-oriented Lutheranism on piety, spirituality, charity, and social concerns finds a close parallel in the consensual type of religion portrayed by Allen and Spilka.

On the other hand, there are those who find fault with this intrinsic/ extrinsic dichotomy. Despite elaborate and exhaustive factor analysis of religious responses, King and Hunt (1972:31) failed to isolate any kind of intrinsic factor, and the responses that should have been clustered together under the extrinsic heading were scattered across a number of other factors. Furthermore, Allport's distinction suggests that "*only* altruistic attidudes *can* follow from religious beliefs (otherwise the belief is inauthentic, extrinsic religion)" (Stark and Glock, 1968:19), which leads to the position that religious people who show prejudice or a general lack of altruism are not "truly" religious.

Theoretically, it would seem to be most parsimonious to consider the relation between "consensual," "extrinsic," or "law-oriented" religion and prejudice as the expression of a general conservatism. At the most, the impact of religious orientations on social attitudes is to rationalize them: "habits of conformity, acquiescence, conservatism, and closemindedness may generalise from religion to social judgements, which lie in the same general sphere of values and commitments" (Dittes, 1969:633). In other words, religion does not by itself cause prejudice, although it might well make the holding of prejudicial views more congenial. "The reason why churchgoers on average are more prejudiced than nonchurchgoers is not because religion instills prejudice. It is rather that a large number of people, by virtue of their psychological make-up, require for their economy of living both prejudice and religion . . ." (Allport, 1966:451).

Allport's psychological interpretation is given a sociological treatment by Middleton (1973:46), who sees the relation between conservative religion and prejudice as a response to feelings of anomie. In other words, an individual's experience of anomie causes him to be disposed toward a certain type of religiosity and toward racially prejudiced views. Hoge and Carroll (1973:75) detect "status concerns" rather than anomie behind the relationship, but nevertheless agree that the main determinants of prejudice are not religious beliefs so much as personal rigidity and personal need for unchanging cognitive and social structures. This makes more comprehensible the higher prejudice shown by occasional church attenders, among whom a concern for social status (symbolized in some respects by this occasional conformity) is strongest. This thesis is substantiated in a study by Strickland and Weddell (1972) who found that Unitarians were both "extrinsic" in their religious orientation and *low* on racial prejudice, whereas Baptists were both more intrinsic in their religious orientation and more prejudiced. In this case, the liberalism of the Unitarians and the conservatism of the Baptists seemed to be the more important factor.

In sum, then, religion *is* often associated quite strongly with racial prejudice, and certain forms of religiosity (emphasizing particularism and conservatism) are almost invariably associated with prejudice. However, this is not as much a matter of religion causing prejudice as a matter of this kind of religiosity and racial bigotry being part of the same constellation of social attitudes. These social attitudes, in turn, are probably grounded in experiences that have to do with anomie or status loss, which create a fairly strong need for stability and authoritarian attitudes.

CONCLUSION

The conclusions that can be drawn about the relationship between religion and racial discrimination and prejudice must be tentative. However, broad patterns are vaguely discernible. On the basis of the evidence presented in this chapter, it is possible to conclude that although ethnicity and religion no longer work as closely to structure group cleavages in the United States, ethnicity, with its religious rationalization, is still important in the private sphere of family and friends. Religion has also helped create a set of parallel ethnic institutions, within which internal social mobility is possible and power struggles occur, but which probably have the overall effect of weakening the social position of the various ethnic groups and perpetuating their position of subordination. Although virulent feelings of ethnic hostility are no longer widespread, the continued salience of ethnic differences associated with a Protestant/ Catholic division is evident in social, economic and political life.

As far as race is concerned, the American churches have undergone considerable desegregation at the denominational level (as, for example, in the abolition of the black Central Jurisdiction of the Methodist Church) but are still markedly segregated at the local level. The churches are among the most racist of all American institutions. At the individual level, sociological research has failed to make clear the relationship between religion and prejudice. Even if churchgoers are more prejudiced than those who do not attend church, it is those who attend very frequently who are the least prejudiced of all. In his prejudice, the occasional attender conforms to a historical pattern of feelings of white,

Anglo-Saxon superiority. In showing little racial prejudice, the nonattender and the very frequent attender have clearly selected their values from outside the dominant American tradition. The association between religion and racial prejudice is strongest of all where different religious positions are distinguished not by attendance but by theological attitude. There is a strong association between conservative theological attitude, localism, and racial prejudice, all part of the same, general, subculture.

16

RELIGION
AND POLITICAL CONFLICT

INTRODUCTION

Politics in industrial societies means access to and influence over the state: that is, the tax collector, the courts, the police, the military and so on. Political power in Western societies is generally believed to be competitive, fragmented and diffused: everybody has some power and nobody can have too much power. Political institutions comprise legislative assemblies, parties, lobbies and interest groups, and political processes include election campaigns, voting, party caucusing, lobbying and demonstrations. This view of politics is heavily influenced by a democratic pluralist model of political behavior in which all are considered equal before the law, office-holders are thought to be responsive to the electorate, freedom of speech and association prevail, and no one group exercises permanent control over the state.

The interaction between religion and political processes is the subject of this chapter and Chapter 17. The relation between church and state has already been addressed, in Chapter 10, but in these two chapters the emphasis is on the role of religion in political conflict. Unfortunately, there is considerable debate as to the nature of political conflict in modern Western societies. Many commentators are highly skeptical about the validity of the democratic pluralist model presented at the beginning of this chapter. They point to the exercise of unchecked and largely invisible power, the concentration of power in elites, and the increasing autonomy of the state, and suggest that much of the party squabbling and electioneering are the "ephemera" and "surface play" of politics (Birnbaum, 1969:41).

The conflict model, which guides our thinking in Part IV of this book, assumes that, ultimately, political power is closely associated with material forces, with the control over the means of production. "The economic and political life of capitalist societies is *primarily* determined by the relationship, born of the capitalist mode of production, between [capitalist employers and industrial wage-earners]. Here are . . . the social forces whose confrontation most powerfully shapes the social climate and the political system of advanced capitalism. In fact, the political process in these societies is mainly about the confrontation of these forces, and is intended to sanction the terms of the relationship between them" (Miliband, 1969:16). If this is true, a great deal of contemporary American and British politics is indeed "surface play" concealing rather than reflecting the actual struggle for power.

This chapter assumes neither the pluralist nor the conflict model to be absolutely valid. Instead, the relation of religion to politics is considered in the light of both models, for they each have something to say about modern political systems and processes. The "ephemera" of politics— elections for political party candidates and so on—are heavily influenced by religious considerations. The first task of this chapter is, then, to examine the relation between religious identification and party preference to assess the extent to which religious divisions shape political conflicts at this surface level. In this section, it is particularly important to distinguish the effect of religion on party preference from that of social class, for a conflict theorist would be especially interested in the link between religious conflict and that emanating from material interests. A second task is to examine the effect of religious *attitudes* on political opinions. Here the issue is whether or not religion attenuates or intensifies class-based political conflicts. Do religious and class interests push voters in the same direction or do they contradict and weaken each other?

In the Marxian model, the existence of status groups like religious communities is very important because insofar as such groups define themselves in opposition to other status groups rather than as part of a more inclusive working class (defined in opposition to a ruling class), the development of class consciousness and a critique of the capitalist system is effectively blocked. These status groups are ways in which people protect themselves from inequality and lack of control over their lives and what they produce; but they are the product of a "false consciousness" because they represent, not just an ideological accommodation to the existing political order, but the structural isolation of one section of the labor force from another. Given this, the extent to which religio-ethnic subcultures crosscut class ties and weaken political solidarity is of especial interest. So also is the final topic of this chapter, Marx's famous thesis that religion is an opiate for the masses, causing them to desert their true, class-determined political interests. If the data show that the more religious of the working class are also the more conservative, and if the data show that the teachings and programs of the churches have the net effect of legitimizing elite political values and weakening class solidarity, then the opiate thesis is confirmed.

There would be little point in investigating the association between religion and political conflict if they were thought to be unrelated. But in no Western society is this true. No political party in either the United States or the United Kingdom approaches being formally linked to a church. However, American Catholics do tend to vote Democrat, whereas Protestants prefer the Republican Party. In the United Kingdom, there are historical associations between the Church of England and the Conservative Party, between the Free Churches and the Liberal Party, and between the Catholic Church and the Labor Party.

THE DEVELOPMENT OF RELIGION AND POLITICS
IN THE UNITED STATES

The ties that exist today between party and denomination in the United States can be understood fully only by looking at the past. Alliances between religious groups and political factions were in evidence in the United States well before the Civil War. The more establishment-minded Episcopalians and Congregationalists supported the Federalists and Whigs, and the more evangelical and democratic Methodists and Baptists, as well as the few Catholics, sided with the Jeffersonians. By the time of the Civil War, the Methodists and Baptists had begun to rise in social status and to set themselves more and more apart from the growing Catholic population. They aligned themselves more closely with the Republicans, the party of the country. The Republicans, in their turn, identified themselves even more closely with the "old stock" Protestantism, and found themselves in frequent opposition to the newer Catholic elements. Together with their subsequent loss of the South, this seemed to consign the Republican Party to a permanent minority position. It is an irony, as Hamilton (1972:539) has noted, "that the party that needed to encourage assimilation, that had to break down the ethnic barriers in order to maintain its electoral chances repeatedly found itself engaged in campaigns that had just the opposite effect."

The Democratic Party, meanwhile, solicited the support of the Catholic immigrants by displaying a greater tolerance of newcomers and less zeal in attempting to impose upon them the moral values of a Protestant middle class. By allying themselves with the Democratic party, the Catholics were probably helped in their effort to reconcile the communal values of their church with their new society's norms of individual, secular achievement. In view of this alignment, it is not surprising that the strongest supporters of the Democratic Party have been the Irish Catholics, the greatest numbers of whom entered the country between the Civil War and the turn of the century (Greeley, 1971:73).[1]

MODERN POLITICS AND RELIGION

The frequent references by contemporary journalists to "the Catholic vote" indicate that, in the popular mind, at least, religion and politics are still closely associated. Modern survey research makes it possible to examine this relationship in unprecedented detail. Unfortunately, although both religion and politics are multidimensional, both have been treated rather simplistically in the research carried out so far. Religion is usually measured simply by avowed affiliation, and sometimes by stated theological position. Such measurements are occasionally refined by adding a gauge of strength of religiosity, such as frequency of attendance. Political behavior is measured most often by party preference or avowed party registration, seldom by voting results. Although these are indeed rough measures, and could doubtless be improved upon, they do provide new insights into the relation between religion and politics, and a new measure of confidence in interpreting this relation, which is the main aim of this part of the chapter.[2]

American history teaches that Protestants vote Republican and Catholics and Jews vote Democrat. This association persists, as the following table indicates.

[1] "An analysis of voting returns in a number of states in the 1864 presidential election indicates relationships between various social factors and party presidential choice similar to those which differentiated Democrats and Whigs in the 1840s and were to distinguish Republicans and Democrats following the war. Lincoln's support came disproportionately from Protestants of New England and Anglo-Saxon background living in rural areas and small towns and 'the wealthier residential districts of the greater cities.' Catholics, those of non-Anglo-Saxon recent immigrant background, particularly the Germans and those living in the poorer districts of the larger cities, were disposed to vote for McClellan, the Democratic candidate" (Lipset, 1964:82).

[2] The following discussion concentrates on voting in presidential elections. The relation between religion and party identification is much stronger at the state and local level than it is at the national level (Lipset, 1964:90).

TABLE 16:1

PRESIDENTIAL CANDIDATE PREFERENCE BY MAJOR RELIGIOUS GROUP

	Carter (Democrat)	*Ford (Republican)*
Protestant	46%	54%
Catholic	55	45
Jew	68	32
Other	59	41

(New York Times/CBS Poll, Nov. 1976. New York Times, 11/4/76)

Catholics *are* more likely to support the Democratic candidate than Prot-estants, but the table shows how misleading it is to talk of "the Catholic vote," or any kind of religious bloc voting. Only the Jews approach two-thirds support for a candidate; the other two major faiths are almost evenly divided. However, slight as it is, the association between faith and party persists. The 1976 poll also showed that support for the presiden-tial candidates varied by income, occupation, education and race: the well-to-do, for example, were much more likely to support Ford. It is well known that such demographic characteristics are also related to religion (see Chapter 14). This raises the possibility that some of the variation in voting that appears to be due to religious differences is actually the product of other social forces. It is important, then, to con-trol for voters' non-religious characteristics in trying to assess the precise impact of religion on political behavior.

Using data gathered by the Survey Research Center at the University of Michigan in 1960, 1964, 1968 and 1972, Knoke (1976:27) was able to isolate the precise impact of religious affiliation on party identification. To carry out the analysis, he converted party identification into a five-point scale consisting of (1) strong Democrat; (2) not-so-strong Democrat and Independent-leaning-to-Democrat; (3) Independent; (4) not-so-strong Republican and Independent-leaning-to-Republican; (5) strong Republican. Republican preference was scored high. Thus, in the follow-ing table, a deviation above the mean indicates Republican leaning, and a deviation below the mean indicates Democratic preference.

This table confirms the existence of a religious factor in party identifi-cation and shows that alignments formed in the nineteenth century per-sist. The Jews are the most consistently Democratic group and exhibit the strongest support. Indeed, if they occupied a position in the stratifi-cation system comparable to that of the population as a whole, they would be even more Democratic than they are now. The Jews are fol-lowed in loyalty to the Democratic Party by the Catholics. The most Democratic of all Protestant groups are the Baptists and Neo-

TABLE 16:2

**STRUCTURAL COEFFICIENTS FOR REGRESSION
OF PARTY IDENTIFICATION ON
13 RELIGIOUS GROUPS, NET OF OCCUPATION, EDUCATION,
AND INCOME, FOR WHITES, 1960–1972**

Religious Group	*Year*			
	1960	*1964*	*1968*	*1972*
Presbyterian	.83	.61	.55	.46
Episcopalian [a]	1.16	1.08	.39	.43
Nontraditional	.75	.29	.52	.29
Methodist	.23	.17	.25	.30
Lutheran	.16	.20	.12	.20
Neo-fundamentalist	.27	.00	.01	.04
None [b]	.25	−.10	−.18	−.60
Pietistic	−.09	.58	−.01	−.13
General Protestant	−.23	−.03	.31	.02
Other Religions	−.07	−.59	−.04	−.03
Baptist	−.30	−.33	−.02	−.01
Catholic	−.62	−.31	−.35	−.36
Jew	−.54	−.67	−.97	−.87
Grand Mean	2.83	2.62	2.80	2.97

[a] = Mormons, Christian Scientists, Unitarians, Quakers
[b] = Disciples of Christ, "Christian"

Fundamentalists. But their pro-Democratic showing might be due to their heavy concentration in the South. Most Protestant groups, as expected, prefer the Republican Party, Episcopalians showing the greatest deviation from the mean in this regard. They are followed by the Presbyterians and the nontraditional group—among whom the Mormons are prominent. Lutherans and Methodists are more middle-of-the-road politically, but they show a slight but steady inclination to identify themselves as Republicans.

Identification with a political party tends to be stronger among the more devout, although there is some variation in the strength of this relationship from one year to another. This provides further support to the argument that religious factors are influential in determining party preferences. For example, Protestants who attend church frequently are more likely than Protestants who attend church infrequently to identify with the Republican Party. Similarly, Catholics who attend church frequently are more likely than Catholics who attend infrequently to identify with the Democrat Party. The relationship between frequency of attendance and political behavior is stronger among Protestants than among Catholics. The reason for this is that Catholic norms prescribing church attendance are much stronger than church attendance norms among Protestants. There is, therefore, much greater variation in church attendance within the Protestant group as a whole (Knoke, 1976:32).

Notice that Table 16.2 controls for socioeconomic status. The traditional association of Catholics with *both* lower-status jobs and the Democratic Party always raises the question of whether Catholics prefer Democratic candidates not because they are Catholics but because they occupy low status occupations and therefore feel drawn toward the liberal/left party. The table clearly shows that even when occupation of head of household, educational level, and total family income are controlled for, religious differences in party preference remain. In other words, the preference of, say, Episcopalians, for the Republican Party is not solely due to the higher social class of members of that denomination.

Of course, both socioeconomic status and religion are influences on party preference. It is noteworthy, however, that "there are greater party preference differences between ethnocultural groups of similar social status than there are between status groups of the same ethnocultural group" (Nie, *et al.*, 1976:223). In other words, religion is a more powerful influence on party preference than class. For the election years covered in Knoke's (1976:28) analysis (1960, 1964, 1968, and 1972), occupation, income and education *combined* at no time contributed more than four percent of the variance in party identification explained—in 1972 the combined SES effect was only 0.8 percent. Religious identification, for the same years contributed 13 percent (1960), 10 percent (1964), 7 percent (1968) and 4 percent (1972). Using a data set covering the years 1952–1972 from the same source as Knoke, Fee (1976:82) draws the same conclusion: religion is as good as any other predictor of party preference. Furthermore, the correlation of religion with party preference is about half that of party identification *with all other social characteristics (except race) taken together*. Although the net impact of religion declined during the 1960s from the high point it reached during the Kennedy/Nixon Presidential race, religion and ethnicity continue to make the greatest difference to modern party preferences (Hamilton, 1972:217).

Table 16.2 shows that during the 1960s there were some minor changes in the political alignments of the various religious groups. Episcopalian support for the Republicans, for example, weakened. The period between 1955 and 1970 was one of considerable political upheaval in the United States. One consequence of this was a shift in party alignments, mostly a movement away from both the Democratic and

Republican camps and toward the category of Independent as people expressed their disillusionment with party politics. Not surprisingly, this upheaval has also affected the relationship between religion and politics.

Nie *et al.*, (1976:240) distilled data from fifteen National Opinion Research Center surveys conducted between 1952 and 1972, and the results of their analysis are shown in Table 16.3. As the proportion of various religious groups in the population has not been constant over that time period, it was necessary to hold population distribution constant while computing any changes in party identification that might have taken place. For example, in Table 16.3 the first group in the left-hand column (high status northern white Protestants) grew from being 20 percent of the population in 1952 to 22.4 percent in 1972. On the basis of this population growth, the increase from 9.8 percent to 11.5 percent of the Democratic identifiers is 0.5 percent more than would have been expected. In other words, this group contributed that much more to the Democratic coalition that would have been expected on the basis of their population growth alone.

TABLE   16:3

SOURCE OF PARTY IDENTIFIERS, 1950s AND 1970s

Group	Democratic Identifiers			Republican Identifiers		
	1950s	1970s	Deviation	1950s	1970s	Deviation
High-Status Northern White Protestants	9.8	11.5	+ .5	36.1	38.1	−2.3
Lower and Middle Status Northern White Protestants	18.9	18.3	+3.7	32.6	22.3	−2.8
Border South White Protestants	5.2	7.8	+ .8	4.2	7.7	+2.1
Southern White Protestants, Middle Status and Above	12.4	8.6	−6.9	4.1	11.2	+6.1
Lower Status Southern White Protestants	17.3	11.8	−2.7	4.1	5.4	+2.0
Catholics	20.3	20.8	− .3	12.4	12.0	− .5
Jews	5.0	3.6	− .2	.9	.8	− .1
Blacks	11.2	17.7	+4.3	5.6	2.5	−4.2
	100	100		100	100	

This table says a great deal about the shifting religio-political alignments in the United States from 1952 to 1972. First, there have been sizable Republican gains in the solidly Protestant white South. During the 1960s, the Republican Party made considerable inroads into the once uniformly Democratic South, the result of, among other things, the migration of a new middle class (mainly Republican) population into the industrialized regions of the South and the support given by the northern-dominated Democratic Party to the civil rights movement. In 1972, the white southerners, overwhelmingly Protestant, split their party identification as follows: 47 percent Democrat, 18 percent Republican, and 35 percent Independent (Nie, *et al.*, 1976: 218). By this measure alone, the traditional association between Protestantism and Republicanism has not been weakened, and may, in fact, have been strengthened. Data that would be useful here but are not available are those on denominational affiliation. It would be interesting to know if these new southern Republicans belong to denominations that are traditionally Republican, such as the Episcopalians and the Presbyterians, and if the southerners who remain Democrat belong to the Baptists or similar denominations.

Second, the loyalty of northern white Protestants to the Republican Party has weakened. In 1952, 43 percent of this group identified themselves as Republicans, 31 percent as Democrats, and 26 percent as Independents. By 1972, these proportions were 33 percent, 27 percent, and 39 percent, respectively. The rate of decline of northern white Protestant support for the Republican Party was higher among the higher status members (Nie, *et al.*, 1976:224).

Third, Catholics have shown an increasing disposition to identify themselves as Independents. In 1952, they were 55 percent Democrat, 19 percent Republican, and 27 percent Independent. By 1972, they were 47 percent Democrat, 15 percent Republican, and 38 percent Independent. Elsewhere, however, Nie *et al.* (1976:231) point out that the extent to which Catholics are more likely than the general population to identify themselves as Democrats *increased* during this period. In other words, their shift into the Independent category was less than that of the general population.

The movement of Catholics away from preference for the Democratic Party reflects both their changing social status and the variety of political orientations subsumed under the title Catholic. Those Catholics who have a historical loyalty to the Democratic Party–although their loyalty seems to be weakening–are in fact a very mixed group. There is the Catholicism of the paternalistic, big-city political machine in which the Democratic Party plays the role of father and employer. There is the Catholicism of the white ethnics, in which the Democratic Party is the defender of the working man against the demands of minorities such as blacks, women, and the young. There is the Catholicism of the trade unions, in which the Democratic Party is the provider of welfare benefits, social security, and jobs.

There is also an emphasis upon personal salvation among many of today's Catholics, an asceticism and anti-intellectualism that make them appear much like the Protestants who support the rather conservative Democratic Party of the South or even the American Independent Party and who are alienated by the liberal politics of the northern Democratic Party. This is one reason why Catholics show a very weak correlation between theological liberalism and political liberalism (see Henriot, 1970). Catholics are not "pure" liberals, in other words. They express strong disapproval of riots, school busing, and marijuana smoking and take a hard line on capital punishment. But at the same time, they support programs for the elimination of poverty, family assistance, the control of industrial pollution, and a speed-up in racial integration programs (Greeley, 1974b:212–30). Given the liberalism of the Democratic Party under McGovern, the discrediting of the Republican Party under Nixon, and a general disaffection with political institutions in general, including political parties, it is not too surprising that some Catholics should have moved into the Independent category. Those Catholics who have been most loyal to the Democratic Party are the Irish and Polish Catholics, who have been almost as strongly Democratic as Jews (Fee, 1976:83). Close behind are the Slavs, who maintained an 80 percent Democratic voting record between 1956 and 1968 (Levy and Kramer, 1972:169).

Fourth, although overwhelmingly Protestant (all but about 2 percent), blacks are also heavily Democratic. Until 1934, the black vote was decidedly Republican, the party of the Great Emancipator. During the New Deal, however, blacks began to switch their votes. Lyndon Johnson garnered 97 percent of the black vote in 1964, and Jimmy Carter received 83 percent in 1976. In 1970, all but about 6 percent of American blacks considered themselves Democrats (Nie *et al.*, 1976:227). The only variation in black support for the Democrats is in voter turnout. When blacks become disaffected politically, they do not switch their votes to the Republican camp but abstain (Levy and Kramer, 1972:48).

A fifth conclusion that may be drawn from the preceding table is that Jewish support for the Democratic Party weakened slightly between 1952 and 1972. Jews who leave the ranks of the Democrats tend to drift into the Independent rather than the Republican category. Although Jews became less Democratic, religion became more important as a predictor of their partisanship (Fee, 1976:88). Parenti (1966:261) has suggested that the Jews' support for the Democratic Party is due, in part, to the greater toleration the Democrats have shown toward minority groups. The location of white Catholics, blacks, and Jews in the Democratic camp is undoubtedly due to their common identity as minority groups in American society. But the Democratic loyalty of the Jews is also attributed to the fact that Judaism has managed to sustain a strong moral commitment that is free of the guilt that is more characteristic of Protestants, and that might have obstructed the Democrats' efforts to expand opportunities for well-being and pleasure. Jews have been very active in the left-wing of the Democratic Party. The liberal Americans for Democratic Action is 35 percent Jewish (Grupp, 1973:403).

The traditional patterns of religious affiliation and party preference have therefore persisted into the 1970s, but there have been some slight changes in strength of party loyalties. Broadly speaking, Catholics and Jews are still strongly Democrat and Protestants strongly Republican. However, all three groups have shown a recent tendency to place themselves in the Independent category. The Protestants seem to have shown a slightly greater tendency to do this, but overall, the shift has been a uniform one, so the relative Democrat/Catholic and Republican/Protestant associations have remained the same (Fee, 1976:83). Unfortunately, the 1960s were *also* a time when party preference came to signify less and less. In the 1968 and 1972 Presidential elections, one of every four persons voted for a candidate of a party other than the one with which he or she was identified. If Independents are added to these cross-voters, then in 1972, 51 percent either voted against their own party's candidate or were Independent, with no party ties to guide them.

Party loyalties have a significance of their own in determining voting behavior. Thus, although Catholics have traditionally been Democrat, this is not solely a matter of religion "causing" party preference or party voting. Religious affiliation and party loyalty are coproducers of voting practices and the association between church membership and party membership is to many people "natural" and taken for granted. But what happens when religious affiliation and party loyalty work at cross-purposes? Many people were faced with this question in 1960 when the Catholic John Kennedy ran as Democratic candidate against the Protestant Richard Nixon, the Republicans' choice. Most of the electorate escaped this dilemma. Catholics could vote Democrat for a Catholic candidate: Protestants could vote Republican for a Protestant candidate. However, Protestant Democratic voters and those Catholics who had built a loyalty to the Republican Party were placed in a dilemma. The 1960 election thus provided some measure of the importance of religious affiliation in relation to traditional party loyalties and of the salience of the religious factor in modern American politics.

Converse (1966:106) has shown that vote switching did indeed occur in 1960, which suggests that for many people religious considerations outweighed party loyalties. Using panel data, Converse tested the impact of religiosity on voting by investigating how many Protestants who had identified themselves as Democrats in 1958 switched to Nixon in 1960, presumably because of Kennedy's Catholicism. Reasoning that the more devout Protestant Democrats would be more likely to be anti-Catholic than the less devout, Converse constructed a measure of degree of religiosity. He measured frequency of church attendance and amount of "identification with the Protestant community," the latter being a measure of the sense of proximity and common interest an individual feels with his fellow Protestants. In Table 16.4, adapted from Converse (1966:119), "the cell entry in each cage is the decrement in the Democratic proportion of the two-party vote proportion which could have been expected on the basis of the distribution of party identifications shown by individuals in the cell in 1958."

TABLE 16:4

**1960 DEVIATIONS OF PRESIDENTIAL VOTE PARTISANSHIP
FROM 1958 EXPECTATIONS OF
WHITE PROTESTANTS BY REGION, HEAD'S OCCUPATION,
AND TWO TYPES OF RELIGIOUS INVOLVEMENT**

| | *Church Attendance* | |
Head's Occupation	*Regular/Often*	*Seldom/Never*
Non-South		
Professional or business	−11%	−13%
Clerical or blue collar	−15	− 2
South		
Professional or business	−25	−16
Clerical or blue collar	−36	−13

| | *Identification with Protestant Community* | |
Head's Occupation	*High*	*Low*
Non-South		
Professional or business	−13%	−12%
Clerical or blue collar	−17	− 5
South		
Professional or business	−24	−15
Clerical or blue collar	−32	−20

The table clearly shows that vote-switching was quite extensive, and occurred in all categories. By and large, the more religious voters were more likely to switch votes. Vote-switchers were more common among the lower-status Protestants and among Protestants in the South. The shift of the greatest magnitude was among those southerners who combined low social status with strong religiosity. For example, 36 percent fewer of the clerical and blue-collar workers residing in the South who attended church regularly voted for the Democratic candidate than would have been expected on the basis of 1958 party affiliations. The overall conclusion must be that religion, or at least Protestant/Catholic differences, played a significant part in determining presidential support and that the religious identification of a candidate can be the cause of a significant departure of voters from party loyalties.

Although the Kennedy-Nixon battle was touted as a highly unusual one because of its religious overtones, it was not the first time religion had played an important part in a presidential election campaign, nor was it the first time that vote-switching for religious reasons had occurred. The Democrats put forward a Catholic candidate in 1928, Alfred Smith, and he failed to attract the usual measure of support fot the Democratic Party. It has become customary to attribute his defeat to his Catholicism, especially since the 1920s were a period of considerable anti-Catholicism and the campaign was marked by expressions of religious hostility. It is true that there was much more to Smith than his religion to possibly alienate normally Democratic voters, especially in the South: he was opposed to Prohibition, he was Irish, he carried a big-city image, and he was somewhat of a liberal (see Silva, 1962). However, his religion did become a big issue during the campaign, and large numbers of voters did desert the party. It would be naive to suppose that fear of having a Catholic in the White House played no part in this vote switching.

However, there is good reason to believe that by the time of the Kennedy-Nixon campaign, the religious issue had come to play a smaller part in elections. In the intervening years, the Catholic community as a whole had structurally assimilated in terms of wealth, jobs, and education, and was to a lesser extent seen as an alien group. It is hard to compare the impact of religion on the 1928 and 1960 elections, for so many factors play a part in deciding the vote. However, looking at Wisconsin alone (for which comparable data are available), Baggeley (1962) found that religion made 60 percentage points difference in the voting in 1928 but only 26 percentage points difference in 1960. Although these data from the North may not be generalizable to the more traditionally anti-Catholic South, they clearly suggest a decline in purely religious voting and a reassertion of other loyalties such as those to one's class. The Catholicism of a candidate is perhaps less important now: in the 1968 presidential election, two Irish Catholics, Robert Kennedy and Eugene McCarthy, were candidates for the Democratic presidential nomination, and a Polish Catholic, Edmund Muskie, received the Democratic nomination for vice-president.

The impact of religion on normal political activism also seems to be declining. The political orientation of Protestant and Catholic delegates to the political conventions of 1972 showed more similarities than differences, and "tended toward traditional political styles: toward moderate, eclectic, ideological views and toward party solidarity as well as policy interests" (Kirkpatrick, 1976:360–61). It is unlikely that religion played much part in the selection of delegates. Catholics, who comprised 21 percent of the delegates, were slightly under represented but so, too, were Protestants, who comprised 56 percent. Jews, at 7 percent, and Atheists and Agnostics, at 15 percent, were over represented.

Religious considerations have by no means altogether disappeared from national politics. In the 1976 presidential campaign, the evangelical Protestantism of Jimmy Carter, a Southern Baptist, became a political issue. The Carter victory was substantially due to the swing of Protestant voters in general, not just evangelicals. Protestants gave Carter a seven-point higher percentage of their vote than they usually do for a Democratic presidential candidate. However, Carter's share of the vote among Catholics dropped by six percentage points and by between five and ten percentage points among Jews (*Christian Century*, 12/3/76:60).

What general conclusions can be drawn concerning the relationship between religion and political conflict in the United States? First of all, it must be noted that the extent to which the split between the conservative party of the right (the Republicans) and the liberal party of the left (the Democrats) really articulates fundamental social cleavages in American society is very much open to debate. Although it is undeniable that there are occupational groups in the United States, the political parties are not uniformly aligned with them. The manual laborer is by no means loyal to the party of the left, and many middle-class people vote Democrat. In fact, both parties are coalitions and include both mass and elite members. Consequently, party conflict in the United States is only minimally an expression of class conflict.

The influence of religion on political conflict has been to obscure class polarities. Almost from the beginning, the lines of cleavage in the United States have been as much religious, ethnic, and racial as they have been class. By orienting themselves to these vertical cleavages, coalition parties have crosscut class ties. Thus, white-collar workers, who would normally vote Republican, if they are also Catholic, will be led to vote Democrat. Blue-collar workers, who would normally vote Democrat, are encouraged, if they are Protestant, to vote Republican. Only under conditions such as these could the situation described by Hamilton (1972:319) arise, in which half of the working class white Protestants living in small towns identify themselves as Republican—the party of the rich and well-born. Lipset (1964:98) notes that a majority of working-class people in the high-status Episcopalian, Presbyterian, and Congregationalist denominations vote Republican. The implication is that working-class members of predominantly higher-status churches are strongly influenced by the modal opinion of the group "or, perhaps, that the workers who adhere to such denominations do so in part because they are 'upwardly mobile,' that they seek to identify with the more privileged class." The cross-cutting ties of religion and class have helped perpetuate the division, formed at the turn of the century, between the unskilled Catholic Democratic voter and the skilled Protestant Republican voter—a conflict between natives and aliens that was legitimized both politically¯and religiously. In Marxian terms, American society has not yet reached the final stage of the capitalist era, for the proletariat and the bourgeoisie have not been forced into an increasingly violent confrontation with each other. Rather, society remains fragmented on such bases as language, ethnicity, region, race and religion.

This thesis is partially confirmed by Johnson's (1962; 1964; 1966) studies of the relation between theological position (rather than denominational affiliation) and party preference. In some respects, the division between evangelical, Fundamentalist, or conservative Protestantism and Modernist or liberal Protestants is more meaningful today than the denominational affiliations that it crosscuts. It may well be that religion is better measured by theological position than by religious affiliation. And it is known that theological conservatives and liberals differ on political and social issues such as welfare programs, public morality, and law enforcement (see Dredger, 1974).

In two separate studies, Johnson was able to demonstrate that theological orientation has significant effects on voting preference, effects independent of and sometimes contradicting the impact of class. His conclusions were as follows: first, for theological liberals, Republicanism is inversely related to frequency of church attendance among *both* white-collar workers and blue-collar workers. In other words, the more often theological liberals attend church, the less likely are they to vote Republican. Second, for theological fundamentalists, Republicanism is positively related to frequency of church attendance among both white-collar and blue-collar workers. In other words, the more often a fundamentalist attends church, the more likely that person is to vote Republican.

Third, although there are class differences in voting (for example, white-collar workers are more inclined to vote Republican) theological differences are also important. For example, blue-collar *fundamentalists* who attend church frequently are more likely to vote Republican than blue-collar *liberals* who attend church frequently. Fourth, cross pressures from religion and class are exerted on frequently-attending white-collar workers who are theologically liberal and frequently-attending blue-collar workers who are theologically fundamentalist. Johnson found that there was less difference between these two groups with regard to Republican voting than would have been expected on the basis of class alone and concluded that they had been "pushed together" by the cross pressures. Fifth, frequently-attending white-collar workers who are fundamentalists and frequently-attending blue-collar workers who are theological liberals are not cross pressured. The differences between them as far as their disposition to vote Republican is concerned is much larger than would be expected on the basis of class alone. In other words, theological attitudes reduce class-based political differences by making white-collar workers less Republican and blue-collar workers less Democrat. Sixth, although the separate effects of theological attitudes is to push the classes closer together in voting preference, the *combined* effect of religion is to reinforce a long-established conservatism among the middle class and weaken liberalism among the working class. Blue-collar churchgoers, most of whom hear a conservative theology preached, are much less likely to vote Democrat than nonchurchgoers and those few who are theologically liberal. But there are only a few middle class people with liberal theologies who are switching out of *their* class to counterbalance this.

Johnson's conclusions have been challenged by Anderson (1966) and Rojek (1973). Johnson (1967) has convincingly rebutted Anderson's critique, but there is enough contrary evidence in Rojek's Appalachian data to keep the issue open.[3] For example, Rojek found that white-collar fundamentalists, who ought to have been the most strongly Republican group, where one of the weakest. However, he did find that theological conservatism and Republican preference among blue-collar workers are positively associated. In other words, conservative theology tends to draw blue-collar workers toward the Republican camp. The question

---

[3] In a replication of Johnson's Oregon study in a rural county in Illinois, Anderson (1966) failed to substantiate Johnson's findings. Party preference went very much by class, and the theological split between liberals and fundamentalists had little impact on party preference. But the meaning of a liberal/fundamentalist split in a rural mid-western county (where liberals are few in number) is uncertain. Anderson's failure to find any connection between theology and party preference might well be due to the lack of theological variation. Furthermore, Anderson classified the denominations in his sample as liberal not (as Johnson did), on the basis of the theological position of the pastor, but on the basis of whether or not it belonged to the National Council of Churches. "Since a great many local congregations of denominations participating in the NCC are theologically conservative, and since rural areas contain a disproportionate number of such churches, it is very likely that most if not all of the churches Anderson classifies as liberal are in fact conservative" (Johnson, 1967:434).

which remains unsettled is the net effect of these conflicting pressures of class and religion. Are more blue-collar workers Republican by virtue of their religion than are white-collar workers Democratic because of their religion? Unfortunately, this issue will only be resolved when we know what proportion of the blue-collar vote is affected by religious attitudes, and for this we need larger surveys than Johnson's.

Religious and political beliefs and attitudes combine to form quite distinct subcultures in the United States. These subcultures cut across the lines that connect class position to party preference, moderating the influence of purely economic interests on political behavior. The result of these multiple cleavages is to mute the intensity of the conflict that would follow from their superimposition. This is not to say the support which the church members give to the respective parties is the result of a consciously shared decision. It is more likely to be the residue of reactions to common experiences; it is the social history of a group that leads its members to give their loyalty to one particular party. Specific religious attitudes probably no more than help interpret and legitimize sentiments already formed. The implication is that religion does not have a direct impact on political action. This can be illustrated by considering the relation between religious fundamentalism and political conservatism. Religious fundamentalism, so closely associated with right-wing political beliefs (see Orum, 1968; Jorstad, 1970), is not a direct cause of political action so much as "a concomitant cultural phenomenon, with its own impetus. . . . This is not to deny the independent effects of fundamentalist beliefs, but rather to blunt the edge of religious determinism as it might be applied mechanistically to extremist political movements. Fundamentalist religious belief, seen culturally in America, is also traditional religious belief. Traditional religious belief is the symbolic center of a traditional style of life" (Lipset and Raab, 1970:392). Religion and politics are, in other words, part of the same "cultural baggage."

A religio-political subculture survives because its members know each other and meet frequently. This is why the communal aspect of religion best predicts political behavior (Wuthnow, 1973:121). For example, vote switching by Protestant blue-collar workers from Democrat to Republican in the Kennedy/Nixon election of 1960 was most common among those who had a strong communal sense of their religion (Anderson, 1970:171). Actually, religion influences political life through both its theological and its communal aspects. Catholics are politically liberal for communal reasons—they have experienced being a minority group; they are liberal largely in spite of their theology. Elite Protestants are liberal because of their beliefs. Jews are liberal because of both theology and communal experiences. As Catholics become more assimilated and as the communal dimension of Catholicism becomes less important, Catholics might begin to move closer to the political position of Protestants and the religious factor might thereby become less important. As long as religion is associated with ethnic, language, regional and other segmental ties, however, it will continue to weaken the tie between class and politics.

RELIGION AND POLITICAL CONFLICT
IN THE UNITED KINGDOM

The association between religion and politics is not nearly so strong in the United Kingdom as it is in the United States. For example, just as many members of the Church of England (long known as "The Conservative Party at prayer") prefer the Labour Party (44 percent) as the Conservative Party (41 percent).[4] As in the United States, Catholics tend to support the party of the left: 62 percent prefer the Labour Party, 24 percent the Conservative. But the most significant difference between the two countries is the sizable group of people in the United Kingdom who have no church affiliation; about half of these people support the Labour Party. (Butler and Stokes, 1974:156; see also Bochel and Denver, 1970:208; Sissons, 1973:224; Berry, 1970:50)

In the United Kingdom, class and religious lines tend to overlap. Upper- and middle-class Britons are both Anglican and Tory; the working class is both irreligious and Labour. Much of the apparent variation in party preference by religion is in fact the result of differences in social class, although a religious factor does persist and there is evidence of vote switching on religious grounds (Butler and Stokes, 1974:160). As in the United States, the net effect of this vote switching is conservative: the tendency of working-class Anglicans (especially the regular attenders) to support the party of the middle class, combined with the solidarity of middle-class Anglicans in support of "their" party, although less significant today than formerly, contributes to a weakening of class politics in the United Kingdom.[5]

---

[4]This reflects more than anything else the fact that many Britons identify themselves as Anglican rather freely. Controlling for the relationship between Anglicanism and voting by frequency of attendance reveals that the regularly church-attending Anglican is "overwhelmingly likely to be Conservative: the purely nominal Anglican . . . in most cases Labour" (Butler and Stokes, 1974:158).

[5]This is not to say that religion "causes" politics. There has long been an association between the Church of England and the establishment, and many working class people habitually conform to the Church, just as they habitually conform to all middle class norms and leadership.

RELIGION AND POLITICS IN CANADA

It is generally agreed that in Canada, "religion is the greatest source of polarization for political parties" (Schwartz, 1974:579). It is more important than, for instance, social class in explaining voting behavior (McDonald, 1969:129). Since the turn of the century, the pattern has been for the Catholics to support the Liberal Party (and, more recently, the *Creditistes*), the Jews to support the New Democratic Party and the Liberal Party, and the Protestants to support the Conservative Party (and, more recently, the Social Credit Party) (Mol, 1976:250). Although only a small minority of Catholics have shifted to the *Creditistes*, all of that party's support does come from the Catholic community, and although only a small minority of the nation's Protestants support the Social Credit Party, its chief support does come from fundamentalist and dissident Protestant sects and some Anglicans, especially in the western provinces. Also, although in all regions of the country Catholics give most of their support to the Liberal Party, sometimes as much as 22 percent above the regional average (Meisel, 1973:3), the Liberal Party itself is well balanced in terms of religious representation. The pattern of voting by religious identification is shown in Table 16.5, which is adapted from data derived from a national survey taken soon after the 1965 election (Schwartz, 1974:580).

TABLE 16:5

RELIGION AND VOTING IN CANADA IN 1965

	Liberal	Conservative	NDP	Social Credit	Creditistes
Roman Catholic	57%	22%	31%	6%	100%
Ukranian Catholic	1	2	3	—	—
United Church	17	35	24	26	—
Anglican	10	18	13	21	—
Presbyterian	3	9	3	9	—
Baptist	3	3	2	—	—
Lutheran	1	3	3	11	—
Greek Orthodox	*	*	1	4	—
Other Protestant	3	5	4	20	—
Jewish	2	*	3	—	—
None	2	3	5	2	—

*less than one percent

Commentators (such as Laponce, 1969:203; Schwartz, 1974:580; Anderson, 1966) agree that despite the close ties between ethnicity and religion in Canada, religion does have an independent impact on political behavior, although why it takes this form is not clear. The alignment of the Catholics with the Liberals may be due to that party's firmer stand on civil rights, and it may have something to do with the historical association between Protestants and the Conservative Party. It is interesting to note, however, that devout Catholics and clerics are more likely to be Conservative (Schwartz, 1974:582), which reflects a more traditional and European pattern than that found in the United States.

Religion continues to be important in Canadian politics despite alleged secularization. This is because religion is one among a number of factors such as language, country of origin, region, and education, that break up the Canadian people into different subcommunities. There are no signs that this kind of division is diminishing in importance.

RELIGION AS AN AGENT OF DE-POLITICIZATION

To a conflict theorist, data on the cross-cutting effects of religion and class on political behavior are confirmation of the Marxian notion that religion is "the opiate of the masses," for they show that religion lessens the likelihood that the lower classes will act politically to further their economic interests. Marx was not surprised that modern Christianity—and especially Protestantism, with its *"cultus* of the abstract man," or intense individualism—appealed to the bourgeoisie, for it harmonized fully with their political and economic interests. Although he did not claim that the bourgeoisie deliberately imposed their religious ideas on the proletariat, he explained the existence of similar religious ideas among the working class as a function of the superior power of the capitalist class to disseminate and legitimate ideas congenial to them, and as a function of the alienated condition of the proletariat, which made them receptive to such ideas.[6]

In Marx's view, religion is a "perverse world consciousness" for both capitalist and worker because it obscures the inescapable fact of the conflicting economic interests in society and "the changes required to alter the course of society in the direction of objective class interests" (Anderson, 1974:135). *Any* set of beliefs that inhibits the spread of knowledge about the experiences workers share as a result of their common

[6]Evidence presented in Chapters 10 and 11 shows that the churches legitimize dominant political and economic values. These values—individualism, private property, legalism, equality of opportunity—are the values of the upper and middle classes.

relation to the means of production—in short, anything that reduces class awareness—would be "an opiate." However, inasmuch as the obscuring of class conflict works to the benefit of the capitalist class and to the disadvantage of the proletariate, the idea of religion as a pleasurable but harmful drug has been applied most often to the working class.

Marx argued that religion, in spiritualizing the differences between people brings about a condition of *de-politicization*.

> It is a situation in which, while conflict and tension exist in the hierarchy, the conflict has not become openly political. The conflicting segments or ranks are not organized for conflict; no one attempts to alter the shape of the hierarchy. While subordinates may complain about the treatment they receive from those above them, they do not propose to move to a position of equality with them, or to reverse the positions in the hierarchy (Becker, 1967:240–41).

In other words, they do not propose to alter the distribution of power. This condition can be brought about in two ways. First, religion denies political conflict by providing a set of spiritual values that supplant the economic values over which political conflict takes place. This is called *transvaluation*. Second, religion denies political conflict by stressing the importance of the individual over society, the insignificance of social arrangements and plans, and the irrelevance of group conflict beside the paramount importance of the condition of the individual. This is known as *individuation*.

Transvaluation

Transvaluation is the substitution of spiritual values for material values, inner, or spiritual, equality is stressed above economic or political inequality. It stems from Christian dualism, which sees man as sharply separated into spiritual and secular (or material) realms—the proper sphere of action of the Church being the former. Transvaluation consoles and compensates the under privileged by substituting a hierarchy based on one's state of grace for hierarchies based on birth, possessions, and power.

There are a number of consequences of adopting this view:

1. The scarce resources that are normally the focus of political struggle are deemed worthless and the world of politics thereby becomes irrelevant. For example, the Catholic Church has traditionally taken the position that the political life of the community is not its concern. In Underwood's (1957:307) predominantly Catholic "Paper City," the area of public life the Church defined as political and therefore irrelevant

included most of the important economic issues of urban living: housing for low-income people; tax policies and welfare expenditures of the local government; collective bargaining of labor and management in the city; extension of union activities; expansion of political participation in the community; reform or change of the political and governmental structure of the city; economic instability of an inflationary or deflationary nature in the community.

2. Energies that might have been directed at self-liberation of the poor are channeled into "an overabundance of small congregations for a surplus number of untrained preachers who are always seeking a position. . . ." (Washington, 1964:54). In other words, energies are directed at attempts to achieve upward mobility and power within the religious community itself rather than in the world at large.

3. False links between social classes are forged by the idea that fellow church members are "really" equal on spiritual terms, despite the social differences that separate them. Thus, in Blauner's (1958:36) view, the rhetoric of equal involvement in religious organizations has greatly inhibited the formation of class consciousness among the workers of America, especially in the South.[7]

4. In "rising above" politics, the church legitimizes the status quo. For example, Moore (1974:58) describes how English Methodists

> tried hard to observe a "no politics" rule; this did not mean that men should have no political views but that the expression of these views should not create strife in the life of the Church. What the no politics rule usually meant was the Conservative or Liberal views could be expressed in sermons or speeches without being identified as "political" whereas radical or socialist ideas were seen as political or disruptive.

The Gastonia, North Carolina, mill-village churches studied by Pope (1965:159) in the 1920s made an even stronger effort to stay out of politics. Although these efforts were "almost always disguised in terms of the general welfare of the community," the mill officials had final supervision over them.

5. Religious beliefs that promise an imminent end to earthly suffering and the advent of an age when all spiritual worthies will rank equal also achieve a kind of transvaluation, and can engender a strong sense of political futility, particularly if they teach that believers "should live

---

[7]The idea that religion fosters the mingling of classes within the church is also false. Church leadership like political leadership everywhere, tends to be heavily concentrated among the better-off members of the congregation. Few congregations are models of participatory democracy. Decision-making tends to be confined to a small minority of higher status members.

loosely in relation to wordly structures" (Kauffman and Harder, 1975:151). It is noteworthy that, at least in modern societies, the belief that the present dispensation will soon end and be succeeded by an age in which present social roles will be reversed, rarely leads to political radicalism. Schwartz's (1970:109) discovery that Seventh-Day Adventists show little interest in radical politics is probably something that could be said of all millenial groups that appeal to the poor. Far from being rebellious, they teach obedience to constituted authority; they are hostile to groups that are politically radical. Adventism will at least encourage the belief that the social order and the unfolding of history are God-ordained rather than something for which man is responsible. Although they eschew involvement in politics of any kind, Adventists will also declare a firm loyalty to the state, exhibit a keen desire for recognition from political leaders, and be extremely intolerant of religious heretics and political dissenters. They tend to fuse adventist religion with an equally apocalyptic politics which demands obedience and firmness from all citizens (see Westin, 1963; Jorstad, 1970).[8]

Individuation

A church does not have to explicitly defend the status quo for its teachings to have the effect of muting social protest. It might fail to threaten established institutions simply by showing little awareness of social structure at all. If social structure is recognized, it "is thought of as a simple outgrowth of the impulses, desires, and mental processes of individuals" (Schneider and Dornbusch, 1958:96). The political dimension is treated as a fiction, something that lacks its own laws, development or history. To the extent that religious beliefs exalt the individual, define change in individual rather than social structural terms, and stress the will of the individual as the main determinant of behavior, unfettered by social circumstances, they will de-politicize the consciousness of those who adhere to them, and seriously question the efficacy of political conflict or social reform.

Individuation is present in the idea that what is called politics is actually a moral phenomenon, that parties and programs are not really necessary if the means are there to judge a person's scrupulousness and honesty. Methodists seek to convert politicians in order to make them more honest and loving; Pentecostals seek "spirit-filled" Christians re-

---

[8]The Unification Church combines millenialist religion and apocalyptic politics, propagating conservative policies through several front organizations, such as The International Federation for Victory over Communism. This is not to say that all sects are conservative. Although members of neo-Christian sects like the charismatics tend to be more conservative than the public at large, members of sects such as Scientology, Hare Krishna, Zen, Transcendental Meditation and Satanism tend to be more tolerant of avowed revolutionaries and of alternative life-styles (Wuthnow, 1976b:276).

gardless of their political platform; Hare Krishna devotees are looking for people to lead the country who are filled with that understanding provided uniquely by Krishna Consciousness. All are searching for "an unsullied and accessible realm above politics" and, in effect, are seeking to reduce insoluble conflicts of values to soluble problems of manipulation and interpersonal relationships (Miller, 1961:106). They put people above party.

Individuation is also manifest in the inspirational literature exemplified by the writings of Norman Vincent Peale. Although Peale's readership is probably mainly lower-middle class, a version of his ideas is very widespread. Peale treats politics as a game or contest in which "the rules are no part of your action; none of your power [is] directed toward the invention of the game or any games" (Meyer, 1960:264). He tells his readers how to get on by playing the game within the rules and by manipulating available strategies, and promotes an idea of freedom that is confined to personal relationships, individual expression, and self-directed activity. There is no cognizance of class or of competing economic interests except those that are manifest at the level of individual opportunities.

It is appropriate to recall here the remarks made about the socialising function of sects in Chapter 14, for much the same could be said of some of the religions of the working class as far as politics are concerned. In their emphasis on the attainment of individual respectability through self-improvement, they socialise their membership into not only the economic but also the political ways of the middle classes. Thus, in some respects religion has undoubtedly served to enhance the political capabilities of those on the periphery of the political system. For example, there is good reason to believe that English Methodism, in its stress on tight organizational control at the grass-roots level, self-discipline, and spiritual equality, instructed its membership in more democratic ideas and techniques and enable them individually to participate more fully in political affairs (Thompson, 1963:365). However, Methodism appealed only to the aristocracy of the working class—those about to enter the middle class—and to them it brought a liberalism that was decaying in the face of the growing socialist movement. The individualism of Protestantism has not, then, been without political effect on its working-class adherents, but that effect was hardly calculated to foster a sense of class awareness.[9]

[9]The question of the political implications of Methodism has not been resolved (see Semmel, 1973). Although there are grounds for being skeptical of Wesley's impact on the politics of the working class, the vivid picture he painted of a troubled and persecuted people must have helped generate some feeling of solidarity and independence among his followers. Many chapels enjoyed considerable autonomy, and they must have provided training in organizational skills which would later prove useful in political life (Thompson, 1963:391–400; Hill, 1973a:183–204).

AMELIORATIVE REFORM

The conflict model does not preclude the idea of religion promoting class consciousness and radical social change, nor does it rule out the possibility of the church being engaged in social reform. However, it does assume that all social reform will be class-oriented, or represent genuine social structural change. The churches have frequently involved themselves in social reform movements. However, most of these have been oriented toward adapting the working class more fully to the demands of the capitalist system by ameliorating its negative effects. In the Marxian view, such reform movements serve equally the function of opiate because they give the illusion of change while affecting no real redistribution of power. It is significant that the churches have rarely supported movements of radical reform such as socialism.

The nineteenth century revivalists have been given credit for bringing about several major social reforms. In many ways, these people were latter-day Puritans, channeling their intense moralism into crusades for social betterment, such as temperance, slavery abolition, and numerous attempts to improve the lot of the poor. However, they were conspicuous for their obsession with moral problems, such as drinking, and for their view that the the only hope of social reform is the regeneration of the individual. They failed to associate the growing problems of the industrial cities with the capitalist system as a whole.[10] In McLoughlin's (1959:414) view, revivalists such as Moody and Sunday who received most of their support from business interests, were exploited by "a combination of naive religious reformers and astute local business interests and their political henchmen."[11]

Working alongside the revivalists in the cities were other reform movements, such as missions and settlement houses, which often developed into full-fledged established sects, such as William Booth's Salvation Army. The Salvation Army appealed specifically to the urban proletariat untouched by the churches, whose middle-class ways Booth clearly disdained. Booth energetically set about alleviating the horrors of

[10]The impulse for ameliorative reform draws upon the "private" side of American Protestantism which argues that "saving the souls of individuals is the task of the Christian, and . . . that changing the hearts of individuals [will] solve social problems." This more private side of Protestantism has "been the majority side from the beginning," dominating the more "public" Protestantism. The public Protestantism holds that "social and economic forces are so strong that they oppress humans and take away their freedom; therefore social reform is needed to attain the redemption of individuals" (Hoge, 1976:25).

[11]In England, Moody was patronized by Lord Shaftsbury, who believed that "if the poor man did his duty in obedience, humility, sobriety, and piety, then the rich and well-born would take care of him" (McLoughlin, 1959:180).

working class inner-city life. However, he did not challenge dominant political arrangements but concentrated instead, on controlling "the consumption of alcohol, and tobacco, particularly the former, and various forms of indulgence such as luxuries, amusements, entertainment, [and] fashion" (Robertson, 1968:65). Later, Catherine Booth declared specifically that the "Salvation Army benefits the State by creating a RESPECT FOR THE LAW."

The YMCA served a similar purpose. Its reformist zeal was lent to any organization that seemed to offer a chance for lower-income groups to become more like the middle class, through vocational training, night schools, and "programs of character and skill development (for both social and psychological purposes) to persons who could otherwise not afford them" (Zald, 1970:69). The YMCA was originally financed by the railroad magnates, who considered it "as good business, resulting in improved morals and better employees" (Zald, 1970:59). Rich industrialists such as Philip Armour and Cyrus McCormack contributed generously to Moody's revivals and his Home Missions, and B. F. Jacobs funded the Sunday Schools Union, which "mirrored the country's values and produced a pious and knowledgeable laity" (Ahlstrom, 1975, II:199). Moody told *his* backers that "there could be no better investment for the capitalists of Chicago than to put the saving salt of the Gospels into those dark homes" (McLoughlin, 1959:27).[12] This sentiment lives on in the breast of many employees today. Earle, et al., (1976:26) found that the mill managers of Gastonia still consider the most important service the churches provide for Gastonia is in building "employability" into their congregations—inculcating traits of punctuality, industry, sobriety and obedience.

Radical political reform never received the support of the churches. The major attempt by the churches to implement social reform–the Social Gospel–never adopted a position from which it could really criticize the capitalist system.

A large wing of the social movement was consistently conservative in its analysis and prescription. The conservative social Christians looked at current social unrest with fear and horror; they devoted a major part of their energies to pointing out the ends of socialism. Usually they were at least skeptical of trade unions and some of them were overtly hostile. The solutions they urged, ranging from

[12]"The gospel of Horatio Alger had no better prophet than Moody. He told a Boston audience that a man who really wanted to work would work for anything. . . . If he served faithfully enough, he would become indispensable to his employer, and then his star would rise. . . . Only those who would not work would starve" (Weisberger, 1966:224).

consumers' cooperatives to savings banks, involved no practical challenge to contemporary economic assumptions (May, 1949:163).[13]

In England, the estrangement between radical politics and religion become obvious as early as the 1840s (Campbell, 1971:48). England's equivalent of the Social Gospel, Christian Socialism, was caustically described by Marx (1955:89) as "the holy water with which the priest consecrates the heart burnings of the aristocrat." It was led by an "upper-middle-class elite," and was highly paternalistic, more concerned to avoid rather than promote socialism (Jones, 1968:24). Early leaders like Frederick Maurice and Charles Kingsley were fiercely anti-democratic (Kitson-Clarke, 1973:307). Their proposals were mainly intended to show that respect and friendship were possible between people of different classes (Inglis, 1963:171).[14]

Although the argument is often made that many Protestant denominations fostered the growth of more democratic politics and thus stimulated political reform, there is serious question as to whether or not this was really so. Moore's (1974:184) opinion is that the influence of Methodism on the rise of the Labour Party was "mainly negative." By the time the Labour Party began to edge toward power in England, at the turn of the century, the urban working class had become totally alienated from the churches, with their formalism, conservative politics, dependence on the wealthy for support, the remoteness of their clergy, and advocacy of submission rather than critical analysis.[15]

There was even less connection between socialism (even unionism) and the churches in the United States, especially in the South. Pope (1965:201) found that southern ministers in the 1920s were uniformly opposed to unionization, and that union organizers were quick to realize that ministers were among their worst enemies. Ministers took no stand on such issues as the regulation of wages, and working conditions, contenting themselves with appealing to the better nature of the contending

[13]Leaders of the Social Gospel movement, such as Washington Gladden, sought state regulation of working hours, factory inspections, taxation of inheritance, and the regulation of monopolies. He believed that the orderly processes of the market place were being disrupted by unethical behavior on both sides—the "morally depraved" and "improvident" working class and the "corrupt" and "unChristian" capitalist.

[14]A concern to "improve" the working class is also evident in Sabbatarianism. Its chief purpose was to teach middle class norms to the laboring population. "The working man rises up to the spirit of the day, dresses up in his Sunday best and marks the day by a special decorum in his behavior. One day in seven he lives out of his class. . ." (Homan, 1970:86).

[15]Moore (1974:45) reports that most of the union leaders in the Durham, England coalfields were Methodists, but they promoted a view of society as a functioning whole, not as one of contending classes. Mine owners, too, were often Methodists, interested in social reforms and anxious to play down conflicts between themselves and labor. The rise of class politics in the 1920s, culminating in the General Strike of 1926, destroyed this link between unionism religion for good.

parties. A study of Gastonia, North Carolina in the later 1960s, designed as a follow-up to Pope's original work, reported two kinds of changes in this regard. First, there was less consensus among ministers on opposition to organized labor—although the churches continued to be heavily promanagement. The churches remain part of a general subculture in which paternalism and suspiciousness toward unions are strong themes, despite (or perhaps because of) some advances which unions have made in the area. Ministers were now more inclined to support the principle of unionism while disapproving of actual unions as corrupt, violent and too powerful. They also were likely to disagree that unions were necessary in their particular community (Earle, et. al., 1970:216).

Second, the churches do not encourage the view that unionism is a real economic issue. Labor-management relations, in so far as they are addressed at all, are viewed in ethical terms: they are to be improved by more righteous living. The churches and the world of work have moved further apart, and religion is seen as being less relevant to economic and political issues (Earle et. al., 1976:222).[16] The laity have perhaps, become more anxious for change and more disdainful of merely ambulatory services such as soup kitchens, but they still emphasize their mission of helping individuals change their ways rather than helping society change its institutions. The unions, for their part, are much more likely to have the confidence to challenge too close a relation between minister and mill (Earle, et. al., 1976:205). Despite these changes, Blauner's (1958:35) view remains substantially correct: it is almost impossible to exaggerate "the role of religion as a mechanism which allowed the work force to adapt to the changed conditions of life, and thus thwarted the development of movements of radical protest."[17]

CONCLUSION

The conflict model views the urban industrial proletariat as the driving political force in any fundamental restructuring of society, and sees all genuine political conflict as class conflict. For many reasons, the increasing class conflict and political instability that Marx predicted have

[16]"What then for the carryover of religion into the affairs of the mill, the insurance company, city politics, and the like? Alas: there is little energy left for such things; little experience to suggest that workers can influence managers; so many complex social and economic questions that seem foreign to the Bible, that it might just be useless to talk about such things" (Earle, et. al., 1976:18).

[17]Pope (1965:29) believed that the "greatest contribution of the churches to the industrial revolution in the South undoubtedly lay in the labor discipline they provided through the moral supervision of the workers. . . . methods used in helping convert an atomistic assemblage of rural individualists into a disciplined labor force, amenable to a high degree of social control, consisted of the inculcation of personal virtues (stability, honesty, sobriety, industry), provision of a center for community integration other than the mill itself, and emotional escape from the difficulties of life in the mill village."

not eventuated: "the worker in capitalist society is individualist rather than collectivist, privatised and home-centered rather than discontented and desirous of change" (Anderson, 1974:283). It has been the purpose of this chapter to show that much of this weak class consciousness is due to the religious factor in social life.

It seems, then, that religion had little or no contact, either in the United States or in the United Kingdom, with principal movement for social reform of the abuses of industrial capitalism. Conservative churchmen did not feel concerned with these kinds of issues at all, and the liberal churchmen, seeking to bring church and society into ever better adjustment, favored liberal reforms. By offering reformist solutions to deep-seated problems, these liberal churchmen separated industrial conflict from its underlying political conflict. It is significant that the strongest church support for trade unions in England came in the 1870s, when the unions functioned much more as friendly societies than as political machines. The emergence of a more militant unionism, and its growing link with socialism, made the churches much more circumspect in their support for labor organizations. Much of the reformism of the late nineteenth century was aimed at eliminating the need for politics altogether. The answer to the tensions and conflicts of industrial capitalism was said to be the better adaptation of the individual to the laws of God. Especially in the United States, reform movements were typically moralistic, aiming at breaking any solidaristic opposition to existing conditions of inequality by holding out to the ablest and most ambitious of the disadvantaged the change to improve themselves. These reforms offered the disprivileged the means of better competition; the unequal were given a chance to be unequal but superior.

The emergence of a "class for itself" as a political force is inhibited wherever nonclass factors intrude. This has clearly been the case in the United States, where religious loyalties and beliefs have been a major influence on political behavior. Although there has been some association among class, religion and voting, this has not offset the crosscutting effect of religion, which has weakened class consciousness and attenuated class politics. This effect manifests itself not only in data on party preference and voting, and in the apolitical orientation of the churches, also in the social reformism of the churches, which has been assimilative and not class oriented. The various "moralistic binges" (abolition, Temperance, nativism, and anti-Communism) in which the churches, but also in the social reformism of the churches, which has been assimilative and not class oriented. The various "moralistic binges" (abolition, Temperance, nativism, and anti-Communism) in which the sought to end politics entirely by denying the existence of power blocs—with the effect, however, of giving elites an efficient means for preserving the power they already possess. The churches have legitimated a democratic system that overwhelmingly favors the bourgeoisie (Collins, 1975:394), and the working class has been given a political choice only within the system.

17

RELIGION
AS AN AGENT OF CHANGE

INTRODUCTION

Marx's thinking on religion was dominated by the idea that religion reflects a condition of alienation, in which man had "not yet found himself." Marx believed that the love, goodness, wisdom, and creativity of man had been projected outwardly onto a biblical god. This image had then come to appear an external and independent being who condemns man for his lack of love, his evil, his ignorance, and his impotence. Man was thus divided against himself—in other words, alienated. Marx also believed that religion mystified man's condition, preventing him from seeing either the full extent of his misery or the possibility of becoming free from that misery.

As an "illusory happiness" religion, for Marx, stands in the way of true self-realization and functions as "the opium of the people," detaching them from the real contradictions of social life. For this reason, Marx's sociology is associated most often with the idea that religion is an agent of social control and a conservative force. But Marx (1955:102) was well aware of the revolutionary potential of religious ideas, and nowhere did he claim that religion must always have stabilizing consequences. He believed, for example, that "the chiliastic dream visions" of Christianity offered "a very convenient starting point" for the property-less in their fight against their feudal overlords. Other sociologists, not all of them Marxists, share this view, and argue that religious movements can act as "catalysts of history, crystallising in acute form social discontents and aspirations, and marking the moments of social structural collapse, and sometimes heralding, or even promoting, social reintegration" (Wilson, 1970:71).

An adequate assessment of this other side of the Marxian perspective on religion would entail a wide-ranging historical and comparative survey of modern Western societies, and the part played by religious protest movements in changing them, but such an undertaking is not feasible here. This chapter can only present a few examples of the kind of analysis to which such a perspective leads. First, it is necessary to stipulate the conditions under which religion will operate as an impetus to radical social change. Second, as a means of examining the thesis in some detail, the impact of black religion on the struggle for liberation by black people will be assessed. Third, having looked at the contribution of black religion to the struggle for racial equality and individual freedom, it is fitting to examine the role of white church people in the movement. A brief historical survey will reveal that although white churches have not been absent from the civil rights movement, only a small proportion of the clergy and an even smaller minority of the laity have contributed their support. The fourth task will be to find out what this minority looks like: who are the most active ministers?

The civil rights campaign, which has aimed at achieving equal rights for all racial and ethnic groups, has not, of course, been the only movement for social change in the United States in recent years. The war in Vietnam produced a severe crisis in the political life of the nation. Members of all three major faiths engaged in the movement against the war, but in this chapter the focus will be upon the nature of Catholic and Jewish engagement. In the antiwar movement, a Catholic Left sought to break down the dichotomy between Christian person-to-person morality and the political world of expedience and self-interest. In the same movement, and in the leftist critiques of capitalism, Jews continued their tradition of involvement in movements of political reform.

THE CONDITIONS FOR RADICAL RELIGIOUS ACTION

It is wrong to assume that a movement of religious dissent is also a movement of political protest. The function of many sects is to accommodate powerless groups to their condition of subordination in the secular world. Under certain conditions, however, religion can operate as an inspiration for radical social action aimed at fundamental social change. Just what these conditions are is not yet precisely known, but they probably include the following:

1. In religious movements, people express their discontent in religious and not political terms and espouse religious and not political values. Religion cannot operate as a stimulus for political change if religion and politics are altogether separate. Not even modern Western societies have reached this degree of structural differentiation, but the degree to which political and religious spheres are mixed in a society does vary, not only from one society to another but also from one part of a society to another. To the extent that they are undifferentiated, religious protest will also be political protest.

2. The closer the alliance between one specific denomination and the State, the closer religious protest comes to being political protest. For example, European sectarianism carries political overtones that are not found as readily in the United States, because the ties between the State and the established church are still close in many European societies. American blacks, too, have a tendency to fuse religious and political protest, because they have been confronted by white churches and a State run by whites linked together in dominion over them.

In general, the American experience has been for sects to accommodate quite easily to the status quo and become denominations. Despite being larger and better organized, a denomination is less of a political threat to the State than a sect. Sects demand exclusive commitment, which either redefines politics (the struggle of Good and Evil) or derogates political allegiances. The denomination, on the other hand, sees political and religious allegiances as more or less coterminous, or as entirely separate but compatible. Only in sectarianism (particularly through the social premiums and discipline the sect is able to impose), can new values be internalized and a really new self-image and group identity be formed. The sect is the only social form capable of breaking through the established social order.

3. People are not typically driven to sectarianism or religious protest by their political frustrations. However, it is reasonable to suppose that religious protest will be more likely to carry political overtones if secular opportunities for expressing grievances and bringing about social change have been closed off. Ironically, religious movements that spring up where political dissent is discouraged often have a political character "read into" them by the authorities. Consequently, they assume a political character not only in the eyes of the general public but also in their own eyes.

4. The revolutionary potential of a religious movement also has a lot to do with the received ideas upon which it draws. For example, Judaism and its Christian off-spring have been dynamic religions, not passively receptive of the social order, at least compared with Eastern religions which stress either orderly adaptation to or radical rejection of the empirical world. The prophetic tradition in Judeo-Christian thought has

fueled a religious radicalism that is easily translated into political rev-olutionism: "the very idea of the dawn of a millenial kingdom on earth always contained a revolutionary tendency" (Mannheim, 1936:211). The ingathering of God's people is an idea much more congenial to political radicalism than the alternative theme of personal salvation, which is also found within Christianity.

Actually, there are several revolutionary themes within the Judeo-Christian tradition. They include (1) the death and resurrection of Christ and the early realization of a heavenly Kingdom by him; (2) apocalyptic thinking fostered by the persecution of the early Christians, with its images of chosenness, release, and overturning; (3) the promise of eventual triumph over earthly suffering; (4) the vision of a future Golden Age, which is to be based on the principle of God's dominion and not on that of demonic powers; (5) the egalitarian message of grace and salvation for all, regardless of social condition; (6) the post-Aquinas teaching that tyrants can be rightfully usurped; (7) the exodus theme, with its message of liberation and deliverance; (8) the pilgrim people idea, with its message of temporary suffering and necessary sojourn in a world of troubles; (9) the idea of divine judgment, with its implication that all human institutions are corrupt and frail; and (10) the idea of God as Lord, whose domain is entirely separate from that of Ceasar's.

Religion fosters political radicalism to the extent that it enhances class consciousness. For example, class and religious identification may coin-cide, heightening the visibility of class divisions; religious agencies may lay the groundwork for class-benevolent societies and trade unions; and religious teachings may provide the means by which an individual can distance himself from a given social reality and imagine some better alternative. The true chiliast is an activist: he is not content with mere prophecies and speculations. "He is not actually concerned with the millenium to come: what is important for him is that it happened here and now, and that it arose from mundane existence, as a sudden swing over into another kind of existence" (Mannheim, 1936:217).

A connection between religious and political radicalism can be de-tected as far back as the original band of Christians, who drew upon a prophetic tradition (described in the Old Testament) to resist their Roman overlords. Political radicalism is also associated with the Protes-tant Reformers (see Williams, 1962), especially the Anabaptists, who wished not merely to *reform* the Church but to break it down entirely and begin anew, and whose occupation of Munster in 1534–35 was broken only by a bloody seige and the death of their leader, John of Leiden (see Bax, 1903; Cohn, 1970:252–271). The Anabaptists were communists. They established free, voluntary communities, admitted newcomers only after confessional baptism, and maintained loyalty by strict discipline. They were severely ascetic and rejected the materialism of those around them as well as the commerce and technology to which it gave rise. By refusing to pay taxes and evading conscription, they directly contradicted the authority of the State.

The radical wing of the Reformation in England, including groups like the Diggers, the Levellers and the Fifth Monarchy Men, were also politically radical (see Petergorsky, 1940). George Fox, the Quaker, also combined political and religious dissent, rejecting the hierarchy not only of the churches but of the political world as well, determined not to "bow and scrape" to anyone (Hubbard, 1974:24). Many of these religious dissenters found their way to the United States. However, the absence of any established church and the high rates of social and geographical mobility in the new country ensured that no ready connection between religious and political dissent would be made there.

The reforms which the denominations in the United States have supported have not been radical, and they have done little to promote the rise of political consciousness among the burgeoning urban and factory-employed class (see Chapters 11 and 16). However, the rise of working-class politics has not been entirely without religious inspiration. A few denominations did display sympathy for unionism, and some union leaders legitimated their criticism of the factory system and their labor agitation by invoking Protestant reformers such as Thomas Munzer and John of Leiden. Union leaders also drew upon the perfectionist theology of Finney and Moody to criticize the evils of the factory system and make a case for large-scale reforms (Gutman, 1968:158). Miller (1958:210) argues, with some justice, that "the credit for ending the long hours of work in the steel industry belongs to the churches of America," as does the elimination of child labor.

As in England, the association between unionism and religion seems to have been strongest during the beginnings of the union movement. Church leaders saw unionism as a means of recapturing some of the social solidarity of the old agrarian way of life, and supported its aims by invoking Christian ideal of brotherhood and charity. This kind of unionism was congenial to the churches because it was a turning back. By the turn of the century, after the labor wars of the 1880's and 1890's, the language of labor leaders and political radicals was more secular and the churches' support for unionism had weakened.

The reform efforts of the churches during the first half of the twentieth century have already been described in Chapter 11. Although many denominational leaders were active in the progressive reforms of the Social Gospel and the New Deal, very few extended their critique to question the foundations of capitalism itself. However, a minority did keep the association between radicalism and religion alive, especially during the Depression. The Fellowship of Socialist Christians (with

Reinhold Niebuhr and John C. Bennett among its leaders) attacked the New Deal as too cautious. A poll conducted in 1934 of 20,000 Protestant ministers and Jewish rabbis found 28 percent supporting socialism as the way to bring about the ideal society. In the cities the proportion supporting socialist reforms ran as high as 50 percent (Miller, 1958:101).

The most radical of recent decades, the 1960s, saw the mainstream denominations taking a largely reactive role. Those most involved in social movements during that decade seem either to have been irreligious or to have found satisfaction for their religious needs outside the mainstream churches. During this time, when the left-wing became more visible and gained more support than at any previous time except the 1930s and the 1890s, the churches did not change their liberal, reformist orientation toward such matters as poverty, unemployment, and the alienation of the factory work-force. While American politics began to resonate for the first time with criticisms of the *successes* of capitalism, the churches continued their attacks on its failures. While many were beginning to bemoan overproduction, the churches were still puzzling over underproduction. The link between the left and the churches was extremely tenuous. Those church people who did become involved in attempts at radical change tended to be highly unorthodox. As Hoge (1974:152) notes: "the periods of greatest political activism" are usually "the periods of lowest traditional religious orthodoxy and participation," simply because a general radicalizing trend will affect both political institutions and the churches.

Seeds of radical social change in the 1960s should not be sought in the orthodox denominations, then, but on the fringes of orthodoxy. It is of interest that the 1960s witnessed a ferment of religious experimentation as well as political protest. Innovations took the form not only of many new religious movements but of attempts to radically reform the denominations. For example, many American theologians (especially those affiliated in some way with university campuses) began condemning the religious institutions of which they were a part for being enslaving, for busying the laity with self-justifying activities, and for causing them to celebrate material rather than spiritual values.

Impulses for social change *did* emanate from the churches during the 1960s, then, but only from those parts of the church that were hemselves undergoing change. Theological radicals, attacking the elitism, rigidity, conservatism, and lack of responsiveness of the orthodox denominations, pointed the way to significant and potentially radical changes:

1. A "secular" and "de-mythologized" "death of God" theology condemned the other-worldly, transcendental, and individualistic elements in Chris-

tianity and called for the realization of Christian values in the structures of this world.

2. A new "situation ethics" arose to question the traditional, legalistic, and static system of morality as being oppressive and alienating.
3. The authority of seminaries and colleges was challenged by demands for curriculum reforms and greater student autonomy.
4. Demands were made that the churches become more deeply committed to the civil rights movement and show greater concern for social issues.
5. Traditional church structures were criticized for being impersonal, elitist, and out of date.

The churches responded vigorously and positively to many of these demands, and in so doing moved closer to the movements of political reform that had inspired them. However, their position remained essentially a reactive one. There was little sense of denominations being in the vanguard of change.

BLACK RELIGION AND BLACK LIBERATION

As black people have struggled to emancipate themselves from servitude, the role of the black church has been the subject of continual debate. It is beyond dispute that religion has always been very important in the black community. Some see the black church as "an involuntary (or at least semiinvoluntary) communal association that resembles the phenomenon of a state church" (Nelson, 1971:10), providing solace, comfort, and stability. Others see it as a voluntary association committed to the goals of equality and freedom—as a "spearhead of reform" (Fichter, 1965a:1087). The ambiguity of black religion provides an excellent opportunity to look at the kinds of arguments that are made for and against the idea that religion can instigate fundamental social change.

Not all the arguments about the political role of black religion can be presented here, but some of the points of contention that are found most frequently can be described. In the following discussion of eight topics, the arguments for the liberating role of religion will be presented first; counterarguments will then be advanced.

The Impact of African Survivals

For: The slaves were not entirely stripped of their African culture. Among other things, they brought with them religious ideas from Africa. These ideas, modified by the experience of slavery and placed in contact with Christian ideas, kept alive a sense of pride and independence when most of the other sources of black social strength had been destroyed by enslavement.

Against: The significance of the African survivals for slave life is unclear. Washington (1972:32) does not agree that there were African survivals of significance. Genovese (1974:205–19) documents several survivals but is not convinced that they had a positive effect on the emancipation of slaves. For example, the "witchdoctors," or conjurors who ministered to the slaves, were believed to be powerless in the white community, and their practical magic offered no challenge to the system of slavery or the means to make one when the time became ripe.

The Freedom Message of the Gospel

For: Many slaves became converted to Christianity, especially Baptism. The Baptists taught that all individuals have freedom of spiritual opportunity; that leadership is measured by the experience of Spirit Baptism, not education or birth; and that individual congregations should be run democratically. Add to these ideas the highly emotional rites of adult baptism and conversion, and it is not difficult to see in slave Christianity a religion both egalitarian and sustaining in times of trouble (Washington, 1972:41; Genovese, 1974:238).

Against: Although it is true that both Baptists and Methodists stressed equality and freedom, both denominations also supported the system of slavery. The teachings to which slaves were actually exposed were designed to "test their purity by the intensity of their feelings." These teachings focused upon moral purity and humility as the message of Jesus. "Christianity was equated with honesty, charity, obedience, industry, truthfulness and kindness" (Washington, 1964:196). Through this message, which was disseminated in specially prepared catechisms, sermons, and programs of instruction, "missionaries frankly tried to substitute for the fear of corporal punishment, or the love of reward, a Christian conscience of duty as an incentive to promote docility, honesty and fidelity among slaves" (Sernett, 1975:76). Thus, a religion with the potential for liberation could be made to serve the purpose of social control.

Lack of Political Freedom

For: Religious dissent will become associated with political protest if a minority group has little opportunity to openly express its grievances. This is so manifestly true of blacks that some have argued that black religion *must* have had a political character. Thus, while pointing to heaven, the black preacher was actually giving hope for improvement in this world; while urging redemption, he was raising the sense of black pride and self-worth; while generating emotional heat in Spirit Baptism, he was providing the catharsis necessary to maintain the black community as a cohesive unit. The black preacher was also fond of using the analogy of the Jews in bondage to the Romans to portray the condition of blacks, and his congregation was fond of singing spirituals, which were songs of protest "in acceptable and thinly veiled form" (Washington, 1964:287; see also Wilmore, 1972:72).

Against: Whether or not black religion contained covert political messages is much debated. Liberating slogans are not hard to find in black religion, but alternative interpretations are equally plausible. It is too easy to equate cries of "freedom" and "the New Jerusalem" with political slogans of the same meaning. And the meaning of the spirituals is not clear. While to some they are a barely concealed cry for political emancipation, to others they are exclusively "otherworldly in outlook" (Frazier, 1974:19). The slaves relied heavily on their preachers for solace and moral guidance, but true chiliasm was virtually absent, partly because at no time were the slaves threatened as a group or subjected to sudden crises or rapid social change (Genovese, 1974:274). The difficulty here is that it is too easy to read back into religious symbols meanings that were never there for the slaves.

Autonomy Achieved in Independent Denominations

For: Once blacks began to run their own denominations, they acquired the organizational skills and the sense of independence they needed to prepare for the struggle for liberation (see May and Nicholson, 1933:289–92). For example, African Methodist Episcopal Zion ministers were active in the abolitionist movement and inspired the presentation of the first emancipation petition to the House of Representatives in 1800 (Wilmore, 1972:122). After Emancipation, a considerable number of black ministers moved into political office; "a still larger number used their pulpits to politicize their congregations but did not themselves actively seek office" (Nelsen and Nelsen, 1975:32).

Against: The black denominations secured some autonomy for blacks, but has this always been oriented to change? Perhaps not, because their autonomy made it less likely that blacks would seriously challenge segregation in such a way as to endanger their existence (Lincoln, 1974:108). At the turn of the century, W.E.B. DuBois (1971:77) sardonically noted that the black denominations concerned themselves most with raising funds, maintaining their membership, organizing amusements and recreations, maintaining moral standards, and engaging in charity work. They gave social concerns a low priority. Heavily financed by whites and often split along class lines, the black denominations do not seem to have been very active in instigating social change.

Black Religion Helped Mobilize Slave Revolts

For: The beginnings of concerted militancy against white dominion can be traced to the African Society, formed in 1780, which was a forerunner of the African Methodist Episcopal Church (Washington, 1972:51). The class system of the African Methodist Association of Charleston was used for recruitment and communication during Denmark Vesey's revolt (Wilmore, 1972:83). Apprehensive about the potential militancy of black religion, whites passed laws in the early 1800s that prohibited independent meetings or "hush-arbor" religion.

Against: It is true that cases of direct religious inspiration for slave revolts can be found: Nat Turner, an "exhorter," is a conspicuous example. Counterarguments concern not so much the evidence of religious connections with slave revolts as the political effects of the revolts themselves. It is well known that, in the short run at least, revolts were counter-productive, and led to much closer control over all aspects of slave life (Genovese, 1974:186).

Black Religion Inspired Nationalism

For: The most extreme form of black politics is nationalism—the ideal of a self-governing nation of ex-slaves. One kind of nationalism is the back-to-Africa movement, and there is much in black religion to keep this ideal alive: the Christian theme of the Promised Land; the story of Exodus; and the idea of blacks having their roots in the pre-Mosaic Middle East. Marcus Garvey, who organized the most ambitious back-to-Africa movement, in the 1920s, founded his own African Orthodox Church to mobilize religious sentiment behind his cause.

The Black Muslims represent another kind of black nationalism, one that is aimed more at self-determination within the United States. The Muslims achieved considerable public attention during the 1960s because their hostility toward whites and their demands for black self-determination resonated so well with the emerging theme of Black Power.

Against: The black denominations, although active in missionizing in Africa, have never supported the back-to-Africa movement and bitterly opposed Marcus Garvey. The Black Muslims are a relatively small group, they are outside the mainstream of black religion, and they are significant not so much for their nationalism (which has always been secondary) as for their strict ethical demands. As much as any black religion can be, the Muslims have always been highly individualistic, enjoining strict morality as the path to self-improvement.

The Work of the Churches in the Civil Rights Movement

For: The impact of the black churches in civil rights organizations such as the National Association for the Advancement of Colored Peoples (NAACP), the Congress of Racial Equality (CORE), the Southern Christian Leadership Conference (SCLC), and the Student Non-Violent Co-ordinating Committee (SNCC) is clearly reflected in their mixture of energized protest and faith in the ultimate goodness of the majority of whites, and is personified in the figure of Martin Luther King. Individual church people were prominent in rallies and marches; individual congregations gave food and shelter to civil rights workers; and denominations allocated funds to support civil rights groups and issued public pronouncements in support of the civil rights movement.[1]

Against: Although black ministers and their congregations did help mobilize civil rights workers, they adhered strictly to the position that racial discrimination was above all a matter of evil or badness, that such evils were individual failings and not the fault of the system, and that moral persuasion, rather than power should form the basis of the movement. Furthermore, although their *moral* support for the movement is well documented, in practice "those church leaders associated with SCLC seldom involved themselves beyond the matter of financial support for the movement" (Lincoln, 1974:108).

The churches' role diminished in proportion to the growth in power of more militant groups, such as the Black Panther Party, which reflected the overall secularization of the civil rights movement during the 1960s. The orthodox black denominations condemned the Black Panthers and other groups that did not adhere strictly to nonviolent tactics. Many black church leaders opposed James Forman's "reparations" demands in 1969, and those who did support them treated them as a call for better opportunities for blacks to compete in the American economy rather than as a challenge to the distribution of power and wealth.

Blacks Who Are Religious Are Likely To Be Involved in Social Action

For: The radical impulse in black religion is reflected in the fact that those blacks who do involve themselves in the civil rights struggle tend to

---

[1]A "Black Theology" appeared in the 1960s rejecting both resignation and accommodation on the part of blacks (see Cone, 1969). As the civil rights struggle became more violent, more and more black churchmen dismissed the idea of an integrated church in an integrated society as "morally bankrupt" (Nelsen and Nelsen, 1975:126). They focused, instead, on the way in which black religion could serve to increase blacks' political power and social freedom.

have strong religious commitment. There is a liberal, progressive black religion that continues to stimulate militancy among its adherents (Nelsen and Nelsen, 1975:144; see also Alston, 1972b).

Against: Survey research shows that whatever the disporportion of church people on the barricades, the more religious the individual, the less likely he or she is to favor militancy on behalf of civil rights (Marx, 1969:98; Schuman and Hatchett, 1974:88). Thus, if there is a progressive side to modern black religion, there is also a highly individualistic side, which fosters political indifference or caution among blacks.

Black religion would therefore appear to be *both* an opiate and an inspiration for its people. However, a Marxian sociologist would not necessarily agree that the more liberal, progressive side of black religion is really change-oriented. To the extent that it aims at equality of opportunity for blacks, it socializes them into the capitalist system and leaves the structure of economic inequalities in that system untouched. Very few black clergy have rejected the materialist and capitalist values of America or advocated any radical alternative. Reform has therefore been channeled into badly needed welfare measures, which, however, do little more than ameliorate the conditions of black people. The churches failed to follow Malcolm X in his shift leftward or endorse the anticapitalist programs of the Black Panther Party.

WHITE CHURCHES AND THE CIVIL RIGHTS MOVEMENT

The very first white opponents to slavery were religious leaders in Pennsylvania, who spoke out against the system as early as the 1670s. Mainly Quakers, Mennonites and Dunkers, these early abolitionists based their opposition on the principles of equality and freedom. What they claimed for themselves they claimed for all others. Thus, although the contribution of the white churches to the defense of the racial status quo is easily documented (see Chapter 15), so too is their part in bringing about fundamental changes in this area.

Churchmen, mainly Congregationalists and Presbyterians, dominated the abolitionist movement from the very beginning in the early years of the nineteenth century. Revivalists such as Charles Finney and Theodore Weld played an especially important role. Tied to no particular denomination, traveling from town to town, highly dramatic in their preaching, and utterly convinced that all social evils would be eliminated through personal salvation, they helped mobilize white middle-class support behind the abolitionist movement. They did not link slavery to the economic system, but they did point loudly and insistently to the evils inherent in the slave-master relationship. The emancipation of the slaves was very much the work of the churches.[2]

In the present century, the struggle to realize the promise of racial equality has also occupied the churches, but in many varied ways. The cutting edge of the mainstream denominations' civil rights effort has been the Federal Council (later, National Council) of Churches. The FCC, which began to agitate for equal (if still separate) facilities for all races soon after its inception in 1908, has always been considered a radical group (Calvert, 1970:29).

But although the *policy* of the mainstream Protestant denominations before the Second World War was progressive, their actions fell far short of what was needed. For example, although the FCC condemned lynching throughout the 1930s, it at no time endorsed specific legislative proposals for the only effective preventative—making lynching a federal crime. "A questionnaire of 1935, answered by some five thousand ministers, revealed only 3.3% had worked against lynching by preaching and writing to their congressmen in favor of a federal law" (Miller, 1958:133). Not until 1939 did the FCC begin to attack segregation itself. The NCC continued to formulate progressive race relations policies after the Second World War, but it played no part in the birth of the modern civil rights movement in the 1950s. Despite the furor created by civil rights actions, especially in the South, the NCC gave no institutional support to the 1957 or 1960 civil rights acts when these were pending in Congress (Pratt, 1972:150).

It took sustained, violent and highly publicized resistance to civil rights groups (such as the jailing of Martin Luther King in Birmingham, Alabama, in 1963) to summon forth a more concerted and active effort on the part of Protestants. In 1963, the most progressive of the denominations, the Presbyterians, established a new Commission on Religion and Race to mobilize members' civil rights actions, an example that the NCC followed in the same year. As the civil rights struggle intensified during the 1960s, the NCC grew more militant, publicly supporting demonstrations and marches. It was a vocal supporter of the Civil Rights Act of 1964 and the Voter Registration Act of 1965, and its representatives were the only whites involved in the organization of the March on Washington in 1963. The NCC was responsible for the funding of the highly controversial Delta Ministry in Mississippi in 1964. In 1967, the old Commission on Religion and Race was replaced by a new Depart-

[2]"It is impossible to conceive of the antislavery movement minus the religious elements. The crusade drew its inspiration from the Christian ethic, its major leaders from the clergy, its rank and file members from the Christian laymen, and its greatest organized support from the churches" (Miller, 1958:9).

ment of Racial Justice, which enjoyed more sweeping powers and a bigger budget.

Although the National Council of Churches became known in the 1960s for its commitment to the goal of racial justice and equal opportunity for black people, and although it had clearly demonstrated its readiness to support direct-action tactics to achieve that goal, it was, ironically, more liberal than the denominations it claimed to represent, and much more liberal than the many Protestant groups it did *not* represent (such as the Southern Baptists). It was the more liberal Protestants who attended NCC General Board meetings the most conscientiously. NCC staff members tended to be recruited from the more liberal denominations, and it was these denominations that tended to give most generously to the coffers of the NCC. In short, the outlook and policies of the NCC reflected more the attitudes of its professional staff than the laity for whom they worked (Pratt, 1972:82). In the late 1960s, the NCC began to suffer a decline in income owing to its liberalism. Council leaders began to reason that, in their concern to issue ethical pronouncements and promote the civil rights struggle, the spiritual side of the Council's work had been neglected. As a result, pronouncements were toned down, a less ambitious agenda for social change was drawn up, and a greater cooperation with local and regional committees was encouraged.

The major religious bloc outside the NCC, the Catholic Church, did not commit its institutional strength to the civil rights effort. The Catholic clergy, both individually and through diocesan committees, expressed their support for various civil rights strategies, and individual Catholics became prominent in many civil rights campaigns, but the public associations of the Catholic Church, as reflected in the press, remained with "the established, the dignified, and the 'respectable' men and institutions of American society" (Osborne, 1967:241). By the late 1960s the Catholic Church, like the NCC, began to support the more moderate civil rights organizations. It is noteworthy, for example, that the United States Conference of Catholic Bishops intervened on behalf of the largely Mexican-American United Farm Worker's Union in 1973 in advance even of the AFL-CIO.

The civil rights movement shifted further to the political left as the 1960s wore on, and many of the more liberal Protestant denominations followed it. It is highly significant that one of the most strident demands of the entire decade, James Forman's Black Manifesto, in which he demanded "reparations" of $500 million from whites, was aimed at what he considered to be the most vulnerable and sympathetic of American institutions—the liberal denominations. Forman's manifesto was initially presented to the interfaith, interracial, heavily middle-class, and liberal Riverside Church in New York City in 1969.

Many of the liberal denominations were sympathetic to Forman's demands, although they were offended by the stridency with which he presented them. In response, the NCC began to channel more funds into the Interreligious Foundation for Community Organization, the National Committee of Black Churchmen, and the Black Economic Development Conference, as well as setting up affirmative action programs within its own administration. The denominations thus began at last to attack the problem of institutional as well as individual racism.[3]

The civil rights movement did not consist solely of marches and demonstrations by highly publicized organizations such as SNCC. Much effort, time, and money were expended in setting up community organizations in inner-city areas for the purpose of alleviating racial tensions caused by poor housing, inadequate health facilities, segregated schooling, and unemployment. By virtue of their strong interest in community stability and in preventing the fragmentation and impoverishment of neighborhoods, the churches would seem to have had a vested interest in such organizations, an interest they were well suited to pursue by using existing parochial and congregational structures.

The movement of whites to the suburbs accelerated greatly during the 1950s, and many community organizations were formed on the edge of ghettos to try to half a process that not only perpetuated racial discrimination but, by reducing the proportion of middle-income dwellers in the city, exacerbated the fiscal crisis of the cities. The churches played a prominent part in many of these organizations at a time when their integrationist goal was shared by only a few (Fainstein, 1974:145; see also Hadden and Longino, 1975).[4]

The record is clear, then, that at both the national and local levels, denominations, congregations, and individual church members con-

---

[3]The Disciples of Christ, not the most liberal of NCC denominations, condemned Forman's "racism, violence, separatism, extortion and revenge" but at the same time doubled the funding for its urban crisis "reconciliation" program. It also redeployed $30 million of congregational and headquarters money to minority group needs. Furthermore, it agreed that one-fifth of its staff should be non-white, voted to invest in minority businesses, and created an Urban Affairs Commission to deal with inner-city problems (Christian Century, 4/24/1974). The Southern Baptists, however, were shocked by Forman's demands, one spokesman labeling it the work of a "fanatical fringe" (Kelsey, 1973:244).

[4]The Organization for the Southwest Community of Chicago (OSCC), established in 1959, is an example of church-sponsored community organizations. Including 36 of the area's 67 churches, OSCC provided a forum where whites and blacks could meet, funded low interest loans to encourage people to stay in the area and improve their homes, mounted pickets against landlords who allowed their property to deteriorate, lobbied against city agencies which failed to enforce housing, health and safety regulations, and publicly condemned real estate agents thought to be engaged in block-busting (see Fish, 1966).

tributed a great deal to the struggle for civil rights. But there is considerable evidence that such action was confined to a small minority of church members and did not represent the dispositions of the majority (Pratt, 1972:109; Hadden, 1969:84). The activist ministers and laity were a highly visible minority and gave the impression that the churches were behind the movement wholeheartedly, but close examination of the opinions of the ordinary church member tells a different story. The greater the religiosity of the typical white church member, the *less* militant he or she was likely to be (Eckhardt, 1970:199). The activist ministers, in particular, seemed to be a "new breed," different from the laity they served. In fact, they resembled rather closely the old supporters of the Social Gospel, but, like their predecessors, they were a distinctive minority (see Garrett, 1973). It is of considerable interest, then, to examine how they differed from those around them.

CLERGY ATTITUDES TOWARD CIVIL RIGHTS ACTIVISM

By the time the civil rights movement had reached national proportions and become a matter of bitter confrontation between blacks and whites, the majority of Protestant clergymen had come to support it. Few of the ministers polled in 1964 were opposed to demonstrations and marches in the cause of civil rights—only 8 percent of the Methodists and Missouri Synod Lutherans, 6 percent of the American Baptists, 5 percent of the Episcopalians and American Lutherans, and 4 percent of the Presbyterians (Hadden, 1969:104). By 1968, Protestant ministers (two-thirds of them, at least) had come to accept the Black Power movement as "probably necessary" (Stark, 1971:113).

Although in general they supported civil rights campaigns and expressed dissatisfaction with their own denomination's contribution to the cause, Protestant ministers were not sure that clergymen should actually become personally involved in the struggle. Only one third of the 1964 sample sympathized with ministers who manned the barricades (Hadden, 1969:109). Again, there were variations by denomination. Support for involvement by ministers in the California farm workers' unionization campaign was as high as two thirds of Methodist ministers but as low as one tenth of Southern Baptist ministers (Quinley, 1974:107).[5] In fact, very few California ministers did become involved in the unionization work. Only 26 percent reported having made a public statement about it,

---

[5] Nearly half the Southern Baptist ministers disapprove of ministerial involvement in union affairs in any capacity, compared with just nine percent of Presbyterian ministers (Leiffer, 1969:114).

22 percent had delivered a sermon on the topic, 17 percent had signed a petition, 13 percent had written to a public official, 11 percent had organized a study group within their church to discuss the issue, and only 5 percent had actually marched on the picket line or traveled to Delano, the center of the strike. The most active ministers were Presbyterians and Congregationalists (Quinley, 1974:117), as they seem to have been in the civil rights movement as a whole.

LAY ATTITUDES TOWARD DENOMINATIONAL INVOLVEMENT IN CIVIL RIGHTS CAMPAIGNS

Most lay people are not looking for their church to be prophetic (see Glock et al., 1967), and in most congregations there is a notable absence of "preaching, teaching, and discussion about issues besetting local communities and the world" (Brewer, 1967:9). They look to the church to provide the principles which they can apply themselves as they think fit in particular situations. Most of all, they see the most important function of their religion as being to provide "the strength and courage for dealing with the trials and problems of life" (Johnson and Cornell, 1972:51). Just over half those interviewed in 1968 believed that their church should not pronounce on social issues at all (Gallup, 1972:2120). Within each denomination, including the Catholic Church, the same kind of antipathy to adopting political positions has been discovered (Hoge, 1973:181; Hoge, 1976:49,104; Fukuyama, 1972:89; Kersten, 1970:32; Sweetser, 1974:24,69).[6] Black church members are much more likely than whites to support their denomination speaking out on social and political issues, especially the younger ones (Nelsen and Nelsen, 1975:89).

The largest of the white Protestant denominations, the Southern Baptists, probably exemplifies the position of most mainstream Protestant churches. Southern Baptists have been unwilling to mount a concerted social-action program in the past, the single major exception being its Temperance crusade. Its political action has been directed at moral reform, intended to secure the continued independence of the churches, and directed much more at the restraint on individual freedoms by the state than that imposed by corporations. The Southern Baptist Conven-

[6]Nine out of ten Episcopalians feel their minister has the right to urge them to vote, but only one in ten feel he has the right to tell them who to vote for (Glock et al., 1967:124). "The typical churchgoer is not primarily interested in the accomplishment of social action or social betterment goals but in friendliness and fellowship, the chance to meet 'good' people and associate with them" (Wood, 1970:1066). Thus, for example, the United Presbyterian laity (relatively liberal) "adhere to a middle class view of religion and society, stressing support of the *status quo* and the relevance of the church to personal and family life, not to broader social or political questions" (Hoge, 1970:56).

tion indirectly criticized the civil rights movement during the 1960s by condemning the attendant violence—which the Baptists usually attributed to the demonstrators rather than the police.[7] The various denominations do, of course, differ in their ideas about the appropriateness of organized political action. Theological (not class) differences explain most of the variance. The more conservative the theology, the greater the opposition to political involvement (Hoge, 1970:72).

Both Protestant and Catholic laity take a more conservative attitude toward civil rights campaigns than their clergy (Hadden, 1969:127; National Opinion Research Center, 1972:124; Sweetser, 1974:66). Ministers feel, quite correctly, that they are usually more liberal on civil rights issues than their congregation (Quinley, 1974:174).

Ironically, many denominations have taken firm public stands on civil rights issues in a clear attempt to influence the political process, despite the aloofness of the laity. Wood (1970:1061) found that, by 1966, all the mainstream denominations had made general statements supporting integration, and a third of these had moved beyond words to action, providing sanctions against local or regional units that refused to integrate. Even the conservative Lutherans have occasionally entered the civil rights arena. However, lay Lutherans have largely remained oblivious of these pronouncements (Kersten, 1970:137). The same is true of other church people, both Protestant and Catholic (Schroeder, 1964:172; Obenhaus, 1963:117; Rosten, 1975:387; Johnson and Cornell, 1972:26; see also Wood, 1975). The vast majority of lay people are disinterested in church involvement in civil rights work and are opposed to those attempts of which they are aware.

CONFLICT BETWEEN CLERGY AND LAITY

In the light of the foregoing discussion, it comes as no surprise to learn that conflict often arises between a pastor and his flock over the question of civil rights work. The pastor is most likely to see the church as a voluntary association geared for social-action programs, whereas the laity is more likely to see it as a community for the preservation of moral (and individual) values (Hoge, 1973:181). Of course, in some denominations, such as the United Church, this conflict is barely evident (Campbell and Fukuyama, 1970:63), but for most denominations the spectacle of ministers on the barricades has sparked acrimonious debate. Conflict also occurs in the Catholic Church: 72 percent of the priests, but only 30 percent of the laity in one Chicago study approved of the use of

---

[7]One prominent Southern Baptist described the 1963 March on Washington as the work of "restive Negroes" who had been stirred up by Communist agitators (Kelsey, 1973:241).

parish facilities for community action programs. Differences of a similar magnitude separate priests and laity on the question of ministers making pronouncements from the pulpit (Sweetser, 1974:24,69).

Even more tension is created if a minister actually becomes involved in demonstrations and marches (Hadden, 1969:135; Kersten, 1970:127). In a study of the 1957 Little Rock school desegregation fight, Campbell and Pettigrew (1959:65) report that the ministers most active in the integrationist cause suffered reductions in churchgiving, received many requests for membership transfer, saw their attendance fall, and suffered verbal and written abuse. Similarly, in a 1964 school desegregation campaign in Cleveland, at least 12 of the 231 ministers who became involved were fired, 2 others resigned, and 4 were demoted (Hadden, 1969:125). In June, 1963, five months after 28 Methodist clergymen in Mississippi issued a manifesto opposing racial discrimination and pleading for freedom for ministers to speak out on racial issues, only 9 of the signers remained with the congregation they were serving when the manifesto was published (Bailey, 1964:150–51). It is not surprising, then, that 60 percent of a sample of Southern Methodist ministers were found to be suffering the effects of role strain—the race issue being the most frequent cause (Bailey, 1972:108).[8] Nor is it surprising that denominations suffered organizational strain as a result of their participation in the civil rights movement. All the Protestant denominations that actively and publicly supported the NCC's progressive stand on civil rights lost members during the 1960s, especially those with members in the South. There were several schisms as a result of disagreements over civil rights policies (see Wood, 1972).

Yet truly radical political activism is extremely rare among ministers. Only about 4 percent can be classified as "radical left activists"— ministers for whom there is no difference between pastoral and social concerns. Even among those who have actually engaged in civil disobedience, there is "little evidence of acceptance of confrontation politics . . . or government ownership of big business" (Quinley, 1974:149). If the bulk of even activist ministers hardly qualify as political radicals, they *do*, however, comprise a distinctive minority within the churches. What kind of minister are they?

THE "NEW BREED" OF CLERGYMEN

The 1960s seemed to energize ministers in a new way behind the cause of racial justice or in a way that was sufficient, at least, to encour-

---

[8]Not all activist ministers suffered in this way. In a survey of largely northern Protestant church members, Johnson and Cornell (1972:17) found that only one percent reported having reduced their contributions as a result of their church's social action programs.

age talk of a "new breed" of ministers. The clear implication was that these activist ministers were quite unlike their more traditional colleagues—and research has shown this to be so.

One generalization that can be made with much confidence is that activist ministers tended not to be parish ministers at all, but the occupants of staff positions in denominations, missions, and agencies or of chaplaincies or campus mininstries, where they were free of parish control (Martin, 1972:43; Bailey, 1972:94; Hadden, 1969:70). Their activism was probably not the consequence of their nonparish situation, but was more likely to have been an accompaniment to it. That is, the seminarian likely to be liberal on civil rights was also likely to shy away from a normal parish ministry and to relish the freedom a nonparish post affords (Hoge, 1973:182; Hammond, 1965:135). Interestingly, this was true also the religious radicals of the 1930s. They, too, tended to be "seminary professors, church press editors, episcopal officers, agency heads and the like" (Miller, 1958:115).

Activist ministers were, on average, younger than ministers who did not get involved (Stuhr, 1972:55; Hadden, 1969:170).[9] There are a number of ways of explaining this other than the simple assertion that ministers, like everyone else, get more conservative as they grow older. Age may actually reflect length of incumbency (Campbell and Pettigrew, 1959:90; Stuhr, 1972:55; see also Gibbs, 1969). A long tenure means that friendship networks have been established and roots put down, which makes it difficult for the minister to take part in disruptive and change-oriented programs. The fewer the close friends a minister has in the community, the more likely he is to be politically active (Quinley, 1974:143).

It is also possible that the age factor actually reflects a greater willingness to take risks, something that normally manifests itself at the beginning of a career (Martin, 1972:30). Perhaps much more likely is the idea that age reflects differences in seminary training: the younger ministers have been exposed to more liberal, action-oriented seminary training and have inculcated a different image of the pastor's role (Hoge, 1973:184; Campbell and Pettigrew, 1959:90). The more activist ministers do tend to have more "modern" ideas of the minister's job, stressing above all the role of the minister as an organizer (Nelsen, 1973:384). Black ministers who are both young and theologically liberal tend to be more activist than their older and more conservative colleagues (Johnstone, 1969:82).

In most denominations, the more liberal the clergyman theologically, the more liberal he is politically. Moreover, ministers, in contrast with laypeople, are quite likely to translate their liberal attitudes into action

[9]The activist ministers in Quinley's (1974:141) sample were a little older. Their average age was in the late 30's.

(Kersten, 1970:214; Bailey, 1972:94; Stuhr, 1972:59; Quinley, 1974:142; Stark, 1971:97).

Activist ministers tend to take as their primary reference group not the congregation they serve, but their ministerial colleagues. Frequency of contact with and support from fellow ministers is an important factor in the social activism of clergymen (Martin, 1972:30; Quinley, 1974:142).

Ministers are much more likely to be activists if they belong to a more episcopalian denomination; they are less likely to be activist if they are subject to close congregational control. This is true even where theology, region of the country, and size of the denomination are held constant (Wood, 1970:1065; Wood, 1975:204).

A minister's liberal sentiments tend not to be translated into action unless he feels he has the support of his congregation (Hadden, 1969:170; Quinley, 1974:142; see also Blume, 1970).

Ministers of congregations in which the average level of education is high are more likely to be active (Quinley, 1974:142; see also Gibbs, 1969), probably because such congregations are likely to be more liberal. The same interpretation can be given to the positive association between size of congregation and the activism of the minister: the large congregations can afford to hire seminary trained ministers, who tend to be more liberal.

The more activist clergy tend to come from liberal denominations such as the United Church, the Episcopalians, the Presbyterians and the Methodists; ministers from the Baptist, Lutheran, and Brethren denominations tend to be underrepresented among the ranks of activist clergy (Hadden, 1969:124; Stuhr, 1972:54; see also Blume, 1970). Furthermore, ministers were much more likely to join the civil rights movement if their denomination had publicly supported the cause (Hadden, 1969:170).

This, then, is what the "new breed" of clergymen that emerged during the 1960s looked like. These ministers were alike in urging that authority in social institutions be shared, in their appeal for open communication, in their desire that the church become involved in community affairs, and in their concern that the church make itself relevant to current social problems (Hall and Schneider, 1973:65). However, not only was this group of ministers somewhat removed from the laity by virtue of the positions they held, and not only were they distant from the laity theologically, they were also only a very small minority of the ministry—no more than about 12 percent (Stark, 1971:118). What is more, it is precisely this group who were most likely to express regret at having entered the ministry and were most likely to be thinking of leaving it (Judd et al., 1970:44). Reform was thus invested in a small, rather unusual group of professionals, whose commitment to institutional religion was weak at best. This is not, of course, to deny that clergymen were overrepresented in the civil rights movement. The point is that the net impact of the churches was not prophetic but priestly, not liberal but conservative. The two faces of religion are again made apparent: a religion oriented to the preservation of things as they are, and a religion motivated by a desire to change the world in order to conform to values that are realized only imperfectly at present. The intense energy channeled into reform can, if the times are ripe, disturb the equilibrium that the religious factor normally maintains.

THE CATHOLIC RESISTANCE

Churchmen were also prominent in that other great movement of social dissent in the 1960s, the campaign against the war in Vietnam. The most radical church group in the movement was the one that came to be known as the Catholic Resistance. This group had no formal structure and no real leaders, but its acknowledged spokesmen were the Berrigan brothers.[10]

Although pacifism is not unknown among Catholics (Dorothy Day and Peter Maurin of the *Catholic Worker* had long argued the Catholic pacifist position), the stance of the Catholic Church is better reflected in the fact that only 223 of the 53,345 conscientious objectors during the Second World War were Catholics. The Catholic Resistance grew out of a tradition of personal radicalism articulated by the *Catholic Worker*. According to this tradition, the evils of society were to be tackled by a combination of nonviolence and strong belief in the dignity of each individual—a kind of revolution by conscience. The idealism of President Kennedy, the formation of organizations such as the Peace Corps, the successes of the civil rights movement, and the ferment generated by Vatican II, did a great deal not only to intensify this personalized radicalism but also, among a few, to channel it more in the direction of political action. Thus, the Catholic Resistance began by denouncing the evils of war and witnessing to the truth, but gradually moved in the 1960s to the advocacy of more fundamental structural changes in American society, an advocacy that became more strident only after the

[10]Philip, a Josephite, had been earlier engaged in the civil rights movement (the Josephites were founded to help Freedmen), but he was also an early opponent of the war in Vietnam. He joined the Catholic Peace Fellowship in 1964. Daniel, a Jesuit, had been impressed by the worker-priest movement in France during a visit there in the 1950s, and was seriously disillusioned by the Pope's disbandment of the movement. Daniel helped organize Clergy and Laymen Concerned About Vietnam in 1965.

apparent failure of liberal politics with McCarthy's defeat at the Democratic Convention in 1968.

The Catholic Resistance is perhaps best known for its "raids" on the offices of the Selective Service System, the first of which took place as early as 1966. Initially, the emphasis was on moral witness and civil disobedience. The raiders would wait for the police and the FBI to arrive at the scene of the crime and arrest them, preferably with the press also in attendance. By 1967, both Berrigan brothers had been in jail, Philip for a draft board raid in Baltimore, Daniel for his part in a demonstration at the Pentagon that was not authorized by a permit.

Gradually, the Catholic Resistance became more radical. The Berrigans began to attack the churches for offering only comfort and security to the rich and for being concerned with politics only when the institutional interests of the church were at stake. They also criticized liberal Catholics for defining reform simply in terms of Americanizing the Catholic Church or making it conform more closely to a false model of democracy. They increasingly linked the civil rights and antiwar movements to a general critique of American capitalism.[11] The Berrigans were constantly condemned for their peace efforts and were repeatedly sanctioned by their superiors. Yet they played a major part in the escalation of the antiwar movement: between 1967 and 1971 the Catholic Resistance was responsible for over thirty draft board raids (Nelson and Ostrow, 1972:55).

The Catholic Resistance eventually broke up, its leaders in jail and the war unended. Its membership had rarely exceeded a few hundred, although its sympathizers must have numbered many more. It is impossible to assess the impact of the Resistance on the Catholic Church itself, except to guess that it must have been quite small.[12] However, it had a major impact on the antiwar movement because it operated as a link between established institutions, such as the Church, and the more extreme political opposition to the war, such as the Students for a Democratic Society (SDS) and the Weathermen. The peace activists (especially the activists rather than the sympathizers) were drawn from the more liberal end of the theological spectrum, and it is uncertain what proportion of either Catholics or Protestants were liberals at that time (Bolton, 1973:559).

[11] At his trial for the Catonsville draft board raid, Philip Berrigan declared: "we have lost confidence in the institutions of this country, including our own churches. . . . We have lost confidence because we do not believe any longer that these institutions are reformable" (quoted in Nelson and Ostrow, 1972:55).

[12] Despite the highly publicized activity of the Catholic Resistance, Catholics polled in 1968 were only slightly more in favor of pulling out of Vietnam than were Protestants (Hamilton, 1975:195).

THE CHURCHES AND THE NEW LEFT

The most radical movements of the 1960s organizations like SDS and the Weathermen and more fleeting coalitions such as the National Mobilization Committee to End the War in Vietnam, were overwhelmingly secular. Their ideology was a changing mixture of Marxism, Leninism, Maoism, anarchism, and socialism, and their driving force was a student population, the majority of whom did not profess any religious allegiance. The real cutting edge of reform in the 1960s was, therefore, almost totally secular.

There were two exceptions to this pattern. One, a cluster of new religious groups, such as Hare Krishna and the Christian World Liberation Front, espoused counter-cultural values and showed greater than average tolerance for political radicalism (Wuthnow, 1976b:276). The Christian World Liberation Front combined apocalyptic fervor with an identification of Jesus as a revolutionary. The following appeared as a full-page notice in the second issue of the CWLF newspaper, *Right On* (quoted in Heinz, 1976:153–54).

Reward

Jesus, Alias: the Messiah, Son of God, King of Kings, Lord of Lords, Prince of Peace, etc.
Notorious Leader of a world-wide liberation movement.
Wanted for the following charges:
  Practicing medicine and distribution of food without a licence
  Interfering with businessmen in the Temple
  Associating with known criminals, radicals, subversives, prostitutes, and street people.
  Claiming to have authority to make people God's children.
Appearance unknown. Rumoured to have no regard for conventional dress standards. Hangs around slum areas, few rich friends, often sneaks out into the desert. He has a group of devoted followers, formerly known as apostles, now called freemen (from his saying: You will know the truth and the truth shall set you free). Beware—This man is extremely dangerous. His insidiously inflamatory message is particularly effective with young people who haven't been taught to ignore him yet. He changes men and sets them free.

WARNING: HE IS STILL AT LARGE!

This CWLF propaganda combined the age-old theme of Jesus the subversive, the rebel come to bring freedom from oppression and constraint, with the modern terminology of the New Left and the bureaucratic jargon of the forces of social control. Although it is not possible to say whether people first developed an interest in radical politics and then an interest in counter-cultural religion, or the reverse, the data do suggest that the two were often mutually supportive. Of course, a real political challenge could only have developed had such groups expanded enormously in membership and influence. So far, this has not happened, but the fusion of religion and radical politics in groups such as the CWLF was clear enough.

The other exception was a small band of liberal Protestants and, most visible of all, Jews. Jews were present in radical organizations and active in marches and rallies out of all proportion to their numbers in the population. The Free Speech Movement, which began at Berkeley in 1964, was 32 percent Jewish on a campus where Jews made up 20 percent of the student body, and at least 35 percent of the students involved in the Mississippi Freedom Summer Project in 1964 were Jewish (Porter and Dreier, 1973:xxi–xxii).

Jews have a long history of support for left-wing causes. Jewish unions were the backbone of the Socialist Party at the turn of the century, and at one time one third of the American Communist Party was Jewish (Porter and Dreier, 1973:xviii). Furthermore, the Jews of the New Left did not seem as hesitant as the Jews of the Old Left in making their Jewishness known. Left-wing Jews had often changed their names or written under pseudonyms in the 1930s, but the Jewishness of Mark Rudd, Abbie Hoffman, and Jerry Rubin was undeniable.

It would seem, then, that the radicalism and internationalism that many Jewish immigrants brought to the United States was alive and well. It would also seem that there is something about the Jewish faith that is conducive to leftist and radical politics. Yet, two facts suggest caution in adopting either of these conclusions. First, during the 1950s the reform wing of the Jewish community became much preoccupied with the problem of assimilation. Always a concern for the Jew, assimilation became an important issue after the depredations of Joseph McCarthy (which prompted many Jews to question anew how well they were accepted in the American melting pot), especially as more and more Jews began to enter income categories that would entitle them to full participation in American life. The reform priorities of the Jewish community during the 1950s were, therefore, the liberal ones of securing civil rights and religious freedom. Their efforts in these directions were epitomized by the Anti-Defamation League of B'nai Brith, a decidedly liberal organization later repudiated by the radical Jews. The traditional Jewish link with left-wing politics thus seemed to have broken. Second, the Jewish radicalism of the 1960s seems to have been more a case of radicals-who-happened-to-be-Jews than anything else. The lack of public concern about their Jewishness that distinguished the Jewish students of the 1960's from the Jews of the Old Left, although partly the result of a decline in anti-Semitism, seems to suggest that the radical Jews were "singularly unself-conscious about their Jewishness" (Porter and Dreier, 1973:xxiii). In fact, the Jews who were active in radical politics had little knowledge of Jewish religious history (they were *not* modeling themselves on the ancient Israelites); they seemed unconcerned about the possible disappearance of the Yiddish culture; and far from identifying with the Jewish community and its way of life, they rejected the materialism and status-striving of its mainly middle-class members. The 1967 Israeli War and the appearance of anti-Semitism among New Left radicals and blacks helped reawaken a sense of Jewishness among these individuals (and gave rise to organizations such as the Radical Zionist Alliance), but there is little evidence to suggest that their involvement in radical politics was at any time prompted by specifically religious considerations. Jewish radicalism seems to have been a secular phenomenon: the radical Jews were the children of professional, well-educated, politically liberal, humanistically oriented parents who just happened to be Jews.

CONCLUSION

It is appropriate to conclude this consideration of the involvement of the churches in social reform movements on this rather ambiguous note. There are two sources of ambiguity in regard to these issues which only more research can resolve. First, although the involvement of religious people and religious institutions in social-reform movements is undeniable, the extent to which this is attributable to their religious faith and the extent to which it is attributable to other social characteristics they possess, is not yet decided. The youth of activist ministers, the marginality of Jews, and the higher education of the more supportive laity all cast doubt on the impact of religion per se on the impulse to engage in social reform. Second, although the contribution of the churches to social reform cannot be denied, it is unusual for the churches to take the lead in social reform. Once an issue has been forced upon the public's attention, however, the churches often play a role in establishing the framework within which the problem is viewed and solutions sought. By the same token, although the vast majority of church people have not been involved in social-reform movements and have by and large disapproved of such efforts, it has often been the case that the majority of those people who do attempt important social reforms are church people. The most plausible explanation of this puzzle, of course, is that religion operates *both* as a conservatizing and stabilizing force *and* as a potentially liberating, even revolutionary, force.

Part V

SECULARIZATION

18

SECULARIZATION:
THE NATURE OF THE TRENDS

INTRODUCTION

It is a fairly widespread notion that religion is on the decline in the West. It is the purpose of this chapter to see how far the sociological evidence confirms this idea. Unfortunately, it is not a simple matter to decide whether or not religion is declining. The word religion is of such uncertain meaning that it can decline in one sense but not in another (see Shiner, 1967). For example, the spread of atheism signifies a decline in religion only if it is identified with a particular belief; lower rates of attendance betoken a less religious people only if that particular rite is important; the rise of anticlericalism is noteworthy only if the organizational survival of the churches is considered essential. More troublesome is the fact that one person's "decay" might be another person's "growth." The separation of Church from State, seen by some as a weakening of religion, might be seen by others as a necessary withdrawal from temporal concerns; falling rates of attendance, an obvious sign of weakness to many, are seen by others as an inevitable and necessary abandonment of empty rituals; the bureaucratization of the church, heard by many as its death knell, is greeted by others as a timely adoption of more efficient means of attaining denominational goals. The problem is that "there is no unitary process called 'secularisation' arising in reaction to a set of characteristics labelled 'religious' " (Martin, 1969:16).

There is also the problem that the concept of secularization is susceptible to use as propaganda, as a means of "reading into" changes in religion its gradual demise. Indeed, some would argue that value judgments are inherent in that concept (see, for example, Martin, 1969). However, despite its varied meanings and the ideological dangers attendant on its use, the concept of secularization would appear to be indispensable to the modern sociologist. There can hardly be any question that there has been a decline in the influence of religious institutions in the modern West, and also a decline in the number of people for whom transcendental concerns are an everyday affair. The concept should not be abandoned, but the assumptions underlying its use should be made explicit—and this must be done before a discussion of trends can begin.

Whether secularization is used to refer to a decline or merely to change depends a great deal on which definition of religion is favored. If a substantive, exclusivist definition is used, then it is appropriate to speak of the presence or absence of religion. It is valid to speak of discredited beliefs disappearing and of empty practices being discontinued. In this sense, secularization clearly refers to a decline in the "amount" of religion.

If a functional definition of religion is used, it is illogical to refer to the decline of religion, for religion is to be found wherever a person's search for the ultimate leads him. And as this search is an essential part of the human's sociality, it cannot be thought of as disappearing while human life exists.

> What is generally called secularisation and the decline of religion appear as the decline of the external control system of religion and the decline of traditional religious belief. But religion, as that symbolic form through which man comes to terms with the antinomies of his being, has not declined, indeed cannot decline unless man's nature ceases to be problematic to him (Bellah, 1971:50).

From this point of view, it is quite valid to speak of changes in the institution of religion ("the external control system of religion") and even the discrediting of beliefs (such as a decline in the belief in hell). But these changes merely indicate that religion has been "relocated" and is now to be found, for instance, in sensitivity training groups, in the "civil religion" of the State, or in new religious movements. Or it may be the cause that religion survives, in essence, in the ethical systems that have their foundation in religious beliefs.

The meaning given to the term secularization thus depends on the definition of religion with which one begins. This is not the place to enter into debates about the proper definition of religion. However, the functionalist definition would seem to entail difficult problems of analysis. For example, functionalists seem to so define religion as to enable them to plead that "true" religion has never declined and that "anything jettisoned over the last two centuries, like belief in witches or belief in devils or belief in Noah's flood, was the dropping of the irrelevant, or of noxious clutter, and has not touched the gold of religious faith and practice" (Chadwick, 1975:4). The implication is that the loss of the sense of transcendence or the belief that there is a providence at work in the lives of people is of no consequence. Such a conclusion would seem to be both unreasonable and unconfirmed. There are difficulties in separating change from decline, but surely it can be done. The churches have been engaged in a "perpetual task of adjusting religious understanding of the world to new knowledge about the world" (Chadwick, 1975:15), but this does not mean that all such changes have no secular significance. Although the churches might integrate evolutionary theories into their theology, the diminished belief in miracles that might result is surely both change and decline.

Secularization will be taken to mean the process whereby (1) beliefs concerning the supernatural and the practices associated with them are discredited and (2) the institution of religion loses social influence. It is a process in which fewer and fewer of life's decisions are made with reference to the transcendental. The precise boundaries between this process and mere change in religion are hard to locate, for "it is often easier to be sure that a process is happening than to define precisely what the process contains and how it happens" (Chadwick, 1975:2). Much confusion is sown by labeling changes as "declines" when in fact they may only be changes. Giving greater control to the laity, liberalizing dietary taboos, updating liturgies, discarding traditional dress, bureaucratizing the administration—all of these are changes that might or might not be secular, depending on whether or not they lead to a diminished sense of transcendence in the lives of individuals and weaken the social power of the church.

In a sense, this whole book is an attempt to describe the changing impact of religion on society. However, changes over time are the special subject of this chapter.

THE DECLINE IN RELIGIOUS BELIEF

Secularization means that less credence is given to religious beliefs. Has the belief in a God, Supreme Being, or Creator, in life after death or a world of spirits disappeared? The evidence suggests that such beliefs are as firm today as they ever were: 94 percent of Americans polled in 1975 expressed a belief in God (Gallup, 1976:13); as late as 1968, about 75 percent of the American population were convinced of the possibility of life after death (Hertel and Nelsen, 1974:413).

Short-run fluctuations in religious belief have occurred. The young displayed increased skepticism during the highly political 1960s, when those under thirty-one certain there is no life after death increased by 4 percentage points (Hertel and Nelsen, 1974:416). However, these fluctuations are the result of specific generational effects rather than long-term changes. Indeed, by 1973, the gap between prevalence of religious belief among those under 35 and prevalence of belief among those over 35 had widened, but this was attributable to events taking place in the 1960s. Most of those in the over 35 age group in 1973 would have reached adulthood and completed their period of primary socialization prior to the a-religious 1960s (Wuthnow, 1976c:858).

Hoge (1974:55), analyzing replication studies of college students, concludes that there has been no consistent decline in religious belief. Highs reached in the 1920s, were followed by lows in the 1930s. These were followed by highs in the 1950s, which in turn were followed by lows in the 1960s.

The widespread belief in God conceals wide differences between denominations. It is significant that the denominations that show the greatest uncertainty about the nature (even the existence) of God—for example, the United Church—show the lowest rates of attendance and the highest rates of decline in attendance in recent years. A decline in religious belief seems to be accompanied by a decline in institutional commitment. "While the churches continue to be organised on the basis of traditional orthodoxy, persons who lack the beliefs which are needed to make such organisations meaningful are falling away from religious institutions: a general corrosion of commitment presently accompanies the acceptance of a modernised, liberal theology" (Stark and Glock, 1968:213). Members of the more liberal denominations tend not to believe in life after death, the Second Coming of Christ, miracles, or the virgin birth. Their present membership seems to be a way station to irreligion. Faith remains strong among the more conservative denominations—which, incidentally, are growing relative to their liberal competitors. However, the success of the conservatives does not mean they appeal to disaffected liberals (who are more likely to leave the church altogether), but reflects rather their higher fertility rates and lower drop-out rates. The net result of changes in religious belief in the United States, however, is that new believers and disbelievers more or less balance each other. Hence the proportion of those who believe in God remains constant at around 95 percent.

CHURCH ATTENDANCE

Attendance at church, or some other meeting place for worship, would appear to be a more reliable measure of religiosity than belief.

Attendance is observable, repeated, quantifiable, and relatively unambiguous. Of course, it is not quite that simple. The different faiths and denominations attribute widely different meanings to the act of worship and to regular attendance at meetings. Thus, it should not be supposed that Catholics are more religious than Protestants because 16 percent fewer Protestants than Catholics attend church weekly: the norms prescribing regular attendance happen to be stronger for Catholics than for Protestants, who express their religiosity in other ways.

American survey data on church attendance gathered over the past thirty years show a steady increase in attendance until the 1960's, followed by a decline and then, more recently, a slight increase once more. In 1940, 37 percent of the adult population reported weekly attendance at church. By 1961, this had risen to 47 percent, from which point it declined to its 1975 figure of 40 percent (Gallup, 1976:26).

The steady rise of church attendance in the 1950s, together with the popularity of revivalists such as Billy Graham and inspirational literature such as that of Norman Vincent Peale, gave rise to talk of a new Awakening, of a religious revival in America (see Eckhardt, 1958; Herberg, 1960). "Between 1945 and 1953 the yearly distribution of Bibles rose 140 percent, reaching the incredible figure of nearly 10 million Bibles a year by 1953" (Miller, 1975:66). In 1953, one out of every ten books sold was religious.

Did Americans become more religious during this period? There are grounds for supposing that the 1950s saw Americans being religious in a different *way* rather than being more religious. The rise of church attendance seems tied much more closely to demographic changes than to changes in religious knowledge or commitment (see Herberg, 1960; Wilson, 1966). For example, the 1950s saw an enormous increase in the size of the middle class. Churchgoing being a more middle-class thing to do, it is reasonable to suppose that the rise of the proportion of middle class people in the population will raise church-attendance rates. The 1950s also witnessed a shift to the right that placed a premium on outward social conformity, adherence to "the American Way," and hostility to "atheistic Communism"—all of which encouraged public professions of piety.

The high rates of church attendance in the 1950s are also attributable to the "familism" of that decade. The upswing in church attendance coincided with an increase in the number of American families with children—the result of the postwar "baby boom." Inasmuch as churchgoing habits are greatly influenced by the demands of children, it is probable that the rise in church attendance during the 1950s was due not so much to increased religiosity as to the increase in the number of parents with young children (see Berger and Nash, 1962; Nash, 1968).[1]

Commentators who doubted the authenticity of the 1950s "revival" can draw encouragement from the decline that set in during the 1960s. On the other hand, those who saw the high rates of attendance during the 1950s as a genuine return to religion are skeptical about the alleged decline of the 1960s, and can look with comfort to the fact that this decline was halted in the early 1970s. There is little justification for arguing that the 1960s finally initiated the long-term disappearance of church attendance as a social custom. The 1960s were certainly a time when many people, especially Catholics, dropped the churchgoing habit. But because this decade was a time of general dissatisfaction with all social institutions, a decline in commitment to the established church cannot be taken as positive evidence of a decline in religion. Younger Americans especially became disaffected with political, economic, familial, and educational institutions, and even rejected many institutions of the leisure sphere, such as big-time college athletics and professional sports. They located most social evils in established institutions, in bureaucracies and in hierarchies, and experimented with alternative communities and lifestyles (Hoge, 1974:47). It comes as no surprise, then, that regular church attendance should have declined during this period. It is significant that once the turmoil died down, the Vietnam War ended, and a recession set in, the decline in attendance rates halted.

The fluctuations in church attendance between 1950 and 1970 can thus be accounted for by short-run factors, and do not indicate long-term trends in either direction. Churchgoing habits seem to have fluctuated in this way throughout the present century—high rates in the 1920s, lows in the 1930s, highs in the 1950s, and lows in the 1960s.[2]

The proportion of Catholics regularly attending church is still higher than that of Protestants. However, Catholics contributed more to the decline that took place in the 1960s: between 1964 and 1974 the Protestant attendance rate dropped by only one percentage point, whereas the Catholic rate dropped by 16 points. In consequence, the two faiths are becoming more alike in their churchgoing habits: 24 percentage points separated them in 1966, but only 11 in 1974 (Gallup, 1975:1). There is no solid evidence as to why Catholics should have experienced a faster decline than Protestants. There is little doubt that the Second Vatican

---

[1]During the 1950s, the churches displayed an intense interest in the family. "Family-life agencies prospered, drawing on the skills of psychiatrists, educators, sociologists and lawyers. A considerable family-life journalism flourished. Pre-marital counselling took on a new self-consciousness. Pastors, rabbis and priests affiliated with colleges enjoyed heavy business. Husbands, wives, and husbands-and-wives could attend conferences, belong to special clubs, and go on special retreats" (Meyer, 1968:230).

[2]During the Great Depression, "the churches suffered along with the rest of the nation. Membership dropped, budgets were slashed, benevolent and missionary enterprises set adrift, ministers fired, and chapels closed" (Miller, 1958:63).

Council, which eased some of the demands on Catholics, has something to do with it, and it probably also has something to do with lay resistance to the pope's firm stand on the sinfulness of artificial birth control. After the encyclical of 1968, there must have been many Catholics who, without in any way diminishing their faith, could no longer participate as conscientiously in the outward forms of their religion.

That just under half the adult population in the United States is to be found in a place of worship at least once a week—more than at any time in the country's history—makes it difficult to argue that America is a secularizing society. It is, of course, possible to argue that high rates of church attendance do not necessarily mean intense religiosity. The increasing subordination of distinctively religious values in American society, and the suspicion that much of this churchgoing lacks distinctive content or special meaning (as when one is urged to "go to the church of your choice"), places in question the real significance of these attendance figures. Wilson (1966:91) argues that a large part of this churchgoing is explained by the fact that "going to church is one of the values of American life, [and] having a faith is expected of upright citizens." In other words, churchgoing is a national as much as a religious value.

In contrast to the United States, the United Kingdom has experienced quite a decline in church attendance.[3] A national religious census conducted in 1851 reported that at least 36 percent of the population appeared in church at least once on census day (see Pickering, 1967). This figure had dropped to about 25 percent by 1900 and was down to 15 percent in 1965 (Argyle and Beit-Hallahmi, 1975:11). The decline in attendance appears to have taken place in waves, first among the working class and later, in the twentieth century, among the middle class. The Church of England suffered the first losses; the decline of the Free Churches did not begin until the early twentieth century. Until very recently, Catholics maintained high rates of attendance, but lately there has been a marked decline; between 1955 and 1975 regular Mass attendance among the total Catholic population in England and Wales dropped from 76 percent to 32 percent (*America*, 1/31/76).

It is clear that regular churchgoing has for some time been the practice of only a very small minority of the British population. In view of this fact, it is surprising to discover that the vast majority of British people still prefer to baptize their children, get married in a church, and have a religious funeral. Infant baptism is not a rite that all denominations find meaningful, but those that do find many British people still desirous of solemnizing the birth of their children. For example, 46.5 percent of all live births in 1973 were solemnized by baptism in the

---

[3]In Canada, church attendance rates have almost halved in recent years, but they have not yet fallen to English levels. Weekly church attendance was reported by 39 percent of the adult population in 1974, down from 61 percent in 1951 (Mol, 1976:242).

Church of England alone. The continued popularity of baptism is hard to account for in view of the low attendance figures, but it probably has something to do with social conventions that are only indirectly religious.

> No legal sanction attaches to Christening, but there are fairly explicit moral sanctions, exemplified in part in the duties laid down for godparents. There are also sanctions of a more secular kind. There are still sectors of English society where it is the "done thing" to have a child received into the Church by the administration of baptism. For a parent to neglect to have this performed is regarded as a dereliction of duty, leaving the child without a formally bestowed name, without an assigned place in the social universe and without the putative support of godparents in the social and economic as well as the moral sense (Firth et al., 1970:220).

These sanctions, which find popular expression in the idea that bad luck will accrue to a child who has not been baptized, are all the more powerful because they concern an unwitting and helpless infant.

Religious marriages are even more common than infant baptisms, partly because most religious denominations include this rite in their liturgy. All but 2.6 percent of the marriages in 1844 were celebrated in a church or chapel (Paul, 1973:185). There has been a decline since then, but the rate is still much higher than church-attendance rates would indicate. In 1967, 45 percent of all marriages were solemnized in the Church of England, 11.0 percent in a Catholic church and another 9.4 percent in other places of worship—in other words, about two thirds of all marriages. Although this proportion had fallen to about half by 1973, the discrepancy between people's desire to be married by a minister and their willingness to listen to his sermons every week remained large (Wilson, 1976:24).

The explanation for the continued high rate of religious marriages may be the lack of drama and tension in civil marriages, which is crucial when establishing a new family unit means more and more that the couple will be isolated and left to fend for themselves in many ways. As beginning new families becomes costlier, perhaps the need for a more dramatic rite of passage increases. The popularity of church weddings may also be due to more widespread affluence. The customary features of the marriage celebration—the gifts, the limousines, the reception, and the dress—are insufficient to make the day as distinctive and memorable in a society where gift giving, eating out, and automobile rides are routine, and where one's best attire is no longer reserved for special occasions. In an affluent society, no excuse is needed for conspicuous consumption. The only thing left by which to set the marriage ceremony apart—the only thing money cannot buy—is the pomp and circumstance of a church wedding (Wilson, 1966:70).

In the United Kingdom, the mixture of low weekly attendance rates and high rates of participation in rites of passage suggests that both practices have altered meanings. Attendance appears to be less and less the performance of an obligation and a way of ensuring the living of a Christian life, and more and more a purely voluntary, occasional, and individualistic means of securing personal enhancement and comfort. In the United States the churches actually "sell" themselves as a kind of "service station" standing ready to provide routine spiritual "tune-ups." The rites of passage, meanwhile, seem to carry a much heavier burden of extrareligious meanings than they once did, and are valued for their dramatic, expressive, and integrative functions as much as for their theological meaning. They no longer impinge on people's lives in the sense of disseminating knowledge or exemplifying moral standards. Instead, they provide a kind of instant ceremonial to order, with no questions asked. The public continues to assign to organized religion a special circumscribed place as the repository of values, but increasingly takes the view that it should be safely insulated and restricted to ceremonial occasions so that it does not interfere with the mundane business of day-to-day living.

CHURCH MEMBERSHIP

There are all sorts of problems in using membership figures to measure religiosity. Apart from the obvious fact that not all religious people bother to join a denomination, the interpretation of the membership figures that are compiled is problematic: denominations differ widely in their definition of membership; they change their criteria from year to year; they do not update their figures frequently; they devote limited resources and personnel to the task of enumeration; and many do not gather (or at least make public) membership figures at all. Measuring changes in religiosity on the basis of membership figures is thus a hazardous business indeed.

Long-range historical data indicate that church membership in the United States rose in the nineteenth century from a low of about 6 percent in 1800 to about 35 percent in 1900, and peaked in 1936 at 77 percent (Littell, 1962:32; Demerath, 1968:353; Gallup, 1976:31). A decline in church membership set in during the 1960s, the first period in American history when there was an overall net loss in church membership. The first to experience the decline were the more liberal denominations, such as the United Church, the Presbyterians, and the Methodists (Kelley, 1972:6). But in 1970 the Catholic Church reported its first drop in membership. The overall rate of decline would have been greater had not some of these losses been compensated for by gains in membership among the more conservative denominations, such as the Southern Baptists, the Christian Churches, and the Mormons, and among some of the newer sects, such as the Pentecostals, the Holiness groups, the Jehovah's witnesses, and the Seventh Day Adventists. It is too soon to see to what extent this decline is the beginning of a trend. There are good enough reasons, however, to attribute it to short-term factors such as the political turmoil of the 1960s, during which many people became disaffected with the liberal denominations (either because they were doing too much or not enough for civil rights) and the more conservative groups became more popular.

In the United Kingdom, the trends in church membership have been quite different. The Church of England has experienced a considerable loss of members, whether the criterion of membership is infant baptism, Sunday school attendance, Confirmation, Easter Communion or membership in the Electoral Roll (Beeson, 1973:42; Church of England Yearbook, 1976:180). By the last measure (admittedly the strictest) membership fell 33 percent between 1924 and 1954 and a further 29 percent between 1954 and 1964. The Free Churches too have experienced an absolute decline in membership, with Congregationalists and Presbyterians suffering the most. In fact, the decline of these two denominations has been faster than that of the Church of England (Currie and Gilbert, 1972:449). The proportion of Catholics in the population doubled between 1851 and 1966, but this increase was due less to people converting to that faith than to the higher fertility of Catholics and immigration from Ireland (Martin, 1972:229).

CHURCH GIVING

The amount of their annual income Americans give to their church has been remarkably consistent. In 1929, the figure was 1.9 percent. Even during the Depression, the figure did not drop below 1.1 percent, and by 1965 it had climbed back up to 1.3 percent (Demerath, 1968:365). In 1975, Americans gave $11.68 billion to their churches, a 7.6 percent increase from the year before (about equal to the inflation rate), just under half of all charitable bequests, and seven times the amount of money they gave to political parties (*Christianity Today*, 7/4/76:52; Swanson, 1968:811).[4]

However, other signs suggest that the financial support of the churches is not solid. Between 1963 and 1973, the per capita contributions of Catholics dropped by 31 percent (allowing for inflation). Be-

[4]The norms guiding church giving are not uniform. For example, in 1965 the Free Methodists reported an annual giving rate of $358 a person, but the United Methodists gave only $59 per person (Gaustad, 1968:124).

tween 1970 and 1972 the value of construction of new religious buildings decreased by 33.2 percent (Wuthnow, 1976c:852). In the United Kingdom, figures that report changes in giving over time are not available. Giving to the Church of England equals the average American rate (Argyle and Beit-Hallahmi, 1975:4), but, in contrast with church giving in the United States, it has failed to keep pace with the high inflation rates of recent decades (Church of England Yearbook, 1976:158).

ATTITUDES TOWARD RELIGION

One obvious meaning of secularization is that people come to think that religion is no longer important in their society. Religion loses its "presence" as a social force, it becomes less "visible," less public. As religion becomes more and more private, it enters the arena of "free choice of the use of time, energy, and wealth in which the end products of the economy are marketed for consumers" (Wilson, 1976:40). As religion loses its institutional force, it becomes a mere diversion, a leisure-time pursuit to be contracted into as needed, and a means of escape from the "real" world of social and political obligations.

The importance of looking at how significant religion is felt to be is that there is a difference between religiosity as measured by an aggregate of believers and religiosity as measured by the institutional "presence" of religion. Thus in England, where only 15 percent of the population regularly attend church, 81 percent feel it is "very" or "quite" important that Britain remain a Christian country (Independent Television Authority, 1970:17); 69 percent feel that in order to live a good life, a person must have some kind of religious belief (Independent Television Authority, 1970:26). The Church is obviously able to make its presence felt long after people have ceased to internalize its ethic or attend its worship services.

Yet, recent poll data suggest that more and more English people believe that the influence of religion is waning (Social Surveys, 1974). This is not as clearly as the case in the United States, although there have been some recent fluctuations. In 1957, at the height of the "religious revival," only 14 percent of the American population thought that religion was losing its influence; 69 percent believed it to be increasing. However, after the upheavals of the 1960s the proportion thinking religion to be losing its influence shot up to 75 percent. The return tt political normalcy in the early 1970s reversed this trend, and, by 1975, the proportion believing religion to be on the increase had risen to 39 percent (Gallup, 1976:57).

Other measures of the perceived importance of religion support the secularization thesis. Religion contributes little to Americans' sense of well-being. Life satisfaction is most closely associated with congenial spare time activities, with a happy family life, with good health, and with a comfortable standard of living. Religion (together with the national government) ranks low on the list of life domains thought to contribute to a sense of well-being (Campbell et al., 1976:76).

Some notion of people's attitudes toward religion is also conveyed by how they regard its representative, the minister. It is easy to contrast the prestige of the seventeenth century New England divine (often the best-educated man in his community and probably a political official as well) with the prestige of the minister of today, who has to compete with the professional politician, the scientist, and the businessman for social status. There can be little doubt that a decline in prestige has taken place. But in the short span of time covered by survey data, this is only barely hinted at. A 1947 survey ranked ministers thirteenth in an occupational prestige hierarchy (with architects eighteenth); a replication carried out in 1963 found that ministers had slipped to seventeenth (while architects climbed to fourteenth (see Hoge et al., 1964)—hardly a significant change.[5] In the United Kingdom, the Anglican clergy, formerly linked with the minor landed gentry, are now more likely to be grouped in the public mind with university lecturers (Towler, 1969:445), but they have certainly not slipped into the social obscurity the low attendance figures would imply.

Three other changes in the ministry are relevant to the secularization thesis. First, with the exception of a very few denominations, there has been a decline in the number of people entering the ministry and an increase in the number leaving it (Bonifield, 1970:209; Rosten, 1975:391; *America*, 2/28/76; Paul, 1973:169; Wilson, 1976:27; Fichter, 1974b:21–22). Second, at least in the Church of England, the quality of entrants is declining, and their average age is rising (see Coxon, 1967). Third, their income is falling: between 1963 and 1973 the income of American Protestant clergy rose by about 50 percent, while that of professionals like accountants was increasing by 70 percent (Bonn, 1975:245). Curiously, while many denominations experience an increasing shortage of ministers, which reduces the supply, in relation to comparative occupations, ministerial salaries fall, not rise. United Presbyterian ministers are now paid on a par with elementary school teachers; Methodists receive, on average, a thousand dollars less a year, and American Baptist ministers are paid little more than manual laborers (Bonifield, 1970:212). Within specific denominations, there is little or no relation between demand/supply ratios and salary, so the declining

[5]Ministers themselves do not share this view. They believe that their profession does carry less prestige than it once did (Leiffer, 1969:140). They also believe that their pay scales have been unfairly allowed to slip behind those of comparable professions (Bonifield, 1970:211).

pay of ministers has to do with how low they are evaluated in general. Thus, the "United Presbyterian minister receives the highest income among the Protestant clergy while he is also in more plentiful supply (relative to the demand for his services) than his brethren in other denominations" (Bonifield, 1970:209).[6]

STRUCTURAL DIFFERENTIATION

Religion loses influence if it becomes something set apart, divorced from other concerns, an increasingly specialized agency performing an ever narrowing set of services. The concept "structural differentiation" refers to the gradual dissociation of the major institutional spheres (the family, the polity, the economy, religion, law, education, and so on) from one another, the emergence of highly specialized collectivities and roles, and the appearance of relatively specific and autonomous symbolic and organizational frameworks. In the process, social institutions become disembedded from kinship, territorial, and other ascriptive units. This process means that religion, as a social institution, becomes less pervasive and more a separate compartment of life. From a condition in which religious ideas permeate other, barely distinguishable institutions, such as the family, work, and politics, the position of religion is radically altered; it becomes possible to speak of specifically religious roles, organizations, and norms, and a specifically religious culture independent of (and often competing with) science and political ideologies. At the same time, the idea of a hierarchy of values, at the apex of which are religious values, is replaced by the idea of different compartments of life, each with its own set of values.

Some sociologists (such as Parsons, 1963; O'Dea, 1968:93) regard structural differentiation as a "purification" of faith because it means that religion becomes freed of its "nonreligious" trappings, such as education, and the accretions it has collected in its history, such as vested interests in property. Consequently, they do not consider structural differentiation a decline in religion at all, for it is a way in which religious needs can be met more "efficiently." In this view, structural differentiation does not mean a weakening of control on the part of religion be-

[6]The social status of an occupation is measured not only by the prestige given to it or by how much it pays, but also by the qualities attached to it by others, the difficulty of entering it, and the rate of turnover of those who do gain entrance. By these measures, the Anglican clergy are clearly declining in status. Their average age is increasing, the age-at-entry is rising, the level of education of entrants is falling, and the turnover rate is higher than it has ever been before (Wilson, 1966:79–80; Paul, 1964:21). The Catholic clergy in England are undergoing a "massive aging process" and the Church is now top-heavy with aged clergy. In 1975, 35 percent of Catholic priests in England were over sixty (*Sunday Times*, 5/18/75).

cause social institutions remain highly interdependent: "its legitimating or guiding function is exercised as fully, however indirectly, as it is in less differentiated societies" (Fenn, 1974:153).[7]

The idea that structural differentiation does not weaken the impact of religious institutions on society must surely be rejected. It is difficult to see how religion can sustain its traditional role of maintaining cultural integration if "the religious argument" is one among many. It is also difficult to see how religion can continue to have the same impact on life if the increasing specialization of institutions means that more and more social activities are altogether untouched by religion. And the fact of institutional interdependence is not convincing evidence of the impact of modern religion. An *indirect* influence is, after all, weaker because it is contingent on the operation of intervening, nonreligious variables.

Evidence of the structural differentiation of religion is not hard to find: five examples follow.

1. The most obvious meaning of structural differentiation is that it entails a division of labor, the implication of which for religion is that occupational life is increasingly freed from religious considerations. Not only have religious monopolies on production and consumption long since disappeared, but social networks increasingly bear the stamp of the workplace rather than the church. Although friendships are still more likely to be formed around religious and ethnic ties than anything else, younger Americans are increasingly choosing their friends and associates from among those they work with rather than those they pray with (Laumann, 1973:108).

2. The days when the churches had a virtual monopoly on learning have gone. Religious schools have been displaced by secular schools; the amount of time spent on religious instruction in schools has been curtailed or eliminated altogether, and attendance at Sunday schools has declined markedly.

3. The differentiation of a secular State in the United States can be traced back to the Revolution. The principal architects of the Constitution were deists or agnostics, who were largely influenced by Enlightenment secularity (Morgan, 1968:23). The actual separation of Church and State has run an uncertain course in the United States, but the institutional independence has been largely maintained. The growth of the secular State in England began as long ago as the seventeenth century, when the idea began to take hold that the State was sanctioned not

---

[7]The Parsonian position is supported by evidence showing the level of religious practices to be unrelated to the degree of structural differentiation in a society. The United States and Belgium are both highly differentiated societies, but they record high levels of church attendance. On the other hand, the country with the highest church attendance rates of all, Ireland, is relatively undifferentiated. Low levels of weekly attendance are found in the Scandinavian countries which have medium levels of differentiation (Mol, 1972:16).

supernaturally but by a kind of contract engaged in for the mutual protection of property. It is important to note that the separation of Church and State is not necessarily a sign of secularization—as its advocates are quick to point out. It is conceivable that a church entirely free from political entanglements is thereby more religious. Yet, it is hard not to believe that where Church and State are separate the impact of religion on political decision-making is bound to be less, especially if many religions are tolerated. A State that remains aloof from religious squabbles will be a State untouched by spiritual considerations.

4. The religious foundations of morality and thence of law are gradually collapsing. Reflecting a shift from a society perceived as a moral order to one seen primarily as a technical order, the courts are concerning themselves more and more with technical matters (such as traffic safety) and finance (for example, taxes) and less and less with moral issues such as adultery and blasphemy. Cases are decided on purely legal bases, or on grounds provided by rationally trained experts, who make little reference to religion. In addition, religious justifications for legal proceedings are no longer considered important: there has, for example, been a decline in the number of people opting to use the religious oath.

In the area of morals, behavior once considered the province of the churches is now treated with indifference (for example, dress styles), is no longer considered proper for the church to decide (for example, usury) or is a topic on which the churches' position is hotly debated from the point of view of a secular ethic. The churches have lost moral influence as they have lost moral certainty: "although the Church still preaches against sin, just what Churchmen now consider to be sin in some respects has changed" (Wilson, 1976:17). When the churches do speak out on moral issues, they tend to do so after the general opinion on the matter has become clear—in which case they function to legitimate and interpret decisions already made. The result is that church people are seeing their faith less and less as a distinctive (and perhaps odd) set of fundamentals and more and more as a vague and comforting underpinning for the norms by which they would in any case live. Although most people probably still see Christian teachings as "the distant and final authority for right behaviour . . . very few think that God acts in any way as a direct agent of retribution for those in breach of moral regulations" (Gorer, 1965:88).[8]

---

[8]The Scriptures have become part of American folklore, but they have lost much of their religious meaning. For example, the majority of church members interviewed in one mid-West community were familiar with the parable of the good Samaritan, and recognized that it was a lesson in helping those in distress. However, none of those interviewed were aware of, or could articulate, the theological significance of this tale. Not one of them "expressed the idea that the way the Samaritan gave of himself to the injured man paralleled God's outpouring of himself to man with no expectation of return" (Obenhaus, 1963:78).

In the process of secularization, an ethics without supernatural foundation has emerged. The connection between religion and morality has not been severed, but the priorities have been reversed. The sense of religiousness has been transfered to the scrupulous ethical behavior to which it was supposed to lead. In other words, rather than morality being identified with religion, religion is identified with morality. A religious person is identifiable by his honesty; being honest is what it means to be religious. In deciding who is "truly religious" today, most people select moral acts such as not drinking or not gambling; or acts of self-abnegation, such as helping the sick; or consistent behavior patterns, such as "dealing straight" (King and Hunt, 1972:9).

5. At one time, the Church was the principal agent of charity in the community, to be turned to in times of personal distress and community disaster. These social-welfare functions have been relinquished by the Church and taken over by specialized agencies. The poor now look not to church charities but to unemployment benefits; the sick (although they might still offer a prayer) think first of going to the physician (Argyle and Beit-Hallahmi, 1975:141). Consequently, the clergyman has relinquished many of his roles to the physician, the lawyer, the social worker, the teacher, and the psychiatrist.

CONCLUSION

Secularization is so complex and the data so sparse, that general conclusions can be drawn only in the most tentative fashion. The following conclusions seem to be reasonable.

1. The polls show that just under half of the United States population but only 15 percent of the United Kingdom population attend church every week. This marks an increase followed by a steady rate of attendance in the United States, and the culmination of a slow but steady decline in the United Kingdom. Levels of giving in both countries have remained constant.

2. There is no evidence with which to assess changes in belief over time in the United Kingdom, but religious beliefs are certainly less widespread than those in the United States. Historically, the lower rates of overt agnosticism and atheism in the United States might have something to do with the lack of an Established Church. In other words, it is less important for American dissidents to assert lack of religious conformity in order to make a political statement. In the United States, subscription to simple and basic tenets of Christian orthodoxy, such as the existence of God and divinity of Christ, has remained constant or even risen a little. But there is slightly less belief in other aspects of orthodoxy, such as life after death, especially among the young. There is

evidence that rejection of orthodoxy is associated with diminished denominational commitment.

3. There is very little evidence on this matter, but at least there is none to deny that a kind of "folk" or "common" religion survives in modern Western societies, even in the midst of rational lifestyles. Furthermore, religious institutions have not yet lost their legitimacy as vital social agencies, even though this legitimacy is rather vague and implicit. The idea that religion and the Church is a "good thing" is as strong in England, where beliefs and practices are low, as it is in the United States, where they are more common. Furthermore, the blandness of American religion is not necessarily a sign of secularity. Weak denominational ties are the price paid for religious tolerance. Paradoxically, the central place of religion in American society is contingent upon its vacuity.

4. The 1960s, during which secular political movements dominated center stage in both the United States and the United Kingdom, appear to have had little effect on the conviction of those who already believe. But they do seem to have produced a slightly higher proportion of those who might be labeled atheists.

5. The much publicized "secular theologies" and writings about the "death of God" seem to have been confined to a very small proportion of church people, most of them situated on college campuses. Moreover, the movement was short-lived. In any case, there is some doubt as to whether this should in fact be seen as a secularizing trend, or as in any way assisting such a trend.

6. Most of the data introduced into the secularization debate are general inventories of religious belief and practices, having little to do with the consequences of religiosity for individual or organizational behavior. Strength of commitment, the structural location of believers, the ethical consequences of church membership—none of this is indicated by the data. *i.e., salience not quantified.*

7. Finally, changes do not necessarily mean decline. The "search for ultimacy" is indeed permanent; the need for belief is always there. There is no evidence to suggest that the needs to which religion speaks have disappeared or been satisfied. The 1960's witnessed considerable disenchantment with traditional religious forms, much experimentation, and a great deal of wandering in search of new means of finding and establishing personal identities. But this unrest often led to the discovery of new "signals of transcendence" (Berger, 1969:65), in response to which new religions were formed.

19

THE CAUSES
OF SECULARIZATION

INTRODUCTION

Secularization is so complex that no single or master cause is conceivable. A number of major social transformations have been linked to the decline of religion, including the rise of science, the emergence of the nation-state, and the growth of industrial capitalism. These developments are interconnected so closely that trying to establish some causal priority among them is meaningless. They form part of a general intellectual and social development that began with the Enlightenment, a period when the faith in reason, with its empirical, pragmatic orientation to the world, began to replace faith in revelation or tradition. At that time, life began to be organized increasingly "through a division and coordination of activities on the basis of an exact study of men's relations with each other, with their tools and their environment, for the purposes of achieving greater efficiency and productivity" (Freund, 1968:19). The rise of science, the emergence of the secular State, and the spread of capitalism are the principal manifestations of this process of rationalization.

THE GROWTH OF SCIENCE

The growth of the scientific world view means that the natural (and, later, the social) world becomes the object of systematic scrutiny, for the purposes of which canons of procedure are agreed upon. Science is also the name given to the body of knowledge that accumulates as a result of empirical research. The scientific world view is largely incompatible with a belief that there are supernatural powers. To the scientist, the natural world consists of objects that are lawfully related. The laws that relate them can be discovered by controlled investigation, and the knowledge thus gained can be used to acquire dominion over nature. Ideas about the sacredness of nature and about natural objects being connected to (or a manifestation of) an underlying supernatural reality that is not open to empirical investigation are antithetical to science. Science is valued not only for its practicality but also for its universalism, impartiality, and skepticism. The contrast between religion and science is one of values as well as technique.

In many fields of human concern, scientific procedures have almost completely taken over as guides to human affairs. The study of nature is now the province of a completely secular body of physical sciences. The application of scientific findings is now the job of the technologist, the engineer, the physicist, and the chemist. Education has largely been freed from religious control, and religious teachings are replaced by science and civics courses. Sunday school attendance declines as a purely secular childhood training (informed by the new social sciences) becomes more sophisticated. Science is now part of "the Establishment," and religion's place in it is uncertain; the scientist is the expert to whom all turn for problem solving.

The impetus for the growth of science comes not only from its proven success as the source of material abundance and physical well-being, but also from an internal dynamic. In other words, science is a logically closed and *self-aggrandizing* system. It defines its own problems and its own criteria of evaluation. Problems that do not fit the rational-empirical model are not considered real problems. In consequence, many human concerns have to be redefined in order to be amenable to scientific analysis. Having done this, the scientist is able either to solve the real problem or to explain his failure to do so in scientific terms.

The conflict between religion and science has been drawn so vividly, and the "victories" of science over religion publicized so well, that it is customary to look upon the relation between religion and science as a war that religion is losing (see, for example, White, 1896). However, this is a simplistic view, for a number of reasons:

1. It exaggerates the power of science to reduce human problems to a rational-empirical framework: there is by no means uniform acceptance of the idea that all problems are nothing but technical problems. Indeed, many would hold that the really crucial issues—suffering, injustice, and loneliness, among others—are precisely those that cannot be defined in scientific terms.

2. The imagery of warfare pits the impartial and objective scientist against the committed, subjective true believer. In fact, the scientist, like the churchman, is committed to a set of values of his own (which are accepted as a matter of faith), and his mode of operation rarely approaches the detached impartiality suggested by the popular stereotype of him.

3. Scientific arguments do not necessarily contradict religious interpretations of events. The advance of science does not have to mean the retreat of religion. For example, the empirical observation that cancer is caused by cigarette smoking does not rule out the idea that getting cancer results from leading a sinful life.

4. The increasing reliance of a society on technology does not necessarily mean a decline in religiosity, for the fruits of technology can be enjoyed by many when the knowledge used to obtain them is confined to a few. It is as well not to exaggerate the technical knowledge of the person in the street, even in a highly technological age. The principles by which something like a television set works are as incomprehensible to the average person as are the workings of the oracle.

5. The attempt to synthesize Scriptures with Darwinism, and the appearance of movements such as Christian Science and Scientology, might seem to be a sign of the capitulation of religion to science, but this is not so. In either case, the goal is to transcend science rather than imitate it—to find some common scheme that can accommodate both science and religion.

6. The idea that science must necessarily eliminate religion exaggerates the extent to which religion caters to the need for empirical knowledge. Religious ritual and religious experience do not rest upon or convey truth statements as much as ideas about right order and right feeling. In reality, religion provides very little factual information, and rests not upon the accuracy of its factual statements as much as upon the emotional and expressive satisfactions it affords. It is for this reason that Durkheim (1975:37) was right when he said, "if we go back to the arguments, each in turn, which science musters against religion, we see that thought they may be strong enough to entrench the unbeliever yet further in his opinion, there is not one of them capable of converting a believer."

Yet the idea that science and religion are not necessarily incompatible can be taken too far. The growth of science certainly undercuts the position of religion in many spheres of life. Granted that religion may cater primarily to emotional and expressive needs, the continual disconfirmation of religious theses will tend to diminish the sense of transcendence upon which religious sentiments rest. In other words, although science does not have a direct impact on the authenticity of religious experiences, it does tend to weaken the sense of "other reality" which is the foundation of religious experience.[1]

THE BIRTH OF THE NATION-STATE

The nation-state, which began to appear in the sixteenth century, is both a reflection and a further instigator of secularization.

> In our era, the image of the modern state is that of a *rationalising* force. By virtue of this rational force the modern state is able to transform and validate the varied political structures out of which it has emerged. . . . In fine, the process generally described as the rise of the "modern state" may, from the sociological perspective, be seen as the transformation of various forms of nonrational power to more rational ones (Berger, 1971:25).

In post-Enlightenment Europe, the State became increasingly divorced from the Church, and political affairs were gradually removed from the domain of religion.

The modern State is characterized above all by its use of rational-legal administration in which rules of impersonalism and universalism in the interests of citizenship rights have supplanted rules of personal loyalty and ascription. The regulatory State, legitimated by more rational ideas such as the social contract, and using formal standards of justice to oversee the expansion of the capitalist economy, fostered the growth of large-scale government bureaucracies that were far removed from the influence of the Church. Later developments, such as the extension of the franchise and the rise of the welfare state, make the individual less and less likely to turn to the Church even in times of distress, let alone find satisfaction there.

The rise of the secular State, which "exerts no pressure in favour of one religion rather than another religion, . . . in which no social or educational pressure is exerted in favour of one religion rather than another religion or no religion, . . . wholly detached from religious (or irreligious) teaching or practice," was inspired by the liberal ideas about the rights of man made popular by Locke, especially the right of freedom of conscience.

---

[1]"The increasing intellectualization and rationalization [in modern societies] do *not* . . . indicate an increased and general knowledge of the conditions under which one lives. It means something else, namely, the knowledge or belief that if one wished one *could* learn it at any time. Hence, it means that principally there are no mysterious incalculable forces that come into play, but rather that one can, in principle, master all things by calculation. This means that the world is disenchanted" (Weber, 1946:139).

If the right to be irreligious is won, then the institutions, privileges and customs of a State and society must be dismantled, sufficiently dismantled at least, to prevent the State or society exercising pressure upon the individual to be religious if he wishes not to be religious. The liberal State, carried on logically, must be the secular State (Chadwick, 1975:27).

Thus, democratic principles promise the individual a voice in policy making and thereby tend to undermine the authority of the Church. Furthermore, once democratic forms have been established, alternative channels of social protest are available.

THE SPREAD OF CAPITALISM

The growth of the capitalist market economy "has been an overwhelmingly powerful force of secularization" (Roth, 1976: 264). Ironically, the growth of capitalism was fueled by a religious movement. The contribution of the Protestant Reformation to the origins of modern capitalism is well known. Other factors were certainly involved in this momentous change: the accumulation of a large mass of "free" laborers; technological developments; the breakdown of status-group monopolies on production and consumption as the result of nationalism; and the development of new capital through the import of raw materials and precious metals (see Tawney, 1947). However, the set of motives referred to as the spirit of capitalism owed much to the rationalizing spirit of the Protestant Reformers.

The Reformers tried to eliminate sacramentalism, the less routine miracles, and the world of intercessors populated by angels and spirits. Their almost fanatical concern with self-control, discipline, organization, and practical affairs brought about a "demystification of the world" and encouraged the idea that man could, by his own knowledge and industry, achieve dominion over the natural world. As a result of the Reformation, "man took the center of the stage, even though it was still believed that God had written the script in his life-span man was to act out. But like the author of a play, God was no longer of importance to its performance, and was not responsible for it" (Wilson, 1976:12). Unwittingly, the Reformers set in motion the process whereby humans changed from spiritual beings who in order to survive must give attention to economic affairs, to economic actors who in their prudence take occasional and casual precautions to assure their spiritual well being.

Calvin taught that one's occupation, however mundane, was one's "calling" in life, and was rich with religious significance as the expression of God's will on earth. Although good works could not earn salvation, a life organized systematically and successfully around the production of good works could be interpreted as an external sign of inward grace. In this inner-worldly asceticism, Calvin's followers found a convenient legitimation for an acquisitive, innovative orientation to work and accumulation that, in contrast with pre-Reformation capitalism, recognized the importance of careful, methodical work "in the world." Appropriately capitalist attitudes were thus given religious sanction.

Capitalism expanded markets, increased the average size of firms, depersonalized work relations, increased the reliance on machine power, reduced more and more areas of life to matters of calculation and planned performance, and encouraged an economizing attitude toward human relationships in the interests of greater material productivity. These changes gradually eliminated the original religious motivation for economic activity. As Weber (1930:181) observed, "The Puritan wanted to work in a calling; we are forced to." Whether it is the realm of production, where industriousness, self-control, and dedication to career are important virtues, or the realm of consumption, where prodigality and display are the important virtues, the modern economic system is completely mundane, the "transcendent ethic has vanished" (Bell, 1973:78).

Industrial capitalism is self-aggrandizing. As it expands, the number of social strata dominated by its rationalism increases and the number of people open to charismatic appeals falls. Furthermore, the functional specialization that is a central part of the rationalization of the economy increases the number of satisfying secular roles available. The Church is no longer one of the most attractive organizations in which to work.

The precise relationship of these processes to one another—the growth of science and technology, the emergence of the nation-state, and the spread of capitalism—is the subject of great debate, which cannot be entered into here (see Green, 1959). For Marx, the leading factor was the growth of an increasingly complex market system and its intrusion into more and more spheres of social life. Weber saw rationalization as pushing ahead primarily in the area of administration. They were in agreement, however, that mature capitalism is "a world in which religion is replaced by a social organisation in which technological rationality reigns supreme" (Giddens, 1971:215).

THE LOSS OF COMMUNITY

To some scholars, it is not so much the rationalization process that leads directly to a decline in religion, but the loss of community that rationalization causes. The assumption is that because religion is the community expressed in sacred terms, religion will disappear if community is lost. This thesis seems to apply particularly well to England. The industrial revolution in England saw the breakdown of groups in which a sense of community was strong: family, village, small town, and region were broken up by the rise of industry and the urbanization that accompanied it. The mobility demanded by the industrial system and the concentration of people mainly on the basis of their occupation disrupted the traditional ties of the country life and made redundant the role of the Church as the source of stability and continuity.

The features of urban living are now familiar: diverse and transient populations, impersonal and utilitarian relationships, fragile and unstable communities. In England, where the growth of large towns was followed by a decline in religious attendance, urbanization as much as industrialization led to a weakening of traditional religious forms. This decline was felt most acutely by the Church of England, whose traditional parish system was quite unable to cope with urban living.[2] The Free Churches were only slightly more successful in building an urban base. The Methodists, for example, found that their circuit system did not work well in the cities (Inglis, 1963:90). The significance of urbanization is that it freed more and more people from the traditional controls of the Church as practiced in the stable, closed, rural community.

The growth of England's urban population was openly referred to as a threat to internal peace and stability, and the necessity of reimposing religious controls on the laboring classes was frequently discussed. It is for this reason that many Anglicans cautiously approved of Wesley's ministrations among the poor. Methodism, described by Thompson (1966:365) as "the desolate inner landscape of Utilitarianism," enjoined a frugal and industrious life that promised to socialize rural migrants into the new discipline of the factory system and cope with the anarchy of the towns. However, only a small portion of working-class people were drawn into the Methodist fold, and these individuals tended to be skilled workers, anxious to learn the ways of the middle class to which they aspired. By 1851, when Methodists constituted about 10 percent of the English population, most of its members were middle class (Inglis, 1963:9).

Other attempts by Victorian churchmen to combat growing secularity in the urban proletariat were no more successful. Between 1809 and 1820, the English Parliament, for the first time in its history, voted funds to endow and increase Anglican benefices in the cities (Inglis, 1963:7), but the new churches were not patronized. The pew-rent system (long

[2]The Church of England has found that "the greater the density of population, the poorer the results (per 1,000 of the population) on the whole in baptisms, confirmation and Easter communicant figures" (Paul, 1973:55).

thought to be the chief reason why so few poor people attended church) was finally abolished around 1900, but no increase in working-class attendance resulted. The Salvation Army (tacitly supported by the Church of England) was more successful in bringing religion to the masses, but only a small minority of the working class actually enlisted in William Booth's legions (Inglis, 1963:196).

Loss of community becomes a plausible reason for the decline of religion if the moral, rather than the cognitive, dimension of religion is emphasized. After all, going to church is a ritual that might appear to rest on belief and that, being discontinued, might be supposed to indicate a decline in that belief. However, it is probably more accurate to say that people sometimes make ritual and then the ritual needs explanation. In this case, it is the disturbance of the ritual that is important; the discrediting of the beliefs is secondary. This might explain why, ironically enough, it was among those least exposed to scientific challenges to religion that the churchgoing habit disappeared first.

The estrangement of most of the working class "from the benevolent god of Christianity seems to have been founded on their perception of the obvious injustice of the world—hence on a moral feeling rather than on mere positivistic belief" (Roth, 1976:262). The middle class, who were exposed the most to science, retained the churchgoing habit the longest. They simply assimilated Darwinism and Biblical criticism into a modified Christianity that had room for evolutionary theory and for the Social Gospel. Thus,

> it is not the case that men first stopped believing in God and the authority of the Church, and then subsequently started behaving differently. It seems clear that men first of all lost any over-all social agreement as to the right way to live together, and so ceased to be able to make sense of any claims to moral authority. Consequently, they could not find intelligible the claims to authority which were advanced on the part of the Church (MacIntyre, 1967:54).

The antipathy that the urban proletariat showed toward religious institutions and their officials preceded rather than followed their loss of faith (Campbell, 1971:21). The Church lost its hold because the practical imperatives by which the industrial worker was guided demanded a morality that the Church was unable to provide (Roth, 1976:264). The Church seemed to be incapable of doing anything more than enrolling those working-class people who were prepared to adapt themselves to middle-class ways. The world to which the laboring city dwellers were exposed was increasingly one of "conveyor belts, time-and-motion studies, and bureaucratic organisation." The moral prescriptions of Christianity, geared to a settled world of face-to-face contacts and "the intimacies of the family courtship, friendship and neighbourliness," began to seem anachronistic (Wilson, 1976:6).

William Booth, founder of the Salvation Army, noted perceptively that the conflict between the middle-class churchman and the unchurched industrial worker was actually a moral conflict. Between them, he maintained, there was "an incompatibility of moral temper. The average working man of today thinks more of his rights and wrongs than of his duties and his failure to perform them" (quoted in Inglis, 1963:335). Working people continued to defer to religious institutions to a large degree and to practice a kind of private religion, but they now looked upon the Church as the representative of a group enjoying unjust advantages over them. Thus it is that the socialist movement, toward which the urban population was increasingly drawn, did not actually attack religion as such (for many socialists found in it valuable ideas of justice, freedom, and communism). Rather, it attacked the churches "because they were pillars of the structure which must be destroyed" (Chadwick, 1975:85). The mass of the urban proletariat has never been known for its positive atheism or its militantly antireligious stance. Instead, they have tended to be a-religious, accepting everyday realities, reluctant to impose any kind of systematic coherence on their lives, and finding significance chiefly in the everyday round. Theirs is a more local, private world, in which general questions about the meaning of the universe are irrelevant, and the organizational apparatus of formal religion unimportant.

THE AMERICAN CASE

The religious factor is more important in the United States than in the United Kingdom: all of the indexes show that Americans are more religious than the British. The United States would appear to be an anomaly—a highly advanced industrial society, subject to the very same forces which have secularized Britain, but maintaining a level of religiosity higher than at any other time in its history. It is difficult to resolve this puzzle with the evidence at hand, but the answer might well be found in a closer look at what the high rates of religious observance in the United States actually signify.

Americans regularly attend church in great numbers despite considerable ignorance about the teachings of their faith. For example, although 40 percent of all adult Americans attend church once a week, only 35 percent are able to name the four Gospels. In contrast, 61 percent of Britons can name the Gospels, but only 15 percent attend church weekly. Nor does religious history seem to loom very large for Americans: when asked to name the most important event in the world, they place the birth of Christ fourteenth (equal with the Wright brothers' invention of the airplane) and rank Columbus' discovery of America first (Herberg, 1960:2). The ethical consequences of their faith are also of minor importance: the most committed church members are those who reject the idea that their faith has ethical consequences (Stark and Glock, 1968:214). Finally, with a few exceptions, American religion is almost devoid of denominational content. Religious warfare is confined to a fringe, as for most people one denomination seems to be about as good as another. How can this be explained?

In a society where an Established Church is absent, where pluralism is a strongly held value, where there is negligible class conflict, and where voluntary associations are an important means of status affirmation, church attendance seems to have achieved its popularity because it is a sign of respectability and community belongingness. High rates of church attendance in a society not otherwise marked by piety in practical affairs suggest that Americans have not moved away from religion as have the English, but have *taken it over*. This process has taken two forms: first, religion has assumed a national role as a sign of "Americanism" (see Herberg, 1960); second, religion has become a matter of personal preference rather than an obligation, a commodity to be consumed as desired (Wilson, 1966:94). Neither of these ideas is particularly religious, but both are clearly American. In a sense, then, religion has been secularized, absorbed into the mundane world of modern industrial capitalism.

The vacuity of American religion is partly the creation of pluralism itself. Religious beliefs, which are farthest removed from sense experience, are especially dependent on social unanimity for their continuing plausibility: the impact of competing beliefs will be to reduce the credibility of each belief. Where many truths are tolerated, no claim to absolute truth will be credible. Where many religions are tolerated, there is the option of no religion at all. In a pluralistic system, the churches are forced to become marketing agencies and their teachings and practices must take on the character of commodities for sale. The need to market their "product" makes the churches extremely sensitive to changing consumer preferences. And, of course, this concern with marketability makes it increasingly difficult for them "to maintain the religious tradition as unchanging verity" (Berger, 1967:137), and punctures the mystery of the Church.

Pluralism also means an increase in the number of organizations to which it is possible (even necessary) to belong. This means that the Church is only one among many outlets for an individual's energies and aspirations. Even as first among equals, religion loses its ability to define social situations or to set events within its own frame of reference. To speak of the religious "side" of an issue, or of "the churches' view," is already to undermine fatally the claim of the Church to absolute truth. At best, the Church becomes a follower, legitimating decisions already made by demonstrating how they fit into its perspective. The mass media have accelerated this trend: although they have not created the arguments over religion, they have sharpened, magnified, and diffused them (Chadwick, 1975:43).

The argument that pluralism is a secularizing force has great merit, but it must not be carried too far. The marginality of the Church does not in itself necessitate a further weakening of that position. It is an error to suppose that toleration of other faiths is tantamount to admitting the falsity of one's own beliefs. In Protestantism, where the individual is concerned above all else with his own relationship with God, this is decidedly not the case. It is more accurate to say that pluralism is a facilitating condition of secularization: it helps further the trend once it is under way.

All the social forces adduced to explain secularization are common to the United States and the United Kingdom—indeed, to all modern Western societies. In each society, the scientist and technologist reign, the State is purely secular, education is almost entirely free from church control, business enterprises are measured pragmatically, and bureaucracies encage the working population. In England, the impact of these forces has been to create and intensify class conflict in a highly urbanized setting. There can be little question that the decline of religion in England is associated with the rise of this industrial class warfare and the decline of middle-class hegemony. The vestiges of religion that remain in England in the more traditional and ceremonial events merely reflects this waning hegemony.

In the United States, an entirely different situation prevails. Frequent public religious observances are the practice of almost half the entire population. A "civil religion" suffuses political life to an extent not found in England, where, ironically enough, there remains an Established Church. On the other hand, these religious observances appear to be of a somewhat vacuous kind. Specific religious loyalties and commitments are found only among a few, religious knowledge and awareness is minimal, and, more important, the ethical consequences of this religiosity are extremely difficult to locate. In study after study cited in this book, the decline of the religious factor is announced: it is no longer as influential in regard to who an individual marries, how many children she has, where she goes to college and for how long, what kind of job she gets, how successful she is at that job, who she votes for, and how she gets on with ethnic and racial minorities. All of this would seem to point to a secularity as profound as that found in many other modern societies. There are several explanations for this anomaly.

First, the relatively high attendance rates *do* accurately reflect religiosity, religious faith *is* important in such areas as economics, politics, community affairs, and kinship, but the research to date has not detected this. Given the enormous problems of isolating the religious factor and given its neglect in most contemporary sociological research, there is a possibility that this is so. In any case, in the complete absence of the needed data, there is no way of saying that the impact of religion is *less* today than it was at the turn of the century, even if it is low today.

Second, it might be that modern religion belongs in the private sphere. This means that religion might well have lost much of its public, institutional salience, but that it remains potent at the level of individual preference. Most of the research reported in this book and much of the talk of secularization in the United States ignores this possibility. However, it is hard to see how something that has become a personal preference, confined, perhaps, to the home or relegated in importance to attendance at the Kiwanis once a week, has not at the same time "lost" something. Traditionally, religion has been attached to concepts such as "the ultimate" or "the absolute": the thesis of privatization implies a loss of this kind of transcendence.

Third, it is possible that there has indeed occurred a separation of religion and other social institutions in the United States and that much of American religiosity is vacuous. However, this does not necessarily mean that total commitment or an all-embracing religiosity is a thing of the past or might not once again become a dominant feature of American society. There are many groups on the margins of society, in the counter-culture or in the underground who do articulate this kind of total commitment, and the 1960s witnessed a proliferation of such groups and a popularization of their message. It might well be that the flourishing of these groups signals a return to transcendence. This is the topic of the concluding section of this chapter.

Because of these three options, any firm statement about secularization in the United States if virtually a matter of faith. However, the "hard data" used in this book to measure secularization—the data on the consequences of religion—would seem to clearly indicate a decline. This conclusion assumes, however, that all the secularizing processes discussed above are given, and this is not the case. For one thing, the churches themselves do not sit idly by and watch these forces at work. The next section will describe one of the most important forms of adjustment they have made.

THE ECUMENICAL MOVEMENT:
A RESPONSE TO SECULARIZATION

The churches are not the passive victims of secularization. They actively respond to the challenges industrial capitalism has presented to their position of authority. One very important response has been the ecumenical movement, in which distinct denominations draw closer together in different degrees of collaboration and contact. The contemporary period in church history has been referred to as "the ecumenical era" (Cavert, 1968:7);, so profound has been the movement in this direction. This section will explore some of the options the churches have taken up as they seek to respond to declining membership and institutional strength.

Ecumenicism has a number of meanings. It can range from mere inter-board cooperation (in which, for example, mission boards in two different denominations collaborate in their work) through federation (in which separate denominations formalize their joint endeavors under a corporate body) to organic union (in which separate denominations surrender their separate identities and become one united church). The modern trend of ecumenicism reverses the nineteenth-century pattern of denominational division. The modern zeal for alliances contrasts starkly with the bitter religious rivalries and schisms of the last century. Why has this movement occurred?

The Melting Pot Theory

Ecumenicism can be explained quite simply by pointing to the decline of the social differences that many of the old denominational boundaries followed (see Lee, 1960). Thus, as class differences disappear, denominations identified with specific status groups also vanish; as ethnic loyalties weaken and language barriers are broken down, ethnic churches are no longer needed. Unfortunately, this theory ignores the fact that denominations acquire an autonomy and momentum just as political parties do. Their members build specific loyalties to the denomination, which last far longer than the original social causes of the separate church. The model also fails to recognize that America is hardly the melting pot it is commonly pictured as. Ethnic loyalties remain very strong. This theory, which is based almost entirely upon assumptions about assimilation, cannot account for ecumenicism.

The Pluralist Theory

The ecumenical movement can be accounted for with a "market model." According to this model, the necessity to collaborate is given by the need to rationalise competition itself in the pluralistic situation. The competitive system is established once it has become impossible to utilise the political machinery of the society for the elimination of religious rivals. The forces of this market then tend toward a system free competition very similar to that of laissez-faire capitalism (Berger, 1967:140).

In other words, the chief consequence of pluralism is to increase the amount of competition among religious bodies. Such competition, in religious institutions as well as in economic institutions, tends to move all the competitors toward a common form, so that each is guaranteed a share of the market. This increased similarity, plus the costs of competition, encourages the formation of cartels—or ecumenical bodies. Pluralism thus leads to ecumenicism; competitiveness encourages the standardization of the product.

This model is quite suggestive, but there are two problems associated with it. First, it does not explain why the pluralism of the nineteenth century led to repeated division, and the pluralism of the twentieth century has given rise to mergers. Second, competition among denominations in a social climate that encourages equality of opportunity might well make for greater similarity among them. However, it must also be acknowledged that competition has a logic of its own, and it may function to *maintain* the interest in and affiliation with specific denominations, because this is the only distinctiveness religious faith has. In other words, if producers of very similar products are competing for the same customers in an open market and if the good is not that important to everyday life, the differences in packaging become very important (Wilson, 1968:78). Thus, as theological differences decline and as the impact of religion on major institutions weakens, denominations' boundaries might well become more and not less salient. This salience might make a difference in the kind of ecumenical strategy adopted, even if it does not put a halt to ecumenicism altogether. If competition increases the salience of "packaging" while standardization of the product takes place, federation is the strategy most likely to be adopted, for under it the same product but a different package can be achieved at the same time.

The Secularization Model

Ecumenicism can be accounted for by looking upon it as an adjustment by the denominations to institutional weakness. This model does not contradict the market model, but to pluralism must be added secularization. When one is faced with totally alien faiths, or no faith at all, the finer points of a religion begin to seem irrelevant. Historically, ecumenicism occurred first where the churches' struggles were hardest, where their resources were fewest, and in areas of church life where tradition was weakest—for example, foreign and home missions. Ecumenicism can thus be seen as a defensive move by the churches to prevent the weakening of the impact of the churches on other faiths and on society at large.

This model of ecumenicism assumes that "organisations amalgamate when they are weak rather than when they are strong, since alliance means compromise and amendment of commitment" (Wilson, 1966:126). Accordingly, ecumenicism reflects a desire, through efficient planning and organization, to reduce wasteful competition, maintain funding levels by making joint, broader appeals, save on building costs by erecting community churches, make coordination of effort easier by adopting common administrative procedures, give clergy greater security of tenure by pooling employment training and deployment, and protect the churches' position politically by setting up a single lobby. These are the actions of organizations which are becoming weaker.

In this model, ecumenicism is tied directly to declining institutional strength, as measured by falling membership relative to the general population and diminished social influence. For instance, the English Methodist union in 1932 can clearly be seen as a reaction to a decline in membership that began in the 1880s and became most rapid in the 1920s. Currie (1968:100) argues that this kind of merger is most likely when a denomination recruits fewer members but is also losing fewer, which means that the hard core has been reached. "This hard core is more loyal, but proselytises less, and secures less frontal growth. The slowing up of the organisational process accompanies a shift of emphasis from frontal to lateral growth, and increases organisational pressure for the transition to a superdenomination." Lateral growth is especially likely to happen where the average age of the membership is increasing, where greater geographical mobility strengthens the desire of the membership to have more congregations available to them, and where there is some notion of optimum size for the denomination. For instance, in the case of the Methodists, there seems to have been some idea of the size of the "Methodist World" and the number of separate Methodist groups that could compete in it effectively. As that world contracted, so did the number of viable groups.

The Development of Ecumenicism

The nineteenth century of religious divisions has become the twentieth century of religious union. Actually, this is an oversimplification, as some form of cooperation among denominations can be traced back well into the last century. The revivalists sought to transcend denominational boundaries, as did many voluntary bodies, such as the American Bible

Society, the American Sunday School Union, the American Anti-Slavery Society, the American Peace Society, and the YMCA. The growth of these agencies was greatly encouraged by the distinctively American idea that religious faith is above all something to be used. In fact, the mission agencies became so powerful and so caught up in the spirit of cooperation that ties between denominations became stronger than those within them; "home missions specialists [communicated] across denominational lines as [did] foreign missions specialists and other agency personnel in the fields of education, publicity, and social action" (Winter, 1968:43).

THE NATIONAL COUNCIL OF CHURCHES. Coordination among agencies in different denominations and the pooling of resources for mission work developed over time in response to practical needs. This development led to much more formal efforts to create an organization that would coordinate interdenominational work across a whole range of tasks. The first step in this direction was taken in 1908 with the formation of the Federal Council of Churches. Altogether, twenty-nine separate Protestant denominations joined the Council, including the black African Methodist Episcopal Church, African Methodist Episcopal Zion Church, and the National Baptist Convention, but excluding the Lutherans and the Southern Baptists. The FCC was formed mainly to develop and implement a new social creed with which the member denominations could cope with the problems of the new urban industrial society then in the making—albeit its early efforts were given a considerable boost by the cooperative demands made by the First World War.

In 1951, the FCC became the National Council of Churches. Previously independent cooperative ventures in the fields of missions, education, stewardship, and mass communications were absorbed by the new council, and the United, Augustana, and Danish Evangelical Lutheran Churches joined, raising the membership to 143,000 congregations (Cavert, 1970:29). Between 1951 and 1968, ten more denominations joined, but the Southern Baptists, American Lutherans, Missouri-Synod Lutherans, Churches of Christ, Unitarians, and Christian Scientists remained outside.

Today, the NCC is represented at the grass-roots level by over 1,000 local councils. They have been set up to facilitate denominational cooperation in community programs and to help establish and publicize the churches' common position on issues such as drinking, gambling, and obscenity. These local councils have tried to encourage "comity," the process whereby "churches develop joint planning and strategy in order to avoid overlapping and overlooking" (Lee, 1960:169). Comity has become highly rationalized: it "routinely involves the use of census data, real estate and demographic projections, as well as survey data gathered by the research departments of the denominational bureaucracies themselves" (Berger, 1967:142). Most comity arrangements consist of covenants by the various denominations on "territorial rights" in a community, whereby each denomination has exclusive first claim on newcomers to a given residential area. Comity also results in agreements not to overchurch the total community in the interests of keeping the local congregation of each denomination at a viable size.[3]

THE WORLD COUNCIL OF CHURCHES. Federations of churches have also been attempted at the international level. Organized efforts at international church cooperation can be traced back at least to the International Missionary Council formed in 1910, but the first assembly of what is now known as the World Council of Churches was not held until 1948. Even more than national federations, international ecumenicism concentrates on the practical side of church work—its motto being "doctrine divides, service unites." The WCC has reflected the same concerns as the Canadian Council of Churches, the British Council of Churches, and the NCC in America: (1) missionary work in the non-Christian world, (2) practical work in disaster relief and charity, and (3) doctrinal agreement. It need hardly be said that the first two have progressed much more smoothly than the last.

UNIONS. The most fundamental form of ecumenicism is the denominational merger, in which separate denominations lose their identities and merge into one "super-denomination." This means either a mutual recognition of ministries and intercommunion or, more completely, a full, organic union. This kind of merger can be either intraconfessional (as was the union of Methodists in the 1930s) or interconfessional (as was the formation of the United Church of Canada in 1925 out of the Presbyterian, Methodist, and Congregational denominations).

This form of ecumenicism has become increasingly common. Thus, although the number of church members in the United States has increased enormously, the number of separate denominations and sects has remained at about 280. In 1906, there was one religious group for every 170,500 adult church members; by 1926 this figure had reached 207,000, and by 1956 it was up to 400,000 (Lee, 1960:75). Unlike the nineteenth century, growth in membership in the present century has not been accompanied by the multiplication of groups. The merger movement is concealed to some extent by the apparent diversity of American religion, which can be misleading. For example, there are 22 separate Methodist denominations and sects, but one of them contains seven eighths of all Methodists in the United States (Lee, 1960:75). The

[3]An alternative to comity arrangements is the community church, which is independent of but affiliated with several denominations and which is intended to serve the entire Protestant community within a given area.

merger movement, prominent in which have been unions of formerly divided Methodists (1939), Congregationalists (1957), Presbyterians (1958), and Lutherans (1960, and again in 1962) continues unabated. In 1972, the United Church and the Disciples of Christ formally commissioned a committee to arrange their eventual reunion, and the Presbyterian Church in the United States and the United Presbyterian Church have begun discussions on a merger. In Canada, conversations about a possible Anglican-United union began in 1972. In England, the Congregational Church and the Presbyterian Church joined in 1972 to form the United Reformed Church.

THE CONSULTATION ON CHURCH UNION. There is a pattern to these mergers. Two denominations are most likely to merge if they are of common doctrinal, historical and ethnic origins, if there are ecclesiastical similarities between them, and if they are geographically complementary. These same factors are responsible for the most amibitious merger attempt of all—the Consultation on Church Union, begun by Presbyterians, Episcopalians, Methodists, and officials of the United Church in 1960. Official negotiations commenced in 1962, when the Disciples of Christ joined. In 1966, the COCU was joined by the Presbyterian Church in the United States and the AMEC. The next year, the AMEZC joined, together with another black denomination, the Christian Methodist Episcopal Church. This kind of merger is more sweeping than any previously envisaged, and negotiations are moving very slowly. It is the latest in a long line of efforts stretching back to the Faith and Order movement of the 1920s, to achieve some kind of permanent *rapprochement* among the mainstream Protestant denominations.

INTERFAITH ECUMENICISM. The ecumenical strategies described so far have concerned only Protestant denominations. Ecumenicalism between *faiths* has proceeded much more cautiously. Catholic attitudes have been guided by papal encyclicals such as *Mortalium Animos* (1928), which warned the faithful against participation in religiously-mixed gatherings. Protestants have been protected against Catholics by watchdogs such as the Evangelical Alliance. Protestant and Catholic leaders have occasionally cooperated in charity work and in war efforts, but such enterprises have steered well clear of theological and ecclesiastical issues.

During the 1960s, however, intial moves were made to improve relations between Protestants and Catholics. The Catholic Church sent its first official observers to the WCC assembly in 1961. Protestants were present as observers at the Second Vatican Council (1962–65). The Council both symbolized and furthered a new ecumenical spirit among Catholics, and the hierarchy of the Church moved closer to the position that church divisions are harmful not only to Protestants but to Catholics as well. The Decree on Ecumenicism issued by the Council "virtually liquidated the Counter Reformation begun some 400 years before by the Council of Trent" (Cavert, 1970:288).[4]

Vatican II fundamentally altered Protestant/Catholic relations at the institutional level, effecting a major reorientation of the two faiths to each other. But did the ecumenical pronouncements emanating from the Council reflect a continuing trend, and did they represent the opinions of the rank and file? Both these questions must be answered in the negative. Although the ecumenical spirit has been much in evidence in recent years, there are few signs that denominational and interfaith divisions are about the disappear. There is a long history of intense religious hostility to be overcome before Protestants and Catholics can move closer together. Furthermore, the Fundamentalist/Modernist division within Protestantism is sufficiently strong to have caused the more conservative denominations to refuse membership in ventures such as the NCC and the COCU and to establish their own National Association of Evangelicals (1942). Similarly, the more evangelical groups in Canada have refused to join the more liberal Canadian Council of Churches.

The significance of the COCU in the trend toward superdenominations should not be overestimated. The COCU gathered initial strength during the late 1950s and early 1960s, when the WASP values it largely represents had not come under the serious challenge they were to meet in the mid-1960s. The civil rights movement seriously disturbed the sense of community that had inspired the original proposal. The incorporation of some of the major black denominations into the COCU in the 1960s did not prevent the eruption of serious tensions within the Union over the respective merits of racial integration and separatism. Moreover, the COCU overestimated the level of consensus among church members. The COCU was first proposed during a time of liberal optimism about the benefits of planning, efficient administration, and teamwork. During the 1960s, these assumptions were vigorously questioned, particularly by the less pragmatic young, who were more sceptical about the benefits of large-scale bureaucracies and social planning. The temporary but influential popularity of secular theology, with its enthusiasm for the "secular city" and the churches' part in it, led to a questioning of the liberal Protestantism endorsed by most of the de-

[4]Vatican II initiated a number of ecumenical moves, including (1) the proclamation of a new goal of restoring church unity, based not merely on mutual toleration but on cooperation; (2) public support for the work of the World Council of Churches; (3) an admission of the "ecclesiastical reality" of non-Catholic denominations; (4) a clarification of the doctrine of the hierarchy of truths—in other words, a more open admission that some Catholic truths are more negotiable than others; (5) a renunciation of Catholic "triumphalism" in which the Church claims to be above reform; and (6) approval of the Decree on Ecumenicism.

nominations taking part in the consultations. By 1970, the original drive of the COCU had been slowed. The tumult of the 1960s and the accompanying shift in values—the rediscovery of romanticism, the renewed quest for community, the popularity of Eastern religions and an eclectic mysticism, and the rejection of "bigger-is-better" formulas for progress—combined to render the COCU anachronistic, the symbol not of an inevitable development but of a passing phase, a reminder of the native, pragmatic optimism of the 1950s.

Attitudes Toward Ecumenicism

There exists today a "folk ecumenicism," which is practiced not only by those who are religious without being interested in denominational rivalries, but also by those who seem to take a delight in combining the insights and practices of a variety of different denominations, and even faiths, in a mix of their own. There has also emerged a common-core or "mainstream" Protestantism in which there is broad consensus on doctrine (such as the nature of the Trinity), a common ethos of fellowship, social humanitarianism, a pragmatic temper, respect for opinions of the laity, common organizational forms, similar architecture and considerable movement among different denominations for the sake of convenience. But what do these two approaches have to do with the ecumenicism already described? Very little at all, it seems.

A fifth of the Protestant laity have never even heard of the National Council of Churches. An overwhelming majority of those who have looked favorably on its work and goals (Johnson and Cornell, 1972:108). About half of American Protestants are in favor of the merger of all Protestant denominations into one body. There is some slight variation among the denominations in the support given to merger movements (Kelley, 1972:346):

PERCENTAGE ANSWERING "YES" TO THE QUESTION, "WOULD YOU LIKE TO SEE ALL PROTESTANTS UNITED IN ONE DENOMINATION?"

Baptist	Episcopalian	Methodist	Congregationalist	Sectarian
56	47	58	49	30

There are no surprises in this table: of the groups represented, those closest to the theological "middle" show the greater willingness, and those groups located at either end of the spectrum, both liberal and conservative, show the least. Kelley found that there was much more scepticism about the possibility of true ecumenicism among different faiths, as the following table shows:

RESPONSES TO THE STATEMENT, "UNITY AMONG PROTESTANTS, ROMAN CATHOLICS AND EASTERN ORTHODOX CHURCHES WILL ALWAYS BE IMPOSSIBLE"

	Bapt.	*Episc.*	*Meth.*	*Congreg.*	*Sectarian*	*Jew*	*Cath.*
Disagree	19	33	32	30	22	12	48
Agree	64	43	47	48	72	54	30
Don't Know	17	24	21	22	6	34	22
	100						

Theological position thus makes a bigger difference in attitudes toward interfaith ecumenicism. The more theologically liberal church members are likely to be more in favor of moves toward unity. In line with this general liberalism, supporters of ecumenicism in both the Protestant and Catholic faiths are also likely to favor involvement of the church in social and political affairs (Kelley, 1971:8).

More practical considerations govern the clergyman's support for ecumenicism. The "eventual union" of all Protestant denominations receives the support of only 29 percent of Quinley's (1974:91) sample of California clergymen. However, 60 percent said they would favor the merger of their local church with one of another denomination if this became financially necessary. Ecumenical support of this rather practical kind emanates from the younger clergy in both the Protestant (Hadden, 1969:58) and Catholic (Fichter, 1968:40) faiths.

Ecumenical activity among ministers themselves seems to be rather uncommon. Lenski (1963:290), reporting before Vatican II, records little contact or cooperation among the clergy of different churches in Detroit. "Only 19% of the white Protestant clergy and 5% of the Negro Protestant clergy said they had spoken with any member of the Catholic clergy during the preceding month. Only 16% of the Catholic clergy reported conversations with a Protestant minister." No contacts were reported between Catholic priests and Jewish rabbis. Since Vatican II, the practice of admitting Catholic priests to state and local councils of churches has spread. For example, a 1972 survey of Chicago's Catholic priests found 68 percent of them participating in local ministerial organizations (Sweetser, 1972:31). However, there is little evidence on just how far this practice has spread, or how effective it is as an ecumenical tool.[5]

[5]None of the branches of Judaism have joined in the ecumenical movement (Glazer, 1972:158).

Not very much is known about the attitudes of laypeople in England toward ecumenicism. It is certain that a major impediment to ecumenicism in England is the established position of the Church of England, whose top functionaries are political appointees. Many non-Anglicans feel that union is impossible while this connection endures.

As in the United States, the clergy in England tend to favor ecumenicism more than the laity. Voting in the 1972 Church of England General Synod showed that 63 percent of the House of Laity favored eventual Protestant/Catholic union, compared with 66 percent of the clergy and 85 percent of the bishops (Paul, 1973:195). Not surprisingly, High Church Anglicans favor union with the Catholic Church the most; Broad Church Anglicans look in the opposite direction, toward the Methodists (Bryman, 1974:472). In general, ecumenicism receives substantial but not overwhelming support from the English people. Data from a 1967 survey show that 64 percent of the Anglicans and 58 percent of the Nonconformists support the idea of having one Protestant body. The same survey showed that 52 percent of the Anglicans and 62 percent of the Catholics approved of negotiations to end interfaith differences (Brothers, 1971:48).

IS ECUMENICISM A RESPONSE TO SECULARIZATION?

The existence of a powerful ecumenical movement that is helping reshape Western religion cannot be denied. The formation of the various national councils of churches and, later, the World Council of Churches, as well as the many mergers that have taken place since 1900, show that the denominations within Protestantism, and (less rapidly) Protestants and Catholics, are moving closer together. Only Judaism has divorced itself from the movement. Among both clergy and laity there is considerable support for moves toward union.

The question of whether or not ecumenicism is actually a response to secularization remains to be answered. Ecumenicism does seem to function in this way in the United Kingdom. The Methodist reunion of the 1930s, the negotiations between Anglicans and Methodists during the 1960s, and the merger of the Congregationalists and Presbyterians in 1972 seem to have been prompted by a sense of the declining numerical strength of each denomination and the need to operate more efficiently and economically in the face of this decline. It is frequently debated whether the denominations are declining because they are ecumenical (on the grounds that the rather bland result of merger is unappealing) or whether they are ecumenical because they are declining. In all probability, neither position is correct: both ecumenicism and decline are "symptoms of an underlying process which makes for diminishing effectiveness in gaining and retaining members while it also, more or less independently, creates a receptivity to possibilities of co-operation with other groups. . . ." (Kelley, 1972:97).

In the United States, it is not as clear that ecumenicism is a response to secularization. Church membership in America has increased during the period of federation and merger at a faster rate than it did during the nineteenth century. There is no correlation between declining membership and mergers. The Depression, for example, which caused a downturn in membership, did not stimulate ecumenicism. Indeed, poorer attendance rates and the desire of denominations to keep church functionaries in their jobs seemed to intensify denominational rivalries (Cavert, 1970:59).

The waxing and waning of the rate of mergers seems to have had less to do with the rise and fall of membership and more to do with changing sentiments regarding pluralism. The United States has undergone periodic intensifications of nativism, during which the urge to unite and eliminate denominational boundaries (especially if these are drawn along ethnic lines) has increased. The strength of ecumenicism is related not as much to absolute membership numbers as to changes in the importance attached to subgroup identities. There is no necessary cumulative development in this process as the secularization model would suggest, and associating mergers with periods of nativism makes it possible to account for ecumenicalism even if overall membership remains constant, or even rises.

Ecumenicism is certainly a form of adjustment by the denominations, but there are ways of looking at this strategy other than as a response to institutional weakness. First, it is possible that the pre-1960s mergers were typically sought as a means of greater institutional power and economic rationality, not because the concerned denominations felt weaker, but because they had come increasingly under the domination of bureaucrats for whom development and success are measured in precisely those terms. Mergers among denominations, as in business, are just another way to grow.

Second, it might well be that ecumenicism is a class movement, that it reflects a social division between mainstream Protestantism and the evangelical lower classes. The National Council of Churches has consistently sought to enforce a liberal, middle class social policy on its members. Significantly, not only have conservative denominations such as the Southern Baptists refused to join the NCC, but an opposing body, the National Association of Evangelicals, has arisen to regroup the fundamentalist denominations. Much of the work done by the various interdenominational agencies can be seen, as much as anything else, as a way of effecting political and theological alignments. The liberal activism of the NCC during the 1960s alienated many of the more conservative church members, and income began to decline sharply in 1969, forcing cutbacks in staff and closer attention to the complaints of donors who had withheld or reduced support. Conservatives and liberals in each denomination use the agencies to strengthen their overall position within the Protestant community. The liberals in one denomination, through the work of liberal agencies, feel closer to the liberals in another denomination than to the conservatives in their own. No doubt some of the comity arrangements *have* been inspired by strategic weaknesses within separate denominations in, say, a new community. But the secularization model does not seem to be very useful in explaining ecumenicism in the United States as a whole. The ecumenical movement in the United States, though possibly inspired to some extent by a seige mentality, is also much more aggressive and self-confident, and is built more upon the image of the business trust than ecumenicism in England with its sectarian self-image.

OTHER RESPONSES TO SECULARIZATION

The most typical response of the mainstream denominations to the rationalization of society has been to exploit the bureaucratic and technological developments associated with it in the interests of remaining relevant, useful, and expansionary. Not all of the denominations have gone about this in the same way, but some of the more popular options can be listed:

1. Denominations have become increasingly bureaucratized, mainly in the interests of recruitment and fund raising, and have come to resemble closely business corporations or government agencies (see Winter, 1968; Paul, 1973).

2. A process of "de-structuration" has taken place—a "deliberate process of abandoning old forms and procedures," such as discarding traditional dress, modernizing liturgies, and adopting new symbols (Wilson, 1976:85).

3. Religion has become increasingly personalized. The denomination preaching an evangelical religion that places overwhelming emphasis on personal morality and stresses freedom of religious choice and the responsibility of each individual for the state of his soul has become increasingly popular. This has furthered the process whereby religion withdraws from the public, institutional sphere and becomes located entirely within the private, individual sphere. The continued popularity of the intensely individualistic "positive thinking" Christian literature further enhances this personalism. Individual achievement, for some, and the Ark, for others, are the most important contemporary symbols. Religion continues to provide a context of meaning for the individual,

satisfying needs for comfort and reassurance, but it has ceased to function as a basis for social cohesion and integration.

4. Many denominations have formulated a situational ethics which contrasts with the old legalism. Designed to shift the Church closer to secular views on ethical behavior, situation ethics stresses the importance of social contexts and the relativity of ethical systems.

5. The denominations have involved themselves more and more in ameliorative reform in an attempt to keep abreast of changing society. However, they have been relegated to a supporting role in reform efforts, and the kind of reform about which they have been most enthusiastic has been that designed to free the individual to better compete as an individual. Thus, the lot of the poor, blacks, and women is thought to be improved if restraints on their freedom and inequalities of opportunity are swept away. The denominations harness the image of "God's New Israel," but in an evolutionary way. The improved future will be more of the same.

6. Finally, some of the denominations have responded to social change by a strategy of purification, a return to simple, basic principles in teaching and liturgy—an attempt to gain strength by the adoption of a more "sectarian" posture. Kelley (1972) argues that in the secular climate of the late 1960s this strategy seemed to work best. The more theologically conservative denominations refused to compete with secular organizations, shunned mergers with more liberal organizations, and avoided bureaucratizing their administration. Instead, they concentrated on the one "product" they could offer that secular organizations could not—salvation. In this they seemed to be successful, for while the more liberal denominations (who did choose to compete, with their own social action programs) lost members, the more conservative denominations (who went back to first principles) picked up members.

Most of these strategies—a mixture of rolling with the punches, aggressive exploitation of secularity, and direct challenge to rationalization—are in themselves rationalizing. They show the denominations fighting and coping with rationalization in highly rational terms. They are chiefly adaptive reactions. However, they do not exhaust the range of responses, nor do they promise to be very significant as alternatives to rationalization. To find alternatives, we must return to where this book began—in the religious underground.

THE NEW RELIGIOUS CONSCIOUSNESS

The more profound religious responses to rationalization take the form of social movements and sectarian groups, the members of which see themselves as engaged in a reformation of consciousness. These movements are in fact part of the general movement of reaction against some of the crises and contradictions of modernity, the chief of which are the following:

1. The rationalization of means, and the expansion of wealth to which it leads, does not necessarily lead to an increase in happiness. In fact, it might well lead to a lowering in the quality of life through pollution, resource scarcity, and nuclear war.
2. The domination of nature and fellow beings in the interests of pure instrumentalism, the repressive control of technical reason, is not self-evidently good. Science and technology pose serious threats to the autonomy of the individual and his sense of freedom.
3. Social inequities exist amidst affluence and abundant, productive capacities, despite a rhetoric of justice and freedom.

The mainstream denominations have been aware of some of these crises, but their response has remained firmly within the world view responsible for them. However, there has been a response that offers a fundamental challenge to the utilitarian individualism and technical reason causing these crises. There has been a movement away from future-oriented individualism and toward a search for meaning in the present, in which heavy emphasis is placed on subjective experience. This is manifest, for example, in the neo-Pentecostal revolt against reason, expertise, scholarship, formal training, and education. Although there is a privatism here, there is also a fundamental critique of American institutions. There is a belief in the unity of all beings, a sense of unity between the divine and the human that runs counter to the individualism of the utilitarian system. There is a faith that "nature, social relationships, and personal feelings [can] now be treated as ends rather than means, [can] be liberated from the repressive control of technical reason" (Bellah, 1976:338). In this movement, which draws partly on Eastern philosophies, "the distinction between a natural realm and a supernatural realm fades to make way for a more multiplex concept of reality which can contain many kinds of reality. The traditional emphasis upon dogma and Biblical revelation is replaced by an emphasis upon personal religious experience" (Wuthnow, 1976b:85).

Groups that espouse these kinds of belief are not trying to modernize the churches; they wish to escape modernity. Because the mainstream denominations have lost their place as the locus of imaginative advance, because they have lost their legitimation as a means of finding the new (this function is now popularly ascribed to the artist or the scientist), a liberation from the contradictions of modernization will emanate only from the marginal groups that espouse a truly prophetic religion. It is they, and only they, who hold out a promise for fresh religious insights and for fresh and liberating knowledge.

Will this promise be fulfilled? This is impossible to say, but there are a number of reasons why one should be skeptical about the transformative potential of this new religious consciousness.

1. In view of the extensive media coverage of groups such as Scientology, Hare Krishna, and the Children of God, their membership remains very small. Even in the San Francisco Bay area, where these groups have been most active and where there is a highly receptive population, only about one in four have ever heard of them, and of those few who *had* heard of them, no more than 13 percent were attracted to them (Wuthnow, 1976b:269). It *is* worth noting that most of those attracted to such movements tend to be young and well educated (Wuthnow, 1976b:287). It is no bar to the future consequences of such movements that their present membership is small because, of course, all transformative movements have had small beginnings. However, it is also true that many young people spend a period of their lives in religious experimentation, only to return to the denomination of their origin. To say that small beginnings do not necessarily betoken failure assumes that the way religion promoted social change in the past will continue. But this assumption is not warranted—which is the second reason for us to be skeptical about these movements.

2. The idea that fringe groups in modern societies contain the seeds of significant social change follows from the knowledge that religious movements have done this in the past. But the West "appears to have passed beyond the point at which religious teaching and practice can exercise formative influence over whole societies, or any significant segment of them" (Wilson, 1976:96). The fringe groups may well signify little more than transient and volatile gestures of defiance toward the prevailing trend of secularization.

3. There is also reason to be skeptical of the transformative potential of the new religious consciousness simply because it seems to present no real challenge to prevailing modes of thought. The new religious movements

> are not so much the progenitors of a counter-culture, as random anti-cultural assertions. What is called the "counter-culture" is indeed little more than a range of phenomena from the hippies, flower people, speed freaks, Jesus people, Hare Krishna devotees, and the rest, who do not represent a culture at all, but just congeries of options in a plural society—a diverse set of options "out" (Wilson, 1976:110).

In their intense individualism, the new religious movements seem to stand not only against the prevailing culture but against all culture. They are yet another manifestation of "the highly privatised preference that reduces religion to the significance of pushpin, poetry and popcorn" and add nothing to the prospective reintegration of society around a new set of values (Wilson, 1976:96). The sects which draw on Christian teachings offer a sense of community, participation, and euphoria not present in the more formal denominations. But there is nothing here to challenge the established order. Poor organization, limited resources and privatism combine with small membership to render them socially ineffective in the here and now, whatever their ultimate fate.

4. Finally, it has to be recognized that marginal religious groups have never been the sole cause of radical change. The effectiveness of the fringe groups has been greatly diminished by the loss of the sense of transcendence in everyday life. This loss has occurred because the shared sentiments and affective ties people have are diffuse and weak. Perhaps a renewal of a sense of transcendence will come about only when these ties are renewed, but until then, these groups must remain on the margin. It is their religious message, combined with reconstituted social relationships, that is the condition for change.

APPENDIX

THE MEASUREMENT
OF RELIGIOSITY

INTRODUCTION

The increasingly technical problem of measuring religiosity deserves a separate discussion. Throughout this book, problems of measurement have cropped up. Frequently, uncertainty about the relation of religion to some other aspect of social life has been reduced to the question, "What do you mean by religion?" Common terms such as "preference," "identification," "affiliation," and "membership" are used to indicate religiosity, and simple and superficial signs of religiosity, such as church attendance, are made to stand for the total religious experience. Yet it is common sense that these terms mean different things. "While questions of 'membership' refer largely to formal institutional affiliation and social allegiance, questions of 'preference' may refer more to personal orientations of values and beliefs, which would not necessarily coincide with existing institutional membership" (Finner, 1970:273). An individual may clearly be religious in one sense and not in another. For example, church yearbooks show that 60 percent of the American population are members of a church, but opinion pollsters find that between 95 percent and 97 percent of the population have a religious preference. Similar discrepancies exist between attendance and membership (see Bultena, 1949).

The misleading character of measurements of religiosity has been recognized for a long time. Figures provided by denominations have always been unreliable. At first, this was due to lack of techniques and resources, but modern churches have failed to avail themselves of sophisticated enumeration methods. Furthermore, the pressure to show growth in membership leads some denominations to inflate their numbers. Others keep no membership records at all—or at least none they make public. Survey researchers have done little better: often, their survey of religious groups is incomplete. But the chief reason for poor measurement is the kind of question asked, which is usually confined to a simple identification question, with perhaps an attendance frequency question thrown in as well.

These are the technical difficulties. There are also conceptual problems. Many denominations are not specific about what kind of commitment is to count as membership. The Church of England, for instance, does not specify whether membership includes (1) those who have been baptized, (2) those who have been confirmed, (3) those who have received Holy Communion at least three times in the past year, (4) those who are on the Electoral Roll, or some combination of these. The Catholic Church, like the Church of England, has a broad, inclusive definition of membership that embraces many different degrees of religious commitment. The other denominations tend to be more exclusive in their ideas about who is and who is not a member, but they are not assiduous in their maintenance of membership rolls, and departed members are not conscientiously pruned from them. Furthermore, it is not unknown for denominations to change their conception of what it means to be a member. For example, the surge in church membership in the United States between 1890 and 1910 was due to no religious revival, but to the fact that several denominations admitted children onto the membership rolls for the first time.

Measuring religiosity with only one index is obviously misleading. So too is using the same index in different settings as if it means the same thing. For example, the significance of churchgoing varies from one denomination to another. Catholics tend to be more church-oriented than most Protestants. Regular worship-service attendance, going to Mass, making confession, and other church-related rituals are central to their faith. But the fact that they attend church more frequently than the average Protestant does not mean they are more religious, but only that they are religious in a different way.

A measurement of religion must also tap ways of being religious that are not tied closely to institutional religion. There are many ways of being religious other than by joining a denomination or attending church regularly. There is widespread agreement, among church members and non-members alike, that neither lack of membership nor non-attendance betokens irreligion (Campbell and Fukuyama, 1970:61; Sissons, 1973:162).

> Irrespective . . . of whether or not they themselves take much part in organised religious activities, people do not necessarily seem to think that a man who only goes to church or chapel on special occasions is therefore, and for that reason alone, unlikely to hold perfectly orthodox Christian beliefs; nor do they always feel that the assiduous church- or chapel-goer is necessarily more "religious" than those who hardly ever visit a place of worship (Gorer, 1965:85).

It comes as no surprise, then, to learn that of those who identify themselves as Catholics, 38 percent do not receive Holy Communion every month, 4 percent are not in the habit of making their Easter duty, and 13 percent report having missed Mass at least once during the four previous Sundays (Moberg, 1971:556).

Religion is clearly not a homogeneous whole. Individuals who are religious in one respect might not be in another. This is convincing evidence that religion is multidimensional. The gradual recognition of this fact, and concerted efforts to identify and measure these dimensions, represents one of the most significant advances in the recent sociology of religion.

THE DIMENSIONS OF RELIGION

Formal attempts to list and measure the dimensions of religiosity began to appear in the 1960s. In 1961, Fukuyama (1961) proposed a fourfold classification of religiosity, consisting of organizational activity, doctrinal knowledge, doctrinal adherence, and extent of involvement in extrachurch life. About the same time, Lenski (1963) was engaged in a secondary analysis of Detroit-Area survey data in which he used four dimensions: *associationalism*, or frequency of attendance at corporate worship services; *communalism*, which was measured by religious endogamy and choice of friends by religion; *orthodoxy* of belief, measured by acceptance of the prescribed doctrines of the Judeo-Christian faith; and *devotionalism*, which means private prayer and reference to the Divine in making everyday decisions. Lenski's dimensions, particularly the distinction between communal and associational religion, have proved very useful. But the study of the dimensionality of religion has been influenced most by the work of Glock and Stark (1965). They note the similarities between their scheme and Lenski's. They propose a ritualism dimension that parallels Lenski's associational dimension; they suggest an experiential dimension much like Lenski's devotionalism; and their belief dimension is identical to his. However, unlike either Lenski or Fukuyama, they formulate a knowledge dimension. On the other hand, whereas the two earlier authors obviously feel the communal side of religion is important, Glock and Stark ignore this. Glock and Stark's scheme of dimension is frequently used and much discussed. It is therefore worth examining in detail.

The *experiential* dimension of religiosity is "all those feelings, perceptions and sensations which are experienced by an actor or defined by a religious group as involving some communication, however slight, with a divine essence" (Glock and Stark, 1965:20). In a later work (Stark and Glock, 1968:43–66), the authors describe this dimension in more detail, giving some examples:

1. The confirming experience: a sudden feeling, knowing, or intuition that one's beliefs are true. This can take the form of a generalized sense of sacredness (as felt during ritual) or a specific awareness of the presence of the divinity (as felt when alone with nature).
2. The responsive experience: a feeling that the divine has taken specific notice of one's existence, as in the feeling of having been saved, having undergone a miraculous cure, or having been divinely protected from some disaster.
3. The ecstatic experience: a feeling of deep intimacy with the Holy (often with sexual overtones), which may be likened to possession or intoxication, and may take the form of seizures.
4. The revelational experience: the sense of having been taken into the confidence of the Deity or of being tuned to the infinite.

The *belief* dimension means more than simply the sheer number of beliefs assented to. There has been a tendency, beginning with Lenski's formulation of orthodoxy, to use orthodox Judeo-Christian tenets as the base line in measuring this dimension, a person being considered more religious the closer his beliefs approximate those tenets. Stark and Glock follow this rule. They include statements of the following kind, strong assent to which means a high score on the belief dimension.

1. I believe in a personal God.
2. I am absolutely sure that God exists.
3. Jesus was not mortal.
4. I believe in miracles.
5. I believe that there is life after death.
6. I believe in the existence of the Devil.
7. I believe a child is born into the world already guilty of sin.
8. I believe that faith in Christ as Savior is absolutely necessary to salvation.

9. The Bible is God's truth.
10. Receiving Holy Baptism, Holy Communion, church membership, and regular prayers are essential to salvation.

The proposition is that the greater the proportion of these beliefs held, and the more firmly they are held, the more accurate it is to describe the individual as religious. There are obvious difficulties in using these items to measure the belief dimension. It could be argued that they measure only how good (that is, how orthodox) a Christian individual is. It is possible for a Congregationalist, or even a Christian Scientist, not to mention a Buddhist, to disagree with these statements and still have strong religious beliefs. *Some* measure of belief is obviously necessary, but it is questionable that the measure can be as content-specific as the list of items given by Stark and Glock. This is a difficult issue and will be taken up again below.

The *ritual* dimension measures more than simple attendance at worship services. The kind of items included under this heading are:

1. church attendance
2. watching religious services on television or hearing them on the radio
3. attendance at Holy Communion or the Lord's Supper
4. attendance at midweek services or study groups
5. financial support
6. saying grace at meal times
7. Bible reading
8. private prayer

The main problems with this kind of list are that it says nothing about how these various activities fit together—they are not all of equal importance to people of different denominations—and it says nothing about how the meaning of these activities varies from one individual to another. However, as long as these shortcomings are borne in mind, the necessity of some such list has to be acknowledged.

The *knowledge* dimension is independent of the belief dimension, although they both concern the ideational side of religion. It is possible to believe without having extensive knowledge, and it is possible to know without believing. The measurement of the knowledge dimension usually involves some kind of simple test, most often scriptural knowledge, but sometimes also of church history. Stark and Glock's scheme measures knowledge of the Ten Commandments, the correct identification of the Old Testament prophets from a list of biblical names, and the correct identification of statements as being from the Bible.

Lenski found that many social variables (such as degree of racial prejudice) were affected more by communal than by associational religiosity. Nevertheless, Stark and Glock (1968) do not suggest a communal dimension, although, curiously, they did write a chapter on the church as a "moral community," which seems to suggest the same thing. For example, they seek to measure the extent of an individual's friendship ties within the congregation, the proportion of an individual's friends who are fellow church members, and the extent to which an individual's voluntary-association memberships are confined to church-related associations. In other words, like Lenski, they are trying to measure how much an individual's religion constitutes a community for him. It seems that Stark and Glock are aware of the importance of communalism, but do not consider it a dimension of religiosity equal to belief and practice.

Stark and Glock (1968:179) conclude that belief is the most important dimension of religion, on the grounds that it has the highest average intercorrelation with the other indexes. But it is important to remember that the dimensions are nevertheless independent of one another. Although a correlation of .70 is considered necessary to suggest that two dimensions are measuring the same thing, the highest intercorrelation reported is .57. The independence of the dimensions is confirmed by factor analysis, in which it was found that no "item had its maximum loading on a factor in which an item from another dimension also had its maximum loading" (Stark and Glock, 1968:181).

If these are the dimensions of religion, how are they to be measured? This question can be answered only by looking at actual questionnaire items and at the construction of indexes. It is not possible to follow this exercise completely, but some idea of the more important suggestions for specific item-measures for each dimension can be gained by looking at Faulkner and DeJong's (1966) study. The following items measure commitment on the various dimensions. *Each item is expressed in the fashion that indicates the strongest religiosity*, although on the questionnaire each consists of a scale ranging from strong to weak religiosity.

1. *Ideological*
   a. The world will come to an end according to God's will.
   b. The deity is a Divine God, creator of the universe, who knows my innermost thoughts and feelings, and to whom one day I shall be accountable.
   c. God's forgiveness comes only after repentence.
   d. God acts and continues to act in the history of mankind.
   e. The Bible is God's word, and all it says is true.

2. *Intellectual*
   a. The story of creation as recorded in Genesis is literally true.
   b. I believe the report of miracles in the Bible; that is, they occurred through a setting aside of the natural laws by a higher power.
   c. Religious truth is higher than any other form of truth.
   d. Name at least three of the four Gospels.

3. *Ritualism*
   a. It is impossible for an individual to develop a well-rounded religious life apart from the institutional church.

   b. I spend more than one hour a week reading the Bible.
   c. I have attended at least three of the past four Sabbath worship services.
   d. Prayer is a regular part of my behavior.
   e. A marriage ceremony should be performed only by a religious official.
4. *Experiential*
   a. My religious commitment gives to my life a purpose it would not other-wise have.
   b. I frequently or occasionally feel close to the Divine.
   c. Religion offers me a sense of security in the face of death that would not otherwise be possible.
   d. Religion provides me with an interpretation of this existence that could not be discovered by reason alone.
   e. Faith, meaning putting full confidence in the things we hope for and being certain of things we cannot see, is essential to one's religious life.

5. *Consequences*
   a. Nonessential businesses should not be open on the Sabbath.
   b. Sexual intercourse before marriage is wrong.
   c. It is better to vote for a political candidate who is affiliated with a religious organization.
   d. Cheating on your income tax is wrong.

Faulkner and DeJong administered these items to a sample of college students in the North. Like Stark and Glock, they found that (1) the dimensions were independent of one another; (2) they were positively related; and (3) the belief dimension was the most important. Clayton (1968) replicated Faulkner and DeJong's study using students from the South who were attending more religious colleges, and confirmed the earlier findings. Using roughly comparable dimensions, Campbell and Fukuyama (1970) surveyed members of the United Church. They too found the dimensions to be independent and positively related; they also found the belief dimension to be the most important. Amalgamating the schemes of Glock and Stark (1965) and Lenski (1963), Kersten (1970:53) arrived at identical conclusions. Finney (1970:277) found that the dimensions emerged with particular clarity among those who not only declared a religious preference but were also church members. There is considerable evidence, then, that religion is multidimensional and that certain dimensions of religion consistently appear.

SOME PROBLEMS WITH THE MEASUREMENT OF RELIGIOUS DIMENSIONS

Despite this apparent success in uncovering dimensions of religion, there is widespread recognition that severe problems attend the use of this type of measurement.

1. The most important dimension is obviously that of belief—it occurs with the most frequency and has the most internal consistency. However, this fact may be misleading, on two counts. First, the studies

cited above have been confined to Jews and Christians, two faiths in which religious belief is central; it is not clear how generalizable these results are to faiths in which experience or ritual are paramount. Second, the items used to measure belief do not measure belief in general but rather closeness to Judeo-Christian orthodoxy. It is not surprising, then, that Southern Baptists score higher on the belief dimension that members of the United Church. This hardly indicates that members of the United Church are less religious than Southern Baptists; it merely suggests that they believe something different. Clearly, measuring belief makes sense only when the content-specific nature of the items is made perfectly plain. It is inconceivable that the same items could measure strength of belief in widely separate religious traditions.

2. Stark and Glock and Faulkner and DeJong all recognize that the *salience* of beliefs is as important as their number, but they do not provide any way of measuring it.

3. There are serious questions about the face validity of the items used by Faulkner and DeJong (1966) and Clayton (1968) to measure the knowledge, ritual and experience dimensions. They seem to measure not actual knowledge, practice, and experience but beliefs *about* these aspects of religion (see Weigert and Thomas, 1969). For example, under the heading of knowledge, Faulkner and DeJong include "I believe in the report of miracles in the Bible." Under the heading of ritualism is included "Do you feel it is possible for an individual to develop a well-rounded religious life apart from the church?" Under the heading of experience, respondents, instead of being required to report actual experiences, are asked how important or how highly valued such experiences are. Admittedly, dimensions such as experience and ritual are hard to measure, and it *is* useful to have information about how much people value this side of religion, but reports about experiences cannot substitute for the actual experiences.

4. The assumption underlying these schemes is that the dimensions, though independent, should intercorrelate. Using Faulkner and DeJong's own data, Cardwell (1971) has shown that this is more the case with some denominations than with others. The dimensions, when highly intercorrelated, add up to a measure of Catholicism, in Cardwell's opinion. Of course, this means that those who are furthest away from the Catholic faith are judged less religious. This raises serious questions about how well the multidimensional scheme can be used to compare different denominations.

5. The belief dimension looms large in all the studies cited above. This has led some to argue that religion is not multidimensional at all, but consists merely of different ramifications of a central belief dimension. In a large-scale study of college students, Clayton and Gadden (1974:140), using factor analysis to cluster the items suggested by Faulk-

ner and DeJong, found that four dimensions factored out—belief, knowledge, ritual, and experience. However, the belief dimension alone accounted for 83 percent of the variance. They conclude that knowing an individual's score on the belief dimension is a safe way of predicting his position on the other dimensions. They suggest that more work be done on refining the belief dimension than on developing others. Their position is supported by Gibbs and Crader (1970) who, in reanalyzing Glock and Stark's original data, found that the intercorrelations between dimensions were so high as to suggest that the different dimensions were all measuring the same thing. Their position is contradicted, however, by Longino and Hadden (1976) who, in factor-analyzing the belief dimension alone, found no internal variation, based on the items normally used.

6. In their original version of the religious dimensions, Glock and Stark suggested a consequences dimension, which would identify the effects of religiosity on an individual's day-to-day life, not only because the idea of "works" is important theologically, but also because ethics are thought to be an essential part of religion. In their 1968 version, however, Stark and Glock (1968:16) dropped this dimension on the grounds that "it is not entirely clear the extent to which religious consequences are a part of religious commitment or simply follow from it." The status of this dimension is unclear at the present time. and this is a problem that will be taken up again in the conclusion.

Although there are many critics of Glock and Stark's dimensions, few advocate a return to one-dimensional concepts of religion. Most propose dimensions of their own (see, for example, Fichter, 1969; O'Dea, 1970; Lazerwitz, 1973; Maranell, 1974; Davidson, 1975; Himmelfarb, 1975). All these schemes overlap, and the intended improvements are far from obvious. All of the authors seem to be saying much the same kind of thing, but how the pie is sliced and where individual item-measures are placed varies widely. "Different authors used different labels for tantalisingly similar ideas; and similar labels for different ideas" (King and Hunt, 1972:8). This kind of confusion has led some sociologists to abandon the more intuitive method begun by Glock and Stark and to suggest a method that seems to allow the facts to speak more clearly for themselves—the factor-analytic method.

THE FACTOR-ANALYTIC METHOD OF DISCOVERING RELIGIOUS DIMENSIONS

Factor analysis is one method of escaping the biases that are built into the multidimensional approach. The hazard of intuiting dimensions, and then formulating items to measure these dimensions, is that they will be "found," whether or not they are there. The advantage of factor analysis is that the location of items that correlate more highly with each other than with all the items as a whole is not influenced by the intuitive ideas of the researcher. Factor analysis is a technique for determining how much various items hang together and can be treated the same for the purposes of measurement. It is a way of locating and identifying fundamental properties underlying whatever tests, scales, and measures are used to investigate a phenomenon. A factor is to be seen as a strictly hypothetical entity rather than as something objective and real. For example, through factor analysis of intelligence tests, it is possible to see that underlying intelligence are a number of factors, such as verbal ability and numerical ability, that are related but independent. Of course, only those items can cluster together that are actually included in the study, and this is the decision of the investigator. Moreover, once factors have emerged, their naming and interpretation must also be carried out. But this method does seem to leave less room for seeing only what one wants to see in the items.

The factor analysis of religious dimensions owes most to the work of King and Hunt. In a series of studies (King, 1967; King, 1969; King and Hunt, 1972; King and Hunt, 1975), they have factor-analyzed responses to many questionnaire items. These items have been drawn from various sources—the work of Lenski and Glock and Stark, the suggestions of clergy and laypeople, other sociological surveys, pretest questionnaires, the authors' own reading, and church experiences. The repeated surveys more or less confirm one another, providing a list of, not five, but eight, separate dimensions.

These dimensions, reported fully in King and Hunt (1972), together with the number of items included within each dimension and an example of an item, are as follows:

1. *Creedal assent*: consisting of seven items, such as "I believe in eternal life." This dimension is similar in many ways to Lenski's orthodoxy and Glock and Stark's belief dimensions, but the authors claim that it lacks the bias of previous schemes toward the liberal-fundamentalist axis.
2. *Devotionalism:* comprises five items, such as "How often do you pray privately in places other than the church?" This dimension is similar to Lenski's devotionalism dimension and constitutes part of Glock's practice dimension.
3. *Congregational involvement:* consists of church attendance, organizational activity, and financial support.
4. *Knowledge:* basically a list of test items, such as correctly identifying the Old Testament prophets from a set of names.
5. *Orientation to religion:* not so much a way of being religious as an orientation toward religion and the Church. Two subdimensions are distinguishable:
   a. Growth and striving: made up of six items, such as "I try hard to grow in understanding of what it means to live as a child of God."

     b. Extrinsic religiosity: consists of five items, such as "Church membership has helped me to meet the right kinds of people."
6. *Salience:* consists of two subdimensions:
     a. Behavior: comprises seven items, such as "How often in the last year have you shared with another church member the problems and joys of trying to live a life of faith in God?"
     b. Cognition: made up of five items, such as "My religious beliefs are what really lie behind my whole approach to life."

Although the use of a different method has certainly added to the complexity of the concept of religiosity, not too much is new about the factor-analytic scheme, except perhaps in regard to emphasis. Creedal assent, devotionalism, congregational involvement, and knowledge all tap long-recognized aspects of religiosity. An orientation-to-religion factor has been anticipated by those critics of previous schemes who suggest, for example, that not only amount of knowledge but also the attitude toward knowledge itself is integral to religiosity. The "extrinsic" subdimension is a nice substantiation of the view of many commentators that there is a very important "social" side to modern religiosity. Finally, even Glock and Stark in their original formulation raise the question of saliency, and here it establishes itself as an independent factor.

At the present time, there is no way of judging whether or not the factor-analytic method is the preferable method of formulating religious dimensions. Like the other approaches, this one has attendant problems. First of all, the factor-analytic method will be only as good as the items included in it, and these are the product of the individual researcher. For example, there seems to be consensus among users of a variety of methods that regular, frequent private prayers to which importance is attached and which are thought to produce results are a sure sign of high religiosity, but the wording, scaling, and positioning of an item that will measure this remains problematic. Second, most of the studies that have used the factor-analytic method have been confined to church members. This has the result of virtually eliminating church activity and the importance given to church membership as a variable. But it has a more important consequence, which is to increase the likelihood that respondents to surveys will make subtle distinctions, especially if the investigator provides them with the opportunity for doing so, because it is among church members that such sophistication is to be expected (Dittes, 1969:610). Keene (1967a; 1967b) substantiates this criticism. In a study of Baha'i members alone, he found that there appear to be five dimensions of religiosity, which closely resemble those of Glock and Stark. Later, in a study embracing not only Baha'i but also Jews, Catholics, and Protestants, as well as those not affiliated with any church at all, he found that there emerged a single factor on which a whole cluster of items loaded, and a number of smaller factors that trailed off.

These findings suggest that whenever a small homogeneous sample is used, a number of small factors will emerge; when a large diverse sample is used, a large principal factor will appear. Nudelman's (1971) analysis of Stark and Glock's (1968) data seems to support this contention. Using data from Stark and Glock's large, diverse sample and employing the factor-analytic technique on the original items, regardless of dimension, Nudelman found only two factors. One, which he called "devotion," included items of private prayer, belief, and experience, and accounted for 50 percent of the variance. Another, which he called "participation," included measures of communalism, ritualism, and knowledge, and accounted for 26 percent of the variance. Once again, among factor analysts, as among those who employ more intuitive methods, there are those who question the multidimensionality of religion.

CONCLUSION

Only the most tentative conclusions can be drawn from this brief review of some of the attempts to construct a measure of religiosity:

1. The argument for multidimensionality is by no means won, but the weight of the evidence would seem to support it. Few now dispute the contention that there are several different "sides" to religion. There is, however, the feeling that belief is by far the most important dimension of the Judeo-Christian tradition of religion.

2. At the present time, there is no way of determining the respective merits of the intuitive and factor-analytic methods of discovering dimensions of religion. Indeed, there need be no resolution as long as a reasonable degree of congruence between them exists.

3. There is continuing debate over whether or not "consequences" is a dimension of religion or an effect of religion. On one side, it is argued that the consequences of religion cannot be included as part of religion because this would preclude asking questions about the impact of religion on social behavior. On the other side is the argument that many, if not most, religious groups include the extent of behavior change resulting from the acceptance of religious injunctions as an important measure of religiosity. An integral part of the Catholic religion, for example, is the connection between faith and morals: "this is what one believes, and this is how one acts in order to be a good Catholic" (Devine, 1975:78). However, it might be that these differences are more apparent than real. Both parties to this argument are interested chiefly in the relation between religious beliefs, practices, and experiences, on the one hand, and a person's behavior in other social contexts, on the other. Those who would seek to include consequences within religion are no less aware of the variable relation between, for example, beliefs (which

contain value statements and thereby imply a course of action) and consequences. Another kind of resolution to this dilemma is suggested by DeJong et al. (1976) who argue that individual consequences should be included as part of religion, and social consequences should be treated as the effect of religion.

4. Commitment to values is an important aspect of religion, yet is touched by none of the dimensions. Questions on values framed in a religious context should be explored as possible future items.

5. Whichever technique is used, there is still the strong suggestion in all the studies cited that it is really conformity to orthodox church religion that is being measured. The various techniques therefore make sense only within a given definition of what religion is, and this point should always be made clear.

It is hard for a person who reviews these studies of religiosity to escape the feeling that the property-space ideas about religion are not yet really settled. The whole idea of measurement connotes equal units and cumulativeness, yet the dimensions, however arrived at, seem to often to be a cluster of discrete items, themselves often scaled items that do not really add up. The process is like adding apples and oranges. As presently conceived, the dimensions would not appear to be true dimensions, in the sense of being a property amenable to a single measurement.

Verbit (1970) has pointed out that the dimensions presently employed should best be considered as components of religion, each of which, in turn, has a number of true dimensions. In other words, the idea of dimensions should suggest a way of measuring religiosity rather than a distinctive class of religious behaviors. Verbit therefore proposes that the existing dimensions—ritual, doctrine, emotion, knowledge, ethics, and community—be treated as components of religion (much like the elements in chemistry), each of which can be measured along four true dimensions—content, frequency, intensity, and centrality.

> "Content" refers to the specific elements of a person's religious repertoire: it betokens what he believes, feels, does, knows and joins. . . . "Frequency" refers to the *amounts* of various religious behaviours that an individual incorporates into his normal routines. . . . "Intensity" measures the degree of *determination* or consistency with which a man sticks to his position. . . . "centrality" has to do with the *importance* that a person attributes to a given act or tenet or feeling within the total religious system (Verbit, 1970:27).

Under this analytical scheme, any given religious behavior, such as private prayer, is first classified (for example, it might be included under ritual, but it could also be grouped under emotion if accompanied and given meaning by intense feelings) and then measured. It would be necessary to know, for instance, which prayers were said about what, how often and how regularly they were said, how strictly the individual adhered to prayer norms, and how important this act was to him. This kind of analysis is, of course, much more complex. The six components and four dimensions render up a twenty-four cell matrix, but this might well be what is necessary to properly conceptualize the phenomenon of religiosity and provide the researcher with an instrument subtle enough to allow for the many and varied manifestations of the religious spirit.

These studies must, of course, go on. Their true test, however, comes when they are employed to account for variation in religious and social behavior, and it is in this context that they must always be judged.

BIBLIOGRAPHY

ABERLE, DAVID. 1966. The Peyote Religion Among the Navaho. Chicago: Aldine Publishing Co.

ABRAMS, RAY. 1969. Preachers Present Arms: The Role of the American Churches and Clergy in World Wars I and II, with Some Observations on the War in Vietnam. Scottsdale, Pa.: Herald Press.

ABRAMSON, HAROLD. 1973. Ethnic Diversity in Catholic America. New York: John Wiley.
———. 1975. "The religioethnic factor and the American experience: Another look at the three-generation hypothesis." Ethnicity 2:163–77.

ADAMS, JAMES. 1970. The Growing Church Lobby in Washington. Grand Rapids, Mich.: Eerdmans.

ADORNO, THEODORE. 1974. "The stars down to Earth: The Los Angeles Times astrology column." Telos 19:13–90.

AHLSTROM, SYDNEY. [1972] 1975. A Religious History of the American People, 2 vols. Garden City, N.Y.: Doubleday, Image Books.

ALFRED, RANDALL. 1976. "The Church of Satan." Pp. 180–202 in Charles Glock and Robert Bellah (eds.), The New Religious Consciousness. Berkeley: University of California Press.

ALLEN, R. O. AND BERNARD SPILKA. 1967. "Committed and consensual religion: A specification of religion-prejudice relationships." Journal for the Scientific Study of Religion 6:191–206.

ALLINSMITH, W. AND B. ALLINSMITH. 1948. "Religious affiliation and political-economic attitudes." Public Opinion Quarterly 12:377–89.

ALLISON, J. 1969. "Religious conversion: Regression and progression in an adolescent experience." Journal for the Scientific Study of Religion 8:23–38.

ALLPORT, GORDON. 1966. "The religious context of prejudice." Journal for the Scientific Study of Religion 5:447–57.

ALSTON, JOHN. 1972a. "Review of the polls." Journal for the Scientific Study of Religion 11:180–86.

———1972b. "Religiosity and black militancy: A reappraisal." Journal for the Scientific Study of Religion 11:252–61.

ALSTON, JOHN, WILLIAM MCINTOSH, AND LOUISE WRIGHT. 1976. "Extent of interfaith marriage among white Americans." Sociological Analysis 37:261–64.

ANDERS, SARAH. 1955. "Religious behavior of church families." Marriage and Family Living 17:54–57.

ANDERSON, CHARLES. 1968. "Religious communality among white Protestants, Catholics and Mormons." Social Forces 46:501–8.

———1970. White Protestant Americans: From National Origins to Religious Group. Englewood Cliffs, N.J.: Prentice-Hall.

ANDERSON, DONALD. 1966. "Ascetic Protestantism and political preferences." Review of Religious Research 7:167–71.

ANDERSON, GRACE. 1966. "Voting behavior and the ethnic-religious variable: A study of a federal election in Hamilton, Ontario." Canadian Journal of Economics and Political Science 32:27–37.

APPEL, JOHN. 1970. "American Negro and immigrant experiences: Similarities and differences." Pp. 339–47 in Leonard Dinnerstein and Frederic Jaher (eds.), The Aliens: A History of Ethnic Minorities in America. New York: Appleton-Century-Crofts.

ARGYLE, MICHAEL AND BENJAMIN BEIT-HALLAHMI. 1975. The Social Psychology of Religion. Boston: Routledge & Kegan Paul.

ASHBROOK, JAMES. 1966. "The relationship of church members to church organization." Journal for the Scientific Study of Religion 5:397–420.

BABCHUK, NORMAN, HARRY CROCKETT, JR., AND JOHN BALLWEG. 1967. "Change in religious affiliation and family stability." Social Forces 45:551–55.

BAGGELEY, ANDREW. 1962. "Religious influences in Wisconsin voting, 1928–1960." American Political Science Review 56:66–70.

BAGLEY, CHRISTOPHER. 1970. "Relation of religion and racial prejudice in Europe." Journal for the Scientific Study of Religion 9:219–25.

BAHR, HOWARD. 1970. "Aging and religious disaffiliation." Social Forces 49:59–71.

BAILEY, DONALD. 1972. Factors Affecting Racial Attitudes and Overt Behavior of Seminary Trained Methodist Ministers: A Panel Study. Ph.D. dissertation, Emory University.

BAILEY, KENNETH. 1964. Southern White Protestantism in the Twentieth Century. New York: Harper & Row.

BALK, ALFRED. 1968. The Religion Business. Richmond: John Knox Press.

BALSWICK, JACK. 1974. "The Jesus people movement: A generational interpretation." Journal of Social Issues 30:23–42.

BALTZELL, E. DIGBY. 1964. The Protestant Establishment: Aristocracy and Caste in America. New York: Random House.

BARTON, ALLEN. 1971. "Selected problems in the study of religious development." Pp. 837–55 in Merton Strommen (ed.), Research on Religious Development. New York: Hawthorne Books.

Bax, Ernest Belfort. 1903. Rise and Fall of the Anabaptists. New York: Macmillan.

Becker, Howard. 1967. "Whose side are we on?" Social Problems 14:239–47.

Beckford, James. 1972. "The embryonic stage of a religious sect's development: The Jehovah's witnesses." Pp. 11–32 in Michael Hill (ed.), Sociological Yearbook of Religion in Britain. London: SCM Press.

Beckford, James. 1975a. "Two contrasting types of sectarian organization." Pp. 70–85 in Roy Wallis (ed.), Sectarianism: Analyses of Religious and Non-Religious Sects. New York: John Wiley.

———. 1975b. The Trumpet of Prophecy: A Sociological Study of the Jehovah's Witnesses. New York: John Wiley.

———. 1976. "New wines in new bottles: A departure from the church-sect conceptual tradition." Social Compass 23:71–85.

Beeson, Trevor. 1973. The Church of England in Crisis. London: Davis-Poynter.

Bell, Daniel. 1971. "Religion in the sixties." Social Research 38:447–97.

———. 1973. The Coming of Post-Industrial Society: A Venture in Social Forecasting. New York: Basic Books.

———. 1976. The Cultural Contradictions of Capitalism. New York: Basic Books.

Bellah, Robert. 1970. Beyond Belief. New York: Harper & Row.

———. 1975. The Broken Covenant: American Civil Religion in Time of Trial. New York: Seabury Press.

Bendix, Reinhard. 1962. Max Weber: An Intellectual Portrait. Garden City, N.Y.: Doubleday, Anchor Books.

Bennett, John. 1967. The Hutterian Brethren. Stanford, Calif.: Stanford University Press.

Berger, Brigitte. 1971. Societies in Change: An Introduction to Comparative Sociology. New York: Basic Books.

Berger, Peter. 1958. "Sectarianism and religious sociation." American Journal of Sociology 64:41–44.

———. 1961. Noise of Solemn Assemblies: Christian Commitment and the Religious Establishment in America. Garden City, N.Y.: Doubleday.

———. 1963. "A market model for the analysis of ecumenicity." Social Research 30:77–90.

———1967. The Sacred Canopy: Elements of a Sociological Theory of Religion. Garden City, N.Y.: Doubleday.

———. 1969. A Rumor of Angels: Modern Society and the Rediscovery of the Supernatural. New York: Doubleday and Co.

———. 1974. "Second thoughts on substantive versus functional definitions of religion." Journal for the Scientific Study of Religion 13:125–34.

Berger, Peter and Brigitte Berger. 1975. Sociology: A Biographical Approach. New York: Basic Books.

Berger, Peter and D. Nash. 1962. "Church commitment in an American suburb—An analysis of the decision to join." Archives de Sociologie des Religions 13:105–20.

Berger, Stephen. 1971. "The sects and the breakthrough into the modern world: On the centrality of the sects in Weber's Protestant Ethic thesis." Sociological Quarterly 12:486–89.

BERGSON, HENRI. 1935. The Two Sources of Morality and Religion. Trans. K. Ashley Audra and Cloudesley Brereton. New York: Henry Holt.

BERRY, DAVID. 1970. The Sociology of Grass Roots Politics: A Study of Party Membership. London: St. Martin's.

BESANCENEY, PAUL. 1970. Interfaith Marriages. New Haven: College and Universities Press.

BIANCHI, EUGENE. 1970. "John XXIII, Vatican II and American Catholicism." Annals 387:30–40.

BIBBY, REGINALD AND MERLIN BRINKERHOFF. 1973. "The circulation of the saints: A study of people who join conservative churches." Journal for the Scientific Study of Religion 12:273–84.

———. 1974a. When proselytizing fails: An organizational analysis." Sociological Analysis 35:189–200.

———. 1974b. "Sources of religious involvement: Issues for future empirical investigation." Review of Religious Research 15:71–79.

BIRNBAUM, NORMAN. 1969. The Crisis in Industrial Society. New York: Oxford University Press.

———. 1973. "Beyond Marx in the sociology of religion?" Pp. 5–70 in Charles Glock and Phillip Hammond (eds.), Beyond the Classics? Essays in the Scientific Study of Religion. New York: Harper & Row.

BLACKWELL, JAMES. 1975. The Black Community: Diversity and Unity. New York: Harper & Row.

———. 1976. "The power basis of ethnic conflict in American society." Pp. 179–96 in Lewis Coser (ed.), The Uses of Controversy in Sociology. New York: Free Press.

BLAUNER, ROBERT. 1958. "Industrialization and labor response: The case of the South." Berkeley Publications in Society and Institutions 4:29–43.

———. 1966. "Death and Social Structure." Psychiatry 29:378–94.

BLAZER, DAN AND ERDMAN PALMORE. 1976. "Religion and aging in a longitudinal panel." Gerontologist 16:82–85.

BLIZZARD, SAMUEL. 1956a. "The minister's dilemma." Christian Century, April 25:508–9.

———. 1956b. "Role conflicts of the urban Protestant parish minister." City Church 7:13–15.

———. 1958. "The Protestant parish minister's integrating role." Religious Education 53:374–80.

BLOCH-HOELL, NILS. 1964. The Pentecostal Movement. London: Allen & Unwin.

BLOOD, ROBERT. 1972. The Family. New York: Free Press.

BLUM, B. S. AND J. H. MANN. 1960. "The effect of religious membership on religious prejudice." Journal of Social Psychology 52:97–101.

BLUME, NORMAN. 1970. "Clergymen and social action." Sociology and Social Research 54:237–48.

BOCHEL, J. M. AND D. T. DENVER. 1970. "Religion and voting: A critical review and a new analysis." Political Studies 18:205–19.

BODE, JERRY. 1970. "Status and mobility of Catholics vis-a-vis several Protestant denominations: More evidence." Sociological Quarterly 11:103–11.

———. 1972. "Status and mobility of church members and non-members." Sociology and Social Research 57:55–61.

BOLTON, CHARLES. 1972. "Alienation and action: A study of peace-group volunteers." American Journal of Sociology 78:537–61.

BONIFIELD, WILLIAM. 1970. "The minister in the labor market." Pp. 209–220 in Phillip Hammond and Benton Johnson (eds.), American Mosaic: Social Patterns of Religion in the United States. New York: Random House.

BONN, ROBERT. 1975. "Ministerial income—1973." Pp. 246–51 in Yearbook of American and Canadian Churches. Nashville: Abingdon Press.

BOUMA, GARY. 1970. "Assessing the impact of religion: A critical review." Sociological Analysis 31:172–79.

———. 1973. "Beyond Lenski: A critical review of recent 'Protestant Ethic' research." Journal for the Scientific Study of Religion 12:141–56.

BOURQUE, LINDA. 1969. "Social correlates of transcendental experiences." Sociological Analysis 30:151–63.

BOUVIER, LEON. 1972. "Catholics and contraception." Journal of Marriage and the Family 34:514–22.

BOUVIER, LEON AND S. L. N. RAO. 1975. Socioreligious Factors in Fertility Decline. Cambridge, Mass.: Ballinger.

BOYD, MALCOLM. 1969. The Underground Church. Baltimore: Penguin.

BRAUDE, LEE. 1961. "Professional autonomy and the role of the layman." Social Forces 39:297–301.

BRESSLER, MARVIN AND CHARLES WESTOFF. 1963. "Catholic education, economic values, and achievement." American Journal of Sociology 69:225–33.

BREWER, EARL. 1952. "Sect and church in Methodism." Social Forces 30:400–8.

———. 1967. Protestant Parish: A Case Study of Rural and Urban Parish Patterns. Atlanta: Communicative Arts Press.

BROOM, LEONARD AND NORVAL GLENN. 1966. "Religious differences in reported attitudes and behavior." Sociological Analysis 27:187–209.

BROTHERS, JOAN. 1971. Religious Institutions. London: Longmans.

BROWN, ROGER. 1967. The Ecumenical Revolution: An Interpretation of the Catholic-Protestant Dialogue. Garden City, N.Y.: Doubleday.

———. 1969. "Secular ecumenicism: The direction of the future." Pp. 395–422 in Donald Cutler (ed.), The Religious Situation: 1969. Boston: Beacon Press.

BRYMAN, ALAN. 1974. "Churchmanship and ecumenicism." Journal of Ecumenical Studies 11:467–76.

BUDD, SUSAN. 1973. Sociologists and Religion. London: Collier-Macmillan.

BULTENA, LOUIS. 1944. "Rural churches and community integration." Rural Sociology 9:257–64.

———. 1949. "Church membership and church attendance in Madison, Wisconsin." American Sociological Review 14:384–89.

BUMPASS, LARRY. 1970. "The trend of interfaith marriage in the United States." Social Biology 17:253–59.

BUMPASS, LARRY AND JAMES SWEET. 1972. "Differentials in marital instability: 1970." American Sociological Review 37:754–66.

BURCHINAL, LEE. 1957. "Marital satisfaction and religious behavior." American Sociological Review 22:306–10.

BURCK, C. G. 1976. "Group profile of the Fortune 500 chief executive." Fortune 93:172–77.

BURKETT, S. R. AND M. WHITE. 1974. "Hellfire and delinquency: Another look." Journal for the Scientific Study of Religion 13:455–62.

BURRIDGE, KENELM. 1969. New Heaven, New Earth: A Study of Millenarian Activities. New York: Schocken Books.

BUTLER, DAVID AND DONALD STOKES. 1969. Political Change in Britain: Forces Shaping Electoral Choice. New York: St. Martin's Press.

———. 1974. Political Change in Britain: The Evolution of Electoral Choice. (2nd ed.) New York: St. Martin's Press.

CAMPBELL, ANGUS, PHILIP CONVERSE AND WILLARD RODGERS. 1971. White Attitudes toward Black People. Ann Arbor, Mich.: Institute for Social Research.

———. 1976. The Quality of American Life: Perceptions, Evaluations and Satisfactions. New York: Russell Sage.

CAMPBELL, COLIN. 1971. Toward a Sociology of Irreligion. London: Macmillan.

———. 1972. "The cult, the cultic milieu and secularization." Pp. 119–36 in Michael Hill (ed.), Sociological Yearbook of Religion in Britain. London: SCM Press.

CAMPBELL, ERNEST Q. AND THOMAS PETTIGREW. 1959. Christians in Racial Crisis: A Study of Little Rock's Ministry. Washington, D.C.: Public Affairs Press.

CAMPBELL, THOMAS AND YOSHIO FUKUYAMA. 1970. The Fragmented Laymen. Philadelphia: Pilgrim Press.

CAMPOLO, ANTHONY. 1971. A Denomination Looks at Itself. Valley Forge, Pa.: Judson Press.

CANTRIL, HADLEY. [1941]. 1963. The Psychology of Social Movements. New York: John Wiley and Sons. (Science Editions.)

CAPORALE, ROCCO AND ANTONIO GRUMELLI. 1971. The Culture of Unbelief. Berkeley and Los Angeles: University of California Press.

CARDEN, MAREN. 1969. Oneida: Utopian Community to Modern Corporation. Baltimore: Johns Hopkins.

CARDWELL, JERRY. 1971. "Multidimensional measurements of interfaith commitment." Pacific Sociological Review 14:79–88.

CARLOS, SERGE. 1970. "Religious participation and the urban-suburban continuum." American Journal of Sociology 75:742–59.

CARROLL, JACKSON. 1971. "Structural effects of professional schools on professional socialization: The case of Protestant clergymen." Social Forces 50:61–74.

CAVERT, SAMUEL. 1968. The American Churches and the Ecumenical Movement, 1900–1968. New York: Association Press.

———. 1970. Church Cooperation and Unity in America: A Historical Review, 1900–1970. New York: Association Press.

CHADWICK, OWEN. 1975. The Secularization of the European Mind in the Nineteenth Century. Cambridge: Cambridge University Press.

CHAMBERLAYNE, JOHN. 1964. "From sect to church in British Methodism." British Journal of Sociology 15:139–49.

CHERRY, CONRAD. 1971. God's New Israel: Religious Interpretations of American Destiny. Englewood Cliffs, N.J.: Prentice-Hall.

CHURCH INFORMATION OFFICE. 1975. Church of England Yearbook. London: Church Information Office.

CLAYTON, RICHARD. 1968. "Religiosity in 5-D: A Southern test." Social Forces 47:80–83.

————. 1973. "Religiosity and attitudes towards induced abortion: An elaboration of relationship." Sociological Analysis 34:26–39.

CLAYTON, RICHARD AND JAMES GLADDEN. 1974. "The five dimensions of religiosity: Toward demythologizing a sacred artifact." Journal for the Scientific Study of Religion 13:135–44.

CLELLAND, DONALD, THOMAS HOOD, C. M. LIPSEY, AND RONALD WIMBERLEY. 1974. "In the company of the converted: Characteristics of a Billy Graham crusade audience." Sociological Analysis 35:45–56.

CLINE, V. B. AND J. M. RICHARDS. 1965. "A factor analytic study of religious beliefs and behavior." Journal of Personality and Social Psychology 1:569–78.

COHN, NORMAN. 1970. The Pursuit of the Millenium: Revolutionary Millenarians and Mystical Anarchists of the Middle Ages. (revised and expanded edition) New York: Oxford University Press.

COLE, G. STEWART. 1931. History of Fundamentalism. New York: R. R. Smith.

COLEMAN, JAMES. 1964. "Social cleavage and religious conflict." Pp. 90–100 in Earl Raab (ed.), Religious Conflict in America. New York: Doubleday.

COLLINS, RANDALL. 1975. Conflict Sociology: Toward an Explanatory Science. New York: Academic Press.

CONE, JAMES H. 1969. Black Theology and Black Power. New York: Seabury Press.

CONVERSE, PHILIP. 1966. "Religion and politics: The 1960 election." Pp. 96–124 in Angus Campbell (ed.), Elections and the Political Order. New York: John Wiley.

COOPER, LEE. 1974. " 'Publish' or perish: Negro Jehovah's witnesses' adaptation in the ghetto." Pp. 700–21 in Irving Zaretsky and Mark Leone (eds.), Religious Movements in Contemporary America. Princeton, N.J.: Princeton University Press.

COXON, ANTHONY. 1967. "Patterns of occupational recruitment: The Anglican ministry." Sociology 1:73–80.

CROCKETT, HARRY. 1969. "Change in religious affiliation and family stability: A second study." Journal of Marriage and the Family 3:464–68.

CROOG, SYDNEY AND JAMES TEELE. 1967. "Religious identity and church attendance of sons of religious intermarriages." American Sociological Review 32:93–103.

CROSS, WHITNEY. [1950] 1965. The Burned-Over District: The Social and Intellectual History of Enthusiastic Religion in Western New York, 1800–1950. New York: Harper & Row, Torchbooks.

CRYSDALE, STEWART. 1965. The Changing Church in Canada: Beliefs and Social Attitudes of United Church People. Toronto: Board of Evangelism and Social Service, United Church.

CURRIE, ROBERT. 1968. Methodism Divided: A Study in the Sociology of Ecumenicalism. London: Faber & Faber.

CURRIE, ROBERT AND ALAN GILBERT. 1972. "Religion." Pp. 407–50 in A. Halsey (ed.), Trends in British Society Since 1900: A Guide to the Changing Social Structure of Britain. London: Macmillan.

CURRY, LEROND. 1972. Protestant-Catholic Relations in America: World War I through Vatican II. Lexington, Ky.: University of Kentucky Press.

DALY, MARGARET. 1970. "Women and the Catholic church." Pp. 124–38 in Robin Morgan (ed.), Sisterhood is Powerful. New York: Vintage Books.

———. [1968] 1973. The Church and the Second Sex. Boston: Beacon Press.

DANER, FRANCINE. 1976. The American Children of Krsna: A Study of the Hare Krsna Movement. New York: Holt, Rinehart & Winston.

DAVIDSON, JAMES. 1969. "Protestant and Catholic perceptions of church structure." Social Forces 47:314–22.

———. 1972. "Religious belief as an independent variable." Journal for the Scientific Study of Religion 11:65–75.

———. 1975. "Glock's model of religious commitment: Assessing some different approaches and results." Review of Religious Research 16:83–93.

DAVIS, JAMES. 1932. "A study of Protestant boards of control." American Journal of Sociology 38:418–31.

DAVIS, KINGSLEY AND WILBERT MOORE. 1945. "Some principles of social stratification." American Sociological Review 10:242–49.

DAVIS, REX AND JAMES RICHARDSON. 1976. "The organization and functioning of the Children of God." Sociological Analysis 37:321–39.

DEJONG, GORDON, JOSEPH FAULKNER, AND REX WARLAND. 1976. "Dimensions of religiosity reconsidered: Evidence from a cross-cultural study." Social Forces 54:866–89.

DEMERATH, NICHOLAS J., III. 1965. Social Class in American Protestantism. Chicago: Rand McNally.

———. 1968. "Trends and anti-trends in religious change." Pp. 349–448 in Eleanor Sheldon and Wilbert Moore (eds.), Indicators of Social Change. New York: Russell Sage.

———1974. A Tottering Transcendence: Civil vs. Cultic Aspects of the Sacred. Indianapolis: Bobbs-Merrill.

DEVINE, GEORGE. 1975. American Catholicsm: Where Do We Go from Here? Englewood Cliffs, N.J.: Prentice-Hall.

DIAMOND, ROBERT. 1970. "A self-portrait of the chief executive: The Fortune 500-Yankelovich survey." Fortune 81:181,320,323.

DIERENFIELD, R.B. 1967. "The impact of the Supreme Court decisions on religion in public schools." Religious Education 62:445–51.

DILLINGHAM, HARRY. 1965. "Protestant religion and social status." American Journal of Sociology 70:416–22.

DITTES, JAMES. 1967. "Review article: Christian beliefs and anti-Semitism." Review of Religious Research 8:183–87.

———. 1969. "Psychology of religion." Pp. 602–59 in Gardner Lindzey and Elliot Aronson (eds.), Handbook of Social Psychology, 5. Reading, Mass.: Addison-Wesley.

DOMHOFF, G. WILLIAM. 1967. Who Rules America? Englewood Cliffs, N.J.: Prentice-Hall.

DOUGLAS, MARY. [1966]. 1970a. Purity and Danger: An Analysis of Concepts of Pollution and Taboo. Baltimore: Penguin.

———. 1970b. Natural Symbols: Explorations in Cosmology. New York: Random House, Pantheon.

———1975. Implicit Meanings: Essays in Anthropology. Boston: Routledge & Kegan Paul.

DRIEDGER, LEO. 1974. "Doctrinal belief: A major factor in the differential perception of social issues." Sociological Quarterly 15:66–80.

DU BOIS, W. E. [1899]. 1971. "The function of the Negro church." Pp. 77–81 in Hart Nelsen, Raytha Yokeley and Anne Nelsen (eds.), The Black Church in America. New York: Basic Books.

DURKHEIM, EMILE. [1915] 1965. The Elementary Forms of the Religious Life. New York: Free Press.
———. 1975. Durkheim on Religion. Ed. W. S. F. Pickering. London: Routledge & Kegan Paul.

DYNES, RUSSELL. 1956. "Rurality, migration and sectarianism." Rural Sociology 21:25–28.
———. 1957. "The consequences of sectarianism for social participation." Social Forces 35:311–34.
———.1959. "The relation of community characteristics to religious organizations and behavior." Pp. 253–68 in Marvin Sussman (ed.), Community Structure and Analysis. New York: Thomas Y. Crowell.

EARLE, JOHN, DEAN KNUDSEN, AND DONALD SHRIVER. 1976. Spindles and Spires: A Re-Study of Religion and Social Change in Gastonia. Atlanta: John Knox Press.

EBONY. 1974. Ebony Handbook. Chicago: Johnson.

ECKARDT, A. ROY. 1958. The Surge of Piety in America: An Appraisal. New York: Association Press.

ECKHARDT, K. W. 1970. "Religiosity and civil rights militancy." Review of Religious Research 11:197–203.

EDWARDS, HARRY. 1968. "Black Muslim and Negro Christian family relationships." Journal of Marriage and the Family 30:604–11.

EISENSTADT, SHMUEL N. 1968. "Charisma and institution building: Max Weber and modern sociology." Pp. ix–lvi in Shmuel N. Eisenstadt (ed.), Max Weber on Charisma and Institution Building. Chicago: University of Chicago Press.

EISTER, ALLAN. 1957. "Religious institutions in complex societies." American Sociological Review 22:387–91.
———. 1973. "H. Richard Niebuhr and the paradox of religious organization: A radical critique." Pp. 355–408 in Charles Glock and Philip Hammond (eds.), Beyond the Classics? Essays in the Scientific Study of Religion. New York: Harper & Row.

ELAZAR, D. 1961. "Churches as molders of American politics." American Behavioral Scientist 4:15–18.

ELIADE, MIRCEA. 1959. The Sacred and the Profane: The Nature of Religion. New York: Harcourt, Brace & World.

ELINSON, HOWARD. 1965. "The implications of Pentecostal religion for intellectualism, politics and race relations." American Journal of Sociology 70:403–15.

ELKIND, DAVID. 1964. "Age changes in the meaning of religious identity." Review of Religious Research 6:36–40.
———. 1971. "The development of religious understanding in children and adolescents." Pp. 658–85 in Merton Strommen (ed.), Research on Religious Development. New York: Hawthorne Books.

ELLWOOD, ROBERT, JR. 1973. Religious and Spiritual Groups in Modern America. Englewood Cliffs, N.J.: Prentice-Hall.

ELZEY, WAYNE. 1975. "Liminality and symbiosis in popular American Protestantism." Journal of the American Academy of Religion XLIII:741–56.

ESTUS, CHARLES AND MICHAEL OVERINGTON. 1970. "The meaning and end of religiosity." American Journal of Sociology 75:760–78.

EVANS-PRITCHARD, E. E. 1965. Theories of Primitive Religion. Oxford: The Clarendon Press.

FAIRCHILD, ROY AND JOHN C. WYNN. 1961. Families in the Church: A Protestant Survey. New York: Association Press.

FALLDING, HAROLD. 1972. "Canada." Pp. 101–15 in Hans Mol (ed.), Western Religion: A Country by Country Sociological Inquiry. The Hague: Mouton.

———. 1974. The Sociology of Religion: An Explanation of the Unity and Diversity in Religion. Toronto: McGraw-Hill Ryerson.

FAULKNER, J. E. AND GORDON DEJONG. 1966. "Religiosity in 5-D: An empirical analysis." Social Forces 45:246–54.

FEATHERMAN, DAVID. 1971. "The socio-economic achievement of white religio-ethnic sub-groups: Social and psychological explanations." American Sociological Review 36:207–22.

FEE, JOAN. 1976. "Political continuity and change." Pp. 76–102 in Andrew Greeley, William McCready, and Kathleen McCourt (eds.), Catholic Schools in a Declining Church. Kansas City: Sheed & Ward.

FENN, RICHARD. 1970. "The process of secularization: A post-Parsonian view." Journal for the Scientific Study of Religion 9:117–36.

———. 1974. "Religion and the legitimation of social systems." Pp. 143–61 in Allan Eister (ed.), Changing Perspectives in the Scientific Study of Religion. New York: Wiley-Interscience.

FICHTER, JOSEPH. 1951. Dynamics of a City Church. Chicago: University of Chicago Press.

———. 1961. Religion as an Occupation: A Study in the Sociology of Professions. Notre Dame, Ind.: University of Notre Dame Press.

———. 1965. Priests and People. New York: Sheed & Ward.

———. 1969. "Sociological measurement of religiosity." Review of Religious Research 10:169–77.

———. 1973. One Man Research: Reminiscences of a Catholic Sociologist. New York: John Wiley.

———. 1974a. "Liberal and conservative Catholic Pentecostals." Social Compass 21:303–10.

———. 1974b. Organization Man in the Church. Cambridge, Mass.: Schenkman Publishing Co.

———. 1975. The Catholic Cult of the Paraclete. New York: Sheed & Ward.

FINNER, STEPHEN. 1970. "Religious membership and religious preference: Equal indicators of religiosity." Journal for the Scientific Study of Religion 9:273–79.

FINNEY, JOHN. 1971. The Religious Commitment of American Women. Ph.D. dissertation, University of Wisconsin, Madison.

FIRTH, RAYMOND. 1970. Families and Their Relatives: Kinship in a Middle-Class Sector of London. New York: Humanities Press.

FISCHLER, CLAUDE. 1974. "Astrology and French society: The dialectic of archaism and modernity." Pp. 281–93 in Edward Tiryakian (ed.), On the Margin of the Visible: Sociology, the Esoteric and the Occult. New York: Wiley-Interscience.

FISH, JOHN ET. AL.. 1966. On the Edge of the Ghetto: A Study of Church Involvement in Community Organization. Chicago: University of Chicago Divinity School.

FORD, THOMAS. 1960. "Status, residence and fundamentalist religious belief in the southern Appalachians." Social Forces 39:41–49.

FORSTER, PETER. 1972. "Secularization and the English context." Sociological Review 20:153–68.

FOX, W. S. AND ELTON JACKSON. 1973. "Protestant-Catholic differences in educational achievement and persistence in school." Journal for the Scientific Study of Religion 12:65–84.

FRAZIER, E. FRANKLIN. [1963] 1974. The Negro Church in America. New York: Schocken Books.

FREEDMAN, RONALD, PASCAL WHELPTON, AND JOHN SMIF. 1961. "Socio-economic factors in religious differentials in fertility." American Sociological Review 26:608–14.

FREUND, JULIEN. 1968. The Sociology of Max Weber. Trans. Mary Ilford. New York: Vintage Books.

FRY, JOHN. 1975. The Trivialization of the United Presbyterian Church. New York: Harper & Row.

FUKUYAMA, YOSHIO. 1961. "The major dimensions of church membership." Review of Religious Research 2:154–61.

————. 1972. The Ministry in Transition: A Case Study of Theological Education. University Park, Pa.: Pennsylvania State University Press.

FURNISS, NORMAN. 1954. The Fundamentalist Controversy, 1918–1931. New Haven: Yale University Press.

GALBRAITH, JOHN. 1967. The New Industrial State. Boston: Houghton Mifflin.

GALLUP, GEORGE. 1972. The Gallup Poll: Public Opinion, 1935–1971, Vol. 3. New York: Random House.

GALLUP, GEORGE AND JOHN DAVIES. 1971. Religion in America, 1971. Princeton, N.J.: Gallup International.

GALLUP POLL. 1974a. "More millions claim seeing UFO's." Current Opinion 2:7.

————. 1974b. "Public opinion referendum." Pp. 1–17 of Report No. 113, Gallup Opinion Index. Princeton, N.J.: American Institute of Public Opinion.

————. 1975. Religion in America: 1975. Princeton, N.J.: Gallup International.

————. 1976a. Religion in America: 1976. Princeton, N.J.: Gallup International.

————. 1976b. "Thirty-two million look to stars for help in conducting daily affairs." Pp. 25–27 in Gallup Poll Index, 1976. Princeton, N.J.: American Institute of Public Opinion.

————. 1977. "Widespread segregation found in nation's churches." Gallup Poll Release, April 7, 1977. Chicago: Field Enterprises.

GARRETT, WILLIAM. 1973. "Politicized clergy: A sociological interpretation of the 'New Breed.'" Journal for the Scientific Study of Religion 12:383–99.

GARRISON, VIVIAN. 1974. "Sectarianism and psychosocial adjustment: A controlled comparison of Puerto Rican Pentecostals and Catholics." Pp. 298–329 in Irving Zaretsky and Mark Leone (eds.), Religious Movements in Contemporary America. Princeton, N.J.: Princeton University Press.

GAUSTAD, EDWIN. 1968. "American's institutions of faith." Pp. 111–30. in William McLoughlin and Robert Bellah (eds.), Religion in America. Boston: Beacon Press.

———. 1969. "Churches of Christ in America." Pp. 1013–33 in Donald Cutler (ed.), The Religious Situation: 1969. Boston: Beacon Press.

GEERTZ, CLIFFORD. 1973. The Interpretation of Cultures. New York: Basic Books.

GENOVESE, EUGENE. 1974. Roll, Jordan, Roll: The World the Slaves Made. New York: Pantheon.

GERLACH, LUTHER AND VIRGINIA HINE. 1970. People, Power and Change: Movements of Social Transformation. Indianapolis: Bobbs-Merrill.

GERSTNER, JOHN. 1975. "The theological boundaries of evangelical faith." Pp. 21–37 in David Wells and John Woodbridge (eds.), The Evangelicals: What They Believe, Who They Are, Where They Are Going. New York: Abingdon.

GIBBS, D. J. AND K. CRADER. 1970. "A criticism of two recent attempts to scale Glock's and Stark's dimensions of religiosity." Sociological Analysis 31:107–14.

GIDDENS, ANTHONY. 1971. Capitalism and Modern Social Theory: An Analysis of the Writings of Marx, Durkheim and Max Weber. Cambridge: Cambridge University Press.

———. 1975. The Class Structure of the Advanced Societies. New York: Harper Torchbooks.

GLASSE, JAMES. 1968. Profession: Minister. Nashville, Tenn.: Abingdon.

GLAZER, NATHAN. 1970. Remembering the Answers: Essays on the American Student Revolt. New York: Basic Books.

———. 1972. American Judaism. Chicago: University of Chicago Press.

GLENN, NORVAL AND RUTH HYLAND. 1967. "Religious preference and worldly success: Some evidence from national surveys." American Sociological Review 32:73–86.

GLOCK, CHARLES, BENJAMIN RINGER, AND EARL BABBIE. 1967. To Comfort and to Challenge: A Dilemma of the Contemporary Church. Berkeley and Los Angeles: University of California Press.

GLOCK, CHARLES AND RODNEY STARK. 1966. Christian Beliefs and Anti-Semitism. New York: Harper & Row.

GOCKEL, GALEN. 1969. "Income and religious affiliation: A regression analysis." American Journal of Sociology 74:632–47.

GOLDSCHMIDT, WALTER. 1944. "Class denominationalism in rural California churches." American Journal of Sociology 49:348–55.

GOLDSTEIN, B. AND R. L. EICHHORN. 1961. "The changing Protestant Ethic: Rural patterns in health, work and leisure." American Sociological Review 26:557–65.

GOLDSTEIN, SIDNEY. 1969. "Socio-economic differentials among religious groups in the United States." American Journal of Sociology 74:612–31.

———. 1974. "American Jewry, 1970: A demographic profile." Pp. 93–162 in Marshall Sklare (ed.), The Jew in American Society. New York: Behrman House.

GOLDSTEIN, SIDNEY AND CALVIN GOLDSCHNEIDER. 1968. Jewish Americans. Englewood Cliffs, N.J.: Prentice-Hall.

GOODE, ERICH. 1966. "Social class and church participation." American Journal of Sociology 72:102–11.

———. 1968. "Class styles in religious sociation." British Journal of Sociology 19:1–16.

GORDON, ALBERT. 1964. Intermarriage: Interfaith, Interracial, Interethnic. Boston: Beacon Press.

————. 1967. The Nature of Conversion: A Study of Forty-Five Men and Women Who Changed Their Religion. Boston: Beacon Press.

GORER, GEOFREY. 1955. Exploring English Character. London: Cresset Press.

————. 1965. Death, Grief and Mourning in Comtemporary Britain. London: Cresset Press.

GORSUCH, R. L. AND D. ALESHIRE. 1974. "Christian faith and ethnic prejudice: A review and interpretation of research." Journal for the Scientific Study of Religion 13:281–307.

GRAHAM, BILLY. 1975. "Jesus and the liberated woman." Pp. 421–28 in Kenneth Hammeger (ed.), Confronting the Issues: Sex Roles, Marriage and the Family. Boston: Allyn & Bacon.

GREBLER, LEO, JOAN MOORE, AND RALPH GRUZMAN. 1970. The Mexican-American People: The Nation's Second Largest Minority. New York: Free Press.

GREELEY, ANDREW. 1963. Religion and Career: A Study of College Students. New York: Sheed & Ward.

————. 1970. "Religious intermarriage in a denominational society." American Journal of Sociology 75:949–52.

————. 1971. Why Can't They Be Like Us?: America's White Ethnic Groups. New York: Dutton.

————. 1972. The Denominational Society: A Sociological Approach to Religion in America. Glenview, Ill.: Scott, Foresman.

————. 1974a. Ecstasy: A Way of Knowing. Englewood Cliffs, N.J.: Prentice-Hall.

————. 1974b. Ethnicity in the United States: A Preliminary Reconnaissance. New York: John Wiley.

————. 1975. The Sociology of the Paranormal: A Reconnaissance. Sage Research Papers in the Social Sciences (Studies in Religion and Ethnicity Series No. 90–023). Beverly Hills, Calif.: Sage Publications.

————. 1977. The American Catholic: A Social Portrait. New York: Basic Books.

GREELEY, ANDREW AND GALEN GOCKEL. 1971. "The religious effects of parochial education." Pp. 265–301 in Merton Strommen (ed.), Research on Religious Development. New York: Hawthorne Books.

GREELEY, ANDREW, WILLIAM McCREADY, AND KATHLEEN McCOURT. 1976. Catholic Schools in a Declining Church. Kansas City: Sheed & Ward.

GREELEY, ANDREW AND PETER ROSSI. 1966. The Education of Catholic Americans. Chicago: Aldine.

GREEN, ROBERT (ED.) 1959. Protestantism and Capitalism: The Weber Thesis and its Critiques. Boston: Heath.

GRUPP, F. AND R. NEWMAN. 1973. "Religious preference and membership of the John Birch Society and Americans for Democratic Action." Journal for the Scientific Study of Religion 12:401–13.

GUEST, AVERY AND JAMES WEED. 1976. "Ethnic residential segregation: Patterns of change." American Journal of Sociology 81:1088–111.

GUSFIELD, JOSEPH. [1963] 1969. Symbolic Crusade: Status Politics and the American Temperance Movement. Urbana, Ill.: University of Illinois Press.

GUTMAN, HERBERT. 1968. "Protestantism and the American labor movement:

The Christian spirit in the Gilded Age." Pp. 139–73 in Alfred Chandler (ed.), Dissent. DeKalb, Ill.: University of Northern Illinois Press.

HACKETT, ALICE. 1967. 70 Years of Best Sellers, 1895–1965. New York: Bowker.

HADDEN, JEFFREY. 1969. The Gathering Storm in the Churches: The Widening Gap Between Clergy and Laymen. Garden City, N.Y.: Doubleday.

HADDEN, JEFFREY AND CHARLES LONGINO, JR. 1974. Gideon's Gang: A Case Study the Church in Social Action. Philadelphia: Pilgrim Press.

HAGSTROM, W. 1957. "The Protestant clergy as a profession: Status and prospects." Berkeley Publications in Society and Institutions 3:54–69.

HALL, DOUGLAS AND BENJAMIN SCHNEIDER. 1973. Organizational Climates and Careers: The Work Lives of Priests. New York: Seminar Press.

HAMILTON, RICHARD. 1972. Class and Politics in the United States. New York: John Wiley.

———. 1975. Restraining Myths: Critical Studies of United States Social Structure and Politics. New York: John Wiley.

HAMMOND, PHILIP. 1974. "Religious pluralism and Durkheim's integration thesis." Pp. 115–42 in Allan Eister (ed.), Changing Perspectives in the Scientific Study of Religion. New York: John Wiley.

———. 1976. "The sociology of American civil religion: A bibliographical essay." Sociological Analysis 37:169–82.

HAMMOND, PHILLIP AND ROBERT MITCHELL. 1965. "The segmentation of radicalism—The case of the Protestant campus ministries." American Journal of Sociology 71:133–43.

HARPER, CHARLES. 1974. "Spirit-filled Catholics: Some biographical comparisons." Social Compass 21:311–24.

HARRELL, DAVID JR. 1971. White Sects and Black Men in the Recent South. Nashville: Vanderbilt University Press.

———. 1975. All Things Are Possible: The Healing and Charismatic Revivals in Modern America. Bloomington, Ind.: Indiana University Press.

HARRIS POLL. 1974. "Most believe in Devil but not demonism." Current Opinion 2:65.

HARRISON, MICHAEL. 1974a. "Sources of recruitment to Catholic Pentecostalism." Journal for the Scientific Study of Religion 13:49–64.

———. 1974b. "Preparation for life in the spirit." Urban Life and Culture 2:387–414.

———. 1975. "The maintenance of enthusiasm: Involvement in a new religious movement." Sociological Analysis 36:150–60.

HARRISON, PAUL. 1959. Authority and Power in the Free Church Tradition: A Social Case Study of the American Baptist Convention. Princeton, N.J.: Princeton University Press.

HARTMAN, PATRICIA. 1976. "Social dimensions of occult participation: The Gnostic study." British Journal of Sociology 27:169–83.

HAWTHORNE, HARRY. 1955. The Doukhobors of British Columbia. Vancouver: University of British Columbia Press.

HEINZ, DONALD. 1976. "The Christian World Liberation Front." Pp. 143–61 in Charles Glock and Robert Bellah (eds.), The New Religious Consciousness. Berkeley: University of California Press.

HEISS, JEROLD. 1960. "Premarital characteristics of the religiously intermarried in an urban area." American Sociological Review 25:47–55.

―――. 1961. "Interfaith marriage and marital outcome." Marriage and Family Living 23:228–33.

HENRIOT, PETER. 1970. "Political vs. religious liberalism among Catholics." Pp. 289–305 in William Liu and Nathaniel Pallone (eds.), Catholics/USA: Perspectives on Social Change. New York: John Wiley.

HERBERG, WILL. 1960. Protestant-Catholic-Jew: An Essay in American Religious Sociology. Garden City, N.Y.: Doubleday, Anchor Books.

HERTEL, BRADLEY, GERRY HENDERSHOT, AND JAMES GRIMM. 1974. "Religion and attitudes toward avocation: A study of nurses and social workers." Journal for the Scientific Study of Religion 13:23–34.

HERTEL, BRADLEY AND HART NELSEN. 1974. "Are we entering a post-Christian era?: Religious beliefs and attendance in America, 1957–1968." Journal for the Scientific Study of Religion 13:409–19.

HIGGINS, PAUL AND GARY ALBRECHT. 1977. "Hellfire and delinquency revisited." Social Forces 55:952–58.

HILL, CAROLE. 1973. "Black healing practices in the rural South." Journal of Popular Culture 6:849–53.

HILL, CHRISTOPHER. 1970. "Some aspects of race and religion in Britain." Pp. 30–44 in David Martin and Michael Hill (eds.), Sociological Yearbook of Religion in Britain. London: SCM Press.

HILL, MICHAEL. 1973a. A Sociology of Religion. New York: Basic Books.

―――. 1973b. The Religious Order: A Study of Virtuoso Religion and its Legitimation in the Nineteenth-Century Church of England. London: Heinemann Educational Books.

HILL, SAMUEL. 1966. Southern Churches in Crisis. New York: Holt, Rinehart & Winston.

HIMMELFARB, HAROLD. 1975. "Measuring religious involvement." Social Forces 53:606–18.

HINE, VIRGINIA. 1974. "Deprivation and disorganization theories of social movements." Pp. 646–64 in Irving Zaretsky and Mark Leone (eds.), Religious Movements in Contemporary America. Princeton, N.J.: Princeton University Press.

HININGS, ROBIN AND BRUCE FOSTER. 1973. "The organization structure of churches: A preliminary model." Sociology 7:93–106.

HIRSCHI, TRAVIS AND RODNEY STARK. 1969. "Hellfire and delinquency." Social Problems 17:202–13.

HODGE, ROBERT, PAUL SIEGAL, AND PETER ROSSI. 1964. "Occupational prestige in the United States, 1925–1963." American Journal of Sociology 70:286–302.

HOGE, DEAN. 1974. Commitment on Campus. Philadelphia: Westminister Press.

―――. 1976. Division in the Protestant House: The Basic Reasons Behind Intra-Church Conflict. Philadelphia: Westminister Press.

HOGE, DEAN AND J. W. CARROLL. 1973. "Religiosity and prejudice in northern and southern churches." Journal for the Scientific Study of Religion 12:181–97.

―――. 1975. "Christian beliefs, nonreligious factors and anti-Semitism." Social Forces 53:581–94.

HOGGART, RICHARD. 1958. The Uses of Literacy: Aspects of Working Class Life, with Special Reference to Publications and Entertainment. London: Chatto and Windus.

HOLLENWEGER, WALTER. 1972. The Pentecostals: The Charismatic Movement in the Churches. Minneapolis: Augsburg Publishing House.

HOLT, JOHN. 1940. "Holiness religion: Cultural shock and social reorganization." American Sociological Review 5:740–47.

HOMAN, ROGER. 1970. "Sunday observance and social class." Pp. 78–92 in David Martin and Michael Hill (eds.), Sociological Yearbook of Religion in Britain. London: SCM Press.

HOSTETLER, JOHN. 1963. Amish Society. Baltimore: Johns Hopkins.

———. 1974. Hutterite Society. Baltimore: Johns Hopkins.

HOSTETLER, JOHN AND GERTRUDE HUNTINGTON. 1967. The Hutterites in North America. New York: Holt, Rinehart & Winston.

HOULT, THOMAS. 1950. "Economic class consciousness in American Protestantism." American Sociological Review 15:97–100.

HUBBARD, GEOFFREY. 1974. Quaker by Convincement. Baltimore: Penguin.

HUBER, JOAN AND WILLIAM FORM. 1973. Income and Ideology: An Analysis of the American Political Formula. New York: Free Press.

HUNT, LARRY AND JANET HUNT. 1975. "A religious factor in secular achievement among blacks: The case of Catholicism." Social Forces 53:595–605.

HUNT, RICHARD AND MORTON KING. 1971. "The intrinsic-extrinsic concept: A review and evaluation." Journal for the Scientific Study of Religion 10:339–56.

HUNTER, ALBERT. 1974. Symbolic Communities: The Persistence and Change of Chicago's Local Communities. Chicago: University of Chicago Press.

INDEPENDENT TELEVISION AUTHORITY. 1970. Religion in Britain and Northern Ireland: A Survey of Public Attitudes. London: Independent Television Publications.

INGLIS, KENNETH. 1963. Churches and the Working Class in Victorian England. London: Routledge & Kegan Paul.

ISAMBERT, FRANCOIS. 1972. "France." Pp. 175–87 in Hans Mol (ed.), Western Religion: A Country by Country Sociological Inquiry. The Hague: Mouton.

ISICHEI, ELIZABETH. 1964. "From sect to denomination in Quakerism." British Journal of Sociology 15:207–22.

———. 1968. "Organisation and power in the Society of Friends." Pp. 182–213 in Bryan Wilson (ed.), Patterns of Sectarianism. London: Heinemann.

JACKSON, ELTON, WILLIAM FOX, AND HARRY CROCKETT, JR. 1970. "Religion and occupational achievement." American Sociological Review 35:48–63.

JAHODA, GUSTAV. 1969. The Psychology of Superstition. London: Allen Lane.

JARVIS, PETER. 1975. "The parish ministry as a semi-profession." Sociological Review 23:911–22.

JOHNSON, BENTON. 1961. "Do Holiness sects socialize in dominant values?" Social Forces 39:309–16.

———. 1962. "Ascetic Protestantism and political preference." Public Opinion Quarterly 26:35–46.

———. 1963. "On church and sect." American Sociological Review 28:539–49.

———. 1964. "Ascetic Protestantism and political preference in the deep South." American Journal of Sociology 69:359–66.

———. 1966. "Theology and party preference among Protestant clergymen." American Sociological Review 31:200–07.

———. 1967. "Theology and the position of pastors on public issues." American Sociological Review 32:433–42.

————. 1971. "Church-sect revisited." Journal for the Scientific Study of Religion 10:124–37.

JOHNSON, BRUCE. 1974. "The Democratic mirage: Notes toward a theory of American politics." Pp. 184–226 in Herbert Reid (ed.), Up the Mainstream: A Critique of Ideology in American Politics and Everyday Life. New York: David McKay Co.

JOHNSON, DOUGLAS AND GEORGE CORNELL. 1972. Punctured Preconceptions: What North American Christians Think About Their Church. New York: Friendship Press.

JOHNSON, WELDON. 1971. "The religious crusade: Revival or ritual." American Journal of Sociology 76:873–90.

JOHNSTONE, RONALD. 1969. "Negro preachers take sides." Review of Religious Research 11:81–89.

————. 1975. Religion and Society in Interaction: The Sociology of Religion. Englewood Cliffs, N.J.: Prentice-Hall.

JONES, PETER D'A. 1968. The Christian Socialist Revival, 1877–1914: Religion, Class and Social Conscience in Late-Victorian England. Princeton, N.J.: Princeton University Press.

JORSTAD, ERLING. 1970. The Politics of Doomsday: Fundamentalists of the Far Right. Nashville: Abingdon.

JUD, GERALD, EDGAR MILLS, AND GENEVIEVE WALTERS BURCH. 1970. Ex-Pastors: Why Men Leave the Parish Ministry. Boston: Pilgrim Press.

JUDAH, J. STILLSON. 1974. Hare Krishna and the Counterculture. New York: John Wiley.

KALBACH, W. E. AND W. W. McVEY. 1976. "Religious composition of the Canadian population." Pp. 221–40 in Stewart Crysdale and Les Wheatcroft (eds.), Religion in Canadian Society. Toronto: Macmillan of Canada.

KANE, STEPHEN. 1974. "Ritual possession in a southern Appalachian religious sect." Journal of American Folklore 87:293–302.

KANTER, ROSABETH. 1972. Commitment and Community: Communes and Utopias in Sociological Perspective. Cambridge, Mass.: Harvard University Press.

KARSON, MARC. 1974. "Catholic anti-socialism." Pp. 164–84 in John Laslett and S.M. Lipset (eds.), Failure of a Dream? Essays in the History of American Socialism. Garden City, N.Y.: Doubleday.

KAUFFMAN, J. HOWARD AND L. HARDER. 1975. Anabaptists Four Centuries Later: A Profile of Five Mennonite and Brethren in Christ Denominations. Scottsdale, Pa.: Herald Press.

KEENE, JAMES. 1967a. "Baha'i world faith: A redefinition of religion." Journal for the Scientific Study of Religion 6:221–35.

————. 1967b. "Religious behavior and neuroticism, spontaneity, worldmindedness." Sociometry 30:137–57.

KEHRER, GUNTER. 1972. "Germany: The federal republic." Pp. 189–212 in Hans Mol (ed.), Western Religion: A Country by Country Sociological Inquiry. The Hague: Mouton.

KELLEY, DEAN. 1972. Why the Conservative Churches are Growing: A Study in the Sociology of Religion. New York: Harper & Row.

KELLEY, JAMES. 1971. "Sources of support for ecumenism: A sociological study." Journal of Ecumenical Studies 8:1–9.

————. 1972. "Attitudes toward ecumenicism: An empirical investigation." Journal of Ecumenical Studies 9:341–51.

KELSEY, GEORGE. 1973. Social Ethics Among Southern Baptists, 1917–1969. Metuchen, N.J.: Scarecrow Press.

KERSTEN, LAWRENCE. 1970. The Lutheran Ethic: The Impact of Religion on Laymen and Clergy. Detroit: Wayne State University Press.

KING, MORTON. 1967. "Measuring the religious variable: Nine proposed dimensions." Journal for the Scientific Study of Religion 6:173–85.

————. 1969. "Measuring the religious variable: Amended findings." Journal for the Scientific Study of Religion 8:321–23.

KING, MORTON AND RICHARD HUNT. 1972. Measuring religious dimensions: Studies in congregational involvement. Southern Methodist University Studies in Social Science. Dallas: Southern Methodist University.

————. 1975. "Measuring the religious variable: A national replication." Journal for the Scientific Study of Religion 14:13–22.

KINZER, DONALD. 1964. An Episode in anti-Catholicism: The American Protective Association. Seattle: University of Washington Press.

KIRKPATRICK, JEANNE. 1976. The New Presidential Elite: Men and Women in National Politics. New York: Russell Sage and the 20th Century Fund.

KITSON-CLARK, G. 1973. Churchmen and the Condition of England, 1832–1885: A Study in the Development of Social Ideas and Practice from the Old Regime to the Modern State. London: Methuen.

KLOETZLI, WALTER. 1961. The City Church: Death or Renewal. Philadelphia: Muhlenberg Press.

KNOKE, DAVID. 1974a. "Religion, stratification and politics: America in the 1960's." American Journal of Political Science 18:331–45.

————. 1974b. "Religious involvement and political behavior." Sociological Quarterly 15:51–65.

————. 1976. Change and Continuity in American Politics: The Social Bases of Political Parties. Baltimore: Johns Hopkins.

KNUDTEN, RICHARD AND MARY KNUDTEN. 1971. "Juvenile delinquency, crime and religion." Review of Religious Research 12:130–52.

KORNBLUM, WILLIAM. 1974. Blue Collar Community. Chicago: University of Chicago Press.

KOSA, JOHN. 1970. "The emergence of a Catholic middle class." Pp. 15–24 in William Liu and Nathaniel Pallone (eds.), Catholics/USA: Perspectives on Social Change. New York: John Wiley.

KRICKUS, RICHARD. 1976. Pursuing the American Dream: White Ethnics and the New Populism. Bloomington, Ind.: Indiana University Press.

KUNZ, PHILIP. 1963. "Religious influences on paternal discipline and achievement demands." Marriage and Family Living 25:224–25.

LAMANNA, RICHARD AND JAY COAKLEY. 1969. "The Catholic Church and the Negro." Pp. 147–93 in Philip Gleason (ed.), Contemporary Catholicism in the United States. Notre Dame, Ind.: University of Notre Dame Press.

LANDIS, JUDSON. 1960. "Religiousness, family religion and family values in Protestant, Catholic and Jewish families." Marriage and Family Living 60:341–47.

LAPONCE, J. A. 1969. "Ethnicity, religion and politics in Canada: A comparative analysis of survey and census data." Pp. 187–216 in Mattei Dogan and Stein Rokkan (eds.), Quantitative Ecological Analysis in the Social Sciences. Cambridge, Mass.: M.I.T. Press.

LARSON, MARTIN AND C. STANLEY LOWELL. 1969. The Churches: Their Riches, Revenues and Immunities: An Analysis of Tax-Exempt Property. New York: Robert C. Luce.

LAUER, ROBERT. 1975. "Occupational and religious mobility in a small city." Sociological Quarterly 16:380–92.

LAUMANN, EDWARD O. 1973. The Bonds of Pluralism: The Form and Substance of Urban Social Networks. New York: John Wiley.

LAZERWITZ, BERNARD. 1961. "Some factors associated with variation in church attendance." Social Forces 39:301–9.

———. 1964. "Religion and social structure in the United States." Pp. 426–39 in Louis Schneider (ed.), Religion, Culture and Society. New York: John Wiley.

———. 1971. "Intermarriage and conversion: A guide for future research." Jewish Journal of Sociology 13:41–64.

———. 1973. "Religious identification and its ethnic correlates: A multivariate model." Social Forces 52:204–20.

LAZERWITZ, BERNARD AND L. ROWITZ. 1964. "The three-generation hypothesis." American Journal of Sociology 69:529–38.

LEE, ROBERT. 1960. The Social Sources of Church Unity. New York: Abingdon.

LEE, ROBERT AND RUSSELL GALLOWAY. 1969. The Schizophrenic Church: Conflict over Community Organization. Philadelphia: Westminster Press.

LEFEVER, HARRY. 1971. Ghetto Religion: A Study of the Religious Structures and Styles of a Poor White Community in Atlanta,, Georgia. Ph.D. dissertation, Emory University.

LEIFFER, MURRAY. 1960. The Role of the District Superintendent in the Methodist Church. Evanston, Ill.: Northwestern University Bureau of Social and Religious Research.

———. 1969. Changing Expectations and Ethics in the Professional Ministry: A Research Report on the Attitudes of Ministers in Five Protestant Denominations. Evanston, Ill.: Northwestern University, Bureau of Social and Religious Research.

LENSKI, GERHARD. 1963. The Religious Factor: A Sociological Study of Religion's Impact on Politics, Economics, and Family Life. Garden City, N.Y.: Doubleday, Anchor Books.

LEVY, MARK AND MICHAEL KRAMER. 1972. The Ethnic Factor: How America's Minorities Decide Elections. New York: Simon & Schuster.

LEWIS, LIONEL. 1963. "Knowledge, danger, certainty and the theory of magic." American Journal of Sociology 69:7–12.

LEWY, GUENTER. 1973. Religion and Revolution. London: Oxford University Press.

LINCOLN, C. ERIC. 1973. The Black Muslims in America. Boston: Beacon Press.

———. 1974. The Black Church Since Frazier. New York: Schocken Books.

LIPSET, SEYMOUR MARTIN. 1963. The First New Nation: The United States in Historical and Comparative Perspective. New York: Basic Books.

———. 1964. "Religion and politics in the American past and present." Pp. 69–126 in Robert Lee and Martin Marty (eds.), Religion and Society in Conflict. New York: Oxford University Press.

———. 1975. "The paradox of American politics." Public Interest No. 41, 142–65.

LIPSET, SEYMOUR MARTIN AND EARL RAAB. 1970. The Politics of Unreason: Right-Wing Extremism in America, 1790–1970. New York: Harper & Row.

LOFLAND, JOHN. 1966. Doomsday Cult: A Study of Conversion, Proselytization, and Maintenance of Faith. Englewood Cliffs, N.J.: Prentice-Hall.

LONGINO, CHARLES AND JEFFREY HADDEN. 1976. "Dimensionality of belief among mainstream Protestant clergy." Social Forces 55:30–42.

LUCKMANN, THOMAS. 1967. The Invisible Religion: The Transformation of Symbols in Industrial Society. New York: Macmillan.

McCORMICK, E. PATRICK. 1975. Attitudes Toward Abortion: Experiences of Selected Black and White Women. Lexington, Mass.: Lexington Books.

McCREADY, WILLIAM AND ANDREW GREELEY. 1976. The Ultimate Values of the American Population. Beverley Hills, Calif.: Sage Publications.

McDONALD, LYNN. 1969. "Religion and voting: A study of the 1968 Canadian federal election in Ontario." Canadian Review of Sociology and Anthropology 6:129–44.

McEVOY, JAMES, III. 1971. Radicals or Conservatives? The Contemporary American Right. Chicago: Rand McNally.

McGUIRE, MEREDITH. 1972. "Toward a sociological investigation of the 'Underground Church.'" Review of Religious Research 14:41–47.

———. 1974. "An interpretive comparison of elements of the Pentecostal and Underground Church movements in American Catholicism." Sociological Analysis 35:57–65.

MACINTYRE, ALISDAIR. 1967. Secularisation and Moral Change. London: Oxford University Press.

McLEOD, HUGH. 1974. Class and Religion in a Late Victorian City. London: Croom Helm.

McLOUGHLIN, WILLIAM. 1959. Modern Revivalism. New York: Ronald Press.

———. 1960. Billy Graham. New York: Ronald Press.

———. 1968. "Is there a third force in Christendom?" Pp. 45–72 in William McLoughlin and Robert Bellah (eds.), Religion in America. Boston: Beacon Press.

MACK, RAYMOND. 1956. "The Protestant Ethic, level of aspiration and social mobility." American Sociological Review 21:295–300.

MAKLER, HARRY. 1963. "Centralization/decentralization in formal organizations: A case study of American Protestant denominations." Review of Religious Research 5:5–11.

MALINOWSKI, BRONISLAW. [1925]. 1948. Magic, Science and Religion and Other Essays. Boston: Society for the Propagation of Christian Knowledge.

MANNHEIM, KARL. 1936. Ideology and Utopia: An Introduction to the Sociology of Knowledge. New York: Harcourt, Brace.

MARANELL, GARY. 1974. Responses to Religion: Studies in the Social Psychology of Religious Beliefs. Lawrence, Kans.: University of Kansas Press.

MARTIN, DAVID. 1967. A Sociology of English Religion. London: SCM Press.

———. 1969. The Religious and the Secular. London: Routledge & Kegan Paul.

———. 1972. "Great Britain: England." Pp. 229–47 in Hans Mol (ed.), Western Religion: A Country by Country Sociological Inquiry. The Hague: Mouton.

MARTIN, WILLIAM. 1972. Christians in Conflict. Chicago: Center for the Scientific Study of Religion.

MARTY, MARTIN. 1970. The Righteous Empire: The Protestant Experience in America. New York: Dial Press.

———. 1976. A Nation of Behavers. Chicago: University of Chicago Press.

MARTY, MARTIN, STUART ROSENBERG, AND ANDREW GREELEY. 1968. What Do We Believe? The Stance of Religion in America. New York: Meredith Press.

MARX, GARY. 1967. "Religion: Opiate or inspiration of civil rights militancy among Negroes?" American Sociological Review 32:64–73.

MARX, KARL AND FREDERICK ENGELS. 1955. On Religion. Moscow: Foreign Languages Publishing House.

MASS OBSERVATION. 1948. Puzzled People. London: Victor Gollancz.

MAUSS, MARCEL. [1950] 1972. A General Theory of Magic. Trans. Robert Brain. London: Routledge & Kegan Paul.

MAY, HENRY. [1949] 1972. The Protestant Churches and Industrial America. New York: Harper & Row Torchbooks.

MAYER, ALBERT AND HARRY SHARP. 1962. "Religious preference and worldly success." American Sociological Review 27:218–27.

MAYOR, STEPHEN. 1967. The Churches and the Labour Movement. London: Independent Press.

MAYS, BENJAMIN AND JOSEPH NICHOLSON. 1933. The Negro's Church. New York: Institute of Social and Religious Research.

MEAD, SIDNEY. 1975. The Nation with the Soul of a Church. New York: Harper Forum Books.

MEANS, RICHARD. 1966. "Protestantism and economic institutions: Auxiliary theories to Weber's Protestant Ethic." Social Forces 44:372–81.

MEHL, ROGER. 1970. The Sociology of Protestantism. Trans. James Farley. Philadelphia: Westminster Press.

MEISEL, JOHN. 1973. Working Papers in Canadian Politics. Montreal: McGill-Queen's University Press.

METZ, DONALD. 1967. New Congregations: Security and Mission in Conflict. Philadelphia: Westminster Press.

MEYER, DONALD. 1960. The Protestant Search for Political Realism, 1919–1941. Berkeley and Los Angeles: University of California Press.

———. 1966. The Positive Thinkers: A Study of the American Quest for Health, Wealth and Personal Power from Mary Baker Eddy to Norman Vincent Peale. Garden City, N.Y.: Doubleday, Anchor Books.

———. 1968. "Churches and families." Pp. 230–48 in William McLoughlin and Robert Bellah (eds.), Religion in America. Boston: Beacon Press.

MIDDLETON, RUSSELL. 1973. "Do Christian beliefs cause anti-Semitism?" American Sociological Review 38:33–61.

MILIBAND, RALPH. 1969. The State in Capitalist Society: An Analysis of the Western System of Power. New York: Basic Books.

MILLER, DOUGLAS. 1975. "Popular religion in the 1950's: Norman Vincent Peale and Billy Graham." Journal of Popular Culture 9:66–76.

MILLER, ROBERT MOATS. 1958. American Protestantism and Social Issues, 1919–1939. Chapel Hill, N.C.: University of North Carolina Press.

MILLER, WILLIAM. 1961. "Religion and political attitudes." Pp. 81–118 in James Ward and A. Leland Jamison (eds.), Religion in American Life. Vol. 2. Princeton, N.J.: Princeton University Press.

MOBERG, DAVID. 1962. The Church as a Social Institution: The Sociology of American Religion. Englewood Cliffs, N.J.: Prentice-Hall.

————. 1965. "Religiosity and old age." Gerontologist 5:78–87.

————. 1971. "Religious practices." Pp. 551–98 in Merton Strommen (ed.), Research on Religious Development. New York: Hawthorne Books.

MOL, HANS. 1972. "Introduction." Pp. 1–25 in Hans Mol (ed.), Western Religion: A Country by Country Sociological Inquiry. The Hague: Mouton.

————. 1976. "Correlates of churchgoing in Canada." Pp. 241–54 in Stewart Crysdale and Les Wheatcroft (eds.), Religion in Canadian Society. Toronto: Macmillan of Canada.

MONAHAN, THOMAS. 1971. "The extent of interdenominational marriage in the United States." Journal for the Scientific Study of Religion 10:85–92.

————. 1973. "Some dimensions of interreligious marriages in Indiana, 1962–1967." Social Forces 52:195–203.

MONAHAN, THOMAS AND M. M. KEPHART. 1954. "Divorce and desertion by religious and mixed religious groups." American Journal of Sociology 59:454–65.

MOORE, JOHN, 1973. "The Catholic Pentecostal movement." Pp. 73–90 in Michael Hill (ed.), Sociological Yearbook of Religion in Britain. London: SCM Press.

MOORE, ROBERT. 1974. Pit-Men, Preachers and Politics: The Effect of Methodism in a Durham Mining Community. London: Cambridge University Press.

————. 1975. "Religion as a source of variation in working class images of society." Pp. 35–44 in Martin Bulmer (ed.), Working Class Images of Society. Boston: Routledge & Kegan Paul.

MORGAN, RICHARD. 1968. The Politics of Religious Conflict: Church and State in America. New York: Pegasus.

MORRIS, JAMES. 1973. The Preachers. New York: St. Martin's.

MUELLER, CHARLES AND WELDON JOHNSON. 1975. "Socioeconomic status and religious participation." American Sociological Review 40:785–800.

MUELLER, SAMUEL AND ANGELA LANE. 1972. "Tabulations from the 1957 current population survey on religion." Journal for the Scientific Study of Religion 11:76–98.

MYERS, GUSTAVUS. 1960. The History of Bigotry in the United States. Ed. Henry Christman. New York: Capricorn Books.

NASH, DENNISON. 1968. "A little child shall lead them: A statistical test of an hypothesis that children were the source of the American 'Religious Revival.' " Journal for the Scientific Study of Religion 7:238–40.

NASH, DENNISON AND PETER BERGER. 1962. "The child, the family and religious revival in suburbia." Journal for the Scientific Study of Religion 2:85–93.

NATIONAL OPINION RESEARCH CENTER. 1972. Catholic Priests in the U.S.: Sociological Investigations. Washington, D.C.: U.S. Catholic Conference.

NEILL, STEPHEN. 1960. Anglicanism. Baltimore: Penguin Books.

NELSEN, HART. 1972. "Sectarianism, world view and anomie." Social Forces 51:226–33.

————. 1976. "Musical pews: Rural and urban models of occupational and religious mobility." Sociology and Social Research 60:279–89.

NELSEN, HART AND H. D. ALLEN. 1974. "Ethnicity, Americanisation and religious attendance." American Journal of Sociology 79:906–22.

NELSEN, HART, THOMAS MADRON, AND RAYTHA YOKELEY. 1975. "Black religion's Promethean motif: Orthodoxy and militancy." American Journal of Sociology 81:139–46.

NELSEN, HART AND ANNE KUSENES NELSEN. 1975. The Black Church in the Sixties. Lexington, Ky.: University of Kentucky Press.

NELSEN, HART AND H. P. WHITT. 1972. "Religion and the migrant to the city: A test of Holt's cultural shock theory." Social Forces 50:379–84.

NELSEN, HART, RAYTHA YOKELEY, AND THOMAS MADRON. 1971. "Rural-urban differences in religiosity." Rural Sociology 36:389–96.

————. 1973. "Ministerial roles and social actionist stance: Protestant clergy and protest in the sixties." American Sociological Review 38:375–86.

NELSON, BENJAMIN. 1973. "Weber's Protestant Ethic: Its origins, wanderings, and foreseeable futures." Pp. 71–130 in Charles Glock and Phillip Hammond (eds.), Beyond the Classics? Essays in the Scientific Study of Religion. New York: Harper & Row.

NELSON, GEOFFREY. 1969. Spiritualism and Society. London: Routledge and Kegan Paul.

NELSON, JACK AND RONALD OSTROW. 1972. The FBI and the Berrigans: The Making of a Conspiracy. New York: Coward, McCann & Geoghegan.

NEWMAN, WILLIAM. 1976. "Religion in suburban America." Pp. 265–78 in Barry Schwartz (eds.), The Changing Face of the Suburbs. Chicago: University of Chicago Press.

NIE, NORMAN, SIDNEY VERBA, AND JOHN PETROCIK. 1976. The Changing American Voter. Cambridge, Mass.: Harvard University Press.

NIEBUHR, H. RICHARD. [1929]. 1957. The Social Sournes of Denominationalism. York: Meridian Books.

NISBET, ROBERT. 1966. The Sociological Tradition. New York: Basic Books.

NOEL, D. L. AND A. PINKNEY. 1964. "Correlates of prejudice: Some racial differences and similarities." American Journal of Sociology 69:609–22.

NORDHOFF, CHARLES. [1875] 1961. The Communistic Societies of the United States. New York: Hillary House Publishers.

NORMAN, EDWARD. 1976. Church and Society in England, 1770–1970. Oxford: Clarendon Press.

NOTTINGHAM, ELIZABETH. 1971. Religion: A Sociological View. New York: Random House.

NUDELMAN, A. E.. 1971. "Dimensions of religiosity." Review of Religious Research 13:42–56.

OBENHAUS, VICTOR. 1963. The Church and Faith in Mid-America. Philadelphia: Westminster Press.

O'CONNOR, EDWARD. 1971. The Pentecostal Movement in the Catholic Church. Notre Dame, Inc.: Ave Maria Press.

————. 1968. The Catholic Crisis. Boston: Beacon Press.

————. 1970. "The sociology of religion reconsidered." Sociological Analysis 31:145–52.

O'DEA, THOMAS. 1957. The Mormons. Chicago: University of Chicago Press.

————. 1966. The Sociology of Religion. Englewood Cliffs, N.J.: Prentice-Hall.

O'DEA, THOMAS AND RENATO POBLETE. 1970. "Anomie and the 'quest for community': The formation of sects among the Puerto Ricans of New York." Pp. 180–200 in Thomas O'Dea, Sociology and the Study of Religion: Theory, Research, Interpretation. New York: Basic Books.

ORUM, ANTHONY. 1970. "Religion and the rise of the radical white: The case of southern Wallace support in 1968." Social Science Quarterly 51:674–88.

OSBORNE, WILLIAM. 1967. The Segregated Covenant: Race Relations and the American Catholic New York: Herder & Herder.

PARENTI, MICHAEL. 1967. "Political values and religious cultures: Jews, Catholics, and Protestants." Journal for the Scientific Study of Religion 6:259–69.

PARSONS, ANNE. 1965. "The Pentecostal immigrants: A study of an ethnic central city church." Journal for the Scientific Study of Religion 4:183–97.

PARSONS, TALCOTT. 1954. Essays in Sociological Theory (Revised Edition). Glencoe, Ill.: Free Press.

————. 1960. Structure and Process in Modern Society. Glencoe, Ill.: Free Press.

————. 1963. "Christianity and modern industrial society." Pp. 33–70 in Edward Tiryakian (ed.), Sociological Theory, Values and Socio-Cultural Change. Glencoe Ill.: Free Press.

PATTISON, E. MANSELL. 1974. "Ideological support for the marginal middle class: Faith healing and glossolalia." Pp. 418–58 in Irving Zaretsky and Mark Leone (eds.), Religious Movements in Contemporary America. Princeton, N.J.: Princeton University Press.

PAUL, LESLIE. 1964. The Deployment and Payment of the Clergy. London: Church Information Office.

————. 1973. A Church by Daylight: A Reappraisement of the Church of England. London: Geoffrey Chapman.

PETERGORSKY, D. W. 1940. Left-Wing Democracy in the English Civil War. London: Victor Gallancz.

PETERS, VICTOR. [1965] 1971. All Things Common: The Hutterian Way of Life. New York: Harper & Row, Torchbooks.

PETERSEN, DONALD AND ARMAND MAUSS. 1973. "The cross and the commune: An interpretation of the Jesus People." Pp. 261–80 in Charles Glock (ed.), Religion in Sociological Perspective: Essays in the Empirical Study of Religion. Belmont, Calif.: Wadsworth.

PETERSEN, LARRY AND ARMAND MAUSS. 1976. "Religion and the 'right to life': Correlates of opposition to abortion." Sociological Analysis 37:243–54.

PFEFFER, LEO. 1974. "The legitimation of marginal religions in the United States." Pp. 9–26 in Irving Zaretsky and Mark Leone (eds.), Religious Movements in Contemporary America. Princeton, N.J.: Princeton University Press.

PHOTIADIS, JOHN. 1965. "The American business creed and denominational identification." Social Forces 44:92–100.

PICKERING, W. S. F.. 1967. "The 1851 religious census—A useless experiment?" British Journal of Sociology 18:382–407.

PLOCH, DONALD. 1974. "Religion as an independent variable: A critique of some major research." Pp. 275–94 in Allan Eister (ed.), Changing Perspectives in the Scientific Study of Religion. New York: Wiley-Interscience.

PLOWMAN, EDWARD. 1975. "The deepening rift in the charismatic movement." Christianity Today, October 10:52–54.

POGGIE, JOHN AND CARL GERSUNG. 1972. "Risk and ritual: An interpretation of fishermen's folklore in a New England community." Journal of American Folklore 85:66–72.

POGGIE, JOHN, RICHARD POLLNAC, AND CARL GERSUNG. 1976. "Risk as a basis for taboos among fishermen in southern New England." Journal for the Scientific Study of Religion 15:257–62.

POPE, LISTON. [1942] 1965. Millhands and Preachers (2nd ed.). New Haven: Yale University Press.

PRATT, HENRY. 1972. The Liberalization of American Protestantism: A Case Study in Complex Organizations. Detroit: Wayne State University Press.

QUINLEY, HAROLD. 1974. The Prophetic Clergy: Social Activism among Protestant Ministers. New York: John Wiley.

REDEKOP, CALVIN. 1969. The Old Colony Mennonites: Dilemmas of Ethnic Minority Life. Baltimore: Johns Hopkins.

REIMER, D. 1965. White Protestantism and the Negro. New York: Oxford University Press.

RHODES, LEWIS AND CHARLES NAM. 1970. "The religious context of educational expectations." American Sociological Review 35:253–65.

RIESELBACH, LEROY. 1973. Congressional Politics. New York: McGraw-Hill.

RIESMAN, DAVID. 1961. The Lonely Crowd. New Haven: Yale University Press.

RIGHTS MAGAZINE. 1963. "A study of religious discrimination by social clubs." Pp. 95–102 in Raymond Mack (ed.), Race, Class and Power. New York: American Book Co.

ROBBINS, THOMAS, DICK ANTHONY, AND THOMAS CURTIS. 1975. "Youth culture religious movements: Evaluating the integrative hypothesis." Sociological Quarterly 16:48–64.

ROBBINS, THOMAS, DICK ANTHONY, MADELEINE DOUCAS, AND THOMAS CURTIS. 1976. "The last civil religion: Reverend Moon and the Unification Church." Sociological Analysis 37:111–25.

ROBERTSON, ROLAND. 1968. "The Salvation Army: The persistence of sectarianism." Pp. 49–105 in Bryan Wilson (ed.), Patterns of Sectarianism. London: Heinemann.

———. 1970. The Sociological Interpretation of Religion. Oxford: Basil Blackwell.

ROJEK, DEAN. 1973. "Protestant Ethic and political preference." Social Forces 52:168–77.

ROOF, WADE. 1974a. "Explaining traditional religion in contemporary society." Pp. 295–314 in Allan Eister (ed.), Changing Perspectives in the Scientific Study of Religion. New York: Wiley-Interscience.

————. 1974b. "Religious orthodoxy and minority prejudice: Causal relationship or reflection of localistic world view?" American Journal of Sociology 80:643–64.

————. 1976. "Traditional religion in contemporary society: A theory of local-cosmopolitan plausibility." American Sociological Review 41:195–208.

ROSENBERG, BRUCE. 1974. "The psychology of the spiritual sermon." Pp. 135–49 in Irving Zaretsky and Mark Leone (eds.), Religious Movements in Contemporary America. Princeton, N.J.: Princeton University Press.

ROSSIDES, DANIEL. 1976. The American Class System: An Introduction to Social Stratification. Boston: Houghton Mifflin.

ROSTEN, LEO. 1975. Religions of America: Ferment and Faith in an Age of Crisis: A New Guide and Almanac. New York: Simon & Schuster.

ROTH, GUENTHER. 1975. "Socio-historical model and developmental theory: Charismatic community, charisma of reason and the counter-culture." American Sociological Review 40:148–57.

————. 1976. "Religion and revolutionary beliefs: Sociological and historical dimensions in Max Weber's work—In memory of Ivan Vallier (1927–1974)." Social Forces 55:257–72.

RUDGE, PETER. 1968. Ministry and Management: The Study of Ecclesiastical Administration. London: Tavistock.

RUETHER, ROSEMARY. 1970. The Radical Kingdom: The Western Experience of Messianic Hope. New York: Harper & Row.

RUNCIMAN, WALTER. 1966. Relative Deprivation and Social Justice. Berkeley: University of California Press.

RUPPEL, HOWARD. 1969. "Religiosity and premarital sexual permissiveness: A methodological note." Sociological Analysis 30:176–88.

————. 1970. "Religiosity and premarital sexual permissiveness." Journal of Marriage and the Family 32:647–55.

RYDER, NORMAN. 1973. "Recent trends and group differences in fertility." Pp. 57–68 in Charles Westoff et al. (eds.), Toward the End of Growth: Population in America. Englewood Cliffs, N.J.: Prentice-Hall.

RYDER, NORMAN AND CHARLES WESTOFF. 1971. Reproduction in the United States: 1965. Princeton, N.J.: Princeton University Press.

SCANZONI, JOHN. 1971. The Black Family in Modern Society. Boston: Allyn & Bacon.

————. 1975. Sex Roles, Life Styles and Childbearing: Changing Patterns in Marriage and the Family. New York: Free Press.

SCHNEIDER, LOUIS AND SANFORD DORNBUSCH. 1958. Popular Religion: Inspirational Books in America. Chicago: University of Chicago Press.

SCHROEDER, W. WIDICK AND VICTOR OBENHAUS. 1964. Religion in American Culture: Unity and Diversity in a Midwestern County. New York: Free Press.

SCHUMAN, HOWARD. 1971. "The religious factor in Detroit." American Sociological Review 36:30–38.

SCHUMAN, HOWARD AND SHIRLEY HATCHETT. 1974. Black Racial Attitudes: Trends and Complexities. Ann Arbor, Mich.: Institute for Social Research.

SCHWARTZ, MILDRED. 1974. "Canadian voting behavior." Pp. 543–618 in Richard Rose (ed.), Electoral Behavior: A Comparative Handbook. New York: Free Press.

SEGGAR, JOHN AND PHILLIP KUNZ. 1972. "Conversion: Evaluation of a step-like process for problem-solving." Review of Religious Research. 13:178–84.

SEMMEL, BERNARD. 1973. The Methodist Revolution. New York: Basic Books.

SERNETT, MILTON. 1975. Black Religion and American Evangelicalism: White Protestants, Plantation Missions, and the Flowering of Negro Christianity, 1787–1865. Metuchen, N.J.: Scarecrow Press.

SHIBUTANI, TAMOTSU AND KIAN KWAN. 1965. Ethnic Stratification: A Comparative Approach. London: Macmillan.

SHILS, EDWARD. 1975. Center and Periphery: Essays in Macrosociology. Chicago: University of Chicago Press.

SHINER, LARRY. 1967. "The concept of secularization in empirical research." Journal for the Scientific Study of Religion 6:207–20.

SILVA, RUTH. 1962. Rum, Religion and Votes: 1928 Re-examined. University Park, Pa.: Pennsylvania State University Press.

SIMMONDS, ROBERT, JAMES RICHARDSON, AND MARY HARDER. 1974. "Organizational aspects of a Jesus movement." Social Compass 21:269–81.

SISSONS, PETER. 1973. The Social Significance of Church Membership in the Burgh of Falkirk. Edinburgh: Church of Scotland.

SKIDMORE, WILLIAM. 1975. Theoretical Thinking in Sociology. Cambridge: Cambridge University Press.

SKLARE, MARSHALL. 1971. America's Jews. New York: Random House.

SKLARE, MARSHALL AND JOSEPH GREENBLUM. 1967. Jewish Identity on the Suburban Frontier: A Study of Group Survival in the Open Society. New York: Basic Books.

SMELSER, NEIL. 1962. Theory of Collective Behavior. New York: Free Press.

SMITH, JAMES AND GIDEON SJOBERG. 1961. "The origins and career patterns of leading Protestant clergymen." Social Forces 39:290–96.

SMITH, ROCKWELL, CLIFFORD BLACK, BARBARA HOFFMAN, AND S. BURKETT MILNER. 1974. Sociological Studies of an Occupation: The Ministry. Evanston, Ill.: The Murray and Dorothy Leiffer Bureau of Social and Religious Research.

SMITH, TIMOTHY. 1957. Revivalism and Social Reform in Mid-Nineteenth-Century America. New York: Abingdon.

SNOOK, JOHN. 1973. Going Further: Life-and-Death Religion in America. Englewood Cliffs, N.J.: Prentice-Hall.

SNOW, LOUDELL. 1973. " 'I was born just exactly with the gift': An interview with a voodoo practitioner." Journal of American Folklore 86:272–81.

SOCIAL SURVEYS (GALLUP). 1965. Television and Religion. London: Gallup.

———. 1974. "British Shun Mysticism." Current Opinion 2:36.

SOMBART, WERNER. 1951. The Jews and Modern Capitalism. Trans. M. Epstein. Glencoe, Ill.: Free Press.

SORAUF, FRANK. 1976. The Wall of Separation: The Constitutional Politics of Church and State. Princeton, N.J.: Princeton University Press.

SPILKA, BERNARD AND J. REYNOLDS. 1965. "Religion and prejudice: A factor-analytical study." Review of Religious Research 6:163–68.

STARK, RODNEY. 1972. "The economics of piety: Religious commitment and social class." Pp. 483–503 in Gerald Thielbar and Saul Feldman (eds.), Issues in Social Inequality. Boston: Little Brown.

————. 1973. "Age and faith: A changing outlook or an old process?" Pp. 48–58 in Charles Glock (ed.), Religion in Sociological Perspective: Essays in the Empirical Study of Religion. Belmont, Calif.: Wadsworth.

STARK, RODNEY, BRUCE FOSTER, CHARLES GLOCK, AND HAROLD QUINLEY. 1971. Wayward Shepherds: Prejudice and the Protestant Crergy. New Ycrk: Harper & Row.

STARK, RODNEY AND CHARLES GLOCK. 1968. American Piety: The Nature of Religious Commitment. Berkeley and Los Angeles: University of California Press.
————. 1973. "Prejudice and the churches." Pp. 88–101 in Charles Glock (ed.), Religion in Sociological Perspective: Essays in the Empirical Study of Religion. Belmont, Calif.: Wadsworth.

STEELE, ROBERT. 1970. Storming Heaven: The Lives and Turmoils of Minnie Kennedy and Aimee Semple McPherson. New York: Morrow.

STEEMAN, THEODORE. 1969. "The underground church: The forms and dynamics of change in contemporary Catholicism." Pp. 713–48 in Donald Cutler (ed.), Religious Situation: 1969. Boston: Beacon Press.

STEINBERG, STEPHEN. 1974. The Academic Melting Pot: Catholics and Jews in American Higher Education. New York: McGraw-Hill.

STONE, DAVID. 1975. "Another look at 'the religious complexion of Canada.' " Pp. 252–58 in Yearbook of American and Canadian Churches. Nashville: Abingdon.

STROUT, CUSHING. 1974. The New Heaven and New Earth: Political Religion in America. New York: Harper & Row.

STUHR, WALTER. 1972. The Public Style: A Study of Community Participation of Protestant Ministers. Chicago: Center for the Scientific Study of Religion.

SWANSON, GUY. 1967. Religion and Regime: A Sociological Account of the Reformation. Ann Arbor, Mich.: University of Michigan Press.
————. 1968. "Modern secularity: Its meaning, sources and interpretation." Pp. 801–34 in Donald Cutler (ed.), Religious Situation: 1968. Boston: Beacon Press.

SWATOS, WILLIAM, JR. 1976. "Weber or Troeltsch? Methodology, syndrome, and the development of church-sect theory." Journal for the Scientific Study of Religion 15:129–44.

SWEETSER, THOMAS. 1974. The Catholic Parish: Shifting Membership in a Changing Church. Chicago: Center for the Scientific Study of Religion.

TAEUBER, KARL AND ALMA TAEUBER. 1964. "The Negro as an immigrant group." American Journal of Sociology 69:374–82.

TAKAYAMA, K. PETER. 1975. "Formal polity and change of structure: Denominational assemblies." Sociological Analysis 36:17–28.

TAMBIAH, S.J. 1968. "The magical power of words." Man (New Series) 3:175–208.
————. 1973. "The form and meaning of magical acts: A point of view." Pp. 199–229 in Robin Horton and Ruth Finnegan (eds.), Modes of Thought: Essays on Thinking in Western and Non-Western Societies. London: Faber & Faber.

TAMNEY, JOSEPH. 1970. "The social psychology of conversion." Pp. 399–418 in William Liu and Nathaniel Pallone (eds.), Catholics/USA: Perspectives on Social Change. New York: John Wiley.

TAPP, ROBERT. 1973. Religion among the Unitarian Universalists. New York: Seminar Press.

TATRO, CHARLOTTE. 1974. "Cross my palm with silver: Fortune telling as an occupational way of life." Pp. 286–99 in Clifton Bryant (ed.), Deviant Behavior: Occupational and Organizational Bases. Chicago: Rand McNally.

TAWNEY, R. H.. [1926] 1947. Religion and the Rise of Capitalism. New York: Penguin.

THOMAS, KEITH. 1973. Religion and the Decline of Magic: Studies in Popular Beliefs in Sixteenth- and Seventeenth-Century England. Baltimore: Penguin.

THOMAS, MICHAEL. 1972. "American civil religion: An empirical study." Social Forces 51:218–25.

TIRYAKIAN, EDWARD. 1962. Sociologism and Existentialism: Two Perspectives on the Individual and Society. Englewood Cliffs, N.J.: Prentice-Hall.

TOMASSON, RICHARD. 1970. "Religion is irrelevant in Sweden." Pp. 111–27 in Jeffrey Hadden (ed.), Religion in Transition. New Brunswick, N.J.: Transaction Books.

TOWLER, ROBERT. 1969. "The social status of the Anglican minister." Pp. 443–50 in Roland Robertson (ed.), The Sociology of Religion: Selected Readings. Baltimore: Penguin.

———. 1974. Homo Religiosus: Sociological Problems in the Study of Religion. London: Constable.

TOWLER, ROBERT AND AUDREY CHAMBERLAIN. 1973. "Common religion." Pp. 1–16 in Michael Hill (ed.), Sociological Yearbook of Religion in Britain. London: SCM Press.

TRAVISANO, RICHARD. 1969. "Alternation and conversion as qualitatively different transformations." Pp. 594–606 in Gregory Stone and Harvey Faberman (eds.), Social Psychology Through Symbolic Interaction. Waltham, Mass.: Ginn-Blaisdell.

TRENT, JAMES AND JENETTE GOLDS. 1967. Catholics in College: Religious Commitment and the Intellectual Life. Chicago: University of Chicago Press.

TROELTSCH, ERNST. 1931. The Social Teachings of the Christian Churches (Two Vols.) Trans. Olive Wyon. New York: Macmillan.

TRUZZI, MARCELLO. 1972. "The occult revival as popular culture." Sociological Quarterly 13:16–36.

———. 1974. "Towards a sociology of the occult: Notes on modern witchcraft." Pp. 628–45 in Irving Zaretsky and Mark Leone (eds.), Religious Movements in Contemporary America. Princeton, N.J.: Princeton University Press.

TURNER, JONATHAN. 1974. The Structure of Sociological Theory. Homewood, Ill.: Dorsey.

TURNER, VICTOR. 1974. "Metaphors of anti-structure in religious culture." Pp. 63–84 in Allan Eister (ed.), Changing Perspectives in the Scientific Study of Religion. New York: Wiley-Interscience.

TYGART, CLARENCE. 1973. "Social movement participation: Clergy and the anti-Vietnam war movement." Sociological Analysis 34:202–11.

TYLER, ALICE. [1944] 1962. Freedom's Ferment: Phases of American Social History from the Colonial Period to the Outbreak of the Civil War. New York: Harper, Torchbooks.

TYLER, LAWRENCE. 1966. "The Protestant Ethic among the Black Muslims." Phylon 27:5–14.

UNDERHILL, RALPH. 1975. "Economic and political antecedents of monotheism: A cross-cultural study." American Journal of Sociology 80:841–61.

UNDERWOOD, KENNETH. 1957. Protestant and Catholic. Boston: Beacon Press.

UNITED STATES EQUAL OPPORTUNITY COMMISSION. 1968. Hearings on Discrimination in White Collar Employment: "Restricted Membership" at the Managerial Level—Exclusion of Jews from the Executive Suite. Washington, D.C.: U.S. Government Printing Office.

VAN ROY, RALPH, FRANK BEAN, AND JAMES WOOD. 1973. "Social mobility and doctrinal orthodoxy." Journal for the Scientific Study of Religion 12:427–40.

VERBIT, MERVIN. 1970. "The components and dimensions of religious behavior: Toward a reconceptualization of religiosity." Pp. 24–38 in Phillip Hammon and Benton Johnson (eds.), American Mosaic: Social Patterns of Religion in the United States. New York: Random House.

VERNON, GLENN. 1968a. "The religious 'nones': A neglected category." Journal for the Scientific Study of Religion 7:219–29.

———. 1968b. "Marital characteristics of religious independents." Review of Religious Research 9:162–70.

VIDICH, ARTHUR AND JOSEPH BENSMAN. [1958] 1960. Small Town in Mass Society: Class, Power and Religion in a Rural Community. Garden City, N.Y.: Doubleday, Anchor Books.

VINCENT, CLARK. 1964. "Interfaith marriages." Pp. 50–59 in Earl Raab (ed.), Religious Conflict in America. New York: Doubleday.

VOGT, EZRA AND RODNEY HYMAN. 1959. Water-Witching, USA. Chicago: University of Chicago Press.

WACH, JOACHIM. [1944] 1962. The Sociology of Religion. Chicago: University of Chicago Press.

WALLACE, ANTHONY. 1966. Religion: An Anthropological View. New York: Random House.

WALLIS, ROY. 1973. "The sectarianism of Scientology." Pp. 136–55 in Michael Hill (ed.), Sociological Yearbook of Religion in Britain. London: SCM Press.

———. 1974. "Ideology, authority and the development of cultic movements." Social Research 41:299–327.

———. 1975a. "The Aetherius Society: A case study in the formation of a mystagogic congregation." Pp. 17–34 in Roy Wallis (ed.), Sectarianism. New York: John Wiley.

———. 1975b. "The cult and its transformation." Pp. 35–52 in Roy Wallis (ed.), Sectarianism. New York: John Wiley.

———. 1975c. "Societal reaction to Scientology: A study in the sociology of deviant religion." Pp. 86–116 in Roy Wallis (ed.), Sectarianism. New York: John Wiley.

———. 1975d. "Therapeutic cult to religious sect." Sociology 9:89–100.

WARBURTON, T. RENNIE. 1969. "Holiness religion: An anomaly of sectarian typologies." Journal for the Scientific Study of Religion 8:130–39.

WARD, CONOR. 1965. Priests and People: A Study in the Sociology of Religion. Liverpool: Liverpool University Press.

———. 1972. "Ireland." Pp. 295–303 in Hans Mol (ed.), Western Religion: A Country by Country Sociological Inquiry. The Hague: Mouton.

WARNER, WILLIAM LLOYD. 1961. Family of God: A Symbolic Study of Christian Life in America. New Haven: Yale University Press.

WARREN, B. L. 1970. "Socio-economic achievement and religion: The American case." Sociological Inquiry 40:130–55.

WASHINGTON, JOSEPH. 1964. Black Religion: The Negro and Christianity in the United States. Boston: Beacon Press.

———. 1972. Black Sects and Cults. Garden City, N.Y.: Doubleday.

WEBER, MAX. 1930. The Protestant Ethic and the Spirit of Capitalism. Trans Talcott Parsons; foreward by R.H. Tawney. London: George Allen & Unwin.

———. 1946. From Max Weber: Essays in Sociology. Trans. and ed. Hans Gerth and C. Wright Mills. New York: Oxford University Press.

———. [1947] 1964. The Theory of Social and Economic Organization. Ed. with an introduction by Talcott Parsons. Glencoe, Ill.: Free Press.

———. 1965. The Sociology of Religion. Trans. Ephraim Fischoff. London: Methuen.

WEIGERT, ANDREW AND DARWIN THOMAS. 1969. "Religiosity in 5-D: A critical note." Social Forces 48:260–63.

WEISBERGER, BERNARD. [1958] 1966. They Gathered at the River: The Story of the Great Revivalists and Their Impact on Religion in America. Chicago: Quadrangle.

WESTIN, ALAN.. 1963. "The John Birch Society." Pp. 239–68 in Daniel Bell (ed.), The Radical Right. Garden City, N.Y.: Doubleday, Anchor Books.

WESTOFF, CHARLES AND LARRY BUMPASS. 1973. "The revolution in birth control practices of U.S. Roman Catholics." Science 179:41–44.

WESTOFF, CHARLES, ROBERT POTTER, JR., AND PHILIP SAGI. 1963. The Third Child: A Study in the Prediction of Fertility. Princeton, N.J.: Princeton University Press.

WESTOFF, CHARLES AND NORMAN RYDER. 1970. "Conception control among American Catholics." Pp. 257–68 in William Liu and Nathaniel Pallone (eds.), Catholics/USA: Perspectives on Social Change. New York: John Wiley.

WHITMAN, FREDERICK. 1968. "Revivalism as institutionalized behavior: Analysis of the social base of a Billy Graham crusade." Social Science Quarterly 49:115–27.

WHITE, ANDREW. 1896. A History of the Warfare of Science with Theology in Christendom (2 vols.). New York: Appleton-Century-Crofts.

WHITLEY, OLIVER. 1959. The Trumpet Call of Reformation. St. Louis: Bethany Press.

WHITTEN, N. E.. 1962. "Contemporary patterns of malign occultism among Negroes in North America." Journal of American Folklore 75:311–25.

WHITWORTH, JOHN. 1975. God's Blueprints: A Sociological Study of Three Utopian Sects. Boston: Routledge & Kegan Paul.

WHYTE, WILLIAM. 1957. The Organization Man. Garden City, N.Y.: Doubleday, Anchor Books.

WILENSKY, HAROLD AND JACK LADINSKY. 1967. "From religious community to occupational group: Structural assimilation among professors, lawyers and engineers." American Sociological Review 32:541–61.

WILLIAMS, GEORGE. 1962. The Radical Reformation. London: Weidenfeld & Nicholson.

WILLIAMS, J. PAUL. 1969. What Americans Believe and How They Worship (3rd. ed). New York: Harper & Row.

WILLIAMS, MELVIN. 1974. Community in a Black Pentecostal Church: An Anthropological Study. Pittsburgh: University of Pittsburgh Press.

WILLIAMS, ROBIN. 1960. American Society: A Sociological Interpretation. New York: Knopf.

WILMORE, GAYRAUD, JR. 1972. Black Religion and Black Radicalism. New York: Doubleday.

WILSON, BRYAN. 1961. Sects and Society: The Sociology of Three Religious Groups in Britain. London: Heinemann.

———. 1966. Religion in Secular Society: A Sociological Comment. London: C. A. Watts.

———. 1967. "The Exclusive Brethren: A case study in the evolution of sectarian ideology." Pp. 287–344 in Bryan Wilson (ed.), Patterns of Sectarianism. London: Heinemann.

———. 1968. "Religion and the churches in contemporary America." Pp. 73–110 in William McLoughlin and Robert Bellah (eds.), Religion in America. Boston: Beacon Press.

———. 1970. Religious Sects: A Sociological Study. London: Weidenfeld and Nicholson.

———. 1973. Magic and the Millenium: A Sociological Study of Religious Movements of Protest among Tribal and Third-World Peoples. New York: Harper & Row.

———. 1976. Contemporary Transformations of Religion. London: Oxford University Press.

WIMBERLEY, RONALD. 1976. "Testing the civil religion hypothesis." Sociological Analysis 37:341–52.

WIMBERLEY, RONALD, DONALD CLELLAND, THOMAS HOOD, AND C. M. LIPSEY. 1976. "The civil religious dimension: Is it there?" Social Forces 54:890–900.

WIMBERLEY, RONALD, THOMAS HOOD, C. M. LIPSEY, DONALD CLELLAND, AND MARGUERITE HAY. 1975. "Conversion in a Billy Graham crusade: Spontaneous event or ritual performance?" Sociological Quarterly 16:162–70.

WINGROVE, C. RAY AND JON ALSTON. 1974. "Cohort analysis of church attendance, 1939–1969." Social Forces 53:324–31.

WINTER, GIBSON. 1961. The Suburban Captivity of the Churches. Garden City, N.Y.: Doubleday.

———. 1968. Religious Identity: The Formal Organization and Informal Power Structure of the Major Faiths in the United States Today. New York: Macmillan.

WINTER, J. ALAN. 1974. "Elective affinities between religious beliefs and ideologies of management in two eras." American Journal of Sociology 79:1134–50.

WOOD, JAMES. 1970. "Authority and controversial policy: The churches and civil rights." American Sociological Review 35:1057–69.

———. 1972. "Unanticipated consequences of organisational coalitions: Ecumenical co-operation and civil rights policy." Social Forces 51:512–23.

———. 1975. "Legitimate control and 'organisational transcendence.'" Social Forces 54:199–211.

WOOD, JAMES AND MAYER ZALD. 1966. "Aspects of racial integration in the Methodist Church: Sources of resistance to organizational policy." Social Forces 45:255–65.

WUTHNOW, ROBERT. 1973. "Religious commitment and conservatism: In search of an elusive relationship." Pp. 117–32 in Charles Glock (ed.), Religion in Sociological Perspective: Essays in the Empirical Study of Religion. Belmont, Calif.: Wadsworth.

———. 1976a. "Astrology and marginality." Journal for the Scientific Study of Religion 15:157–68.

———. 1976b. The Consciousness Reformation. Berkeley and Los Angeles: University of California Press.

———. 1976c. "Recent patterns of secularization: A problem of generations?" American Sociological Review 41:850–67.

YINGER, J. MILTON. 1960. "Contraculture and subculture." American Sociological Review 25:625–35.

———. 1968. "A research note on interfaith marriage statistics." Journal for the Scientific Study of Religion 7:97–103.

———. 1970. The Scientific Study of Religion. New York: Macmillan.

YEARBOOK OF THE AMERICAN AND CANADIAN CHURCHES. 1975. Nashville: Abingdon.

ZABLOCKI, BENJAMIN. 1971. The Joyful Community: An Account of the Bruderhof, a Communal Movement Now in Its Third Generation. Baltimore: Penguin.

ZALD, MAYER. 1970. Organization Change: The Political Economy of the YMCA. Chicago: University of Chicago Press.

ZALD, MAYER AND ROBERTA ASH. 1966. "Social movement organizations: Growth, decay and change." Social Forces 44:327–40.

ZARETSKY, IRVING. 1974. "In the beginning was the Word: The relationship of language to social organisation in Spiritualist Churches." Pp. 166–222 in Irving Zaretsky and Mark Leone (eds.), Religious Movements in Contemporary America. Princeton, N.J.: Princeton University Press.

INDEX